The PRC Enterprise Bankruptcy Law

The People's Work in Progress

The PRC Enterprise Bankruptcy Law

The People's Work in Progress

DERYCK A. PALMER AND
JOHN J. RAPISARDI

* * *

SCOTT J. GREENBERG AND SAMUEL S. CAVIOR
CONTRIBUTING EDITORS

Beard Books
Washington, D.C.

ISBN 1-58798-297-8

Printed in the United States of America.

PREFACE

We wish to thank Professor Shuguang Li and Alan C.W. Tang who regularly made themselves available to answer many of our questions in learning and understanding the intricacies of Chinese insolvency and general business practices. Professor Li, who is at the China University of Political Science and Law, was very much involved in the drafting process of the Enterprise Bankruptcy Law. Alan Tang, who is head of Restructuring, Investigation and Insolvency Services at Grant Thornton (Hong Kong), is the author of one of the few definitive sources available in English on insolvency law in China, upon which we relied in our research. Another person to whom we are indebted is Xingxiang Zhang, a Legal Policy Counsel for GE (China), who took the time to provide valuable comments to early and late draft manuscripts.

We owe much gratitude to our associates Scott Greenberg and Sam Cavior. As "contributing editors" they each played an important role in researching and drafting at different stages, and their respective contributions made this book possible.

Our colleagues, Binghao Zhao and Wendy Kane, also lent invaluable assistance to us, for which we owe our heartfelt thanks. In addition, we thank our legal assistants, Angela Williams and Valerie Jorgovan, who helped coordinate the many trips to China necessary to make this book happen.

Finally, a special note of thanks must go to a former colleague of ours, Johnson Ng. Johnson was the original pioneer in assisting us in reviewing and commenting upon the initial drafts of the proposed Chinese bankruptcy law in 2001 and 2002. Many of the memoranda that he wrote in analyzing the proposed law in its nascent stage helped launch this project.

Our ambition through this work has been to assist in the further refinement and understanding of what is a remarkable and impressive piece of legislation. We hope that those coming new to this law (whether as academic, student, investor or other) will find this book to be a useful guide and resource.

Deryck A. Palmer
John J. Rapisardi
Cadwalader, Wickersham & Taft LLP

FOREWORD

I am very pleased to introduce The PRC Enterprise Bankruptcy Law: The People's Work in Progress as the first major Western work to be published on the new Enterprise Bankruptcy Law of the People's Republic of China, which became effective June 1, 2007. This book might be destined to become a key resource for Western investors seeking to understand the Chinese system and for Chinese practitioners (lawyers, administrators, judges and legislators) seeking to understand our new bankruptcy processes from the U.S. perspective.

As observers of its drafting and implementation may know, the Enterprise Bankruptcy Law represents the fruition of more than twelve years of effort by my colleagues and countrymen to establish a unified system of insolvency law to serve as one of the pillars of the market economic structure in China. We have developed a modern law that addresses many of the needs of our rapidly growing economy and the concerns of the Chinese people. Among its many advances, the law expands the availability of bankruptcy solutions to more legal entities than before, encourages the rescue and rehabilitation of distressed businesses, enables more efficient disposition of resources, protects creditors' lawful interests and reduces the cost of capital, while also protecting the workers of the nation. A comprehensive understanding of the new law will be critical to both domestic Chinese and international businesses and investors seeking to operate in China's emerging markets. Effective implementation and administration of the law, however, will require courts, practitioners and parties in interest to become familiar with new concepts and processes. I believe that this book provides valuable insight and guidance to aid in that goal.

I have known the authors, Deryck A. Palmer since 1999 and John J. Rapisardi since 2005. Over the years, their unflagging faith in the development of the Chinese legal infrastructure and their thoughtful commentary on the Enterprise Bankruptcy Law at stages of drafting have been an invaluable resource for myself and my fellow drafters, and it has been my pleasure to consider them friends of the Chinese community of insolvency law professionals.

Of course, in developing the new law, we drafters took guidance from many established bankruptcy systems and legal traditions—and not just the United States—in order to ensure that our bankruptcy law would have the world's best practices as well as Chinese characteristics. Deryck's and John's long and close involvement with the development of the new law, however, and their extensive experience with U.S. bankruptcy law uniquely qualifies them to undertake this careful, in-depth analysis of the Enterprise Bankruptcy Law from an American perspective. This book, I believe, offers insights, practical considerations and useful recommendations regarding the potential operation and implementation of the new law. Its clear discussions of individual provisions provide a good understanding of the new law as a whole, while its comparative structure allows practitioners and academics alike to examine the law through the prism of the bankruptcy system of the United States.

As the title of this book notes, the Enterprise Bankruptcy Law is a work in progress that continues to evolve even now. Indeed, in the near future the Supreme People's Court will promulgate an official explanation with respect to many aspects of the new law. Furthermore, we will begin to see the new law in application as liquidation and reorganization cases are tried—a process that has already begun. No doubt, Deryck and John will continue to update and supplement this volume as the law is honed and lessons are learned from practical experience.

In the meantime, I believe this book is an excellent resource for all who are interested in the development of insolvency law in China. I have had the honor to review advance drafts of this book and to contribute my comments to the authors where appropriate, and I recommend this work as the cornerstone for any library on the Enterprise Bankruptcy Law of the People's Republic of China.

Professor Shuguang Li
China University of Political
Science and Law, Beijing
September 2008

Contents

Introduction

The long-standing effort of the People's Republic of China ("PRC") to develop and enhance its position in the world as an economic superpower took a major step forward in August 2006, when its National People's Congress passed the *Enterprise Bankruptcy Law of the People's Republic of China* (the "Enterprise Bankruptcy Law"). The new law, which became effective on June 1, 2007, implements sweeping reforms to China's bankruptcy law regime, and advances the country's goal to become a full-fledged member of the World Trade Organization.

When examining the provisions of this groundbreaking legislation, it becomes evident that China, already the world's second-largest economy,[1] is indeed serious about transitioning to a market-based economy. By most measures, China's economy has experienced a recent surge that is unprecedented for the country. For example, in 2007, China overtook America for the first time in its share of the world's exports.[2] China's economy grew at a startling 11.9% and 11.5% in the second and third quarters of 2007, the fastest pace in more than a decade.[3] Since October 2007, the *renminbi* (RMB)[4] has climbed at an annual rate of 13% against the U.S. dollar, its fastest rise since 2005.[5] However, as China's robust economic growth begins inevitably to slow, it is expected that bankruptcies under the new law will grow exponentially. Indeed, there are some who expect a slowdown in a variety of Chinese industries following the 2008 Summer Olympics in Beijing. The economic

---

[1] Based on gross domestic product (purchasing power parity) valuations by the International Monetary Fund, as reported in its *World Economic Outlook Database (April 2008 Edition)*, available at *http://www.imf.org/external/pubs/ft/weo/2008/01/weodata/index.aspx* (last visited June 11, 2008).

[2] *See WTO: China overtakes US as second biggest exporter*, Chinadaily.com, Apr. 12, 2007, available at *http://www.chinadaily.com.cn/china/2007-04/12/content_849420.htm* (last visited June 3, 2008); *see also* Press Release, *WTO: developing, transition economies cushion trade slowdown* (Apr. 17, 2008), at Appendix Table 4 (Merchandise trade: leading exporters and importers, 2007), available at *http://www.wto.org/english/news_e/pres08_e/pr520_e.htm* (last visited June 11, 2008).

[3] *See* Keith Bradsher, *Slowing Marginally, China's Economy Sets 11.5% Growth Pace*, N.Y. Times, Oct. 25, 2007, at C4; David Barboza, *China's Growth Accelerates to 11.9%, and Food Prices Spur Inflation*, N.Y. Times, July 19, 2007, at C3.

[4] RMB is the official currency of the People's Republic of China.

[5] *See Revaluation by Stealth: China is allowing its currency to rise more rapidly. Why?*, The Economist, Jan. 12, 2008, at 69.

downturn and increased bankruptcy filings in a recession will mean that the new law in the future will play a critical role in China's ability to sustain its global economic stature.

Compared to prior law, the Enterprise Bankruptcy Law provides much greater investor certainty by establishing a road map for investors and lenders as to how their money may be recovered in the event of financial distress. A resulting increase in the availability of foreign credit ultimately should lower the cost of borrowing for Chinese companies, and also aid China in weathering economic downturns. Furthermore, the new law allows for reorganization, a process that should permit the restructuring of troubled enterprises in a more coherent manner. As a result, more Chinese companies will be able to survive rather than be liquidated—and thereby preserve jobs for workers.

The Enterprise Bankruptcy Law provides foreign investors with a new opportunity to explore potential markets and promote business development in China. According to a report prepared in 2007 by Deloitte and the Australian Society of Accountants—Hong Kong Branch, directors and senior management of foreign companies expressed confidence in the Enterprise Bankruptcy Law as a positive measure for the Chinese economy. More than two-thirds of interviewees believe that, with the full implementation of the Enterprise Bankruptcy Law, they would increase foreign investment in China over the next three years.[6]

Adoption of the Enterprise Bankruptcy Law was the culmination of China's twelve-year effort to update and improve its bankruptcy laws. Beginning with a review of the existing legal framework in China, the process involved intensive study of the insolvency and restructuring laws and practices of many developed nations, including (in part) the United States, the United Kingdom, France, Germany, Italy, Russia, the Netherlands, Australia, Japan, South Korea, and Thailand. To varying degrees, the influence of each of these various models is apparent in the Enterprise Bankruptcy Law; this book shall focus on the new law's many similarities to U.S. law in particular.

The process of formulating the Enterprise Bankruptcy Law has also exposed the Chinese legislature to the fairly recent phenomenon of drafting laws that take into account the market aspect of the socialist market economy. Many believe that, through the many drafts and iterations of the

---

[6]*See* China's New Bankruptcy Law Boosts Business and Investor Confidence, *http://www.deloitte.com/dtt/press_release/0,1014,sid%253D7062%2526cid%253D162453,00.html* (last visited June 3, 2008).

Enterprise Bankruptcy Law, the Chinese government has found better ways of integrating the interests of the state, the debtors, the creditors, and the Chinese workers.

Passage of the Enterprise Bankruptcy Law was delayed in the final years of the process, in large part because academics and government officials had not resolved how best to provide for the payment of employee claims. Under prior law, in certain circumstances, unsecured employee claims were entitled to be paid out of encumbered assets ahead of the claims of lenders secured thereby. Indeed, the last draft of the new law prior to enactment adopted the same scheme. As a result of a major compromise, however, the enacted law provides that only those labor claims that accrued prior to the adoption of the law on August 27, 2006, will be entitled to such priority over secured claims, which otherwise are now entitled to full priority over labor claims. It is important to note, however, that this compromise between employee claims and secured claims is not applicable in the proceedings of those state-owned enterprises ("SOEs") that are enrolled in an existing "Policy Bankruptcy" program, which are explicitly exempted from the effects of the Enterprise Bankruptcy Law.

Notwithstanding the exception for certain SOEs covered under the "Policy Bankruptcy" program, the Enterprise Bankruptcy Law is perhaps most notable for providing a unified law that will apply equally to SOEs and non-SOEs (with certain minor exceptions). By contrast, the prior Chinese insolvency laws and regulations failed to cover more than 4.9 million domestic private enterprises. This is a new development in Chinese bankruptcy law that should level the playing field across the government/private sector divide, and make it easier for all companies to obtain credit in a competitive market. Especially with respect to non-SOEs (of which there are now many, including publicly held companies as well as former SOEs that have been privatized), the new law offers an avenue for improving financial performance by restructuring and reducing outstanding debt.

The driving force behind China's willingness to finally adopt sweeping bankruptcy reform arose out of the need to address the consequences of its socialist state-directed economy, in which national banks freely lent money to SOEs to ensure maximum employment of workers, often without regard to the borrowers' efficiency, need, or financial strength. The net result of such a system is an economy filled with inefficient companies and saddled with "non-performing loans" ("NPLs"). Economists estimate that the total amount of NPLs ranges anywhere from $410 billion to $815 billion as of mid-2003, with the amount steadily increasing every year.[7]

Among other notable features of the Enterprise Bankruptcy Law are provisions that:

- allow the debtor to file a voluntary bankruptcy application and then choose either reorganization, conciliation, or liquidation;[8]
- allow creditors to file an involuntary bankruptcy application, and also seek either reorganization or liquidation;[9]
- remove the requirement of government approval for filing bankruptcy applications;[10]
- prescribe the appointment of an administrator to oversee the bankruptcy, but also allow for the debtor to request permission to manage its affairs and property (*i.e.*, to act as a debtor in possession);[11]
- allow for the filing of a plan of reorganization similar in concept to a plan under chapter 11 of the U.S. Bankruptcy Code;[12]
- allow for "cramdown" of certain creditors who do not consent to the proposed plan of reorganization;[13]
- acknowledge the concept of "debtor-in-possession" loans;[14]
- impose an "automatic stay" against creditors that temporarily prevents them from enforcing their rights against the debtor, including via litigation commenced pre-bankruptcy;[15]
- set forth the procedure for creditors to file claims, as well as provide for convening meetings of creditors and forming a creditors' committee;[16]

---

[7] Weitseng Chen, *WTO: Time's Up for Chinese Banks*, 7 Chi. J. Int'l L. 239, 240–41 (2006).

[8] Enterprise Bankruptcy Law, chs. VIII, IX and X.

[9] *Id.*, art 7.

[10] *Id.*

[11] *Id.*, arts. 22, 73.

[12] *Id.*, arts. 79, 81.

[13] *Id.*, art. 87.

[14] *Id.*, art. 75.

[15] *Id.*, arts. 19–21, 75.

[16] *Id.*, chs. VI, VII.

- give the debtor the choice to dissolve or continue performance of executory contracts, and the ability to recover preferential and fraudulent pre-bankruptcy transfers to creditors;[17]
- limit the value of secured claims to the value of collateral;[18]
- allow auctions and assets sales in certain cases;[19]
- allow suppliers who shipped goods to the debtor pre-bankruptcy to take back such goods that are still on delivery; and[20]
- allow for the setoff of claims, and specify circumstances where setoff would not be appropriate.[21]

The Enterprise Bankruptcy Law gives new flexibility to a greater universe of debtors by providing for reorganization as well as liquidation, and clarifies and strengthens the rights of both debtors and creditors in bankruptcy. Nevertheless, bankruptcy reform in China remains very much a work in progress. Many provisions under the new law—with respect to creditors' rights and remedies, as well as the debtor's abilities in attempting to reorganize—would benefit from clarification or further development. In addition, entirely absent from the new law are provisions (or exceptions from provisions) relating to asset securitization transactions (*e.g.*, repurchase agreements, swap agreements, securities contracts, forward contracts, commodity contracts, and master netting agreements), along with other areas of bankruptcy law.

Recognizing that various "market economy countries have complete bankruptcy legal systems[,] while China has a relatively short history of bankruptcy law legislation," one of the goals of the drafters of the Enterprise Bankruptcy Law was to "pay attention to combining the international experience with the specific situation of China."[22] In order to benefit from the historical and comparative experience of other developed and developing nations, the process of redeveloping China's bankruptcy law has involved the

---

[17] *Id.*, arts. 18, 31–34.

[18] *Id.*, arts. 109–110.

[19] *Id.*, art. 112.

[20] *Id.*, art. 39.

[21] *Id.*, art. 40.

[22] *Explanations on PRC Enterprise Bankruptcy Law (Draft)*, 10th Sess. Standing Comm., Nat'l People's Cong. (June 21, 2004) (statement of Jia Zhijie, Vice Chairman, Fin'l and Econ. Comm., Nat'l People's Cong.) (hereinafter "2004 Draft Explanation").

earnest study by Chinese academics and legislators of varied bankruptcy law systems from around the world.

Certainly, the passage of the Enterprise Bankruptcy Law represents a dramatic step toward creating a legal infrastructure capable of responding to the needs of China's growing economy, as well as the problems that typically accompany such growth. Still, the authors hold that the success of this new law will depend upon fair and consistent application by the courts throughout China, an aspiration that the authors acknowledge is made much more difficult by the influence that local governments outside of China's larger cities likely will exert over the bankruptcy process. There are many foreign investors and skeptics who will be following how the courts apply this new law in the first waves of bankruptcy filings.

It is expected that the Supreme People's Court will promulgate rules, regulations, and "explanations" in the near term that will settle the many practical uncertainties engendered by ambiguities in the language of the Enterprise Bankruptcy Law. To be sure, implementation of the new law will take many years; judges, administrators, and other professionals will become increasingly familiar with both the law and the complex commercial problems it will be called upon to address. During that time, foreign investors can be expected to assess whether the gains represented by the new law are dissipated by subsequent legislation, and whether China's courts are applying the law in a fair and consistent manner.

In order to better understand the Enterprise Bankruptcy Law, we provide some context out of which the law arose and how it compares to the U.S. bankruptcy model. In Chapter One, we discuss the structure of the Chinese government and its court system and the principal forms of commercial enterprise that exist in China. In order to understand the origins of the new law, we review in detail in Chapter Two the bankruptcy laws that were passed in 1986 and in 1991. In Chapter Three, we address general concepts regarding obtaining collateral and enforcing creditor remedies in China. In Chapters Four through Nine we provide an overview of the Enterprise Bankruptcy Law and a detailed analysis of its provisions. We also provide a comparison of important provisions under the new law to comparative sections in the U.S. Bankruptcy Code to assist the reader in understanding how these provisions work. Finally in Chapter Ten, we discuss cross-border issues relating to foreign insolvency proceedings in China, specifically with reference to the UNCITRAL *Model Law on Cross-Border Insolvency*.

A note about translation: the analysis of Chinese law presented in this book is based on translations of Chinese statutes, regulations, and other materials. Readers are cautioned to look to the original Chinese text of such sources for definitive interpretations of the law. Lastly, nothing contained in this book should be considered as the rendering of legal advice, and readers are responsible for obtaining such advice from their own legal counsel. This book is intended for educational and informational purposes only.

CHAPTER ONE: Bankruptcy Law in the People's Republic of China

Before analyzing the Enterprise Bankruptcy Law, it will be helpful first to understand the context in which bankruptcy law has developed in the PRC, as well as the basics of both the PRC legal system and the bankruptcy laws that led up to the enactment of the new law.

1.1 The March Toward a Market Economy

The PRC was founded in 1949 by the Communist Party of China. Espousing the doctrine of historical determinism, which provided that the Party was the primary means of transforming China from a feudalistic society into a Communist utopian society, the new government established a state-planned economic system in which the "whole people" owned all assets and means of production. Commercial and industrial enterprises were owned and operated directly or indirectly by the state, which took on the role of providing for the livelihoods and well-being of the nation's workers from "cradle to grave."

Although concepts of enterprise insolvency and bankruptcy existed in China before 1949,[1] they became *non sequiturs* in the new regime. The old laws had been abolished, and the very idea of the failure of SOEs was incompatible with doctrine. Some SOEs experiencing economic difficulties may have been merged into other entities, or even quietly wound down; as a practical matter, however, they were most often simply supported and allowed to carry on because they played an integral social-services role in the fabric of society.

After enduring disastrous economic policies in the 1950s and 1960s, and following President Nixon's visit in 1971, the PRC gradually opened its doors again to the world. When Deng Xiaoping came to power in 1978, he set in motion economic reforms to replace the Communist utopian ideal with "market socialism"—a more pragmatic market-driven model that nonetheless still featured strong centralized control over the economy and government. Since then, the PRC's average annual economic growth rate has

---

[1] *See, generally, Qing Bankruptcy Law* (1906); *Guomindang Bankruptcy Law* (1935).

been approximately 10%, fueled in part by foreign investment that continues to increase annually.[2]

In conjunction with encouraging the growth of the private sector during this period, the PRC government also attempted to reform its state sector. The new spirit of economic reform led some to acknowledge the reality that many SOEs were insolvent and inefficiently operated, and that a way was needed to address the problems of unprofitable businesses. To rescue poorly managed, money-losing SOEs and unlock the value of their underutilized assets, China began a process of "systematic transformation" of SOEs into private enterprises, and has allowed foreign investors to participate.

As the flow of foreign investment into China increased, the legal infrastructure for investment also grew. Where once special regulations were enacted on an *ad hoc* basis by local authorities, a national infrastructure for foreign investment enterprises and domestic enterprises alike began to take shape. These innovations continue to become simultaneously more robust and unified on one hand, and more broad-based on the other. For example, in 1980, China had no private property rights and no explicit private enterprise ownership. Since then, however, China has engaged in sustained and prodigious legislative development, as characterized by more than 400 national laws, 2,700 state decrees, and 10,000 administrative regulations and local provisions. These measures include a new Property Law[3] and amendments to the Constitution of the PRC that recognize and provide for protection of private property rights for the first time since the beginning of the Communist era.

Many of the most recent developments are clearly the result of China's efforts to comply with the membership requirements of the World Trade Organization ("WTO"), which it joined at the end of 2001. In 2002, the PRC government claimed that, after reviewing 2,300 laws and regulations, it had abolished 830 of them and amended 325.[4]

As the following table demonstrates, the Enterprise Bankruptcy Law is but one among the most recent of the many new market-economy laws that

---

[2] Foreign direct investment in China has increased from $3.5 billion in 1990 to more than $60 billion in 2004 and $72 billion in 2005. GDP Growth 1952–2007, *http://www/chinability.com/GDP.htm*; FDI Inflows in US$ Billion, 1984–2005, *http://www/chinability.com/FDI.htm* (updated as of May 4, 2008; last visited June 3, 2008).

[3] Promulgated by the Nat'l People's Cong., Mar. 16, 2007, effective Oct. 1, 2007.

[4] Statement of Xie Feng, Chinese Embassy Spokesperson (July 22, 2002).

have been enacted in China. It is against the context of this paradigm shift in the PRC's economic foundation that development of modern bankruptcy laws in China should be viewed.

30 Years of New PRC Laws	
1979	Sino-Foreign Equity Joint Ventures Law
1985	Foreign Economic Contracts Law (repealed by Contract Law)
1986	General Principles of Civil Law
1986	Wholly Foreign-Owned Enterprises Law
1986	Enterprise Bankruptcy Law (Trial Implementation)
1988	State-Owned Enterprises Law
1988	Sino-Foreign Cooperative Joint Ventures Law
1989	Administrative Litigation Law
1990	Sino-Foreign Equity Joint Ventures Law (amended)
1991	Civil Procedure Law (revised)
1993	Company Law
1993	Unfair Competition Law
1994	Arbitration Law
1995	Commercial Banking Law
1995	Insurance Law
1995	Secured Interests Law
1996	Foreign Investment Enterprises Liquidation Procedures
1996	Procedures for Administration of the Provision of Security to Foreign Entities by Domestic Institutions Inside China
1998	Implementing Rules Regarding Procedures for Administration of the Provision of Security to Foreign Entities by Domestic Institutions Inside China
1998	Securities Law
1999	Contract Law
2000	Opinion of the Supreme People's Court on Several Issues Concerning the Application of the Secured Interests Law
2000	Wholly Foreign-Owned Enterprises Law (amended)
2000	Sino-Foreign Cooperative Joint Ventures Law (amended)
2001	Sino-Foreign Equity Joint Ventures Law (amended)
2001	Trust Law

30 Years of New PRC Laws	
2002	Explanation of the Supreme People's Court on Several Issues Concerning Trial of Enterprise Bankruptcy Cases
2002	Provisional Regulations on Restructuring State-Owned Enterprises Using Foreign Investment
2003	Provisional Regulations on Acquisition of Domestic Enterprises by Foreign Investors
2003	Provisional Regulations on Administration of the Transfer State-Owned Assets and Equity of Enterprises
2005	Regulations on Non-Performing Asset Disposal by Foreign Investment Enterprises
2005	Company Law (amended)
2005	Securities Law (amended)
2005	Measures on Administration of Strategic Investment by Foreign Investors in Listed Companies
2006	Measures on Administration of Takeover of Listed Companies
2006	*Enterprise Bankruptcy Law*
2007	Civil Procedure Law (amended)
2007	Labor Dispute Mediation and Arbitration Law
2007	Labor Contract Law
2007	Antimonopoly Law
2007	Property Law

1.2 Chinese Legislative Institutions and the Legislative Process

1.2.1 Legislative Institutions

At the national level, the legislative functions of government are performed by the National People's Congress ("NPC"), its Standing Committee, and the State Council (including its various ministries and commissions). Local governments are permitted to enact regulations to address local needs, provided that they are consistent with national legislation; these functions are performed by institutions that largely mirror the national legislative organizational structure.

1.2.1.1 National People's Congress

The NPC is the "highest organ of State power," with direct supervision over the State Council, the Supreme People's Court, the Supreme People's

Procuratorate, and the Central Military Commission.[5] The NPC is a single-chamber body composed of approximately 3,000 delegates from the country's twenty-three provinces,[6] five autonomous regions,[7] four municipalities under the direct supervision of the central government,[8] and the armed forces.[9]

The NPC meets once a year to hear testimony on and examine the work reports submitted by the Standing Committee of the NPC, the State Council, the Supreme People's Court and the Supreme People's Procuratorate. During that time, the NPC also examines and approves the yearly state budget, as well as plans for the national economy and for social development.

Pursuant to the PRC Constitution, the NPC is also vested with China's legislative power.[10] Its functions include amending the Constitution, supervising its implementation and enforcement, and enacting and amending "basic laws."[11] Other functions of the NPC include electing the President and Vice-President of the PRC; ratifying the President's choices for Premier, Vice-Premiers of the State Council, and Ministers; and electing the President of the Supreme People's Court, the Procurator-General of the Supreme People's Procuratorate, and the Chairman of the Central Military Commission. When the NPC is in session, most decisions are made by the Presidium, a group of some 200 members.

1.2.1.2 Standing Committee of the NPC

Consisting of approximately 150–200 members appointed by each new NPC at its first session, the Standing Committee of the NPC today exercises

---

[5] *Constitution of the People's Republic of China*, adopted Dec. 4, 1982, as amended (hereinafter the "PRC Constitution"), arts. 57, 63.

[6] This number includes Taiwan.

[7] The five autonomous regions (Inner Mongolia, Ningxia, Xinjiang, Tibet, and Guangxi Zhuang) have the same status as provinces.

[8] These municipalities are Beijing, Shanghai, Tianjin and Chongqing.

[9] PRC Const., art. 59.

[10] *Id.*, art. 58. The NPC also has final authority over the judiciary and executive branches of government, and is empowered to approve the establishment of provinces, autonomous regions, and municipalities under the direct supervision of the central government; establish special administrative regions; and declare war and mobilize the armed forces.

[11] The term "basic law" has not been officially defined, but generally refers to national legislation that has a significant impact on fundamental rights and obligations, including legislation such as the major codes. The significance of any distinction is unclear, however, given that other bodies (including the NPC's Standing Committee and the State Council) have taken the lead in developing laws and regulations that significantly affect fundamental rights and obligations.

most of the NPC's legislative powers, and is thus the supreme legislative body of the PRC. Meeting approximately six times each year, the Standing Committee is responsible for the interpretation and enforcement of the PRC Constitution,[12] as well as the enactment, interpretation, and amendment of the laws.[13] Since the beginning of the "Open Door" era in 1979, the Standing Committee has enacted more than 400 laws.[14]

The *Rules of Procedure of the National People's Congress of the People's Republic of China*[15] and the Legislation Law of the People's Republic of China[16] set forth the national-level legislative process. Any NPC delegate may introduce a legislative proposal,[17] which requires the support of thirty-eight other NPC delegates in order to be formally submitted for consideration. Upon submission, the proposal is sent to special committees of the NPC for examination and discussion. Normally, the bill is then sent to the Legislative Affairs Committee (a working committee of the Standing Committee), which researches the subject, recommends any necessary changes, and finalizes the draft for submission either to the Standing Committee or directly to the NPC. If adopted by a majority vote, the proposal will be promulgated into law by Order of the President of the PRC.

1.2.1.3 State Council

Notwithstanding the role of the Standing Committee of the NPC, the State Council (sometimes referred to as the Central People's Government) is *de facto* the most powerful legislative body in the PRC. Technically the "executive agency" of the NPC, the State Council supervises the various ministries, bureaus, commissions, and local governments as the highest organ of state administration. But it also has power under the PRC Constitution

---

[12] In the PRC, interpretation of the Constitution is the purview of the NPC and the Standing Committee rather than the courts. *See* PRC Const., art. 67.

[13] *Id.*, arts. 65, 66, 67. The Standing Committee is not empowered to amend the Constitution or to enact "basic laws" (which instead are enacted by the NPC), but it may amend such laws and pass other regulations, and interpret all. The Standing Committee also supervises the People's Courts and the appointment of judges.

[14] In addition, the standing committees of local people's congresses throughout the country have enacted thousands of local rules and regulations.

[15] Promulgated by the Nat'l People's Cong., Apr. 4, 1989.

[16] Promulgated by the Nat'l People's Cong., Mar. 15, 2000 (hereinafter the "Legislation Law").

[17] PRC Const., art. 72. In addition, the Presidium of the NPC, the Standing Committee, the State Council, and the Supreme People's Court may submit bills.

to issue administrative rules and regulations, orders, and directives within the jurisdiction of its various subsidiary departments,[18] which amounts to legislation by administrative fiat.[19]

Such "administrative regulations" have the power of law, prevailing over provincial laws and other local regulations, and are subordinate only to the PRC Constitution, the basic laws of the NPC, and the national laws of the Standing Committee. The State Council and its departments have issued thousands of administrative regulations, and more than 70% of the bills considered by the NPC or the Standing Committee are initiated or drafted by the State Council.

The State Council's subsidiary departments include a General Office and twenty-seven ministries and commissions that administrate various aspects of the central government. The most important ministries and commissions within the context of this book's discussion include the MOF, the Ministry of Commerce ("MOFCOM"),[20] the People's Bank of China, and the State Development and Reform Commission.

In addition, more than forty specialized organizations are administrated by the State Council, despite the fact that they are not components of the State Council. Many of these operate almost as ministries, and include the State-owned Asset Supervision and Administration Commission ("SASAC"), the State Administration of Industry and Commerce ("SAIC"), the China Securities Regulatory Commission, the China Insurance Regulatory Commission, and the China Banking Regulatory Commission. In addition, several state bureaus are administered by the State Council's various ministries and commissions, including the SAFE.

The State Council reports to the NPC at its annual session, and to the Standing Committee at all other times. It is headed by the Premier, and is composed of Vice-Premiers, State Councilors, Ministers, Chief Commissioners, the Auditor-General, and the Secretary-General, all of whom are appointed by the NPC or the Standing Committee.

---

[18] PRC Const., arts. 89, 90.

[19] Seemingly by design, the language of Chinese laws is often vague or ambiguous, leaving opportunities for administrative agencies to issue implementing rules and regulations that supplement and interpret the law as the agency deems necessary and appropriate. Notably, some administrative regulations reflecting internal rules or policy directives about interpretation and implementation sometimes remain confidential and unpublished, and may not be disclosed to foreign parties.

[20] Previously incarnated as MOFTEC.

1.2.2 China's Courts

The judicial system of the PRC, collectively known as the "People's Courts," was originally established in the early 1950s, but thereafter has been reorganized pursuant to the Organic Law of the People's Courts.[21] The People's Courts today may be grouped into four categories: (i) the Supreme People's Court; (ii) local courts of various levels; (iii) military courts; and (iv) specialty courts.[22]

The Supreme People's Court is the highest court in the land.[23] In addition to functioning as the final court of appeal, the Supreme People's Court has jurisdiction (albeit rarely exercised) as a court of first instance with respect to civil and commercial cases of great national significance. The Supreme People's Court also has authority to issue judicial interpretations on the application of laws.

The local courts of the PRC include more than 3,000 Basic People's Courts, approximately 375 Intermediate People's Courts, and thirty-one Higher People's Courts.[24] The Basic People's Courts are the lowest level in the court system. Established at the county level, they hear civil disputes as courts of first instance unless otherwise provided by law. The Intermediate People's Courts, established at the major-municipal and prefectural levels, have original jurisdiction with respect to major cases involving foreign nationals, cases of significance within their respective jurisdictional territories, and other cases as may be designated by the Supreme People's Court. The Higher People's Courts, established at the provincial level and in China's autonomous regions (as well as in the four municipalities governed directly by the central government), may exercise jurisdiction as courts of first instance with respect to matters that are of significance within their respective jurisdictional territories.

---

[21] Adopted by the Nat'l People's Cong., July 1, 1979; revised 1983, 1986, and 2006.

[22] *See* PRC Const., art. 124. This discussion does not consider the People's Procuratorates, which are organized under the revised *Organic Law of the People's Procuratorates*, adopted by the Nat'l People's Cong., July 1, 1979. Generally, the procuratorates are entrusted with supervision of the courts and administrative tribunals, investigation and prosecution of illegal conduct of government officials, and investigation and prosecution of threats to public security.

[23] PRC Const., art. 127.

[24] *Organic Law of the People's Courts, art. 2; see also Civil Procedure Law of the People's Republic of China*, ch. II, section I.

Specialty courts handle maritime, railroad, and traffic matters (among other areas of responsibility). In contrast to the United States, China lacks bankruptcy courts or judges that specialize in bankruptcy law. Instead, bankruptcy cases or proceedings are filed and heard just like any other civil matters, and they normally are handled by the Basic People's Courts or Intermediate People's Courts. In some provinces, however, China recently has begun to establish divisions within the People's Court that are to specialize in bankruptcy law.[25]

1.2.3 Interpretation of Laws

The Chinese legal system is a civil-law system (with "Chinese characteristics," as the Chinese say), rather than a common-law system as in the United States or the United Kingdom. Thus, no doctrine of judicial precedent exists, and case law is not binding upon (and is seldom referred to in) court judgments. Instead, the Chinese legal system relies heavily on legal codes and related administrative guidance for the implementation of statutes. Very often, however, Chinese laws are drafted in general principles and vague terms.

Interpretation of such laws is carried out by government agencies (and increasingly, by the People's Supreme Court) pursuant to delegation of the Standing Committee's power.[26] The following definitions of interpretations may be useful in understanding this relationship.

"Legislative interpretation" – The Standing Committee of the NPC may interpret the Constitution, the basic laws enacted by the NPC, and its own national laws. Likewise, the standing committees of provincial people's congresses may interpret and resolve issues regarding application of their own local regulations and rules.

"Administrative interpretation" – The State Council may interpret administrative laws in connection with problems arising from their actual application (other than in an adjudicative context).

---

[25] *See* Annabel Allen, *Critique: China's Draft Bankruptcy Law*, AsiaLaw, May 2005 (reporting establishment of bankruptcy courts in southern China and in larger cities such as Beijing and Shanghai).

[26] The Standing Committee is granted power to interpret statutes by Article 67(4) of the PRC Constitution; *see also* ch. IV of the Legislation Law. Such power is delegated pursuant to the *Resolution on Strengthening the Work of Interpretation of Laws*, adopted by the Standing Comm., Nat'l People's Cong., June 10, 1981.

"Judicial interpretation" – The Supreme People's Court and the Supreme People's Procuratorate may interpret laws within the context of trial and procuratorial work, respectively.

Although judicial interpretations are not legislation *per se*, they have the effect of law on lower courts.[27] The Supreme People's Court often has used this power to issue judicial interpretations on certain laws to guide their implementation, sometimes shortly after the laws become effective. A judicial interpretation of the Enterprise Bankruptcy Law is reportedly in process.

1.3 The Chinese Banking System and the NPL Market in China

China's economy continues to surge ahead, led by exports and capital investment, and is now the second largest economy in the world. With China's rapid economic development, substantial effort has been devoted to reforming China's banking system in recent years. The People's Bank of China is the central bank and the foundation of the banking system. As of January 1, 2007, China had three policy banks (established for the purposes of policy lending, as opposed to commercial lending), four state-owned commercial banks,[28] thirteen shareholding commercial banks, 112 city commercial banks, and 626 credit cooperatives and other financial institutions.

China's state-owned commercial banks have been the mainstay of the state's financial system and have played an important role in economic development, primarily as channels for raising and allocating capital. In addition, the state-owned banks in the past also operated as entities engaged in policy lending. In 1995, the Chinese government introduced the Commercial Banking Law to commercialize the operations of the four state-owned banks. At the same time, China was facing the significant and increasing problems of non-performing loans, which were beginning to undermine the stability of the banking system and the efficient operation of markets. In fact, the vast majority of the NPLs were extended by China's four state-owned commercial banks to SOEs. It was evident to the Chinese government that working out NPLs would be a critical and necessary step for banking reform in China.

---

[27] Several Provisions on Judicial Interpretation, issued by the Supreme People's Court, June 23, 1997, art. 4.

[28] The "Big Four" state-owned commercial banks are Bank of China ("BOC"), China Construction Bank ("CCB"), Agricultural Bank of China ("ABC"), and Industrial and Commercial Bank of China ("ICBC").

In 1999, to address the NPL situation, the Chinese government established Asset Management Companies ("AMCs") for the integrated management and disposal of the NPLs. The four government-authorized AMCs were Cinda, Huarong, Great Wall and Orient. AMCs purchased non-performing loans in the amount of 1.4 trillion RMB at book value from five state banks.[29] According to statistics released by the China Banking Regulatory Commission ("CBRC"), from their establishment in 1999 to the end of 2006, the four Chinese AMCs had disposed of NPLs of 1,210.282 billion RMB. An aggregate of 211 billion RMB of cash was recovered.

Meanwhile, a number of governmental authorities, including the State Administration of Foreign Exchange ("SAFE"), the National Development and Reform Commission ("NDRC"), Ministry of Foreign Trade and Economic Cooperation ("MOFTEC"), Ministry of Finance ("MOF") and others, promulgated a series of rules and regulations related to foreign investment in the NPL market in China.

In October 2001, the Ministry of Finance, the People's Bank of China and MOFTEC jointly released the *Interim Provisions on Drawing Foreign Capital into the Asset Restructuring and Disposal by Financial Asset Management Companies* (the "AMC Provisions"). According to the AMC Provisions, AMCs may restructure and dispose of the assets they possess by drawing on foreign capital. It is clear that the emphasis of the AMC Provisions was to encourage and facilitate foreign capital investment in the NPLs, introduce more sophisticated management techniques, and to promote innovation within the enterprises and the reform of state-owned enterprises in order to establish a more modern enterprise system for disposal of the NPLs.

In the past, foreign investors that purchased NPL portfolios from the Chinese NPL market often entrusted the domestic AMCs with oversight of the NPLs. Foreign investors, however, increasingly preferred a larger role in dealing with the NPLs and, to that end, have often entered into project-based joint venture companies with AMCs for the acquisition and disposal of specific NPL portfolios. It should be noted that only the Ministry of

---

[29] Specifically, Cinda purchased NPLs in the amount of 394.4 billion RMB from CCB and State Development Bank; Huarong purchased NPLs in the amount of 407.7 billion RMB from ICBC; Great Wall purchased NPLs in the amount of 345.8 billion RMB from ABC; and Orient purchased NPLs in the amount of 267.4 billion RMB from BOC.

Commerce at its headquarters has the power to approve the establishment of such a joint venture.[30]

China allows foreign investors to acquire NPL portfolios through an overseas special-purpose vehicle ("SPV") directly. In its *Circular of Relevant Issues on the Control of Foreign Exchanges relating to the Use of Foreign Capital for Non-performing Asset Disposal of Financial Asset Management Companies,*[31] SAFE has set out rules for wiring acquisition payments into China and the disposal of proceeds out of China. Also, the People's Bank of China and State Taxation Bureau have issued regulations concerning domestic collections bank accounts for overseas SPVs operating in China established for the disposal of NPLs, and related taxation issues.

Finally, it is significant that the Chinese government has played an active part in the macro-regulation of NPL markets through the implementation of measures on transnational acquisitions of NPLs. Specifically, according to the *Circular Concerning the Regulation of the Archival Filing Administration of Alienating Bad Claims to Foreign Parties by Financial Institutions,*[32] foreign investors are restricted from purchasing three categories of NPLs: (i) any NPL with, or guaranteed by, the Chinese government at any level or its administrative department as the debtor, (ii) any NPL of any enterprise falling within the prohibited category of the *Catalog of Industries for Guiding Foreign Investment*[33] or involving any industry of national security, and (iii) any other NPL forbidden by laws and regulations from being sold to foreign parties. Moreover, the Circular requires foreign investors to pay the sale price in its entirety for those NPLs that may be purchased by foreign investors. For foreign investors, this means that they will have to face a higher threshold to enter the Chinese NPL market.

1.4 Commercial Enterprises in the PRC

The commercial landscape of the PRC once reflected more closely the country's socialistic roots than it does today. At one time, all of China's companies were owned by the state; as a result, the early development of the bankruptcy system focused primarily on liquidation of SOEs. Accompanying the development of an increasingly market-oriented economy, however, was the emergence of business

---

[30] *See Circular on Strengthening the Administration of Examination and Approval of Utilizing Foreign Investment for Bad Asset Disposal*, promulgated by the General Office, Ministry of Commerce, Apr. 29, 2005.

[31] Promulgated by the SAFE, Dec. 17, 2004.

[32] Issued by the NDRC and SAFE, Feb. 1, 2007.

[33] Promulgated by the NDRC and MOFCOM, revised Nov. 7, 2007, effective Dec. 1, 2007.

entities other than SOEs, including various forms of private enterprises with domestic and/or foreign investment. The Enterprise Bankruptcy Law addresses this wider array of enterprises in China that may have need of its provisions.

1.4.1 Legal Persons

One of the basic concepts in Chinese company law is that of the "legal person" (as opposed to a natural person). *The General Principals of Civil Law of the People's Republic of China* (the "GPCL")[34] defines a legal person as "an organization which possesses . . . capacity for civil acts and which, in accordance with law, independently enjoys civil rights and assumes civil obligations."[35] The GPCL further provides that a legal person must:

(1) be established according to law;
(2) possess necessary capital or property;
(3) have its own name, organizational structure, and premises; and
(4) be able to assume civil liability independently.[36]

In short, legal persons under Chinese law may own assets, sue, and be sued in their own name. PRC law recognizes various types of organizations as having legal personhood, including government agencies, institutions, certain associations, and "enterprise legal persons." Partnerships and sole proprietorships do not qualify as legal persons under the GPCL, which treats them under the chapter devoted to "Citizens (Natural Persons)" rather than the separate chapter devoted to "Legal Persons."[37]

The capacity of a legal person for civil acts and obligations begins upon its establishment and ends upon its dissolution. Several laws govern the various types of legal persons, and related regulations govern the procedures for their establishment. In general, however, legal persons come into existence on the date they are registered with the SAIC.

1.4.2 Enterprise Legal Persons

For purposes of our discussion, the most important category of legal persons is the "enterprise legal person." An enterprise legal person is any

---

[34] Promulgated by the Nat'l People's Cong., Apr. 12, 1986, effective Jan. 1, 1987.

[35] GPCL, art. 36.

[36] *Id.*, art. 37.

[37] *See* GPCL, chs. II and III. This book generally will not address entities that are not enterprise legal persons and therefore not eligible to be debtors under Article 2 of the Enterprise Bankruptcy Law, such as sole proprietorships and partnerships.

commercial or industrial enterprise that is a state-owned, collectively-owned,[38] or privately-owned legal person that has received all necessary governmental approvals and is registered with the SAIC. Private enterprises having legal person status generally take the form of limited liability companies and companies limited by shares. Furthermore, the GPCL acknowledges two broad categories of enterprise legal persons: those that are domestic, and those with foreign investment.[39]

1.4.2.1 State-Owned Enterprises

According to the *State-Owned Enterprise Law of the People's Republic of China* (the "SOE Law"),[40] an SOE is "a socialist commodity production and operation unit that shall, in accordance with law, make its own managerial decisions, take full responsibility for its own profits and losses, and practice independent accounting."[41] SOEs are limited liability companies inasmuch as, technically, they bear civil liability only to the extent of the property that the state has entrusted to their operation and management.[42]

Thousands of SOEs exist in China, each of which was formed and is directly or indirectly supervised by the central, provincial, or other local governments. As discussed in section 2.4, many require some restructuring.

1.4.2.2 Business Forms Under the Company Law

The *Company Law of the People's Republic of China* (the "Company Law")[43] provides the basic legal framework for the formation of private enterprises[44]

---

[38] *See* Alan Tang, *Insolvency in China and Hong Kong: A Practitioner's Perspective* 193 (Sweet & Maxwell Asia 2005). Collectively-owned enterprises are industrial enterprises where the means of production are owned by collectives, rather than by the state. These include urban and rural enterprises that were formerly privately owned but have been registered by the industrial and commercial administration agency as collective units capable of raising funds from the public. *Id.*

[39] GPCL, art. 41. *See also Provisions Concerning Enterprise Registration Classifications*, issued jointly by the State Statistics Bureau and the SAIC, Aug. 28, 1998 (providing for three categories, instead of two, by dividing non-domestic enterprises into enterprises with investment from Hong Kong, Macau, and Taiwan and enterprises with investment from other foreign sources).

[40] Adopted by the Nat'l People's Cong., Apr. 13, 1988.

[41] SOE Law, art. 2.

[42] GPCL, art. 48.

[43] Adopted by the Standing Comm., Nat'l People's Cong., Dec. 29, 1993, effective July 1, 1994; amended Dec. 25, 1999, Aug. 28, 2004, and Oct. 27, 2005.

[44] "Private enterprise" applies here in the sense of market-oriented and non state-owned. As will be discussed, certain types of such private enterprise may be public companies.

in China. The law contemplates two forms of company—the limited liability company ("LLC") and the company limited by shares ("CLS," also known as a joint stock company). These forms are similar in many respects, including in providing limited liability for investors and in their corporate governance structures and processes.[45] The Company Law also permits conversion of SOEs into LLCs and CLSs.

The Company Law applies to domestic companies and to companies with foreign investment registered in the PRC alike, although the latter also are subject to many other laws and regulations.

1.4.2.2.1 Limited Liability Companies

A limited liability company is defined in the Company Law as an enterprise with legal person status that meets certain minimum requirements for registered capital (depending on the type of business engaged in by the company), and in which the liability of each investor is limited to its capital contribution.[46] Furthermore, an LLC must have at least two, but not more than fifty, investors.[47] No limitation on foreign investment has been established.

Although LLC investors are typically called shareholders, the capital of an LLC is not divided into individual shares of equal value, and the company does not issue shares; thus, an LLC cannot apply for listing on a public exchange without first converting to the CLS form (as will be discussed). Instead, an investor's interest is represented by certificates evidencing its percentage holding in the company. Transferring interests from an investor to a non-investor requires the consent of a majority of the owners.

1.4.2.2.2 Foreign Investment Enterprises

Companies in China with some degree of foreign direct investment are known as foreign investment enterprises ("FIEs"), and typically take one of three principal forms.[48] The formation, structure, and operation of such foreign investment LLCs are subject to additional laws and regulations, many

[45] One of the major differences is that a CLS may issue shares to the public and list shares on public exchanges.

[46] Company Law, art. 3.

[47] Exceptions to this rule are SOEs and foreign investment enterprises, which may have as few as one investor.

[48] Certain other forms will be discussed in this Section.

of which will be discussed in this section.[49] In addition, FIEs are subject to several other special laws and regulations regarding (in part) foreign exchange controls, tax treatment, labor relations, and market access.[50]

Equity Joint Ventures

An equity joint venture ("EJV") is an LLC formed by one or more Chinese parties, together with one or more foreign parties, in accordance with the *Sino-Foreign Equity Joint Ventures Law of the People's Republic of China* (the "EJV Law")[51] and its implementing regulations (the "EJV Regulations").[52] The parties enter into a joint venture contract and contribute capital in the form of cash, equipment, know-how, and property rights. Such investments are not necessarily made in monetary terms; typically, the Chinese party contributes labor and premises. The venture attains legal person status upon approval of the joint venture contract and related documents by the relevant economic and trade authorities, and subsequent registration of the enterprise by the SAIC.

Profits and losses are shared by the parties according to the proportion of their respective contributions to the equity of the company, and the liability of any party is limited to its subscribed capital.[53] Foreign participation of at least 25% is required to enjoy policies favorable to foreign investors, but generally there is no upper limit unless set by specific regulation.

Cooperative Joint Ventures

A cooperative joint venture ("CJV") is a company formed by one or more Chinese parties, together with one or more foreign parties,

---

[49] In fact, the laws and regulations governing the three principal forms of FIE actually predate the Company Law, which expressly provides that it applies to LLCs with foreign investment subject to the rules and regulations governing FIEs. *See* Company Law, art. 18.

[50] For example, FIEs must comply with the *Catalog of Industry Guidelines for Foreign Investment*, which sets forth categories of industries in which foreign participation is prohibited, restricted, permitted, or encouraged. Some areas in the non-prohibited categories are reserved exclusively for joint ventures.

[51] Adopted by the Nat'l People's Cong., July 1, 1979; amended Apr. 4, 1990 and Mar. 15, 2001.

[52] *Detailed Rules for the Implementation of the Sino-Foreign Equity Joint Ventures Law of the People's Republic of China*, promulgated by the State Council, Sept. 20, 1983; amended Jan. 15, 1986, Dec. 21, 1987, and July 21, 2001.

[53] EJV Law, art. 4.

in accordance with the *Sino-Foreign Cooperative Joint Ventures Law of the People's Republic of China* (the "CJV Law")[54] and its implementing regulations (the "CJV Regulations").[55] The parties may seek to establish a CJV for many of the same reasons as an EJV, but the CJV form offers greater flexibility in two major respects. First, the parties may decide to structure the venture as something similar to a partnership, in which they simply cooperate in connection with a specific project, or else as an incorporated venture with characteristics similar to an EJV. Second, the parties may agree by means of their joint venture contract to share the profits and losses in any manner they choose, rather than strictly according to the ratio of their capital contributions.

Where the CJV takes the first form, the investing parties own the venture's assets and share its liabilities according to their contracted terms, but the venture has neither legal person status nor limited liability.[56] Where the CJV takes the latter form (i.e., similar to an EJV), however, the venture may obtain legal person status once registered as an LLC.[57] In practice, the majority of CJVs are established as LLCs.

Even where the CJV takes the LLC form, however, profits and losses are shared according to the terms of the joint venture contract between the parties, which need not allocate according to the ratio of the parties' capital contributions.[58] This feature, which results in CJVs sometimes being called "contractual" joint ventures, imparts a degree of flexibility that EJVs (and other LLCs) do not enjoy. In practice, the foreign party generally receives a higher proportion of profits in the early years, while the Chinese party becomes the owner of the venture's assets upon its termination.

---

[54] Adopted by the Nat'l People's Cong., Apr. 16, 1998; revised by the Standing Comm., Nat'l People's Cong., Oct. 31, 2000.

[55] *Detailed Rules for the Implementation of the Sino-Foreign Cooperative Joint Ventures Law of the People's Republic of China*, issued by MOFTEC, Sept. 4, 1995; *Interpretation of the Implementation of Certain Articles of the Detailed Rules for the Implementation of the Sino-Foreign Cooperative Joint Ventures Law of the People's Republic of China*, issued by MOFTEC, Oct. 22, 1996.

[56] CJV Law, art. 2; CJV Regulations, art. 14. Thus, not all FIEs are LLCs, because some CJVs may not have legal person status. In addition, FIEs may also take other forms, such as the company limited by shares (as will be discussed).

[57] CJV Regulations, art. 14.

[58] CJV Law, arts. 2, 22.

Wholly Foreign-Owned Enterprises

A wholly foreign-owned enterprise ("WFOE") is an enterprise legal person established within Chinese territory in accordance with the *Wholly Foreign-Owned Enterprises Law of the People's Republic of China* (the "WFOE Law")[59] and its implementing regulations (the "WFOE Regulations"),[60] with registered capital provided entirely by one or more foreign investors. A WFOE generally takes the form of a LLC, but it also can take other forms with governmental authorization. Where the WFOE is an LLC, the foreign party's liability is limited to its subscribed investment.[61]

1.4.2.2.3 Companies Limited by Shares

The second corporate form provided for in the Company Law is the CLS, otherwise known as a joint stock company. A CLS is a limited-liability enterprise similar in concept to the public corporation familiar in many Western legal systems. Compared to LLCs, CLSs require more registered capital, and other requirements for formation and governance are generally more restrictive. Total capital is divided into shares of equivalent value, and allocated to a theoretically unlimited number of shareholders. The company is liable for its debts to the extent of its assets, and shareholder liability is limited to the extent of individual shareholdings.[62]

Foreign Investment Companies Limited by Shares

In addition to the foregoing company forms, several other business forms also are available to foreign investors, including the foreign investment company limited by shares ("FICLS").[63] According to the *Provisional Regulations on Issues Concerning Establishment of Foreign Investment Companies Limited by Shares* (the "FICLS Regulations"),[64] a FICLS is a combination of the CLS and the EJV in that its total capital is divided into shares of equal

---

[59] Adopted by the Nat'l People's Cong., Apr. 12, 1986; revised Oct. 31, 2000. Enterprises established by Hong Kong, Macau, or Taiwan entities or by Chinese citizens abroad are covered. PRC branches established by foreign enterprises are explicitly excluded.

[60] *Detailed Rules for the Implementation of the Law of the People's Republic of China on Foreign Investment Enterprises,* approved by the State Council, Oct. 28, 1990; revised Apr. 12, 2001.

[61] WFOE Law, art. 8; WFOE Regulations, art. 19. Foreign investors are prohibited from acting to "harm the social order or public interest of China." WFOE Law, art. 4.

[62] Company Law, art. 3.

[63] Other forms, not discussed here, include the foreign investment holding company.

[64] Promulgated by MOFTEC, Jan. 10, 1995.

value that are issued to Chinese and foreign shareholders, whose liability is limited to the extent of their holdings.[65]

The FICLS Regulations permit existing FIEs with a three-year record of profitability to be converted to an FICLS upon approval by MOFCOM. Other PRC laws and policies concerning foreign investment continue to apply after conversion. The FICLS Regulations also permit SOEs to be converted, as long as they have been operating profitably for three of the preceding five years. Foreign shareholders must purchase at least 25% of the shares representing the company's registered capital in freely convertible foreign currency, and the scope and purpose of the FICLS must not be inconsistent with state policy concerning foreign investment enterprises.

[65] FICLS Regulations, art. 2. This article also requires 25% of registered capital to be held by foreign investors. Investment from Hong Kong, Macau, and Taiwan is treated in the same way as foreign investment. *Id.*, art. 27.

CHAPTER TWO: Bankruptcy Law in the PRC Prior to 2007

One of the principal improvements achieved by the enactment and implementation of the Enterprise Bankruptcy Law is the unification of the diverse statutory bases of Chinese bankruptcy law into a single code generally applicable to almost all business entities in every part of the PRC.[1] Prior to enactment and implementation of the Enterprise Bankruptcy Law, China operated under several parallel bankruptcy regimes, each applicable to only certain types of entities and often limited to specific geographic areas. In broad strokes, these separate bankruptcy law systems may be considered as follows.

- The primary bankruptcy statute was the previous *Enterprise Bankruptcy Law of the People's Republic of China (Trial Implementation)* enacted in 1986 (the "1986 Bankruptcy Law"),[2] which applied only to SOEs. In addition, in 1991, a short chapter on bankruptcy applicable to non-SOEs with legal-person status was added to the *Civil Procedure Law of the People's Republic of China* (the "CPL").[3] Together, and as complemented by several judicial interpretations issued by the Supreme People's Court, these two laws provided a liquidation model of bankruptcy.
- Chinese bankruptcy law also began developing on another experimental track in 1994, when the State Council initiated a pilot program for the reorganization of industrial SOEs in certain regions. The program, which came to be known as the "Policy Bankruptcy" program, was eventually extended nationwide and survives the implementation of the Enterprise Bankruptcy Law. The Policy Bankruptcy program was intended largely to protect workers of bankrupt SOEs through resettlement, retraining and priority treatment of their claims.

[1] This book does not address the subjects of insolvency and bankruptcy under the laws of Hong Kong, which continue in force, or of the Republic of China (Taiwan).

[2] Adopted by the Standing Comm., Nat'l People's Cong., Dec. 2, 1986, effective Oct. 1, 1988; repealed June 1, 2007.

[3] Adopted by the Nat'l People's Cong., Apr. 9, 1991, effective same.

- In addition, in 1996, MOFTEC promulgated the *Foreign Investment Enterprises Liquidation Procedures,* addressing the liquidation and dissolution of solvent FIEs. In practice, however, FIEs were handled under the rubric of the subsequently promulgated *Provisions on Several Issues Regarding the Hearing of Enterprise Bankruptcy Proceedings* (the "2002 Explanation").[4,5] Also, the Company Law included provisions for liquidation of solvent companies formed under that law.[6] Essentially, these laws provided for cases of insolvent debtors to fall under proceedings governed by the bankruptcy provisions of the CPL.[7]
- Article 71 of the *Commercial Bank Law of the People's Republic of China*[8] provides that if a commercial bank is unable to pay its debts as they fall due, then the People's Court shall (after obtaining the consent of the China Banking Regulatory Commission) declare it bankrupt. A similar provision is included in the *Insurance Law of the People's Republic of China*[9] (requiring approval from the China Insurance Regulatory Commission).
- Additional local regulations on bankruptcy were enacted on the provincial, prefectural, or municipal level that were applicable to enterprises variously solvent and insolvent, and to foreign and domestic entities alike. These include the *Guangdong Province Company Bankruptcy Regulations,*[10] the *Shenzhen Special Economic Zone Enterprise Bankruptcy Regulations,*[11] and the *Beijing Municipality Liquidation Provisions of Foreign Investment Enterprises.*[12]

A bankruptcy law regime consisting of such a collection of concurrently active bankruptcy statutes, regulations, explanations, and territorial rules

---

[4] *Interpretation No. 23 [2002] of the Supreme People's Court,* adopted at the 1,232nd meeting of the Judicial Committee, Supreme People's Court, July 18, 2002; promulgated by the Supreme People's Court, July 30, 2002, effective Sept. 1, 2002.

[5] *See* Tang, *supra* Chapter One, note 38, at 569.

[6] *See* Company Law, ch. X.

[7] *See, e.g.,* Company Law, arts. 188, 191.

[8] Adopted by the Nat'l People's Cong., May 10, 1995; amended Dec. 27, 2003 (hereinafter the "Commercial Bank Law").

[9] Adopted by the Standing Comm., Nat'l People's Cong., June 30, 1995, revised Oct. 28, 2002 (hereinafter the "Insurance Law").

[10] Drafted by the Standing Comm. Guangdong People's Cong., Aug. 1993.

[11] Enacted by the Standing Comm. Shenzhen People's Cong., Nov. 10, 1993.

[12] Adopted by the Standing Comm. Beijing People's Cong., Aug. 14, 1993.

variously applicable to SOEs and other entities inevitably created an environment of uncertainty in practice. Due to the lack of specialized courts and judges to handle bankruptcy matters, courts throughout the country attempted to implement these diverse bankruptcy laws at their own discretion, and with little centralized guidance.

The 1986 Bankruptcy Law, which applied only to SOEs, dictated a basic division between SOEs and non-SOEs.[13] This division was carried through to the bankruptcy provisions of the CPL as well, which applied to enterprise legal persons (*e.g.*, collectively owned enterprises, EJVs, CJVs, and WFOEs), but explicitly not to SOEs.[14] Thus, under prior bankruptcy law, SOEs fell under the scope of only the 1986 Bankruptcy Law, while private enterprises (if covered at all) came under the scope of the CPL.

By contrast, the Enterprise Bankruptcy Law does not distinguish between SOEs and non-SOEs. Instead, Article 2 of the new law applies to *all* enterprise legal persons. Thus, with a few limited exceptions, most companies would fall within the scope of the new law, regardless of whether it is state-owned.

Former Bankruptcy Regime:

SOEs	**Non-SOEs**	**Financial Institutions**
Enterprise Bankruptcy Law (for Trial Implementation) (1986) "Policy Bankruptcy" Program (1994)	Civil Procedure Law Chapter XIX: Procedures for Bankruptcy of Enterprise Legal Persons (1991)	Commercial Bank Law (Art.71) Insurance Law (Art.86) Securities Law (Art.153)

Now: A Unified Enterprise Bankruptcy Law

Enterprise Bankruptcy Law: Applies Equally to All Enterprise Legal Persons

[13] 1986 Bankruptcy Law, art. 2.

[14] *See* CPL, art. 206 ("The bankruptcy debt repayment process for state-owned enterprises shall be governed by the *Enterprise Bankruptcy Law of the People's Republic of China (For Trial Implementation).*").

2.1 The 1986 Bankruptcy Law

In 1984, delegates to the NPC began discussing the possibility of reintroducing a bankruptcy law to address the problems facing many SOEs. A year later, a draft had been prepared, and by the end of 1986 the first bankruptcy law of Communist China had been adopted by the Standing Committee, becoming effective on November 1, 1988. Although the 1986 Bankruptcy Law contained just forty-three articles in six chapters and provided a framework primarily for the liquidation of SOEs, it nevertheless represented a major step forward at the time.

2.1.1 Initiating a Bankruptcy Case

2.1.1.1 Eligible and Ineligible Entities

As noted previously, only SOEs were eligible to be debtors under the 1986 Bankruptcy Law. Additionally, the 1986 Bankruptcy Law excluded certain entities from being liquidated by explicitly providing that they "shall not be declared bankrupt." Such entities included (i) "public utility enterprises and enterprises that have an important relationship to the national economy and the people's livelihood, for which the relevant government departments grant subsidies or adopt other measures to assist the repayment of debts," and (ii) "enterprises that have obtained guarantees for the repayment of debts within six months from the date of the application for bankruptcy."[15]

2.1.1.2 Two Ways to Commence a Case

Under the 1986 Bankruptcy Law, a bankruptcy case could be commenced either through a voluntary petition by the debtor or an involuntary petition by the debtor's creditors. Under Article 7, creditors could seek to have the debtor declared bankrupt if the debtor was "unable to repay debts that are due." The debtor, too, could file a bankruptcy application if it was "unable to repay debts that are due," but *only* after receiving permission to do so from the "superior department" in charge.[16] Article 7 was to be read together with Article 3, which provided additional factors for the court to consider, such as whether the losses of the debtor were serious and/or were incurred due to poor management.

---

[15] 1986 Bankruptcy Law, art. 3.

[16] *Id.*, art. 8.

In the context of an involuntary filing under the 1986 Bankruptcy Law, the burden of showing the debtor's inability to repay due debts appears to have rested with the creditor. Article 7 provided "when the creditor is submitting the bankruptcy application, it should provide relevant evidence relating to the amount of the claim and to the inability of the debtor to repay the debts that are due." It is unclear what type of evidence was required to be submitted.

The 1986 Bankruptcy Law also did not provide a clear threshold for when a debtor is "unable to repay debts due." The 2002 Explanation addressed this threshold by explaining that a debtor is "unable to repay debts that are due" when the period for the repayment of debts has expired and the debtor "obviously lacks the capacity to repay the debts."[17] Unfortunately, what constituted an "obvious" lack of capacity was not made clear. The 2002 Explanation provided a presumption, however, where the debtor ceased and had not resumed paying its debts.[18]

2.1.1.3 SOEs Contesting an Involuntary Petition

In the event that a creditor initiated a bankruptcy case against an SOE, the involuntary debtor was not without recourse. As Article 9 of the 2002 Explanation clarified, the debtor was allowed to contest the involuntary filing ("if the debtor dissents"). If "the court finds such dissent reasonable," then the court will inform the creditor(s) to bring a civil lawsuit first and will decline the application for bankruptcy.[19] The success of the debtor's dissent was thus subject to the discretion of the People's Court.

2.1.1.4 Involuntary Petition Allows for Possible Reorganization of SOE

Although the 1986 Bankruptcy Law contained a reorganization feature, it was so limited that it could be exercised only by the government, and then only in involuntary cases. Article 17 provided that after a case had been commenced by creditors of an SOE, the government department in charge of the involuntary debtor "may, within three months after the People's Court has accepted the case, apply to carry out reorganization of the enterprise,"

---

[17] 2002 Explanation, art. 31.

[18] *Id.*

[19] *Id.*, art. 9.

and that the period of reorganization cannot exceed two years.[20] Thus, with respect to SOEs against which creditors filed an involuntary petition, the government could intervene and suspend the bankruptcy case by applying for reorganization.

The 1986 Bankruptcy Law did not, however, provide much guidance in the application of this limited reorganization concept. After an application for reorganization was submitted by the government department in charge of the debtor, the SOE was to submit a draft settlement agreement to a meeting of creditors. The agreement was to stipulate the period in which the debtor would repay its debts. Pursuant to Article 19, if this settlement agreement was "recognized by the People's Court," the bankruptcy case would be suspended. As an alternative, Article 21 provided the court with the ability to terminate the reorganization and liquidate the SOE.

2.1.2 Implementation

Chapter V of the 1986 Bankruptcy Law, entitled "Bankruptcy Declarations and Bankruptcy Liquidations," contained 20 articles devoted to the circumstances under which the People's Court could declare an enterprise bankrupt, and provided the procedures for liquidation. Under the 1986 Bankruptcy Law, all bankruptcy cases began as liquidations and proceeded as such, unless the government's reorganization option was invoked.

2.1.2.1 Liquidation Teams

Pursuant to Article 24 of the 1986 Bankruptcy Law, within fifteen days after an enterprise was declared bankrupt, the People's Court was to establish a "liquidation team" to take over management of the bankrupt enterprise. Once established, the liquidation team was responsible for "the keeping, putting into order, appraisal, disposition and distribution of the bankruptcy property."[21] The purpose of establishing the liquidation team was to oversee an orderly liquidation of the enterprise's assets. The liquidation team was further mandated to "carry out necessary civil actions in accordance with the law."[22]

Article 24 provided that the members of the liquidation team were to be designated by the People's Court from among "the superior departments

---

[20] 1986 Bankruptcy Law, art. 17.

[21] *Id.*, art. 24.

[22] *Id.*

in charge, government finance departments, and other relevant departments and professional personnel." In practice, all members of the liquidation team were government representatives; by contrast, the Enterprise Bankruptcy Law envisions the participation of non-governmental professionals (*e.g.*, attorneys, consultants, and bankers) in the bankruptcy process, in the role of "administrator." Article 24 of the 1986 Bankruptcy Law also allowed the liquidation team to hire "necessary work personnel," and required the team to report on its work to the People's Court.

2.1.2.2 Satisfaction of Claims

Pursuant to Article 32 of the 1986 Bankruptcy Law, secured creditors were to be repaid with priority to the extent of their security, and would receive an unsecured "bankruptcy claim" to the extent the obligation exceeded the value of the collateral. Much like under the U.S. Bankruptcy Code, a secured creditor's treatment under the 1986 Bankruptcy Law was bifurcated: the creditor maintained a secured claim to the extent of the value of the underlying collateral, as well as an unsecured deficiency claim to the extent the claim exceeded the value of the collateral.[23]

Despite the language of the 1986 Bankruptcy Law providing priority to secured creditors, this was not reflected in real-word practice due to the passage of later legislation concerning certain employee claims,[24] as will be discussed.

Article 37 of the 1986 Bankruptcy Law set forth the priority scheme for repayment of claims, providing that bankruptcy expenses were to be paid first. Those expenses, similar to administrative expenses under the U.S. Bankruptcy Code, could include expenses incurred by management in the sale and distribution of estate property (including expenses of hiring personnel),

---

[23] Technically, Article 28 exempted "property that already constitutes security collateral" from the bankruptcy estate. It may be argued that, although the 1986 Bankruptcy Law clearly provides for repayment of what is commonly thought of as secured claims, secured creditors did not hold such claims in the bankruptcy proceeding, and participated only to the extent of their unsecured deficiency claims. Article 28 also provided that excess value in collateral is included in the bankruptcy estate.

[24] *See* Wang Weiguo, *Liability and Liquidation Order in PRC Bankruptcy Legislation*, INSOL Electronic Newsletter, July 2006 (noting that, since 1994, the workers of SOEs have enjoyed a special priority according to provisions issued by the central government, which state that assets shall not be used to pay creditors until the workers are "well paid," including not only unpaid claims but also rehabilitation allowance).

and the litigation expenses of the bankruptcy case. After deduction of such administrative expenses, the 1986 Bankruptcy Law gave priority to wages and labor insurance expenses owed by the bankrupt enterprise. Next priority was given to the taxes owed by the bankrupt enterprise. Finally, the 1986 Bankruptcy Law provided for distribution to holders of unsecured "bankruptcy claims" (defined by Article 30 as claims "not secured with property and claims secured with property for which the priority right to receive repayment has been abandoned"). Where remaining estate assets were insufficient to satisfy a particular class of claims, the law provided for *pro rata* distribution within the class.[25]

2.1.3 *Other Provisions of the 1986 Bankruptcy Law*

Although the 1986 Bankruptcy Law focused primarily on the orderly liquidation of assets, it is worth noting that the law also included a host of complex concepts found in Western law, including those presented in the following table.

Article	Subject	Provided:
Article 26	Executory Contracts	The liquidation team may terminate or continue to perform "executory" contracts, and the termination of such contracts gives rise to an unsecured bankruptcy claim.
Article 28	Property of the Estate	Includes all property operated and managed at time of declaration of bankruptcy, anything obtained during the case, and other property rights exercisable by debtor; explicitly excludes security collateral.
Article 31	Acceleration and Unmatured Interest	Claims not due at time of filing are accelerated; unmatured interest is not allowed.
Article 32	Secured Claims	Repayment priority for prepetition secured claims; bifurcation of claims between secured and unsecured portions based on underlying value of collateral.
Article 33	Setoff	Setoff against monies owed by the debtor.
Article 34	Administrative Priority	Priority for expenses of bankruptcy case administration and disposition of debtor's assets.

[25] 1986 Bankruptcy Law, art. 37.

Article	Subject	Provided:
Article 35	Avoidance Actions	Certain actions of the debtor declared null and void if carried out in the six months prior to case commencement.
Article 36	Asset Sales	Sale of assets as a whole or piecemeal.
Article 37	Distribution of Property	Priority scheme to satisfy claims, including pro rata distribution within a class if remaining assets are insufficient to satisfy all claims.

The 1986 Bankruptcy Law was explicitly repealed by Article 136 of the Enterprise Bankruptcy Law, effective as of June 1, 2007.

2.2 Chapter XIX of the 1991 Civil Procedure Law

In 1991, at the request of the Supreme People's Court, a section addressing enterprise bankruptcy was added to the CPL. Contained in the eight articles of Chapter XIX of the CPL,[26] these bankruptcy provisions address and apply only to non-SOEs that qualify as enterprise legal persons. Article 206 of the CPL states that the provisions of Chapter XIX do not apply to "enterprises without legal personality, individual business, leaseholding farm households and individual partnership." Article 206 also provided explicitly that these provisions were not applicable to SOEs, which would be governed by the 1986 Bankruptcy Law.

Under the Chapter XIX provisions, an eligible entity could apply to the People's Court to have itself declared bankrupt, or a creditor could also apply. The CPL provided that "[i]f an enterprise legal person is in serious losses and is unable to repay debts that are due, its creditors may apply to the People's Court for declaring the debtor's bankruptcy repayment; the debtor may also file at the People's Court to declare bankruptcy repayment."[27]

Certain provisions of the CPL mirrored provisions found in the 1986 Bankruptcy Law, including those providing for the notification of known creditors, the formation of a liquidation team, and the first-priority status of wages and labor insurance expenses (after payment of bankruptcy fees).

Chapter XIX contained little guidance regarding the procedures and rights of parties involved in a bankruptcy case, and the vagueness of its provisions suggested a high potential for difficulty in application. In addition,

[26] Chapter XIX is entitled "Procedures for Bankruptcy of Enterprise Legal Persons."

[27] CPL, art. 199.

the CPL addressed only liquidation and conciliation as remedies, and did not provide for any form of reorganization of non-SOEs. Prior to the June 2007 effective date of the Enterprise Bankruptcy Law, reorganization was an exclusive privilege of SOEs in involuntary cases, and stood within the exclusive control of their supervising agencies.

Chapter XIX of the CPL was explicitly deleted pursuant to Article XIX of the *Decision on Amending the Civil Procedure Law of the People's Republic of China.*[28]

2.3 The 2002 Explanation

The Supreme People's Court issued several judicial interpretations in connection with the 1986 Bankruptcy Law and Chapter XIX of the CPL. Of these, the most important and comprehensive was the 2002 Explanation, which provided an extensive set of rules to guide the correct application of the 1986 Bankruptcy Law and Chapter XIX, and to govern "the trial of enterprise bankruptcy cases."[29]

The 106 articles of the 2002 Explanation covered, in part:

- the jurisdiction of courts over enterprise bankruptcy cases;
- the informational requirements for bankruptcy applications;
- the procedures for asserting claims and the various kinds of claims;
- the procedures for convening and conducting meetings of creditors;
- the composition and duties of liquidation teams;
- the definition of estate property;
- the payment of bankruptcy expenses; and
- the procedures for distribution of estate property.

In addition, the 2002 Explanation provided for a kind of automatic stay (injunction)—to the extent that the People's Court was to "suspend other civil execution procedures against the debtor's properties" after the acceptance of an enterprise bankruptcy case—and provided further detail as to when execution procedures could be enjoined.[30] Moreover, the 2002 Explanation provided for transfer of pending lawsuits (not in the appeal stage) commenced

---

[28] Adopted by the Standing Comm., Nat'l People's Cong., Oct. 28, 2007, effective Apr. 1, 2008.

[29] 2002 Explanation, preamble.

[30] *See id.*, art. 20.

by the debtor as plaintiff, to the People's Court presiding over the bankruptcy case.[31]

Article 25 of the 2002 Explanation provided that "[a]fter the People's Court has accepted an enterprise bankruptcy case, and before the bankruptcy proceedings are terminated, the debtor may apply to the People's Court for conciliation," a process by which the debtor and its creditors arrange a compromise and settlement of the debtor's debts. If a conciliation agreement were approved by the People's Court before the court issued "an order on bankruptcy declaration," the bankruptcy cases were to be suspended.[32]

Article 28 of the 2002 Explanation also reiterated a concept expressed in Chapter IV of the 1986 Bankruptcy Law allowing the government to apply for reorganization of an SOE if an involuntary bankruptcy had been commenced by creditors. Article 28 specifically provided that "the application for reorganization shall be proposed before the debtor is declared bankrupt."

2.4 Labor Issues and the "Policy Bankruptcy" Program

As part of its efforts to shift to a market-based economy, China has taken many steps to address the problems faced by SOEs and encourage them to become self-sustaining market participants. Many SOEs (especially old, heavy-industry enterprises), however, have not been able to make the transition to the burgeoning consumer-oriented economy, raising the specter of large-scale unemployment and social unrest. Given the PRC's legacy of a paternalistic "low income but full employment" philosophy in connection with economic planning and social welfare,[33] as well as the inevitability of labor dislocation due to the ongoing rationalization of the nation's economy, the "proper" treatment of labor claims had been an especially problematic issue in the development of bankruptcy law in the PRC.

Workers at SOEs have long endured low (and sometimes sporadic) wages because of the counterbalancing expectation that their livelihoods and basic needs will be taken care of by the state throughout the entirety of their lives, essentially "from cradle to grave." Were these expectations to be betrayed on any significant scale, the resulting dislocation of workers could

---

[31] *See id.*, art. 19.

[32] *Id.*, art. 25.

[33] *See* Tang, *supra* Chapter One, note 38, at 534.

result in unmanageable levels of social and political unrest. It is not hard to understand why the PRC expressed a strong interest in seeing that employees and their claims receive not only retraining but also superior treatment in the event of an enterprise bankruptcy or reorganization.

Because of this societal need, the 1986 Bankruptcy Law, while embodying a willingness to explore the idea of enterprise bankruptcy, simultaneously provided that "[t]he State through various means shall appropriately arrange for the reemployment of the staff and workers of bankrupt enterprises, and shall guarantee their basic living needs prior to reemployment."[34] The 1986 Bankruptcy Law further noted that specific measures would be separately promulgated by the State Council to ensure that labor interests were accorded appropriate priority.[35]

In fact, beginning in 1994, the State Council issued a series of circulars establishing and then expanding a "Capital Structure Optimization Program" for testing bankruptcy under the provisions of the 1986 Bankruptcy Law. Initially applicable to industrial SOEs in eighteen pilot cities,[36] the number of test cities for this "Policy Bankruptcy" program (as it came to be known) was increased in 1996 and again in 1997, and by 1999 the program was extended "to all cities in the country."[37] The program expires in 2008.[38]

The Policy Bankruptcy program was initially intended to provide a mechanism for satisfying obligations related to the resettlement of workers of bankrupted SOEs. The principal methods include the sale of assets such as land-use rights ("LURs"), either in stand-alone sales or as part of the liquidation of the enterprise, as well as the merger of debtor SOEs into healthier SOEs.[39] Beyond serving merely as a test of the 1986 Bankruptcy Law, however, Policy Bankruptcy is now acknowledged to be "a special policy,

---

[34] 1986 Bankruptcy Law, art. 4.

[35] *Id.*

[36] *State Council Circular No. 59* (Oct. 25, 1994).

[37] Tang, *supra* Chapter One, note 38, at 217.

[38] *State Council Circular No. 3* (Jan. 16, 2006) ("no policy bankruptcy shall be implemented after 2008").

[39] *See* Tang, *supra* Chapter One, note 38, at 216 (discussing *State Council Circular No. 113* (1994) and *State Council Circular No. 130* (1995)). For most participating SOEs, land-use rights are the only remaining assets of value. *See id.* at 549. State-owned banks may also be subjected to less onerous regulations regarding the writing-off of bad loans to SOEs participating in the program. *State Council Circular No. 3*.

different from commercial bankruptcy, intended to solve SOE financial distress" in particular industries.[40]

Generally, the Policy Bankruptcy program makes clear that, in any SOE bankruptcy:

- it is the responsibility of the local government to ensure that all measures are taken first to settle workers of the bankrupt enterprise properly and preserve social stability;
- LURs of the bankrupt enterprise are to be disposed of by way of either auction or tender, and the proceeds used first to resettle all workers and employees of the enterprise properly; and
- if the proceeds from disposal of LURs are insufficient to settle labor-related obligations, then additional assets and proceeds are to be transferred to the estate for such purpose.[41]

The program further provides that assets are not to be used to pay creditors until the workers are paid, noting that "labour rehabilitation and pension expenses are priority claims to land-use rights even if such land-use rights have been mortgaged by the SOE, for example to banks."[42] By thus providing for labor-related obligations to be paid with priority out of the proceeds of collateral, the State Council fundamentally altered the priority scheme established in the 1986 Bankruptcy Law, Chapter XIX of the CPL, and the 2002 Explanation.[43]

As will be discussed in Section 4.3.3.3 below, the proper relationship between labor claims and the interests of secured creditors was a hotly contested issue that delayed the enactment of the Enterprise Bankruptcy Law for quite some time. Some early drafts of the law contemplated establishing a general priority of labor claims over collateral. Ultimately, while acknowledging the need for some special treatment for labor claims even in non-Policy

---

[40] *Id.* The program focuses on "supporting the revitalization of the old-industry zone in the Eastern China Area and the economic structure adjustment of the Central and Western China Areas, supporting SOE reform and distress relief in military industries and the closing-up and bankruptcy of depleted coal mines, and handling the remaining work in the closing-up and bankruptcy of distressed enterprises in the non-ferrous metals industry." *Id.*

[41] Tang, *supra* Chapter One, note 38, at 550–51.

[42] *State Council Circular No. 492* (1996).

[43] It should be noted that this special treatment was not available to all SOEs, but only to those enrolled in the Policy Bankruptcy program. All other SOEs were subject to the 1986 Bankruptcy Law.

Bankruptcy cases, the new law limits such treatment to claims arising prior to the date of its enactment, and otherwise reaffirms the protected status of secured claims. It is important to note, however, that SOEs participating in the Policy Bankruptcy program are explicitly carved out from the scope of the Enterprise Bankruptcy Law;[44] as a result, their bankruptcies will continue to be administered under the Policy Bankruptcy program until it expires.

As of 2006, 2,116 SOEs were covered by the Policy Bankruptcy program remaining to be processed, owing an aggregate 227.16 billion RMB (approximately $28.15 billion at the time) to state-owned financial institutions. Their bankruptcies are anticipated to affect an aggregate 3.51 million employees.[45] But it is unrealistic to expect that all of these proceedings will be completed by the time the program expires in 2008, and it is not clear at this time what will be done about them at that point. One possibility is that such SOEs will become subject to the Enterprise Bankruptcy Law. Alternatively, remaining participants may be subjected to "administrative closure" and similar winding-up procedures, and the government may subsidize distributions on account of employee claims and other claims to the extent necessary.[46]

---

[44] *See* Enterprise Bankruptcy Law, art. 133.

[45] *State Council Circular No. 3.*

[46] *See* Francesco Guerrerain & Richard McGregor, *Struggling China State Companies Win Stay of Execution*, Financial Times, Sept. 25, 2006, at 9.

CHAPTER THREE: Property, Collateral, and Creditor's Remedies in the PRC

3.1 Lending in China

Commercial lending and borrowing are highly regulated in the PRC. Variations in treatment depend on factors such as the nature of the borrower and the lender, as well as the currency and proposed use of the loan. In particular, the borrowing of foreign exchange by domestic enterprises from international sources is subject to a greater degree of regulation than domestic borrowing in order to exert centralized control over the process of utilizing foreign capital to aid China's economic development. Loans from foreign sources are subject to quotas and other forms of state planning with respect to the use of foreign capital at both the national and various regional levels.

The ability of Chinese enterprises to borrow funds from abroad is largely governed at the national level by the *Rules of the PRC on Foreign Exchange Control* (the "Forex Regulations")[1] and its implementing regulations, which apply to all transactions involving foreign exchange conducted by all parties in China (including individuals, enterprises, and governmental bodies).[2] SAFE is primarily responsible for interpreting and administering the Forex Regulations. In addition, commercial borrowing from international sources is subject to the *Administrative Measures on International Commercial Loan Borrowing by Domestic Institutions* (the "Commercial Loan Measures")[3] and the *Provisional Measures on the Management of Foreign Loans* (the "Foreign Loan Measures"),[4] as well as many *ad hoc* rules on specific transactions in special zones, overseas listing transactions, and the like.

Under this regulatory framework, the foreign debt of organizations in the PRC must be registered with the various foreign exchange control

---

[1] Promulgated by the State Council, Jan. 29, 1996; revised Jan. 14, 1997.

[2] Forex Regulations, art. 4. The Forex Regulations define "foreign exchange" to include (among other elements) foreign currency, instruments of payment denominated in foreign currency (including negotiable instruments), and securities denominated in foreign currency (including government bonds, company bonds, shares, and the like).

[3] Promulgated by the SAFE, Sept. 24, 1997 (replacing previous measures of 1991).

[4] Promulgated jointly by the SAFE, MOF, and the State Commission of Development and Planning, Jan. 8, 2003 (repealing certain provisions of the Commercial Loan Measures in order to comply with WTO requirements).

departments of the State Council (chiefly SAFE), which either directly or indirectly approve and supervise the borrowing activities, and which also monitor, collect, and publish data on foreign debt.[5]

3.1.1 International Borrowing by Organizations Resident in China

International commercial loans are borrowings by "organizations resident in China" from financial institutions, enterprises, other organizations, or individuals abroad (or in Hong Kong, Macau, and Taiwan) for which repayment obligations are denominated in foreign currency. These include (in part) loans from foreign banks and other financial institutions, enterprises, and natural persons; bonds issued overseas; various forms of trade financing; international finance leasing; and non-resident foreign currency deposits.

"Organizations resident in China" include domestic financial institutions and enterprises, government authorities, and public institutions and organizations. They now also include FIEs and foreign-funded financial institutions in China, which was not the case under the Commercial Loan Measures prior to the Foreign Loan Measures. As a result of this change in status, when domestic Chinese enterprises borrow foreign exchange from a foreign-funded financial institution resident in China, it is not considered an international borrowing; foreign-funded financial institutions resident in China may lend foreign exchange to other Chinese residents without obtaining the same approvals necessary for international commercial loans. On the other hand, a foreign-funded financial institution resident in China is considered to be engaged in international borrowing (and thus will be subject to the control of PRC foreign exchange authorities) when obtaining foreign exchange loans and guarantees from its own overseas affiliates.[6]

As noted, borrowers resident in China must obtain approval from SAFE in order to borrow and use funds from abroad.[7] Furthermore, all international commercial loan agreements must be registered, and will become effective

---

[5] Forex Regulations, art. 25.

[6] In addition, pursuant to the *Measures on Administration of Foreign Debts Owed by Foreign Banks in China*, issued jointly by the People's Bank of China, China Banking Regulatory Commission, and State Development and Reform Commission, May 27, 2004, foreign-funded banks must apply annually for a grant with respect to the foreign debt quota for the year.

[7] Commercial Loan Measures, art. 4.

only upon such registration.[8] Applications for approval and registration are made to the foreign exchange bureaus of SAFE. Upon successful registration, the borrower is issued a foreign debt registration certificate. In addition to approval and registration, borrowers must report to SAFE annually on the use of loan proceeds during the previous year. Any change from the approved use of funds must have received the approval of the original approving agency.[9]

3.1.2 Borrowing by FIEs

In addition to being generally subject to the regulations applicable to organizations resident in China, FIEs also are subject to other requirements specific to FIEs. The Foreign Loan Measures and other regulations set forth, in general terms, restrictions on borrowing by FIEs.

3.1.2.1 Foreign Borrowing

The aggregate foreign borrowings of an FIE generally are limited to the difference between the company's registered capital and its "total investment." Total investment, which is set forth in each FIE's articles of association, reflects the investment/leverage ratio of registered capital to possible debt, which varies with the size of registered capital. If foreign borrowing exceeds the allowed amount, then total investment is subject to re-examination by the original approving agency.

These restrictions are not applicable to FIEs that qualify as "foreign invested investment companies," which may incur more debt.[10] An FIE with \$30 million to \$100 million of registered capital may incur up to four times the amount of its paid-in registered capital; an FIE with more than \$100

---

[8] Foreign Loan Measures, arts. 22, 40; *see also Provisional Measures for Statistics on and Monitoring of Foreign Debt*, promulgated by the State Administration for Exchange Control, Aug. 27, 1987; Forex Regulations, art. 22 (FIEs must notify SAFE of any foreign currency denominated loans received from lenders abroad); *Tentative Procedures for Foreign Debt Administration*, enacted by the SAFE, Mar. 1, 2003 (providing tighter registration standards for FIEs, including the requirement that foreign debt agreements will not be effective until registered with SAFE).

[9] Borrowers are prohibited from depositing or making direct payments of foreign funds abroad, or converting foreign funds into RMB, without specific approval.

[10] To qualify, an investment company must (i) have had assets during the preceding year of not less than \$400 million and have established other FIEs (for which its paid-in capital exceeded \$10 million) or (ii) have good credit, the wherewithal to establish an investment company, and have established more than ten FIEs (for which its total paid-in capital exceeded \$30 million).

million of registered capital may incur up to six times its paid-in registered capital.

3.1.2.2 Domestic Borrowing

Aside from international commercial loans, FIEs may borrow funds from domestic institutions, such as PRC banks and designated foreign exchange banks in China.

Where the domestic lending institution is a PRC bank, the loan will be subject to the *General Provisions of Loans of the People's Bank of China* (the "Lending General Provisions")[11] in addition to the regulations discussed earlier. With respect to FIEs, the Lending General Provisions provide (in part) that: the FIE may not borrow if it has invested more than 50% of its net asset value in other companies; loans may be used only as specified in the loan agreement (and in no event for investing in other companies, speculating in real estate or securities, or for further lending to other parties); and the interest rate must conform to the limits prescribed by the PBOC.[12]

FIEs also may borrow from Chinese foreign exchange banks, pursuant to the *Notice on Improvement of the Administration of RMB Loans Secured by Foreign Exchange.*[13] As the name of the regulation suggests, FIEs may borrow RMB-denominated funds by offering foreign currency as collateral. Alternatively, the loans may be secured by "credit guarantees" provided by foreign financial institutions in the form of unconditional, irrevocable, and non-transferable letters of credit (including standby letters of credit). Such borrowings may be used only for working capital or to invest in fixed assets, and explicitly *not* to purchase foreign exchange. The term of the loan may not exceed five years, and the amount may not exceed the value of the collateral currency (adjustments in the amount of the loan and/or collateral may be required from time to time due to exchange rate fluctuations). Borrowers must have their registered capital fully paid-in (and not reduced or withdrawn).

Inter-company loans are not permitted in the PRC unless the articles of association of the lending party authorizes lending. Generally, only financial institutions are authorized to lend in China. Thus, for instance, the Chinese venturor in an EJV or CJV (or its holding company or subsidiaries) likely

---

[11] *Order No. 2* promulgated by the PBOC, June 28, 1996.

[12] *See also* Contract Law, art. 204.

[13] Issued by the PBOC, July 15, 1999.

is not capable of legally lending funds to the joint venture (or providing a guarantee to the joint venture or its creditors). Likewise, an FIE is not able to lend funds to other entities unless lending has been approved in the scope of its business.

3.1.3 Consequences of Unapproved Lending

Loan agreements that are not approved by the relevant governmental authorities are void. The consequences of the failure to obtain necessary approvals and registration include (i) refusal by the foreign exchange bureaus of SAFE to register the debt, (ii) refusal by PRC banks to open foreign exchange accounts for the parties, and (iii) prohibition against PRC banks from remitting payments of principal and interest.

Likewise, *ultra vires* lending by domestic enterprises is void. Where the lender lacks the corporate capacity to lend, enforcement of the loan in the People's Courts will not be possible.

In other words, where funds are loaned without an approved loan agreement or outside the lender's corporate capacities, the lender may have no legal means to recover the funds out of Chinese banks or in Chinese courts.[14] Where the loan agreement is void, any related security agreement will also be void.[15]

3.2 Taking and Perfecting Security

The taking of security for financial obligations is not a new concept in the PRC. The GPCL sets forth several ways in which obligations may be secured,[16] and the *Opinion on Several Problems in the Implementation of the General Principles of Civil Law* (the "Civil Law Explanation")[17] explains that claimholders with a security interest over their claims take priority over unsecured obligees (except as otherwise provided by law).[18] As discussed in Section 9.3.1 below, the Enterprise Bankruptcy Law explicitly permits the granting of security interests in connection with loans to the debtor during

---

[14] *See Circular of the State Council on Strengthening the Administration of the Obtaining of International Commercial Loans* (Jan. 12, 1989); *Procedures for Administration of Taking Out International Commercial Loans by Organizations in China*, issued by the SAFE, Jan. 1, 1998.

[15] *See* Property Law, art. 172; Secured Interests Law, art. 5.

[16] The GPCL provides for guarantees, pledges, deposits, and liens. *See* GPCL, art. 89.

[17] Issued by the Supreme People's Court, Jan. 26, 1988, effective same.

[18] Civil Law Explanation, art. 60.

the "reorganization period," presumably subject to all other applicable laws and regulations.

Since 1995, the granting of security has been governed principally by the *Secured Interests Law of the People's Republic of China* (the "Secured Interests Law"),[19] which provides for the protection of creditors through the use of guarantees, mortgages, pledges, liens, and security deposits.[20] Various other national laws also contain provisions relating to security for obligations, such as the Commercial Bank Law[21] and the *Contract Law of the People's Republic of China*,[22] and certain regional authorities also have enacted mortgage regulations.[23]

Most recently, the new Property Law includes a chapter on "Real Rights for Security" that covers the granting of mortgages, pledges, and liens. Its provisions are very similar to those in the Secured Interests Law and other statutes, and presumably will prevail where any conflict arises.

3.2.1 Forms of Security

As in the West, the significance under PRC law of being secured is that the secured creditor is entitled to priority of payment from specific collateral (or the proceeds thereof).[24] Although PRC law provides for guarantees, mortgages, pledges, liens, and security deposits as forms of security, the first three of these are the typical forms used for loan transactions.

---

[19] Promulgated by the Standing Comm., Nat'l People's Cong., June 30, 1995, effective Oct. 1, 1995.

[20] Secured Interests Law, art. 2 and (generally) chs. I through VI.

[21] Commercial Bank Law, art. 36.

[22] Adopted by the Nat'l People's Cong., Mar. 15, 1999, effective Oct. 1, 1999 (hereinafter the "Contract Law"), art. 198.

[23] *See, e.g., Provisional Regulations of Shanghai Municipality on RMB Mortgage Loan Administration*, enacted by the PBOC, Shanghai Branch, June 9, 1988; *Provisional Regulations of Shanghai Municipality on Foreign Exchange Mortgage Loan Administration*, enacted by the State Foreign Exchange Administrative Bureau, June 9, 1988; *Regulations of Guangdong Province on Mortgage Loan Administration*, enacted by the Guangdong Provincial People's Government, Dec. 20, 1992. These regional regulations generally govern the giving of security interests in certain kinds of property by domestic enterprise legal persons to financial institutions, requiring written contracts and imposing limitations in the form of borrowing ratios, agency approvals, and the like.

[24] *See, e.g.*, Property Law, art. 170; Secured Interests Law, art. 33; Civil Law Explanation, art. 60.

3.2.1.1 Guarantees

A guarantee is defined by the Secured Interests Law to be "the act of a guarantor, pursuant to an agreement between the guarantor and the creditor, in performing the obligations of or bearing liability for a debtor when that debtor fails to perform its obligations."[25] Guarantees can be given only pursuant to a written contract,[26] specifying (among other measures): the principal obligation; the term for repayment; the "mode" of the guarantee (either general or joint and several); the "scope" of the guarantee (*i.e.*, whether the guarantee covers only the principal obligation or also any interest, damages); and the duration of the guarantee.[27] The absence of such terms does not invalidate the contract.

Under a general guarantee, the guarantor may refuse liability where a dispute over the debtor's obligation has not been finally determined by judicial or arbitral proceedings and where the obligation has not yet been found to be incapable of satisfaction by execution against the debtor's property.[28] Under a joint and several guarantee, the guarantor is liable upon the debtor's failure to perform.[29] Where the guarantee contract is silent or ambiguous as to mode, the guarantee is deemed to be of the joint-and-several variety.[30] In either instance, the parties to the guarantee contract may seek indemnification from each other.[31]

Where the guarantee contract does not specify the duration of the guarantee, the guarantee is deemed to endure for only six months after the maturity of the obligation; unless the creditor initiates collection efforts (litigation or arbitration) within the agreed or statutory period, the guarantor will be excused from liability.[32]

Where an obligation is secured by both a guarantee and a mortgage or pledge of property, the guarantor's liability is limited to such portion of

---

[25] Secured Interests Law, art. 6.

[26] *Id.*, art. 13.

[27] *Id.*, art. 15.

[28] *Id.*, art. 17. The guarantor may assert such defense even if the debtor waives its objections, *id.*, art. 20, but may not refuse liability if the debtor cannot be located or collection efforts are stayed in bankruptcy proceedings. *Id.*, art. 17.

[29] *Id.*, art. 18.

[30] *Id.*, art. 19.

[31] *Id.*, art. 31.

[32] *Id.*, arts. 25, 26.

the obligation as is not covered by the mortgage or pledge (even if the other secured creditor abandons its security interest in property).[33]

3.2.1.2 Mortgages and Pledges

The other major forms of contractual security in China are (i) a mortgage on real property and (ii) a mortgage on or pledge of personal property. A mortgage is a form of security by which the debtor or a third party designates property as collateral for a creditor's claim without transferring possession of the property.[34] When the debtor fails to pay his debt, the secured creditor has the right to initiate collection proceedings with respect to the mortgaged property, and receive either the property or the proceeds from its sale.[35]

The Secured Interests Law and the Property Law both specify categories of property that may be mortgaged and categories that may not. The following table describes mortgageable property under both statutes.

Under the Secured Interests Law[36]	Under the Property Law[37]
• Buildings and other fixtures on land; • Land-use rights with respect to state-owned land, buildings, and other fixtures; • Land-use rights with respect to barren mountains, barren valleys, waste hills, and waste sands for which the mortgagor has lawfully contracted, with the contract counterparty's consent; • Equipment, means of transport, and other property owned by the mortgagor or by the state (for which the mortgagor has the lawful right to dispose); and • Other property that may be mortgaged according to law.	• Buildings and other fixtures on land; • Land-use rights with respect to construction land; • Contracted management rights with respect to barren land and the like obtained by means of bid invitation, auction, and public consultation; • Present and future manufacturing facilities, raw materials, semi-manufactured goods, and products; • Buildings, vessels, and aircraft under construction; • Means of communications and transportation; and • Properties other than those that may not be mortgaged according to any law or administrative regulation.

[33] *Id.*, art. 28. The new Property Law provides similarly as between a mortgagee who waives his security interest and other providers of security. *See* Property Law, art. 194.

[34] Property Law, art. 179; Secured Interests Law, art. 33.

[35] Property Law, art. 179; Secured Interests Law, art. 33.

[36] Secured Interests Law, art. 34.

[37] Property Law, art. 180.

With some exceptions for buildings under construction, the Secured Interests Law did not allow security interests to be granted in a changing pool of assets or future assets; that is to say, assignments by way of security and floating charges over accounts were not recognized.[38] This may no longer be the case under the new Property Law, however, which provides that "[u]pon the written agreement between the parties concerned, an enterprise . . . may mortgage the manufacturing facilities, raw materials, semi-manufactured goods and products it has already owned *or is going to own* . . . ."[39] The new Property Law also provides that accounts receivable are pledgeable property.[40] It is hoped that the Supreme People's Court will clarify the status of floating charges in the judicial interpretation of the Property Law that it reportedly has started preparing.

Non-mortgageable property includes land itself; land-use rights with respect to collectively owned land (such as farmland, homesteads, and land allocated for personal/private use) unless otherwise prescribed by law; public-interest facilities (such as educational, medical, and public health facilities); property with unclear or disputed ownership or use rights; property that has been attached, arrested, or otherwise lawfully seized; and other property which may not be mortgaged according to law.[41]

Mortgages can be given only pursuant to a written contract,[42] specifying (in part) the principal obligation; the term for repayment; the designation, amount, quality, location, and ownership and usufructary status of the collateral; and the "scope" of the security (*i.e.*, whether the collateral secures only the principal obligation or also any interest,

---

[38] G. Griffiths, *International Acquisition Finance: Law and Practice*, § 6.53, at 173 (Oxford University Press 2006).

[39] Property Law, art. 181 (emphasis added). Where this occurs, the Property Law further provides that the mortgagor is to register the mortgage (although such registration does not trigger effectiveness). *Id.*, art. 189. Furthermore, without registration, "the right to mortgage shall not challenge any bona fide third party." In any event, registration "shall not challenge the buyer which has paid a reasonable price in normal business operations and has obtained the property under mortgage." *Id.*

[40] *See* Property Law, arts. 223, 228.

[41] Property Law, art. 184; Secured Interests Law, art. 37. It is not clear whether the Property Law represents an expansion or contraction of the universe of mortgageable property, or whether it is simply a new formulation of the list in the Secured Interests Law.

[42] Property Law, art. 185; Secured Interests Law, art. 38. Such requirement is similar to the limitations imposed by statutes of frauds in common-law legal systems.

damages, and/or the like).[43] Mortgages for certain kinds of property must be registered with the appropriate registration authority, and such mortgages are effective from the date of such registration.[44] Otherwise, registration is optional, and mortgages are effective from the date of execution of the mortgage contract.[45]

A pledge differs from a mortgage in that a mortgagor retains possession of the mortgaged collateral, while a pledgor gives up possession of pledged collateral to the pledgee.[46] In addition to ordinary kinds of personal property, mortgageable personal property presumably also is pledgeable, but pledgeable property also includes negotiable instruments such as bank drafts, checks, promissory notes, bonds, deposit certificates, warehouse receipts, bills of lading, lawfully transferable shares of stock, and lawfully transferable exclusive intellectual property rights (*e.g.*, trademarks, patents, and copyrights).[47]

Like mortgages, pledges also can be given only pursuant to a written contract[48] that specifies similar information.[49] Generally, however, no registration is required (or provided for), and the pledge is effective upon delivery of the collateral.[50] In the case of pledged securities or intellectual property rights, however, the pledge becomes effective only upon registration with the appropriate authorities.[51] Neither mortgages nor pledges entail a transfer of proprietary rights; in fact, it is expressly prohibited to so provide in the contracts.[52]

---

[43] Property Law, art. 185; Secured Interests Law, art. 39.

[44] Property Law, arts. 180, 187 (mandatory registration with respect to buildings and other fixtures, land-use rights with respect to construction land, rights to contracted management of barren land and the like, and buildings under construction); Secured Interests Law, arts. 41, 42 (mandatory registration with respect to land-use rights for unimproved land; real property consisting of buildings in towns and villages; woodlands; vessels and vehicles; and equipment and similar industrial property). The appropriate registration authorities typically are local in nature, and vary with the type of property involved.

[45] Property Law, art. 188; Secured Interests Law, art. 43.

[46] *Compare* Property Law, art. 179 *with* art. 208; Secured Interests Law, art. 33 *with* art. 63.

[47] Property Law, art. 223 (also listing fund units and accounts receivable); Secured Interests Law, art. 75.

[48] Property Law, art. 210; Secured Interests Law, art. 64.

[49] Property Law, art. 210; Secured Interests Law, art. 65.

[50] Property Law, arts. 212, 224; Secured Interests Law, arts. 64, 76.

[51] Property Law, arts. 226–228 (regarding registration of pledges of accounts receivable); Secured Interests Law, arts. 78, 79. Pledges of stock may be subject to additional requirements under applicable laws and regulations governing transfers of stock.

[52] *See* Property Law, arts. 186, 211; Secured Interests Law, arts. 40, 66.

3.2.2 Perfection of Security Interests

Registration of security interests is tantamount to perfection, as illustrated by Article 43 of the Secured Interests Law, which provides that a mortgagee cannot assert its security interest as against a third party unless the mortgage is registered—even if such registration is optional.[53] It is not clear whether this effect is limited to competing secured creditors, or instead applies broadly to all third parties. Presumably, failure to perfect would result in at least the security interest being inferior to the properly perfected interest of another secured creditor.

Where two mortgages have been given with respect to the same collateral, the registered mortgage takes priority. Where both are registered, the first in time is first in right; if they are contemporaneous, the mortgagees take *pro rata*. Where registration is not required and neither mortgage is registered, the creditor with the earlier effective date takes priority (or if contemporaneous, then *pro rata*).[54] Where a mortgage and a pledge have been registered with respect to the same collateral, the mortgage takes priority, but where there is a mortgage and a lien on the same property, the lien takes priority.[55]

From a practical perspective, it must be noted that registration of security interests is a local matter regulated at provincial, county, municipal, and other levels, and that China lacks transparent and easily navigated systems for public recordation or the relatively simplified perfection of liens (as provided, for instance, under the Uniform Commercial Code in the U.S.).

3.2.3 Security Given to Foreign Parties

Security given by domestic PRC parties to foreign parties is subject to approval by and registration with SAFE.[56] The Foreign Loan Measures

---

[53] *See* Secured Interests Law, art. 43; *see also* Property Law, arts. 188, 189.

[54] Property Law, art. 199; Secured Interests Law, art. 54. Where registration is required and neither mortgage is registered, both mortgages presumably are ineffective to begin with under the Secured Interests Law; the Property Law, however, provides for *pro rata* treatment.

[55] J. Hartley and L. Leung, *Country Q and A: China*, PLC Cross-Border Finance: Secured Lending Handbook 2007/08, 33 (Practical Law Company 2008).

[56] *See Tentative Procedures for Foreign Debt Administration*, promulgated by the SAFE, Jan. 8, 2003; Foreign Loan Measures, arts. 19, 22, 40; *Administrative Measures on Security Given to Foreign Parties by Domestic Institutions*, adopted by the PBOC, Sept. 25, 1996; Forex Regulations, art. 24; *Interpretation of the Secured Interests Law*, issued by the Supreme People's Court, Dec. 8, 2000, art. 6(1). Some observers have noted that true free-market systems do not require governmental approval of private transactions such as the granting of security interests.

provide that security contracts with foreign parties will take effect only upon registration, and security given without approval and registration is invalid.

With particular respect to guarantees, the *Administrative Measures on Security Given to Foreign Parties by Domestic Institutions* (the "Security Measures") provide that SAFE is charged with approving and registering all guarantees issued by PRC companies to foreign creditors, including FIEs and foreign-funded financial institutions, except in connection with short-term financing (*i.e.*, for less than one year). To obtain approval, PRC companies must meet certain liquidity and asset/liability levels. Furthermore, only a limited number of PRC companies (such as financial institutions) are authorized in their articles of association to provide guarantees.

3.3 Collecting Debts in the PRC

The GCPL provides creditors with the right "to demand that the debtor fulfill its obligations as specified by the loan agreement or according to legal provisions."[57] The GPCL and other PRC law, however, do not do more, such as allow for any form of self-help. Outside of a bankruptcy proceeding, creditors' remedies are essentially as follows.

3.3.1 Debt Recovery by the Unsecured Creditor

In the first instance, where (i) an unsecured creditor's claim involves only the repayment of money, (ii) the creditor is not involved in any other disputes with the debtor, and (iii) service of a payment order on the debtor is practicable, the creditor may petition a court of competent jurisdiction to issue a payment order against the debtor. Such payment order is not a court judgment, however, and is unenforceable if the debtor does not pay.

Therefore, creditors must usually litigate (or arbitrate, if the contract so provides and/or the parties agree), and then seek to enforce the court judgment (or arbitration award) if successful. Execution on court judgments is principally governed by the CPL, which sets forth general principles regarding the procedures for application and transfer of judgments for execution, as well as the enforcement measures that courts may take.[58] In addition, the *Opinion on Implementation of the Civil Procedure Law of the People's Republic of*

---

[57] GPCL, art. 82.

[58] *See* CPL, arts. 210, 216–218. In addition, Part IV of the CPL governs civil actions involving foreign parties (nationals, enterprises, and organizations), providing that they have the same rights and obligations in the People's Courts as PRC parties.

China[59] provides more guidance than the CPL itself, but it still leaves many practical issues unaddressed. The most comprehensive guidance for execution is to be found in the 137 articles of the *Certain Provisions Concerning the Execution Work of the People's Court (for Trial Implementation)* (the "Execution Provisions").[60]

Generally, application can be made to the court for execution once all appeals have been exhausted. The Execution Provisions provide that, where both parties are legal persons or organizations, such application must be made within six months, and the court is obliged to decide whether to accept the application within seven days. If the application is accepted, then the execution-related functions of the court usually are carried out by its enforcement division (as opposed to the adjudicatory division, as established in most Chinese courts).

The enforcement division is responsible for compelling judgment debtors to comply with executable documents. Under the Execution Provisions, executable documents include civil judgments, arbitration awards, and mediation settlements, as well as other documents for the recovery of debt or property having legal effect under Chinese law. In carrying out the execution of judgments, the enforcement division is empowered to take a number of coercive measures, including making inquiries to financial institutions about a debtor's assets, sealing and seizing property (including the debtor's equity interests in other companies), and auctioning off seized property.

3.3.2 Debt Recovery by the Secured Creditor

Notwithstanding secured creditors' superior position with respect to unsecured creditors generally, secured creditors in the PRC must apply to the People's Court in order to enforce their security interests against the debtor's property.

Upon default by the debtor, a mortgagee has the right to have its claim satisfied out of the mortgaged property, but it *cannot* simply foreclose on the property, because automatic transfer of title is specifically prohibited by PRC law and any contractual provision that purports to do so is void.[61] Likewise, a pledgee cannot simply claim title to the pledged property already in its possession. The Secured Interests Law and the Property Law both provide that

---

[59] Issued by the Supreme People's Court, July 14, 1992, effective same.

[60] Issued by the Supreme People's Court, June 11, 1998, effective July 18, 1998.

[61] *See* Property Law, arts. 186, 211; Secured Interests Law, arts. 40, 66.

the secured creditor must agree with the debtor on the method of disposing of mortgaged or pledged property.[62] If the parties are unable to agree on the disposition of property to satisfy the creditor's claim, however, then (under the Secured Interests Law) the creditor may initiate legal proceedings for a disposition order, which may grant title to the collateral to the creditor, who may then seek to enforce the order,[63] or (under the Property Law) the creditor may simply have the court liquidate the property (through auction or other sale) and distribute the proceeds, avoiding a time-consuming lawsuit.[64]

In addition to these procedural difficulties in enforcing a mortgage or other security, the creditor must first be sure that the security has been duly registered with the appropriate authorities. As a practical matter, it is more difficult for foreign creditors to enforce their rights, as both the security interest and the underlying debt must be registered with and approved by SAFE. As a result, secured creditors may pursue settlement of the debt rather than enforcement measures.

The enforcement procedure itself is no different for secured creditors than for unsecured creditors. As noted earlier, the judgment specifies the amount of the debt owed, and the enforcement division compels the debtor to satisfy its debt. Failing that, the enforcement division will dispose of the collateral through auction or forced sale, and apply the proceeds to settle the secured creditor's claim. Any surplus is returned to the debtor.

---

[62] *See* Property Law, arts. 195, 219; Secured Interests Law, arts. 53, 71.

[63] *See* Secured Interests Law, arts. 53.

[64] *See* Property Law, arts. 195.

CHAPTER FOUR: Overview of the Enterprise Bankruptcy Law

4.1 The Need for Bankruptcy Reform

The 1986 Bankruptcy Law was groundbreaking legislation. Not only was it China's first bankruptcy statute under the Communist regime, but it also implemented many fairly sophisticated restructuring concepts regarding property of the estate, the assumption and rejection of executory contracts, acceleration of debt, unmatured interest, priority of secured claims, setoff, avoidance powers, asset sales, and procedures for the distribution of property.

As already noted, however, the 1986 Bankruptcy Law required governmental approval prior to filing a bankruptcy application, which was a cumbersome process subject to delay. In addition, the 1986 Bankruptcy Law provided for reorganization only in very limited circumstances, and was implemented only on a trial basis from the very outset. In the years following the implementation of the 1986 Bankruptcy Law, the rapid pace of economic reform in China began to expose serious financial problems and the limited ability of existing law to address them. Subsequent legislation and rulemaking relating to the Policy Bankruptcy program represented a recognition of (and reaction to) some of those problems,[1] but those developments arguably whittled away the promise of the 1986 Bankruptcy Law. In the meantime, the volume of non-performing loans granted by the major state-owned banks to bolster money-losing SOEs continued to accumulate,[2] and it became apparent that China's insolvency and bankruptcy landscape was in need of improvement beyond the innovations represented by the 1986 Bankruptcy Law.

An official review of the 1986 Bankruptcy Law was commenced in 1994, and a first draft of a revised law was prepared in 1995, followed by the preparation and discussion of several additional drafts. The Asian financial

[1] As discussed in Section 2.4 above, the Policy Bankruptcy program was initiated by the State Council in 1994 to protect workers of troubled industrial, mining and military SOEs in certain regions, through resettlement and priority treatment of their claims, beyond the provisions of the 1986 Bankruptcy Law. More than 2,000 SOEs currently participate in the program.

[2] Recent reports suggest that the current amount of outstanding nonperforming loans from the four major Chinese state-owned banks may be in excess of $300 billion.

crisis of 1997–98, followed by the infamous collapse and bankruptcy of Guangdong International Trust and Investment Corporation ("GITIC") in 1998–99, dramatically punctuated the need for more robust laws on economic issues, including insolvency and bankruptcy. Nevertheless, a stalemate over political considerations relating to employment, social welfare, and social stability effectively halted the drafting process in 1998.

The process caught its second wind in 2003, and by June 2004 the first draft of a renewed proposed bankruptcy law was submitted to the Standing Committee for consideration and approval. Further revised drafts were considered in October 2004 and during 2005. The last draft went through its last round of deliberations and was approved by the Standing Committee of the National People's Congress on August 27, 2006, becoming effective on June 1, 2007.

4.2 General Contours of the Enterprise Bankruptcy Law

The Enterprise Bankruptcy Law is much more extensive than prior law, and represents a significant expansion in the Chinese bankruptcy and restructuring framework in at least four major respects. First, as alluded to earlier, governmental approval to file a bankruptcy application is no longer necessary. Second, unlike the 1986 Bankruptcy Law (which applied only to SOEs) and Chapter XIX of the CPL (which applied only to non-SOE enterprise legal persons), the Enterprise Bankruptcy Law applies to both SOEs and non-SOE enterprise legal persons alike.[3] Third, recognizing the limitations of the liquidation-oriented prior law, the new law provides more-liberal access to the reorganization process. Fourth, the new law reflects a practical compromise with respect to the proceeds of collateral that tries to balance the socioeconomic interests implicated in the zero-sum relationship between secured claims and labor claims.

The Enterprise Bankruptcy Law consists of 136 articles organized into 12 chapters (compared to the 43 articles and 6 chapters of the 1986 Bankruptcy

---

[3] It is important to note, however, that not all SOEs are covered, and not all non-SOEs are eligible under the Enterprise Bankruptcy Law. Proceedings under the Policy Bankruptcy program will proceed pursuant to existing measures, which require bankruptcy estates to satisfy employees first, rather than creditors. *See* Enterprise Bankruptcy Law, art. 133. These bankruptcies are expected to be phased out in 2008. Other entities not eligible to be debtors include partnerships, their partners, sole proprietorships, their investors, certain other profit-making organizations, and natural persons engaged in industry or commerce, although the liquidation of some of these entities may be guided by the new law. *See id.*, art. 135.

Law and the 8 articles of Chapter XIX of the CPL). The following chart categorizes the components of the law.

Chapter	**Title**	**Subject(s)**
Chapter I (Articles 1–6)	General Provisions	Eligible entities; jurisdiction of the courts; standards for filing a bankruptcy proceeding; and other procedural matters.
Chapter II (Articles 7–21)	Application and Acceptance	Applications that may be filed; types of evidence that must be submitted with each application; and process by which the People's Court accepts or denies applications.
Chapter III (Articles 22–29)	The Administrator	Eligibility of persons to serve; administrator's duties; and standards for performance.
Chapter IV (Articles 30–40)	The Debtor's Property	Formation of the bankruptcy estate; avoidance of fraudulent or preferential transfers; redemption of collateral; reclamation; and setoff.
Chapter V (Articles 41–43)	Bankruptcy Expenses and Common-Interest Debts	Administrative costs of the bankruptcy proceeding.
Chapter VI (Articles 44–58)	Assertion of Claims	Procedure by which creditors may assert their claims.
Chapter VII (Articles 59–69)	The Creditors' Meeting	Selection of a creditors' committee; and committee's responsibilities.
Chapter VIII (Articles 70–94)	Reorganization	Procedures for reorganization application; reorganization period; formulation and approval of reorganization plan; and implementation of reorganization plan.
Chapter IX (Articles 95–106)	Conciliation	Process for the debtor and its creditors to settle debts through a court-approved "conciliation agreement."
Chapter X (Articles 107–124)	Bankruptcy Liquidation	Declaration of bankruptcy; priority of claims; appraisal and distribution of assets; and conclusion and winding down of bankruptcy proceeding.
Chapter XI (Articles 125–131)	Legal Liabilities	Liabilities of persons involved in the bankruptcy proceeding (*e.g.*, directors and managers of the debtor-enterprise).

Chapter	Title	Subject(s)
Chapter XII (Articles 132–136)	Supplementary Provisions	Treatment of employee claims; eligibility of commercial banks and insurance companies; and applicability of liquidation provisions as model for treatment of otherwise ineligible entities.

Many underpinnings of the provisions of the new law (and indeed, even the 1986 Bankruptcy Law) can be found, in one form or another and to varying degrees, in the U.S. Bankruptcy Code—and, more specifically, in chapter 11 thereof. Some of the comparable provisions are summarized in the following table, and will be discussed in further detail in the chapters to follow.

Comparison of U.S. Bankruptcy Code and Enterprise Bankruptcy Law

U.S. Bankruptcy Code	Enterprise Bankruptcy Law
Who May be a Debtor: varies for chapters 7, 9, 11, 12, 13 and 15; generally, insurance companies and banks are not eligible. Section 109.	Enterprise Legal Person. Article 2.
Eligibility for chapter 11: no requirement to demonstrate insolvency; stockbrokers and commodity brokers are not eligible. Section 109.	Must establish inability to pay debts as they mature or have insufficient assets to pay debts; with respect to an application for reorganization, the court must be satisfied reorganization is necessary.
Debtor allowed to operate business in the ordinary course. Sections 1107 and 1108.	In a reorganization, debtor may "manage its affairs" under administrator's supervision. Article 73.
Duties and powers of debtor in possession/ trustee. Section 1106.	Duties and powers of administrator. Article 25.
Executory contracts. Section 365.	Executory contracts. Article 18.
Appointment of Trustee. Section 1104. Conversion to chapter 7 / Dismissal of bankruptcy case. Section 1112.	Termination of Reorganization Procedure. Article 78.
Treatment of Administrative Claims. Section 503(b)/507(a).	Bankruptcy Expenses and Common-Interest Debts. Articles 41–43.
Debtor in Possession Financing. Section 364.	Loans permitted during Reorganization Period. Article 75.
Creation of Bankruptcy Estate. Section 541.	The Debtor's Property. Article 30.

U.S. Bankruptcy Code	Enterprise Bankruptcy Law
Automatic Stay enjoining all acts and actions against debtor and debtor's property. Section 362.	Suspension of acts against debtor's property. Article 19. Suspension of litigation (may resume after administrator takes over). Article 20.
Venue. 28 U.S.C. § 1408. Location of chapter 11 case: domicile, or principal place of business/assets in the U.S. during 180 days prior to filing (or greatest portion thereof), or district where bankruptcy case of an affiliate is pending.	Venue. Article 3. Location of case: debtor's domicile (place of main business office or company registration).
Preferences. Section 547. Recovery of transfers, made within ninety days prior to filing, on account of antecedent debt and giving advantage to preferred creditor.	Avoidance of Payments. Article 32. Avoidance of transfers made to creditors by insolvent debtor within six months prior to filing.
Fraudulent Conveyances. Section 548. Avoidance of transfers made within two years prior to filing either with the intention to defraud creditors or by an insolvent debtor for less than reasonably equivalent value.	Fraudulent Transfers. Avoidance of certain transactions made within one year prior to filing. Article 31. Avoidance of actions to hide assets or fabricate debts. Article 33.
Time Deadline to File Claims. Section 501/Bankruptcy Rules 3001/3007.	Time Deadlines. Articles 45 & 48. Filing Written Claims. Article 49.
Doctrine of Excusable Neglect.	Eliminated in enacted law.
Unmatured Interest Not Allowed on Unsecured Claims. Section 502(b).	No Unmatured Interest on Claims. Article 46.
Obligations of Joint Debtors. Section 509.	Rights of Creditors against Joint Debtors. Article 52.
Creditors' Meeting. Section 341.	Creditors Allowed to Attend Creditors' Meeting. Article 59. Timing of Creditors' Meeting. Article 62. What Can Occur at Meeting. Article 61. Governance at Creditors' Meeting. Articles 60, 61, 64.
Appointment of Creditors' Committee. Section 1102. Ordinarily, holders of seven largest unsecured claims are appointed. Committee may be expanded, including to accommodate small business creditors with disproportionately large claims.	Appointment of Creditors' Committee. No greater than nine members, with one representative of labor claims required. Article 67. Secured creditors not eligible to vote on liquidation or conciliation plans. Article 59.

U.S. Bankruptcy Code	Enterprise Bankruptcy Law
Powers/Duties of Creditors' Committee. Section 1103. Oversees/monitors case.	Powers/Duties of Creditors' Committee. Article 68. Supervises management, disposal, and distribution of debtor's property. Proposes convention of creditors' meeting. Exercises other functions consigned by the creditors' meeting.
Contents of Plan of Reorganization. Section 1123.	Contents of Plan. Article 81.
Classification of Claims. Section 1122. Claims in same class must be similar. Business justification for separation of similar claims. Convenience claims allowed.	Classification. Article 82. Separate voting groups for secured claims, labor claims, taxes, and unsecured claims. "Sub-group of small-amount claims" allowed.
Voting on Plan. Section 1126. By class. More than one-half in number of claims voting, and at least two-thirds in amount of claims voting.	Voting Requirements. Article 84. By voting group. More than one-half in number of creditors present at the creditors' meeting, and more than two-thirds in total amount of claims.
Cramdown. Section 1129(b). Plan of reorganization may be confirmed by the court notwithstanding non-acceptance by a class of creditors, if all provisions of section 1129(a) other than 1129(a)(8) are met, and the plan— does not discriminate unfairly between similarly situated claims; and is fair and equitable with respect to each impaired, non-accepting class.	Cramdown. Article 87. Plan of reorganization may be approved by the court notwithstanding non-acceptance by a group of creditors, if the plan provides for— secured claims to be fully paid by collateral (unless such group accepts lesser treatment); labor claims and tax claims to be fully paid (unless such groups accept lesser treatment); unsecured claims to be paid no less than under bankruptcy liquidation (unless such group accepts lesser treatment); equity interest holders' interests to be adjusted fairly and equitably (unless such group accepts lesser treatment); members of the same group to be treated fairly, equally, and according to the priority prescribed in Article 113; and the operation scheme of the debtor is feasible.

U.S. Bankruptcy Code	Enterprise Bankruptcy Law
Exclusive Time to File a Plan. Section 1121. 120 days from the order for relief. Can be extended for "cause," but not beyond 18 months.	Time to File a Plan. Article 79. Six months from the order allowing reorganization. Can be extended for an additional three months upon "reasonable grounds."

Some of the following key issues in the Enterprise Bankruptcy Law are addressed in its first several provisions.

- Article 1 – Purpose. Article 1 provides that the law "is formulated in order to regularize the enterprise bankruptcy procedures, fairly dispose of credits and debts, protect the lawful rights and interests of creditors and debtors, and maintain the order of the socialist market economy."[4]
- Article 2 – Eligibility. In order to be a debtor under the new law, an entity must be "an enterprise legal person" that "is unable to pay off the debts as they become due, and its assets are insufficient to pay off all of its debts or it is obviously lacking in the capability to repay the debts."
- Article 3 – Venue. Proceedings are proper before the People's Court that sits in the debtor's domicile.
- Article 5 – Foreign Proceedings. Article 5 provides that proceedings initiated under the new law will cover property of the debtor outside of China, and that the People's Court shall review requests for recognition and enforcement of foreign judgments and orders involving a debtor's property within China. Further, the People's Court will enforce such judgment or order if it "neither violates the basic principles of the law of the People's Republic of China, nor impairs the national sovereignty and security and public interests of the society or the lawful rights and interests of the creditors in the territory of the People's Republic of China."
- Article 6 – Employees. Article 6 provides that the People's Court "shall protect the lawful rights and interests of the employees of

[4] In addition, reminiscent of goals expressed in the legislative history of the U.S. Bankruptcy Code, the Enterprise Bankruptcy Law is intended to "maximize the earnings of creditors and maintain the overall social interests and increase the possibility of passing the reorganization plan." 2004 Draft Explanation.

the enterprise" when deciding bankruptcy proceedings, and furthermore, the court shall "enforce legal responsibilities of the management personnel."

- Article 7 – Three Types of Relief. The new law provides for three forms of relief: (i) reorganization, (ii) conciliation, and (iii) liquidation, as will be discussed in the following section.

4.3 Three Alternatives: Reorganization, Conciliation, and Liquidation

As noted, one of the breakthrough achievements of the Enterprise Bankruptcy Law is that it expands and refines the alternatives available for dealing with financially and/or operationally distressed entities in China. Where prior PRC law provided what was essentially a liquidation-oriented approach (albeit containing the concept of conciliation by agreement with creditors, as well as a very limited possibility of reorganization), the new law explicitly delineates three alternative routes for the bankruptcy process: (i) reorganization, (ii) conciliation, and (iii) liquidation.

Road Map of Bankruptcy Procedures

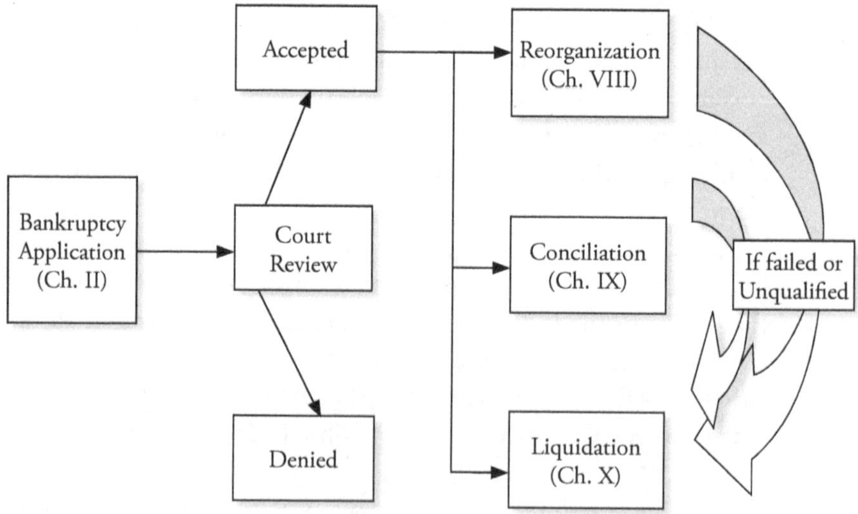

4.3.1 Reorganization

Chapter VIII of the Enterprise Bankruptcy Law contains "reorganization" provisions in twenty-five articles, discussed in detail in Chapter Nine of this book. The following chart summarizes some of the key differences between the 1986 Bankruptcy Law and the new law with respect to reorganization.

Reorganization Measures

	1986 Bankruptcy Law	Enterprise Bankruptcy Law
Applicable Scope	Limited to involuntary bankruptcy proceedings of SOEs.	Bankruptcy proceedings of any enterprise legal person eligible to be a debtor.
Permitted Applicants	Limited to governmental department responsible for SOE-debtor.	Debtors; Creditors; Shareholders; Financial Regulatory Authorities.
Duration of Reorganization	Up to two years.	Six months to file plan, with possible extension of three months, generally followed by voting within thirty days and court approval within the next forty days.
Implementation of Reorganization Plan	Adopted by governmental department responsible for SOE-debtor.	Adopted by creditors' meeting, and confirmed by the People's Court.

4.3.2 Conciliation

Chapter IX of the Enterprise Bankruptcy Law contains "conciliation" provisions in twelve articles, presenting a process by which the debtor and its creditors may agree to a compromise and settlement of the debtor's debts as an alternative to liquidation or a drawn-out reorganization proceeding. In this context, conciliation is an arrangement, outside of bankruptcy, by a debtor and its creditors for payment or rescheduling of the debtor's obligations.

4.3.2.1 Application for and Acceptance of Conciliation Procedure

Pursuant to Article 95 of the Enterprise Bankruptcy Law, "[t]he debtor may . . . apply to the People's Court for conciliation directly, or apply to the People's Court for conciliation after the bankruptcy application is accepted but before the bankruptcy of the debtor is declared by the People's Court." It appears that only the debtor (and not its creditors) may apply for conciliation; in order to do so, the debtor must submit a proposed conciliation agreement.[5]

Upon verifying that the application complies with the provisions of the new law, the court shall issue an order permitting the conciliation procedure, give public notice of the order, and call for a creditors' meeting to be convened.[6] The Enterprise Bankruptcy Law unfortunately does not set forth the standards for determining whether a conciliation application complies with or violates the new law.

Secured creditors (stayed by Article 19 from exercising their rights upon acceptance of the case) regain the ability to exercise their rights "from the date the People's Court makes a ruling of conciliation."[7] As a practical matter, this timing may be premature from the perspective of the administrator and/or debtor, inasmuch as they likely would prefer to avoid the distraction of foreclosure actions when dealing with questions about and adjustments to the proposed conciliation agreement (as will be discussed). Secured creditors also may be able to strip the debtor of operational assets needed for the debtor to fulfill the proposed conciliation agreement, as well as obtain recoveries that could violate the distribution priorities established with respect to certain employee obligations (in the event that the conciliation attempt fails and the debtor is liquidated).

4.3.2.2 Adoption of the Conciliation Agreement by Creditors

Once called by the court, a creditors' meeting shall convene to vote on the conciliation agreement. In order to pass, more than half of the unsecured creditors present and eligible to vote and possessing more than two-thirds in amount of the unsecured claims must vote in favor of the agreement.[8]

If the conciliation agreement is passed by the creditors' meeting, then the court shall issue an order acknowledging the agreement and suspending the bankruptcy proceeding, and it shall instruct the administrator to suspend performance of his duties.[9] The administrator is to transfer the debtor's property and business to the debtor, and then submit a report concerning the performance of his duties to the court.[10] Once acknowledged by the

[5] Enterprise Bankruptcy Law, art. 95.

[6] *Id.*, art. 96.

[7] *Id.*

[8] *Id.*, art. 97.

[9] *Id.*, art. 98.

[10] *Id.*, art. 98.

court, the conciliation agreement shall be binding on the debtor and all pre-application creditors,[11] and the debtor shall pay off its debts according to the conciliation agreement.[12]

In the event that the debtor reaches unanimous agreement with all creditors concerning disposal of credits and its debt, the debtor "may request the People's Court to acknowledge the agreement and conclude the bankruptcy procedures."[13]

If the proposed conciliation agreement is not adopted by the creditors' meeting, or the conciliation agreement adopted by the creditors is not acknowledged by the People's Court, then the court shall issue an order declaring the debtor bankrupt.[14] The new law does not specify grounds or standards for the People's Court to acknowledge, or refuse to acknowledge, a conciliation agreement adopted by creditors.

If a conciliation agreement that has been acknowledged by the court is determined later to have been obtained by the debtor's fraud or other unlawful conduct, then the agreement shall be invalidated and the debtor declared bankrupt.[15] Furthermore, if the debtor refuses or is unable to pay off its debts according to the conciliation agreement, then the creditors may request that the court declare the debtor bankrupt, whereupon "the People's Court shall rule to terminate the implementation of the conciliation agreement and declare the debtor bankrupt."[16] If this happens, the payments already received by the conciliating creditors would "remain valid," but unpaid portions of the claims would be considered bankruptcy claims.[17]

4.3.2.3 Discharge

Article 106 of the Enterprise Bankruptcy Law provides that "[w]ith respect to debts that have been reduced or exempted according to the conciliation agreement, the debtor shall be exempted from the repayment liability upon completion of the implementation of the conciliation

---

[11] *Id.*, art. 100.

[12] *Id.*, art. 102.

[13] *Id.*, art. 105.

[14] *Id.*, art. 99.

[15] *Id.*, art. 103.

[16] *Id.*, art. 104.

[17] *Id.* Creditors who received distributions under the invalidated conciliation agreement then may receive distributions on their remaining bankruptcy claims "only if other creditors have been repaid to the same proportion."

agreement."[18] Once payments are made by the debtor pursuant to the terms of the conciliation agreement, therefore, the debtor is discharged from pre-bankruptcy obligations to creditors.

The conciliation alternative seemingly was provided to offer debtors an accelerated process for settling and reducing unsecured debt where it may not be necessary to utilize the more-elaborate procedures contained in the reorganization chapter. Indeed, a debtor choosing conciliation would probably be seeking to improve its financial performance simply by adjusting the unsecured liabilities on its balance sheet, rather than (also) effecting operational changes. In contrast, the reorganization option would be preferable if the debtor (i) needed postpetition financing, (ii) needed to cram down on unsecured debt, or (iii) would benefit from rejecting unprofitable contracts, recovering fraudulent conveyances and preferences, or the like.

4.3.3 Bankruptcy Liquidation

Chapter X of the Enterprise Bankruptcy Law establishes bankruptcy liquidation provisions in its eighteen articles. Although parties may seek liquidation upon acceptance of a bankruptcy application by the People's Court (*i.e.*, at the outset of the bankruptcy case), the new law also provides for liquidation as the ultimate resolution either where no successful application for conciliation or reorganization is made, or where an attempt at conciliation or reorganization has failed. The immediate precursor to liquidation is the formal declaration of bankruptcy by the People's Court, which may be precipitated by the occurrence of myriad disqualifying events in the context of either conciliation or reorganization.

4.3.3.1 Declaration of Bankruptcy

Rather than requiring the filing of an application specifically for liquidation, Chapter X simply provides that "[i]f the People's Court declares the debtor bankrupt in accordance with this Law, it shall, within five days after the ruling is made, serve the ruling on the debtor and administrator."[19] The court will then notify creditors (whose addresses are known) within ten days and make a public announcement of the bankruptcy order.[20]

---

[18] *Id.*, art. 106.

[19] *Id.*, art. 107.

[20] *Id.*

The new law's concept of being declared bankrupt has no close counterpart in current U.S. bankruptcy law,[21] although it is found in the prior formulation of Chinese bankruptcy law. The 1986 Bankruptcy Law made a distinction between obtaining approval of a bankruptcy application and declaration of bankruptcy. Approval of the bankruptcy application occurred at the beginning of the process, allowing the bankruptcy case to commence; on the other hand, declaration of bankruptcy could occur either immediately thereafter or when liquidation became inevitable.[22] This distinction has been carried over to the Enterprise Bankruptcy Law. Pursuant to Article 93 of the new law, with respect to reorganization (and as was discussed with respect to conciliation), the People's Court is to declare the debtor bankrupt when the debtor is unable (or fails) to carry out its non-liquidating alternatives.

The only way for a debtor to avoid being declared bankrupt (other than successfully contesting an application for involuntary liquidation) is for the People's Court to conclude the bankruptcy procedures because either: (i) the debtor pays off the debts that are currently due, or (ii) a third party pays off the debts that are currently due for the debtor, or guarantees all the debtor's debts in full.[23]

4.3.3.2 Plan of Disposal; Asset Sales

In a liquidation, the administrator is responsible for drafting a plan for the disposal of estate property. Once the proposed plan of disposal is submitted to and adopted by the creditors' meeting (or approved by the court, if the creditors' meeting is unable to resolve the matter),[24] the administrator shall dispose of the property in accordance with the plan.[25]

With respect to liquidation of assets, Article 112 provides that "[t]he pricing and sale of the bankruptcy estate shall be conducted through an auction, unless otherwise decided by resolutions of the creditors' meeting. The bankrupt enterprise may be wholly or partially sold after pricing. . . . [and] [i]ntangible assets and other assets may be sold separately. Any property that is not allowed to be sold through auction or is subject to transfer restrictions under the provisions of the law or regulations shall be disposed of

---

[21] Douglass G. Boshkoff and Yongxin Song, *China's New Enterprise Bankruptcy Law: A Translation and Brief Introduction*, 61 Am. Bankr. L.J. 359, 361 (1987).

[22] 1986 Bankruptcy Law, art. 23.

[23] Enterprise Bankruptcy Law, art. 108.

[24] *See id.*, art. 65.

[25] *Id.*, art. 111.

in accordance with the relevant provisions of the law or regulations."[26] These sale provisions are set forth only in the context of the liquidation chapter of the new law. The flexibility that asset sales may provide to a debtor could increase its chances of achieving a successful reorganization. Therefore, it is advisable for the authorities to consider including asset sales provisions in the reorganization section of the new law (*i.e.*, Chapter VIII).

Regardless of whether sale of PRC assets occur in the context of a liquidation of a bankrupt enterprise pursuant to Article 112 or a reorganization pursuant to future provisions, that sale presumably still would be subject to other regulations, especially with respect to foreign investors.[27]

4.3.3.3 Plan of Distribution; Priority Scheme

In addition to liquidating the estate, the administrator is responsible for devising a plan for distribution of the liquidated estate.[28] The plan must set forth the following elements: (1) the name and domicile of creditors receiving distributions under the plan; (2) the amount of claims participating in the distribution; (3) the amount of estate value available for distribution; (4) the priority, proportion, and amount of distributions; and (5) the method(s) of distribution.[29] The plan is submitted first to the creditors' meeting for adoption, and then to the court for confirmation.[30]

Article 113 is the primary provision that sets out the priority by which unsecured claims are to be satisfied out of the liquidated estate. Following payment of bankruptcy expenses and common-interest debts, the estate is to be distributed to satisfy labor claims, followed by tax claims, and then general bankruptcy claims.[31] With respect to contingent claims and claims relating to pending litigation, the administrator shall reserve distribution shares to

---

[26] *Id.*, art. 112.

[27] *See, e.g., Provisional Regulations on Administration of the Transfer of State-Owned Assets and Equity of Enterprises*, issued jointly by the SASAC and MOF, Dec. 31, 2003, effective Feb. 1, 2004; *Provisional Regulations on Acquisition of Domestic Enterprises by Foreign Investors*, issued jointly by MOFTEC, the State Administration of Taxation, SAIC, and SAFE, Mar. 7, 2003, effective Apr. 12, 2003; *Provisional Regulations on Restructuring State-Owned Enterprises Using Foreign Investment*, promulgated by the State Economic and Trade Commission, MOF, SAIC, and SAFE, Nov. 8, 2002, effective Jan. 1, 2003.

[28] Enterprise Bankruptcy Law, art. 115.

[29] *Id.*, art. 115.

[30] *Id.*, arts. 115, 116. Note that secured credotors are not entitled to vote on liquidation plans. *See id.*, art. 59.

[31] *Id.*, art. 113.

Liquidation Priorities of the Enterprise Bankruptcy Law

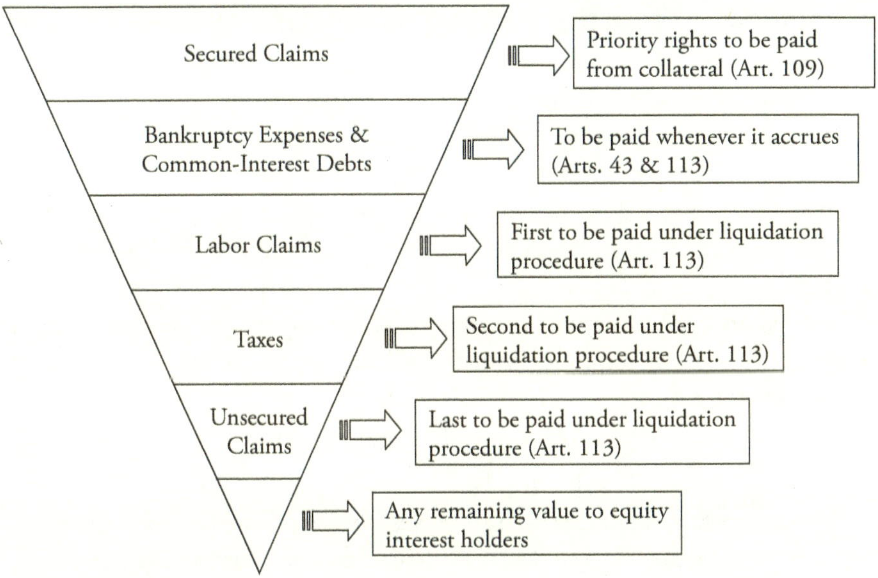

Labor claims that were incurred before Aug. 27, 2006 may be satisfied with proceeds from the sale of encumbered assets, with priority over secured creditors, to the extent they cannot be satisfied from unencumbered sources.

settle such accounts.[32] As was the case under the prior law, the Enterprise Bankruptcy Law provides that when assets are insufficient to meet all of the repayment needs of a class of claims, the property will be distributed on a *pro rata* basis within the class.[33]

Despite the fact that equity interests are not addressed in Article 113, they presumably would receive any residual value after distributions to claimholders.[34] Likewise, secured claims are not addressed in Article 113; nevertheless, the liquidation chapter provides elsewhere that "[a]ny holder of security interests in specific property of the bankrupt has the priority right to

---

[32] *Id.*, arts. 117, 119. These distribution shares are subject to reallocation if not collected within certain periods of time.

[33] *Id.*, art. 113.

[34] Note, however, that no provisions in the liquidation chapter or in the sections dealing with the creditors' meetings provide for voting by equity interest holders on a liquidation plan.

be repaid by such particular property."[35] Despite this measure, the priority of secured claims is still vulnerable in certain circumstances under the new law.

Although the 1986 Bankruptcy Law provided that the claims of secured creditors in SOE proceedings were to be satisfied prior to labor claims, State Council circulars subsequently provided that labor claims are to be paid out of collateral when necessary.[36] This priority scheme was incorporated into the second draft of the Enterprise Bankruptcy Law during its development, but was then removed in the following draft. The correct priority between secured claims and labor claims continued to be the subject of much debate, as drafters strove to balance the business-oriented goals of the new law with social and political concerns over mass layoffs and the possible lack of compensation or protection for workers. Ultimately, the new law was enacted with a compromise, set forth in Article 132.

Under Article 132 of the law, collateral used to secure claims—

> shall be used, prior to the repayment to the holders of security interests in such specific properties, to pay off the portions of wages, the subsidies for medical treatment and disability, and the pensions for the disabled and the families of the deceased which are due and unpaid, the fees for the basic pension insurance and the basic medical insurance which should have been paid into the individual accounts of the employees and which are unpaid, and other compensations payable to the employees under the laws and administrative regulations, which in each case is incurred prior to the promulgation date hereof and has not been paid off in full through the liquidation procedure as provided in Article 113 hereof.[37]

Thus, to the extent they cannot be satisfied from the liquidated estate, labor claims under the Enterprise Bankruptcy Law of the kind enumerated here will be repaid with the proceeds of secured creditors' collateral ahead of secured claims, *but* only *if* such labor claims were incurred *before* August 27, 2006 (the promulgation date of the new law). Labor claims incurred on or after August 27, 2006, will not enjoy this priority over secured claims. Note,

---

[35] Enterprise Bankruptcy Law, art. 109.

[36] *See* Chapter Two, *supra.*

[37] Enterprise Bankruptcy Law, art. 132.

however, that SOEs enrolled in the Policy Bankruptcy program are exempt from this amended priority scheme.

The following table summarizes the new law's compromise treatment of labor claims and secured claims.

Cases filed under:	**Labor Claims incurred BEFORE Aug. 27, 2006**	**Labor Claims incurred ON/AFTER Aug. 27, 2006**
1986 Bankruptcy Law; 1991 Civil Procedure Law	In practice, notwithstanding statutes, Labor Claims take priority over Secured Claims.	In practice, notwithstanding statutes, Labor Claims take priority over Secured Claims.
Policy Bankruptcy program	Labor Claims take priority over Secured Claims.	Labor Claims take priority over Secured Claims through 2008; status thereafter unclear.
Enterprise Bankruptcy Law	Labor Claims take priority over Secured Claims.	**Secured Claims take priority over Labor Claims.**

4.3.3.4 Termination of Bankruptcy Proceeding

Where the bankruptcy estate has no assets, or upon final distribution of estate assets and submission of a report thereof to the court, the administrator shall apply to the People's Court for termination of the bankruptcy proceeding.[38] The court shall make its determination within the following fifteen days.[39] Within ten days after the People's Court orders the termination of the proceeding, the administrator shall arrange for the cancellation of the debtor's business registration with the appropriate authorities.[40] The administrator's duties shall then be concluded, unless pending litigation or arbitration exists.[41] No explicit provision has been made under the new law for discharge of liabilities in the liquidation context.

---

[38] *Id.*, art. 120.

[39] *Id.*

[40] *Id.*, art. 121.

[41] *Id.*, art. 122.

CHAPTER FIVE: Commencing a Bankruptcy Proceeding

5.1 Who May Be a Debtor

5.1.1 Entities: SOE and Non-SOE Distinction

As previously noted, one of the major innovations of the Enterprise Bankruptcy Law is that its application is not limited to SOEs. Unlike its counterpart in the 1986 Bankruptcy Law, Article 2 of the Enterprise Bankruptcy Law makes no distinction between SOEs and non-SOEs.[1] It is important to note, however, that the Enterprise Bankruptcy Law—and its reorganization procedure—does not apply to all non-SOEs: the Enterprise Bankruptcy Law is applicable to "dispose" the debts of only enterprise legal persons that are insolvent.[2]

Nevertheless, many other enterprise legal persons that are not SOEs could still qualify to be debtors under the Enterprise Bankruptcy Law. In general contrast to U.S. law, commercial banks, insurance companies, and other financial institutions are able to be considered debtors under the Enterprise Bankruptcy Law, as codified in Article 134.[3]

On the other hand, other types of entities are not eligible to be debtors. These include partnerships, their partners, sole proprietorships, their investors, other profit-making organizations, and natural persons engaged in industry or commerce. Although earlier drafts of the Enterprise Bankruptcy Law provided eligibility to these entities, the law as enacted excludes them.[4] The enacted law also provides that, with respect to the liquidation of non-

---

[1] *Compare* 1986 Bankruptcy Law, art. 2 *with* Enterprise Bankruptcy Law, art. 2.

[2] Enterprise Bankruptcy Law, art. 2; *see also id.*, art. 135. By carving out SOEs enrolled in the Policy Bankruptcy Program, the Enterprise Bankruptcy Law implicitly covers all other SOEs. *See id.*, art. 133.

[3] The State Council's financial regulatory authority may, under Article 134 of the Enterprise Bankruptcy Law, petition for the reorganization or bankruptcy liquidation of such entities. As of this writing, the CBRC has reported that a special ordinance relating to the bankruptcy of banking and financial institutions is being devised. *See China starts legislative procedure on bankruptcy of banking institutions*, Xinhua News, Feb. 8, 2008.

[4] Enterprise Bankruptcy Law, art. 2. Furthermore, personal bankruptcies are not within the scope of the new law, due to the country's underdeveloped systems regarding property registration. *See* 2004 Draft Explanation.

qualifying entities, its liquidation provisions nonetheless "shall apply as reference."[5]

The provisions in the Enterprise Bankruptcy Law setting forth which entities qualify as debtors have their U.S. counterpart in section 109 of the U.S. Bankruptcy Code. Entitled "Who may be a debtor," section 109 defines the eligibility requirements to become a debtor, and states that "only a person that resides or has a domicile, a place of business, or property in the United States, or a municipality," may be eligible as a debtor under U.S. federal bankruptcy law.[6] A "person" is defined under section 101(41) of the U.S. Bankruptcy Code to include individuals, partnerships, and corporations.[7] Unlike the Enterprise Bankruptcy Law, individuals are eligible for bankruptcy under the U.S. Bankruptcy Code.

5.1.2 Prerequisites: Financial Requirements

As a qualifying threshold, Article 2 of the Enterprise Bankruptcy Law provides, in part, that an enterprise legal person is eligible for a bankruptcy proceeding if it "is unable to pay off the debts as they become due, and its assets are insufficient to pay off all of its debts or it is obviously lacking in the capability to repay the debts." Thus, the Enterprise Bankruptcy Law contains an insolvency requirement that encompasses both of the two common formulations of insolvency—"balance sheet" insolvency (in which total liabilities exceed fair value of assets) and "equitable" insolvency (in which the debtor is unable to pay debts as they come due).[8]

---

[5] Enterprise Bankruptcy Law, art. 135. Conversely, certain other laws (such as the Partnership Enterprise Law, Private Education Promotion Law, and Rural Professional Cooperatives Law) now reference the Enterprise Bankruptcy Law on bankruptcy liquidation.

[6] 11 U.S.C. § 109. The U.S. Bankruptcy Code also includes provisions addressing individuals who may qualify for bankruptcy relief under its specific chapters.

[7] Subsections (b), (c), (e), and (f) of section 109 set forth the qualifications for debtor status under chapter 7 (liquidation), chapter 9 (municipalities), chapter 12 (family farmers and fishermen with regular income), and chapter 13 (individuals with regular income). *See* 11 U.S.C. § 109. Subsection (d) designates the qualifications to attain debtor status under chapter 11 (reorganization) of the U.S. Bankruptcy Code. Specifically, railroads and persons that qualify to be debtors under chapter 7 may be debtors under chapter 11; stockbrokers and commodity brokers, however, are specifically excluded from eligibility. *See id.*

[8] In comparison, the U.S. Bankruptcy Code does not require a debtor to be insolvent before commencing a voluntary case under chapter 7 or chapter 11, although one form of insolvency is required to be shown for an involuntary petition. *See id.* § 303(h).

Article 2 goes on, however, to provide specifically that an enterprise legal person may be reorganized under the Enterprise Bankruptcy Law where it "falls within the preceding paragraph, or there is an obvious possibility that it will lose the capability to repay its debts."[9] This modification to the first standard provides a more liberal threshold for access to reorganization; in other words, Article 2 provides that an enterprise seeking to utilize the law's reorganization provisions is allowed to satisfy a lower standard than when it seeks to utilize the law's conciliation or liquidation provisions, for which the new law requires both equitable and balance sheet insolvency. This was established intentionally to enable and encourage debtors to seek reorganization earlier, while a possibility of success still exists.[10]

Furthermore, Article 7 sets an even lower standard of eligibility for reorganization in the involuntary context. Entirely omitting the second element set forth in the first paragraph of Article 2, Article 7 specifies simply that a creditor may file an application for reorganization or liquidation against a debtor if the debtor "is unable to pay off its debts as they become due." This standard also was intentional, designed to address the practical reality that "creditors sometimes are not fully aware of the assets and liabilities of debtors."[11]

Unfortunately, the Enterprise Bankruptcy Law provides no guidance on a number of related issues, including the standard by which to measure a debtor's inability to pay debts, and whether ceasing payment to a single creditor (rather than some greater number) would suffice to meet the threshold, especially for an involuntary application.[12] In fact, previous drafts

---

[9] Enterprise Bankruptcy Law, art. 2.

[10] *See* 2004 Draft Explanation.

[11] *See id.*

[12] The U.S. Bankruptcy Code similarly does not elaborate on the phrase "generally not paying . . . debts as such debts become due" in reference to section 303(h)(1), which provides one of the grounds on which a petition for involuntary relief against a debtor can be granted. Case law in the U.S. uses a multi-factor test that provides some guidance for determining whether an involuntary debtor should be held as "generally not paying" its debts. For example, the concept of "generally" is a comparative one, which should be considered in terms of how many debts are being paid in proportion to the total number of debts. Simply failing to pay one creditor the full amount of the debt due to that creditor does not qualify as "generally" not paying. *See* 2 *Collier on Bankruptcy* ¶ 303.14[1] (Alan N. Resnick & Henry J. Sommer eds., 15th ed. rev. 2008).

of what is now Article 2 provided some definitions for inability to pay debts due; it is not clear why the drafters chose to eliminate them, and it remains to be seen whether the question will be addressed in the anticipated judicial interpretation of the new law.

Whereas an enterprise legal person must meet the mentioned financial requirements to qualify as a debtor under the Enterprise Bankruptcy Law, a debtor under U.S. law can commence a voluntary case to liquidate its operations under chapter 7, or to reorganize under chapter 11, without having to meet any specific requirements, including the need to satisfy a solvency test. Indeed, the provisions of chapter 11 do not even explicitly require that case be filed in "good faith," although courts may dismiss a voluntary case for "cause."[13] American courts have found an implicit requirement of good faith with respect to voluntary commencement of a bankruptcy case, holding that a debtor cannot abuse the bankruptcy process, and that a chapter 11 case commenced in bad faith can be dismissed.[14] Under the U.S. law, voluntary cases are commenced simply by filing a petition with the bankruptcy court under the applicable chapter. Involuntary cases require a petition be filed by at least three creditors that each hold claims that are not contingent and not disputed, and that such claims aggregate at least $12,300 more than the value of any lien on property of the debtor securing such claims.[15]

---

[13] *See generally* 11 U.S.C. § 1112(b). Although not explicitly referenced, courts have held that a lack of good faith in filing a chapter 11 petition establishes cause for dismissal. *See, e.g., In re 299 Jack-Hemp Assocs.*, 20 B.R. 412, 413 (Bankr. S.D.N.Y. 1982) (noting that "what is now impressive judicial gloss that an indispensable ingredient of every petition filed in this court is that it be in good faith"). Determination of good faith is a fact-intensive inquiry that requires an analysis of the individual facts and circumstances of each case. Courts have considered many different factors to articulate a good-faith standard, including whether the chapter 11 filing has a valid reorganization purpose. *See In re SGL Carbon Corp.*, 200 F.3d 154, 163 (3d Cir. 1999).

[14] A large body of U.S. case law addresses bad-faith filings. *See, e.g., In re Liberate Techs.*, 314 B.R. 206 (Bankr. N.D. Cal. 2004); *In re SGL Carbon Corp.*, 200 F.3d 154 (3d Cir. 1999); *Marsch v. Marsch (In re Marsch)*, 36 F.3d 825 (9th Cir. 1994). Courts have found bad faith and dismissed a debtor's chapter 11 case where the debtor uses chapter 11 solely as a litigation tactic or as a means to get out of a valid, arm's-length contract. *See, e.g., In re C-TC 9th Ave. P'ship*, 193 B.R. 650 (Bankr. N.D.N.Y. 1995); *Barclays-American/Business Credit, Inc. v. Radio WBHP, Inc. (In re Dixie Broad., Inc.)*, 871 F.2d 1023 (11th Cir. 1989).

[15] 11 U.S.C. § 303.

5.2 Filing and Acceptance of Bankruptcy Application

In order to commence a bankruptcy proceeding under the Enterprise Bankruptcy Law, an entity must file an application with the People's Court. An application may be filed by either the proposed debtor or its creditor(s); this is similar to the voluntary and involuntary petitions provided for under the U.S. Bankruptcy Code.[16] Pursuant to Article 8, "[a] bankruptcy application letter and relevant evidence shall be submitted in filing a bankruptcy application."

The requirements for the content of the application form filed by the debtor or a creditor are identical. The application must include the basic background of the debtor (and the applicant, if not the same) and the purpose and grounds for the application.[17] Article 8 also includes a catch-all provision that requires the applicant to provide "other information required by the People's Court," which allows the presiding bankruptcy judge to use discretion in determining, on a case-by-case basis, what other financial, factual, and administrative details should be presented to the court.

If the application is filed by the debtor, then the debtor shall also submit "a description of the status of its property, a complete list of debts, a complete list of claims, relevant financial and accounting reports, a proposal on settlement of employees, the payment status of employees' wages and the status of employees' social insurance contribution."[18] When the application is filed by a creditor, however, the debtor is given fifteen days from service of the court's order accepting the proceeding to provide these supplemental materials.[19]

An applicant need not elect reorganization, conciliation, or liquidation (as applicable) at the time of filing its bankruptcy application; it is important to note, however, that nothing in the Enterprise Bankruptcy Law suggests that it may not do so at such time. Indeed, neither the general provisions nor the chapters on reorganization and conciliation specify when a debtor or creditor must apply for reorganization or conciliation (as applicable), other than that it must occur before the debtor is declared bankrupt by the court

---

16 Similar to the U.S. Bankruptcy Code, the Enterprise Bankruptcy Law allows the debtor to contest the filing of an involuntary application. Article 10 allows the debtor to raise an objection within seven days from receipt of notice of the involuntary application.

17 Enterprise Bankruptcy Law, art. 8.

18 *Id.*

19 *Id.*, art. 11.

(which is the step that triggers the liquidation process).[20] Thus, although it appears that liquidation is the default outcome in the absence of an application for reorganization or conciliation being filed and accepted, the Enterprise Bankruptcy Law does not explicitly specify a timeframe in which the court is to make a declaration of the debtor's bankruptcy.

Pursuant to Article 10, the People's Court "shall make a ruling as to whether to accept the bankruptcy application within fifteen days from the date of receipt of the bankruptcy application."[21] In special circumstances, this initial period may be extended for fifteen days with the permission of a superior court.[22] The People's Court shall issue its decision in an order either accepting or rejecting the application. Similar to the 1986 Bankruptcy Law, however, the Enterprise Bankruptcy Law does not provide guidance as to any standard (beyond the eligibility requirements in Article 2) to be applied by a bankruptcy judge in determining whether to accept or reject a bankruptcy application.

If the court accepts an application, then it shall serve its order of acceptance to the debtor within five days after issuing the order.[23] Even after it has accepted an application, the court may make another order rejecting the application if it finds that the debtor does not meet the eligibility requirements of Article 2.[24] Concurrent with issuing an order accepting a bankruptcy application, the court shall designate an administrator, as will be discussed further in Section 6.1.[25] Within twenty-five days after issuing the order, the court shall give notice thereof to all creditors whose addresses are known, and make a public announcement.[26] Such notice and announcement are to include:

- details concerning the identity of the debtor;
- the name and address of the administrator;
- the time and place appointed for the first meeting of creditors;
- the bar date for the filing of claims; and

---

[20] *See id.*, arts. 70, 95.

[21] Note that, for involuntary applications, the People's Court has ten days from the end of the debtor's objection period to make a ruling.

[22] Enterprise Bankruptcy Law, art. 10.

[23] *Id.*, art. 11.

[24] *Id.*, art. 12.

[25] *Id.*, art. 13.

[26] *Id.*, art. 14.

- notice of the requirement that debts owed to the debtor must be paid and property of the debtor must be turned over to the administrator.[27]

If the court rejects an application (whether initially or after first accepting the proceeding), then it shall serve its order of rejection within five days after issuing the order. The applicant may file an appeal with a superior court within ten days after service of the order of rejection.[28]

Insights and Recommendations

- *Set Forth Clear Standards for Involuntary Filing*

Article 7 of the Enterprise Bankruptcy Law allows for an involuntary bankruptcy application to be filed against a debtor by creditors. This ability of creditors to initiate a bankruptcy proceeding against an uncooperative debtor is a good mechanism to include in any bankruptcy law. Despite this, its usefulness may be blunted without clear standards for its application; in addition, these measures may be abused by aggressive creditors in the absence of clear restrictions.

For example, the authors believe that the regulations should specify that an involuntary application may be filed only jointly by a minimum number of creditors representing a minimum amount of debt owed by the debtor, similar to measures under U.S. bankruptcy law described earlier.[29] This statutory language provides clear standards for who can file an involuntary bankruptcy case.

Also, future regulations might subject creditors to monetary sanctions if they are found to have filed an involuntary application in bad faith (*i.e.*, for abusive purposes), but not simply if a reasonable application is denied. Such a requirement that a minimum number of creditors must apply together likely will reduce the possibility of abuse. Without such clearer standards for involuntary applications, creditors may be encouraged to file proceedings simply for leverage, rather than for legitimate business reasons. Judicial interpretation to clarify the language of Article 7 would help the implementation of this provision.

---

[27] *Id.*

[28] *Id.*, art. 12.

[29] 11 U.S.C. § 303.

5.3 Automatic Stay

5.3.1 The Stay with Respect to Pre-Acceptance Claims

Chapter II of the Enterprise Bankruptcy Law provides a mechanism similar to the automatic stay provided for in section 362 of the U.S. Bankruptcy Code. One of the most important concepts in U.S. bankruptcy and reorganization law is the automatic stay, the purpose of which is to give the debtor a "breathing spell" during which the debtor can attempt to reorganize by selling assets, borrowing money, altering its business, and/or negotiating a capital restructuring without confronting the pressure of the seizure of assets and the commencement of lawsuits. The automatic stay is extremely broad in scope, and applies to almost any type of formal or informal action against the debtor (or property of the debtor's estate). Although the Enterprise Bankruptcy Law also provides for an automatic stay that is similar in concept, it is more limited in scope and distinguishes between collection procedures and pending litigation.

Article 16 of the Enterprise Bankruptcy Law delineates the date of cleavage; after the court accepts a bankruptcy application, whether voluntary or involuntary, the debtor may not pay pre-acceptance debts. Article 19 provides that "[a]fter the People's Court accepts the bankruptcy application, any attachment on the debtor's property shall be discharged and any enforcement procedures shall be suspended." This provision presumably is aimed at enjoining creditor efforts to enforce their claims against the debtor's property (*e.g.*, foreclosure).

Similarly, Article 20 provides that "[a]fter the People's Court accepts the bankruptcy application, any commenced and pending civil litigation or arbitration related to the debtor shall be suspended." However, Article 20 goes on to provide that "after the administrator receives and manages the property of the debtor, such litigation or arbitration shall resume." The Enterprise Bankruptcy Law does not specify any procedures for the resumption of pending litigation, such as obtaining prior leave of the People's Court. Generally, however, the new law affirms the concept of adjudicating in a single court all matters touching the debtor's bankruptcy, as reflected in Article 21, which provides that "[a]fter the People's Court accepts the bankruptcy application, any civil litigation related to the debtor can be brought only to the People's Court which has accepted the bankruptcy application."

The Enterprise Bankruptcy Law provides that civil litigation, preserving measures, and other enforcement procedures concerning the debtor shall be automatically stayed when the People's Court accepts the bankruptcy proceeding.[30] It should be noted, however, that this stay takes effect upon the acceptance of the bankruptcy proceeding—not upon the commencement of the process by the filing of an application. In this respect, the Enterprise Bankruptcy Law is similar to now-defunct U.S. law that was replaced in 1978 by the U.S. Bankruptcy Code. The Bankruptcy Act of 1898 did not provide an automatic stay at the very beginning of a case; as a result, creditors were able to engage in collection efforts in the interim until the debtor was able to obtain a stay.

Section 362 of the U.S. Bankruptcy Code provides that the filing of a petition by or against the debtor automatically stays certain actions against the debtor, including "the commencement or continuation ... of a judicial, administrative, or other action or proceeding against the debtor that was or could have been commenced before the commencement of the case under this title, or to recover a claim against the debtor that arose before the commencement of the case."[31] Acts against property of the debtor or the debtor's estate (*e.g.*, any act to obtain possession of property of the debtor's property, to enforce a prepetition judgment, or perfect or enforce certain liens), also are stayed.[32]

5.3.2 Relief From Stay

In the context of a reorganization proceeding, Article 75 of the Enterprise Bankruptcy Law reiterates that, from the time the People's Court accepts an application for reorganization, "the exercise of security rights in specific property of the debtor shall be suspended." The law goes on to provide, however, that where the collateral "will be damaged or the value thereof will decrease dramatically, which is sufficient to damage the rights of the secured creditor, such secured creditor may request to the People's Court for resuming exercise of the security rights."[33] Although this stay of rights and the need to seek relief therefrom echoes concepts found in section 362(d) of the U.S. Bankruptcy Code, the U.S. law provides a more defined set of "cause" for lifting the stay, including the lack of debtor's equity in property that is

---

[30] *See* Enterprise Bankruptcy Law, arts. 19–21, 75.

[31] 11 U.S.C. § 362(a).

[32] *Id.*

[33] Enterprise Bankruptcy Law, art. 75.

not necessary to an effective reorganization as well as the lack of adequate protection.[34]

Insights and Recommendations

- *Specify Duration of Stay and Implement Earlier Effectiveness of Stay*

In Article 19, the Enterprise Bankruptcy Law provides that "[a]fter the People's Court accepts the bankruptcy application, any attachment with respect to the debtor's property shall be lifted and any enforcement procedures shall be suspended." In contrast, Article 20 separately and specifically provides for a stay of litigation or arbitration that is pending at the time that a bankruptcy proceeding is accepted. This second stay appearing under Article 20 is only temporary, however, in that "after the administrator receives and manages the property of the debtor, such litigation or arbitration shall resume."

Consideration should be given to continuing the Article 20 stay of pending litigation for at least the duration of the period of reorganization, so that the administrator and debtor can concentrate their efforts on restructuring the business without the distraction of having to defend (or prosecute) other matters in other forums.

In addition, as discussed previously, both Articles 19 and 20 provide the stay takes effect upon the acceptance by the People's Court of a bankruptcy application. It may be advisable for implementing regulations to provide for the stay to take effect earlier—upon the filing of the application. The earlier effectiveness of the stay is recommended because the filing itself could trigger a frenzy of collection efforts and the commencement of litigation in anticipation of the court's acceptance of the proceeding.

---

[34] 11 U.S.C. § 362(d)(1) and (2).

CHAPTER SIX: Control of Case; Operation of Business

Once the People's Court has accepted a bankruptcy proceeding, the principal parties involved in moving the proceeding along to its conclusion are the administrator, the creditors' meeting, the court, and (upon request and with the court's ratification) the management of the debtor.

6.1 Administrator

Article 13 of the Enterprise Bankruptcy Law provides that, upon accepting a bankruptcy application, the People's Court shall designate an administrator.[1] The concept of an administrator who is charged with duties similar to those of a trustee under the U.S. Bankruptcy Code is new to China's bankruptcy system, and represents a departure from the "liquidation team" concept utilized in the 1986 Bankruptcy Law.

The 1986 Bankruptcy Law provided for a liquidation team to take over management of a debtor. That team usually consisted of government officials, rather than independent organizations, professional agencies, or people with expertise in the debtor's industry.[2] Because the government typically was a major (if not sole) shareholder, major creditor, and also arbiter of the proceeding all at the same time, the members of a liquidation team often (and perhaps inevitably) represented conflicting interests. In contrast, the Enterprise Bankruptcy Law provides that the administrator is appointed by the court, and will be held accountable to the creditors, in part, through the imposition of fiduciary duties of diligence and loyalty.[3]

Similar to the delayed timing for effectiveness of the automatic stay under Articles 19 and 20, however, it is important to note that an administrator is not appointed until the bankruptcy application is accepted by the People's Court. Unlike U.S. measures, no provision has been made under the new law for an interim administrator to take charge of the debtor's assets or to prevent the piecemeal dismemberment of the debtor "on the doorstep" of the courthouse.

---

[1] Enterprise Bankruptcy Law, art. 13.

[2] *See* Section 2.1.2.1 above.

[3] *See* Enterprise Bankruptcy Law, art. 27; *see also* Kevin B. Fisher, *Bankruptcy Reform: China a Safer Bet*, American Banker, No. 67, Vol. 170, Apr. 8, 2005, at 11.

6.1.1 Administrator's Duties

Put simply, the duties of the administrator are to take over all of the debtor's property, manage the debtor's business, and be accountable to the court and representatives of the creditors.[4] Article 25 provides (in relevant part) that the administrator shall perform the following functions:

(1) taking possession of and managing the debtor's property, seal, accounting books, instruments, and other materials;
(2) investigating into the debtor's property and drafting a status report;
(3) making determinations regarding the debtor's internal management affairs;
(4) making determinations regarding the debtor's daily expenses and other necessary expenses;
(5) before the first creditors' meeting, determining whether the debtor's business shall continue operating;
(6) managing and disposing the debtor's property;
(7) participating in legal proceedings on behalf of the debtor;
(8) calling for the creditors' meeting to be convened; and
(9) fulfilling other functions that the People's Court deems appropriate.

Of particular interest is the requirement that the administrator must determine, by the time of the first meeting of creditors, whether the debtor's business shall continue to operate. This determination may be tantamount to a decision about whether to reorganize or liquidate the debtor.

In addition, the administrator is obligated under Article 69 to report to the creditors' committee (once a creditors' committee is established, as will be discussed), with respect to: transferring real property and various other property rights, inventories, business operations, claims or securities; making a loan; giving security; withdrawing a guaranty; assuming an executory contract; and relinquishing rights.

During the period before the first meeting of creditors, *i.e.*, before a creditors' committee is formed, Article 26 provides that the administrator must obtain court approval of its decision to continue or terminate the

[4] Enterprise Bankruptcy Law, art. 25.

debtor's business operations.[5] Notwithstanding that the administrator's duties are delineated in the Enterprise Bankruptcy Law, it is clear that the level of the administrator's involvement in any particular bankruptcy case will be guided, in large part, by the differing roles that an administrator may be expected to undertake, depending upon the type of bankruptcy proceeding that is pending. For example, an administrator liquidating all of a debtor's assets in a liquidation case might be expected to have a more prominent role than an administrator supervising a debtor in possession in a reorganization case.

6.1.2 Eligibility and Selection

The power to select the administrator was a contentious issue during deliberations over the new law. The July 2004 draft provided that the administrator initially designated by the court could be replaced by creditors at the first creditors' meeting. In the final enacted draft, however, the creditors may only request that the court dismiss the designated administrator and designate a new one if they believe that the first administrator is not performing its functions.[6] Hopefully, this arrangement will better enable administrators to maintain their independence from creditors.

Article 24 provides that the role of the administrator may be performed by a "liquidation panel" composed of staff from relevant government agencies, institutions, law firms, certified public accountants, bankruptcy liquidation service agencies, or relevant "social intermediary institutions." Alternatively, the People's Court may designate an individual administrator who has the requisite professional knowledge and holds a special practice certificate from a relevant social intermediary institution.[7] Individuals who serve as administrators "shall participate in a professional practice liability insurance plan."[8]

Article 22 provides that additional specific measures regarding designation and compensation of the administrator are to be formulated separately by the

---

[5] In addition, under Article 69, the administrator's reporting obligations are directed to the court even after the first creditors' meeting if a creditors' committee is not established.

[6] *See* Enterprise Bankruptcy Law, art. 22.

[7] *Id.*, art. 24. Article 24 also proscribes appointment of any individual or institution that has been criminally punished for an "intentional offense," has lost its relevant license to practice, or is an interested party in the bankruptcy case, or where the People's Court deems it to be otherwise inappropriate.

[8] *Id.*

Supreme People's Court. Accordingly, the People's Court has promulgated *Provisions on Designating the Administrator in Enterprise Bankruptcy Cases* (the "Designation Provisions") and *Provisions on the Determination of Bankruptcy Administrators' Compensation During the Trial of Enterprise Bankruptcy Cases* (the "Compensation Provisions"), which regulate the processes by which administrators are to be designated and compensated, respectively.

As set forth in the Designation Provisions, administrators are selected by the People's Court from separate registers listing qualified social-intermediary institutes or qualified individuals.[9] The administrator registers are compiled by the Higher People's Courts, unless such court determines that the Intermediate People's Courts under its jurisdiction shall formulate the register.[10] Public announcements regarding application for inclusion in the registers are issued through the media, and contain qualifying criteria, application materials, deadlines for submission, and other information deemed necessary.[11] Individual applicants must reside within the city in which the court is located, and institutional applicants must be registered there.[12] Moreover, the Designation Provisions require law firms, accounting firms, and bankruptcy liquidation firms to submit (in addition to other documentation) a professional certificate, either a business license or a governmental document approving the establishment of the institution, and practicing certificates for professionals employed by the institution.[13]

The Designation Provisions generally permit the designation of a social-intermediary institute to administer a bankruptcy case.[14] In the case of designation of an individual, however, Article 17 of the Designation Provisions permits the court to designate an individual from the administrator register where the bankruptcy case involves clear facts, simple creditor/debtor relationships, and a relative concentration of the debtor's property. In any event, administrators are to be designated in random fashion, *e.g.*, through lotteries.[15]

---

[9] Designation Provisions, arts. 1, 2.

[10] *Id.*, art. 2.

[11] *Id.*, art. 5.

[12] *Id.*, arts. 7, 8.

[13] *Id.*, art. 6.

[14] *Id.*, art. 16.

[15] *Id.*, art. 20.

These new provisions regarding the designation of administrators presuppose the existence of a pool of well-trained professionals in the PRC to take on the administrator's role. As one observer has noted, however, "it is quite obvious that the existing pool of professional talents in bankruptcy and reorganization in the PRC is very limited, and is clearly inadequate to deal with what can be imagined to be an avalanche of new bankruptcy proceedings following the enactment of the [Enterprise Bankruptcy Law]."[16] Although the new law provides that, under Article 28, the administrator may "engage necessary working staff" with the permission of the People's Court, this may be of little aid in the bankruptcy process until the greater market problem is corrected by an expansion of "the existing pool of professional talents."

6.1.3 Comparison to Eligibility and Selection of Trustees Under the U.S. Bankruptcy Code

By way of comparison with the Designation Provisions, in a chapter 7 liquidation under U.S. law, the United States Trustee[17] appoints a "disinterested person" that is a member of a panel of private trustees maintained to serve as interim trustees.[18] Later, the creditors may elect a "disinterested person" to serve as trustee in the case.[19] The primary duty of a chapter 7 trustee is to collect and reduce to money (*i.e.*, liquidate) the property of the debtor's estate for distribution to creditors, in accordance with the best interests of the parties.[20] Note that in a chapter 7 liquidation, the appointment of a trustee is a statutory requirement, and the appointment is made by the U.S. Trustee (rather than the bankruptcy court).[21]

As discussed in Section 6.2 below, in a U.S. chapter 11 case, a trustee is not typically appointed. Instead, the debtor automatically becomes a "debtor in

---

[16] Tang, *supra* Chapter One, note 38, at 643.

[17] The United States Trustee (or "U.S. Trustee") is an office created under the Bankruptcy Reform Act of 1978 as a component of the U.S. Department of Justice. Its functions include, among other things, supervising the administration of bankruptcy cases, providing oversight of private trustees, monitoring the conduct of other parties, ensuring compliance with applicable laws and procedures, identifying and investigating bankruptcy fraud and abuse, and otherwise preserving the integrity of the U.S. bankruptcy system.

[18] 11 U.S.C. § 701.

[19] *Id.* § 702.

[20] *Id.* § 704.

[21] *See id.* § 701.

possession" who fulfills most aspects of the trustee's role.[22] Upon application by a party in interest or the U.S. Trustee, however, the bankruptcy court may order the appointment of a trustee to replace the debtor in possession under certain circumstances.[23] If a trustee is appointed, it must be a private trustee who is elected by creditors, subject to specific procedures.[24] If such trustee later dies, resigns, is removed, or fails to post the required bond, then the U.S. Trustee, with the consultation of the parties in interest, selects a replacement trustee, subject to the court's approval.[25]

To be eligible to serve as a trustee in a chapter 7 or 11 case, a person must be: (i) an individual who is competent to perform the duties of such a trustee, or (ii) a corporation authorized by its corporate charter or bylaws to act as a trustee.[26] In addition, in a case under chapter 7 (or 12 or 13, but not 11), an individual trustee must reside or have an office in the district where the case is pending or in an adjacent district, and a corporate trustee must have an office in at least one of such districts.[27] Furthermore, in all cases, the trustee must also be a "disinterested person,"[28] which generally means that the trustee is not related to the debtor or its bankruptcy case, and does not hold an interest materially adverse to the estate. Relatives of the bankruptcy judge making the appointment and the U.S. Trustee responsible for the case

---

[22] *Id.* § 1107.
[23] *Id.* § 1104(a).
[24] *Id.* § 1104(b).
[25] *Id.* § 1104(d).
[26] *Id.* § 321(a).
[27] *Id.*
[28] *See id.* §§ 701(a)(1), 1104(b), 1202(a), and 1302(a). A "disinterested person" under the U.S. Bankruptcy Code means a person who (i) is not a creditor, an equity security holder, or an insider, (ii) is not and was not a director, officer, or employee of the debtor within two years before the date of the filing of the petition, or (iii) does not have "an interest materially adverse to the interest of the estate or of any class of creditors or equity security holders, by reason of any direct of indirect relationship to, connection with, or interest in, the debtor, or for any other reason." *Id.* § 101(14). Although the concept of an adverse interest is not defined in the U.S. Bankruptcy Code, courts have interpreted it to mean "a competing economic interest tending to diminish estate values or to create a potential to actual dispute in which the estate is a rival claimant." *In re Caldor*, 193 B.R. 165, 171 (Bankr. S.D.N.Y. 1996) (citing *In re Leslie Fay Cos.*, 175 B.R. 525, 533 (Bankr. S.D.N.Y. 1994)); *see also In re CF Holding Corp.*, 164 B.R. 799 (Bankr. D. Conn. 1994) (adverse interest means an interest that would tend to decrease the value of the estate or a predisposition or bias against the estate).

are prohibited from serving as a trustee,[29] as is a person who served as an examiner in the same case.[30]

To qualify as a trustee, the elected or selected trustee must file with the court (within five days after selection and before beginning official duties) "a bond in favor of the United States conditioned on the faithful performance of such official duties."[31] The U.S. Trustee determines the amount and terms of the bond and the sufficiency of the surety on each bond.[32]

6.1.4 Compensation for Administrators

In accordance with Article 28 of the Enterprise Bankruptcy Law, the Compensation Provisions issued by the People's Court set forth guidelines for compensating administrators. Article 2 of the Compensation Provisions sets the ceiling rates of compensation, as determined by percentages against the aggregate value of the debtor's property that is available to satisfy claims.[33] The court may, where it deems necessary, set a cap rate tailored to local circumstances, and that rate is to be published in local media.[34] After accepting a bankruptcy application, the court will determine the aggregate value of the debtor's property, and make a preliminary determination on the administrator's compensation scheme.[35] This compensation scheme may be adjusted when necessary, taking into account such factors as the complexity of the bankruptcy case, as well as risks to and responsibilities of the administrator.[36]

The administrator will be notified of the finalized compensation scheme within three days of the preliminary scheme.[37] The administrator must then

---

[29] Fed. R. Bankr. P. 5002.

[30] 11 U.S.C. § 321(b). An examiner is to be distinguished from a trustee. In a chapter 11 case in which a trustee is not appointed, the court may, in certain circumstances, order the appointment of an examiner in order to "conduct such an investigation of the debtor as is appropriate, including an investigation of any allegations of fraud, dishonesty, incompetence, misconduct, mismanagement, or irregularity in the management of the affairs of the debtor or by current or former management of the debtor." *Id.* § 1104(c). The examiner's duties are generally more limited in scope than a trustee's.

[31] *Id.* § 322(a).

[32] *Id.* § 322(b)(2).

[33] Compensation Provisions, art. 2.

[34] *Id.*

[35] *Id.*, art. 4.

[36] *Id.*, arts. 8, 9.

[37] *Id.*, art. 8.

present the compensation scheme and payment schedule at the first creditors' meeting.[38] Any objections raised by the creditors during the meeting shall be submitted to the court in writing with specific requests, supporting reasons, and corresponding resolutions adopted by the creditors.[39] Within ten days of receipt, the court shall notify the administrator and creditors' committee of the outcome of submitted objections.[40] The compensation scheme will not be adjusted unless the court sustains the creditors' objections.

Before the administrator can collect compensation, it must file an application with the People's Court indicating:

(1) information related to the debtor's property available for paying the compensation;
(2) the time needed to complete the collection and the amount of compensation to be collected; and
(3) details regarding the performance of work in implementing the administrators' role.[41]

The compensation for administrator's services generally enjoys priority in payment.[42] If the debtor's property is insufficient to satisfy the compensation scheme, then the administrator may request that the court terminate the bankruptcy procedure, unless the creditors, administrator, debtor's shareholders, or other related persons pledge to pay the compensation.[43]

Insights and Recommendations

- *Restriction on Foreign Firms Qualifying as Administrators*

One important innovation established by the Enterprise Bankruptcy Law over earlier practice is the introduction of the position of administrator. That innovation, however, did not come without controversy, due to disagreement regarding whether non-resident professionals with relevant experience (*e.g.*, accountants in Hong Kong or international law firms) would be allowed to qualify for designation as administrators. It appears that the Designation Provisions, as discussed earlier, confirm that foreign law firms and accounting

---

[38] *Id.*, art. 6.
[39] *Id.*, art. 17.
[40] *Id.*, art. 18.
[41] *Id.*, art. 11.
[42] *Id.*, art. 12.
[43] *Id.*

firms do not qualify to be listed on the registers. In particular, the Designation Provisions require firms to have professional practicing certificates, which are issued only to native Chinese firms.

The introduction of the administrator also represents an effort to add transparency to the management of the debtor in furtherance of protecting creditors' interests. Notwithstanding that the administrator's goals may be aligned with the interests of creditors, some professionals and scholars have noted that, by operation of the new law, administrators are responsible to the court rather than the creditors. For example, as discussed in section 6.1.2, the right to appoint the administrator rests with the court, and creditors must appeal to the court to replace the administrator.

- *Clarify Administrators' Duties In the Various Roles Played By Administrators*

The various roles that an administrator may play in different possible phases of bankruptcy proceedings will also require the People's Court to further clarify the powers and duties administrators have during each stage, as well as the appropriate qualifications necessary for the administrators to effectively discharge their duties. Under the Enterprise Bankruptcy Law, the administrator takes on a number of roles during the following phases of bankruptcy proceedings, including (i) prior to the creditors' meeting, where the administrator takes on a provisional role; (ii) the period following the creditors' meeting; (iii) the period following approval of a plan of reorganization, where the administrator takes on a plan implementation and oversight role; (iv) during implementation of a settlement plan; and (v) during a liquidation, where the administrator acts as a liquidator.

- *Timing of Appointment of Administrator*

The timing of the administrator's appointment raises an issue similar to (and bound up with) the timing of the effectiveness of the automatic stay. The Enterprise Bankruptcy Law provides for the appointment of the administrator upon acceptance of a bankruptcy application, rather than the filing of the application;[44] this may leave debtors vulnerable to creditors racing

---

[44] *See* Enterprise Bankruptcy Law, art. 13.

to exercise their rights in situations where the debtor's financial situation is deteriorating rapidly. It may be advisable to provide for the appointment of an interim administrator, as is the case under section 701 of the U.S. Bankruptcy Code.

- *Confirm Ability of Administrator to Engage Staff and Provide Guidelines for Their Engagement*

Article 28 of the Enterprise Bankruptcy Law allows the administrator to engage "necessary working staff" with permission of the People's Court. It would be desirable for the anticipated rules and regulations first to clarify whether this article is intended to enable the hiring of professionals and experts (*e.g.*, lawyers, accountants, and financial advisors), and then also to clarify the eligibility, "disinterestedness" standards, selection process, and compensation guidelines to be used in their engagement. In addition, it might be desirable for the regulations to clarify whether the debtor, too, may engage such necessary staff when acting in place of the administrator pursuant to Article 73 of the Enterprise Bankruptcy Law.

- *Committee Retention of Professionals is Advisable*

Similarly, the People's Court also may want to consider allowing the Creditors' Committee, created pursuant to Article 67, to retain its own professionals or to have access to the administrator's (or debtor's) professionals, in order to encourage creditors to join the committee and have peace of mind that they will be able to carry out their functions properly and with proper representation. It may also be desirable to have clarification on the standing of the committee (or the creditors' meeting at large) to take action, for instance when the administrator or debtor refuses or fails to pursue certain actions.[45]

---

[45] *See, e.g.*, *Unsecured Creditors Comm. v. Noyes (In re STN Enters.)*, 779 F.2d 901, 904 (2d Cir. 1985); *Official Comm. of Unsecured Creditors of Cybergenics Corp. v. Chinery*, 330 F.3d 548 (3d Cir. 2003) (holding that, with court approval, a creditors' committee may commence an adversary proceeding on behalf of the debtor when the trustee or debtor in possession unjustifiably fails to do so).

6.2 Debtor in Possession

Article 73 of the Enterprise Bankruptcy Law provides that, in the context of a reorganization proceeding, the debtor itself is allowed to "manage its property and business affairs" with the court's permission. Furthermore, the article specifies that the administrator, "who has received and managed the debtor's property and business according to this Law, shall transfer the property and business affairs to the debtor, and the power of the administrator provided for herein shall be exercised by the debtor."[46] Article 73 also provides, however, that the debtor's management of its business and property is subject to the supervision of the administrator, who thus remains in place. The administrator's continuing role specifically includes supervising the implementation of the reorganization plan[47] and submitting a supervision report to the People's Court.[48]

In contrast, upon commencement of a case under chapter 11 of the U.S. Bankruptcy Code, the debtor continues to operate its business and manage the bankruptcy case as a debtor in possession.[49] That is, with certain exceptions, the debtor "shall have all the rights . . . and powers, and shall perform all the functions and duties . . . of a trustee serving in a case under this chapter,"[50] including operation of the debtor's business.[51] The U.S. Bankruptcy Code provides for the appointment of a trustee to take charge of and operate a debtor's business on request of a party in interest "for cause, including fraud, dishonesty, incompetence, or gross mismanagement of the affairs of the debtor by current management,"

---

[46] Enterprise Bankruptcy Law, art. 73.

[47] *Id.* art. 90.

[48] *Id.* art. 91. While the new law provides that management is subject to the supervision of the administrator, there appear to be no provisions that permit an administrator to remove or request the court to remove management. Where the administrator determines that the debtor is being mismanaged or is refusing the administrator's supervision, the only remedy may be to seek termination of the reorganization procedure pursuant to Article 78.

[49] "Debtor in possession" means "debtor" except when a chapter 11 trustee has been appointed. *See* 11 U.S.C. § 1101(1). The debtor in possession often is referred to by the acronym "DIP."

[50] *Id.* § 1107.

[51] *See id.* § 1108.

or if the appointment of a trustee is in the interest of creditors.[52] In practice, ordering the appointment of a trustee in a chapter 11 case is an extraordinary remedy; debtors in possession are not often displaced. This may be due in part to the fact that, to U.S. thinking, unless the remedy is absolutely necessary, creditors would prefer not to dislodge experienced management, especially in cases in which the debtor seeks to reorganize instead of liquidate. Moreover, as discussed in Section 6.1.3, even where the appointment of a chapter 11 trustee is ordered by the court, it is the creditors who elect the trustee (although the U.S. Trustee may appoint a successor trustee if the elected trustee dies or resigns, is removed, or fails to satisfy a bonding requirement).

On the other hand, contemporary commentary suggests the drafters of the Enterprise Bankruptcy Law decided against the concept of the debtor in possession as it exists under chapter 11 of the U.S. Bankruptcy Code, because they were concerned about entrusting troubled businesses to the same group of managers who may have contributed to bringing the debtor to the precipice

---

[52] *Id.* § 1104(a). The *Bankruptcy Abuse Prevention and Consumer Protection Act of 2005* (the "2005 Amendments") added that a trustee may be appointed "if grounds exist to convert or dismiss the case ... but the court determines that the appointment ... is in the best interests of creditors and the estate." *Id.* § 1104(a)(3). The 2005 Amendments further revised section 1104 by adding the requirement that the U.S. Trustee shall move for the appointment of a trustee if reasonable grounds exist to suspect that current members of the governing body of the debtor, the debtor's chief executive or chief financial officer, or members of the governing body who selected the debtor's chief executive or chief financial officer participated in actual fraud, dishonesty, or criminal conduct in the management of the debtor or the debtor's public financial reporting. *See id.* § 1104(e).

The U.S. Bankruptcy Code does not provide for the court to order the appointment of a trustee on its own motion. Rather, a request must be made by a party in interest or the U.S. Trustee, as well as notice and a hearing. To prevent an abuse of process, however, section 105(a) may be used to give the bankruptcy court authority to order the appointment of a trustee on its own motion. A trustee may be appointed without an evidentiary hearing if the facts in support of such appointment are undisputed. The United States Trustee is required to convene a meeting of creditors for the purpose of electing a chapter 11 trustee in the same manner as in chapter 7 cases if a party in interest makes such a request, and that meeting is to take place not later than thirty days after the court orders appointment of a trustee. *See id.* § 1104(b); *In re Aspen Marine Group, Inc.*, 189 B.R. 859, 861 (Bankr. S.D. Fla. 1995).

of bankruptcy.[53] The new law's disfavor of leaving the debtor in possession is reflected in Article 73, requiring the debtor to apply to the court in order to remain in control.

6.3 Creditor Representatives

6.3.1 Creditors' Meeting Under the Enterprise Bankruptcy Law

Article 59 of the Enterprise Bankruptcy Law provides that "[a] creditor who has lawfully asserted the claim shall be a member of the creditors' meeting and shall have the right to attend the creditors' meeting and vote." Article 59 also provides that creditors whose claims have not been confirmed by the People's Court pursuant to Article 58 may not vote unless the court allows the claims temporarily for that purpose.[54] Secured creditors and other creditors enjoying a statutory priority may not vote with respect to adoption of either a conciliation agreement or a plan of distribution of assets in a liquidation proceeding.[55] Perhaps owing to what often is lost in translation, it is not entirely clear what the new law's reference to the "creditors' meeting" was intended to capture. The creditors' meeting thus refers to a body of creditors as well as an event at which qualified creditors may vote; readers should keep in mind that the term is used in both contexts.

Article 61 sets forth the duties of the creditors' meeting, including investigation into the validity of asserted claims, oversight of the administrator's performance and compensation, selection of the membership of the creditors' committee, determining whether to continue or terminate the debtor's business, determining whether to adopt various plans (*e.g.*, for reorganization, conciliation, appraisal, distribution of liquidated assets), and any other matters the court deems appropriate.

Unless provided otherwise, pursuant to Article 64, resolutions of the creditors' meeting are passed if adopted by more than half in number of the

---

[53] *See* James H.M. Sprayregen, Jonathan P. Friedland, & Yong Wang, *The Middle Kingdom's Chapter 11? China's New Chinese Bankruptcy Law Comes into Sight*, 23-1 Am. Bankr. Inst. J. 34 n.23 (December/January 2005).

[54] Similarly, U.S. Bankruptcy Rule 3018 provides that a court may temporarily allow a claim or interest for the purpose of accepting or rejecting a plan.

[55] Enterprise Bankruptcy Law, art. 59.

creditors present who are eligible to vote and more than half in total amount of unsecured claims eligible to vote (but not necessarily present).[56] Once passed, resolutions are binding on all creditors; dissenting creditors may appeal to the People's Court within fifteen days after a resolution is made if the objectionable resolution breaches relevant laws.[57] If the creditors are unable to pass a resolution with respect to adoption of certain types of plans, then the People's Court shall issue an order deciding the matter,[58] and dissenting creditors may apply for reconsideration within fifteen days (during which period the order shall be stayed).[59]

6.3.2 Creditors' Committee Under the Enterprise Bankruptcy Law

Pursuant to Article 67, the creditors' meeting may establish a creditors' committee consisting of not more than nine creditor representatives, one of whom is to be a representative of the debtor's employees. Article 68 enumerates the duties and powers of the committee, which include the supervision of the management and disposal of the debtor's property, the supervision of the distribution of the bankruptcy estate, and "other duties authorized by the creditors' meeting." In a change from the earliest drafts, the Enterprise Bankruptcy Law as enacted imposes no liability on committee members for negligence in the performance of their role.

6.3.3 Creditors' Committee Under the U.S. Bankruptcy Code

The provisions relating to creditors' committees in the Enterprise Bankruptcy Law have analogs in the U.S. Bankruptcy Code. In a chapter 11 case, the U.S. Trustee is required to appoint a committee of creditors holding

---

[56] This construction of Article 64 is inconsistent with Article 84 of the Enterprise Bankruptcy Law in that secured creditors eligible to vote on a resolution may count for purposes of numerosity, but not amount (since expressly only unsecured claims are counted for amount). Article 84, on the other hand, provides that for purposes of adopting a plan of reorganization, more than half in number of the creditors within each class who are present at the creditors' meeting, representing more than two-thirds in total amount of the claims in that class, must vote in favor of the plan. Thus, secured creditors count for purposes of both numerosity and amount under Article 84. The discrepancy may be a drafting oversight in Article 64.

[57] Enterprise Bankruptcy Law, art. 64.

[58] *Id.* art. 65.

[59] *Id.* art. 66.

unsecured claims as soon as practicable after the order for relief is entered.[60] If creditors organized into a committee prior to the commencement of the case, then such committee may be appointed to serve as the statutory committee provided that it was fairly chosen and is representative of the different kinds of claims to be represented.[61]

Under U.S. law, the committee "shall ordinarily consist of the persons, willing to serve, that hold the seven largest claims against the debtor."[62] No statutory bar exists, however, to having more or fewer than seven members. In commercial cases, the committee usually consists of trade creditors and lending institutions. The U.S. Trustee may, in its discretion, appoint additional committees of creditors or equity security holders as it deems appropriate.[63]

Upon request of a party in interest, the court may order the appointment of additional committees, if necessary, by the U.S. Trustee to ensure adequate representation of creditors and equity security holders.[64] In addition, in a provision added by the Bankruptcy Abuse Prevention and Consumer Protection Act of 2005 (the "2005 Amendments"), upon request of a party in interest and after notice and hearing, the court may order the U.S. Trustee to change the membership of the committee if necessary to ensure adequate representation; for instance, membership may be expanded to include a creditor that is a small business concern (as defined in the Small Business Act) holding claims that are disproportionately large in comparison to its annual gross revenue.[65]

---

[60] 11 U.S.C. § 1102(a)(1). In voluntary cases, the order for relief occurs on the date of the filing of the chapter 11 petition. *See id.* § 301. In involuntary cases, entry of the order for relief may occur days, weeks, or months after the filing date if the filing is contested. *See id.* § 303(h).

[61] *Id.* § 1102(b)(1). Standards for determining whether a prepetition committee was "fairly chosen" are set forth in Bankruptcy Rule 2007(b). *See* Fed. R. Bankr. P. 2007(b).

[62] 11 U.S.C. § 1102(b)(1).

[63] *Id.* § 1102(a)(1).

[64] *Id.* § 1102(a)(2). Other types of committees that may be appropriate include a trade creditors' committee, a secured creditors' committee, a bondholders' committee, and an employees' committee. Nevertheless, a court will be reluctant to appoint such additional committees, due to the additional expense to the debtor's estate, unless the benefits of doing so outweigh the costs. *Albero v. Johns-Manville Corp. (In re Johns-Manville Corp.)*, 68 B.R. 155 (S.D.N.Y. 1986), *appeal dismissed sub nom. Dubin v. SEC*, 824 F.2d 176 (2d Cir. 1987).

[65] *See* 11 U.S.C. § 1102(a)(4).

Although status as an unsecured creditor is a prerequisite for membership on the creditors' committee, it is not alone sufficient. An unsecured creditor also must be a "person" as defined in the U.S. Bankruptcy Code,[66] which excludes most governmental entities.[67] Potential conflicts of interest with the debtor or other unsecured creditors do not automatically preclude committee membership, and courts have held that insiders, competitors, and partially secured creditors may serve on the committee as long as no fiduciary duty is violated and no actual conflict of interest exists.[68]

The appointment of the creditors' committee under section 1102 of the U.S. Bankruptcy Code is intended to ensure that in a chapter 11 case, a body will be formed to represent and protect the interests of unsecured creditors, supervise the debtor or trustee, and serve as the primary negotiating body for the formulation of a plan of reorganization.[69] The committee may, in addition to meeting with the trustee or debtor in possession, investigate the debtor, participate in the formulation of a plan and advise its constituents as to its recommendations, request the appointment of a trustee or examiner, and perform other services in the interest of its constituents.[70] The creditors' committee is a party in interest with the right to appear and be heard on all issues in a chapter 11 case.[71]

---

[66] *See id.* § 101(41).

[67] Governmental entities not excluded include the Federal Deposit Insurance Corporation, the Resolution Trust Corporation, the Pension Benefit Guaranty Corporation, and state employee pension funds. *See id.* §§ 101(41), 1102(b)(1).

[68] *See In re Seascape Cruises, Ltd.*, 131 B.R. 241 (Bankr. S.D. Fla. 1991); *In re Map Int'l, Inc.*, 105 B.R. 5 (Bankr. E.D. Pa. 1989); *In re Vermont Real Estate Inv. Trust*, 20 B.R. 33 (Bankr. D. Vt. 1982).

[69] H.R. Rep. No. 95-595, at 401 (1977), *reprinted in* 1978 U.S.C.C.A.N. 5963, 6357.

[70] *See* 11 U.S.C. § 1103(c)(1)–(5).

[71] *See id.* § 1109(b); *La. World Exposition v. Fed. Ins. Co.*, 858 F.2d 233 (5th Cir. 1988), *reh'g denied (en banc)*, 864 F.2d 1147 (5th Cir. 1989).

CHAPTER SEVEN: *Claims Against the Debtor*

7.1 Categories of Claims

7.1.1 Categories of Claims Under the Enterprise Bankruptcy Law

The Enterprise Bankruptcy Law provides for the classification of claims. Article 82 (in the reorganization chapter) sets out four groups of claims in descending priority: secured claims, labor claims, tax claims, and unsecured claims.[1] Creditors in these groups may participate in the creditors' meeting with respect to a draft reorganization plan, and are classified in these groups for voting purposes. Post-acceptance costs of administration, discussed in Section 7.6 below, are not listed in Article 82. With respect to priority of payment in the liquidation context, these same four groups are specified in the same order, after bankruptcy expenses and common-interest debts are paid.[2]

7.1.2 Categories of Claims Under the U.S. Bankruptcy Code

By contrast, the U.S. Bankruptcy Code groups claims into secured claims, priority unsecured claims, and general unsecured claims. Given the emphasis that the PRC government places on providing for its workers, it should come as no surprise that labor claims comprise their own group of claims, lower in priority only to secured claims. Although the U.S. is not as deferential to workers' claims (inasmuch as there is no separate class for labor claims),[3] the U.S. does afford some priority of payment to the allowed unsecured claims of employees, up to $10,950, for wages, salaries, or commissions.[4] Similarly, tax claims under U.S. law are not classified under a separate class, but are given priority in distribution.[5]

---

[1] In addition, Article 82 also allows the People's Court to establish, under appropriate circumstances, a "sub-group of small-amount claims" in the class of unsecured claims, which concept is similar to section 1122(b) of the U.S. Bankruptcy Code.

[2] *See* Enterprise Bankruptcy Law, art. 113.

[3] The practical implications of dealing with labor claims in China, where such claims may encompass years of back-pay, also are foreign to the U.S. system.

[4] 11 U.S.C. § 507(a)(4).

[5] *See id.* § 507(a)(8).

7.2 Assertion of Claims

7.2.1 Asserting Claims Under the Enterprise Bankruptcy Law

The Enterprise Bankruptcy Law contemplates a system of "asserting claims" that is similar in many ways to the practice of filing proofs of claim under the U.S. Bankruptcy Code.

With the exception of labor claims (*i.e.*, claims for employee wages, medical and disability benefits, workers' compensation, mandatory social insurance fees, and statutory severance fees), Article 48 of the Enterprise Bankruptcy Law requires creditors to assert their claims to the administrator within a time set by the People's Court. Article 49 charges creditors with the burden of providing a written explanation of their claims and supporting evidence, including amount and whether the claims are secured or unsecured. Articles 46 and 47, respectively, provide for the filing of unmatured and contingent claims.

Article 46 also provides that interest (if any) "shall cease to accrue . . . from the date the bankruptcy application is accepted." In contrast to U.S. bankruptcy practice, and without further clarification, this provision appears to apply to secured creditors as well as unsecured creditors.

Under Article 45, the People's Court is to set a bar date that is no less than thirty days and no more than three months after the court's public announcement of acceptance of the bankruptcy application.[6] Under Article 56, if a creditor fails to assert its claim in a timely manner, then it "cannot exercise its rights in the procedures subject to this Law"—most importantly, to participate at creditors' meetings and vote on resolutions (as will be discussed). Nevertheless, such creditor may "make a supplemental assertion before the final distribution of the bankruptcy property" and possibly still receive some distribution on account of its claim (although "no supplemental distribution shall be made available to it with respect to any completed distributions").[7]

Pursuant to Article 57, upon receiving the written materials and evidence in support of creditors' claims, the administrator is to examine the validity of the claims and prepare and make available to interested parties a record that

---

[6] Earlier drafts of the Enterprise Bankruptcy Law provided that creditors could apply for an extension when unable to timely assert claims due to "irresistible causes or other just causes," a concept presumably similar to "excusable neglect" under U.S. case law. This provision is not present in the law as enacted.

[7] Enterprise Bankruptcy Law, art. 56.

is functionally the equivalent of a claims register under U.S. proceedings. Under Article 58, the administrator is required to submit the claims register and claims materials for investigation at the first creditors' meeting. Where the debtor and creditors have no objection to particular claims, the People's Court shall "confirm" those claims by order; otherwise, the parties may litigate the claims before the court. The Enterprise Bankruptcy Law does not provide details regarding the timing and procedure for this claims-reconciliation process.

7.2.2 Asserting Claims Under the U.S. Bankruptcy Code

The provisions governing the claims assertion process under the Enterprise Bankruptcy Law should be familiar to those who have had exposure to the U.S. bankruptcy system. Pursuant to section 521(a)(1) of the U.S. Bankruptcy Code and Bankruptcy Rule 1007, the debtor is required to file schedules of assets, liabilities, current income and expenditures, executory contracts, unexpired leases, and a statement of its financial affairs within the first fifteen days after filing its petition. Under U.S. law, however, the time limit is generally extended by the bankruptcy court pursuant to a motion filed by the debtor on the first day of the bankruptcy case.

In order to assess the size of claims against the estate and formulate its plan, a debtor under U.S. law typically requests a deadline or "bar date" for the filing of claims pursuant to Bankruptcy Rule 3003(c). The bankruptcy court will fix (and, for cause shown, may extend) the time within which proofs of claims or interests may be filed. The debtor serves to all known creditors a notice of the bar date; to account for unknown creditors, the debtor also typically publishes notice in a national newspaper.

A creditor must file a proof of claim if: it disagrees with the amount for which it has been scheduled in the debtor's schedules; the claim does not appear on a schedule of liabilities; or the claim is scheduled as contingent, unliquidated, or disputed.[8] Creditors who fail to file a proof of claim in a timely manner are not treated as creditors for purposes of voting or distribution. If a creditor misses its applicable bar date, then an extension of the bar date may be granted for cause, and courts will consider "excusable neglect" as a basis for relief.[9]

---

[8] *See* 11 U.S.C. § 501; Fed. R. Bankr. P. 3002(a), 3003(c)(2).

[9] *See* 9 *Collier on Bankruptcy*, *supra* Chapter Five, note 12, at ¶ 3003.03[4][b]; *Pioneer Inv. Servs. Co. v. Brunswick Assocs. Ltd. P'ship*, 507 U.S. 380 (1993).

The proof of claim filed by a creditor is *prima facie* evidence of the validity and amount of the creditor's claim,[10] which will be "deemed allowed" under section 502(a) of the U.S. Bankruptcy Code and serve as the basis for the estate's distribution to the creditor unless a party in interest objects.[11] In the event an objection is filed against a proof of claim, section 502(b) states that the court must determine the amount of the claim as of the date of the bankruptcy petition, and further lists factors the court must consider when deciding to allow or disallow claims or parts of claims.[12] In particular, section 502(b) disallows claims for unmatured interest on unsecured claims, among other concerns.[13]

7.3 Assignment of Claims

As a general matter, under U.S. law, claims may be sold and assigned by creditors to third parties. The U.S. Bankruptcy Code and the Bankruptcy Rules contain few provisions specifically relating to claims trading.[14] Bankruptcy courts, however, have used their inherent equitable powers (as well as powers under the U.S. Bankruptcy Code) to regulate claims trading. In doing so, they have articulated two primary concerns: (i) that claims trading may constitute an abuse of the reorganization process when used to gain control of a company to the detriment of other creditors and equity interest holders,[15] and (ii) that claims trading by "insiders" without proper disclosure may violate their fiduciary duties to the bankruptcy estate.[16]

The Enterprise Bankruptcy Law contains only one provision addressing transfers, but it applies to equity interests rather than claims. Article 77 provides that "[d]uring the reorganization period, the directors, supervisors or

---

[10] *See* Fed. R. Bankr. P. 3001(f).

[11] 11 U.S.C. § 502(a).

[12] *See id.* § 502(b).

[13] *See id.* § 502(b)(2).

[14] For instance, Bankruptcy Rule 3001 sets forth certain rules for filing notice of transferred claims in some circumstances. *See* Fed. R. Bankr. P. 3001(e).

[15] *See, e.g., In re Allegheny Int'l, Inc.*, 118 B.R. 282 (Bankr. W.D. Pa. 1990) (finding bad faith where claims were purchased in order to obtain a blocking position and prevent acceptance of debtor's plan of reorganization).

[16] *See, e.g., id.; Citicorp Venture Capital, Ltd. v. Comm. of Creditors Holding Unsecured Claims (In re Papercraft Corp.)*, 211 B.R. 813 (W.D. Pa. 1997) (finding inequitable conduct where insider purchased claims at discount).

senior management staff of the debtor shall not transfer their equity interests in the debtor to a third party without consent by the People's Court." With the exception of this one provision prohibiting insiders from divesting their interests in the debtor,[17] the Enterprise Bankruptcy Law does not contain any other provisions addressing the assignment or transfer of claims or interests to third parties. It remains possible that the anticipated judicial interpretation will address such open issues.

7.4 Estimating Claims

Often, a creditor may have a claim against a debtor without knowing the full extent of the claim, either in terms of liability, amount, or both. In Article 47, the Enterprise Bankruptcy Law explicitly acknowledges the possibility of contingent claims by providing that "[a]ny claim which is conditional, subject to any time limit or under any pending litigation or arbitration may be asserted by the creditor." As noted in Section 6.3.1 above, the Enterprise Bankruptcy Law also provides, in Article 59, that the People's Court may "temporarily" confirm the amount of a claim to enable the creditor to vote on resolutions of the creditors' meeting; presumably, such temporary claim allowance involves assignment of some value to otherwise objectionable claims. The new law does not, however, explicitly call for (or provide any mechanism for) assessing or assigning the value of contingent claims or claims that may be objectionable for not asserting an amount.

By contrast, section 502(c) of the U.S. Bankruptcy Code provides that a court must "estimate" any contingent or unliquidated claim when fixing or liquidating such claim would unduly delay the administration of the case. While section 502(c) expressly states that claims shall be estimated for the purposes of allowance (so that an estimated claim would be an allowed claim for all purposes in the bankruptcy case), courts may estimate claims for other limited purposes, such as establishing claims reserves,[18] determining whether

---

[17] Article 77 is presumably intended to curb trading on inside information, and possibly also to ensure that the fiduciary duties of insiders remain aligned with personal interests. Notably, however, Article 77 is limited to prohibiting transfers by insiders "during the reorganization period," and the Enterprise Bankruptcy Law does not contain analogous provisions in its chapters on conciliation or liquidation.

[18] *See, e.g., In re Adelphia Commc'ns Corp.*, 368 B.R. 140, 279 (Bankr. S.D.N.Y. 2007) (estimating claim for purposes of establishing claim reserve).

and to what extent a claimant may vote to accept or reject a plan,[19] and confirming a plan.[20] Courts are granted broad discretion to use whatever method is best suited to the particular circumstances to estimate claims.[21]

7.5 Issues Relating to Secured Claims

7.5.1 Secured Claims Under the Enterprise Bankruptcy Law

The classification and treatment of secured claims in the Enterprise Bankruptcy Law is set forth in several provisions:

- Article 37, which applies to all proceedings, provides that the administrator may "take back any collateral pledged or withheld by paying off debts or providing security acceptable to the creditors." The provision also limits the debtor's payment or substitute security to "the then-current market value of the collateral pledged or withheld."
- Article 46, which also applies to all proceedings, provides that where interest is applicable, "interest shall cease to accrue . . . from the date the bankruptcy application is accepted." Such treatment would seem to apply to secured as well as unsecured debts.
- Article 75, which applies only to reorganization proceedings, provides that "the exercise of security rights in specific property of the debtor shall be suspended," but the secured creditor may seek leave of the court to exercise its rights "if the likelihood exists that the collateral will be damaged or the value thereof will decrease dramatically, which is sufficient to damage the rights of the secured creditor."
- Article 87(1), which applies only to reorganization proceedings, provides that in order to obtain court approval of a plan of reorganization over the objection of the voting group of secured creditors, the plan must provide that secured claims "will be fully

[19] *See* Fed. R. Bankr. P. 3018(a) ("[T]he court after notice and hearing may temporarily allow the claim or interest in an amount which the court deems proper for the purpose of accepting or rejecting a plan.").

[20] *See* 28 U.S.C. § 157(b)(2)(B) (listing core bankruptcy proceedings to include "estimation of claims or interests for the purposes of confirming a plan").

[21] *See In re Thomson McKinnon Securities, Inc.*, 191 B.R. 976, 979 (Bankr. S.D.N.Y. 1996) (collecting cases, and noting nearly unfettered discretion afforded a judge as estimator of claims).

paid off" with respect to collateral, and any losses incurred by the delay in repayment and diminution in value of the secured creditor's security interest will be compensated fairly.

- Article 109, which applies only to liquidation proceedings, affirms for "[a]ny holder of security interests in specific property of the bankrupt" its "priority right to be repaid by such particular property." Where the collateral is insufficient to fully repay such secured creditor, Article 110 provides that "the unpaid portion of such secured claim shall become an ordinary [*i.e.*, unsecured] claim."

The classification and treatment of secured claims in the Enterprise Bankruptcy Law represent a departure from prior law (*i.e.*, the 1986 Bankruptcy Law as modified by the State Council Circulars establishing the Policy Bankruptcy program). By expressly providing for secured claims to be paid first in priority in most cases, even before labor claims, the new law acknowledges that the rights of secured creditors in collateral should not be compromised by allowing proceeds from collateral to be distributed with priority to labor claims, as previously permitted under the Policy Bankruptcy program.

The treatment of secured claims in the Enterprise Bankruptcy Law also includes the U.S. concept of an unsecured "deficiency claim"; however, the concept appears only in the liquidation provisions and not in the reorganization provisions of the law. Under Article 110 of the Enterprise Bankruptcy Law, a secured creditor is allowed a secured claim for up to the value of the collateral, and an unsecured deficiency claim to the extent that the value of the collateral is less than the amount of the secured claim. Further, under Article 75, secured creditors may petition the court to exercise their rights as secured creditors where there exists a likelihood of damage to or a decrease in the value of collateral.

Article 46 of the Enterprise Bankruptcy Law contains a provision similar to U.S. law that stops the accrual of interest on unsecured debt after the commencement of a bankruptcy proceeding. Article 46, however, goes further than U.S. law insofar as it does not appear limited to unsecured debt. Namely, without specifying whether it relates to secured or unsecured debt, Article 46 provides that "interest shall cease to accrue . . . from the date the bankruptcy application is accepted."

7.5.2 Secured Claims Under the U.S. Bankruptcy Code

The provisions of the Enterprise Bankruptcy Law relating to secured claims encompass some concepts regarding secured creditors' rights that are similar to those found in U.S. bankruptcy laws. Under U.S. law, a secured claim stems from a right to the specific property, or collateral, securing the claim. In contemplation of situations in which the value of such collateral may have decreased after credit is extended by the creditor, the U.S. Bankruptcy Code provides several important protections for the secured creditor.

The first of these is the bifurcation of the claim, under section 506(a) of the U.S. Bankruptcy Code, into two parts: (i) a secured claim (to the extent of the value of the collateral) and (ii) an unsecured "deficiency" claim (for the excess that is not secured).

The second is the granting to the creditor, under section 1111(b) of the U.S. Bankruptcy Code, of a choice to have its claim secured in its entire amount (notwithstanding the current valuation of the collateral) rather than bifurcated under section 506(a). That is, where the debtor will retain the collateral under its plan of reorganization, the creditor is entitled to have the entire amount of its claim treated as a secured claim, even if the value of the collateral is less than the amount of the debt, so that the creditor (rather than the debtor) may receive the benefit of the enhanced value if the collateral appreciates in value.[22] Section 1111(b) thus addresses the issue of "lien stripping," in which a secured creditor's lien is "stripped down"; to the

---

[22] The U.S. Congress enacted section 1111(b)(1)(A) to overrule legislatively the decision of *Great Nat'l Life Ins. Co. v. Pine Gate Assocs., Ltd. (In re Pine Gate Assocs., Ltd.)*, 2 Bankr. Ct. Dec. 1478 (Bankr. N.D. Ga. 1976), a case under the Bankruptcy Act of 1898. In *Pine Gate*, the court permitted the debtor to pay the secured creditor the appraised value of its collateral security (an amount lower than the amount of the aggregate mortgage debt) in full satisfaction of its mortgage and to retain the property, as well as the benefit of any subsequent appreciation in the property's value. The *Pine Gate* decision left the U.S. lending industry in fear that bankruptcy courts would, as a general rule, value their collateral security at its lowest amount and then allow the debtor to retain ownership and all opportunity for appreciation in the value of the property by giving the mortgage creditor only the appraisal value. Consequently, the intent of section 1111(b) was to increase the leverage of undersecured creditors, particularly in cases where the debtor has only one major asset, by giving them the opportunity to assert their unsecured deficiency claim or, in the alternative, to elect fully secured status under the debtor's plan.

extent that the creditor's claim exceeds the value of the collateral, the creditor is given the option to choose which treatment it prefers.[23]

The third is the accrual of postpetition interest on secured debt and the allowance of fees, costs and charges for oversecured creditors. Section 506(b) of the U.S. Bankruptcy Code explicitly provides that interest, and any reasonable fees, costs or charges provided for by agreement between the parties, shall be allowed with respect to a secured claim to the extent that it is oversecured.[24] In other words, during the period of time that the secured creditor is prevented from realizing on its collateral due to the bankruptcy proceeding, interest continues to accrue on principal until the total amount of principal plus interest equals the total fair market value of collateral. This accrual of interest, and allowance of other charges provided for under the security agreement, for oversecured claims compensates the secured creditor for the delay of foreclosing on its collateral. Conversely, under certain circumstances, the secured creditor's collateral may be "surcharged" pursuant to section 506(c) for "the reasonable and necessary costs and expenses" of preserving or disposing of the collateral to the extent the secured creditor benefits from such actions.

7.5.3 Adequate Protection

A secured creditor who is concerned about the value of its collateral may seek "adequate protection," a term of art under U.S. bankruptcy law for a measure intended to protect the claim holder from a decrease in the value of its interest in property resulting from the imposition of the automatic stay, the debtor's use of the property, or the granting of a lien against the property

---

[23] In *Dewsnup v. Timm*, the U.S. Supreme Court ruled that a lien can be voided under section 506(d) of the U.S. Bankruptcy Code only to the extent that the underlying claim is not allowed, rather than merely because a portion of the claim is deemed unsecured pursuant to section 506(a). 502 U.S. 410, 415–17 (1992). Nevertheless, the decision was limited to its facts, and the Court noted that it "would allow other facts to await their legal resolution on another day." *Id.* at 416–17. Some courts have permitted lien-stripping in chapter 11 cases. *See, e.g., In re 680 Fifth Ave. Assocs.*, 156 B.R. 726 (Bankr. S.D.N.Y.), *aff'd*, 169 B.R. 22 (S.D.N.Y. 1993), *aff'd*, 29 F.3d 95 (2d Cir. 1994) (recognizing the debtors ability to strip liens in a chapter 11 case).

[24] Interest also may be paid on unsecured debt if the debtor is solvent. *See* 11 U.S.C. § 726(a)(5); *see also United Sav. Ass'n. of Tex. v. Timbers of Inwood Forest Assocs., Ltd.*, 484 U.S. 365, 379 (1988) (section 726(a)(5) "requires no more than that undersecured creditors receive postpetition interest from a solvent debtor on equal terms with unsecured creditors rather than ahead of them—which, where the debtor is solvent, involves no hardship").

to secure postpetition financing. A party with an interest in property of the debtor's estate may, at any time during the case, request the bankruptcy court to prohibit or condition the debtor's use of such property as may be necessary to adequately protect that party's interest in the property. Section 361 of the U.S. Bankruptcy Code provides three nonexclusive examples of adequate protection: periodic cash payments, additional or replacement liens, and the "indubitable equivalent" of an entity's interest in the property. As previously discussed, a party may seek relief from the automatic stay if adequate protection is lacking.

The Enterprise Bankruptcy Law provides for a limited form of "adequate protection" under certain circumstances. Under Article 37, which applies to reorganizations, liquidations and conciliations, "the administrator may take back any collateral pledged or withheld by paying off debts or providing security acceptable to the creditors." The amount paid or the alternate security is "limited to the value up to the then-current market value of the collateral pledged or withheld if the value of the collateral pledged or withheld is lower than the amount of the secured claims."[25] In addition, Article 75, which allows a secured creditor to request leave to resume the previously suspended exercise of security rights "if the likelihood exists that the collateral will be damaged or the value thereof will decrease dramatically, which is sufficient to damage the rights of the secured creditor," may also serve as the basis for an adequate protection demand with respect to collateral that remains in the debtor's possession.

7.6 Payment of Administrative Expenses

7.6.1 Post-Acceptance Costs and Expenses Under the Enterprise Bankruptcy Law

Like the U.S. Bankruptcy Code regarding "administrative expenses," the Enterprise Bankruptcy Law makes provision for payment of the costs and expenses of post-acceptance case administration and operation of the debtor's business. The Enterprise Bankruptcy Law, however, makes a distinction between "bankruptcy expenses" on one hand and "common-interest debts" on the other.

As set forth in Article 41 of the Enterprise Bankruptcy Law, bankruptcy expenses include the proceeding acceptance fee, expenditures

[25] Enterprise Bankruptcy Law, art. 37.

for the appraisal, management and distribution of estate property, compensation for the administrator, and expenditures in performance of the administrator's duties and for his professionals and staff. As set forth in Article 42, common-interest debts include (in part) obligations arising from the administrator's enforcement of an executory contract, as well as employee wages and social insurance fees to be paid in connection with the continuing operation of the debtor's business after the court accepts the bankruptcy proceeding.

Pursuant to Article 43 of the Enterprise Bankruptcy Law, bankruptcy expenses and common-interest debts alike "shall be paid off from time to time out of the debtor's properties," that is, as they come due. Consistent with this provision, Article 113 in the law's liquidation chapter provides for the priority of these costs ahead of the enumerated types of bankruptcy claims. Articles 81 and 87 in the reorganization chapter, however, are silent as to the required payment of bankruptcy expenses and common-interest debts; presumably, this was an oversight that will be corrected through judicial interpretation.

Where the debtor has insufficient assets to satisfy both the bankruptcy expenses and common-interest debts, Article 43 provides that the bankruptcy expenses shall have priority, with *pro rata* payment among the common-interest debts. Where the assets are insufficient to satisfy even the bankruptcy expenses, Article 43 provides for the administrator to apply to the court for termination of the bankruptcy proceeding.

7.6.2 Administrative Expenses Under the U.S. Bankruptcy Code

Section 503(b) of the U.S. Bankruptcy Code provides that administrative expenses include: (i) the "actual, necessary costs and expenses of preserving the estate"; (ii) certain taxes; (iii) compensation and reimbursement for services rendered by a trustee, examiner, or other officer of the court; (iv) expenses incurred by a creditor in connection with the filing of an involuntary petition, the recovery of property of the estate transferred or concealed by the debtor, the prosecution of a criminal offense related to the bankruptcy case; and (v) expenses incurred by a creditor, and indenture trustee, an equity security holder, or certain *ad hoc* committees in making a substantial contribution to a reorganization or municipal bankruptcy case.

In addition to granting a second priority in payment to the administrative expenses allowed under section 503(b), section 507(a) of the U.S. Bankruptcy

Code grants priority payment to the following expenses and claims: (i) domestic support obligations (relevant where the debtor is an individual natural person); (ii) expenses of an appointed bankruptcy trustee; (iii) claims arising in the ordinary course of business during the gap period between the commencement of an involuntary case and the appointment of a trustee or the order for relief; (iv) certain wages, salaries and commissions earned within 180 days of the petition date, limited to $10,950 for each individual or corporation; (v) certain contributions to an employee benefit plan, limited to $10,950 multiplied by the number of employees covered by each such plan; (vi) allowed unsecured claims of grain producers; (vii) allowed unsecured claims arising from deposits in connection with the lease, purchase or rental of property; (viii) certain income tax claims, property tax claims, employment tax claims, excise tax claims, customs duties claims, and tax penalty claims; (ix) claims based on Federal Deposit Insurance Corporation commitments to maintain capital of insured banks; and (x) claims for death or injury arising from the debtor's operation of a motor vehicle or vessel while intoxicated.

7.7 Reclamation and Setoff Rights

7.7.1 Reclamation Rights

Article 39 of the Enterprise Bankruptcy Law provides that "if a seller has shipped purchased goods to the debtor-purchaser but the debtor has not yet received the goods and has not made full payment, the seller may recover the purchased goods in transit."[26] This is similar to the concept of reclamation under U.S. law. Two important differences exist, however—unlike the U.S. Bankruptcy Code, the Enterprise Bankruptcy Law does not impose any time limitations for defining eligible transactions, nor does it have an insolvency requirement.

Section 546(c) of the U.S. Bankruptcy Code provides that a seller of goods who has sold goods to the debtor in the ordinary course of the seller's business may reclaim the goods (by satisfying certain demand requirements) where the debtor received the goods within forty-five days before the commencement of its bankruptcy case and while it was insolvent.[27] Even where the seller fails to make proper demand, the seller is entitled to an administrative expense

[26] In addition, "the administrator may make full payment and request the seller to deliver the purchased goods." *Id.* art. 39.

[27] *See* 11 U.S.C. § 546(c).

for the value of goods delivered to the debtor within twenty days before case commencement.[28]

7.7.2 Setoff Rights

Under Article 40 of the Enterprise Bankruptcy Law, creditors who owe debts to the debtor may "make a setoff claim to the administrator" (*i.e.*, demand the administrator to offset them). A creditor may not assert a right of setoff, however, if the creditor "acquires claims against the debtor from others after the bankruptcy application is accepted" or incurs certain debts to the debtor "knowing that the debtor is unable to pay off debts as they become due or has filed a bankruptcy application."[29]

Under U.S. law, setoff of mutual prepetition obligations is a matter of state-law rights; section 553 of the U.S. Bankruptcy Code provides that such rights are not affected by the federal bankruptcy law except in specified circumstances indicative of manipulation.[30] Thus, for instance, a creditor may not assert a right of setoff if (i) the obligations to be offset are not both prepetition obligations, (ii) the creditor acquired the obligations postpetition, or (iii) the creditor acquired the obligations for the purpose of setoff.[31] Recoupment, which is an equitable doctrine under U.S. law allowing postpetition obligations to be offset against prepetition obligations arising from the same transaction,[32] is not addressed in the Enterprise Bankruptcy Law.

---

[28] *See id.* § 503(b)(9). Moreover, under U.S. law, if the debtor/purchaser has not filed for bankruptcy, a creditor/vendor's reclamation rights are governed by the Uniform Commercial Code (the "UCC"), which has been adopted by most states. Under section 2-702(2) of the UCC, a seller may reclaim goods if (i) the buyer received the goods on credit, (ii) the goods were received while the buyer was insolvent, and (iii) the seller makes a demand for return of the goods within ten days after receipt. Specifically, under the UCC, a debtor/purchaser is "insolvent" if it (i) is has generally ceased to pay debts in the ordinary course of business other than as a result of good faith dispute; (ii) is unable to pay debts as they become due; or (iii) is insolvent within the meaning of federal bankruptcy law. UCC § 1-201. The seller's reclamation rights can be diminished if the seller's reclamation right is "subject to the rights of a buyer in ordinary course or other good-faith purchaser." UCC § 2-702(3).

[29] Enterprise Bankruptcy Law, art. 40.

[30] *See* 11 U.S.C. § 553.

[31] *Id.*

[32] *See Ashland Petroleum Co. v. Appel (In re B&L Oil Co.)*, 782 F.2d 155 (10th Cir. 1986) (discussing both setoff and recoupment).

Insights and Recommendations

- *Clarify Whether Interest Ceases to Accrue for All Debt, and Whether Costs and Expenses Are Allowed for Oversecured Claims*

As noted above, Article 46 of the Enterprise Bankruptcy Law provides that interest on debt stops accruing after acceptance of a bankruptcy proceeding, without specifying whether interest will be permitted to continue to accrue on secured debts. If Article 46 is intended or interpreted to mean that secured claims are not entitled to the accrual of interest to the extent of any oversecurity for a claim, then it would represent a major difference from Western legal traditions in the treatment (and, indeed, the very concept) of a secured claim.[33] Moreover, the interests of secured creditors under the Enterprise Bankruptcy Law would benefit from regulations allowing oversecured creditors to recover the fees, costs and charges provided for under the security agreement, similar to section 506(b) of the U.S. Bankruptcy Code.

- *Guidance Is Needed as to Forms of Adequate Protection and the Extent of Deficiency Claims for Secured Creditors in Reorganization Cases*

By permitting a secured creditor to seek court permission to exercise its rights against collateral where there is a likelihood of damage or diminution in value, Article 75 of the Enterprise Bankruptcy Law offers a treatment similar to the concept of adequate protection for secured creditors under U.S. law. However, clarification on how a secured creditor can exercise its rights in this regard would be helpful. In addition, the following concepts which are found in U.S. law but are absent in the Enterprise Bankruptcy Law would clarify some familiar rights of secured creditors:

  - allowing interest to accrue, and reasonable fees and other costs allowed by agreement, with respect to secured claims if the value of collateral exceeds debt;[34]

---

[33] Note that under the Secured Interests Law and the Property Law discussed in Chapter 2 above, the security agreement between lender and borrower may set forth whether interest is within the "scope" of security.

[34] *See* 11 U.S.C. § 506(b) and below at Section 9.5.

- granting a secured creditor "superpriority administrative expense" status to the extent the value of collateral declines during the pendency of the bankruptcy case;[35] and
- "surcharging" collateral if the administrator expends estate funds to preserve collateral for the benefit of secured lenders.[36]

Article 37 limits secured claims to the value of collateral, and applies in both Chapter VIII reorganizations and Chapter X liquidations. Article 110 provides that, if a secured creditor who seeks repayment from collateral securing the claim is not fully repaid, "the unpaid portion of such secured claim shall become an ordinary claim." Thus, Article 110 grants secured creditors an unsecured deficiency claim to the extent that collateral does not satisfy the full claim. But because Article 110 is within the Chapter X liquidation section of the Enterprise Bankruptcy Law, and no analog appears in the reorganization chapter of the law, it would appear that this provision and the concept of unsecured deficiency claims for secured creditors only applies in liquidations and not reorganizations.

As will be seen later, Article 87(1) in the reorganization chapter of the Enterprise Bankruptcy Law provides that, if the voting group of secured creditors does not consent to a plan of reorganization, the plan may be approved over its objection if secured claims will be "fully paid off" and "losses incurred by the delay of the repayment will be compensated fairly and the security interests have not suffered substantial damages." In construing Article 87(1), a court might find that, if the value of the collateral does not

[35] Under certain circumstances, the U.S. Bankruptcy Code provides that a secured creditor is entitled to receive an administrative expense with priority over all other administrative expenses if adequate protection previously granted for the creditor's secured claim later proves to have been inadequate. Pursuant to section 507(b)(2), a creditor must satisfy several requirements in order to receive such superpriority status: (i) the debtor must have provided adequate protection that turned out to be inadequate; (ii) the creditor must have an allowable administrative expense claim under sections 507(a)(2) and 503(b); and (iii) the claim must have arisen from (a) the automatic stay under section 362, (b) the use, sale, or lease of the collateral under section 363, or (c) the granting of a lien under section 364(d). *See* 11 U.S.C. § 507(b).

[36] *See id.* § 506(c). Although not provided in the Enterprise Bankruptcy Law itself, a concept similar to surcharging appears in the regulation governing compensation of bankruptcy administrators, which provides that where the administrator renders service in maintaining, selling and delivering collateral, it may seek remuneration from secured creditors. *See* Compensation Provisions, art. 13.

exceed the total debt owed to the secured creditor, awarding an unsecured deficiency claim to the secured creditor constitutes fair compensation for damages from the delay in repayment to that creditor. However, there are no statutory assurances that a court would award an unsecured deficiency claim under such a scenario. Thus, if the value of a secured creditor's collateral is significantly lower than the amount of accrued debt, the debtor may have an incentive in a reorganization proceeding to force a cramdown, pay off the secured claim at the reduced market value of the collateral, and retain the collateral, since (strictly as a statutory matter) the undersecured creditor would not be entitled to an unsecured deficiency claim (excess of debt over collateral value) with which to block a reorganization plan.[37] As discussed in Section 7.5.2, the U.S. system addresses this issue of "lien stripping" by permitting an undersecured creditor to elect whether to assert a deficiency claim or be given fully secured status under a plan.

Article 110 may benefit from the addition of a mechanism similar to section 1111(b) of the U.S. Bankruptcy Code, which allows secured creditors to choose how their claims are to be treated in connection with the lien stripping that is otherwise effected by Article 37, and grants secured creditors the option of using the unsecured deficiency claim as a method to block a plan of reorganization. As the law exists now, the secured creditor's right to a deficiency claim in a reorganization proceeding is subject to the court's discretion.

- *Application of Provisions Dealing with Disputed Claims to the Reorganization Chapter*

Article 118 of the Enterprise Bankruptcy Law provides that distributions that are returned from the creditor and are still unaccepted after two months following the announcement of a final distribution shall be deemed abandoned by the creditor and distributed to other creditors. Article 119 provides that, with respect to disputed claims associated with pending litigation or arbitration, the administrator shall set aside a claims reserve. If those claims do not become liquidated within two years following the conclusion of the

---

[37] Note, however, that the court may be able to award such a deficiency claim as "fair compensation" under Article 87 of the Enterprise Bankruptcy Law.

bankruptcy proceedings, however, the claims reserve shall be distributed to other creditors.[38]

Although both of these provisions are helpful mechanisms for dealing with disputed claims, they appear only in Chapter X of the Enterprise Bankruptcy Law, dealing with liquidations. It might be beneficial to have these provisions apply to the reorganization procedures of Chapter VIII as well.

- *Apply Payment of Bankruptcy Expenses and Common-Interest Debts to Reorganization Proceedings*

Finally, as is provided in Article 113 in the liquidation chapter of the Enterprise Bankruptcy Law, the reorganization chapter too should include a requirement for payment of expenses for bankruptcy and common-interest debts, including debts incurred "for the continuing operation of the debtor."[39]

---

[38] *See* Enterprise Bankruptcy Law, art. 119.

[39] *Id.*, art. 42.

CHAPTER EIGHT: Assets and Rights of the Debtor

8.1 Property of the Estate

8.1.1 Property of the Estate Under the Enterprise Bankruptcy Law

Analogous to section 541 of the U.S. Bankruptcy Code, Article 30 of the Enterprise Bankruptcy Law defines property of the bankruptcy estate. It provides that "[a]ll the property owned by the debtor at the time when the bankruptcy application is accepted and the property that the debtor acquires after the acceptance of the bankruptcy application but prior to the conclusion of the bankruptcy procedures constitute the debtor's property," and appears intended to be as broad as possible.[1] Article 17 requires "debtors of the debtor or holders of property of the debtor" to "pay off their debts or deliver the property," respectively, and to make such payment or turnover to the administrator rather than the debtor.

In addition, the Enterprise Bankruptcy Law provides for the recovery of various assets by the administrator for the benefit of the bankruptcy estate. As discussed in Section 8.3.1 below, such recovered assets include the fruits of avoidances (Articles 31, 32, 33, and 34), certain transfers to insiders (Article 36), and even pending capital contributions from investors (Article 35).

8.1.2 Property of the Estate Under the U.S. Bankruptcy Code

The breadth of what is intended to comprise property of the estate should be familiar to those who have practiced under the U.S. bankruptcy laws. Section 541 of the U.S. Bankruptcy Code defines property of the estate, in part, as "all legal or equitable interests of the debtor in property as of the commencement of the case."[2] Section 541 property includes all kinds of property, both tangible and intangible (including contract rights and causes of action), wherever located and by whomever held. The definition of "property of the estate" is intentionally broad to allow the bankruptcy court an opportunity to administer all of the debtor's property, regardless of how tangential the debtor's interest in it might be. Section 541 also enumerates items which do not constitute property of the estate. Examples

---

[1] Enterprise Bankruptcy Law, art. 30.

[2] 11 U.S.C. § 541(a)(1).

of such property include interests that the debtor holds in trust or escrow for another person, rights in a contract that has been terminated prior to the commencement of the bankruptcy case, and any property in which the debtor holds only legal title but no beneficial interest.[3]

8.2 Executory Contracts

8.2.1 Assumption/Rejection Under the Enterprise Bankruptcy Law

Article 18 of the Enterprise Bankruptcy Law provides that after the People's Court accepts a bankruptcy application, with respect to a contract made prior to such acceptance that remains unfulfilled on both sides, the administrator "shall have the power to decide whether to reject or assume such contract." This provision follows the concepts of assumption and rejection of executory contracts found in U.S. bankruptcy law.

The Enterprise Bankruptcy Law provides a time limit for the administrator (or the debtor, where permitted) to decide to assume or reject executory contracts. If the administrator does not notify the contract counterparty within two months after acceptance of the bankruptcy filing (or thirty days after receiving a demand from the counterparty for a determination), then the contract is deemed rejected.[4] If the administrator decides to assume the contract, then the counterparty is entitled to demand security—what seemingly amounts to adequate assurance of future performance as required under the U.S. Bankruptcy Code—and, if the administrator fails to do so, the contract is deemed rejected.[5]

Where the contract is rejected, the counterparty may assert a claim for damages.[6] Where the contract is assumed, obligations arising thereunder constitute common-interest debts of the estate.[7]

---

[3] *Id.* § 541(b).

[4] Enterprise Bankruptcy Law, art. 18.

[5] *Id.* It is not clear whether this "security" concept, which appears to reflect the concept of adequate assurance of future performance found in section 365(b)(1)(C) of the U.S. Bankruptcy Code, is broad enough to cover the curing of defaults and compensation for actual pecuniary loss arising from defaults. *See* 11 U.S.C. § 365(b)(1)(A), (B).

[6] Enterprise Bankruptcy Law, art. 53. Unlike the U.S. Bankruptcy Code, the Enterprise Bankruptcy Law does not prescribe limitations on certain types of damages claims, *see, e.g.*, 11 U.S.C. § 502(b)(6) (termination of lease), § 502(b)(7) (termination of employment contract), and does not explicitly provide for such damages claims to be treated as prepetition claims. *See id.* § 365(g).

[7] *See* Enterprise Bankruptcy Law, art. 42. No provision suggests that a common-interest debt (or bankruptcy expense, or other postpetition claim) results where the contract is rejected.

8.2.2 Assumption/Rejection Under the U.S. Bankruptcy Code

Section 365(a) of the U.S. Bankruptcy Code authorizes a trustee (or debtor in possession) to assume or reject an executory contract or unexpired lease, subject to the approval of the bankruptcy court. The term "executory contract" is not defined in the U.S. Bankruptcy Code, but generally is held to mean a contract as to which material performance remains due to some extent on both sides.[8] This section provides the debtor with a powerful tool, allowing the debtor to shed burdensome contracts and leases, as well as keep beneficial contract and lease rights.

Under the U.S. Bankruptcy Code, a trustee generally must assume or reject an unexpired lease or executory contract with all its benefits and burdens, and court approval is required for either assumption or rejection. In order to assume a lease or executory contract, the trustee must establish that, in its business judgment, such assumption is reasonably calculated to be for the net benefit of the estate. In order to reject a lease or executory contract, the trustee must demonstrate that, in its business judgment, the contract is onerous and burdensome. Rejection constitutes a breach of the contract that is deemed to have occurred immediately prior to the date of the filing of the petition, resulting in all damages flowing from the rejection being treated as a prepetition claim.[9] In addition, the U.S. Bankruptcy Code contains special provisions in connection with the termination of certain types of contracts, limiting damages.[10]

When the estate continues to receive benefits under a contract or unexpired lease pending assumption or rejection, the U.S. Bankruptcy Code generally requires the trustee to comply with all lease or contract terms on a current basis.[11] Thus, the nondebtor counterparty is entitled to compensation, and any claims arising after the commencement of the case

---

[8] *See* Vern Countryman, *Executory Contracts in Bankruptcy*, 57 Minn. L. Rev. 439, 460 (1973) (an executory contract is a "contract under which the obligation of both the bankrupt and the other party to the contract are so far unperformed that the failure of either to complete performance would constitute a material breach excusing the performance of the other").

[9] *See* 11 U.S.C. § 365(g).

[10] *See supra* note 6.

[11] *See* 11 U.S.C. § 365(d)(3), (d)(10).

and prior to assumption or rejection are generally treated as administrative expenses.[12]

Prior to the 2005 Amendments, the trustee was able to assume or reject a nonresidential real property lease during the first sixty days of the case, unless the court extended that time for "cause." Courts generally were lenient in extending the time to assume or reject so as not to pressure the trustee into assuming a lease prematurely, which could be seen as the consequences of an unwise assumption followed by rejection being a claim treated as an administrative expense (payable in whole dollars) rather than as a prepetition claim (payable in "bankruptcy" dollars and potentially capped). Pursuant to the 2005 Amendments, however, the trustee has the first 120 days of the case to assume or reject. The court may grant a single ninety-day extension, but no further extensions are possible without the lessor's prior written consent.[13] This amendment has the net effect of limiting the period during which the trustee may elect to assume or reject an unexpired lease of nonresidential real property, and thus may cause improvident assumptions of such leases. It is important to note, however, that the 2005 Amendments also added a new provision that attempts to limit the cost of such rushed decisions by capping the administrative expense claim for damages arising from the subsequent rejection of an assumed commercial lease.[14]

For unexpired leases of other kinds of property and other executory contracts, section 365(d)(2) of the U.S. Bankruptcy Code provides that the trustee may assume or reject at any time before confirmation of a plan of reorganization, although counterparties may seek a court order requiring the trustee to make its determination within some other period of time.

---

[12] Administrative expenses are given priority under section 507 of the U.S. Bankruptcy Code. Administrative expenses include the actual necessary costs and expenses of preserving the estate, including wages, salaries, or commissions for services rendered after the commencement of the case. *See generally id.* § 503(b). With respect to nonresidential (*i.e.*, commercial) real property leases, landlords are entitled to receive the rent provided in the lease during the postpetition period until the lease is assumed or rejected, even if it exceeds the fair rental value of the premises. *See id.* § 365(d)(3); *see also* 3 *Collier on Bankruptcy*, *supra* Chapter Five, note 12, at ¶ 365.04.

[13] *See* 11 U.S.C. § 365(d)(4).

[14] The newly added section 503(b)(7) gives the lessor an administrative expense equal to two years of monetary obligations following the later of rejection or turnover of the premises, and a claim for the balance of the lease term subject to section 502(b)(6). *See id.* § 503(b)(7).

Insights and Recommendations

- *Guidance Is Needed as to Requirement of Court Approval, Limitations on Types of Contracts, and Requirement of Cure of Defaults in Connection with Assumption/Rejection of Executory Contracts*

Although Article 18 of the Enterprise Bankruptcy Law sets forth the rudiments of a system for the assumption or rejection of executory contracts in bankruptcy, official judicial interpretation might have to fill in additional elements "missing" from Article 18. For instance, the new law does not appear to require the approval of the People's Court with respect to the administrator's decision to assume or reject a contract—an important practical check on an otherwise *ad hoc* process. The new law also does not specify any types of contracts that may not be assumed (*e.g.*, personal service contracts; contracts to extend loans or other financing). Also absent is a requirement (similar to that found in the U.S. Bankruptcy Code) that all defaults must be cured and paid in full in connection with assumption of an executory contract.

Additionally, no provision has been made for special circumstances, such as when the debtor is the landlord rather than tenant under an unexpired lease, or is the licensor rather than licensee under an executory contract for intellectual property, as provided in sections 365(h) and (n), respectively, of the U.S. Bankruptcy Code.[15]

8.3 Avoidance Powers

8.3.1 Avoidance Powers Under the Enterprise Bankruptcy Law

The Enterprise Bankruptcy Law contains several provisions that address the avoidance power of the administrator (or the debtor) to recover assets for the benefit of the debtor's estate. Such powers include the ability to avoid certain pre-bankruptcy transactions and pre-bankruptcy transfers to insiders, and even to require investors to complete pending contributions of registered capital.

---

[15] Under section 365(h), where the debtor rejects an unexpired lease of real property for which it is the landlord, the lessee may opt to either treat the lease as terminated or retain its rights under the lease (although the debtor-landlord is relieved of its obligations under the lease). *See id.* § 365(h). Similarly, under section 365(n), where the debtor rejects an executory contract under which it is the licensor of a right to intellectual property, the licensee may opt to either treat the license as terminated or retain its rights thereunder. *See id.* § 365(n).

Article 31 of the Enterprise Bankruptcy Law provides for avoidance of transactions occurring within one year before acceptance of the bankruptcy application that amount to constructive fraud. Such transactions include "(1) transferring property without consideration; (2) dealing at an obviously unreasonable price; (3) providing collateral for any unsecured debt; (4) prepaying any debt before it became due; and (5) giving up claims."[16] Article 31 is roughly analogous to section 548(a)(1)(B) of the U.S. Bankruptcy Code, which condemns certain prepetition transfers as constructively fraudulent transfers, although the PRC law contains no requirement that the debtor was insolvent at the time of, or became insolvent as a result of, the transaction.

Article 32 of the Enterprise Bankruptcy Law provides for avoidance of debt payments made by the debtor (i) during the six months before acceptance of the bankruptcy application, and (ii) while the debtor was eligible for a bankruptcy proceeding under Article 2 (*i.e.*, both equitably and balance-sheet insolvent), unless "the debtor's property benefited from the specific repayment." Article 32 is roughly analogous to section 547(b) of the U.S. Bankruptcy Code, which condemns certain prepetition transfers as "preferences" unless they bestow a corresponding benefit on the bankruptcy estate.

Article 33 of the Enterprise Bankruptcy Law provides that certain other activities of the debtor "shall be null and void," encompassing the hiding or illegal distribution of property "for the purpose of escaping repayment of debt" and the fabrication of debts or recognition of bogus debts. Early drafts of the law omitted the element of *scienter*, which the law as enacted contains, but the law still does not limit the relevant reach-back period for avoidable activities. Article 33 is roughly analogous to section 548(a)(1)(A) of the U.S. Bankruptcy Code, which condemns certain prepetition transfers amounting to actual fraud.

Article 34 of the Enterprise Bankruptcy Law empowers the administrator to recover assets avoided under Articles 31, 32, and 33. The law also enables the administrator to recover certain other assets as well. For instance, with respect to pre-bankruptcy investors who have not fulfilled their capital contribution commitments, Article 35 enables the administrator to require them to deliver the subscribed capital "regardless of the contractual capital contribution schedule." No direct analog exists for this in U.S. bankruptcy law. With

---

[16] Enterprise Bankruptcy Law, art. 31.

respect to "directors, supervisors and senior management personnel" of the debtor, Article 36 enables the administrator to recover "extraordinary income" and any property of the enterprise that such parties have "misappropriated" through abuse of their authority. Although such actions arguably may be viewed as a subset of fraudulent conveyance, this provision has no apparent limit to the reach-back period.

In addition, the Enterprise Bankruptcy Law imposes liability on certain parties *other than the creditors* involved with respect to recovery of certain transfers. Article 128 provides that "[i]f the debtor commits any acts prescribed in the provisions of Article 31, Article 32 and Article 33 of this Law and impairs creditors' interests, the debtor's legal representative and other directly responsible persons shall be liable for compensation in accordance with law." Also, Article 130 provides that the People's Court may impose a fine on the administrator (and presumably also the debtor if it has been authorized to manage the business) if it "fails to perform its duties of loyalty and diligence" in the performance of its duties, and that the administrator "shall be liable for compensation" if its failure "results in any loss to creditors, the debtor or any third party."

8.3.2 Avoidance Powers Under the U.S. Bankruptcy Code

A key feature of U.S. bankruptcy law is the ability of the trustee or debtor in possession, under certain circumstances, to undo prepetition transfers and obligations and recover the property in question for the benefit of the estate. Such "avoidance powers" are important tools in effectuating the equal distribution of a debtor's assets among its general non-priority creditors, one of the underlying principles of U.S. bankruptcy law.[17] As a measure to bolster the avoidance powers, section 502(d)(1) of the U.S. Bankruptcy Code requires the court to disallow any claim of a creditor who has not returned recoverable property to the debtor's estate. Another means to effectuate the trustee's or debtor in possession's avoidance powers is through section 544 of the U.S. Bankruptcy Code, known as the "strong arm" clause. Among other things, the "strong arm" clause confers on the trustee or debtor in possession (i) the rights and powers of a hypothetical creditor who holds a lien of the kind that would take priority over the claims of certain other creditors, and (ii) the status of an actual unsecured creditor in order for the trustee or debtor in possession to avoid any transfer that such unsecured creditor would be

---

[17] 5 *Collier on Bankruptcy*, *supra* Chapter Five, note 12, at ¶ 544.01.

able to avoid under applicable nonbankruptcy law (such as a state fraudulent conveyance statute).[18]

A trustee or debtor in possession may avoid fraudulent conveyances either through the federal fraudulent transfer provisions of the U.S. Bankruptcy Code, or through state fraudulent transfer laws pursuant to section 544. Under section 548 of the U.S. Bankruptcy Code (which is similar to state fraudulent transfer statutes, although the reach-back period under state laws is generally longer), transfers made within two years of the filing of the debtor's bankruptcy petition may be avoided if: (i) the debtor made the transfer with actual intent to hinder, delay, or defraud creditors (*i.e.*, the transfer was actually fraudulent), or (ii) the debtor received less than reasonably equivalent value in exchange for the transfer and the debtor was insolvent or in an unstable financial condition at the time of the transfer (*i.e.*, the transfer was constructively fraudulent).[19] The insolvency requirement under U.S. law contrasts with the PRC law, which does not require the debtor to have been insolvent during the relevant period or to have become insolvent as a result of the transaction. Moreover, since direct evidence of intentional fraud under the actual fraudulent transfer provision generally is unavailable, U.S. courts will consider the existence of certain circumstances as indicative of an actual fraudulent transfer.[20]

In addition to avoiding fraudulent transfers, a trustee or debtor in possession may also avoid certain transactions as preferences under the U.S. Bankruptcy Code. Under section 547(b), in order to qualify as a preference, a transfer must: (i) be to or for the benefit of a creditor; (ii) be for or on account of a debt owed by the debtor before the transfer was made; (iii) be made while the debtor was insolvent; (iv) be made during the ninety days immediately preceding the commencement of the case (or, if to an insider, between ninety days and one year before the filing of the petition); and (v) result in the creditor receiving a greater recovery than it otherwise would receive on account of its claim in a liquidation case. Recognizing that the goal of preference avoidance is to remedy unfair pre-bankruptcy dissolution of the estate—and not to discourage creditors from doing business on credit with

---

[18] 11 U.S.C. § 544(a), (b).

[19] *Id.* § 548(a)(1)(A), (B). "Insolvent" refers to either balance-sheet insolvency or equitable insolvency. *See id.* § 101(32).

[20] *See, e.g., Max Sugarman Funeral Home, Inc. v. A.D.B. Investors*, 926 F.2d 1248 (1st Cir. 1991) (listing certain "badges of fraud" as circumstantial indicia of fraudulent intent).

a struggling debtor—the U.S. Bankruptcy Code provides several exceptions that creditors may use as defenses to avoidance.[21] For example, a transfer that qualifies under the statute as a preference may nonetheless be excepted from avoidance to the extent that (i) the transfer was intended by the debtor and creditor to be a contemporaneous exchange that provides new value to the debtor's estate;[22] (ii) the transfer was made on account of a debt incurred in the ordinary course of the debtor's business, and the payment itself was made in the ordinary course of both parties' business or was made according to ordinary business terms;[23] or (iii) after receiving the preferential transfer, a creditor gives new value to or for the benefit of the debtor.[24]

If a transfer is avoided pursuant to any of the avoidance powers under the U.S. Bankruptcy Code, the trustee or debtor in possession has the earlier of one year from the time the transfer is avoided or until the case is closed or dismissed, to recover the property transferred or the value of such property.[25] Moreover, the trustee or debtor in possession may recover from the initial transferee of such transfer, or any subsequent transferees of the initial transfer.[26] However, section 550(b) does not permit recovery from subsequent transferees that take for value, in good faith, and without knowledge of the voidability of the transfer.[27] Lastly, under section 549(a) of the U.S. Bankruptcy Code, a trustee or debtor in possession also may avoid unauthorized postpetition transfers of property of the estate.[28]

Insights and Recommendations

- *Clarify Solvency Requirement and Reach-Back Period in Avoidance Actions*

In addressing pre-bankruptcy transfers that would be constructively fraudulent, Article 31 of the Enterprise Bankruptcy Law does not require the suspect transfer to have been made while the debtor was insolvent (or to have caused the debtor's insolvency). The scope of Article 31 could benefit

---

[21] *See* 11 U.S.C. § 547(c)(1)–(9).
[22] *Id.* § 547(c)(1).
[23] *Id.* § 547(c)(2).
[24] *Id.* § 547(c)(4).
[25] *Id.* § 550(a), (f).
[26] *Id.* § 550(a).
[27] *Id.* § 550(b).
[28] *Id.* § 549(a).

from clarification by judicial interpretation or similar regulation, *e.g.*, by linking the constructively fraudulent transfer of property to the insolvency of the debtor, in order to avoid giving an inordinate amount of power to the administrator's role. Furthermore, Article 31 provides that securing an unsecured debt within one year before commencement of the bankruptcy case is a constructively fraudulent transfer.

Article 33 of the Enterprise Bankruptcy Law links the concept of actual fraud to the debtor's intent but does not set any limit on how far back the administrator can reach to avoid a transfer. Likewise, in Article 32, the drafters of the new law recognized that it is appropriate to link the avoidability of preferences to the debtor's contemporaneous financial condition. Article 32 provides that the administrator may seek to rescind certain repayments of debt made "while the debtor was in the condition referred to in the first paragraph of Article 2 hereof," *i.e.*, while the debtor was insolvent.[29] Given the controversial and often contentious nature of preference actions (at least in the U.S. experience), however, it may be advisable for rules or interpretation to expand upon or clarify the statutory-preference exception to provide greater detail than merely to state that a repayment is avoidable "unless the debtor's property benefited from the specific repayment."[30]

- *Develop Additional Avoidance Concepts*

It also would be desirable (although perhaps necessarily in conjunction with further development of PRC laws on commercial and secured transactions) for the Enterprise Bankruptcy Law to include measures similar to section 544 of the U.S. Bankruptcy Code. This provision establishes that the trustee has the right to avoid any transfer by (or obligation of) the debtor that creditors otherwise would be able to avoid under non-bankruptcy law.[31] Section 544 also gives the trustee a special status as a hypothetical creditor who holds a lien of the kind that would take priority over the claims of certain other creditors.[32] This last power may be particularly useful in China, where the lack of coordinated standards for public recordation and the perfection of liens has likely resulted in the existence of many "secret" liens.

---

[29] Enterprise Bankruptcy Law, art. 32.

[30] *Id.*

[31] *See* 11 U.S.C. § 544(b).

[32] *See id.* § 544(a).

Finally, to round out the Chinese administrator's "toolbox" of avoidance powers, it might be desirable to see the addition of analogs to section 549 of the U.S. Bankruptcy Code (enabling recovery of unauthorized post-commencement transfers)[33] and section 550 (prescribing, and in some cases limiting, the liability of initial and subsequent recipients of avoided transfers).

[33] Admittedly, Article 16 of the Enterprise Bankruptcy Law provides that "[o]nce the People's Court accepts the bankruptcy application, a pay-off by the debtor of a specific debt shall be invalid," and, as discussed in Section 8.3.1 above, Article 130 provides that the administrator "shall be liable for compensation" if its breach of fiduciary duties "results in any loss to creditors, the debtor or any third party." Nevertheless, the Enterprise Bankruptcy Law contains no specific provision with respect to recovery of unauthorized postpetition payments from the creditors who were illegally paid.

CHAPTER NINE: Reorganization

Chapter VIII of the Enterprise Bankruptcy Law, entitled "Reorganization," is comprised of twenty-five articles, subdivided into three sections: (i) "Application for Reorganization and Period of Reorganization"; (ii) "Proposal and Approval of Reorganization Plan"; and (iii) "Implementation of Reorganization Plan." These provisions govern the process of filing an application for reorganization, enumerate the debtor's rights during the period of reorganization, provide guidance for drafting a plan of reorganization, and detail the procedures for implementing an approved reorganization plan. Chapter VIII of the Enterprise Bankruptcy Law appears to be based largely on the U.S. model of reorganization, found in chapter 11 of the U.S. Bankruptcy Code.

Key Reorganization Points of the Enterprise Bankruptcy Law

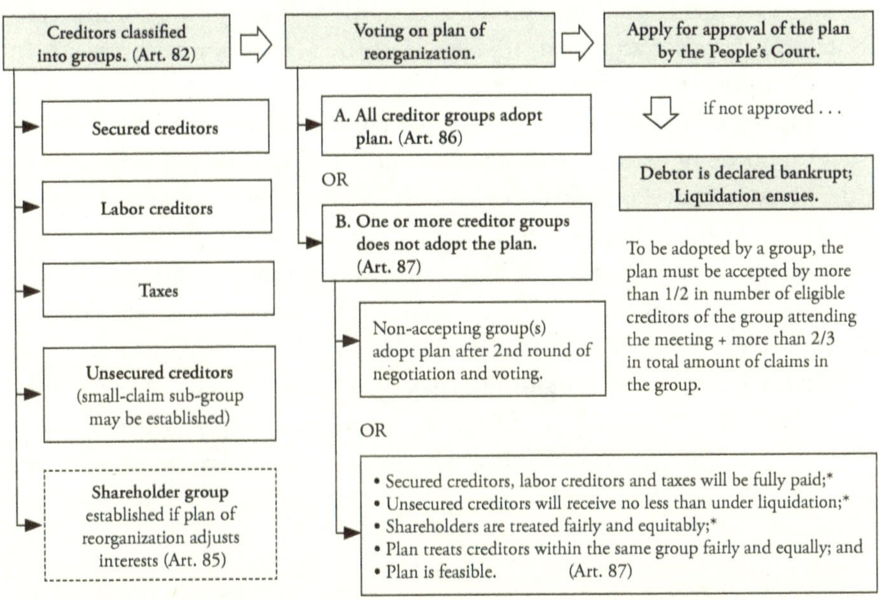

* unless they agree to lesser treatment

9.1 Commencement of a Reorganization

Article 70 of the Enterprise Bankruptcy Law provides that "[t]he debtor or creditors may file an application directly to the People's Court for reorganization of the debtor according to this Law." In other words, as in the United States, a voluntary reorganization case may be filed by the debtor[1] or an involuntary case may be filed by creditors. Under the U.S. Bankruptcy Code, however, the filing of the chapter 11 petition commences the chapter 11 case.[2] By contrast, the filing of the application under the Enterprise Bankruptcy Law only places the issue before the People's Court. As with the application to commence a bankruptcy liquidation, Article 71 of the Enterprise Bankruptcy Law provides that the People's Court will examine the application for reorganization, and issue an order permitting the debtor to undergo the reorganization process, "if it finds that the reorganization application satisfies the requirements [of the Law]." Although a debtor cannot commence a reorganization case in China by the mere filing of a petition, Article 70 of the Enterprise Bankruptcy Law represents a liberalization of access to reorganization because it permits the debtor or its creditors to apply for reorganization *directly* to the People's Court. Under the prior Chinese bankruptcy regime, a reorganization case could occur only if (i) creditors commenced an involuntary case and then (ii) the enterprise's "superior departments in charge" applied for reorganization.[3]

Although Article 2 of the Enterprise Bankruptcy Law generally requires a debtor to demonstrate both balance-sheet and equitable insolvency in order to commence a bankruptcy case, the debtor need only demonstrate any of the insolvency prerequisites to commence a reorganization case.[4] Thus, in determining whether it should allow a reorganization case, the People's Court will consider under Article 2 whether the debtor has demonstrated either balance-sheet insolvency *or* equitable insolvency *or* that "there is an obvious possibility that it will lose the capability to repay its debts."[5] In addition, the People's Court presumably will exercise a level of discretion in determining whether to permit reorganizations to proceed.

---

[1] *See* 11 U.S.C. § 301(a). Any debtor may file a chapter 11 reorganization case except for a domestic or foreign bank (or similar entity), or a foreign insurance company engaged in business in the U.S. *See* 11 U.S.C. § 109(b).

[2] *See id.* § 301(b).

[3] 1986 Bankruptcy Law, art. 3.

[4] *See* Enterprise Bankruptcy Law, art. 2.

[5] *Id.*

Under the U.S. Bankruptcy Code, there is no requirement that the debtor be insolvent.[6] Allowing a solvent debtor to file under chapter 11 encourages the debtor to file early in order to "rehabilitate its business before it is faced with a hopeless situation."[7] For example, in one case a bankruptcy court declined to evaluate the solvency of the debtor in connection with determining whether its plan of reorganization had been proposed in good faith (a requirement for confirmation).[8] The court ruled that "assuming *arguendo* that the debtors are solvent, [the creditor's] claim could have been satisfied through the reorganization process in this court."[9]

As noted, the Enterprise Bankruptcy Law also provides that creditors (as well as debtor) may file an application for reorganization of the debtor.[10] The requirement under the new law presumably is less stringent than that established under the U.S. Bankruptcy Code.[11] Under the Enterprise Bankruptcy Law, a case is not commenced solely by the filing of the application, but instead only by order of the People's Court after examination of the application.

Under the Enterprise Bankruptcy Law, an involuntary bankruptcy liquidation case may be converted into a reorganization case. Article 70 provides that, if an involuntary petition for bankruptcy liquidation is filed by creditors, then the debtor or equity holders representing more than one-

---

[6] *See In re Marshall*, 298 B.R. 670, 683–84 (Bankr. C.D. Cal. 2003); *In re Johns-Manville Corp.*, 36 B.R. 727, 730 (Bankr. S.D.N.Y. 1984). *But see In re SGL Carbon Corp.*, 200 F.3d 154, 164 (3d Cir. 1999) (stating that the "financially healthy" nature of the company was one of the reasons the court decided that the company did not enter chapter 11 in good faith).

[7] *In re SGL Carbon Corp.*, 200 F.3d at 163–64.

[8] *See In re Marshall*, 298 B.R. at 684.

[9] *Id.*

[10] Enterprise Bankruptcy Law, arts. 7, 70.

[11] With respect to the filing of an involuntary chapter 11 case, the U.S. Bankruptcy Code expressly requires that the petition be filed by three or more creditors with undisputed, non-contingent, unsecured claims aggregating at least $13,475 "more than the value of any lien on the property." *See* 11 U.S.C. § 303(a), (b). If fewer than 12 creditors with noncontingent, undisputed claims exist, an involuntary case may be commenced by one or more such creditors with claims aggregating at least $13,475. The aggregate claim amount is adjusted from time to time pursuant to 11 U.S.C. § 104(b). Under the U.S. Bankruptcy Code, the mere filing of the petition commences an involuntary bankruptcy case with immediate consequences for the debtor. The bankruptcy court will grant an order for relief for an involuntary chapter 11 if the debtor does not timely contest the petition. If the debtor contests the involuntary petition, the court will hold a trial to determine whether the order for relief should be granted. *See id.*

tenth of the debtor's "registered capital"[12] may apply to the People's Court to convert the case to a reorganization proceeding after the People's Court accepts the bankruptcy proceeding and before the debtor is declared bankrupt. The procedure is similar to that under the U.S. Bankruptcy Code. If creditors file an involuntary chapter 7 case and the debtor consents to the petition or the court grants relief to the petitioners after a trial, then the debtor may convert the involuntary chapter 7 case to a chapter 11 case.[13] This conversion may occur at any time as an "absolute right," due to the policy that a "debtor should always be given the opportunity to repay his debts."[14]

9.2 Operation of Business

9.2.1 Debtor in Possession Concept Under the Enterprise Bankruptcy Law

As discussed in Section 6.1 above, pursuant to Article 13 of the Enterprise Bankruptcy Law, the People's Court appoints an administrator at the time it decides to accept a bankruptcy application. The court-appointed administrator then performs the following duties:

(1) receiving and managing the debtor's property, seal, accounting books, instruments and other materials;
(2) investigating into the status of the debtor's property and preparing a property status report;
(3) making decisions on the debtor's internal management affairs;
(4) making decisions on the debtor's daily expenses and other necessary expenses;
(5) before the first creditors' meeting, determining whether to continue or terminate the debtor's business operations;
(6) managing and disposing of the debtor's property;
(7) representing the debtor in lawsuits, arbitration or other legal proceedings;
(8) proposing to convene a creditors' meeting;

---

[12] "Registered capital" denotes the equity pledged with the local registration authorities when an enterprise entity is created. China sets the minimum amount of registered capital required for different industries and in different regions. Thus, an involuntary reorganization can be initiated by investors holding more than a certain amount of the debtor's registered capital, upon making the necessary showings and receiving the court's permission.

[13] *See* 11 U.S.C. §§ 303(d), (h) and 706.

[14] *Id.* § 706(a); H.R. Rep. No. 95-595, at 380 (1977).

(9) performing other administrator's duties as deemed appropriate by the People's Court.[15]

Under Article 73, however, upon application, "during the reorganization period, the debtor itself may manage its property and business affairs," albeit "under the supervision of the administrator." The new law does not suggest any standard for consideration of such application by the People's Court. Where the debtor's application is approved, however, the administrator shall return control of the debtor's property and business affairs to the debtor "and the power of the administrator provided for herein shall be exercised by the debtor."[16]

9.2.2 Debtor in Possession Concept Under the U.S. Bankruptcy Code

In contrast to Articles 13 and 73 of the Enterprise Bankruptcy Law, sections 1107 and 1108 of the U.S. Bankruptcy Code allow either a trustee or the debtor (as a "debtor in possession") to operate the debtor's business at the outset of the chapter 11 filing.[17] Upon the filing of a chapter 11 case, the debtor in possession automatically continues to operate and manage the debtor's business and properties.[18] This authority may be terminated only by an order of the court on the request of a party, following required notice and a hearing.[19] As more fully discussed in Section 6.2 above, a debtor in possession may be so displaced, and replaced by a trustee, "for cause, including fraud, dishonesty, incompetence, or gross mismanagement of the affairs of the debtor by current management," or if the appointment of a trustee is in the interest of creditors.[20]

9.3 Postpetition Financing

9.3.1 Financing Under the Enterprise Bankruptcy Law

Generally, postpetition financing is a crucial factor in a debtor's ability to operate its businesses during the pendency of its bankruptcy proceeding and to emerge as a healthy, reorganized entity. Article 75 of the Enterprise Bankruptcy Law provides that "[d]uring the reorganization period, if the debtor

---

[15] Enterprise Bankruptcy Law, art. 25.

[16] *Id.*, art. 73.

[17] *See* 11 U.S.C. §§ 1107, 1108.

[18] *See* § 1108.

[19] *See id.*

[20] *Id.* §§ 1107, 1108.

or the administrator borrows a loan for continuing business, a security interest may be created for such a loan." Thus, the concept of secured postpetition financing is present in the Enterprise Bankruptcy Law, but the law contains no other provisions related to financing during the "reorganization period." Moreover, the law contemplates the availability of postpetition financing only in reorganization proceedings.

9.3.2 Financing Under the U.S. Bankruptcy Code

In contrast to the Enterprise Bankruptcy Law's single general provision for financing "during the reorganization period," section 364 of the U.S. Bankruptcy Code provides a detailed scheme and a variety of special protections for lenders to facilitate the extension of credit to a debtor.[21] Those protections range from priority administrative expense claims to the granting of a lien that may prime an existing lien or liens.

Sections 364(a) and 364(b) of the U.S. Bankruptcy Code authorize a trustee or debtor in possession to obtain unsecured credit and incur unsecured debt as a first-priority administrative expense.[22] If unsecured financing is not available, then section 364(c) authorizes financing on a "superpriority" basis (*i.e.*, having priority over other administrative expenses), secured by a lien on unencumbered property, or secured by a junior lien on property that already is encumbered. If financing pursuant to section 364(c) is not obtainable, then section 364(d) authorizes the court to grant a postpetition lender a lien on encumbered property that is senior or equal to existing liens on the property (a priming lien), so long as adequate protection (as will be discussed) is provided to the existing lienholders.

Insights and Recommendations

- *Clarify Ability to Grant "Priming Liens"*

Troubled companies attempting to reorganize would have much greater flexibility in obtaining necessary postpetition funding if they were able to prime prior secured lenders (or obtain *pari passu* liens) where it could be established that collateral values exceed the value of collateral securing existing lien holders. A prior draft of the Enterprise Bankruptcy Law allowed

---

[21] While postpetition financing typically arises in the reorganization context, section 364 is generally applicable to all proceedings under the U.S. Bankruptcy Code.

[22] *See also* 11 U.S.C. § 503(b)(1).

the debtor to grant new liens to obtain financing to continue operations, but limited the security to unencumbered assets. Given that this restriction was omitted from Article 75 of the law as enacted, priming liens presumably are not forbidden. Further regulations should clarify the requirements for such liens.

9.4 Asset Sales

9.4.1 Sale of Assets Under the Enterprise Bankruptcy Law

The Enterprise Bankruptcy Law does not contain analogous sale provisions in the reorganization context. The only reference to asset sales contained in the Enterprise Bankruptcy Law appears in the liquidation chapter, where Article 112 barely does more than acknowledge the concept of selling assets in an auction.

9.4.2 Sale of Assets Under the U.S. Bankruptcy Code

Under section 363(c) of the U.S. Bankruptcy Code, a debtor is authorized to use, sell, or lease property of the estate in the ordinary course of business without bankruptcy court approval. In addition, section 363(b) allows the debtor to use, sell, or lease property of the estate outside the ordinary course of business "after notice and a hearing."[23] These provisions recognize that a debtor may need to sell assets to further the restructuring of its business (*e.g.*, to shed non-core assets or to create liquidity). A typical "363 asset sale" process includes the marketing of the assets, the negotiation and execution of a "stalking horse" agreement to set a floor price, the establishment of bidding procedures, an auction, and the approval of the sale by the Bankruptcy Court.

The debtor may also sell property of the estate free and clear of any interests in such property, including liens thereon, under any of the following conditions: (i) applicable non-bankruptcy law permits the sale of such property free and clear of interests; (ii) entities holding interests in such property consent to the sale; (iii) the interest on the property is a lien, and the sale price is greater than the aggregate value of all liens on such property; (iv) the interest is the subject of a *bona fide* dispute; or (v) entities holding interests

[23] *Id.* § 363(b). Notice to creditors must be appropriate under the circumstances, and as long as a similarly appropriate opportunity for a hearing has been given, an actual hearing need not be held if no party in interest has timely requested one. *See id.* § 102(1); Fed. R. Bankr. P. 2002 (providing for twenty days' notice).

in such property could be compelled in a legal or equitable proceeding to accept a money satisfaction of such interests.[24] In recent years, the number of chapter 11 asset sales in bankruptcy has increased markedly in the United States.[25]

Insights and Recommendations

- *Further Guidance on Asset Sales Is Needed*

Incorporating the concepts of notice to creditors and required court approval of non-ordinary course asset sales to the reorganization provisions would add clarity to the Enterprise Bankruptcy Law. When adopted, the regulations hopefully will provide a mechanism for the orderly sale of assets, consistent with the duty to maximize recoveries for the benefit of all creditors. The regulations could specify the amount of notice that must be given to creditors regarding proposed asset sales that are "out of the ordinary course" of a company's business, and the circumstances under which court approval would be required. The regulations could also address the conduct of a public sale or auction (including concepts such as the selection of the "highest or best" offers, and sales "free and clear"). Implementing regulations also may include some guidelines for bid protections, such as break-up fees and expense reimbursements for "stalking horse" bidders, as well as guidelines for the holder of a secured claim to bid in his lien in order to take collateral securing his claim.

9.5 Proposing a Plan of Reorganization

9.5.1 Deadline to File Plan of Reorganization

9.5.1.1 Deadline Under the Enterprise Bankruptcy Law

Article 72 of the Enterprise Bankruptcy Law provides that "[t]he reorganization period shall start from the date when the People's Court rules that the debtor is to be reorganized and end at the termination of the reorganization procedures." To prevent reorganization proceedings from stretching out, previous drafts of the Enterprise Bankruptcy Law provided that the period of reorganization "shall not exceed six months." Although

---

[24] *Id.* § 363(f).

[25] Where a debtor is unable to reorganize, the process of selling off assets may still occur. *See id.* § 1123(a)(5), (b)(4).

this limitation was eliminated in the statute as adopted, the law does provide for a six-month limitation on the time for submission of a plan of reorganization.[26]

Under Article 79 of the Enterprise Bankruptcy Law, the debtor or administrator must submit a reorganization plan within six months from the date of the commencement of the reorganization procedure. This period can be extended for another three months upon request of the debtor or the administrator for a "justifiable reason." Presumably, the determination of what is justifiable is left to the discretion of the People's Court.

Under Article 80 of the Enterprise Bankruptcy Law, either the debtor or the administrator may submit the plan of reorganization, depending on who is in possession of the debtor's property and managing the debtor's business. Unlike the U.S. Bankruptcy Code (which gives the debtor an exclusive period to file a plan of reorganization at the expiration of which another party in interest may file a plan), the Enterprise Bankruptcy Law does not provide for the right of a creditor or other party in interest to file a competing plan. Instead, if no plan is submitted within the allotted time by the debtor or administrator, then the court shall issue an order terminating the reorganization procedure and declaring the debtor bankrupt.[27]

9.5.1.2 Deadline Under the U.S. Bankruptcy Code

Under the U.S. Bankruptcy Code, no time limit is imposed for the duration of a chapter 11 case, and the debtor "may file a plan . . . . at any time in a voluntary case or an involuntary case."[28] During the first 120 days of the case, however, the debtor has the exclusive right to file a plan of reorganization; moreover, during the first 180 days, the debtor has the exclusive right to solicit and obtain acceptances of a plan.[29] The initial 120-day and 180-day exclusive periods may be extended to 18 months and 20 months, respectively, from the commencement of the chapter 11 case.[30] If a trustee is appointed, or if the debtor has not filed and obtained acceptances of

---

[26] *See* Enterprise Bankruptcy Law, art. 79.

[27] *Id.*, art. 79.

[28] 11 U.S.C. § 1121(a). In some instances, plans are negotiated with creditor constituencies prior to the commencement of a chapter 11 case; the debtor is then able to "file a plan with a petition commencing a voluntary case." *Id.* As will be discussed below, "prepackaged" or "prenegotiated" plans, as these are called, facilitate expedited reorganizations.

[29] *Id.* § 1121(b), (c).

[30] *Id.* § 1121(d)(2).

a plan within the exclusive periods, then any party in interest may file a plan.[31] A "party in interest" includes the debtor, the trustee, a creditors' committee, an equity security holders' committee, a creditor, an equity security holder, or an indenture trustee.[32]

"Exclusivity" to file a plan of reorganization (and to solicit acceptances thereof by creditors) gives the debtor an opportunity to control the outcome of the reorganization case, in addition to the leverage to encourage creditors and other parties in interest to work toward a consensual resolution. The limitation on the debtor's exclusive period to file a plan of reorganization, however, provides a limit to the debtor's leverage and motivates the debtor to resolve plan issues rapidly and consensually to minimize the duration of its chapter 11 case.

9.5.2 *Plan Contents and Classification*

9.5.2.1 Plan Contents and Classification Under the Enterprise Bankruptcy Law

Article 81 of the Enterprise Bankruptcy Law states that the proposed plan of reorganization shall contain:

(1) the business operation plan of the reorganized enterprise;
(2) the classification of the claims;
(3) the plan for adjustments to claims;
(4) the plan for repayment of claims;
(5) the time limit for implementing the reorganization plan;
(6) the time limit for supervising the implementation of the plan; and
(7) "other plans that are beneficial to the reorganization of the debtor."

The requirement of these plan elements appears to borrow from the requirements of section 1123 of the U.S. Bankruptcy Code, but not with the level of detail that the U.S. Bankruptcy Code provides.

Article 82 of the Enterprise Bankruptcy Law provides that the plan of reorganization shall classify creditor claims into four groups: (i) secured claims; (ii) labor claims, *i.e.*, claims for "wages, subsidies for medical treatment and disability, and pensions for the disabled and the families of the deceased

---

[31] *Id.* § 1121(c).

[32] *Id.*

which are due and unpaid, fees for basic pension insurance and basic medical insurance . . . and other compensations payable to employees under the laws and administrative regulations"; (iii) tax claims; and (iv) unsecured claims.

Article 82 of the Enterprise Bankruptcy Law also contains a provision that was not included in early drafts of the law, providing that "[i]f necessary, the People's Court may decide to set up a sub-group of small-amount claims in the ordinary claim group to vote on the draft reorganization plan." This new provision appears analogous to section 1122(b) of the U.S. Bankruptcy Code, which allows for the classification of small claims in a separate "convenience class" for voting and distribution purposes based on administrative convenience.[33] How the permitted establishment of a small-claims sub-group would affect the reorganization process (with respect to voting, for instance) remains unclear however.

9.5.2.2 Plan Contents and Classification Under the U.S. Bankruptcy Code

Under section 1123(a) of the U.S. Bankruptcy Code, a plan of reorganization must—

(1) designate classes of claims and interests;
(2) specify unimpaired claims;
(3) specify the treatment of impaired claims;
(4) provide the same treatment for claims in the same class, unless the holder of the claim agrees to less favorable treatment;
(5) provide adequate means to implement the plan, such as, *e.g.*, through a merger of the debtor with one or more entities, a sale of the debtor's property, or an issuance of securities of the debtor;
(6) prohibit the issuance of nonvoting equity securities;
(7) be consistent with the interests of creditors and with public policy with respect to the selection of officers and directors under the plan; and
(8) where the debtor is an individual, provide for payment to creditors from future income as is necessary for the execution of the plan.

---

[33] The effect of establishing a separate "convenience class" of smaller unsecured claims under U.S. law is to encourage creditors with larger claims to voluntarily reduce their claims to fall within the convenience class and to allow the plan proponent to grant cash payments to smaller creditors in exchange for plan acceptance without unfairly discriminating against other creditors. *See, e.g., In re Realty Assocs.*, 53 F. Supp. 1010 (E.D.N.Y. 1943).

Further, section 1123(b) permits, but does not require, a plan of reorganization to do the following:

(1) impair or leave unimpaired any class of claims;
(2) provide for the assumption, rejection, or assignment of executory contracts and unexpired leases;
(3) provide for the settlement or adjustment of any claim or interest;
(4) provide for the sale of all or substantially all of property of the estate;
(5) modify the rights of secured and unsecured creditors; and
(6) include any provision not inconsistent with the provisions of the U.S. Bankruptcy Code.

Unlike the Enterprise Bankruptcy Law's requirement that creditors be classified for purposes of the plan into four specified groups, the U.S. Bankruptcy Code merely requires that a plan classify a "claim or interest" with other "substantially similar" claims or interests.[34] Notably, no requirement exists under U.S. law that all "substantially similar" claims be classed together.[35] "Substantially similar" claims are similar in "kind, species, or character."[36] For example, in one case, the court held that creditors whose claims were secured by different property should not be placed in the same class.[37]

Insights and Recommendations

- *Further Guidance Is Needed on What a Plan Must Include*

Although Article 81 of the Enterprise Bankruptcy Law sets forth certain of the features that either must be or typically are found in a plan of reorganization under the U.S. Bankruptcy Code, the requirements under the Enterprise Bankruptcy Law are not as comprehensive as under U.S. law.

---

[34] 11 U.S.C. § 1122(a).

[35] *Settling States v. Carolina Tobacco Co. (In re Carolina Tobacco Co.)*, 360 B.R. 702, 713 (D. Or. 2007); *but see In re Wabash Valley Power Ass'n, Inc.*, 72 F.3d 1305, 1321 (7th Cir. 1995) (debtor cannot classify claims in such a way as to give certain creditors an unfair advantage in the voting process); *In re Corcoran Hosp. Dist.*, 233 B.R. 449 (Bankr. E.D. Cal. 1999) (separate classification of certain substantially similar claims requires business or economic justification).

[36] *Steelcase Inc. v. Johnston (In re Johnston)*, 21 F.3d 323, 327 (9th Cir. 1994).

[37] *Brady v. Andrew (In re Commercial W. Fin. Corp.)*, 761 F.2d 1329 (9th Cir. 1985). The exception to this rule is if the "different properties are in the same location, purchased at approximately the same time, and thus worth roughly the same amount." *Id.*

By way of example, section 1123(a)(5) of the U.S. Bankruptcy Code sets forth ten subsections with specific examples of providing "adequate means" to implement the debtor's plan. It may be beneficial for later amendments to the Enterprise Bankruptcy Law to lay out some specific ways to implement the debtor's plan, given the relative infancy of the concept of a "reorganization" under the law.

9.6 Lock-Up Agreements; Prepackaged and Prenegotiated Chapter 11 Cases

The U.S. Bankruptcy Code permits a debtor to negotiate a "prepackaged" plan of reorganization with its creditors, and to solicit acceptance of the plan prior to commencing a chapter 11 case. Prepackaged plans minimize the time and expense of a full-fledged chapter 11 case, because the negotiation and acceptance of the plan is accomplished prior to filing the bankruptcy petition. As will be discussed, however, prepackaged plans are not suitable for debtors in certain situations; even if the debtor has negotiated a consensual plan with its key creditor constituencies prior to filing, it may be better for the debtor to commence a chapter 11 case before soliciting approval of the prenegotiated chapter 11 plan.

The Enterprise Bankruptcy Law does not incorporate the concept of a prepackaged plan, but nothing in the law prevents a debtor from prenegotiating a plan before commencing its reorganization case. In addition, because the Enterprise Bankruptcy Law does not include a prohibition against lock-up agreements (discussed below), it may be possible for a debtor to negotiate such agreements with its key constituencies prior to commencing its reorganization case, thereby accomplishing the equivalent of a prepackaged reorganization.

9.6.1 Lock-Up Agreements

Lock-up agreements are a common feature of out-of-court workouts in the United States. They ensure that signatories remain committed, at least contractually, to a negotiated proposal potentially involving many competing creditor or shareholder groups. Without that commitment, the time and resources of workout participants may be wasted if a creditor or creditor group necessary to the success of the workout reneges on an informal agreement in principal.

Many successful restructurings begin outside of court, but ultimately end up as "prepackaged" or "prenegotiated" bankruptcy cases (discussed in sections 9.6.2 and 9.6.3 below). This is typically the case where the company is able to reach an agreement with some or perhaps even all of its creditors concerning the terms of a restructuring, but needs the benefits of the U.S. Bankruptcy Code to implement the necessary adjustments to its balance sheet and capital structure. For instance, if a debtor reaches an agreement with some but not all of its creditors, a bankruptcy filing may be necessary to bind the holdouts to the terms of a proposed restructuring incorporated in a plan of reorganization confirmed by the bankruptcy court.

If the debtor strikes a deal with all of its creditors and decides to file for bankruptcy to complete the workout, it can file a "prepackaged" bankruptcy case. This kind of case involves soliciting creditor votes in favor of a restructuring plan prior to filing a chapter 11 case, and obtaining bankruptcy court authorization to have those votes counted toward confirmation of the plan. Where total consensus is impossible, but the company is able to arrange the cooperation of its significant creditors, it can file a "prenegotiated" chapter 11 case. If so, it will attempt to obtain the participating creditors' commitment to support a plan of reorganization with certain specified terms. That commitment most often takes the form of a lock-up agreement. A "prenegotiated" case often involves the solicitation of creditor votes for a restructuring proposal after filing of the chapter 11 petition.

9.6.1.1 Problems Encountered with Lock-Up Agreements

The relationship between lock-up agreements and bankruptcy law in the U.S. is often an uneasy one. This is so because the U.S. Bankruptcy Code contains rigorous disclosure requirements that must be complied with as part of the plan confirmation process.[38] Votes, or "acceptances," in favor of a chapter 11 plan that were obtained prior to the bankruptcy filing will be valid only if solicitation of the vote complies with any applicable non-bankruptcy law, or if not, was accompanied by disclosure of "adequate information."[39] It may be questionable in some cases whether information imparted to a creditor who signs a pre-bankruptcy lock-up agreement meets this standard.

After filing for bankruptcy, the debtor may solicit votes in favor of a plan only after the creditor or shareholder receives a court-approved

---

[38] As discussed in Section 9.7.1 below, the U.S. Bankruptcy Code requires that every holder of a claim or interest receive a court-approved written disclosure statement containing "adequate information" about a proposed plan before its vote on that plan may be solicited. 11 U.S.C. § 1126(b)(2). Moreover, the court must assess the disclosure statement's adequacy and approve it before transmittal. *See Nelson v. Dalkon Shield Claimants Trust (In re A.H. Robins Co.)*, 1998 U.S. App. LEXIS 21387 (4th Cir. Aug. 31, 1998).

[39] *See* 11. U.S.C. § 1126(b)(1).

disclosure document containing information that the bankruptcy court determines to be adequate. If the court determines that a vote was solicited without disclosure of adequate information or under circumstances that are otherwise improper, it has the power to "designate" (*i.e.*, invalidate) the vote.[40]

Precisely what constitutes "solicitation" of a vote on a plan is not always easy to answer. In many cases, debtors attempting to negotiate the terms of a reorganization plan with multiple creditor groups enter into lock-up agreements with certain major creditors after reaching agreement in principle concerning the acceptable parameters of a plan. A series of court decisions in the United States, beginning with *Trans World Airlines, Inc. v. Texaco, Inc. (In re Texaco, Inc.)*, 81 B.R. 813 (Bankr. S.D.N.Y. 1988), have held that these kinds of agreements are generally enforceable and comply with applicable solicitation requirements. Lock-up agreements typically contain provisions allowing signatories to back out of their commitments where their fiduciary obligations so require or the plan actually proposed by the debtor is materially different than what was agreed.

There are other shortcomings and problems encountered in the process of attempting to "lock-up" creditors to either a prepackaged or prenegotiated chapter 11 case, but there are also many benefits, including (i) providing more certainty to the ability of the debtor to successfully reorganize and emerge from a chapter 11 proceeding, (ii) reducing the amount of time (and thus the costs) the debtor must spend in chapter 11, and (iii) allowing parties to confer prior to a chapter 11 filing and attempt to work out many issues that might otherwise be litigated in the chapter 11 proceeding, thereby potentially avoiding outcomes that would be unsatisfactory to all. As practitioners under the Enterprise Bankruptcy Law encounter new and challenging cases, some situations may lend themselves to the implementation of a similar approach, using a lock-up to streamline the issues that may arise during the case. The lesson to be learned from the experience of using lock-up agreements in the United States is that their successful implementation is often case-specific.

---

[40] Section 1126(e) of the U.S. Bankruptcy Code provides that "[o]n request of a party in interest, and after notice and a hearing, the court may designate any entity whose acceptance or rejection of such plan was not in good faith, or was not solicited or procured in good faith or in accordance with the provisions of this title. 11 U.S.C. § 1126(e).

9.6.2 Prepackaged Cases

In a "prepackaged" chapter 11 case, the debtor files the case after soliciting and receiving the votes necessary to confirm the proposed plan of reorganization. In order to accomplish this, the debtor must negotiate with its key creditors prior to the filing of the petition, reach agreement on the terms of a proposed plan of reorganization, and solicit acceptances of the plan. The U.S. Bankruptcy Code expressly provides for solicitation and voting on a chapter 11 plan prior to commencement of a case,[41] filing a chapter 11 plan together with the debtor's petition,[42] and counting votes solicited prepetition.[43]

Although the time spent under the supervision of the bankruptcy court in a prepackaged case can be quite short,[44] the period of time leading up to the commencement of the prepackaged chapter 11 case can be quite long. Negotiations leading up to the development of a plan of reorganization can take many months, and may bog down indefinitely in the absence a supervising court to assist and influence the parties to come to an agreement. In addition, if the case involves regulatory review of plan documents (depending on the debtor's industry), an extended exchange of comments and revisions may transpire, which can cause significant delays.

Nevertheless, at the time that a prepackaged case is finally commenced, the debtor is able to report to its suppliers and customers that the ultimate outcome—a confirmed plan—is more or less assured, thereby reducing apprehension. Moreover, trade creditors often are less concerned about the prospect of a prepackaged case because they generally receive full recovery of their claims.[45] Finally, once commenced, a prepackaged chapter 11 case is usually less contentious than a traditional chapter 11 case.

A prepackaged chapter 11 case is an option only where the debtor's financial distress is traceable primarily to burdensome levels of debt and the debtor does not need a comprehensive restructuring of its business operations. Because a prepackaged chapter 11 case is dependent on a negotiated agreement with key creditor constituencies prior to case commencement, this option

---

[41] *See* Fed. R. Bankr. P. 3018(b).

[42] *See* 11 U.S.C. § 1121(a).

[43] *See id.* § 1126(b).

[44] Prepackaged cases have lasted less than thirty days, although forty-five to ninety days is more typical.

[45] This is due to the difficulty of soliciting these creditors outside of bankruptcy, as well as to assure their goodwill and cooperation.

generally requires that the debtor's debt be in the hands of a stable group of creditors. If the debt is actively traded, however, negotiations are much more difficult, if not impossible. Moreover, even if the debt is held by a stable group of creditors during the negotiation period, the process can unravel quickly if creditors subsequently sell their claims prior to the formal vote on the plan. For these reasons, a successful prepackaged case depends on having a creditor body that is committed to the plan and willing to restrict its ability to sell and transfer claims.

9.6.3 Prenegotiated Cases

A prenegotiated chapter 11 case is similar to a prepackaged case in that negotiations with major creditor constituencies occur prior to commencement of the case, and the debtor typically files its plan of reorganization at the time that it files its bankruptcy petition. As opposed to a prepackaged chapter 11 case, however, in a prenegotiated case, solicitation of creditors for acceptance of the plan takes place after commencement and after court approval of the debtor's disclosure statement. Through a prenegotiated chapter 11 case, the complications of prepetition solicitation can be avoided while retaining many of the advantages of a prepackaged case, and the time in bankruptcy can still be as little as sixty to ninety days.[46]

The principal disadvantage of the prenegotiated chapter 11 case is that the debtor commences its chapter 11 case with no assurance that its proposed plan will be accepted by the required majorities of creditors. However, lock-up agreements could be entered into with key constituents in order to assure the debtor of support by such constituencies.[47]

9.6.4 Prepackaged and Prenegotiated Reorganization Cases Under the Enterprise Bankruptcy Law

Despite the fairly common practice of using prepackaged and prenegotiated reorganization cases in the U.S. in certain circumstances, and the inclusion of certain provisions in the U.S. Bankruptcy Code allowing for such use, no provisions appear in the Enterprise Bankruptcy Law that address

---

[46] Bankruptcy Rule 2002 requires twenty-five days' notice of the deadline for filing objections to a disclosure statement, and the same notice of the hearing to consider approval of a disclosure statement. The extent of the solicitation period varies depending on the number of holders of claims and interest, and whether these claims are based on public securities. A thirty-day voting period is usually sufficient, and shorter periods have been used.

[47] *See* Section 9.6.1 above for a more fulsome discussion of lock-up agreements.

prepackaged or prenegotiated cases. However, it should also be noted that there is nothing in the Enterprise Bankruptcy Law that would seem to prohibit the practice of a prepackaged or prenegotiated case. One procedural difference that might make implementation of such a case more challenging under the Enterprise Bankruptcy Law, however, is that unlike under the U.S. Bankruptcy Code, an administrator is designated when the People's Court rules to accept a bankruptcy application.[48] Therefore, even if the representatives of the company were able to negotiate some sort of "prepackaged" or "prenegotiated" deal with creditors prior to applying for reorganization, such a negotiated deal likely would need to have the support or approval of the administrator as part of the debtors' application to manage its property and business affairs by itself under the supervision of the administrator.[49] Despite this extra procedural step of seeking the administrator's approval of a "prepackaged" or "prenegotiated" deal, the benefits of exploring these types of cases and allowing parties to reach agreement prior to filing the bankruptcy case may prove useful as more cases are tested under the Enterprise Bankruptcy Law.

9.7 Acceptance of a Plan of Reorganization

9.7.1 Disclosure and Solicitation

Article 84 of the Enterprise Bankruptcy Law provides that "[t]he People's Court shall hold a creditors' meeting within thirty days from the date of receipt of the draft reorganization plan to vote on the draft reorganization plan," and that at such meeting, "[t]he debtor or administrator shall explain the draft reorganization plan to the creditors' meeting and answer inquiries." The Enterprise Bankruptcy Law provides nothing further regarding disclosure about the draft reorganization plan or solicitation of votes.

By contrast, section 1125 of the U.S. Bankruptcy Code requires that, prior to soliciting acceptances from impaired creditors, the debtor must file and obtain court approval of a disclosure statement describing, in part, the proposed plan of reorganization and its treatment of claims.[50] At the court hearing to consider approval of the disclosure statement, parties in interest may object to its contents and request modifications. Under the U.S. Bankruptcy Code, the disclosure statement must provide the debtor's impaired creditors

---

[48] Enterprise Bankruptcy Law, art. 13.

[49] *Id.*, art. 73.

[50] *See also* Fed. R. Bankr. P. 3016(c).

with "adequate information" permitting an "informed judgment" regarding the proposed plan. In that regard, section 1125 provides:

> "[A]dequate information" means information of a kind, and in sufficient detail, as far as is reasonably practicable in light of the nature and history of the debtor and the condition of the debtor's books and records, including a discussion of the potential material Federal tax consequences of the plan to the debtor, any successor to the debtor, and a hypothetical investor typical of the holders of claims or interests in the case, that would enable such a hypothetical investor of the relevant class to make an informed judgment about the plan.[51]

The determination of whether a disclosure statement contains adequate information is to be made on a case-by-case basis, focusing on the unique facts and circumstances of each case.[52] A disclosure statement generally contains the following types of information:

(1) the circumstances that gave rise to the filing of the bankruptcy petition;
(2) a complete description of available assets and their value;
(3) the anticipated future of the debtor;
(4) the source of the information provided in the disclosure statement;
(5) a disclaimer, which typically indicates that no statements or information concerning the debtor or its assets or securities are authorized other than those set forth in the disclosure statement;
(6) the condition and performance of the debtor while in chapter 11;

---

[51] 11 U.S.C. § 1125(a)(1).

[52] *See Quality Inns Int'l, Inc. v. L.B.H. Assoc. Ltd.*, 1990 WL 116761, *2 (4th Cir. July 26, 1990) (holding that "[t]he adequacy of a disclosure statement is determined on a case by case basis in light of the particular facts and circumstances"); *In re Cardinal Congregate I*, 121 B.R. 760, 765 (Bankr. S.D. Ohio 1990) (holding that "the precise information [of a disclosure statement] required will be governed by the facts and circumstances presented in each case"); *In re Scioto Valley Mortgage Co.*, 88 B.R. 168, 170 (Bankr S.D. Ohio 1988) (holding that "[a] determination as to what constitutes adequate information in any particular instance must occur on a case-by-case basis under the facts and circumstances presented"); *In re Phoenix Petroleum Co.*, 278 B.R. 385, 393 (Bankr. E.D. Pa. 2001) (holding that in a chapter 11 bankruptcy case, for purposes of a disclosure statement, "the determination of what is adequate information is subjective and made on a case by case basis").

(7) information regarding claims against the debtor's estate;
(8) a liquidation analysis setting forth the estimated return that creditors would receive in a liquidation under chapter 7;
(9) the accounting and valuation methods used to produce the financial information in the disclosure statement;
(10) information regarding the future management of the debtor, including the amount of compensation to be paid to any insiders, directors, and/or officers;
(11) a summary of the plan of reorganization, including a description of each class of claims or interests and a statement indicating whether or not such class is impaired under the plan, as well as a projection of the percentage recovery anticipated for each class;
(12) an estimate of all administrative expenses, including attorneys' fees and accountants' fees;
(13) the collectibility of any accounts receivable;
(14) any financial information, valuations, and *pro forma* projections that would be relevant to creditors' determinations of whether to accept or reject the plan;
(15) information relevant to the risks being taken by the creditors and interest holders;
(16) the actual or projected value that can be obtained from avoidable transfers;
(17) the existence, likelihood, and possible success of non-bankruptcy litigation;
(18) the tax consequences of the plan;
(19) the relationship of the debtor with its affiliates; and
(20) identification of those facts favoring the settlement of claims being implemented by the plan.[53]

Under the U.S. Bankruptcy Code, the court does not conduct a valuation of the debtor or an appraisal of the debtor's assets before approving the disclosure statement.[54] Creditors objecting to the disclosure statement may object only to the adequacy of the information provided, and then only for the objecting creditor's particular class.[55]

---

[53] *See, e.g., Scioto Valley*, 88 B.R. at 170–71.

[54] 11 U.S.C. § 1125(b).

[55] *See Scioto Valley*, 88 B.R. at 171; *In re Adana Mortgage Bankers, Inc.*, 14 B.R. 29, 30 (Bankr. N.D. Ga. 1981).

9.7.2 Voting Eligibility Under the Enterprise Bankruptcy Law

Pursuant to Article 79 of the Enterprise Bankruptcy Law, the proposed plan of reorganization shall be submitted to both the People's Court and the creditors' meeting for approval. Pursuant to Article 84, the court will convene a creditors' meeting to vote on the plan within thirty days of the date of receipt of the proposed plan. Under Article 82, voting on the plan is conducted by class.[56] All creditors may vote on the proposed reorganization plan.[57] Allowing all creditors to vote on a proposed reorganization plan is a significant departure from the U.S. Bankruptcy Code, which only permits a creditor to vote on the plan of reorganization if its claim is considered "impaired" under the plan.

Article 85 provides that equity interest holders may send non-voting delegates to the creditors' meeting at which voting on a proposed plan will take place. Article 85 further provides that "[i]f the draft reorganization plan involves matters of adjustment to the investors' rights and interests, an investors' group shall be set up to vote on such matters." Effectively, the Enterprise Bankruptcy Law provides for a class of equity interest holders with the power to vote on a proposed reorganization plan under which they are impaired.

9.7.3 Voting Eligibility Under the U.S. Bankruptcy Code

Section 1124 of the U.S. Bankruptcy Code provides that a claim is impaired unless the plan of reorganization (i) leaves unaltered the legal, equitable, and contractual rights of the holder, or (ii) cures prior defaults, reinstates the maturity of the claim or interest as it existed prior to default, and compensates the holder for damages resulting from a reasonable reliance on a right to receive accelerated payments.[58]

The concept of impairment under the U.S. Bankruptcy Code is critical because it delineates which classes of claims are entitled to vote on a plan. If a class of claims is not entitled to vote, then the debtor may avoid the necessity of soliciting such class and having to potentially satisfy the "cram-

---

[56] *See* Enterprise Bankruptcy Law, arts. 82, 84.

[57] *See id.*, arts. 82, 86.

[58] *See* 11 U.S.C. § 1124. The 2005 Amendments added a new subsection which provides that, upon the occurrence of a default, the claimant must be compensated for actual pecuniary loss suffered from a failure to perform nonmonetary obligations (other than a nonmonetary default under a nonresidential real property lease) in order for the claim to be rendered unimpaired. *See id.* § 1124(2)(D).

down" provisions of the U.S. Bankruptcy Code or other rules such as the "best interests" test.[59]

U.S. courts have ruled that a plan impairs the rights of a creditor if it surrenders excess collateral,[60] cancels a guarantee,[61] modifies shareholder voting rights,[62] or pays employee wages in goods rather than cash.[63] Courts have held that a creditor is entitled to vote on a plan even if it is impaired only in the "slightest fashion,"[64] and some courts have found impairment even where an alteration resulted in the improvement of the holder's economic interest.[65] Under the U.S. Bankruptcy Code, if a debtor is solvent, the prohibition of interest on unmatured unsecured debt is lifted.[66] Namely, unsecured creditors of a solvent debtor are entitled to be paid principal plus interest accruing on principal during the bankruptcy case. If the debtor's plan of reorganization does not provide for the payment in full of principal plus accrued interest to the unsecured creditor in the foregoing circumstance, such creditor is considered to be "impaired" and entitled to vote on the plan of reorganization.[67]

---

[59] Section 1129(a)(7) of the U.S. Bankruptcy Code requires that, for confirmation of a plan where a holder of a claim or interest in an impaired class rejects the plan, each claimant must "receive or retain ... property of a value, as of the effective date of the plan, that is not less than the amount ... received or retained if the debtor were liquidated under chapter 7 of this title." *Id.* § 1129(a)(7).

[60] *In re Sacred Heart Hosp. of Norristown*, 182 B.R. 413, 424 (Bankr. E.D. Pa. 1995) ("Although a secured creditor can be forced to take back its collateral in full payment of its claim ... such treatment most certainly impairs the secured claim.").

[61] *In re Eller Bros., Inc.*, 53 B.R. 10, 12 (Bankr. M.D. Tenn. 1985).

[62] *Acequia v. Clinton (In re Acequia, Inc.)*, 787 F.2d 1352, 1361 (9th Cir. 1986).

[63] *In re Wilhelm*, 101 B.R. 120 (Bankr. W.D. Mo. 1989) (wage claim was impaired where plan proposed to satisfy part of claim through transfer of motor vehicle).

[64] *See, e.g., In re Am. Solar King Corp.*, 90 B.R. 808 (Bankr. W.D. Tex. 1988).

[65] *See, e.g., In re Wilhelm*, 101 B.R. 120 (Bankr. W.D. Mo. 1989); *In re Witt*, 60 B.R. 556 (Bankr. N.D. Iowa 1986).

[66] The U.S. Bankruptcy Code provides that, upon objection, the court shall allow a claim except to the extent "such claim is for unmatured interest." 11 U.S.C. § 502(b)(2). The rule has several exceptions. For example, under the provisions dealing with the distribution of assets under a case under chapter 7, an unsecured creditor is entitled to "payment of interest at the legal rate from the date of the filing of the petition" prior to any distribution of remaining assets to the debtor. *Id.* § 726(a)(5).

[67] *In re Adelphia Commc'ns Corp.*, 368 B.R. 140, 256 (Bankr. S.D.N.Y. 2007) (under a proposed plan in which the debtor would pay less than principal plus accrued interest to a secured creditor where the debtor was found to be solvent, such unsecured creditors were impaired and had the right to vote for or against the plan).

9.7.4 Voting Standards Under the Enterprise Bankruptcy Law

Article 84 provides that "[i]f the draft reorganization plan is passed by more than half of the creditors in a voting group present at the meeting and representing more than two-thirds of the total claims of the group, the draft reorganization plan shall be deemed passed by that group." Thus, acceptance by (i) more than half in number of the creditors in a group present and entitled to vote and (ii) more than two-thirds in amount of the group's confirmed aggregate claim amount (including those present and not present) will carry the group.

Under Article 86 of the Enterprise Bankruptcy Law, the proposed plan is deemed to have been passed and adopted only if "all voting groups" have voted to accept the plan, in which case the administrator or debtor shall file within ten days an application with the People's Court for approval of the plan. Then, within thirty days, "after verifying that the reorganization plan meets the provisions of this Law," the People's Court "shall make a ruling approving the reorganization plan and terminating the reorganization procedures . . . and shall make a public announcement of such ruling."[68]

9.7.5 Voting Standards Under the U.S. Bankruptcy Code

The standards set forth under Article 84 of the Enterprise Bankruptcy Law are similar to the U.S. measure providing that a "class of claims has accepted a plan if such plan has been accepted by creditors . . . that hold at least two-thirds in amount and more than one-half in number of the allowed claims of such class . . . that have accepted or rejected [the] plan."[69] In determining whether an impaired class of claims has voted to accept a proposed plan of reorganization, the tally cannot include "any acceptance of the plan by any insider."[70] The definition of an insider has been applied flexibly. "An insider is one who has a sufficiently close relationship with the debtor that his conduct is made subject to closer scrutiny than those dealing at arms length with the debtor."[71]

Section 1126(a) of the U.S. Bankruptcy Code provides that a holder of a claim allowed under section 502 may accept or reject a plan. Section

---

[68] Enterprise Bankruptcy Law, art. 86.

[69] 11 U.S.C. § 1126(c).

[70] *Id.* § 1129(a)(10).

[71] *In re 9281 Shore Road Owners Corp.*, 187 B.R. 837, 853 (E.D.N.Y. 1995).

502(a) provides that a claim is deemed allowed unless a party in interest objects. A creditor whose claim is objected to is therefore disenfranchised from voting on the plan unless the objection is adjudicated prior to plan voting or a mechanism, such as temporary allowance pursuant to Bankruptcy Rule 3018(a), is provided for. In other words, under the U.S. Bankruptcy Code, only those creditors who actually vote are included in the tabulation for determining acceptance or rejection by the class.[72]

Insights and Recommendations

- *Require Disclosure of Adequate Information Regarding a Proposed Plan*

The Enterprise Bankruptcy Law does not include any disclosure requirements other than the requirement in Article 84 that the debtor or administrator explain the plan at the creditors' meeting convened to vote on the proposed plan. It is hoped that upcoming implementing regulations will require that the administrator or debtor, prior to the Article 84 creditors' meeting, provide creditors with adequate information in written form to enable creditors to make an "informed judgment" on the plan by including some of the informational items listed above in Section 9.7.1.

---

[72] Additionally, "[o]n request of a party in interest, and after notice and a hearing, the court may designate any entity whose acceptance or rejection ... was not in good faith, or was not solicited or procured in good faith." 11 U.S.C. § 1126(e). Entities so designated are excluded from the calculation of acceptances by a class of claims or equity interests. A rejection is not in bad faith when some economic justification exists, and the creditor is not rejecting simply to obtain some unfair advantage over other creditors. *See, e.g., In re Peter Thompson Assocs.*, 155 B.R. 20 (Bankr. D.N.H. 1993); *In re A.D.W., Inc.*, 90 B.R. 645 (Bankr. D.N.J. 1988). A rejection also is not necessarily in bad faith, even if the rejecting creditor would obtain nothing in a liquidation. *See, e.g., In re Landau Boat Co.*, 8 B.R. 432 (Bankr. W.D. Mo. 1981). A rejection may be in bad faith, however, if the rejecting creditor is a business competitor and has the ulterior motive of destroying the debtor's business to further its own business interests. *See, e.g., In re MacLeod Co.*, 63 B.R. 654 (Bankr. S.D. Ohio 1986).
When a plan of reorganization renders a class unimpaired, that class and each holder of a claim or interest in that class are "conclusively presumed" to have accepted the plan. 11 U.S.C. § 1126(f). Thus, solicitation of acceptances from unimpaired classes is not required. Conversely, when a plan of reorganization provides that a class will not receive or retain any interest in property on account of its claim, that class is deemed to have rejected the plan. *Id.* § 1126(g). Accordingly, solicitation of votes from those classes also is not required.

- *Address and Clarify Voting Issues*

Under the U.S. Bankruptcy Code, if a creditor's claim is unimpaired, it has no right to vote—on the principle that if its interests are not impaired by the plan, that creditor should not be able to object to the treatment of other creditors under the plan. Although the Enterprise Bankruptcy Law appears to recognize this principle in permitting equity holders to vote only if their interests are impaired under the plan, it contains no such restriction on the rights of creditors to vote if they are unimpaired. That is, under the Enterprise Bankruptcy Law, all creditors are entitled to vote regardless of impairment. Perhaps forthcoming regulations will limit creditors' voting rights based on impairment. Additionally, it appears that there is no provision, analogous to section 1129(a)(10) of the U.S. Bankruptcy Code, that disqualifies the vote of an "insider" for purposes of determining acceptance or rejection of a plan. In order to prevent insiders from potentially interfering with or tainting the voting process, it might be helpful for regulations to restrict or provide transparency with respect to the votes of "insiders" of a debtor.

9.8 Confirmation or Approval of a Plan of Reorganization

Once a plan is passed by all the voting groups, the plan must be approved by the People's Court. Upon verifying that the adopted plan complies with the provisions of the Enterprise Bankruptcy Law, the court shall issue an order and make a public announcement approving the plan and terminating the reorganization procedure.[73] Where a proposed plan of reorganization is not accepted by all voting groups, however, the proposed plan must satisfy all of the additional requirements set forth in Article 87 of the Enterprise Bankruptcy Law before the court can approve the plan.

Under the U.S. Bankruptcy Code, following the approval by all impaired classes or cramdown over the vote of a dissenting class of creditors, the court must hold a hearing to consider confirmation of the plan, at which parties in interest may object.[74] Where competing plans are presented and meet the requirements for confirmation, the U.S. Bankruptcy Code requires the court to consider the preferences of creditors and equity security holders in determining which plan to confirm.[75]

---

[73] *See* Enterprise Bankruptcy Law, art. 86.

[74] 11 U.S.C. § 1128.

[75] *Id.*

9.8.1 *Requirements for Approval Under the Enterprise Bankruptcy Law*

9.8.1.1 Consensual Plan of Reorganization

As noted in Section 9.7.4 above, under the Enterprise Bankruptcy Law, with respect to a proposed plan that has been accepted by all voting groups, the court shall issue an order approving the plan upon verification that such consensual plan complies with the provisions of the statute. A proposed plan that has been rejected by a voting group after two rounds of voting (or that is not submitted for a second round of voting following a prior rejection and renewed negotiations) can still be approved by the People's Court if the plan satisfies the requirements outlined in Article 87, discussed next in Section 9.8.1.2.

9.8.1.2 Nonconsensual Plan of Reorganization

The Enterprise Bankruptcy Law has requirements that apply in situations where a dissenting group (or groups) of creditors votes against a proposed plan of reorganization. The requirements for acceptance of a proposed plan over the dissent of a voting group[76] are governed by Article 87 of the Enterprise Bankruptcy Law. Article 87 provides that, "[i]f the draft plan of reorganization is not passed in some of the voting groups, the debtor or the administrator may negotiate with such voting groups which did not pass the draft reorganization plan" and then conduct a second round of voting for that group. Any negotiated resolution "shall not impair the interests of the other voting groups."[77] Article 87 of the law further provides:

> If the voting groups which did not pass the draft reorganization plan decline to have the second round of voting or do not pass the reorganization plan in the second round of voting, the debtor or the administrator may request the People's Court to approve the draft reorganization plan provided that the draft reorganization plan satisfies the following conditions:
>
> (1) according to the draft reorganization plan, the claims listed in Article 82, paragraph 1, item (1) hereof [*i.e.*, secured claims] will be fully paid off with respect of

---

[76] The analogous concept under U.S. Bankruptcy Law, called "cramdown," is discussed in Section 9.8.2.2 below.

[77] Enterprise Bankruptcy Law, art. 87.

such specific property, and the losses incurred by the delay of the repayment will be compensated fairly and the security interests have not suffered substantial damage; or the draft reorganization plan has been passed by such voting group;

(2) according to the draft reorganization plan, the claims listed in Article 82, paragraph 1, items (2) and (3) hereof [*i.e.*, labor claims and taxes, respectively] will be fully paid off; or the draft reorganization plan has been passed by the relevant voting groups;

(3) according to the draft reorganization plan, the ordinary claims [*i.e.*, general unsecured claims] will be repaid in a proportion which is not less than the proportion available to them pursuant to the bankruptcy liquidation procedure at the time when the draft reorganization plan is submitted for approval; or the draft reorganization plan has been passed by such voting group;

(4) the adjustment to the investors' rights and interests in the draft reorganization plan is fair and equitable; or the draft reorganization plan has been passed by the investors group;[78]

(5) members within the same voting group are treated fairly and equally under the draft reorganization plan and the repayment priority under the draft reorganization plan does not violate the provisions under Article 113 hereof; and

(6) the business operation plan of the debtor is feasible.

Plan approval under Article 87 thus embodies a "fair and equitable" test, which is clearly applicable at least to voting equity interests, although what is meant by "fair and equitable" under the PRC law is less than completely clear. Unlike the cramdown provisions under the U.S. Bankruptcy Code, the Enterprise Bankruptcy Law in Article 87 may not apply the concept of "fair and equitable" treatment to all groups or classes that vote against the plan. Rather, as provided in Article 87(4), it appears that "fair and equitable"

[78] The "fair and equitable" test as used here appears limited to equity interests, unlike under the U.S. law, where it is applicable to all impaired classes.

explicitly applies only to equity interests voting against the plan. However, in requiring that the plan's repayment priority not violate the hierarchy set forth in Article 113 (*i.e.*, labor claims, taxes, and then unsecured claims), Article 87(5) may impose an "absolute priority" rule applicable to all classes (and thus effectively extend the concept of "fair and equitable" treatment to all voting groups). Article 87(5) also requires that members within each voting group be treated "fairly and equally," which appears to provide an analog to section of 1129(b)(1) of the U.S. Bankruptcy Code's requirement that a plan "not discriminate unfairly," although what is intended is not entirely clear.[79]

Article 87 further requires that secured claims, labor claims and taxes be "fully paid off," which presumably means that such claims are to be paid in full in cash. The only comparable provision under U.S. law is the requirement in section 1129(a)(9)(A) of the U.S. Bankruptcy Code that administrative expense claims be paid in full. Notably, there is no requirement in the PRC plan-related provisions requiring bankruptcy expenses or common-interest debts to be paid in full or as part of the plan; nor is there any provision that could force secured and unsecured creditors to accept a payment of their claims over time, similar to what is permitted under the U.S. Bankruptcy Code's "fair and equitable" test.

The leverage for plan approval provided by the Enterprise Bankruptcy Law to employees and tax authorities under Article 87 is analogous to the priority given to employee and administrative claims under the U.S. law. Section 507 of the U.S. Bankruptcy Code provides that certain expenses and claims have priority over others.[80] Included in this list of priority claims are certain taxes owed by the estate, and certain claims for wages and sales commissions.[81] Because these tax and employee claims are granted priority, a chapter 11 plan generally must provide for their full payment before general unsecured creditors receive any distribution from the debtor's estate.

If the foregoing requirements of Article 87 are satisfied, the People's Court shall issue an order approving the plan of reorganization within thirty days after the debtor's application for cramdown.[82] In the event that the plan of reorganization is not accepted by all voting groups and it fails the Article 87

---

[79] *See* Section 9.8.2.2 below for further discussion of section 1129(b) of the U.S. Bankruptcy Code.

[80] 11 U.S.C. § 507.

[81] *See id.* § 507(a)(4).

[82] Enterprise Bankruptcy Law, art. 87.

cramdown procedure, the People's Court shall terminate the reorganization procedure and declare the debtor bankrupt, effectively converting the Chapter VIII reorganization into a Chapter X bankruptcy liquidation.[83] This contrasts sharply with U.S. law, under which the debtor is not prevented from filing a new plan of reorganization—and, if exclusivity has terminated, creditors also may file their own plan of reorganization.

9.8.2 Requirements for Confirmation Under the U.S. Bankruptcy Code

9.8.2.1 Consensual Plan of Reorganization

The U.S. Bankruptcy Code contains requirements for confirmation of a plan of reorganization that apply to consensual plans (where all classes of creditors vote in favor of a plan). Section 1129 of the U.S. Bankruptcy Code enumerates thirteen requirements governing confirmation of a consensual chapter 11 plan of reorganization:[84]

(1) the plan complies with the applicable provisions of the U.S. Bankruptcy Code;

(2) the plan proponent complies with the applicable provisions of the U.S. Bankruptcy Code;

(3) the plan is proposed in good faith and not by any means forbidden by law;

(4) the court has approved any payment for services or for costs and expenses in connection with the case;

(5) the plan proponent has provided disclosures relating to any individual serving as director or officer of the debtor following plan confirmation, and any insider to be retained by the reorganized debtor;

(6) any governmental regulatory commission has approved any rate change provided for in the plan;

(7) each holder of a claim in an impaired class has either accepted the plan or will receive not less than the amount such holder would have received in a liquidation under chapter 7 of the U.S. Bankruptcy Code;

---

[83] *See id.*

[84] In addition to these requirements, the 2005 Amendments added three new requirements that apply only to debtors that are individuals or are not "a moneyed, business, or commercial corporation or trust." 11 U.S.C § 1129(a)(14)–(16).

(8) each class of claims has accepted the plan or is not impaired under the plan;
(9) the plan provides for full cash payment of administrative expense claims and certain domestic support obligations, wages, and contributions to an employee benefit plan;
(10) at least one impaired class of claims has accepted the plan;
(11) confirmation of the plan is not likely to be followed by a liquidation or another reorganization proceeding;
(12) all bankruptcy fees have been paid; and
(13) the plan provides for the continuation of retiree benefits.[85]

A plan cannot be confirmed unless all of these requirements are satisfied.[86] Among the most important of these requirements are the "best interests of creditors" test and the "feasibility" test:

- The Best Interests of Creditors Test – § 1129(a)(7). To confirm a plan in which any classes are impaired, the plan must provide that each holder in an impaired class has accepted the plan, or will receive or retain under the plan property having a value that is not less than the amount the holder would receive if the debtor were liquidated under chapter 7 of the U.S. Bankruptcy Code. What is important to understand about the "best interests of creditors" test under the U.S. Bankruptcy Code is that it applies to any creditor who dissents or votes in favor of the plan, and is not limited in application to classes or groups of dissenting creditors. As discussed below, the counterpart to the best interests of creditors test is Article 87(3) of the Enterprise Bankruptcy Law.
- Feasibility – § 1129(a)(11). This provision requires that "[c]onfirmation of the plan is not likely to be followed by the liquidation, or the need for further financial reorganization, of the debtor or any successor to the debtor under the plan, unless such liquidation or reorganization is proposed in the plan."[87] Put another way, the plan proponent must demonstrate that it has the ability to generate the funds necessary to make the payments provided

[85] *Id.* § 1129(a). There are several additional requirements that are relevant only where the debtor is an individual or not-for-profit organization.
[86] *See id.*; H.R. Rep. No. 95-595, at 412 (1977), *reprinted in* 1978 U.S.C.C.A.N. 5963, 6368; S. Rep. No. 95-989, at 126 (1978), *reprinted in* 1978 U.S.C.C.A.N. 5787, 5912.
[87] 11 U.S.C. § 1129(a)(11).

for under the plan and operate the reorganized business.[88] Article 87(6) of the Enterprise Bankruptcy Law contains an analogous requirement, as discussed below.

9.8.2.2 Cramdown

Where an impaired class of creditors has voted to reject the plan of reorganization, under section 1129(b)(1) of the U.S. Bankruptcy Code the plan may be "crammed down" over the dissent of the non-consenting class, provided that the plan satisfies the additional requirements that "the plan does not discriminate unfairly, and is fair and equitable" with respect to each impaired dissenting class of creditors.[89]

The "fair and equitable" test is set forth in detail in section 1129(b)(2) of the U.S. Bankruptcy Code, which essentially provides for relative priorities of payment to be preserved by mandating that no junior class or interest may receive anything under a plan unless all dissenting senior classes have received property or payments equal to the value (as of the effective date of the plan) of their allowed claims. Thus, for a plan to be fair and equitable, it must satisfy the "absolute priority" rule. This means that, unless they agree to lesser treatment, senior creditors must be paid in full (receive the present value of their allowed claims) before junior creditors receive any distribution, and unsecured and undersecured creditors' claims must be paid in full before equity interest holders may participate in any recovery. A corollary of the absolute priority rule is that, if junior creditors or equity interest holders will not be satisfied in full, then no creditor may receive more under the plan than the value of its allowed claim.

Under section 1129(b)(2)(A) of the U.S. Bankruptcy Code, a plan is fair and equitable with respect to secured creditors if it provides that (i) the holders of those claims retain the liens securing their claims and receive deferred cash payments, the present value of which (as of the effective date of the plan)

---

[88] Factors considered by courts in determining feasibility include adequacy of capital structure, earning power of business, economic conditions, ability of management, availability of credit, provisions for adequate working capital, and any other factors related to the successful performance of the reorganization plan. *See In re Prussia Assocs.*, 322 B.R. 572, 584 (Bankr. E.D. Pa. 2005); *In re Polytherm Indus., Inc.*, 33 B.R. 823, 830 (W.D. Wis. 1983) (citing *In re Landmark at Plaza Park, Ltd.*, 7 B.R. 653 (Bankr. D.N.J. 1980)).

[89] 11 U.S.C. § 1129(b)(1).

totals at least the value of the liens;[90] or (ii) if the plan provides for the sale of the secured creditors' collateral free and clear of the liens thereon, the liens must attach to the proceeds of the sale and the treatment of those liens must satisfy the requirements of subclause (i) above or subclause (iii) below; or (iii) the secured creditors receive the "indubitable equivalent" of the value of their claims.[91]

With regard to unsecured creditors, under section 1129(b)(2)(B), a plan is fair and equitable if (i) the plan provides that each unsecured creditor receives or retains property of a value (as of the effective date of the plan) equal to the allowed amount of its claim; or (ii) the holder of any claim that is junior to that of the creditor does not receive or retain any property under the plan on account of such junior claim.[92]

With respect to equity interest holders, under section 1129(b)(2)(C), a plan is fair and equitable if (i) the plan provides that each equity interest holder receives or retains property of a value (as of the effective date of the plan) equal to the greatest allowed amount of any liquidation preference to which such equity interest holder is entitled; or (ii) the holder of any claim that is junior to that of the creditor does not receive or retain any property under the plan on account of such junior claim.[93]

The requirement that a plan of reorganization not unfairly discriminate with respect to a dissenting class of creditors in a cramdown plan under the U.S. Bankruptcy Code is the subject of extensive and well-developed case law, and U.S. courts have provided much guidance in this area. A plan does not "discriminate unfairly" if the legal rights of the dissenting class are treated comparably with the rights of other classes who have interconnected

---

[90] The U.S. Bankruptcy Code does not indicate the appropriate rate of interest to be used in calculating such present value. Case law, however, provides that the rate should be based on the prime rate (used by banks when making loans to their most creditworthy customers) plus an upward adjustment for the additional risk of non-payment posed by the particular debtor, rather than (i) a risk-free rate, (ii) the contractual rate previously existing between the debtor and creditor (subject to adjustment), (iii) a "coerced loan" rate (*i.e.*, the rate that the creditor could obtain if it foreclosed on the collateral and made a loan of equivalent risk and duration), or (iv) a rate based on the creditor's cost to borrow the value of the collateral from a third party. *Till v. SCS Credit Corp.*, 541 U.S. 465 (2004). In addition, the value of the collateral means its replacement value. *Assocs. Commercial Corp. v. Rash*, 520 U.S. 953, 960 (1997).

[91] 11 U.S.C. § 1129(b)(2)(A).

[92] *Id.* § 1129(b)(2)(B).

[93] *Id.* § 1129(b)(2)(C).

rights.[94] In determining whether "unfair discrimination" has occurred, courts generally apply four tests that must be satisfied to demonstrate that any discriminatory treatment that may exist is not unfair: "(i) there is a reasonable basis for discriminating, (ii) the debtor cannot consummate the plan without discrimination, (iii) the discrimination is proposed in good faith, and (iv) the degree of discrimination is in direct proportion to its rationale."[95]

Furthermore, to "cram down" a dissenting class of creditors, the plan must be accepted by at least one impaired class of creditors.[96] As mentioned above, only those creditors who are "impaired" by the plan are entitled to vote; those creditors whose claims are unimpaired by the plan are deemed to vote in favor of the plan, and thus are not required to vote on the plan.[97] In this regard, courts generally will not permit a plan proponent to create an impaired class that will vote to accept a plan in order to support a cramdown. Courts generally will prohibit the separate classification of similarly situated claims without a legitimate business purpose as an impermissible attempt to "gerrymander" an affirmative vote.[98] Finally, if the debtor has the requisite

---

[94] *In re Buttonwood Partners, Ltd.*, 111 B.R. 57, 63 (Bankr. S.D.N.Y. 1990).

[95] *Id.* In *Buttonwood Partners*, the dissenting class was made up of one secured creditor. The creditor asserted that the plan discriminated unfairly because a secured creditor with a junior lien was due to receive a higher interest rate on its impaired claim. Applying the first test, the court held that a reasonable basis existed for discrimination or "individualized treatment" because, unlike unsecured claims, each secured claim is unique in that it is either secured by different collateral or, if secured by the same collateral, it frequently has a different priority level. Therefore, each secured claim may be treated according to its distinct characteristics. The court further held that the second test (*i.e.*, whether the debtor can consummate the plan without discrimination), was satisfied because the case had an extensive history and it had not been demonstrated that a plan could be completed without the discriminatory treatment. Under the third test, the court ruled that the parties did engage in good-faith negotiations leading up to the proposal of the plan. The court noted that, during the course of negotiations, the creditor negotiated its treatment under two separate classes together, trading off different benefits in the debtor's treatment of each class. Finally, the insignificant amount of discrimination between the secured claim at issue, as well as the issue of greater return to the junior secured claim (which was also impaired), were justified in the court's decision by the increased risk borne by the junior secured creditor. *Id.*

[96] 11 U.S.C. § 1129(a)(10).

[97] *See id.* § 1126(f). Conversely, a class of claims or interests is deemed not to have accepted a plan if the plan provides that the members of such class will not receive or retain any property on account of their claims or interests; thus, no voting by such members is required. *Id.* § 1126(g).

[98] *See, e.g., Boston Post Road Ltd. P'ship v. F.D.I.C. (In re Boston Post Road Ltd. P'ship)*, 21 F.3d 477 (2d Cir. 1994); *Phoenix Mut. Life Ins. Co. v. Greystone III Joint Venture (In re Greystone III Joint Venture)*, 995 F.2d 1274 (5th Cir. 1991).

votes in favor of its proposed plan and the court is convinced that the plan has met the section 1129 requirements, then the court can confirm the debtor's plan and the debtor can emerge from bankruptcy.

9.8.2.3 "Liquidating" Chapter 11 Plans

It is interesting to note that, although chapter 11 of the U.S. Bankruptcy Code is entitled "Reorganization," the law contemplates the possibility that the debtor may file a plan that results in liquidation—what the legislative history refers to as a "liquidating plan" under chapter 11.[99] As the U.S. Supreme Court has noted, "[c]hapter 11 bankruptcy proceeding ordinarily culminate in the confirmation of a reorganization plan. But in some cases . . . a debtor sells all or substantially all its assets under §363(b)(1) before seeking or receiving plan confirmation. In this scenario, the debtor typically submits for confirmation a plan of liquidation (rather than a traditional plan of reorganization) providing for the distribution of the proceeds resulting the sale."[100] This scenario may also be reached by section 1123(b)(4), which provides that "a plan may . . . provide for the sale of all or substantially all of the property of the estate, and the distribution of the proceeds of such sale among holders of claims or interests."[101]

It may seem counterintuitive that a debtor with no hope or plan of reviving its business affairs would be permitted to liquidate under the U.S. Bankruptcy Code's reorganization chapter; nevertheless, in some circumstances, an efficient liquidating plan in an existing chapter 11 case may offer advantages over liquidation in the chapter 7 context. A greater return from liquidation may be provided for by a chapter 11 case, because existing

---

[99] H.R. Rep. No. 95-595, at 407 (1977), *reprinted in* 1978 U.S.C.C.A.N. 5963, 6363. The term "reorganization" in chapter 11 of the U.S. Bankruptcy Code encompasses the systematic liquidation of a debtor. *See In re Searles Castle Enters., Inc.*, 17 B.R. 440, 442 (B.A.P. 1st Cir. 1982); *In re L.N. Scott Co.*, 13 B.R. 387, 388 (Bankr. E.D. Pa. 1981); 5 *Collier on Bankruptcy*, *supra* Chapter Five, note 12, at ¶¶ 1123.01[5] and 1123.02[4].

[100] *Florida Dept. of Revenue v. Piccadilly Cafeterias, Inc.*, 128 S. Ct. 2326, 2331 n.2 (2008).

[101] Liquidation is also contemplated by section 1123(a), which provides that "a plan shall . . . provide adequate means for the plan's implementation, such as . . . sale of all or any part of the property of the estate . . . or the distribution of all or any part of the property of the estate among those having an interest in such property of the estate." 11 U.S.C. § 1123(a)(5)(D). In addition, section 1129 contemplates the possibility of a liquidating plan when requiring plan feasibility. *See id.* § 1129(a)(11) ("Confirmation of the plan is not likely to be followed by the liquidation, or the need for further financial reorganization, of the debtor or any successor to the debtor under the plan, unless such liquidation or reorganization is proposed in the plan.").

management can remain in place while the business continues to operate and is streamlined and sold in relatively advantageous circumstances, rather than a quick "fire sale." Other advantages may include avoiding the additional cost associated with conversion from chapter 11 (including the appointment of a chapter 7 trustee and the retention of a new group of professionals), as well as potentially favorable tax treatment available under section 1146, such as avoiding the payment of state transfer taxes.[102] On the other hand, the confirmation process for a chapter 11 plan may involve significant costs that might be avoided in chapter 7.

9.8.3 New Value Corollary

Prior to enactment of the U.S. Bankruptcy Code in 1978, a judicial rule commonly called the "new value corollary" or "new value exception" had developed under the former Bankruptcy Act of 1898.[103] This constituted an exception to the "absolute priority" rule described earlier, in that it permitted a debtor's shareholders or partners to make a contribution of new capital as part of a plan of reorganization; in exchange, those shareholders were able to retain some or all of the ownership interest in the reorganized entity, even though some creditors would not be repaid in full under the plan.

Ordinarily, without application of the new value corollary, the absolute priority rule would prevent equity interest holders from retaining any interest in a reorganized company if creditors would not be paid in full and at least one class of impaired claims rejected the proposed plan. This is because the absolute priority rule can be satisfied only if no distribution under the plan or participation right in the reorganized entity is accorded to any creditors or interest holders whose claims or interests are junior to a class of dissenting creditors who will not be paid in full on the plan's effective date.

Under the new value corollary, however, a junior interest holder may retain equity in the property of the debtor over the objection of an

[102] *Id.* § 1146(a) ("The issuance, transfer, or exchange of a security, or the making or delivery of an instrument of transfer under a plan confirmed under section 1129 of this title, may not be taxed under any law imposing a stamp tax or similar tax."). Note, however, that the favorable treatment of section 1146 has been limited to transfers made under a confirmed plan, and does not extend to pre-confirmation sales under section 363. *See Piccadilly Cafeterias*, 128 S. Ct. 2326 (2008).

[103] *See generally Bank of Am. Nat'l Trust & Sav. Ass'n v. 203 N. LaSalle St. P'ship*, 526 U.S. 434, 444–50 (1999) (discussing *Case v. Los Angeles Lumber Prods. Co.*, 308 U.S. 106 (1939)).

impaired senior class so long as the equity interest holder contributes new value to the reorganization. The case law has permitted equity holders to retain an interest under a plan if they offer value that is (i) new, (ii) substantial, (iii) money or money's worth, (iv) necessary for a successful reorganization, and (v) reasonably equivalent to the value or interest received.[104]

Because the new value corollary was recognized in earlier U.S. case law but was not codified in the current U.S. Bankruptcy Code, courts have been divided as to whether the exception survived the codification. The majority of courts that have ruled on the issue have held that the exception has survived; the United States Supreme Court has twice expressly avoided deciding the question.[105] There is no counterpart in the Enterprise Bankruptcy Law to the new value corollary.

Insights and Recommendations

- *Give Further Discretion to the Court to Extend Reorganization Period*

Article 79 of the Enterprise Bankruptcy Law gives the administrator or debtor six months to submit a plan (plus as many as three additional months, with court approval).[106] Unnecessary and value-depriving bankruptcy liquidations could be avoided if the People's Court were granted discretion to further extend the reorganization process, and if the creditors' meeting were given the right to submit a plan after the administrator/debtor's "exclusivity" period expires, rather than directly and forcibly liquidating the company at that point.

- *Develop Technical Terms in Plan-Approval Provisions*

The acceptance requirements for nonconsensual plans under the Enterprise Bankruptcy Law appear to borrow from the plan confirmation requirements under the U.S. Bankruptcy Code, in some cases even using the same language for key concepts, such as "fair and equitable." The legal

---

[104] *Id.*

[105] *See Norwest Bank Worthington v. Ahlers*, 485 U.S. 197, 203 n.3 (1988) ("[O]ur decision today should not be taken as any comment on the continuing vitality of the Los Angeles Lumber exception"); *203 N. LaSalle*, 526 U.S. at 454, 458 (1999) (holding that even if exception existed, it would not save debtor's proposed plan).

[106] *See* Enterprise Bankruptcy Law, art. 79.

concepts of what is "fair and equitable" or "feasible" are highly technical in nature, however, and the jurisprudence on these issues has taken years to develop under the U.S. law. In this regard, it may be useful for the Supreme People's Court to issue interpretative guidelines, or, as applicable, to refer to the U.S. interpretations for guidance.

For example, with respect to Article 87(4), the Enterprise Bankruptcy Law does not make clear how a court should determine that a plan treats holders of equity interests "fairly" and "equitably." As discussed in section 9.8.2.2, under the U.S. Bankruptcy Code, the "fair and equitable" treatment of equity interests requires that each equity interest holder receives at least the greatest allowed amount of any liquidation preference to which such equity interest holder is entitled. In accordance with the "fair and equitable" test under U.S. law, classes senior to equity interest holders cannot receive more than 100% of their claims (plus interest); as such, in reorganizations of solvent debtors, equity interest holders may receive the balance of the equity value remaining in the debtor. Thus, even where the Enterprise Bankruptcy Law provides for the concept of "fair and equitable" treatment of equity interests, the Enterprise Bankruptcy Law would benefit from further clarification of that concept.

- *Apply "Fair and Equitable" Test to All Impaired Creditors*

As discussed above, Article 87(4) of the Enterprise Bankruptcy Law, which provides that "[t]he adjustment to the investors' rights and interests in the draft reorganization plan is fair and equitable" in order to obtain approval of a nonconsensual plan, appears limited to equity interest holders. Article 87(5), however, additionally requires that the plan adhere to the priorities established in Article 113. It remains unclear what Article 87(5) is intended to accomplish, and whether Articles 87(4) and 87(5) together apply a "fair and equitable" test to all creditor groups voting on the plan. Under U.S. law, all impaired classes must be treated fairly and equitably in a cramdown plan. That is, under U.S. law, the concept of "fair and equitable" is not limited just to equity interest holders but also applies to all dissenting impaired creditor groups. Thus, clarification is necessary with respect to whether "fair and equitable" treatment under Article 87 is limited only to equity interests, or instead applies to all creditors and equity interest holders that vote against the plan of reorganization.

- *Clarify the Meaning of "Fully Paid Off"*

As noted, Article 87(1) of the Enterprise Bankruptcy Law only permits the cramdown of secured creditors if the plan provides that those creditors "will be fully paid off with respect to such specific property." In the first instance, the Article would benefit from clarification of what is meant for a secured claim to be "fully paid." Also, it is unclear whether this provision gives secured creditors the ability to repossess collateral or force the liquidation of collateral. If the collateral is necessary for the debtor's ongoing business, then the right of a secured creditor to repossess its collateral might obstruct the reorganization of the debtor. Article 87(1) could be clarified so that secured creditors' claims may be satisfied with other assets, such as deferred payments, substitute liens, and/or equity in the reorganized company.

The concept of "fully paying off" secured creditors under the Enterprise Bankruptcy Law is different from the U.S. concept concerning nonconsensual plan treatment of a dissenting secured creditor class. Under the U.S. law, a plan proponent can force a secured creditor to take a note with interest that can be paid over time at a value of at least the allowed amount of the secured claim. On the other hand, the Enterprise Bankruptcy Law requires the secured claim to be fully paid off, presumably by full payment in cash, which gives leverage to secured creditors. Absent from Article 87(1) is the ability of the debtor to provide the secured creditor with a note equal to 100% of the present value of the secured claim paid over time. The ability of a debtor to "stretch out" payments over time on account of a secured claim gives the debtor a significant amount of leverage. Therefore, clarification of what exactly is meant by the words "fully paid off" will dictate the leverage held by the debtor and secured creditors in negotiating over the terms of treatment of secured claims in a plan.

- *Clarify Whether Secured Creditors Would Be Entitled to Assert Unsecured Deficiency Claims for Plan Purposes*

It is not clear that Article 87 of the Enterprise Bankruptcy Law acknowledges the ability of a secured creditor to assert an unsecured deficiency claim if the value of the collateral securing the claim is less than the total amount of the accrued debt.[107] The ability of the secured creditor to assert a deficiency claim gives the secured creditor leverage in using the unsecured deficiency claim to block a vote in favor of the plan in the unsecured claims group; the amount of leverage, however, will depend on the size of the unsecured deficiency claim.

- *Develop the "Best Interests" Test to Better Protect Unsecured Creditors and Apply the Test to All Impaired Creditors*

Article 87(3) of the Enterprise Bankruptcy Law provides for the approval of a plan of reorganization over a dissenting class of unsecured claims, but it should be noted that the standard for doing so is lower than the standard set forth under the U.S. Bankruptcy Code and results in a different balancing of leverage as between secured creditors, unsecured creditors, and the debtor in connection with negotiating a plan of reorganization.

As discussed earlier, under Article 87(3), a plan may be approved without the consent of the voting group of unsecured creditors if "the ordinary claims will be repaid in a proportion which is not less than the proportion available to them pursuant to the bankruptcy liquidation procedure at the time when the draft reorganization plan is submitted for approval." This appears to be analogous to the "best interests" test set forth in section 1129(a)(7) of the U.S. Bankruptcy Code.[108] Importantly, the "best interests" test under U.S. law is only one of the prerequisites to confirmation of a plan of reorganization in either a consensual or a cramdown situation. Notably, under U.S. law, even if a class accepts a plan of reorganization, the debtor must still establish that the "best interests" test is satisfied with respect to any dissenting creditors within an accepting class. A plan may be crammed down upon a dissenting class of unsecured creditors only if (i) all of the provisions of section 1129(a) are met, including the "best interests"

---

[107] While Article 87 does not appear to address the ability of a secured creditor to vote the "deficiency" or undersecured portion of its claim for purposes of voting for or against the plan, Article 110 of the Enterprise Bankruptcy Law recognizes the concept of a deficiency claim to the extent the "priority right to be repaid" would leave the claim partially unpaid. However, it should be noted that this concept of a deficiency claim is only found in Chapter X of the Enterprise Bankruptcy Law which deals specifically with liquidations, not reorganizations.

[108] The "best interests" test under U.S. law is a prerequisite to confirmation of even a consensual plan of reorganization, inasmuch as it protects dissenting members of accepting classes, ensuring that even if a creditor who rejects the plan is outvoted by the remaining creditors in his class, such creditor will still receive at least as much as he would have received in a liquidation of the debtor.

test, *and* (ii) the plan satisfies the "fair and equitable" test, which requires that such unsecured creditors will receive 100% of the present value of their claims, as of the effective date of the plan, or no holder of any claim that is junior to such unsecured claim receives or retains any property.

Unlike under U.S. law, the "best interests" requirement under the Enterprise Bankruptcy Law appears to be the only prerequisite to confirmation of a plan over a dissenting class of unsecured claims.[109] In essence, the plan can be confirmed notwithstanding rejection of the plan by a dissenting class of unsecured creditors as long as it will pay unsecured creditors as much they would receive in a liquidation of the debtor. In other words, under the Enterprise Bankruptcy Law, a dissenting class of unsecured creditors may be "crammed down" upon if it is established that such creditors will receive the economic equivalent of liquidation value for their claims. Without the ability to dissent to a plan and then force their claims to be paid at 100% of the present value of such claims (which could substantially exceed liquidation value), unsecured creditors have little plan negotiating leverage in the Chinese system.

Additionally, it is recommended that under the Enterprise Bankruptcy Law, the "best interests" test be applied to all creditor and equity interest classes in similar fashion, as is done under U.S. law. Namely, if a creditor votes against a plan, the debtor should be required to satisfy the "best interests" test with respect to that dissenting creditor, even if the rest of its voting group accepts the debtor's plan of reorganization.

Moreover, the provision under Article 87(1) (whereby dissenting secured creditors must be "fully paid off" in order for a nonconsensual plan to be approved) gives far more leverage to the secured creditor group in the plan of reorganization process as compared to the U.S. Bankruptcy Code. That is, under U.S. law, a secured creditor can assert the right to payment in full of its claim through the present value equivalent of a payout over time—not a payment in full in cash, which seems to be allowed under the Enterprise Bankruptcy Law.

It is recommended that the statute be clarified—perhaps so that the leverage points that the U.S. model of cramdown is meant to accomplish may be realized. For example, permitting the debtor to supply a note to secured creditors that "stretches out" the repayment of their secured claims (as opposed

[109] In fact, the Enterprise Bankruptcy Law expressly provides only for the fair and equitable treatment of the rights and interests of equity interest holders. Enterprise Bankruptcy Law, art. 87(4).

to requiring cash payment in full) and requiring a plan of reorganization to pay dissenting unsecured creditors 100% of the present value of their unsecured claims (as opposed to payment of liquidation value), would return some leverage in the plan negotiation process to unsecured creditors.

9.9 Implementation of a Plan of Reorganization

Pursuant to Article 89 of the Enterprise Bankruptcy Law, once a plan of reorganization has been successfully adopted by creditors and approved by the court, "[t]he administrator who has received the debtor's property and business affairs shall transfer the property and business affairs to the debtor," and the debtor "shall be responsible for the implementation of the reorganization plan." Nevertheless, pursuant to Article 90, the administrator continues to "supervise the implementation of the reorganization plan" (as specified by Article 81), and the debtor "shall report to the administrator on the status of implementation of the reorganization plan and the financial status of the debtor."[110]

Pursuant to Article 91, "[t]he People's Court, upon the administrator's application, may rule to extend the supervision period for the implementation of the reorganization plan."[111] At the end of the period, the administrator "shall submit a supervision report to the People's Court"; upon that submission, "the administrator's duty of supervision shall terminate."[112]

9.10 Post-Confirmation Modification of a Plan of Reorganization

Unlike the U.S. Bankruptcy Code, the Enterprise Bankruptcy Law does not appear to include post-confirmation modification provisions. Instead, under the Enterprise Bankruptcy Law, if a debtor is unable or fails to carry out the approved plan, then the court will terminate the plan and declare the debtor bankrupt.[113] Under the U.S. Bankruptcy Code, however, a confirmed reorganization plan may be modified "before substantial consummation" of the plan as long as the modifications meet the statute's provisions in sections 1122 and 1123 (for

---

[110] *Id.*, art. 90. The Enterprise Bankruptcy Law does not address specific implementation-related issues, such as certain tax benefits available under section 1146 of the U.S. Bankruptcy Code (discussed in Section 9.8.2.3 above) or exemptions from securities laws under section 1145 (which are beyond the scope of this book).

[111] *Id.*, art. 91.

[112] *Id.*

[113] *Id.*, art. 93.

classification of claims and plan contents, respectively).[114] In addition, the modification must be justified by the circumstances of the case; the court, after notice and hearing, must confirm the modified plan under section 1129.[115]

9.11 Termination of Reorganization Process

Under the Enterprise Bankruptcy Law, the reorganization process can be terminated in several scenarios. First, Article 79 provides for termination of the reorganization procedure and declaration of the debtor's bankruptcy upon failure of the debtor or administrator to timely submit a proposed plan of reorganization. Second, Article 88 provides the same result of terminating the reorganization proceeding and declaring the debtor bankrupt if the proposed plan is rejected by creditors and fails the cramdown procedure. Third, Article 93 provides for conversion to bankruptcy liquidation upon application of creditors in the event that the reorganized debtor is unable or fails to execute the reorganization plan.

Finally, Article 78 allows the administrator and interested parties, "during the reorganization period," to ask the court to terminate the reorganization procedure in any of the following circumstances: (i) if the management and financial situation of the debtor deteriorates to the point that there is no possibility to save the debtor; (ii) if the debtor commits fraud, maliciously diminishes estate assets, or takes other action disadvantageous to creditors; or (iii) if the debtor's behavior causes the administrator to become unable to perform his duties. These circumstances present a standard similar to the one used in section 1104 of the U.S. Bankruptcy Code for the appointment of a trustee.[116] Given the various scenarios described above that would result in the

---

[114] 11 U.S.C. § 1127(b).

[115] *Id.*

[116] Section 1104(a) provides that the "court shall order the appointment of a trustee" in a chapter 11 case upon the request of any party in interest or the U.S. trustee without regard to the number of shareholders of the debtor or the amount of assets or liabilities of the debtor: (i) for cause, including fraud, dishonesty, incompetence, or gross mismanagement of the affairs of the debtor by current management; (ii) if such appointment is in the interests of creditors, any equity security holders, and other interests of the estate; or (iii) if grounds exist to convert or dismiss the case under section 1112, but the court determines that the appointment of a trustee or an examiner is in the best interests of creditors and the estate. *Id.* § 1104(a). Although section 1104(a) does not terminate the reorganization itself, it does terminate the debtor's authority to operate as a debtor in possession, resulting in displacing the debtor's management as well as its board of directors, parties or managing members (depending upon the type of entity and governance in place for the debtor), passing the power to run the estate to a trustee, and terminating the debtor's exclusivity. Where similar circumstances arise in China, however, the reorganization is likely to be terminated altogether.

termination of the reorganization process under the Enterprise Bankruptcy Law, the reorganization process could be characterized as fragile.

Under the U.S. Bankruptcy Code, either the debtor or a party in interest may ask the court to convert a chapter 11 case to a chapter 7 case.[117] Under section 1112(a), a debtor may convert a chapter 11 case to a chapter 7 case unless (i) the debtor is not a debtor in possession; (ii) the case was commenced as an involuntary chapter 11; or (iii) the case was converted to chapter 11 on the request of a party other than the debtor.[118] Section 1112(b) allows a party in interest to petition the bankruptcy court for conversion or dismissal of a chapter 11 case by establishing "cause" for conversion or dismissal, which includes the significant or continued diminution of the estate's assets.

9.12 Discharge and Releases

9.12.1 Discharge

Articles 92 and 94 of the Enterprise Bankruptcy Law provide, respectively, that "[t]he reorganization plan approved by the People's Court shall be binding on the debtor and all creditors,"[119] and that "[u]pon completion of the implementation of the reorganization plan, the debtor shall not bear repayment liability with respect to debts that have been reduced or released under the reorganization plan."[120] Reading these articles together, the Enterprise Bankruptcy Law discharges the debtor's obligations with regard to claims that are treated under the approved reorganization plan.

The discharge granted to debtors under the Enterprise Bankruptcy Law is similar to the discharge provided under section 1141 of the U.S. Bankruptcy Code.[121] Section 1141(a) provides that confirmation of a plan of reorganization binds the debtor (and essentially all other parties in interest) to the provisions of the plan, regardless of whether such creditor, equity security holder, or other party has accepted the plan. Furthermore, section 1141(c) provides that, except as otherwise provided in the plan or the confirmation order, property dealt with by the plan is thereafter "free and clear" of all claims and interests of creditors, equity security holders, and general partners of the debtors. In this situation, the confirmation of a plan of reorganization has

---

[117] *See* 11 U.S.C. § 1112(a), (b).

[118] *See id.* § 1112(a).

[119] Enterprise Bankruptcy Law, art. 92.

[120] *Id.*, art. 94.

[121] A similar discharge is also provided in the conciliation context. *See id.*, art. 106.

the effect of discharging all prepetition liabilities of the debtor in exchange for the treatment of such liabilities in the manner set forth in the plan, as well as giving the debtor a "fresh start" at operating its business outside the confines of chapter 11.

9.12.2 Third Party Releases

Another issue that is often the source of controversy in U.S. bankruptcy cases involves plans of reorganization that contain "third party releases." In its most basic form, a third party release is a release contained in a debtor's plan of reorganization, and approved by the bankruptcy court, which has the effect of enjoining suits by creditors against third parties that have not filed for bankruptcy under U.S. law and would not otherwise be entitled to a discharge under section 1141(c) (discussed above).

The various federal circuit courts throughout the United States have reached different conclusions regarding the propriety of third party releases approved under the bankruptcy courts' equitable power found in section 105 of the U.S. Bankruptcy Code.[122] Courts that have considered this question have taken different approaches and have focused on the following issues: (i) whether section 524(e) of the U.S. Bankruptcy Code, which states that "discharge of a debt of the debtor does not affect the liability of another entity on, or the property of any other entity for, such debt," bars a bankruptcy court from releasing non-debtors from liability without creditor consent; and (ii) whether the U.S. Congress affirmatively gave bankruptcy courts the power to release third parties from creditors' claims without consent, even if section 524(e) does not expressly preclude such releases.

Even in the limited instances in the United States where bankruptcy courts approve a debtors' plan containing "third party" releases, such a release is typically granted only upon a showing that its inclusion in the plan is "essential" to the reorganization.[123] The lesson learned from the practical experience of attempting to have a bankruptcy court exercise jurisdiction in such a way as to grant a non-debtor party a release from a claim of its creditor,

---

[122] Section 105 provides, in relevant part, "The court may issue any order, process, or judgment that is necessary or appropriate to carry out the provisions of this title." 11 U.S.C. § 105(a).

[123] *See MacArthur v. Johns-Manville Corp.*, 837 F.2d 89, 94 (2nd Cir. 1988) (holding that a release arrangement is essential to reorganization when the reorganization hinges on the debtor being free from indirect suits against parties who would have indemnity or contribution claims against the debtor).

is that such relief is not uniformly accepted and in any event considered drastic. In the cases where such relief is granted, it must be supported by evidence that its inclusion in a plan of reorganization is necessary to the successful implementation of the plan.

CHAPTER TEN: Cross-Border Issues and the UNCITRAL Model Law

10.1 Recognition of Foreign Proceedings

Conducting business in a global economy requires that companies, and those that finance them, must be prepared for the particular risks of international commerce. International insolvency proceedings have become increasingly common with the globalization of the world's economies. In this environment, with assets and creditors dispersed worldwide, adequate mechanisms are needed to distribute a debtor's estate efficiently and equitably. Recognizing this reality, many jurisdictions throughout the world have adopted new bankruptcy laws better designed to address cross-border insolvency issues.

As part of the China's development of a complex commercial code reflecting its status as an important player in the international economy, the Enterprise Bankruptcy Law includes a provision that addresses recognition of foreign proceedings. Article 5 provides that concerned parties may apply to the People's Court for recognition and enforcement of a "judgment or ruling made by a foreign court with respect to a bankruptcy case and involving the debtor's properties located in the territory of the People's Republic of China," which the court shall consider "pursuant to the relevant international treaties signed or entered into by the People's Republic of China or based on the principle of reciprocity." The People's Court shall recognize and enforce the judgment or order if it does not:

(1) breach the fundamental principles of PRC law;
(2) injure the PRC's sovereignty, security, or social interests; or
(3) impair the rights and lawful interests of creditors in the territory of the PRC.[1]

Although this provision may be criticized for offering what appears to be rather broad license for the People's Court to disregard foreign proceedings, it is not unlike the cross-border provisions relating to principles of comity[2]

---

[1] Enterprise Bankruptcy Law, art. 5.

[2] *See* Section 10.3 below for a more fulsome discussion of the principles of comity in the United States and certain other countries.

contained in the bankruptcy laws of other countries, including the United States.[3]

Given the vast amount of foreign investment in the PRC, foreign creditors should be very interested in the receptivity of Chinese courts regarding recognition and enforcement of foreign judgments against assets located in the PRC. At this writing, there are no reported cases of a foreign creditor attempting to use Article 5 of the Enterprise Bankruptcy Law to enforce its rights against collateral located in the PRC. It may be helpful to look to the law and practice existing in China prior to the passage of the Enterprise Bankruptcy Law for a sense of how the People's Courts may react to such attempts by foreign creditors.

10.2 International Principles of Comity

10.2.1 Overview of the Principle of Comity

In enacting provisions such as those found in Article 5 of the Enterprise Bankruptcy Law, many nations are embracing a concept known in the legal world as "comity." Comity is a courtesy among nations "involving . . . mutual recognition of legislative, executive and judicial acts."[4] The U.S. Supreme Court defined the term over a century ago, and that classic definition is still consistently cited today:

> "Comity," in the legal sense, is neither a matter of absolute obligation, on the one hand, nor of mere courtesy and good will, upon the other. But it is the recognition which one nation allows within its territory to the legislative, executive or judicial acts of another nation, having due regard both to international duty and convenience, and to the rights of its own citizens, or of other persons who are under the protection of its laws.[5]

Moreover, international comity is "a willingness to grant a privilege, not as a matter of right, but out of deference and good will."[6] Comity should not be misinterpreted as implying that all laws are subject to some sort of universal jurisdiction. In fact, in many countries, if the foreign law transgresses

---

[3] *See, e.g.*, 11 U.S.C. § 1506 ("Nothing in this chapter prevents the court from refusing to take an action governed by this chapter if the action would be manifestly contrary to the public policy of the United States.").

[4] *Black's Law Dictionary* 284 (8th ed. 2004).

[5] *Hilton v. Guyot*, 159 U.S. 113, 164–65 (1895).

[6] *Id.* at 143.

the forum country's public policy or is prejudicial to its citizens, comity is ignored. To the extent it is observed, however, comity can often encourage international business. In an increasingly interconnected global economy where activity that occurs within the boundaries of one nation may very well have an economic effect in other nations, international comity is essential in international law because it promotes reciprocity in foreign tribunals. As the U.S. Supreme Court noted:

> The expansion of American business and industry will hardly be encouraged if . . . we insist on a parochial concept that all disputes must be resolved under our laws and in our courts. . . . We cannot have trade and commerce in world markets . . . exclusively on our terms, governed by our laws, and resolved in our courts.[7]

Recognizing that business deals often transcend the legal boundaries of just one country, the U.S. Supreme Court recognized that in order to encourage the expansion of American business and industry, U.S. courts must respect and, where appropriate, enforce the laws of foreign nations.

10.2.2 The Principle of Comity in the Bankruptcy Context

The rapid growth in international relationships, both in the marketplace and among the governments of sovereign nations, has led to a substantial increase in the number and complexity of cross-border insolvency situations. A cross-border insolvency case can arise when an entity is placed in a form of insolvency administration in one country, but has assets or debts in other countries. The domestic insolvency laws of each country are likely to be different. The extent to which a nation will recognize and enforce a foreign bankruptcy judgment is important to the development of international business. However, absent a treaty governing the relationship between two sovereign nations, there may be little similarity among nations as to principles for recognizing a foreign judgment. The theory under which one jurisdiction will recognize a judgment made in a foreign jurisdiction is the doctrine of comity.

We briefly highlight below how the concept of "comity" is dealt with in the bankruptcy context by the United States, the European Union, the United Kingdom, France, Germany and Japan.

---

[7] *The Bremen v. Zapata Off-Shore Co.*, 407 U.S. 1, 9 (1972).

United States

As more fully discussed in Section 10.4 below, the 2005 Amendments repealed section 304 of the U.S. Bankruptcy Code and replaced it with an entire new chapter to provide a comprehensive regime that can be invoked in aid of a foreign restructuring proceeding. The new chapter 15, and specifically section 1507(b), codifies the development of international cooperation begun under former section 304, and places a greater emphasis on comity. As one court has noted, "[t]he availability of [the] wide range of relief [automatically available under chapter 15] is effectively a codification of previously existing international 'comity' in the area of insolvency proceedings."[8] Section 1507(b) provides that, in determining whether to provide additional assistance under the U.S. Bankruptcy Code or under other laws of the United States, the court shall consider whether such additional assistance, consistent with the principles of comity, will reasonably assure—

(1) just treatment of all holders of claims against or interests in the debtor's property;

(2) protection of claim holders in the United States against prejudice and inconvenience in the processing of claims in such foreign proceeding;

(3) prevention of preferential or fraudulent dispositions of property of the debtor;

(4) distribution of proceeds of the debtor's property substantially in accordance with the order prescribed by the U.S. Bankruptcy Code; and

(5) if appropriate, the provision of an opportunity for a fresh start for the individual that such foreign proceeding concerns.[9]

Thus, chapter 15 recognizes the principle of comity adopted in U.S. bankruptcy courts and, to the extent properly applied by such courts, will lead to greater consistency and stability in cross-border insolvencies in the United States.

---

[8] *Windt v. Qwest Commc'ns Int'l, Inc.*, 2006 U.S. Dist. LEXIS 75335, *57 (D.N.J. Oct. 17, 2006).

[9] 11 U.S.C. § 1507(b) (emphasis added).

European Union

The *E.U. Regulation on Insolvency Proceedings* (the "E.U. Regulation"), premised on principles of mutual recognition and cooperation, is a mechanism to coordinate insolvency proceedings in the member states of the European Union (except Denmark),[10] embracing both common-law and civil-law countries with considerable differences in their respective insolvency law schemes. Under Article 1.1, the E.U. Regulation governs "collective insolvency proceedings which entail the partial or total divestment of a debtor and the appointment of a liquidator," but specifically does not apply to administrative or other receiverships.[11]

The E.U. Regulation requires insolvency proceedings to be held in the location of a company's "center of main interests" ("COMI"). Although the E.U. Regulation itself does not define COMI, there is a rebuttable presumption that it is the place of the company's registered office.[12] Proceedings covered by the E.U. Regulation will have universal scope and will encompass all of the debtor's assets and affect all creditors, wherever located. The E.U. Regulation also allows secondary proceedings to be commenced in one or more other member states to deal with assets located outside of the country that is the COMI.[13] Under the principle of comity, member states are bound under Article 16 of the E.U. Regulation to recognize both orders commencing proceedings (main or secondary) and judgments handed down in another member state in connection with those proceedings.[14]

United Kingdom

Recognition in the United Kingdom of foreign insolvency tribunals and judgments rendered by such tribunals is not derived from one uniform system of rules, but instead is based loosely on several statutes and common law principles.

---

[10] Samuel L. Bufford, *International Insolvency Case Venue in the European Union: The Parmalat and Daisytek Controversies*, 12 Colum. J. Eur. L. 429, 434 (2006).

[11] *See* E.U. Regulation, Art. 1.1. Insurance undertakings, credit institutions, investment undertakings holding funds or securities for third parties and collective investment undertakings are also specifically excluded from the scope of the Regulation. *Id.*, art. 1.2

[12] *See id.*, art. 3.1.

[13] *See id.*, art. 3.4.

[14] *See id.*, art. 16.

The United Kingdom has three key statutory procedures governing the recognition of foreign insolvency proceedings. First, section 426 of the *Insolvency Act 1986* provides for cooperation between courts exercising jurisdiction in relation to insolvency proceedings. However, this provision is only of limited application because the mandatory language of section 426(4) applies only to countries in the United Kingdom and any other "relevant country or territory." Second, the E.U. Regulation discussed above applies to specified types of transnational insolvency proceedings, including in the U.K. Finally, the U.K. has also adopted the *Cross-Border Insolvency Regulations 2006* ("CBIR"), which implements the United Nations Commission on International Trade Law (UNCITRAL) *Model Law on Cross-Border Insolvency* (discussed more fully in Section 10.4 below).

Specifically, if the bankruptcy proceedings are in another member state of the E.U. (except for Denmark) where the COMI of the entity is located, the trustee (or debtor in possession, as the case may be) in such proceedings has authority to exercise jurisdiction over the debtor's assets within the E.U. (including the U.K.). Alternatively, the trustee can seek assistance in the U.K. where there are insolvency proceedings in a foreign state under the CBIR. Outside of the E.U. or the ambit of the CBIR, the common law principles concerning recognition of foreign insolvency proceedings, continue to apply.[15]

France

There is no specific body of French law on the international recognition of bankruptcy proceedings. France adopts a dichotomous approach concerning the recognition of foreign insolvency proceedings. Because France is a member of the E.U., the E.U. Regulation binds France. As in the U.K., the E.U. Regulation allows a member state's administrator to gain access to French courts and allows those courts to recognize the administrator's powers or the insolvency proceedings in the other member state.

On the other hand, however, in each case where the E.U. Regulation does not apply, French courts apply general principles of applicable French law, which often do not result in comity. Although the attitude of French courts toward insolvency cases is affected by the E.U. Regulation, in the

[15] *See* 2 *Collier International Business Insolvency Guide* ¶ 21.06[6] (Alan N. Resnick & Henry J. Sommer eds., 1st ed. rev. 2007).

absence of the direct application of the E.U. Regulation, French courts give great weight to the principles of the country's own sovereign laws.[16]

Germany

Germany's *Insolvency Act* was amended in 2003 with new sections added to specifically address international insolvencies. As with the U.K. and France, the E.U. regulation covers Germany and governs cross-border insolvency proceedings in relation to other E.U. members. In particular, Germany's courts historically have recognized the importance of extending comity to a foreign bankruptcy proceeding and have uniformly granted comity to insolvency proceedings in Switzerland, the United States and England, among others.[17] Moreover, under the German insolvency statute, foreign insolvency proceedings are recognized automatically without any further procedure of acceptance, unless the foreign country lacks jurisdiction according to German jurisdictional rules and if recognition would be manifestly incompatible with German constitutional rights or other essential principles of German law.[18]

Japan

Previously, Japan's insolvency law rejected the concept of comity, and Japanese courts neither recognized nor gave effect to foreign insolvency proceedings or judgments with respect to property situated in Japan. Practically speaking, however, Japanese courts are "tending to relax the strict attitude toward foreign proceedings."[19] On April 1, 2001, consistent with the principle of comity discussed above, the Japanese *Law on Recognition of and Assistance in Foreign Insolvency Proceeding* ("LRAF") was enacted. LRAF permits a foreign debtor to repatriate its assets out of Japan by abolishing Japan's notorious "territorial policy" and adopting many of the provisions of the UNCITRAL *Model Law on Cross-Border Insolvency.*

Under LRAF, in order to have a foreign judgment recognized within Japan, the trustee (or debtor in possession) must obtain an order from the

---

[16] *See id.* at ¶ 22.08[2][a].

[17] Martin S. Kenney, *et al., Utilizing Cross-Border Insolvency Laws to Attack Fraud: An Analysis of How it Could Work in the British Virgin Islands, the United States, and Germany,* 13 Law & Bus. Rev. Am. 569, 603 (2007).

[18] Alfried Heidbrink, *The New German Rules on International Insolvency Law*, 22-9 Am. Bankr. Inst. J. 16 (2003).

[19] *See* Shoichi Tagashira, *Intraterritorial Effects of Foreign Insolvency Proceedings: An Analysis of "Ancillary" Proceedings in the United States and Japan*, 29 Texas Int'l L.J. 1, 9 (1994).

Tokyo District Court, which is the Japanese court of exclusive jurisdiction for a foreign party seeking to enforce such a judgment within Japan.[20] The Japanese court will issue a recognition order if the following requirements are met:

(1) the debtors' address, residence, or business or other office exists in the country where the relevant foreign insolvency proceeding is pending;
(2) commencement of the foreign insolvency proceeding has been formally ordered; and
(3) none of the following causes for rejection exists:
  (i) the court-determined deposit for the costs of the recognition proceeding has not been paid by the foreign petitioner;
  (ii) it is clear under the foreign proceeding that the effect of such proceeding does not extend to assets located within Japan;
  (iii) providing assistance toward the foreign proceeding violates the public order of Japan;
  (iv) it is clear that no assistance is necessary under LRAF for the foreign insolvency proceeding;
  (v) the foreign representative has failed to report the status of material developments in the foreign insolvency proceeding; or
  (vi) the petition has clearly been filed for illegitimate objectives or in bad faith.[21]

10.3 Existing Law in the PRC and the Enforcement of Foreign Judgments

10.3.1 State of the Law

Prior to the enactment of the Enterprise Bankruptcy Law, the main sources for guidance on foreign bankruptcy proceedings and the enforcement of foreign judgments against assets located in China were the PRC Constitution and the CPL.

The PRC Constitution contains a general proviso stating that any foreign enterprise, economic organization, or individual within Chinese jurisdiction

[20] Mie Fujimoto & Hon. Shinjiro Takagi, *Japan's New Law on Recognition of and Assistance in Foreign Insolvency Proceedings*, 20-6 Am. Bankr. Inst. J. 14 (2001).
[21] *See* LRAF (2001), art. 22.

shall abide by and be subject to Chinese laws, and that their lawful rights and interests shall be protected under Chinese laws.[22] In practice, the PRC government will recognize international conventions and bilateral and multilateral treaties to which it is a party.[23]

While the PRC Constitution provides only vague guidance on recognition of foreign law, the CPL provides greater detail about the recognition and enforcement of foreign court judgments. Article 268 of the CPL provides:

> If a People's Court of the People's Republic of China, after its review in accordance with the international treaties concluded or acceded to by the People's Republic of China or on the principle of reciprocity, considers that the legally effective judgment or order of a foreign court which requires recognition and enforcement does not contradict the basic principles of the law of the People's Republic of China nor violates the state and social, public interest of China, it shall render an order on the recognition of its force.

Such language, with which Article 5 of the Enterprise Bankruptcy Law is consistent, appears encouraging for embracing the spirit of comity. As one expert from the region notes, however, this approach towards recognition and enforcement of foreign judgments has been counterbalanced as a practical matter by a general attitude resulting in the People's Courts often refusing to recognize or execute foreign judgments and rulings in cases over which People's Courts also have jurisdiction. Where a PRC court has ruled on a matter, foreign court rulings may or may not be given equal effect.[24]

Typically, the CPL and relevant treaties set forth the following procedures to be followed by those attempting to have a foreign judgment or ruling recognized in the PRC. The request for recognition should: (i) be made to the appropriate People's Court with jurisdiction over the assets in China, (ii) be made by the creditor in the foreign case or by the foreign court in accordance with any relevant treaty between the foreign country and the PRC, and (iii) the People's Court will then review the request and determine whether the foreign court judgment is consistent with PRC law.[25]

The foreign court judgment then may be recognized by the PRC court if: (i) the judgment has become effective according to the law of the foreign

---

[22] *See* PRC Const., arts. 18, 32.

[23] *See* Tang, *supra* Chapter One, note 38, at 649.

[24] *See id.*, at 651.

[25] *See id.*

country in which the judgment was made and entered;[26] (ii) the local court in China has proper jurisdiction over the matter;[27] (iii) the rights and interests of the litigant have been protected; and (iv) in cases involving the same litigants and the same cause of action, the judgment is in conformity with the principles of PRC law, does not impair PRC sovereignty and security or PRC political and social interests, and *one* of the following requirements is also met: (a) a People's Court has already made a legally effective judgment on the case, (b) the matter is being heard by a People's Court, or (c) a People's Court has recognized the judgment of a court of another country and the judgment has become legally effective in China.[28] After this lengthy process, the court can then decide either to recognize the foreign judgment and issue an order of enforcement, or to deny recognition.

As one expert has noted, in cases where no relevant international treaty exists and reciprocity cannot be proven, the interested party's best approach would be to institute plenary proceedings under PRC law in a court in China.[29] In such case, the foreign creditor should file its suit in the appropriate jurisdiction (*i.e.*, where the assets are located) and file copies of the foreign proceeding's rulings and other relevant filings (in translation).

10.3.2 Practical Implications and the History of Enforcement

Until very recently, the idea of recognizing foreign proceedings or judgments of a domestic debtor attempting to exercise control over property outside of the PRC was not common.

In the latter instance, debtors under the Enterprise Bankruptcy Law cannot take much guidance from the framework of the 1986 Bankruptcy Law with respect to exercising control over assets outside of the PRC. Because the 1986 Bankruptcy Law was crafted to deal with struggling SOEs, which typically had very few assets outside of mainland China, there was seldom an issue of a Chinese debtor attempting to exercise control over extraterritorial property of the estate. The GITIC case (discussed in Section 4.1) was the first high-profile case in which an SOE had significant overseas assets that needed to be reached in the company's bankruptcy. The ultimate result of this new issue for the People's Courts was the addition of Article 73 to the Supreme

---

[26] *See* CPL, art. 267.

[27] *See id.*, arts. 243, 267.

[28] *See id.*, art. 268.

[29] *See* Tang, *supra* Chapter One, note 38, at 652–53.

People's Court's 2002 Explanation, requiring the liquidation panel managing the bankrupt debtor to recover any assets located outside the territory of the PRC.[30]

Of course, recognition in the PRC of foreign judgments arose as an issue even before passage of the Enterprise Bankruptcy Law. A procedural protocol generally must be followed if a foreign administrator or creditor hopes to have a judgment recognized by the applicable People's Court with jurisdiction over the assets against which the foreign party intends to enforce a judgment. As discussed in the introduction to this chapter, the foreign insolvency administrator or creditor may first make an application to the People's Court for recognition of the foreign insolvency proceeding.[31] The foreign party can attempt to do this by providing translated documents outlining the existence of the foreign proceeding, the appointment of the administrator, and a description of the duties and powers of the administrator in the foreign proceeding.[32]

Given China's reluctance, at times, to allow foreign parties to have significant influence over its sovereign laws, one might expect that foreign administrators may run into a host of problems in attempting to enforce judgments in the PRC. Such problems could include local stakeholders refusing to accept the authority of the foreign administrator or refusing to grant such foreigner access to documents, records, or individuals that may be necessary to execute on collateral.

The ability of a foreign enterprise to exercise control over assets in the PRC may be, in large measure, fact-specific. If the foreign party seeks to recover assets within the PRC and that party has no local creditors in China, the matter may be less challenging than a situation in which a foreign creditor is attempting to wrestle control over assets or operations within mainland China, which may have its own local creditors (*e.g.*, employees). In such a scenario, the foreign creditor may run into a more difficult road in attempting to repatriate assets outside of China.

Often, however, a foreign entity operating in China will have local creditors (*e.g.*, employees, trade vendors). Once made aware of the foreign entity's bankruptcy, local creditors may seek to block the foreign administrator from securing and liquidating local assets until the local creditors have been

---

[30] *See* 2002 Explanation.

[31] *See* Tang, *supra* Chapter One, note 38, at 651.

[32] *See id.*, at 653.

paid in full. In this scenario, where claims of foreign creditors also have been made against these assets in China (as part of the overall assets of the company), the foreign administrator will be forced to seek the assistance of the People's Courts to help exercise power over such assets. Success in this process historically has proven to be inconsistent and unreliable. In the event that local creditors will not have 100% of their claims paid (or will not be provided with satisfactory replacement collateral or security), the courts often have proven unwilling to allow assets to be sold and funds repatriated out of China.[33] This becomes particularly troublesome in the context of employee claims for wages and benefits; given the grave concerns regarding unemployment and social unrest, it becomes even less likely that a foreign creditor will be able to shut down operations and eliminate jobs without first settling the wage, pension, and resettlement claims of Chinese employees.

The Enterprise Bankruptcy Law's provision regarding cross-border cooperation appears to be hardly more than a reiteration of the pre-existing standards. But given the importance to the PRC of maintaining the influx of foreign investment and its position as a member of the WTO and participant in the ever-integrating world economy, it may be the passage of the new law itself—more than any development in the content of its cross-border provision—that is the true sign of increased respect for foreign rights in China.

10.4 Chapter 15 and the U.S. Approach to International Restructurings

In the United States, plenary proceedings under chapters 7 and 11 of the U.S. Bankruptcy Code may be used equally by United States debtors having assets in foreign countries and foreign debtors having assets in the United States. Recent cases in which foreign debtors with operations in the U.S. have used chapter 11 proceedings contemporaneously with, or in anticipation of, foreign proceedings include Yukos Oil, Avianca Airlines, and Parmalat.

Until the passage of the 2005 Amendments, which is effective for all cases filed on or after October 17, 2005, a foreign debtor could commence an ancillary case in the United States under section 304 of the U.S. Bankruptcy Code. Section 304 contemplated that the foreign debtors' assets would be administered in a foreign proceeding and, where certain criteria were met, a case ancillary to the foreign proceeding could be utilized to stay litigation against the foreign debtor in the U.S. and permit repatriation of the foreign debtor's U.S. assets.

---

[33] *See id.*, at 663–64.

The 2005 Amendments replaced section 304 in its entirety with a new chapter 15 of the U.S. Bankruptcy Code. Entitled "Ancillary and Other Cross-Border Cases," chapter 15 incorporates the UNCITRAL *Model Law on Cross-Border Insolvency* (the "Model Law"). To date, legislation based on the Model Law also has been adopted in Eritrea (2000), Japan (2000), Mexico (2000), South Africa (2000), Montenegro (2002), Poland (2003), Romania (2003), Serbia (2004), the British Virgin Islands (2005), overseas territories of the United Kingdom (2005), Northern Ireland (2005), and Great Britain (2006).

The express purpose of chapter 15 is to incorporate the Model Law into the U.S. Bankruptcy Code so that an effective mechanism is established for addressing cases of cross-border insolvency through (and while fostering) (i) cooperation between U.S. and foreign courts, (ii) greater legal certainty for trade and investment, (iii) fair and efficient administration of cross-border insolvency cases, (iv) protection and maximization of debtors' assets, and (v) facilitation of the rescue of financially troubled businesses, thereby protecting investment and preserving employment.[34]

Generally, chapter 15 includes provisions addressing the circumstances in which the chapter will apply,[35] how an ancillary case is commenced, recognition of main and nonmain foreign proceedings, parties' rights and interests, notice requirements, jurisdictional issues, discretionary and non-discretionary forms of relief, and the specific means by which the entities involved should engage in communication and cooperation.

A foreign representative may commence a chapter 15 case by filing a "petition for recognition" of a foreign proceeding directly with the U.S. bankruptcy court, accompanied by certified documents and statements affirming the existence of the foreign proceeding. Recognition is subject to bankruptcy court approval, and may be denied if the court finds such relief is "manifestly contrary to the public policy of the United States."[36]

---

[34] 11 U.S.C. § 1501(a).

[35] Chapter 15 applies where (1) assistance is sought in the United States by a foreign court or a foreign representative in connection with a foreign proceeding; (2) assistance is sought in a foreign country in connection with a case under the U.S. Bankruptcy Code; (3) a foreign proceeding and a case under the U.S. Bankruptcy Code with respect to the same debtor are pending concurrently; or (4) creditors or other interested persons in a foreign country have an interest in requesting the commencement of, or participating in, a case or proceeding under the U.S. Bankruptcy Code. 11 U.S.C. § 1501(b)(2).

[36] *Id.* §§ 1506, 1517(a).

The replacement of section 304 of the U.S. Bankruptcy Code by chapter 15 did not drastically alter existing U.S. law regarding ancillary cases; the changes largely codified judicial interpretations of section 304, which gave U.S. courts "authority to open an ancillary proceeding and grant various broad forms of relief to the foreign representative."[37] Conversely, chapter 15 "imposes a rigid procedural structure for recognition of foreign proceedings as either main or nonmain."[38] Courts are required to recognize foreign proceedings simply upon finding that a proper foreign representative has filed a petition for recognition and submitted proper supporting materials.

Upon recognition, a foreign main proceeding will receive certain nondiscretionary relief under the U.S. Bankruptcy Code that previously had been available only through an implementation order of the bankruptcy court.[39] A foreign main proceeding is defined as a "foreign proceeding pending in the country where the debtor has the center of main interests."[40] A foreign nonmain proceeding means any other proceeding "pending in a country where the debtor has an establishment."[41] An establishment is defined as "any place of operations where the debtor carries out a nontransitory economic activity."[42]

Insights and Recommendations

- *Recognition of Rights of Foreign Creditors in the Bankruptcy Process Will Affect Foreign Investment in China*

Multi-jurisdictional and international cases are always challenging, especially where the laws of sovereign nations conflict and national policies

---

[37] *In re Bear Stearns High-Grade Structured Credit Strategies Master Fund, Ltd.*, Chapter 15 Case Nos. 07-12383 and 07-12384 (BRL), 2007 Bankr. LEXIS 2949, *26 (Bankr. S.D.N.Y. Aug. 30, 2007).

[38] *Id.*

[39] Nondiscretionary relief includes the benefits available to debtors under sections 361 (adequate protection), 362 (automatic stay), 363 (sales/use/lease of property), 549 (postpetition transactions), and 552 (postpetition effect of security interest) of the U.S. Bankruptcy Code. In addition, a foreign representative may operate the debtor's business and may exercise the rights/powers of trustee to the extent provided under sections 363 and 552.

[40] 11 U.S.C. § 1502(4). Section 1516(c) provides that "[i]n the absence of evidence to the contrary, the debtor's registered office . . . is presumed to be the center of the debtor's main interests."

[41] *Id.* § 1502(5).

[42] *Id.* § 1502(2).

(*e.g.*, with respect to the employment of local parties) come into play. The PRC has taken a step in the right direction by incorporating Article 5 into the Enterprise Bankruptcy Law. Observers now must wait and see how the judges of the People's Courts will interpret this provision and its underlying principles, and whether the rights of foreign creditors in the PRC will be recognized and respected in situations where Chinese citizens have competing interests. The outcome of these cases may have a significant influence on the appetite of foreign investors to continue to invest large sums of capital in the Chinese economy.

CONCLUSION

The Enterprise Bankruptcy Law has many virtues, which we have analyzed in depth throughout this book. The success of the law will rest upon its fair and consistent application in China's court system, and it will be interesting to see how the Chinese judiciary grapples with what is a very complex commercial statute.

As we noted at the outset, the Enterprise Bankruptcy Law draws in part from the laws of numerous common law countries, such as the United States, Australia and the United Kingdom, as well as civil law countries, such as France, Germany and Japan. Most of these countries have had many decades of experience in the development of their bankruptcy systems, however, and are able to draw upon that deep experience in interpreting and applying their respective insolvency laws. Notably, countries such as the United States have had the benefit of a common law system in developing and refining statutory concepts. It will be incumbent on the Chinese to quickly train as many judges as possible with respect to the new law, but it will be equally important for Chinese legislative bodies to formulate and enact rules and regulations to give the courts proper guidance on the issues and problems that exist, many of which we hope we have identified in this book.

We look forward to observing and commenting upon the development of an increasingly robust bankruptcy system in the PRC in the near future, and welcome readers to share their thoughts and observations with us as further rules, regulations and explanations are issued and applied.

APPENDIX A
The PRC Enterprise Bankruptcy Law

中华人民共和国企业破产法	Enterprise Bankruptcy Law of the People's Republic of China
第一章　总则	**Chapter I　General Provisions**
第一条　为规范企业破产程序，公平清理债权债务，保护债权人和债务人的合法权益，维护社会主义市场经济秩序，制定本法。	**Article 1**　This Law is formulated in order to regularize the enterprise bankruptcy procedures, fairly dispose of credits and debts, protect the lawful rights and interests of creditors and debtors, and maintain the order of the socialist market economy.
第二条　企业法人不能清偿到期债务，并且资产不足以清偿全部债务或者明显缺乏清偿能力的，依照本法规定清理债务。	**Article 2**　If an enterprise legal person is unable to pay off the debts as they become due, and its assets are insufficient to pay off all of its debts or it is obviously lacking in the capability to repay the debts, its debts shall be disposed in accordance with this Law.
企业法人有前款规定情形，或者有明显丧失清偿能力可能的，可以依照本法规定进行重整。	If an enterprise legal person is in any of the conditions set forth in the preceding paragraph, or there is an obvious possibility that it will lose the capability to repay its debts, it may be reorganized pursuant to the provisions hereof.
第三条　破产案件由债务人住所地人民法院管辖。	**Article 3**　A bankruptcy case shall be subject to the jurisdiction of the People's Courts in the place of the debtor's domicile.
第四条　破产案件审理程序，本法没有规定的，适用民事诉讼法的有关规定。	**Article 4**　If this Law is silent as to the trial procedures for bankruptcy cases, the relevant provisions of the Civil Procedures Law shall apply.
第五条　依照本法开始的破产程序，对债务人在中华人民共和国领域外的财产发生效力。	**Article 5**　The bankruptcy procedures initiated pursuant to this Law shall have effect on the debtor's property located outside the territory of the People's Republic of China.
对外国法院作出的发生法律效力的破产案件的判决、裁定，涉及债务人在中华人民共和国领域内	If the People's Court receives an application or request for recognition and enforcement of a legally effective judgment or ruling, made by a foreign

的财产，申请或者请求人民法院承认和执行的，人民法院依照中华人民共和国缔结或者参加的国际条约，或者按照互惠原则进行审查，认为不违反中华人民共和国法律的基本原则，不损害国家主权、安全和社会公共利益，不损害中华人民共和国领域内债权人的合法权益的，裁定承认和执行。	court with respect to a bankruptcy case and involving the debtor's properties located in the territory of the People's Republic of China, the People's Court shall conduct a review thereof pursuant to the relevant international treaties signed or entered into by the People's Republic of China or based on the principle of reciprocity. If, upon review, the People's Court concludes that the judgment or ruling neither violates the basic principles of law of the People's Republic of China, nor impairs the national sovereignty and security and public interests of the society or the lawful rights and interests of the creditors in the territory of the People's Republic of China, a ruling of recognition and enforcement thereof shall be made.
第六条 人民法院审理破产案件，应当依法保障企业职工的合法权益，依法追究破产企业经营管理人员的法律责任。	**Article 6** During trial of a bankruptcy case, the People's Court shall protect the lawful rights and interests of the employees of the enterprise, and enforce legal responsibilities of the management personnel of the bankrupt enterprise, in each case, in accordance with law.
第二章　申请和受理	**Chapter II　Application and Acceptance**
第一节　申 请	**Section I　Application**
第七条 债务人有本法第二条规定的情形，可以向人民法院提出重整、和解或者破产清算申请。	**Article 7** If a debtor falls within Article 2 hereof, such debtor may file an application with the People's Court for reorganization, conciliation or bankruptcy liquidation.
债务人不能清偿到期债务，债权人可以向人民法院提出对债务人进行重整或者破产清算的申请。	If a debtor is unable to pay off its debts as they become due, the creditors may file an application with the People's Court for reorganization or bankruptcy liquidation against the debtor.
企业法人已解散但未清算或者未清算完毕，资产不足以清偿债务的，依法负有清算责任的人应当向人民法院申请破产清算。	If an enterprise legal person has been dissolved without liquidation or the liquidation has not been completed, and its assets are insufficient to pay off the debts, the person who is legally responsible for liquidation shall file an application with the People's Court for bankruptcy liquidation.
第八条 向人民法院提出破产申请，应当提交破产申请书和有关证据。	**Article 8** A bankruptcy application letter and relevant evidence shall be submitted in filing a bankruptcy application with the People's Court.

破产申请书应当载明下列事项： （一）申请人、被申请人的基本情况； （二）申请目的； （三）申请的事实和理由； （四）人民法院认为应当载明的其他事项。	The bankruptcy application letter shall set forth the following information: (1) the basic information of the applicant and the respondent; (2) the purpose of the application; (3) the facts and grounds on which the application is based; (4) other information required by the People's Court.
债务人提出申请的，还应当向人民法院提交财产状况说明、债务清册、债权清册、有关财务会计报告、职工安置预案以及职工工资的支付和社会保险费用的缴纳情况。	If the application is filed by the debtor, the debtor shall also submit to the People's Court a description of the status of its property, a complete list of debts, a complete list of claims, relevant financial and accounting reports, a proposal on settlement of employees, the payment status of employees' wages and the status of employees' social insurance contribution.
第九条 人民法院受理破产申请前，申请人可以请求撤回申请。	**Article 9** The applicant may request to withdraw the application before it is accepted by the People's Court.
第二节 受 理	**Section II Acceptance**
第十条 债权人提出破产申请的，人民法院应当自收到申请之日起五日内通知债务人。债务人对申请有异议的，应当自收到人民法院的通知之日起七日内向人民法院提出。人民法院应当自异议期满之日起十日内裁定是否受理。	**Article 10** If the bankruptcy application is filed by a creditor, the People's Court shall notify the debtor thereof within five days from the date of receipt of the application. If the debtor has an objection to the application, it shall file its objection with the People's Court within seven days from the date of receipt of the notification from the People's Court. The People's Court shall make a ruling as to whether to accept the bankruptcy application within ten days from the expiration of the objection period.
除前款规定的情形外，人民法院应当自收到破产申请之日起十五日内裁定是否受理。	Except for the scenario provided in the preceding paragraph, the People's Court shall make a ruling as to whether to accept the bankruptcy application within fifteen days from the date of receipt of the bankruptcy application.
有特殊情况需要延长前两款规定的裁定受理期限的，经上一级人民法院批准，可以延长十五日。	If an extension of the ruling periods set forth in the two preceding paragraphs is needed under certain special circumstances, upon approval by the immediately superior People's Court, each such period may be extended for another fifteen days.

第十一条 人民法院受理破产申请的，应当自裁定作出之日起五日内送达申请人。	**Article 11** If the People's Court accepts the bankruptcy application, it shall serve the ruling on the applicant within five days from the date when the ruling is made.
债权人提出申请的，人民法院应当自裁定作出之日起五日内送达债务人。债务人应当自裁定送达之日起十五日内，向人民法院提交财产状况说明、债务清册、债权清册、有关财务会计报告以及职工工资的支付和社会保险费用的缴纳情况。	If the application is filed by a creditor, the People's Court shall also serve the ruling on the debtor within five days from the date when the ruling is made. The debtor shall, within fifteen days from the date when such ruling is served, submit to the People's Court a description of the status of its property, a complete list of debts, a complete list of claims, relevant financial and accounting reports, a proposal on settlement of employees, and the payment status of employees' wages and the status of employees' social insurance contribution.
第十二条 人民法院裁定不受理破产申请的，应当自裁定作出之日起五日内送达申请人并说明理由。申请人对裁定不服的，可以自裁定送达之日起十日内向上一级人民法院提起上诉。	**Article 12** If the People's Court rules not to accept the bankruptcy application, it shall serve the ruling, together with an explanation, on the applicant within five days from the date when the ruling is made. If the applicant contests the ruling, it may file an appeal with the immediately superior People's Court within ten days from the date when such ruling is served.
人民法院受理破产申请后至破产宣告前，经审查发现债务人不符合本法第二条规定情形的，可以裁定驳回申请。申请人对裁定不服的，可以自裁定送达之日起十日内向上一级人民法院提起上诉。	If, after the acceptance of the bankruptcy application but prior to a declaration of bankruptcy, the People's Court finds that the debtor does not fall within Article 2 hereof, it may rule to reject the application. If the applicant contests such ruling, it may file an appeal with the immediately superior People's Court within ten days from the date when such ruling is served.
第十三条 人民法院裁定受理破产申请的，应当同时指定管理人。	**Article 13** The People's Court shall designate an administrator when it rules to accept a bankruptcy application.
第十四条 人民法院应当自裁定受理破产申请之日起二十五日内通知已知债权人，并予以公告。	**Article 14** The People's Court shall notify the known creditors and make a public announcement within twenty-five days from the date when it rules to accept the bankruptcy application.
通知和公告应当载明下列事项： （一）申请人、被申请人的名称或者姓名；	The notification and the public announcement shall set forth: (1) the name of the applicant and respondent;

（二） 人民法院受理破产申请的时间； （三） 申报债权的期限、地点和注意事项； （四） 管理人的名称或者姓名及其处理事务的地址； （五） 债务人的债务人或者财产持有人应当向管理人清偿债务或者交付财产的要求； （六） 第一次债权人会议召开的时间和地点； （七） 人民法院认为应当通知和公告的其他事项。	(2) the time of acceptance of the bankruptcy case by the People's Court; (3) the time limit, place and noticeable matters for claim assertion; (4) the name and the business address of the administrator; (5) the requirements that the debtor's debtors or property holders pay off their debts or deliver the property to the administrator; (6) the time and place of the first creditors meeting; and (7) other matters that the People's Court deems necessary to notify and announce.
第十五条 自人民法院受理破产申请的裁定送达债务人之日起至破产程序终结之日，债务人的有关人员承担下列义务：	**Article 15** During the period from the date when the People's Court's ruling to accept the bankruptcy application is served on the debtor through the date when the bankruptcy procedure is concluded, the relevant persons of the debtor shall have the following obligations:
（一） 妥善保管其占有和管理的财产、印章和账簿、文书等资料； （二） 根据人民法院、管理人的要求进行工作，并如实回答询问； （三） 列席债权人会议并如实回答债权人的询问； （四） 未经人民法院许可，不得离开住所地； （五） 不得新任其他企业的董事、监事、高级管理人员。	(1) to appropriately maintain the properties, seals, accounting books, instruments and other materials that are possessed or administrated by them; (2) to work pursuant to the requirements made by the People's Court and the administrator, and answer their inquiries honestly; (3) to attend the creditors' meetings as nonvoting delegates and answer the creditors' inquiries honestly; (4) not to leave the place of domicile without permission from the People's Court; and (5) not to serve as a new director or supervisor or senior management personnel in other enterprises.
前款所称有关人员，是指企业的法定代表人；经人民法院决定，可以包括企业的财务管理人员和其他经营管理人员。	The relevant persons of the debtor referred to in the preceding paragraph means the legal representatives of the enterprise; and upon the decision of the People's Court, those persons may also include the financial management personnel and other operations and management personnel.

第十六条 人民法院受理破产申请后，债务人对个别债权人的债务清偿无效。	**Article 16** Once the People's Court accepts the bankruptcy application, a pay-off by the debtor of a specific debt shall be invalid.
第十七条 人民法院受理破产申请后，债务人的债务人或者财产持有人应当向管理人清偿债务或者交付财产。	**Article 17** After the People's Court accepts the bankruptcy application, the debtor's debtors or property holders shall pay off their debts or deliver the property to the administrator.
债务人的债务人或者财产持有人故意违反前款规定向债务人清偿债务或者交付财产，使债权人受到损失的，不免除其清偿债务或者交付财产的义务。	If any of the debtor's debtors or property holders intentionally violates the provisions under the preceding paragraph by paying off its debts or delivering the property to the debtor and thus causes any losses to the creditors, its obligation to pay off the debts or deliver the property will not be discharged thereby.
第十八条 人民法院受理破产申请后，管理人对破产申请受理前成立而债务人和对方当事人均未履行完毕的合同有权决定解除或者继续履行，并通知对方当事人。管理人自破产申请受理之日起二个月内未通知对方当事人，或者自收到对方当事人催告之日起三十日内未答复的，视为解除合同。	**Article 18** After the People's Court accepts the bankruptcy application, as for an executory contract that was made prior to the acceptance of the bankruptcy application, the administrator shall have the power to decide whether to reject or assume such contract, and to notify the other party thereto. If the administrator does not notify such other party within two months from the date of acceptance of the bankruptcy application, or does not reply within thirty days from the date of receipt of an inquiry by such other party regarding assumption or rejection, such contract shall be deemed rejected.
管理人决定继续履行合同的，对方当事人应当履行；但是，对方当事人有权要求管理人提供担保。管理人不提供担保的，视为解除合同。	If the administrator decides to assume the contract, the other party to such contract shall perform such contract; however, such other party is entitled to ask the administrator to provide security. If the administrator fails to provide security, the contract in question shall be deemed rejected.
第十九条 人民法院受理破产申请后，有关债务人财产的保全措施应当解除，执行程序应当中止。	**Article 19** After the People's Court accepts the bankruptcy application, any attachment with respect to the debtor's property shall be lifted and any enforcement procedures shall be suspended.
第二十条 人民法院受理破产申请后，已经开始而尚未终结的有关债务人的民事诉讼或者仲裁应当中止；在管理人接管债务人的财产后，该诉讼或者仲裁继续进行。	**Article 20** After the People's Court accepts the bankruptcy application, any commenced and pending civil litigation or arbitration related to the debtor shall be suspended; and after the administrator receives and manages the property of the debtor, such litigation or arbitration shall resume.

第二十一条 人民法院受理破产申请后，有关债务人的民事诉讼，只能向受理破产申请的人民法院提起。	**Article 21** After the People's Court accepts the bankruptcy application, any civil litigation related to the debtor can be brought only to the People's Court which has accepted the bankruptcy application.
第三章　管理人	**Chapter III　Administrator**
第二十二条 管理人由人民法院指定。 债权人会议认为管理人不能依法、公正执行职务或者有其他不能胜任职务情形的，可以申请人民法院予以更换。	**Article 22** The administrator shall be designated by the People's Court. If the creditors' meeting determines that the administrator is unable to perform its duties lawfully and fairly or is otherwise not competent for its duties, the creditors' meeting may request the People's Court to replace the administrator.
指定管理人和确定管理人报酬的办法，由最高人民法院规定。	The measures for designating the administrator and setting the administrator's remuneration shall be formulated by the Supreme People's Court.
第二十三条 管理人依照本法规定执行职务，向人民法院报告工作，并接受债权人会议和债权人委员会的监督。	**Article 23** The administrator shall perform its duties pursuant to the provisions herein, report to the People's Court, and be subject to supervision by the creditors' meeting and the creditors' committee.
管理人应当列席债权人会议，向债权人会议报告职务执行情况，并回答询问。	The administrator shall attend the creditors' meetings as a nonvoting delegate, report the status of performance of its duties to the creditors' meeting, and answer inquiries at creditors' meetings.
第二十四条 管理人可以由有关部门、机构的人员组成的清算组或者依法设立的律师事务所、会计师事务所、破产清算事务所等社会中介机构担任。	**Article 24** The position of administrator may be assumed by a liquidation panel composed of personnel from relevant government agencies or institutes, a law firm, an accounting firm, a bankruptcy liquidation service agency or other legally-established social intermediary institutions.
人民法院根据债务人的实际情况，可以在征询有关社会中介机构的意见后，指定该机构具备相关专业知识并取得执业资格的人员担任管理人。	Based on the factual circumstances of the debtor, the People's Court may, after consulting with the relevant social intermediary institution, designate the individual(s) within such intermediary institution who have the required expertise and qualifications to serve as the administrator.

有下列情形之一的，不得担任管理人： （一）因故意犯罪受过刑事处罚； （二）曾被吊销相关专业执业证书； （三）与本案有利害关系； （四）人民法院认为不宜担任管理人的其他情形。	Anyone meeting any of the following conditions shall not serve as the administrator: (1) having been subject to any criminal sanction due to intentional offense; (2) having been disqualified regarding any relevant professional qualification or license; (3) being an interested party in the underlying bankruptcy case; (4) other circumstances which the People's Court finds inappropriate for serving as the administrator.
个人担任管理人的，应当参加执业责任保险。	In the case of an individual who serves as the administrator, he or she shall participate in a professional practice liability insurance plan.
第二十五条 管理人履行下列职责： （一）接管债务人的财产、印章和账簿、文书等资料； （二）调查债务人财产状况，制作财产状况报告； （三）决定债务人的内部管理事务； （四）决定债务人的日常开支和其他必要开支； （五）在第一次债权人会议召开之前，决定继续或者停止债务人的营业； （六）管理和处分债务人的财产； （七）代表债务人参加诉讼、仲裁或者其他法律程序； （八）提议召开债权人会议； （九）人民法院认为管理人应当履行的其他职责。 本法对管理人的职责另有规定的，适用其规定。	**Article 25** The administrator shall perform the following duties: (1) receiving and managing the debtor's property, seal, accounting books, instruments and other materials; (2) investigating into the status of the debtor's property and preparing a property status report; (3) making decisions on the debtor's internal management affairs; (4) making decisions on the debtor's daily expenses and other necessary expenses; (5) before the first creditors meeting, determining whether to continue or terminate the debtor's business operations; (6) managing and disposing of the debtor's property; (7) representing the debtor in lawsuits, arbitration or other legal proceedings; (8) proposing to convene a creditors' meeting; (9) performing other administrator's duties as deemed appropriate by the People's Court. If the duties of the administrator are otherwise provided herein, such other provisions shall apply.

第二十六条 在第一次债权人会议召开之前，管理人决定继续或者停止债务人的营业或者有本法第六十九条规定行为之一的，应当经人民法院许可。	**Article 26** Prior to the first creditors' meeting, if the administrator decides whether to continue or terminate the debtor's business operations, or to take any actions set forth in Article 69 hereof, the decision must be approved by the People's Court.
第二十七条 管理人应当勤勉尽责，忠实执行职务。	**Article 27** The administrator shall perform its duties diligently and loyally.
第二十八条 管理人经人民法院许可，可以聘用必要的工作人员。	**Article 28** The administrator may engage necessary working staff upon the approval of the People's Court.
管理人的报酬由人民法院确定。债权人会议对管理人的报酬有异议的，有权向人民法院提出。	The remuneration of the administrator shall be decided by the People's Court. The creditors' meeting has the right to raise its objection to the remuneration of the administrator, if any, to the People's Court.
第二十九条 管理人没有正当理由不得辞去职务。管理人辞去职务应当经人民法院许可。	**Article 29** The administrator shall not resign from the office without justifiable reasons. The approval of the People's Court is required for the administrator's resignation.
第四章　债务人财产	**Chapter IV　The Debtor's Property**
第三十条 破产申请受理时属于债务人的全部财产，以及破产申请受理后至破产程序终结前债务人取得的财产，为债务人财产。	**Article 30** All the property owned by the debtor at the time when the bankruptcy application is accepted and the property the debtor acquires after the acceptance of the bankruptcy application but prior to the conclusion of the bankruptcy procedures constitutes the debtor's property.
第三十一条 人民法院受理破产申请前一年内，涉及债务人财产的下列行为，管理人有权请求人民法院予以撤销： （一）无偿转让财产的； （二）以明显不合理的价格进行交易的； （三）对没有财产担保的债务提供财产担保的； （四）对未到期的债务提前清偿的； （五）放弃债权的。	**Article 31** If any of the following activities involving the debtor's property occurred within one year prior to the acceptance of the bankruptcy application by the People's Court, the administrator shall have the right to request the People's Court to avoid such activities: (1) transferring property without consideration; (2) dealing at an obviously unreasonable price; (3) providing collateral for any unsecured debt; (4) prepaying any debt before it became due; and (5) giving up claims.

第三十二条 人民法院受理破产申请前六个月内，债务人有本法第二条第一款规定的情形，仍对个别债权人进行清偿的，管理人有权请求人民法院予以撤销。但是，个别清偿使债务人财产受益的除外。	**Article 32** If the debtor paid off any debts within six months prior to the acceptance of the bankruptcy application by the People's Court, while the debtor was in the condition referred to in the first paragraph of Article 2 hereof, the administrator shall have the right to request the People's Court to avoid the repayment unless the debtor's property benefited from the specific repayment.
第三十三条 涉及债务人财产的下列行为无效： （一）为逃避债务而隐匿、转移财产的； （二）虚构债务或者承认不真实的债务的。	**Article 33** Any of the following activities involving the debtor's property shall be null and void: (1) concealing or transferring property for the purpose of escaping repayment of debt; (2) fabricating debts or recognizing false debts.
第三十四条 因本法第三十一条、第三十二条或者第三十三条规定的行为而取得的债务人的财产，管理人有权追回。	**Article 34** The administrator shall have the right to reclaim the debtor's property obtained by anyone as a result of the activities set forth in Articles 31, 32 or 33 hereof.
第三十五条 人民法院受理破产申请后，债务人的出资人尚未完全履行出资义务的，管理人应当要求该出资人缴纳所认缴的出资，而不受出资期限的限制。	**Article 35** After the People's Court accepts the bankruptcy application, if any investor of the debtor has not fully performed its capital contribution obligation, the administrator shall request such investor to make full payment of its committed capital contribution regardless of the contractual capital contribution schedule.
第三十六条 债务人的董事、监事和高级管理人员利用职权从企业获取的非正常收入和侵占的企业财产，管理人应当追回。	**Article 36** The administrator shall recover from the directors, supervisors and senior management personnel any property of the enterprise misappropriated by them and any extraordinary income obtained through the abuse of their positions.
第三十七条 人民法院受理破产申请后，管理人可以通过清偿债务或者提供为债权人接受的担保，取回质物、留置物。	**Article 37** After the People's Court accepts the bankruptcy application, the administrator may take back any collateral pledged or withheld by paying off debts or providing security acceptable to the creditors.
前款规定的债务清偿或者替代担保，在质物或者留置物的价值低于被担保的债权额时，以该质物或者留置物当时的市场价值为限。	The pay-off of debts or the substitute security referred to in the preceding paragraph shall be limited to the value up to the then-current market value of the collateral pledged or withheld if the value of the collateral pledged or withheld is lower than the amount of the secured claims.

第三十八条 人民法院受理破产申请后，债务人占有的不属于债务人的财产，该财产的权利人可以通过管理人取回。但是，本法另有规定的除外。	**Article 38** After the People's Court accepts the bankruptcy application, persons entitled to property possessed by but not belonging to the debtor may take back such property through the administrator, unless otherwise provided for herein.
第三十九条 人民法院受理破产申请时，出卖人已将买卖标的物向作为买受人的债务人发运，债务人尚未收到且未付清全部价款的，出卖人可以取回在运途中的标的物。但是，管理人可以支付全部价款，请求出卖人交付标的物。	**Article 39** At the time when the People's Court accepts the bankruptcy application, if a seller has shipped purchased goods to the debtor-purchaser but the debtor has not yet received the goods and has not made full payment, the seller may recover the purchased goods in transit. However, the administrator may make full payment and request the seller to deliver the purchased goods.
第四十条 债权人在破产申请受理前对债务人负有债务的，可以向管理人主张抵销。但是，有下列情形之一的，不得抵销： （一）债务人的债务人在破产申请受理后取得他人对债务人的债权的； （二）债权人已知债务人有不能清偿到期债务或者破产申请的事实，对债务人负担债务的；但是，债权人因为法律规定或者有破产申请一年前所发生的原因而负担债务的除外； （三）债务人的债务人已知债务人有不能清偿到期债务或者破产申请的事实，对债务人取得债权的；但是，债务人的债务人因为法律规定或者有破产申请一年前所发生的原因而取得债权的除外。	**Article 40** If a creditor owes debts to the debtor before the acceptance of bankruptcy application, the creditor may make a setoff claim to the administrator. However, no setoff shall be made under any of the following circumstances: (1) a debtor of the debtor acquires claims against the debtor from others after the bankruptcy application is accepted; (2) knowing that the debtor is unable to pay off debts as they become due or has filed a bankruptcy application, a creditor incurs debts to the debtor (except for debts borne by the creditor by operation of law or arising from causes occurring one year prior to the bankruptcy application); (3) knowing that the debtor is unable to pay off debts as they become due or has filed a bankruptcy application, a debtor of the debtor acquires claims against the debtor (except for claims acquired by such debtor of the debtor by operation of law or arising from causes occurring one year prior to the bankruptcy application).
第五章　破产费用和共益债务	**Chapter V　Bankruptcy Expenses and Common-Interest Debts**
第四十一条 人民法院受理破产申请后发生的下列费用，为破产费用：	**Article 41** The following expenses incurred after the People's Court accepts the bankruptcy application shall be the bankruptcy expenses:

（一）破产案件的诉讼费用； （二）管理、变价和分配债务人财产的费用； （三）管理人执行职务的费用、报酬和聘用工作人员的费用。	(1) litigation expenses of the bankruptcy case; (2) expenses for management, pricing, and distribution of the debtor's properties; (3) expenses incurred by, and remunerations of, the administrator for performing its duties and the expenses for engaging working staff.
第四十二条 人民法院受理破产申请后发生的下列债务，为共益债务： （一）因管理人或者债务人请求对方当事人履行双方均未履行完毕的合同所产生的债务； （二）债务人财产受无因管理所产生的债务； （三）因债务人不当得利所产生的债务； （四）为债务人继续营业而应支付的劳动报酬和社会保险费用以及由此产生的其他债务； （五）管理人或者相关人员执行职务致人损害所产生的债务； （六）债务人财产致人损害所产生的债务。	**Article 42** The following debts incurred after the People's Court accepts the bankruptcy application shall be the common-interest debts: (1) debts arising from enforcement by the administrator or the debtor of an executory contract against the other party; (2) debts incurred as a result of the non-obligatory management of the debtor's property; (3) debts incurred as a result of the unjust enrichment of the debtor; (4) labor compensation and social insurance fees and other debts incurred for the continuing operation of the debtor; (5) debts incurred as a result of damage to others caused by the administrator or relevant personnel in performing their duties; and (6) debts incurred as a result of damage to others caused by the debtor's properties.
第四十三条 破产费用和共益债务由债务人财产随时清偿。	**Article 43** The bankruptcy expenses and the common-interest debts shall be paid off from time to time out of the debtor's properties.
债务人财产不足以清偿所有破产费用和共益债务的，先行清偿破产费用。	If the debtor's properties are insufficient to pay off all the bankruptcy expenses and all the common-interest debts, the bankruptcy expenses shall be paid off in priority.
债务人财产不足以清偿所有破产费用或者共益债务的，按照比例清偿。	If the debtor's properties are insufficient to pay off all the bankruptcy expenses or all the common-interest debts, such expenses or debts shall be paid off pro rata.
债务人财产不足以清偿破产费用的，管理人应当提请人民法院终结破产程序。人民法院应当自收	If the debtor's properties are insufficient to pay off the bankruptcy expenses, the administrator shall request the People's Court to terminate the bankruptcy procedures.

到请求之日起十五日内裁定终结破产程序，并予以公告。	The People's Court shall make a ruling as to the termination of the bankruptcy procedures within fifteen days from the date of receipt of the request and shall make a public announcement of such ruling.
第六章　债权申报	**Chapter VI　Assertion of Claims**
第四十四条　人民法院受理破产申请时对债务人享有债权的债权人，依照本法规定的程序行使权利。	**Article 44**　A creditor who has a claim against the debtor when the People's Court accepts the bankruptcy application shall exercise its rights in accordance with the procedures provided herein.
第四十五条　人民法院受理破产申请后，应当确定债权人申报债权的期限。债权申报期限自人民法院发布受理破产申请公告之日起计算，最短不得少于三十日，最长不得超过三个月。	**Article 45**　After accepting the bankruptcy application, the People's Court shall set a time limit for the creditors to assert their claims, which shall be no less than thirty days and no more than three months from the date when the People's Court makes a public announcement of the acceptance of the bankruptcy application.
第四十六条　未到期的债权，在破产申请受理时视为到期。	**Article 46**　Claims that are not due shall be deemed as due on the date the bankruptcy application is accepted.
附利息的债权自破产申请受理时起停止计息。	In the case of claims with interest, the interest shall cease to accrue thereon from the date the bankruptcy application is accepted.
第四十七条　附条件、附期限的债权和诉讼、仲裁未决的债权，债权人可以申报。	**Article 47**　Any claim which is conditional, subject to any time limit or under any pending litigation or arbitration may be asserted by the creditor.
第四十八条　债权人应当在人民法院确定的债权申报期限内向管理人申报债权。	**Article 48**　The creditors shall assert their claims to the administrator within the time limit decided by the People's Court.
债务人所欠职工的工资和医疗、伤残补助、抚恤费用，所欠的应当划入职工个人账户的基本养老保险、基本医疗保险费用，以及法律、行政法规规定应当支付给职工的补偿金，不必申报，由管理人调查后列出清单并予以公示。职工对清单记载有异议的，可以要求管理人更正；管理人不予更正的，职工可以向人民法院提起诉讼。	No assertion is required for wages, subsidies for medical treatment and disability, and pensions for the disabled and the families of the deceased which are due and unpaid, fees for basic pension insurance and basic medical insurance which should have been paid into the individual accounts of the employees but which are unpaid, and other compensations payable to employees under the laws and administrative regulations. Instead, the administrator shall list them out and post the list publicly upon investigation and verification. If there is any objection from the employees to the listed items, the employees may ask the administrator to make

	correction; and if the administrator declines to do so, the employees may bring suit before the People's Court.
第四十九条 债权人申报债权时，应当书面说明债权的数额和有无财产担保，并提交有关证据。申报的债权是连带债权的，应当说明。	**Article 49** When asserting a claim, the creditor shall explain in writing the amount of the claim and whether it is secured, and submit relevant evidence. Where a claim being asserted involves a joint claim, it shall be specified.
第五十条 连带债权人可以由其中一人代表全体连带债权人申报债权，也可以共同申报债权。	**Article 50** Joint creditors may assert their claims through one creditor representing all of them, or assert their claims jointly.
第五十一条 债务人的保证人或者其他连带债务人已经代替债务人清偿债务的，以其对债务人的求偿权申报债权。	**Article 51** If a guarantor or other co-debtor of the debtor has paid off debts on behalf of the debtor, such guarantor or co-debtor shall assert its claim based on its right of claim against the debtor.
债务人的保证人或者其他连带债务人尚未代替债务人清偿债务的，以其对债务人的将来求偿权申报债权。但是，债权人已经向管理人申报全部债权的除外。	If the guarantor or other co-debtor of the debtor has not paid off debts on behalf of the debtor, such guarantor or co-debtor shall assert its claim based on its future right of claim against the debtor, except where the creditor has asserted to the administrator all the claims.
第五十二条 连带债务人数人被裁定适用本法规定的程序的，其债权人有权就全部债权分别在各破产案件中申报债权。	**Article 52** If it is ruled that the procedures prescribed herein shall be applied to several co-debtors, their creditor shall be entitled to assert the claims in all the relevant bankruptcy cases with respect to all the claims respectively.
第五十三条 管理人或者债务人依照本法规定解除合同的，对方当事人以因合同解除所产生的损害赔偿请求权申报债权。	**Article 53** If the administrator or the debtor rejects a contract pursuant to the provisions hereof, the other party to the contract shall assert the claims based on the right of claim for damages arising from the rejection of contract.
第五十四条 债务人是委托合同的委托人，被裁定适用本法规定的程序，受托人不知该事实，继续处理委托事务的，受托人以由此产生的请求权申报债权。	**Article 54** If the debtor is the consignor of a consignment contract and has been ruled to be subject to the procedures provided herein, but the consignee continues processing the consigned matters without knowledge of such fact, such consignee shall assert the claim based on the right of claim arising therefrom.

第五十五条 债务人是票据的出票人，被裁定适用本法规定的程序，该票据的付款人继续付款或者承兑的，付款人以由此产生的请求权申报债权。	**Article 55** If the debtor is an issuer of a negotiable instrument and has been ruled to be subject to the procedures provided herein, but the payor under the negotiable instrument continues payment or acceptance, such payor shall assert the claim based on the right of claim arising therefrom.
第五十六条 在人民法院确定的债权申报期限内，债权人未申报债权的，可以在破产财产最后分配前补充申报；但是，此前已进行的分配，不再对其补充分配。为审查和确认补充申报债权的费用，由补充申报人承担。	**Article 56** If a creditor fails to assert within the time limit for claim assertion set by the People's Court, it may make a supplemental assertion before the final distribution of the bankruptcy property; however, no supplemental distribution shall be made available to it with respect to any completed distributions. The creditor who makes the supplemental assertion shall bear the expenses of review and verification of the supplemental claim assertion.
债权人未依照本法规定申报债权的，不得依照本法规定的程序行使权利。	Any creditor who fails to assert its claim pursuant to the provisions hereof cannot exercise its rights in the procedures subject to this Law.
第五十七条 管理人收到债权申报材料后，应当登记造册，对申报的债权进行审查，并编制债权表。	**Article 57** After receiving the materials for claim assertions, the administrator shall register and compile them, examine the asserted claims and prepare a statement of the claims.
债权表和债权申报材料由管理人保存，供利害关系人查阅。	The statement of claims and the materials for claim assertions shall be maintained by the administrator and shall be available to interested parties for examination.
第五十八条 依照本法第五十七条规定编制的债权表，应当提交第一次债权人会议核查。	**Article 58** The statement of claims made in accordance with the provisions of Article 57 hereof shall be submitted to the first creditors' meeting for review and verification.
债务人、债权人对债权表记载的债权无异议的，由人民法院裁定确认。	If the debtor and creditors have no objection to the claims set forth in the statement of claims, they shall be confirmed by the People's Court.
债务人、债权人对债权表记载的债权有异议的，可以向受理破产申请的人民法院提起诉讼。	If the debtor or any of the creditors has an objection to the claims set forth in the statement of claims, the debtor or the creditors may bring suit in the People's Court that has accepted the bankruptcy application.

第七章　债权人会议	**Chapter VII　The Creditors' Meeting**
第一节　一般规定	**Section I　General Provisions**
第五十九条　依法申报债权的债权人为债权人会议的成员，有权参加债权人会议，享有表决权。	**Article 59**　A creditor who has lawfully asserted a claim shall be a member of the creditors' meeting and shall have the right to attend the creditors' meeting and vote.
债权尚未确定的债权人，除人民法院能够为其行使表决权而临时确定债权额的外，不得行使表决权。	Creditors whose claims have not been confirmed shall not exercise the right to vote unless the People's Court confirms the amount of the claim temporarily in order for the creditors to exercise the right to vote.
对债务人的特定财产享有担保权的债权人，未放弃优先受偿权利的，对于本法第六十一条第一款第七项、第十项规定的事项不享有表决权。	If a creditor who has security interests in specific property of the debtor has not given up its priority to claim, such creditor shall not have the right to vote on the matters set forth in Article 61, paragraph 1, items (7) and (10) hereof.
债权人可以委托代理人出席债权人会议，行使表决权。代理人出席债权人会议，应当向人民法院或者债权人会议主席提交债权人的授权委托书。	Creditors may authorize proxies to attend the creditors' meeting and exercise the right to vote. When attending the meeting, a proxy shall submit the creditor's letter of authorization to the People's Court or the chairman of the creditors' meeting.
债权人会议应当有债务人的职工和工会的代表参加，对有关事项发表意见。	Representatives of the employees and the trade union of the debtor shall be present at the creditors' meeting to express their opinions on relevant matters.
第六十条　债权人会议设主席一人，由人民法院从有表决权的债权人中指定。	**Article 60**　The creditors' meeting shall have one chairman, who shall be designated by the People's Court from the creditors with voting rights.
债权人会议主席主持债权人会议。	The chairman of the creditors' meeting shall preside over the creditors' meeting.
第六十一条　债权人会议行使下列职权： （一）核查债权； （二）申请人民法院更换管理人，审查管理人的费用和报酬；	**Article 61**　The creditors' meeting shall exercise the following powers: (1) investigating into the claims; (2) requesting the People's Court to replace the administrator, and reviewing the expenses and remunerations of the administrator;

（三）监督管理人； （四）选任和更换债权人委员会成员； （五）决定继续或者停止债务人的营业； （六）通过重整计划； （七）通过和解协议； （八）通过债务人财产的管理方案； （九）通过破产财产的变价方案； （十）通过破产财产的分配方案； （十一）人民法院认为应当由债权人会议行使的其他职权。	(3) supervising the activities of the administrator; (4) selecting or replacing the members of the creditors' committee; (5) deciding to continue or terminate the debtor's business operations; (6) adopting the reorganization plan; (7) adopting the conciliation agreement; (8) adopting the debtor's property management proposal; (9) adopting the bankruptcy estate pricing proposal; (10) adopting the bankruptcy estate distribution proposal; and (11) other powers that the People's Court deems should be exercised by the creditors' meeting.
债权人会议应当对所议事项的决议作成会议记录。	The creditors' meeting shall make meeting minutes recording the resolutions on the matters discussed.
第六十二条 第一次债权人会议由人民法院召集，自债权申报期限届满之日起十五日内召开。	**Article 62** The first creditors' meeting shall be called by the People's Court, and shall be convened within fifteen days from the expiration date of the time limit on assertion of the claims.
以后的债权人会议，在人民法院认为必要时，或者管理人、债权人委员会、占债权总额四分之一以上的债权人向债权人会议主席提议时召开。	Subsequent creditors' meetings shall be convened at such time as the People's Court deems necessary, or upon the proposal to the chairman of the creditors' meeting by the administrator, the creditors' committee or creditors representing more than one-fourth of the total amount of all the claims.
第六十三条 召开债权人会议，管理人应当提前十五日通知已知的债权人。	**Article 63** The administrator shall notify the known creditors fifteen days in advance of a creditors' meeting.
第六十四条 债权人会议的决议，由出席会议的有表决权的债权人过半数通过，并且其所代表的债权额占无财产担保债权总额的二分之一以上。但是，本法另有规定的除外。	**Article 64** Resolutions of the creditors' meeting shall be adopted by more than half of the creditors with the right to vote present at the meeting, and representing more than half of the total amount of the unsecured claims unless otherwise provided in this Law.

债权人认为债权人会议的决议违反法律规定，损害其利益的，可以自债权人会议作出决议之日起十五日内，请求人民法院裁定撤销该决议，责令债权人会议依法重新作出决议。	If a creditor believes that a resolution of the creditors' meeting is in violation of the law and impairs its interests, such creditor may, within fifteen days after the adoption of such resolution at the creditors' meeting, request the People's Court to revoke the resolution and to order that the creditors' meeting adopt a new resolution in accordance with law.
债权人会议的决议，对于全体债权人均有约束力。	Resolutions of the creditors' meeting shall be binding upon all creditors.
第六十五条 本法第六十一条第一款第八项、第九项所列事项，经债权人会议表决未通过的，由人民法院裁定。	**Article 65** If any matter set forth under Article 61, paragraph 1, items (8) and (9) hereof fails to be determined upon the voting at the creditors' meeting, it shall be subject to the ruling of the People's Court.
本法第六十一条第一款第十项所列事项，经债权人会议二次表决仍未通过的，由人民法院裁定。	If any matter set forth under Article 61, paragraph 1, item (10) hereof fails to be determined upon a second voting at the creditors' meeting, it shall be subject to the ruling of the People's Court.
对前两款规定的裁定，人民法院可以在债权人会议上宣布或者另行通知债权人。	The People's Court may announce at the creditors' meeting or otherwise notify the creditors of the ruling prescribed in the preceding two paragraphs.
第六十六条 债权人对人民法院依照本法第六十五条第一款作出的裁定不服的，债权额占无财产担保债权总额二分之一以上的债权人对人民法院依照本法第六十五条第二款作出的裁定不服的，可以自裁定宣布之日或者收到通知之日起十五日内向该人民法院申请复议。复议期间不停止裁定的执行。	**Article 66** If a creditor contests the ruling made by the People's Court according to first paragraph of Article 65 hereof, or if creditors whose claims comprise more than half of the unsecured claims contest the ruling made by the People's Court according to the second paragraph of Article 65 hereof, they may apply to such People's Court for reconsideration within fifteen days from the date when the ruling is announced or the notice is received. During the reconsideration period, the enforcement of the ruling shall not be suspended.
第二节　债权人委员会	**Section II　The Creditors' Committee**
第六十七条 债权人会议可以决定设立债权人委员会。债权人委员会由债权人会议选任的债权人代表和一名债务人的职工代表或者工会代表组成。债权人委员会成员不得超过九人。债权人委员会成员应当经人民法院书面决定认可。	**Article 67** The creditors' meeting may decide to set up a creditors' committee, which shall comprise the creditors' representatives designated by the creditors' meeting and a representative of the employees or trade union of the debtor. The creditors' committee shall have no more than nine members and all the members shall be recognized by the People's Court in writing.

第六十八条 债权人委员会行使下列职权： (一) 监督债务人财产的管理和处分； (二) 监督破产财产分配； (三) 提议召开债权人会议； (四) 债权人会议委托的其他职权。	**Article 68** The creditors' committee shall perform the following duties: (1) supervising the management and disposal of the debtor's property; (2) supervising the distribution of the bankruptcy estate; (3) proposing the convention of the creditors' meetings; (4) other duties authorized by the creditors' meetings.
债权人委员会执行职务时，有权要求管理人、债务人的有关人员对其职权范围内的事务作出说明或者提供有关文件。	The creditors' committee, when performing its duties, shall be entitled to request the administrator and relevant personnel of the debtor to make explanations or to supply relevant documents on matters within the scope of its duty.
管理人、债务人的有关人员违反本法规定拒绝接受监督的，债权人委员会有权就监督事项请求人民法院作出决定；人民法院应当在五日内作出决定。	If the administrator and relevant personnel of the debtor violate the provisions hereof and refuse to accept supervision, the creditors' committee shall be entitled to request the People's Court to make a decision on the matters under supervision. The People's Court shall make such decision within five days.
第六十九条 管理人实施下列行为，应当及时报告债权人委员会： (一) 涉及土地、房屋等不动产权益的转让； (二) 探矿权、采矿权、知识产权等财产权的转让； (三) 全部库存或者营业的转让； (四) 借款； (五) 设定财产担保； (六) 债权和有价证券的转让； (七) 履行债务人和对方当事人均未履行完毕的合同； (八) 放弃权利； (九) 担保物的取回； (十) 对债权人利益有重大影响的其他财产处分行为。	**Article 69** In conducting any of the following activities, the administrator shall timely report to the creditors' committee: (1) transfers involving interests in land, buildings and other real estate; (2) transfers of mine exploration rights, mining rights, intellectual property rights and other property rights; (3) transfers of all inventories or businesses; (4) borrowings; (5) creation of collateral security; (6) transfers of claims and securities; (7) performance of an executory contract; (8) giving up of rights; (9) taking-back of collateral; and (10) other activities related to the disposal of property which have significant impact on creditors' interests.

未设立债权人委员会的，管理人实施前款规定的行为应当及时报告人民法院。	If no creditors' committee has been set up, the administrator shall timely report to the People's Court in conducting the activities referred to above.
第八章　重 整	**Chapter VIII　Reorganization**
第一节 重整申请和重整期间	**Section I　Application for Reorganization and Period of Reorganization**
第七十条　债务人或者债权人可以依照本法规定，直接向人民法院申请对债务人进行重整。	**Article 70**　The debtor or creditors may file an application directly to the People's Court for reorganization of the debtor according to this Law.
债权人申请对债务人进行破产清算的，在人民法院受理破产申请后、宣告债务人破产前，债务人或者出资额占债务人注册资本十分之一以上的出资人，可以向人民法院申请重整。	If a creditor applies for bankruptcy liquidation of the debtor, the debtor or the investors whose capital contribution represents more than one-tenth of the debtor's registered capital may apply to the People's Court for reorganization after the People's Court accepts the bankruptcy application but before the debtor is declared bankrupt.
第七十一条　人民法院经审查认为重整申请符合本法规定的，应当裁定债务人重整，并予以公告。	**Article 71**　The People's Court shall rule and publicly announce that the debtor is to be reorganized if it finds that the reorganization application satisfies the requirements hereunder.
第七十二条　自人民法院裁定债务人重整之日起至重整程序终止，为重整期间。	**Article 72**　The reorganization period shall start from the date when the People's Court rules that the debtor is to be reorganized and end at the termination of the reorganization procedures.
第七十三条　在重整期间，经债务人申请，人民法院批准，债务人可以在管理人的监督下自行管理财产和营业事务。	**Article 73**　During the reorganization period, the debtor itself may manage its property and business affairs under the supervision of the administrator, after the People's Court approves its application therefor.
有前款规定情形的，依照本法规定已接管债务人财产和营业事务的管理人应当向债务人移交财产和营业事务，本法规定的管理人的职权由债务人行使。	Where the circumstance prescribed in the preceding paragraph occurs, the administrator, who has received and managed the debtor's property and business according to this Law, shall transfer the property and business affairs to the debtor and the power of the administrator provided for herein shall be exercised by the debtor.

第七十四条 管理人负责管理财产和营业事务的，可以聘任债务人的经营管理人员负责营业事务。	**Article 74** If the administrator is responsible for management of the property and business affairs, it may engage the management staff of the debtor to manage the business affairs.
第七十五条 在重整期间，对债务人的特定财产享有的担保权暂停行使。但是，担保物有损坏或者价值明显减少的可能，足以危害担保权人权利的，担保权人可以向人民法院请求恢复行使担保权。	**Article 75** During the reorganization period, the exercise of security rights in specific property of the debtor shall be suspended. However, if the likelihood exists that the collateral will be damaged or the value thereof will decrease dramatically, which is sufficient to damage the rights of the secured creditor, such secured creditor may request to the People's Court for resuming exercise of the security rights.
在重整期间，债务人或者管理人为继续营业而借款的，可以为该借款设定担保。	During the reorganization period, if the debtor or the administrator borrows a loan for continuing business, a security interest may be created for such loan.
第七十六条 债务人合法占有的他人财产，该财产的权利人在重整期间要求取回的，应当符合事先约定的条件。	**Article 76** If the equity owner of property legally possessed by the debtor requests to take back the property during the reorganization period, such equity owner shall satisfy the previously agreed terms and conditions.
第七十七条 在重整期间，债务人的出资人不得请求投资收益分配。	**Article 77** During the reorganization period, the debtor's investors shall not ask for distribution of gain from the investment.
在重整期间，债务人的董事、监事、高级管理人员不得向第三人转让其持有的债务人的股权。但是，经人民法院同意的除外。	During the reorganization period, the directors, supervisors or senior management staff of the debtor shall not transfer their equity interests in the debtor to a third party, without consent by the People's Court.
第七十八条 在重整期间，有下列情形之一的，经管理人或者利害关系人请求，人民法院应当裁定终止重整程序，并宣告债务人破产： （一）债务人的经营状况和财产状况继续恶化，缺乏挽救的可能性； （二）债务人有欺诈、恶意减少债务人财产或者其他显著不利于债权人的行为；	**Article 78** If any of the following events occurs during the reorganization period, upon request of the administrator or an interested party, the People's Court shall rule to terminate the reorganization procedure and declare the debtor bankrupt: (1) the operational and financial condition of the debtor deteriorate continuously, which is impossible to be rescued; (2) the debtor commits fraud, diminishes its property in bad faith or conducts other actions which obviously harm creditors;

（三）由于债务人的行为致使管理人无法执行职务。	(3) the actions of the debtor cause the administrator to be unable to perform its duties.
第二节　重整计划的制定和批准	**Section 2　Proposal and Approval of Reorganization Plan**
第七十九条　债务人或者管理人应当自人民法院裁定债务人重整之日起六个月内，同时向人民法院和债权人会议提交重整计划草案。	**Article 79**　The debtor or administrator shall submit a draft reorganization plan to the People's Court and the creditors' meeting simultaneously within six months from the date the People's Court makes the ruling of reorganizing the debtor.
前款规定的期限届满，经债务人或者管理人请求，有正当理由的，人民法院可以裁定延期三个月。	Upon the expiration of the period referred to in the preceding paragraph and at the request of the debtor or the administrator with justifiable reason, the People's Court may rule to extend the period for three months.
债务人或者管理人未按期提出重整计划草案的，人民法院应当裁定终止重整程序，并宣告债务人破产。	If the debtor or the administrator fails to submit a draft reorganization plan in time, the People's Court shall rule to terminate the reorganization procedure and declare the debtor bankrupt.
第八十条　债务人自行管理财产和营业事务的，由债务人制作重整计划草案。	**Article 80**　Where the debtor itself manages the property and business affairs, the draft reorganization plan shall be prepared by the debtor.
管理人负责管理财产和营业事务的，由管理人制作重整计划草案。	If the administrator is responsible for managing the property and business affairs of the debtor, the draft reorganization plan shall be prepared by the administrator.
第八十一条　重整计划草案应当包括下列内容： （一）债务人的经营方案； （二）债权分类； （三）债权调整方案； （四）债权受偿方案； （五）重整计划的执行期限； （六）重整计划执行的监督期限； （七）有利于债务人重整的其他方案。	**Article 81**　The draft reorganization plan shall contain the following: (1) the business operation plan of the debtor; (2) the classification of claims; (3) the plan for adjustments to claims; (4) the plan for repayment of claims; (5) the time limit for implementing the reorganization plan; (6) the time limit for the supervision of implementation of the reorganization plan; and (7) other plans that are beneficial to the reorganization of the debtor.

第八十二条 下列各类债权的债权人参加讨论重整计划草案的债权人会议，依照下列债权分类，分组对重整计划草案进行表决： （一）对债务人的特定财产享有担保权的债权； （二）债务人所欠职工的工资和医疗、伤残补助、抚恤费用，所欠的应当划入职工个人账户的基本养老保险、基本医疗保险费用，以及法律、行政法规规定应当支付给职工的补偿金； （三）债务人所欠税款； （四）普通债权。	**Article 82** Creditors having the following classified claims shall participate in the creditors' meeting held for discussing the draft reorganization plan, and shall be divided into groups to vote on the draft reorganization plan based on the following classification of the claims: (1) claims with security interests in specific property of the debtor; (2) wages, subsidies for medical treatment and disability, and pensions for the disabled and the families of the deceased which are due and unpaid, fees for basic pension insurance and basic medical insurance which should have been paid into the individual accounts of the employees and which are unpaid, and other compensations payable to employees under the laws and administrative regulations; (3) taxes due but unpaid by the debtor; and (4) ordinary claims.
人民法院在必要时可以决定在普通债权组中设小额债权组对重整计划草案进行表决。	If necessary, the People's Court may decide to set up a sub-group of small-amount claims in the ordinary claim group to vote on the draft reorganization plan.
第八十三条 重整计划不得规定减免债务人欠缴的本法第八十二条第一款第二项规定以外的社会保险费用；该项费用的债权人不参加重整计划草案的表决。	**Article 83** The reorganization plan shall not provide reduction or release of the payments for social insurance expenses other than as provided for in Article 82, paragraph 1, item (2) hereof which are due but unpaid by the debtor; the creditors in respect of such expenses shall not participate in voting on the draft reorganization plan.
第八十四条 人民法院应当自收到重整计划草案之日起三十日内召开债权人会议，对重整计划草案进行表决。	**Article 84** The People's Court shall hold a creditors' meeting within thirty days from the date of receipt of the draft reorganization plan to vote on the draft reorganization plan.
出席会议的同一表决组的债权人过半数同意重整计划草案，并且其所代表的债权额占该组债权总额的三分之二以上的，即为该组通过重整计划草案。	If the draft reorganization plan is passed by more than half of the creditors in a voting group present at the meeting and representing more than two-thirds of the total claims of the group, the draft reorganization plan shall be deemed passed by that group.

债务人或者管理人应当向债权人会议就重整计划草案作出说明，并回答询问。	The debtor or administrator shall explain the draft reorganization plan to the creditors' meeting and answer inquiries.
第八十五条 债务人的出资人代表可以列席讨论重整计划草案的债权人会议。	**Article 85** Representatives of the debtor's investors may attend, without voting right, the creditors' meeting held for discussing the draft reorganization plan.
重整计划草案涉及出资人权益调整事项的，应当设出资人组，对该事项进行表决。	If the draft reorganization plan involves matters of adjustment to the investors' rights and interests, an investors' group shall be set up to vote on such matters.
第八十六条 各表决组均通过重整计划草案时，重整计划即为通过。	**Article 86** If a draft reorganization plan is passed in all voting groups, the reorganization plan shall be deemed passed.
自重整计划通过之日起十日内，债务人或者管理人应当向人民法院提出批准重整计划的申请。人民法院经审查认为符合本法规定的，应当自收到申请之日起三十日内裁定批准，终止重整程序，并予以公告。	Within ten days from the date when the reorganization plan is passed, the debtor or the administrator shall file an application to the People's Court for approval of the reorganization plan; the People's Court, after verifying that the reorganization plan meets the provisions of this Law, shall make a ruling approving the reorganization plan and terminating the reorganization procedures within thirty days from the date of receipt of the application, and shall make a public announcement of such ruling.
第八十七条 部分表决组未通过重整计划草案的，债务人或者管理人可以同未通过重整计划草案的表决组协商。该表决组可以在协商后再表决一次。双方协商的结果不得损害其他表决组的利益。	**Article 87** If the draft plan of reorganization is not passed in some of the voting groups, the debtor or the administrator may negotiate with such voting groups which did not pass the draft reorganization plan. The voting group may conduct a second round of voting after the negotiation. The results reached by the two sides in negotiation shall not impair the interests of the other voting groups.
未通过重整计划草案的表决组拒绝再次表决或者再次表决仍未通过重整计划草案，但重整计划草案符合下列条件的，债务人或者管理人可以申请人民法院批准重整计划草案：	If the voting groups which did not pass the draft reorganization plan decline to have the second round of voting or do not pass the reorganization plan in the second round of voting, the debtor or the administrator may request the People's Court to approve the draft reorganization plan provided that the draft reorganization plan satisfies the following conditions:

(一) 按照重整计划草案，本法第八十二条第一款第一项所列债权就该特定财产将获得全额清偿，其因延期清偿所受的损失将得到公平补偿，并且其担保权未受到实质性损害，或者该表决组已经通过重整计划草案； (二) 按照重整计划草案，本法第八十二条第一款第二项、第三项所列债权将获得全额清偿，或者相应表决组已经通过重整计划草案； (三) 按照重整计划草案，普通债权所获得的清偿比例，不低于其在重整计划草案被提请批准时依照破产清算程序所能获得的清偿比例，或者该表决组已经通过重整计划草案； (四) 重整计划草案对出资人权益的调整公平、公正，或者出资人组已经通过重整计划草案； (五) 重整计划草案公平对待同一表决组的成员，并且所规定的债权清偿顺序不违反本法第一百一十三条的规定； (六) 债务人的经营方案具有可行性。	(1) according to the draft reorganization plan, the claims listed in Article 82, paragraph 1, item (1) hereof will be fully paid off with respect to such specific property, and the losses incurred by the delay of the repayment will be compensated fairly and the security interests have not suffered substantial damage; or the draft reorganization plan has been passed by such voting group; (2) according to the draft reorganization plan, the claims listed in Article 82, paragraph 1, items (2) and (3) hereof will be fully paid off; or the draft reorganization plan has been passed by the relevant voting groups; (3) according to the draft reorganization plan, the ordinary claims will be repaid in a proportion which is not less than the proportion available to them pursuant to the bankruptcy liquidation procedure at the time when the draft reorganization plan is submitted for approval; or the draft reorganization plan has been passed by such voting group; (4) the adjustment to the investors' rights and interests in the draft reorganization plan is fair and equitable; or the draft reorganization plan has been passed by the investors' group; (5) members within the same voting group are treated fairly and equally under the draft reorganization plan and the repayment priority under the draft reorganization plan does not violate the provisions under Article 113 hereof; (6) the business operation plan of the debtor is feasible.
人民法院经审查认为重整计划草案符合前款规定的，应当自收到申请之日起三十日内裁定批准，终止重整程序，并予以公告。	If the People's Court, after examination, finds that the reorganization plan meets the provisions set forth in the preceding paragraph, it shall, within thirty days from the date of receipt the application, rule to approve the reorganization plan and terminate the reorganization procedures, and shall publicly announce the same.
第八十八条 重整计划草案未获得通过且未依照本法第八十七条的	**Article 88** If the draft reorganization plan has been neither passed nor approved pursuant to the provisions

规定获得批准，或者已通过的重整计划未获得批准的，人民法院应当裁定终止重整程序，并宣告债务人破产。	of Article 87 hereof, or has been passed but fails to be approved, the People's Court shall make a ruling terminating the reorganization procedures and declaring the debtor bankrupt.
第三节 重整计划的执行	**Section III Implementation of Reorganization Plan**
第八十九条 重整计划由债务人负责执行。	**Article 89** The debtor shall be responsible for the implementation of the reorganization plan.
人民法院裁定批准重整计划后，已接管财产和营业事务的管理人应当向债务人移交财产和营业事务。	The administrator who has received the debtor's property and business affairs shall transfer the property and business affairs to the debtor after the reorganization plan has been approved in the ruling of the People's Court.
第九十条 自人民法院裁定批准重整计划之日起，在重整计划规定的监督期内，由管理人监督重整计划的执行。	**Article 90** From the date the People's Court makes a ruling to approve the reorganization plan and during the supervision period as provided in the reorganization plan, the administrator shall supervise the implementation of the reorganization plan.
在监督期内，债务人应当向管理人报告重整计划执行情况和债务人财务状况。	During the supervision period, the debtor shall report to the administrator on the status of implementation of the reorganization plan and the financial status of the debtor.
第九十一条 监督期届满时，管理人应当向人民法院提交监督报告。自监督报告提交之日起，管理人的监督职责终止。	**Article 91** Upon expiration of the supervision period, the administrator shall submit a supervision report to the People's Court. The administrator's duty of supervision shall terminate from the date of submitting the supervision report.
管理人向人民法院提交的监督报告，重整计划的利害关系人有权查阅。	The supervision report submitted to the People's Court by the administrator shall be accessible to all interested parties to the reorganization plan.
经管理人申请，人民法院可以裁定延长重整计划执行的监督期限。	The People's Court, upon the administrator's application, may rule to extend the supervision period for the implementation of the reorganization plan.
第九十二条 经人民法院裁定批准的重整计划，对债务人和全体债权人均有约束力。	**Article 92** The reorganization plan approved by the People's Court shall be binding on the debtor and all creditors.

债权人未依照本法规定申报债权的，在重整计划执行期间不得行使权利；在重整计划执行完毕后，可以按照重整计划规定的同类债权的清偿条件行使权利。	Creditors who fail to assert their claims according to the provisions hereof shall not exercise their rights during the implementation period of the reorganization plan; they may exercise their rights according to the repayment terms for the same group of claims as provided in the reorganization plan after the implementation of the reorganization plan has been completed.
债权人对债务人的保证人和其他连带债务人所享有的权利，不受重整计划的影响。	The rights of creditors against a guarantor or other co-debtors of the debtor shall not be affected by the reorganization plan.
第九十三条 债务人不能执行或者不执行重整计划的，人民法院经管理人或者利害关系人请求，应当裁定终止重整计划的执行，并宣告债务人破产。	**Article 93** If the debtor is unable or fails to implement the reorganization plan, upon the request of the administrator or an interested party, the People's Court shall rule to terminate the implementation of the reorganization plan and declare the debtor bankrupt.
人民法院裁定终止重整计划执行的，债权人在重整计划中作出的债权调整的承诺失去效力。债权人因执行重整计划所受的清偿仍然有效，债权未受清偿的部分作为破产债权。	If the People's Court rules to terminate the implementation of the reorganization plan, the undertakings made by creditors as to the adjustment of claims shall no longer be valid. Repayment received by creditors as a result of the implementation of the reorganization plan shall remain valid, while the portion of the claims which have not been repaid shall be treated as bankruptcy claims.
前款规定的债权人，只有在其他同顺位债权人同自己所受的清偿达到同一比例时，才能继续接受分配。	The creditors referred to in the preceding paragraph may continue to receive distributions only if other creditors of the same priority have been repaid to the same proportion.
有本条第一款规定情形的，为重整计划的执行提供的担保继续有效。	In the circumstances referred to in the first paragraph of this Article, collateral provided for the implementation of the reorganization plan shall remain valid.
第九十四条 按照重整计划减免的债务，自重整计划执行完毕时起，债务人不再承担清偿责任。	**Article 94** Upon completion of the implementation of the reorganization plan, the debtor shall not bear repayment liability with respect to debts that have been reduced or released under the reorganization plan.
第九章　和解	**Chapter IX　Conciliation**
第九十五条 债务人可以依照本	**Article 95** The debtor may, in accordance with this

法规定，直接向人民法院申请和解；也可以在人民法院受理破产申请后、宣告债务人破产前，向人民法院申请和解。	Law, apply to the People's Court for conciliation directly, or apply to the People's Court for conciliation after the bankruptcy application is accepted but before the bankruptcy of the debtor is declared by the People's Court.
债务人申请和解，应当提出和解协议草案。	In applying for conciliation, the debtor shall submit a draft conciliation agreement.
第九十六条 人民法院经审查认为和解申请符合本法规定的，应当裁定和解，予以公告，并召集债权人会议讨论和解协议草案。	**Article 96** If the People's Court finds that the conciliation application satisfies the provisions hereof upon examination, it shall make a ruling of conciliation and publicly announce the same, and convene the creditors' meeting to discuss the draft conciliation agreement.
对债务人的特定财产享有担保权的权利人，自人民法院裁定和解之日起可以行使权利。	The holders of security interests in specific property of the debtor may exercise their rights from the day when the People's Court makes a ruling of conciliation.
第九十七条 债权人会议通过和解协议的决议，由出席会议的有表决权的债权人过半数同意，并且其所代表的债权额占无财产担保债权总额的三分之二以上。	**Article 97** The resolution on the conciliation agreement to be passed at the creditors, meeting shall require the consent of more than half of the creditors with voting rights present at the creditors' meeting and representing more than two-thirds of the total amount of unsecured claims.
第九十八条 债权人会议通过和解协议的，由人民法院裁定认可，终止和解程序，并予以公告。管理人应当向债务人移交财产和营业事务，并向人民法院提交执行职务的报告。	**Article 98** If the conciliation agreement is passed at the creditors' meeting, the People's Court shall rule to acknowledge the conciliation agreement and terminate the conciliation procedures and shall publicly announce the same. The administrator shall transfer the property and business affairs to the debtor and submit a report on performance of duties to the People's Court.
第九十九条 和解协议草案经债权人会议表决未获得通过，或者已经债权人会议通过的和解协议未获得人民法院认可的，人民法院应当裁定终止和解程序，并宣告债务人破产。	**Article 99** If the conciliation agreement fails to be passed at the creditors' meeting, or the conciliation agreement passed at the creditors' meeting fails to receive acknowledgement by the People's Court, the People's Court shall rule to terminate the conciliation procedures and declare the debtor bankrupt.
第一百条 经人民法院裁定认可的和解协议，对债务人和全体和解债权人均有约束力。	**Article 100** The conciliation agreement acknowledged by the People's Court shall be binding on the debtor and all the conciliating creditors.

和解债权人是指人民法院受理破产申请时对债务人享有无财产担保债权的人。	Conciliating creditors means the persons who have claims against the debtor which are unsecured by collateral at the time when the People's Court accepts the bankruptcy application.
和解债权人未依照本法规定申报债权的，在和解协议执行期间不得行使权利；在和解协议执行完毕后，可以按照和解协议规定的清偿条件行使权利。	If conciliating creditors fail to assert claims in accordance with the provisions hereof, they shall not exercise their rights during the implementation of the conciliation agreement; they may exercise their rights on the terms of the conciliation agreement after the completion of the performance of the conciliation agreement.
第一百零一条 和解债权人对债务人的保证人和其他连带债务人所享有的权利，不受和解协议的影响。	**Article 101** The rights of conciliating creditors against a guarantor or other co-debtors of the debtor shall not be affected by the conciliation agreement.
第一百零二条 债务人应当按照和解协议规定的条件清偿债务。	**Article 102** The debtor shall pay off its debts on the terms provided for in the conciliation agreement.
第一百零三条 因债务人的欺诈或者其他违法行为而成立的和解协议，人民法院应当裁定无效，并宣告债务人破产。	**Article 103** If any conciliation agreement is entered into as a result of the debtor's fraud or other illegal conduct, the People's Court shall rule it invalid and declare the debtor bankrupt.
有前款规定情形的，和解债权人因执行和解协议所受的清偿，在其他债权人所受清偿同等比例的范围内，不予返还。	In the circumstances set forth in the preceding paragraph, repayments received by conciliating creditors as a result of the implementation of the conciliation agreement shall not be returned to the extent of the proportion of repayments received by other creditors.
第一百零四条 债务人不能执行或者不执行和解协议的，人民法院经和解债权人请求，应当裁定终止和解协议的执行，并宣告债务人破产。	**Article 104** If the debtor is unable or fails to implement the conciliation agreement, upon request of the conciliating creditors, the People's Court shall rule to terminate the implementation of the conciliation agreement and declare the debtor bankrupt.
人民法院裁定终止和解协议执行的，和解债权人在和解协议中作出的债权调整的承诺失去效力。和解债权人因执行和解协议所受的清偿仍然有效，和解债权未受清偿的部分作为破产债权。	If the People's Court rules to terminate the implementation of the conciliation agreement, the undertakings made by the conciliating creditors in the conciliation agreement shall no longer be valid. Repayments received by conciliating creditors as a result of the implementation of the conciliation agreement shall

	remain valid, while the portion of the conciliated claims which have not been repaid shall be treated as bankruptcy claims.
前款规定的债权人，只有在其他债权人同自己所受的清偿达到同一比例时，才能继续接受分配。	The creditors referred to in the preceding paragraph may continue to receive distributions only if other creditors have been repaid to the same proportion.
有本条第一款规定情形的，为和解协议的执行提供的担保继续有效。	In the circumstances referred to in the first paragraph of this Article, collateral provided for the implementation of the conciliation agreement shall remain valid.
第一百零五条 人民法院受理破产申请后，债务人与全体债权人就债权债务的处理自行达成协议的，可以请求人民法院裁定认可，并终结破产程序。	**Article 105** After the People's Court accepts the bankruptcy application, if the debtor reaches an agreement with all the creditors voluntarily concerning the disposal of credits and debts, the debtor may request the People's Court to acknowledge the agreement and conclude the bankruptcy procedures.
第一百零六条 按照和解协议减免的债务，自和解协议执行完毕时起，债务人不再承担清偿责任。	**Article 106** Upon completion of the implementation of the conciliation agreement, the debtor shall not bear repayment liability with respect to debts that have been reduced or released under the conciliation agreement.
第十章 破产清算	**Chapter X Bankruptcy Liquidation**
第一节 破产宣告	**Section I Declaration of Bankruptcy**
第一百零七条 人民法院依照本法规定宣告债务人破产的，应当自裁定作出之日起五日内送达债务人和管理人，自裁定作出之日起十日内通知已知债权人，并予以公告。	**Article 107** If the People's Court declares the debtor bankrupt in accordance with this Law, it shall, within five days after the ruling is made, serve the ruling on the debtor and administrator, and shall, within ten days after the ruling is made, notify the known creditors thereof and publicly announce the same.
债务人被宣告破产后，债务人称为破产人，债务人财产称为破产财产，人民法院受理破产申请时对债务人享有的债权称为破产债权。	After it is declared bankrupt, the debtor shall be called the bankrupt and the debtor's property shall be called the bankruptcy estate. A creditor's claim against the debtor at the time when the People's Court accepts the application for bankruptcy is called a bankruptcy claim.

第一百零八条 破产宣告前，有下列情形之一的，人民法院应当裁定终结破产程序，并予以公告： （一）第三人为债务人提供足额担保或者为债务人清偿全部到期债务的； （二）债务人已清偿全部到期债务的。	**Article 108** Before the bankruptcy declaration, the People's Court shall make a ruling to conclude the bankruptcy procedures and publicly announce the same, if any of the following circumstances occurs: (1) a third party guarantees the full amount of the debtor's debts or pays off for the debtor all of the debts which are due; (2) the debtor pays off all of the debts which are due.
第一百零九条 对破产人的特定财产享有担保权的权利人，对该特定财产享有优先受偿的权利。	**Article 109** Any holder of security interests in specific property of the bankrupt has the priority right to be repaid by such particular property.
第一百一十条 享有本法第一百零九条规定权利的债权人行使优先受偿权利未能完全受偿的，其未受偿的债权作为普通债权；放弃优先受偿权利的，其债权作为普通债权。	**Article 110** If a creditor who enjoys the rights prescribed in the provisions of Article 109 of this Law exercises the priority right to be repaid but is not fully repaid, the unpaid portion of such secured claim shall become an ordinary claim; if any creditor waives its priority right, the creditor's claim shall be become an ordinary claim.
第二节　变价和分配	**Section II　Pricing and Distribution**
第一百一十一条 管理人应当及时拟订破产财产变价方案，提交债权人会议讨论。	**Article 111** The administrator shall timely draft a pricing plan of bankruptcy property and submit it to the creditors' meeting for discussion.
管理人应当按照债权人会议通过的或者人民法院依照本法第六十五条第一款规定裁定的破产财产变价方案，适时变价出售破产财产。	The administrator shall, according to the pricing plan of the bankruptcy estate that has been adopted at the creditors' meeting or that has been confirmed by the People's Court according to the provision under Article 65, paragraph 1 of the Law, price and sell the bankruptcy property in due course.
第一百一十二条 变价出售破产财产应当通过拍卖进行。但是，债权人会议另有决议的除外。	**Article 112** The pricing and sale of the bankruptcy estate shall be conducted through an auction, unless otherwise decided by resolutions of the creditors' meeting.
破产企业可以全部或者部分变价出售。企业变价出售时，可以将其中的无形资产和其他财产单独变价出售。	The bankrupt enterprise may be wholly or partially sold after pricing. If the enterprise is sold after pricing, its intangible assets and other assets may be sold separately.

按照国家规定不能拍卖或者限制转让的财产，应当按照国家规定的方式处理。	Any property that is not allowed to be sold through auction or is subject to transfer restrictions under the provisions of the law or regulations shall be disposed of in accordance with the relevant provisions of the law or regulations.
第一百一十三条 破产财产在优先清偿破产费用和共益债务后，依照下列顺序清偿： （一）破产人所欠职工的工资和医疗、伤残补助、抚恤费用，所欠的应当划入职工个人账户的基本养老保险、基本医疗保险费用，以及法律、行政法规规定应当支付给职工的补偿金； （二）破产人欠缴的除前项规定以外的社会保险费用和破产人所欠税款； （三）普通破产债权。	**Article 113** The bankruptcy estate shall, after the bankruptcy expenses and common-interest debts are repaid in priority, be used for repayment according to the following priority: (1) wages, subsidies for medical treatment and disability, and pensions for the disabled and the families of the deceased which are due and unpaid, fees for basic pension insurance and basic medical insurance which should have been paid into the individual accounts of the employees and which are unpaid, and other compensations payable to employees under the laws and administrative regulations; (2) social insurance fees and taxes other than those prescribed by the previous provision that are due and unpaid; (3) ordinary bankruptcy claims.
破产财产不足以清偿同一顺序的清偿要求的，按照比例分配。	If the bankruptcy estate is insufficient to pay off all claims of the same priority, it shall be distributed on a pro rata basis.
破产企业的董事、监事和高级管理人员的工资按照该企业职工的平均工资计算。	Wages of the directors, supervisors and senior management personnel of the bankrupt enterprise shall be deemed to be the average wages of the employees of such enterprise.
第一百一十四条 破产财产的分配应当以货币分配方式进行。但是，债权人会议另有决议的除外。	**Article 114** Distribution of the bankruptcy estate shall be made in money unless otherwise provided by the creditors' meeting.
第一百一十五条 管理人应当及时拟订破产财产分配方案，提交债权人会议讨论。	**Article 115** The administrator shall work out a distribution plan of the bankruptcy estate in a timely manner and submit it to the creditors' meeting for discussion.

破产财产分配方案应当载明下列事项： （一）参加破产财产分配的债权人名称或者姓名、住所； （二）参加破产财产分配的债权额； （三）可供分配的破产财产数额； （四）破产财产分配的顺序、比例及数额； （五）实施破产财产分配的方法。	The aforementioned distribution plan of the bankruptcy estate shall include the following items: (1) name and domicile of creditors participating in the distribution of the bankruptcy estate; (2) amount of claims participating in the distribution of the bankruptcy estate; (3) amount of the bankruptcy estate available for distribution; (4) the priority, proportion and amount of the bankruptcy estate distribution; (5) the methods for distributing the bankruptcy estate.
债权人会议通过破产财产分配方案后，由管理人将该方案提请人民法院裁定认可。	Upon the adoption of the distribution plan by the creditors' meeting, the administrator shall submit the plan to the People's Court for its ruling and confirmation.
第一百一十六条 破产财产分配方案经人民法院裁定认可后，由管理人执行。	**Article 116** A distribution plan of the bankruptcy estate shall, upon confirmation by the People's Court through its ruling, be implemented by the administrator.
管理人按照破产财产分配方案实施多次分配的，应当公告本次分配的财产额和债权额。	If the administrator makes distribution by installments according to the distribution plan of the bankruptcy estate, it shall announce the amount of property and the amount of claims in each distribution installment.
管理人实施最后分配的，应当在公告中指明，并载明本法第一百一十七条第二款规定的事项。	When making the final distribution installment the administrator shall specify it as such in the announcement and set forth the matters prescribed in Article 117, paragraph 2 hereof.
第一百一十七条 对于附生效条件或者解除条件的债权，管理人应当将其分配额提存。	**Article 117** With respect to any claims subject to any conditions for effectiveness or rescission, the administrator shall set aside its distribution share in advance.
管理人依照前款规定提存的分配额，在最后分配公告日，生效条件未成就或者解除条件成就的，应当分配给其他债权人；在最后分配公告日，生效条件成就或者解除条件未成就的，应当交付给债权人。	As for the distribution share set aside by the administrator in advance in the preceding paragraph, if, on the announcement date of the final distribution, the condition for effectiveness is not satisfied or the condition for rescission is satisfied, such share shall be distributed among the other creditors; if, on the announcement date of the final distribution, the condition for effectiveness is satisfied or the condition for rescission is not satisfied, such share shall be delivered to the creditor in question.

第一百一十八条 债权人未受领的破产财产分配额，管理人应当提存。债权人自最后分配公告之日起满二个月仍不领取的，视为放弃受领分配的权利，管理人或者人民法院应当将提存的分配额分配给其他债权人。	**Article 118** The distribution shares of the bankruptcy estate that have not been collected by creditors shall be set aside by the administrator. If a creditor fails to collect its distribution share within two months from the announcement date of the final distribution, it shall be deemed to have waived the right to collect such shares, and the administrator or the People's Court shall distribute such shares set aside to other creditors.
第一百一十九条 破产财产分配时，对于诉讼或者仲裁未决的债权，管理人应当将其分配额提存。自破产程序终结之日起满二年仍不能受领分配的，人民法院应当将提存的分配额分配给其他债权人。	**Article 119** With respect to claims subject to pending litigation or arbitration during the process of distribution of the bankruptcy estate, the administrator shall set aside the share related to such claims. If such shares cannot be distributed within two years following the conclusion of the bankruptcy procedures, the People's Court shall distribute the shares set aside to the other creditors.
第三节 破产程序的终结	**Section III Conclusion of Bankruptcy Procedures**
第一百二十条 破产人无财产可供分配的，管理人应当请求人民法院裁定终结破产程序。	**Article 120** If the bankrupt has no property for distribution, the administrator shall apply to the People's Court for conclusion of the bankruptcy procedures.
管理人在最后分配完结后，应当及时向人民法院提交破产财产分配报告，并提请人民法院裁定终结破产程序。	After the final distribution of the bankruptcy estate, the administrator shall timely submit to the People's Court a bankruptcy estate distribution report and apply for conclusion of the bankruptcy procedures.
人民法院应当自收到管理人终结破产程序的请求之日起十五日内作出是否终结破产程序的裁定。裁定终结的，应当予以公告。	The People's Court shall, within fifteen days from receipt of the administrator's application, make its ruling on whether to conclude the bankruptcy procedures, and make a public announcement if it rules to conclude the bankruptcy procedures.
第一百二十一条 管理人应当自破产程序终结之日起十日内，持人民法院终结破产程序的裁定，向破产人的原登记机关办理注销登记。	**Article 121** The administrator shall, within ten days from conclusion of the bankruptcy procedures, present the ruling of the People's Court to conclude the bankruptcy procedure to, and de-register the bankrupt enterprise with, the original registration authority.
第一百二十二条 管理人于办理注销登记完毕的次日终止执行职务。但是，存在诉讼或者仲裁未决情况的除外。	**Article 122** The administrator shall terminate his duties starting from the day after it completes the de-registration, unless there is any pending litigation or arbitration.

第一百二十三条 自破产程序依照本法第四十三条第四款或者第一百二十条的规定终结之日起二年内，有下列情形之一的，债权人可以请求人民法院按照破产财产分配方案进行追加分配： (一) 发现有依照本法第三十一条、第三十二条、第三十三条、第三十六条规定应当追回的财产的； (二) 发现破产人有应当供分配的其他财产的。	**Article 123** Within two years after the bankruptcy procedures are concluded according to the provisions in Article 43, paragraph 4 or Article 120 of this Law, creditors are entitled to apply to the People's Court for additional distribution according to the distribution plan of the bankruptcy estate in any of the following circumstances: (1) there exist properties which shall be recovered under the provisions prescribed in Article 31, Article 32, Article 33 and Article 36 hereof; and (2) the bankrupt is found to be in possession of other property that should be distributed.
有前款规定情形，但财产数量不足以支付分配费用的，不再进行追加分配，由人民法院将其上交国库。	Under any of the circumstances provided in the preceding paragraph, if the property discovered is insufficient to cover distribution expenses, the additional distribution shall not be made and such discovered property shall be turned over to the state treasury by the People's Court.
第一百二十四条 破产人的保证人和其他连带债务人，在破产程序终结后，对债权人依照破产清算程序未受清偿的债权，依法继续承担清偿责任。	**Article 124** After conclusion of the bankruptcy procedures, guarantors and other co-debtors of the bankrupt shall remain liable for repayment of any claims of creditors that have not been fully repaid during the bankruptcy liquidation procedure.
第十一章　法律责任	**Chapter XI　Legal Liabilities**
第一百二十五条 企业董事、监事或者高级管理人员违反忠实义务、勤勉义务，致使所在企业破产的，依法承担民事责任。	**Article 125** If any directors, supervisors or senior management personnel of an enterprise breach their duty of loyalty or diligence, resulting in the bankruptcy of the enterprise, they shall bear civil liabilities in accordance with law.
有前款规定情形的人员，自破产程序终结之日起三年内不得担任任何企业的董事、监事、高级管理人员。	Any person involved in the circumstances prescribed in the preceding paragraph cannot, within three years after the conclusion of the bankruptcy procedures, take the position of director, supervisor or senior management personnel at any enterprise.
第一百二十六条 有义务列席债权人会议的债务人的有关人员，经人民法院传唤，无正当理由拒不列席债权人会议的，人民法院	**Article 126** If the debtor's relevant personnel who are obligated to be present at creditors' meetings, after being subpoenaed by the People's Court, refuse to attend such meetings without justifiable reasons, they may be

可以拘传，并依法处以罚款。债务人的有关人员违反本法规定，拒不陈述、回答，或者作虚假陈述、回答的，人民法院可以依法处以罚款。	compelled by the People's Court to be present and subject to fines in accordance with law. If the debtor's relevant personnel, in violation of the provisions hereof, refuse to make presentations or answer inquiries, or make false presentations or answers, the People's Court may impose fines on them in accordance with law.
第一百二十七条 债务人违反本法规定，拒不向人民法院提交或者提交不真实的财产状况说明、债务清册、债权清册、有关财务会计报告以及职工工资的支付情况和社会保险费用的缴纳情况的，人民法院可以对直接责任人员依法处以罚款。	**Article 127** If the debtor, in violation of the provisions of this Law, refuses to submit or falsely submits to the People's Court the description of the status of its property, a complete list of debts, a complete list of claims, relevant financial and accounting reports, the payment status of employees' wages and the status of employees' social insurance contribution, the People's Court may impose a fine upon the persons directly liable in accordance with law.
债务人违反本法规定，拒不向管理人移交财产、印章和账簿、文书等资料的，或者伪造、销毁有关财产证据材料而使财产状况不明的，人民法院可以对直接责任人员依法处以罚款。	If the debtor, in violation of the provisions hereof, refuses to deliver to the administrator the property, seal, accounting books, instruments and other materials, or counterfeits or destroys some evidence related to the property, resulting in uncertainty of the status of property, the People's Court may impose a fine upon the persons directly liable in accordance with law.
第一百二十八条 债务人有本法第三十一条、第三十二条、第三十三条规定的行为，损害债权人利益的，债务人的法定代表人和其他直接责任人员依法承担赔偿责任。	**Article 128** If the debtor commits any acts prescribed in the provisions of Article 31, Article 32 and Article 33 of this Law and impairs creditors' interests, the debtor's legal representative and other directly responsible persons shall be liable for compensation in accordance with law.
第一百二十九条 债务人的有关人员违反本法规定，擅自离开住所地的，人民法院可以予以训诫、拘留，可以依法并处罚款。	**Article 129** If the debtor's personnel, in violation of the provisions hereof, arbitrarily leaves his or her domicile, the People's Court may admonish or detain him or her, and may also impose a fine upon him or her in accordance with law.
第一百三十条 管理人未依照本法规定勤勉尽责，忠实执行职务的，人民法院可以依法处以罚款；给债权人、债务人或者第三人造成损失的，依法承担赔偿责任。	**Article 130** If an administrator fails to perform its duties of loyalty and diligence according to the provisions hereof, the People's Court may impose a fine upon it in accordance with law. If the aforesaid failure results in any loss to creditors, the debtor or any third party, the administrator shall be liable for compensation in accordance with law.

第一百三十一条 违反本法规定，构成犯罪的，依法追究刑事责任。	**Article 131** If any person violates the provisions hereof and such violation constitutes a crime, criminal liabilities will be imposed on such person in accordance with law.
第十二章　附 则	**Chapter XII　Supplementary Provisions**
第一百三十二条 本法施行后，破产人在本法公布之日前所欠职工的工资和医疗、伤残补助、抚恤费用，所欠的应当划入职工个人账户的基本养老保险、基本医疗保险费用，以及法律、行政法规规定应当支付给职工的补偿金，依照本法第一百一十三条的规定清偿后不足以清偿的部分，以本法第一百零九条规定的特定财产优先于对该特定财产享有担保权的权利人受偿。	**Article 132** After this Law becomes effective, the specific properties referenced in Article 109 hereof shall be used, prior to the repayment to the holders of security interests in such specific properties, to pay off the portions of wages, subsidies for medical treatment and disability, and pensions for the disabled and the families of the deceased which are due and unpaid, fees for basic pension insurance and basic medical insurance which should have been paid into the individual accounts of the employees and which are unpaid, and other compensations payable to employees under the laws and administrative regulations, which in each case is incurred prior to the promulgation date hereof and has not been paid off in full through the liquidation procedure provided in Article 113 hereof.
第一百三十三条 在本法施行前国务院规定的期限和范围内的国有企业实施破产的特殊事宜，按照国务院有关规定办理。	**Article 133** Any special matter relating to bankruptcy of a state-owned enterprise within the period and scope prescribed by State Council regulations before this Law becomes effective shall be handled in accordance with the applicable State Council regulations.
第一百三十四条 商业银行、证券公司、保险公司等金融机构有本法第二条规定情形的，国务院金融监督管理机构可以向人民法院提出对该金融机构进行重整或者破产清算的申请。国务院金融监督管理机构依法对出现重大经营风险的金融机构采取接管、托管等措施的，可以向人民法院申请中止以该金融机构为被告或者被执行人的民事诉讼程序或者执行程序。	**Article 134** If any commercial bank, securities company, insurance company or other financial institution falls within Article 2 hereof, the financial regulatory body under the State Council may file an application with the People's Court for reorganization or bankruptcy liquidation of such financial institution. If the financial regulatory body under the State Council adopts measures, in accordance with law, to take over or take custody of such financial institution in substantial business risk, it may apply to the People's Court to suspend the procedures for civil litigation or enforcement against such financial institution.
金融机构实施破产的，国务院可以依据本法和其他有关法律的规定制定实施办法。	For a financial institution to undertake bankruptcy procedures, the State Council may, according to this Law and other relevant laws, formulate corresponding measures for implementation.

第一百三十五条 其他法律规定企业法人以外的组织的清算，属于破产清算的，参照适用本法规定的程序。	**Article 135** For the liquidation of organizations other than enterprise legal persons as prescribed by other laws, which falls within the category of bankruptcy liquidation, the procedures provided under this Law shall apply as reference.
第一百三十六条 本法自2007年6月1日起施行，《中华人民共和国企业破产法(试行)》同时废止。	**Article 136** This Law shall become effective as of June 1, 2007. The *Enterprise Bankruptcy Law of the People's Republic of China (Trial Implementation)* shall be simultaneously abolished.

Please note that the above English text is an unofficial translation of the Chinese statute. While care has been taken in preparing the translation, the authors accept no responsibility for the accuracy of the translation, which should not be used or relied upon as a substitute for detailed legal advice or as a basis for formulating business decisions.

APPENDIX B
The U.S. Bankruptcy Code
(ABRIDGED)

CHAPTER 1—GENERAL PROVISIONS

Sec. 101. Definitions

In this title the following definitions shall apply:

(1) The term "accountant" means accountant authorized under applicable law to practice public accounting, and includes professional accounting association, corporation, or partnership, if so authorized.

(2) The term "affiliate" means—

(A) entity that directly or indirectly owns, controls, or holds with power to vote, 20 percent or more of the outstanding voting securities of the debtor, other than an entity that holds such securities—

(i) in a fiduciary or agency capacity without sole discretionary power to vote such securities; or

(ii) solely to secure a debt, if such entity has not in fact exercised such power to vote;

(B) corporation 20 percent or more of whose outstanding voting securities are directly or indirectly owned, controlled, or held with power to vote, by the debtor, or by an entity that directly or indirectly owns, controls, or holds with power to vote, 20 percent or more of the outstanding voting securities of the debtor, other than an entity that holds such securities—

(i) in a fiduciary or agency capacity without sole discretionary power to vote such securities; or

(ii) solely to secure a debt, if such entity has not in fact exercised such power to vote;

(C) person whose business is operated under a lease or operating agreement by a debtor, or person substantially all of whose property is operated under an operating agreement with the debtor; or

(D) entity that operates the business or substantially all of the property of the debtor under a lease or operating agreement.

(3) The term "assisted person" means any person whose debts consist primarily of consumer debts and the value of whose nonexempt property is less than $150,000.

(4) The term "attorney" means attorney, professional law association, corporation, or partnership, authorized under applicable law to practice law.

(4A) The term "bankruptcy assistance" means any goods or services sold or otherwise provided to an assisted person with the express or implied purpose of providing information, advice, counsel, document preparation, or filing, or attendance at a creditors' meeting or appearing in a case or proceeding on behalf of another or providing legal representation with respect to a case or proceeding under this title.

(5) The term "claim" means—

(A) right to payment, whether or not such right is reduced to judgment, liquidated, unliquidated, fixed, contingent, matured, unmatured, disputed, undisputed, legal, equitable, secured, or unsecured; or

(B) right to an equitable remedy for breach of performance if such breach gives rise to a right to payment, whether or not such right to an equitable remedy is reduced to judgment, fixed, contingent, matured, unmatured, disputed, undisputed, secured, or unsecured.

(6) The term "commodity broker" means futures commission merchant, foreign futures commission merchant, clearing organization, leverage transaction merchant, or commodity options dealer, as defined in section 761 of this title, with respect to which there is a customer, as defined in section 761 of this title.

(7) The term "community claim" means claim that arose before the commencement of the case concerning the debtor for which property of the kind specified in section 541(a)(2) of this title is liable, whether or not there is any such property at the time of the commencement of the case.

(7A) The term "commercial fishing operation" means—

(A) the catching or harvesting of fish, shrimp, lobsters, urchins, seaweed, shellfish, or other aquatic species or products of such species; or

(B) for purposes of section 109 and chapter 12, aquaculture activities consisting of raising for market any species or product described in subparagraph (A).

(7B) The term "commercial fishing vessel" means a vessel used by a family fisherman to carry out a commercial fishing operation.

(8) The term "consumer debt" means debt incurred by an individual primarily for a personal, family, or household purpose.

(9) The term "corporation"—

(A) includes—

(i) association having a power or privilege that a private corporation, but not an individual or a partnership, possesses;

(ii) partnership association organized under a law that makes only the capital subscribed responsible for the debts of such association;

(iii) joint-stock company;

(iv) unincorporated company or association; or

(v) business trust; but

(B) does not include limited partnership.

(10) The term "creditor" means—

(A) entity that has a claim against the debtor that arose at the time of or before the order for relief concerning the debtor;

(B) entity that has a claim against the estate of a kind specified in section 348(d), 502(f), 502(g), 502(h) or 502(i) of this title; or

(C) entity that has a community claim.

(10A) The term "current monthly income"—

(A) means the average monthly income from all sources that the debtor receives (or in a joint case the debtor and the debtor's spouse receive) without regard to whether such income is taxable income, derived during the 6-month period ending on—

(i) the last day of the calendar month immediately preceding the date of the commencement of the case if the debtor files the schedule of current income required by section 521(a)(1)(B)(ii); or

(ii) the date on which current income is determined by the court for purposes of this title if the debtor does not file the schedule of current income required by section 521(a)(1)(B)(ii); and

(B) includes any amount paid by any entity other than the debtor (or in a joint case the debtor and the debtor's spouse), on a regular basis for the household expenses of the debtor or the debtor's dependents (and in a joint case the debtor's spouse if not otherwise a dependent), but excludes benefits received under the Social Security Act, payments to victims of war crimes or crimes against humanity on account of their status as victims of such crimes, and payments to victims of international terrorism (as defined in section 2331 of title 18) or domestic terrorism (as defined in section 2331 of title 18) on account of their status as victims of such terrorism.

(11) The term "custodian" means—

(A) receiver or trustee of any of the property of the debtor, appointed in a case or proceeding not under this title;

(B) assignee under a general assignment for the benefit of the debtor's creditors; or

(C) trustee, receiver, or agent under applicable law, or under a contract, that is appointed or authorized to take charge of property of the debtor for the purpose of enforcing a lien against such property, or for the purpose of general administration of such property for the benefit of the debtor's creditors.

(12) The term "debt" means liability on a claim.

(12A) The term "debt relief agency" means any person who provides any bankruptcy assistance to an assisted person in return for the payment of money or other valuable consideration, or who is a bankruptcy petition preparer under section 110, but does not include—

(A) any person who is an officer, director, employee, or agent of a person who provides such assistance or of the bankruptcy petition preparer;

(B) a nonprofit organization that is exempt from taxation under section 501(c)(3) of the Internal Revenue Code of 1986;

(C) a creditor of such assisted person, to the extent that the creditor is assisting such assisted person to restructure any debt owed by such assisted person to the creditor;

(D) a depository institution (as defined in section 3 of the Federal Deposit Insurance Act) or any Federal credit union or State credit union (as those terms are defined in section 101 of the Federal Credit Union Act), or any affiliate or subsidiary of such depository institution or credit union; or (E) an author, publisher, distributor, or seller of works subject to copyright protection under title 17, when acting in such capacity.

(13) The term "debtor" means person or municipality concerning which a case under this title has been commenced.

(13A) The term "debtor's principal residence"—

(A) means a residential structure, including incidental property, without regard to whether that structure is attached to real property; and

(B) includes an individual condominium or cooperative unit, a mobile or manufactured home, or trailer.

(14) The term "disinterested person" means a person that—

(A) is not a creditor, an equity security holder, or an insider;

(B) is not and was not, within 2 years before the date of the filing of the petition, a director, officer, or employee of the debtor; and

(C) does not have an interest materially adverse to the interest of the estate or of any class of creditors or equity security holders, by reason of any direct or indirect relationship to, connection with, or interest in, the debtor, or for any other reason.

(14A) The term "domestic support obligation" means a debt that accrues before, on, or after the date of the order for relief in a case under this title, including interest that accrues on that debt as provided under applicable nonbankruptcy law notwithstanding any other provision of this title, that is—

(A) owed to or recoverable by—

(i) a spouse, former spouse, or child of the debtor or such child's parent, legal guardian, or responsible relative; or

(ii) a governmental unit;

(B) in the nature of alimony, maintenance, or support (including assistance provided by a governmental unit) of such spouse, former spouse, or child of the debtor or such child's parent, without regard to whether such debt is expressly so designated;

(C) established or subject to establishment before, on, or after the date of the order for relief in a case under this title, by reason of applicable provisions of—

(i) a separation agreement, divorce decree, or property settlement agreement;

(ii) an order of a court of record; or

(iii) a determination made in accordance with applicable nonbankruptcy law by a governmental unit; and

(D) not assigned to a nongovernmental entity, unless that obligation is assigned voluntarily by the spouse, former spouse, child of the debtor, or such child's parent, legal guardian, or responsible relative for the purpose of collecting the debt.

(15) The term "entity" includes person, estate, trust, governmental unit, and United States trustee.

(16) The term "equity security" means—

(A) share in a corporation, whether or not transferable or denominated "stock", or similar security;

(B) interest of a limited partner in a limited partnership; or

(C) warrant or right, other than a right to convert, to purchase, sell, or subscribe to a share, security, or interest of a kind specified in subparagraph (A) or (B) of this paragraph.

(17) The term "equity security holder" means holder of an equity security of the debtor.

(18) The term "family farmer" means—

(A) individual or individual and spouse engaged in a farming operation whose aggregate debts do not exceed $3,237,000 and not less than 50 percent of whose aggregate noncontingent, liquidated debts (excluding a debt for the principal residence of such individual or such individual and spouse unless such debt arises out of a farming operation), on the date the case is filed, arise out of a farming operation owned or operated by such individual or such individual and spouse, and such individual or such individual and spouse receive from such farming operation more than 50 percent of such individual's or such individual and spouse's gross income for—

(i) the taxable year preceding; or

(ii) each of the 2d and 3d taxable years preceding;

the taxable year in which the case concerning such individual or such individual and spouse was filed; or

(B) corporation or partnership in which more than 50 percent of the outstanding stock or equity is held by one family, or by one family and the relatives of the members of such family, and such family or such relatives conduct the farming operation, and

(i) more than 80 percent of the value of its assets consists of assets related to the farming operation;

(ii) its aggregate debts do not exceed $3,237,000 and not less than 50 percent of its aggregate noncontingent, liquidated debts (excluding a debt for one dwelling which is owned by such corporation or partnership and which a shareholder or partner maintains as a principal residence, unless such debt arises out of a farming operation), on the date the case is filed, arise out of the farming operation owned or operated by such corporation or such partnership; and

(iii) if such corporation issues stock, such stock is not publicly traded.

(19) The term "family farmer with regular annual income" means family farmer whose annual income is sufficiently stable and regular to enable such family farmer to make payments under a plan under chapter 12 of this title.

(19A) The term "family fisherman" means—

(A) an individual or individual and spouse engaged in a commercial fishing operation—

(i) whose aggregate debts do not exceed $1,500,000 and not less than 80 percent of whose aggregate noncontingent, liquidated debts (excluding a debt for the principal residence of such individual or such individual and spouse, unless such debt arises out of a commercial fishing operation), on the date the case is filed, arise out of a commercial fishing operation owned or operated by such individual or such individual and spouse; and

(ii) who receive from such commercial fishing operation more than 50 percent of such individual's or such individual's and spouse's gross income for the taxable year preceding the taxable year in which the case concerning such individual or such individual and spouse was filed; or

(B) a corporation or partnership—

(i) in which more than 50 percent of the outstanding stock or equity is held by—

(I) 1 family that conducts the commercial fishing operation; or

(II) 1 family and the relatives of the members of such family, and such family or such relatives conduct the commercial fishing operation; and

(ii) (I) more than 80 percent of the value of its assets consists of assets related to the commercial fishing operation;

(II) its aggregate debts do not exceed $1,500,000 and not less than 80 percent of its aggregate noncontingent, liquidated debts (excluding a debt for 1 dwelling which is owned by such corporation or partnership and which a shareholder or partner maintains as a principal residence, unless such debt arises out of a commercial fishing operation), on the date the case is filed, arise out of a commercial fishing operation owned or operated by such corporation or such partnership; and

(III) if such corporation issues stock, such stock is not publicly traded.

(19B) The term "family fisherman with regular annual income" means a family fisherman whose annual income is sufficiently stable and regular to enable such family fisherman to make payments under a plan under chapter 12 of this title.

(20) The term "farmer" means (except when such term appears in the term "family farmer") person that received more than 80 percent of such person's gross income during the taxable year of such person immediately preceding the taxable year of such person during which the case under this title concerning such person was commenced from a farming operation owned or operated by such person.

(21) The term "farming operation" includes farming, tillage of the soil, dairy farming, ranching, production or raising of crops, poultry, or livestock, and production of poultry or livestock products in an unmanufactured state.

(21A) The term "farmout agreement" means a written agreement in which—

(A) the owner of a right to drill, produce, or operate liquid or gaseous hydrocarbons on property agrees or has agreed to transfer or assign all or a part of such right to another entity; and

(B) such other entity (either directly or through its agents or its assigns), as consideration, agrees to perform drilling, reworking, recompleting, testing, or similar or related operations, to develop or produce liquid or gaseous hydrocarbons on the property.

(21B) The term "Federal depository institutions regulatory agency" means—

(A) with respect to an insured depository institution (as defined in section 3(c)(2) of the Federal Deposit Insurance Act) for which no conservator or receiver has been appointed, the appropriate Federal banking agency (as defined in section 3(q) of such Act);

(B) with respect to an insured credit union (including an insured credit union for which the National Credit Union Administration has been appointed conservator or liquidating agent), the National Credit Union Administration;

(C) with respect to any insured depository institution for which the Resolution Trust Corporation has been appointed conservator or receiver, the Resolution Trust Corporation; and

(D) with respect to any insured depository institution for which the Federal Deposit Insurance Corporation has been appointed conservator or receiver, the Federal Deposit Insurance Corporation.

(22) The term "financial institution" means—

(A) a Federal reserve bank, or an entity that is a commercial or savings bank, industrial savings bank, savings and loan association, trust company, federally-insured credit union, or receiver, liquidating agent, or conservator for such entity and, when any such Federal reserve bank, receiver, liquidating agent, conservator or entity is acting as agent or custodian for a customer (whether or not a "customer", as defined in section 741) in connection with a securities contract (as defined in section 741) such customer; or

(B) in connection with a securities contract (as defined in section 741) an investment company registered under the Investment Company Act of 1940.

(22A) The term "financial participant" means—

(A) an entity that, at the time it enters into a securities contract, commodity contract, swap agreement, repurchase agreement, or forward contract, or at the time of the date of the filing of the petition, has one or more agreements or transactions described in paragraph (1), (2), (3), (4), (5), or (6) of section 561(a) with the debtor or any other entity (other than an affiliate) of a total gross dollar value of not less than $1,000,000,000 in notional or actual principal amount outstanding (aggregated across counterparties) at such time or on any day during the 15-month period preceding the date of the filing of the petition, or has gross mark-to-market positions of not less than $100,000,000 (aggregated across counterparties) in one or more such agreements or transactions with the debtor or any other entity (other than an affiliate) at such time or on any day during the 15-month period preceding the date of the filing of the petition; or

(B) a clearing organization (as defined in section 402 of the Federal Deposit Insurance Corporation Improvement Act of 1991).

(23) The term "foreign proceeding" means a collective judicial or administrative proceeding in a foreign country, including an interim proceeding, under a law relating to insolvency or adjustment of debt in which proceeding the assets and affairs of the debtor are subject to control or supervision by a foreign court, for the purpose of reorganization or liquidation.

(24) The term "foreign representative" means a person or body, including a person or body appointed on an interim basis, authorized in a foreign proceeding to administer the reorganization or the liquidation of the debtor's assets or affairs or to act as a representative of such foreign proceeding.

(25) The term "forward contract" means—

(A) a contract (other than a commodity contract, as defined in section 761) for the purchase, sale, or transfer of a commodity, as defined in section 761(8) of this title, or any similar good, article, service, right, or interest which is presently or in the future becomes the subject of dealing in the forward contract trade, or product or byproduct thereof, with a maturity date more than two days after the date the contract is entered into, including, but not limited to, a repurchase or reverse repurchase transaction (whether or not such repurchase or reverse repurchase transaction is a "repurchase agreement", as defined in this section)[1] consignment, lease, swap, hedge transaction, deposit, loan, option, allocated transaction, unallocated transaction, or any other similar agreement;

(B) any combination of agreements or transactions referred to in subparagraphs (A) and (C);

(C) any option to enter into an agreement or transaction referred to in subparagraph (A) or (B);

(D) a master agreement that provides for an agreement or transaction referred to in subparagraph (A), (B), or (C), together with all supplements to any such master agreement, without regard to whether such master agreement provides for an agreement or transaction that is not a forward contract under this paragraph, except that such master agreement shall be considered to be a forward contract under this paragraph only with respect to each agreement or transaction under such master agreement that is referred to in subparagraph (A), (B), or (C); or

(E) any security agreement or arrangement, or other credit enhancement related to any agreement or transaction referred to in subparagraph (A), (B), (C), or (D), including any guarantee or reimbursement obligation by or to a forward contract merchant or

---

[1] *Sic.* Probably should be followed by a comma.

financial participant in connection with any agreement or transaction referred to in any such subparagraph, but not to exceed the damages in connection with any such agreement or transaction, measured in accordance with section 562.

(26) The term "forward contract merchant" means a Federal reserve bank, or an entity the business of which consists in whole or in part of entering into forward contracts as or with merchants in a commodity (as defined in section 761) or any similar good, article, service, right, or interest which is presently or in the future becomes the subject of dealing in the forward contract trade.

(27) The term "governmental unit" means United States; State; Commonwealth; District; Territory; municipality; foreign state; department, agency, or instrumentality of the United States (but not a United States trustee while serving as a trustee in a case under this title), a State, a Commonwealth, a District, a Territory, a municipality, or a foreign state; or other foreign or domestic government.

(27A) The term "health care business"—

(A) means any public or private entity (without regard to whether that entity is organized for profit or not for profit) that is primarily engaged in offering to the general public facilities and services for—

(i) the diagnosis or treatment of injury, deformity, or disease; and

(ii) surgical, drug treatment, psychiatric, or obstetric care; and

(B) includes—

(i) any—

(I) general or specialized hospital;

(II) ancillary ambulatory, emergency, or surgical treatment facility;

(III) hospice;

(IV) home health agency; and

(V) other health care institution that is similar to an entity referred to in subclause (I), (II), (III), or (IV); and

(ii) any long-term care facility, including any—

(I) skilled nursing facility;

(II) intermediate care facility;

(III) assisted living facility;

(IV) home for the aged;

(V) domiciliary care facility; and

(VI) health care institution that is related to a facility referred to in subclause (I), (II), (III), (IV), or (V), if that institution is primarily engaged in offering room, board, laundry, or personal assistance with activities of daily living and incidentals to activities of daily living.

(27B) The term "incidental property" means, with respect to a debtor's principal residence—

(A) property commonly conveyed with a principal residence in the area where the real property is located;

(B) all easements, rights, appurtenances, fixtures, rents, royalties, mineral rights, oil or gas rights or profits, water rights, escrow funds, or insurance proceeds; and

(C) all replacements or additions.

(28) The term "indenture" means mortgage, deed of trust, or indenture, under which there is outstanding a security, other than a voting-trust certificate, constituting a claim against

the debtor, a claim secured by a lien on any of the debtor's property, or an equity security of the debtor.

(29) The term "indenture trustee" means trustee under an indenture.

(30) The term "individual with regular income" means individual whose income is sufficiently stable and regular to enable such individual to make payments under a plan under chapter 13 of this title, other than a stockbroker or a commodity broker.

(31) The term "insider" includes—

(A) if the debtor is an individual—

(i) relative of the debtor or of a general partner of the debtor;

(ii) partnership in which the debtor is a general partner;

(iii) general partner of the debtor; or

(iv) corporation of which the debtor is a director, officer, or person in control;

(B) if the debtor is a corporation—

(i) director of the debtor;

(ii) officer of the debtor;

(iii) person in control of the debtor;

(iv) partnership in which the debtor is a general partner;

(v) general partner of the debtor; or

(vi) relative of a general partner, director, officer, or person in control of the debtor;

(C) if the debtor is a partnership—

(i) general partner in the debtor;

(ii) relative of a general partner in, general partner of, or person in control of the debtor;

(iii) partnership in which the debtor is a general partner;

(iv) general partner of the debtor; or

(v) person in control of the debtor;

(D) if the debtor is a municipality, elected official of the debtor or relative of an elected official of the debtor;

(E) affiliate, or insider of an affiliate as if such affiliate were the debtor; and

(F) managing agent of the debtor.

(32) The term "insolvent" means—

(A) with reference to an entity other than a partnership and a municipality, financial condition such that the sum of such entity's debts is greater than all of such entity's property, at a fair valuation, exclusive of—

(i) property transferred, concealed, or removed with intent to hinder, delay, or defraud such entity's creditors; and

(ii) property that may be exempted from property of the estate under section 522 of this title;

(B) with reference to a partnership, financial condition such that the sum of such partnership's debts is greater than the aggregate of, at a fair valuation—

(i) all of such partnership's property, exclusive of property of the kind specified in subparagraph (A)(i) of this paragraph; and

(ii) the sum of the excess of the value of each general partner's nonpartnership property, exclusive of property of the kind specified in subparagraph (A) of this paragraph, over such partner's nonpartnership debts; and

(C) with reference to a municipality, financial condition such that the municipality is—
(i) generally not paying its debts as they become due unless such debts are the subject of a bona fide dispute; or
(ii) unable to pay its debts as they become due.

(33) The term "institution-affiliated party"—
(A) with respect to an insured depository institution (as defined in section 3(c)(2) of the Federal Deposit Insurance Act), has the meaning given it in section 3(u) of the Federal Deposit Insurance Act; and
(B) with respect to an insured credit union, has the meaning given it in section 206(r) of the Federal Credit Union Act.

(34) The term "insured credit union" has the meaning given it in section 101(7) of the Federal Credit Union Act.

(35) The term "insured depository institution"—
(A) has the meaning given it in section 3(c)(2) of the Federal Deposit Insurance Act; and
(B) includes an insured credit union (except in the case of paragraphs (23) and (35) of this subsection).

(35A) The term "intellectual property" means—
(A) trade secret;
(B) invention, process, design, or plant protected under title 35;
(C) patent application;
(D) plant variety;
(E) work of authorship protected under title 17; or
(F) mask work protected under chapter 9 of title 17;
to the extent protected by applicable nonbankruptcy law.

(36) The term "judicial lien" means lien obtained by judgment, levy, sequestration, or other legal or equitable process or proceeding.

(37) The term "lien" means charge against or interest in property to secure payment of a debt or performance of an obligation.

(38) The term "margin payment" means, for purposes of the forward contract provisions of this title, payment or deposit of cash, a security or other property, that is commonly known in the forward contract trade as original margin, initial margin, maintenance margin, or variation margin, including mark-to-market payments, or variation payments.

(38A) The term "master netting agreement"—
(A) means an agreement providing for the exercise of rights, including rights of netting, setoff, liquidation, termination, acceleration, or close out, under or in connection with one or more contracts that are described in any one or more of paragraphs (1) through (5) of section 561(a), or any security agreement or arrangement or other credit enhancement related to one or more of the foregoing, including any guarantee or reimbursement obligation related to 1 or more of the foregoing; and
(B) if the agreement contains provisions relating to agreements or transactions that are not contracts described in paragraphs (1) through (5) of section 561(a), shall be deemed to be a master netting agreement only with respect to those agreements or transactions that are described in any one or more of paragraphs (1) through (5) of section 561(a).

(38B) The term "master netting agreement participant" means an entity that, at any time before the date of the filing of the petition, is a party to an outstanding master netting agreement with the debtor.

(39) The term "mask work" has the meaning given it in section 901(a)(2) of title 17.

(39A) The term "median family income" means for any year—

(A) the median family income both calculated and reported by the Bureau of the Census in the then most recent year; and

(B) if not so calculated and reported in the then current year, adjusted annually after such most recent year until the next year in which median family income is both calculated and reported by the Bureau of the Census, to reflect the percentage change in the Consumer Price Index for All Urban Consumers during the period of years occurring after such most recent year and before such current year.

(40) The term "municipality" means political subdivision or public agency or instrumentality of a State.

(40A) The term "patient" means any individual who obtains or receives services from a health care business.

(40B) The term "patient records" means any written document relating to a patient or a record recorded in a magnetic, optical, or other form of electronic medium.

(41) The term "person" includes individual, partnership, and corporation, but does not include governmental unit, except that a governmental unit that—

(A) acquires an asset from a person—

(i) as a result of the operation of a loan guarantee agreement; or

(ii) as receiver or liquidating agent of a person;

(B) is a guarantor of a pension benefit payable by or on behalf of the debtor or an affiliate of the debtor; or

(C) is the legal or beneficial owner of an asset of—

(i) an employee pension benefit plan that is a governmental plan, as defined in section 414(d) of the Internal Revenue Code of 1986; or

(ii) an eligible deferred compensation plan, as defined in section 457(b) of the Internal Revenue Code of 1986;

shall be considered, for purposes of section 1102 of this title, to be a person with respect to such asset or such benefit.

(41A) The term "personally identifiable information" means—

(A) if provided by an individual to the debtor in connection with obtaining a product or a service from the debtor primarily for personal, family, or household purposes—

(i) the first name (or initial) and last name of such individual, whether given at birth or time of adoption, or resulting from a lawful change of name;

(ii) the geographical address of a physical place of residence of such individual;

(iii) an electronic address (including an e-mail address) of such individual;

(iv) a telephone number dedicated to contacting such individual at such physical place of residence;

(v) a social security account number issued to such individual; or

(vi) the account number of a credit card issued to such individual; or

(B) if identified in connection with 1 or more of the items of information specified in subparagraph (A)—

(i) a birth date, the number of a certificate of birth or adoption, or a place of birth; or

(ii) any other information concerning an identified individual that, if disclosed, will result in contacting or identifying such individual physically or electronically.

(42) The term "petition" means petition filed under section 301, 302, 303, or 304 of this title,[2] as the case may be, commencing a case under this title.

(42A) The term "production payment" means a term overriding royalty satisfiable in cash or in kind—

(A) contingent on the production of a liquid or gaseous hydrocarbon from particular real property; and

(B) from a specified volume, or a specified value, from the liquid or gaseous hydrocarbon produced from such property, and determined without regard to production costs.

(43) The term "purchaser" means transferee of a voluntary transfer, and includes immediate or mediate transferee of such a transferee.

(44) The term "railroad" means common carrier by railroad engaged in the transportation of individuals or property or owner of trackage facilities leased by such a common carrier.

(45) The term "relative" means individual related by affinity or consanguinity within the third degree as determined by the common law, or individual in a step or adoptive relationship within such third degree.

(46) The term "repo participant" means an entity that, at any time before the filing of the petition, has an outstanding repurchase agreement with the debtor.

(47) The term "repurchase agreement" (which definition also applies to a reverse repurchase agreement)—

(A) means—

(i) an agreement, including related terms, which provides for the transfer of one or more certificates of deposit, mortgage related securities (as defined in section 3 of the Securities Exchange Act of 1934), mortgage loans, interests in mortgage related securities or mortgage loans, eligible bankers' acceptances, qualified foreign government securities (defined as a security that is a direct obligation of, or that is fully guaranteed by, the central government of a member of the Organization for Economic Cooperation and Development), or securities that are direct obligations of, or that are fully guaranteed by, the United States or any agency of the United States against the transfer of funds by the transferee of such certificates of deposit, eligible bankers' acceptances, securities, mortgage loans, or interests, with a simultaneous agreement by such transferee to transfer to the transferor thereof certificates of deposit, eligible bankers' acceptance, securities, mortgage loans, or interests of the kind described in this clause, at a date certain not later than 1 year after such transfer or on demand, against the transfer of funds;

(ii) any combination of agreements or transactions referred to in clauses (i) and (iii);

(iii) an option to enter into an agreement or transaction referred to in clause (i) or (ii);

(iv) a master agreement that provides for an agreement or transaction referred to

---

[2] *Sic.* Section 304 of this title has been repealed.

in clause (i), (ii), or (iii), together with all supplements to any such master agreement, without regard to whether such master agreement provides for an agreement or transaction that is not a repurchase agreement under this paragraph, except that such master agreement shall be considered to be a repurchase agreement under this paragraph only with respect to each agreement or transaction under the master agreement that is referred to in clause (i), (ii), or (iii); or

(v) any security agreement or arrangement or other credit enhancement related to any agreement or transaction referred to in clause (i), (ii), (iii), or (iv), including any guarantee or reimbursement obligation by or to a repo participant or financial participant in connection with any agreement or transaction referred to in any such clause, but not to exceed the damages in connection with any such agreement or transaction, measured in accordance with section 562 of this title; and

(B) does not include a repurchase obligation under a participation in a commercial mortgage loan.

(48) The term "securities clearing agency" means person that is registered as a clearing agency under section 17A of the Securities Exchange Act of 1934, or exempt from such registration under such section pursuant to an order of the Securities and Exchange Commission, or whose business is confined to the performance of functions of a clearing agency with respect to exempted securities, as defined in section 3(a)(12) of such Act for the purposes of such section 17A.

(48A) The term "securities self regulatory organization" means either a securities association registered with the Securities and Exchange Commission under section 15A of the Securities Exchange Act of 1934 or a national securities exchange registered with the Securities and Exchange Commission under section 6 of the Securities Exchange Act of 1934.

(49) The term "security"—

(A) includes—

(i) note;

(ii) stock;

(iii) treasury stock;

(iv) bond;

(v) debenture;

(vi) collateral trust certificate;

(vii) pre-organization certificate or subscription;

(viii) transferable share;

(ix) voting-trust certificate;

(x) certificate of deposit;

(xi) certificate of deposit for security;

(xii) investment contract or certificate of interest or participation in a profit-sharing agreement or in an oil, gas, or mineral royalty or lease, if such contract or interest is required to be the subject of a registration statement filed with the Securities and Exchange Commission under the provisions of the Securities Act of 1933, or is exempt under section 3(b) of such Act from the requirement to file such a statement;

(xiii) interest of a limited partner in a limited partnership;

(xiv) other claim or interest commonly known as "security"; and

(xv) certificate of interest or participation in, temporary or interim certificate for, receipt for, or warrant or right to subscribe to or purchase or sell, a security; but

(B) does not include—

(i) currency, check, draft, bill of exchange, or bank letter of credit;

(ii) leverage transaction, as defined in section 761 of this title;

(iii) commodity futures contract or forward contract;

(iv) option, warrant, or right to subscribe to or purchase or sell a commodity futures contract;

(v) option to purchase or sell a commodity;

(vi) contract or certificate of a kind specified in subparagraph (A)(xii) of this paragraph that is not required to be the subject of a registration statement filed with the Securities and Exchange Commission and is not exempt under section 3(b) of the Securities Act of 1933 from the requirement to file such a statement; or

(vii) debt or evidence of indebtedness for goods sold and delivered or services rendered.

(50) The term "security agreement" means agreement that creates or provides for a security interest.

(51) The term "security interest" means lien created by an agreement.

(51A) The term "settlement payment" means, for purposes of the forward contract provisions of this title, a preliminary settlement payment, a partial settlement payment, an interim settlement payment, a settlement payment on account, a final settlement payment, a net settlement payment, or any other similar payment commonly used in the forward contract trade.

(51B) The term "single asset real estate" means real property constituting a single property or project, other than residential real property with fewer than 4 residential units, which generates substantially all of the gross income of a debtor who is not a family farmer and on which no substantial business is being conducted by a debtor other than the business of operating the real property and activities incidental.

(51C) The term "small business case" means a case filed under chapter 11 of this title in which the debtor is a small business debtor.

(51D) The term "small business debtor"—

(A) subject to subparagraph (B), means a person engaged in commercial or business activities (including any affiliate of such person that is also a debtor under this title and excluding a person whose primary activity is the business of owning or operating real property or activities incidental thereto) that has aggregate noncontingent liquidated secured and unsecured debts as of the date of the petition or the date of the order for relief in an amount not more than $2,000,000 (excluding debts owed to 1 or more affiliates or insiders) for a case in which the United States trustee has not appointed under section 1102(a)(1) a committee of unsecured creditors or where the court has determined that the committee of unsecured creditors is not sufficiently active and representative to provide effective oversight of the debtor; and

(B) does not include any member of a group of affiliated debtors that has aggregate noncontingent liquidated secured and unsecured debts in an amount greater than $2,000,000 (excluding debt owed to 1 or more affiliates or insiders).

(52) The term "State" includes the District of Columbia and Puerto Rico, except for the purpose of defining who may be a debtor under chapter 9 of this title.

(53) The term "statutory lien" means lien arising solely by force of a statute on specified circumstances or conditions, or lien of distress for rent, whether or not statutory, but does not include security interest or judicial lien, whether or not such interest or lien is provided by or is dependent on a statute and whether or not such interest or lien is made fully effective by statute.

(53A) The term "stockbroker" means person—

(A) with respect to which there is a customer, as defined in section 741 of this title; and

(B) that is engaged in the business of effecting transactions in securities—

(i) for the account of others; or

(ii) with members of the general public, from or for such person's own account.

(53B) The term "swap agreement"—

(A) means—

(i) any agreement, including the terms and conditions incorporated by reference in such agreement, which is—

(I) an interest rate swap, option, future, or forward agreement, including a rate floor, rate cap, rate collar, cross-currency rate swap, and basis swap;

(II) a spot, same day-tomorrow, tomorrow-next, forward, or other foreign exchange, precious metals, or other commodity agreement;

(III) a currency swap, option, future, or forward agreement;

(IV) an equity index or equity swap, option, future, or forward agreement;

(V) a debt index or debt swap, option, future, or forward agreement;

(VI) a total return, credit spread or credit swap, option, future, or forward agreement;

(VII) a commodity index or a commodity swap, option, future, or forward agreement;

(VIII) a weather swap, option, future, or forward agreement;

(IX) an emissions swap, option, future, or forward agreement; or

(X) an inflation swap, option, future, or forward agreement;

(ii) any agreement or transaction that is similar to any other agreement or transaction referred to in this paragraph and that—

(I) is of a type that has been, is presently, or in the future becomes, the subject of recurrent dealings in the swap or other derivatives markets (including terms and conditions incorporated by reference therein); and

(II) is a forward, swap, future, option, or spot transaction on one or more rates, currencies, commodities, equity securities, or other equity instruments, debt securities or other debt instruments, quantitative measures associated with an occurrence, extent of an occurrence, or contingency associated with a financial, commercial, or economic consequence, or economic or financial indices or measures of economic or financial risk or value;

(iii) any combination of agreements or transactions referred to in this subparagraph;

(iv) any option to enter into an agreement or transaction referred to in this subparagraph;

(v) a master agreement that provides for an agreement or transaction referred to in clause (i), (ii), (iii), or (iv), together with all supplements to any such master agreement, and without regard to whether the master agreement contains an agreement or transaction that is not a swap agreement under this paragraph, except that the master agreement shall be considered to be a swap agreement under this paragraph only with respect to each agreement or transaction under the master agreement that is referred to in clause (i), (ii), (iii), or (iv); or

(vi) any security agreement or arrangement or other credit enhancement related to any agreements or transactions referred to in clause (i) through (v), including any guarantee or reimbursement obligation by or to a swap participant or financial participant in connection with any agreement or transaction referred to in any such clause, but not to exceed the damages in connection with any such agreement or transaction, measured in accordance with section 562; and

(B) is applicable for purposes of this title only, and shall not be construed or applied so as to challenge or affect the characterization, definition, or treatment of any swap agreement under any other statute, regulation, or rule, including the Gramm-Leach-Bliley Act, the Legal Certainty for Bank Products Act of 2000, the securities laws (as such term is defined in section 3(a)(47) of the Securities Exchange Act of 1934) and the Commodity Exchange Act.

(53C) The term "swap participant" means an entity that, at any time before the filing of the petition, has an outstanding swap agreement with the debtor.

(56A)[3] The term "term overriding royalty" means an interest in liquid or gaseous hydrocarbons in place or to be produced from particular real property that entitles the owner thereof to a share of production, or the value thereof, for a term limited by time, quantity, or value realized.

(53D) The term "timeshare plan" means and shall include that interest purchased in any arrangement, plan, scheme, or similar device, but not including exchange programs, whether by membership, agreement, tenancy in common, sale, lease, deed, rental agreement, license, right to use agreement, or by any other means, whereby a purchaser, in exchange for consideration, receives a right to use accommodations, facilities, or recreational sites, whether improved or unimproved, for a specific period of time less than a full year during any given year, but not necessarily for consecutive years, and which extends for a period of more than three years. A "timeshare interest" is that interest purchased in a timeshare plan which grants the purchaser the right to use and occupy accommodations, facilities, or recreational sites, whether improved or unimproved, pursuant to a timeshare plan.

(54) The term "transfer" means—

(A) the creation of a lien;

(B) the retention of title as a security interest;

(C) the foreclosure of a debtor's equity of redemption; or

---

[3] *Sic.*

(D) each mode, direct or indirect, absolute or conditional, voluntary or involuntary, of disposing of or parting with—
(i) property; or
(ii) an interest in property.

(54A) The term "uninsured State member bank" means a State member bank (as defined in section 3 of the Federal Deposit Insurance Act) the deposits of which are not insured by the Federal Deposit Insurance Corporation.

(55) The term "United States", when used in a geographical sense, includes all locations where the judicial jurisdiction of the United States extends, including territories and possessions of the United States.

Sec. 102. Rules of construction

In this title—

(1) "after notice and a hearing", or a similar phrase—
(A) means after such notice as is appropriate in the particular circumstances, and such opportunity for a hearing as is appropriate in the particular circumstances; but
(B) authorizes an act without an actual hearing if such notice is given properly and if—
(i) such a hearing is not requested timely by a party in interest; or
(ii) there is insufficient time for a hearing to be commenced before such act must be done, and the court authorizes such act;

(2) "claim against the debtor" includes claim against property of the debtor;

(3) "includes" and "including" are not limiting;

(4) "may not" is prohibitive, and not permissive;

(5) "or" is not exclusive;

(6) "order for relief" means entry of an order for relief;

(7) the singular includes the plural;

(8) a definition, contained in a section of this title that refers to another section of this title, does not, for the purpose of such reference, affect the meaning of a term used in such other section; and

(9) "United States trustee" includes a designee of the United States trustee.

Sec. 103. Applicability of chapters

(a) Except as provided in section 1161 of this title, chapters 1, 3, and 5 of this title apply in a case under chapter 7, 11, 12, or 13 of this title, and this chapter, sections 307, 362(n), 555 through 557, and 559 through 562 apply in a case under chapter 15.

(b) Subchapters I and II of chapter 7 of this title apply only in a case under such chapter.

(c) Subchapter III of chapter 7 of this title applies only in a case under such chapter concerning a stockbroker.

(d) Subchapter IV of chapter 7 of this title applies only in a case under such chapter concerning a commodity broker.

(e) Scope of Application.—Subchapter V of chapter 7 of this title shall apply only in a case under such chapter concerning the liquidation of an uninsured State member bank, or a corporation organized under section 25A of the Federal Reserve Act, which operates, or operates as, a multilateral clearing organization pursuant to section 409 of the Federal Deposit Insurance Corporation Improvement Act of 1991.

(f) Except as provided in section 901 of this title, only chapters 1 and 9 of this title apply in a case under such chapter 9.

(g) Except as provided in section 901 of this title, subchapters I, II, and III of chapter 11 of this title apply only in a case under such chapter.

(h) Subchapter IV of chapter 11 of this title applies only in a case under such chapter concerning a railroad.

(i) Chapter 13 of this title applies only in a case under such chapter.

(j) Chapter 12 of this title applies only in a case under such chapter.

(k) Chapter 15 applies only in a case under such chapter, except that—
(1) sections 1505, 1513, and 1514 apply in all cases under this title; and
(2) section 1509 applies whether or not a case under this title is pending.

Sec. 104. Adjustment of dollar amounts

(a) The Judicial Conference of the United States shall transmit to the Congress and to the President before May 1, 1985, and before May 1 of every sixth year after May 1, 1985, a recommendation for the uniform percentage adjustment of each dollar amount in this title and in section 1930 of title 28.

(b) (1) On April 1, 1998, and at each 3-year interval ending on April 1 thereafter, each dollar amount in effect under sections 101(3), 101(18), 101(19A), 101(51D), 109(e), 303(b), 507(a), 522(d), 522(f)(3) and 522(f)(4), 522(n), 522(p), 522(q), 523(a)(2)(C), 541(b), 547(c)(9), 707(b), 1322(d), 1325(b), and 1326(b)(3) of this title and section 1409(b) of title 28 immediately before such April 1 shall be adjusted—
(A) to reflect the change in the Consumer Price Index for All Urban Consumers, published by the Department of Labor, for the most recent 3-year period ending immediately before January 1 preceding such April 1, and
(B) to round to the nearest $25 the dollar amount that represents such change.

(2) Not later than March 1, 1998, and at each 3-year interval ending on March 1 thereafter, the Judicial Conference of the United States shall publish in the Federal Register the dollar amounts that will become effective on such April 1 under sections 101(3), 101(18), 101(19A), 101(51D), 109(e), 303(b), 507(a), 522(d), 522(f)(3) and 522(f)(4), 522(n), 522(p), 522(q), 523(a)(2)(C), 541(b), 547(c)(9), 707(b), 1322(d), 1325(b), and 1326(b)(3) of this title and section 1409(b) of title 28.

(3) Adjustments made in accordance with paragraph (1) shall not apply with respect to cases commenced before the date of such adjustments.

Sec. 105. Power of court

(a) The court may issue any order, process, or judgment that is necessary or appropriate to carry out the provisions of this title. No provision of this title providing for the raising of an issue by a party in interest shall be construed to preclude the court from, sua sponte, taking any action or making any determination necessary or appropriate to enforce or implement court orders or rules, or to prevent an abuse of process.

(b) Notwithstanding subsection (a) of this section, a court may not appoint a receiver in a case under this title.

(c) The ability of any district judge or other officer or employee of a district court to exercise any of the authority or responsibilities conferred upon the court under this title shall be determined by reference to the provisions relating to such judge, officer, or employee set forth in title 28.

This subsection shall not be interpreted to exclude bankruptcy judges and other officers or employees appointed pursuant to chapter 6 of title 28 from its operation.

(d) The court, on its own motion or on the request of a party in interest—

(1) shall hold such status conferences as are necessary to further the expeditious and economical resolution of the case; and

(2) unless inconsistent with another provision of this title or with applicable Federal Rules of Bankruptcy Procedure, issue an order at any such conference prescribing such limitations and conditions as the court deems appropriate to ensure that the case is handled expeditiously and economically, including an order that—

(A) sets the date by which the trustee must assume or reject an executory contract or unexpired lease; or

(B) in a case under chapter 11 of this title—

(i) sets a date by which the debtor, or trustee if one has been appointed, shall file a disclosure statement and plan;

(ii) sets a date by which the debtor, or trustee if one has been appointed, shall solicit acceptances of a plan;

(iii) sets the date by which a party in interest other than a debtor may file a plan;

(iv) sets a date by which a proponent of a plan, other than the debtor, shall solicit acceptances of such plan;

(v) fixes the scope and format of the notice to be provided regarding the hearing on approval of the disclosure statement; or

(vi) provides that the hearing on approval of the disclosure statement may be combined with the hearing on confirmation of the plan.

Sec. 106. Waiver of sovereign immunity

(a) Notwithstanding an assertion of sovereign immunity, sovereign immunity is abrogated as to a governmental unit to the extent set forth in this section with respect to the following:

(1) Sections 105, 106, 107, 108, 303, 346, 362, 363, 364, 365, 366, 502, 503, 505, 506, 510, 522, 523, 524, 525, 542, 543, 544, 545, 546, 547, 548, 549, 550, 551, 552, 553, 722, 724, 726, 728,[4] 744, 749, 764, 901, 922, 926, 928, 929, 944, 1107, 1141, 1142, 1143, 1146, 1201, 1203, 1205, 1206, 1227, 1231, 1301, 1303, 1305, and 1327 of this title.

(2) The court may hear and determine any issue arising with respect to the application of such sections to governmental units.

(3) The court may issue against a governmental unit an order, process, or judgment under such sections or the Federal Rules of Bankruptcy Procedure, including an order or judgment awarding a money recovery, but not including an award of punitive damages. Such order or judgment for costs or fees under this title or the Federal Rules of Bankruptcy Procedure against any governmental unit shall be consistent with the provisions and limitations of section 2412(d)(2)(A) of title 28.

(4) The enforcement of any such order, process, or judgment against any governmental unit shall be consistent with appropriate nonbankruptcy law applicable to such governmental unit and, in the case of a money judgment against the United States, shall be paid as if it is a judgment rendered by a district court of the United States.

(5) Nothing in this section shall create any substantive claim for relief or cause of action

[4] *Sic.* Section 728 of this title has been repealed.

not otherwise existing under this title, the Federal Rules of Bankruptcy Procedure, or nonbankruptcy law.

(b) A governmental unit that has filed a proof of claim in the case is deemed to have waived sovereign immunity with respect to a claim against such governmental unit that is property of the estate and that arose out of the same transaction or occurrence out of which the claim of such governmental unit arose.

(c) Notwithstanding any assertion of sovereign immunity by a governmental unit, there shall be offset against a claim or interest of a governmental unit any claim against such governmental unit that is property of the estate.

Sec. 107. Public access to papers

(a) Except as provided in subsections (b) and (c) of this section and subject to section 112, a paper filed in a case under this title and the dockets of a bankruptcy court are public records and open to examination by an entity at reasonable times without charge.

(b) On request of a party in interest, the bankruptcy court shall, and on the bankruptcy court's own motion, the bankruptcy court may—

(1) protect an entity with respect to a trade secret or confidential research, development, or commercial information; or

(2) protect a person with respect to scandalous or defamatory matter contained in a paper filed in a case under this title.

(c) (1) The bankruptcy court, for cause, may protect an individual, with respect to the following types of information to the extent the court finds that disclosure of such information would create undue risk of identity theft or other unlawful injury to the individual or the individual's property:

(A) Any means of identification (as defined in section 1028(d) of title 18) contained in a paper filed, or to be filed, in a case under this title.

(B) Other information contained in a paper described in subparagraph (A).

(2) Upon ex parte application demonstrating cause, the court shall provide access to information protected pursuant to paragraph (1) to an entity acting pursuant to the police or regulatory power of a domestic governmental unit.

(3) The United States trustee, bankruptcy administrator, trustee, and any auditor serving under section 586(f) of title 28—

(A) shall have full access to all information contained in any paper filed or submitted in a case under this title; and

(B) shall not disclose information specifically protected by the court under this title.

Sec. 108. Extension of time

(a) If applicable nonbankruptcy law, an order entered in a nonbankruptcy proceeding, or an agreement fixes a period within which the debtor may commence an action, and such period has not expired before the date of the filing of the petition, the trustee may commence such action only before the later of—

(1) the end of such period, including any suspension of such period occurring on or after the commencement of the case; or

(2) two years after the order for relief.

(b) Except as provided in subsection (a) of this section, if applicable nonbankruptcy law, an order entered in a nonbankruptcy proceeding, or an agreement fixes a period within which the debtor or an individual protected under section 1201 or 1301 of this title may file any pleading, demand, notice, or proof of claim or loss, cure a default, or perform any other similar act, and such period has not expired before the date of the filing of the petition, the trustee may only file, cure, or perform, as the case may be, before the later of—

(1) the end of such period, including any suspension of such period occurring on or after the commencement of the case; or

(2) 60 days after the order for relief.

(c) Except- as provided in section 524 of this title, if applicable nonbankruptcy law, an order entered in a nonbankruptcy proceeding, or an agreement fixes a period for commencing or continuing a civil action in a court other than a bankruptcy court on a claim against the debtor, or against an individual with respect to which such individual is protected under section 1201 or 1301 of this title, and such period has not expired before the date of the filing of the petition, then such period does not expire until the later of—

(1) the end of such period, including any suspension of such period occurring on or after the commencement of the case; or

(2) 30 days after notice of the termination or expiration of the stay under section 362, 922, 1201, or 1301 of this title, as the case may be, with respect to such claim.

Sec. 109. Who may be a debtor

(a) Notwithstanding any other provision of this section, only a person that resides or has a domicile, a place of business, or property in the United States, or a municipality, may be a debtor under this title.

(b) A person may be a debtor under chapter 7 of this title only if such person is not—

(1) a railroad;

(2) a domestic insurance company, bank, savings bank, cooperative bank, savings and loan association, building and loan association, homestead association, a New Markets Venture Capital company as defined in section 351 of the Small Business Investment Act of 1958, a small business investment company licensed by the Small Business Administration under section 301 of the Small Business Investment Act of 1958, credit union, or industrial bank or similar institution which is an insured bank as defined in section 3(h) of the Federal Deposit Insurance Act, except that an uninsured State member bank, or a corporation organized under section 25A of the Federal Reserve Act, which operates, or operates as, a multilateral clearing organization pursuant to section 409 of the Federal Deposit Insurance Corporation Improvement Act of 1991 may be a debtor if a petition is filed at the direction of the Board of Governors of the Federal Reserve System; or

(3) (A) a foreign insurance company, engaged in such business in the United States; or

(B) a foreign bank, savings bank, cooperative bank, savings and loan association, building and loan association, or credit union, that has a branch or agency (as defined in section 1(b) of the International Banking Act of 1978[5] in the United States.

(c) An entity may be a debtor under chapter 9 of this title if and only if such entity—

(1) is a municipality;

(2) is specifically authorized, in its capacity as a municipality or by name, to be a debtor

---

[5] *Sic.* Probably should be followed by a closing parenthesis.

under such chapter by State law, or by a governmental officer or organization empowered by State law to authorize such entity to be a debtor under such chapter;

(3) is insolvent;

(4) desires to effect a plan to adjust such debts; and

(5) (A) has obtained the agreement of creditors holding at least a majority in amount of the claims of each class that such entity intends to impair under a plan in a case under such chapter;

(B) has negotiated in good faith with creditors and has failed to obtain the agreement of creditors holding at least a majority in amount of the claims of each class that such entity intends to impair under a plan in a case under such chapter;

(C) is unable to negotiate with creditors because such negotiation is impracticable; or

(D) reasonably believes that a creditor may attempt to obtain a transfer that is avoidable under section 547 of this title.

(d) Only a railroad, a person that may be a debtor under chapter 7 of this title (except a stockbroker or a commodity broker), and an uninsured State member bank, or a corporation organized under section 25A of the Federal Reserve Act, which operates, or operates as, a multilateral clearing organization pursuant to section 409 of the Federal Deposit Insurance Corporation Improvement Act of 1991 may be a debtor under chapter 11 of this title.

(e) Only an individual with regular income that owes, on the date of the filing of the petition, noncontingent, liquidated, unsecured debts of less than $250,000 and noncontingent, liquidated, secured debts of less than $750,000, or an individual with regular income and such individual's spouse, except a stockbroker or a commodity broker, that owe, on the date of the filing of the petition, noncontingent, liquidated, unsecured debts that aggregate less than $250,000 and noncontingent, liquidated, secured debts of less than $750,000 may be a debtor under chapter 13 of this title.

(f) Only a family farmer or family fisherman with regular annual income may be a debtor under chapter 12 of this title.

(g) Notwithstanding any other provision of this section, no individual or family farmer may be a debtor under this title who has been a debtor in a case pending under this title at any time in the preceding 180 days if—

(1) the case was dismissed by the court for willful failure of the debtor to abide by orders of the court, or to appear before the court in proper prosecution of the case; or

(2) the debtor requested and obtained the voluntary dismissal of the case following the filing of a request for relief from the automatic stay provided by section 362 of this title.

(h) (1) Subject to paragraphs (2) and (3), and notwithstanding any other provision of this section, an individual may not be a debtor under this title unless such individual has, during the 180-day period preceding the date of filing of the petition by such individual, received from an approved nonprofit budget and credit counseling agency described in section 111(a) an individual or group briefing (including a briefing conducted by telephone or on the Internet) that outlined the opportunities for available credit counseling and assisted such individual in performing a related budget analysis.

(2) (A) Paragraph (1) shall not apply with respect to a debtor who resides in a district for which the United States trustee (or the bankruptcy administrator, if any) determines that the approved nonprofit budget and credit counseling agencies for such district are not reasonably able to provide adequate services to the additional individuals

who would otherwise seek credit counseling from such agencies by reason of the requirements of paragraph (1).

(B) The United States trustee (or the bankruptcy administrator, if any) who makes a determination described in subparagraph (A) shall review such determination not later than 1 year after the date of such determination, and not less frequently than annually thereafter. Notwithstanding the preceding sentence, a nonprofit budget and credit counseling agency may be disapproved by the United States trustee (or the bankruptcy administrator, if any) at any time.

(3) (A) Subject to subparagraph (B), the requirements of paragraph (1) shall not apply with respect to a debtor who submits to the court a certification that—

(i) describes exigent circumstances that merit a waiver of the requirements of paragraph (1);

(ii) states that the debtor requested credit counseling services from an approved nonprofit budget and credit counseling agency, but was unable to obtain the services referred to in paragraph (1) during the 5-day period beginning on the date on which the debtor made that request; and

(iii) is satisfactory to the court.

(B) With respect to a debtor, an exemption under subparagraph (A) shall cease to apply to that debtor on the date on which the debtor meets the requirements of paragraph (1), but in no case may the exemption apply to that debtor after the date that is 30 days after the debtor files a petition, except that the court, for cause, may order an additional 15 days.

(4) The requirements of paragraph (1) shall not apply with respect to a debtor whom the court determines, after notice and hearing, is unable to complete those requirements because of incapacity, disability, or active military duty in a military combat zone. For the purposes of this paragraph, incapacity means that the debtor is impaired by reason of mental illness or mental deficiency so that he is incapable of realizing and making rational decisions with respect to his financial responsibilities; and "disability" means that the debtor is so physically impaired as to be unable, after reasonable effort, to participate in an in person, telephone, or Internet briefing required under paragraph (1).

Sec. 110. Penalty for persons who negligently or fraudulently prepare bankruptcy petitions

(a) In this section—

(1) "bankruptcy petition preparer" means a person, other than an attorney for the debtor or an employee of such attorney under the direct supervision of such attorney, who prepares for compensation a document for filing; and

(2) "document for filing" means a petition or any other document prepared for filing by a debtor in a United States bankruptcy court or a United States district court in connection with a case under this title.

(b) (1) A bankruptcy petition preparer who prepares a document for filing shall sign the document and print on the document the preparer's name and address. If a bankruptcy petition preparer is not an individual, then an officer, principal, responsible person, or partner of the bankruptcy petition preparer shall be required to—

(A) sign the document for filing; and

(B) print on the document the name and address of that officer, principal, responsible person, or partner.

(2) (A) Before preparing any document for filing or accepting any fees from a debtor, the bankruptcy petition preparer shall provide to the debtor a written notice which shall be on an official form prescribed by the Judicial Conference of the United States in accordance with rule 9009 of the Federal Rules of Bankruptcy Procedure.

(B) The notice under subparagraph (A)—

(i) shall inform the debtor in simple language that a bankruptcy petition preparer is not an attorney and may not practice law or give legal advice;

(ii) may contain a description of examples of legal advice that a bankruptcy petition preparer is not authorized to give, in addition to any advice that the preparer may not give by reason of subsection (e)(2); and

(iii) shall—

(I) be signed by the debtor and, under penalty of perjury, by the bankruptcy petition preparer; and

(II) be filed with any document for filing.

(c) (1) A bankruptcy petition preparer who prepares a document for filing shall place on the document, after the preparer's signature, an identifying number that identifies individuals who prepared the document.

(2) (A) Subject to subparagraph (B), for purposes of this section, the identifying number of a bankruptcy petition preparer shall be the Social Security account number of each individual who prepared the document or assisted in its preparation.

(B) If a bankruptcy petition preparer is not an individual, the identifying number of the bankruptcy petition preparer shall be the Social Security account number of the officer, principal, responsible person, or partner of the bankruptcy petition preparer.

(d) A bankruptcy petition preparer shall, not later than the time at which a document for filing is presented for the debtor's signature, furnish to the debtor a copy of the document.

(e) (1) A bankruptcy petition preparer shall not execute any document on behalf of a debtor.

(2) (A) A bankruptcy petition preparer may not offer a potential bankruptcy debtor any legal advice, including any legal advice described in subparagraph (B).

(B) The legal advice referred to in subparagraph (A) includes advising the debtor—

(i) whether—

(I) to file a petition under this title; or

(II) commencing a case under chapter 7, 11, 12, or 13 is appropriate;

(ii) whether the debtor's debts will be discharged in a case under this title;

(iii) whether the debtor will be able to retain the debtor's home, car, or other property after commencing a case under this title;

(iv) concerning—

(I) the tax consequences of a case brought under this title; or

(II) the dischargeability of tax claims;

(v) whether the debtor may or should promise to repay debts to a creditor or enter into a reaffirmation agreement with a creditor to reaffirm a debt;

(vi) concerning how to characterize the nature of the debtor's interests in property or the debtor's debts; or

(vii) concerning bankruptcy procedures and rights.

(f) A bankruptcy petition preparer shall not use the word "legal" or any similar term in any advertisements, or advertise under any category that includes the word "legal" or any similar term.

(g) A bankruptcy petition preparer shall not collect or receive any payment from the debtor or on behalf of the debtor for the court fees in connection with filing the petition.

(h) (1) The Supreme Court may promulgate rules under section 2075 of title 28, or the Judicial Conference of the United States may prescribe guidelines, for setting a maximum allowable fee chargeable by a bankruptcy petition preparer. A bankruptcy petition preparer shall notify the debtor of any such maximum amount before preparing any document for filing for a debtor or accepting any fee from the debtor.

(2) A declaration under penalty of perjury by the bankruptcy petition preparer shall be filed together with the petition, disclosing any fee received from or on behalf of the debtor within 12 months immediately prior to the filing of the case, and any unpaid fee charged to the debtor. If rules or guidelines setting a maximum fee for services have been promulgated or prescribed under paragraph (1), the declaration under this paragraph shall include a certification that the bankruptcy petition preparer complied with the notification requirement under paragraph (1).

(3) (A) The court shall disallow and order the immediate turnover to the bankruptcy trustee any fee referred to in paragraph (2) found to be in excess of the value of any services—

(i) rendered by the bankruptcy petition preparer during the 12- month period immediately preceding the date of the filing of the petition; or

(ii) found to be in violation of any rule or guideline promulgated or prescribed under paragraph (1).

(B) All fees charged by a bankruptcy petition preparer may be forfeited in any case in which the bankruptcy petition preparer fails to comply with this subsection or subsection (b), (c), (d), (e), (f), or (g).

(C) An individual may exempt any funds recovered under this paragraph under section 522(b).

(4) The debtor, the trustee, a creditor, the United States trustee (or the bankruptcy administrator, if any) or the court, on the initiative of the court, may file a motion for an order under paragraph (2).

(5) A bankruptcy petition preparer shall be fined not more than $500 for each failure to comply with a court order to turn over funds within 30 days of service of such order.

(i) (1) If a bankruptcy petition preparer violates this section or commits any act that the court finds to be fraudulent, unfair, or deceptive, on the motion of the debtor, trustee, United States trustee (or the bankruptcy administrator, if any), and after notice and a hearing, the court shall order the bankruptcy petition preparer to pay to the debtor—

(A) the debtor's actual damages;

(B) the greater of—

(i) $2,000; or

(ii) twice the amount paid by the debtor to the bankruptcy petition preparer for the preparer's services; and

(C) reasonable attorneys' fees and costs in moving for damages under this subsection.

(2) If the trustee or creditor moves for damages on behalf of the debtor under this subsection, the bankruptcy petition preparer shall be ordered to pay the movant the additional amount of $1,000 plus reasonable attorneys' fees and costs incurred.

(j) (1) A debtor for whom a bankruptcy petition preparer has prepared a document for filing, the trustee, a creditor, or the United States trustee in the district in which the bankruptcy petition preparer resides, has conducted business, or the United States trustee in any other district in which the debtor resides may bring a civil action to enjoin a bankruptcy petition preparer from engaging in any conduct in violation of this section or from further acting as a bankruptcy petition preparer.

(2) (A) In an action under paragraph (1), if the court finds that—

(i) a bankruptcy petition preparer has—

(I) engaged in conduct in violation of this section or of any provision of this title;

(II) misrepresented the preparer's experience or education as a bankruptcy petition preparer; or

(III) engaged in any other fraudulent, unfair, or deceptive conduct; and

(ii) injunctive relief is appropriate to prevent the recurrence of such conduct, the court may enjoin the bankruptcy petition preparer from engaging in such conduct.

(B) If the court finds that a bankruptcy petition preparer has continually engaged in conduct described in subclause (I), (II), or (III) of clause (i) and that an injunction prohibiting such conduct would not be sufficient to prevent such person's interference with the proper administration of this title, has not paid a penalty imposed under this section, or failed to disgorge all fees ordered by the court the court may enjoin the person from acting as a bankruptcy petition preparer.

(3) The court, as part of its contempt power, may enjoin a bankruptcy petition preparer that has failed to comply with a previous order issued under this section. The injunction under this paragraph may be issued on the motion of the court, the trustee, or the United States trustee (or the bankruptcy administrator, if any).

(4) The court shall award to a debtor, trustee, or creditor that brings a successful action under this subsection reasonable attorneys' fees and costs of the action, to be paid by the bankruptcy petition preparer.

(k) Nothing in this section shall be construed to permit activities that are otherwise prohibited by law, including rules and laws that prohibit the unauthorized practice of law.

(l) (1) A bankruptcy petition preparer who fails to comply with any provision of subsection (b), (c), (d), (e), (f), (g), or (h) may be fined not more than $500 for each such failure.

(2) The court shall triple the amount of a fine assessed under paragraph (1) in any case in which the court finds that a bankruptcy petition preparer—

(A) advised the debtor to exclude assets or income that should have been included on applicable schedules;

(B) advised the debtor to use a false Social Security account number;

(C) failed to inform the debtor that the debtor was filing for relief under this title; or

(D) prepared a document for filing in a manner that failed to disclose the identity of the bankruptcy petition preparer.

(3) A debtor, trustee, creditor, or United States trustee (or the bankruptcy administrator, if any) may file a motion for an order imposing a fine on the bankruptcy petition preparer for any violation of this section.

(4) (A) Fines imposed under this subsection in judicial districts served by United States trustees shall be paid to the United States trustee, who shall deposit an amount equal

to such fines in a special account of the United States Trustee System Fund referred to in section 586(e)(2) of title 28. Amounts deposited under this subparagraph shall be available to fund the enforcement of this section on a national basis.

(B) Fines imposed under this subsection in judicial districts served by bankruptcy administrators shall be deposited as offsetting receipts to the fund established under section 1931 of title 28, and shall remain available until expended to reimburse any appropriation for the amount paid out of such appropriation for expenses of the operation and maintenance of the courts of the United States.

Sec. 111. Nonprofit budget and credit counseling agencies; financial management instructional courses

(a) The clerk shall maintain a publicly available list of—

(1) nonprofit budget and credit counseling agencies that provide 1 or more services described in section 109(h) currently approved by the United States trustee (or the bankruptcy administrator, if any); and

(2) instructional courses concerning personal financial management currently approved by the United States trustee (or the bankruptcy administrator, if any), as applicable.

(b) The United States trustee (or bankruptcy administrator, if any) shall only approve a nonprofit budget and credit counseling agency or an instructional course concerning personal financial management as follows:

(1) The United States trustee (or bankruptcy administrator, if any) shall have thoroughly reviewed the qualifications of the nonprofit budget and credit counseling agency or of the provider of the instructional course under the standards set forth in this section, and the services or instructional courses that will be offered by such agency or such provider, and may require such agency or such provider that has sought approval to provide information with respect to such review.

(2) The United States trustee (or bankruptcy administrator, if any) shall have determined that such agency or such instructional course fully satisfies the applicable standards set forth in this section.

(3) If a nonprofit budget and credit counseling agency or instructional course did not appear on the approved list for the district under subsection (a) immediately before approval under this section, approval under this subsection of such agency or such instructional course shall be for a probationary period not to exceed 6 months.

(4) At the conclusion of the applicable probationary period under paragraph (3), the United States trustee (or bankruptcy administrator, if any) may only approve for an additional 1-year period, and for successive 1-year periods thereafter, an agency or instructional course that has demonstrated during the probationary or applicable subsequent period of approval that such agency or instructional course—

(A) has met the standards set forth under this section during such period; and

(B) can satisfy such standards in the future.

(5) Not later than 30 days after any final decision under paragraph (4), an interested person may seek judicial review of such decision in the appropriate district court of the United States.

(c) (1) The United States trustee (or the bankruptcy administrator, if any) shall only approve a nonprofit budget and credit counseling agency that demonstrates that it will provide qualified counselors, maintain adequate provision for safekeeping and payment of client funds, provide adequate counseling with respect to client credit problems, and deal responsibly and effectively with other matters relating to the quality, effectiveness, and financial security of the services it provides.

(2) To be approved by the United States trustee (or the bankruptcy administrator, if any), a nonprofit budget and credit counseling agency shall, at a minimum—

(A) have a board of directors the majority of which—

(i) are not employed by such agency; and

(ii) will not directly or indirectly benefit financially from the outcome of the counseling services provided by such agency;

(B) if a fee is charged for counseling services, charge a reasonable fee, and provide services without regard to ability to pay the fee;

(C) provide for safekeeping and payment of client funds, including an annual audit of the trust accounts and appropriate employee bonding;

(D) provide full disclosures to a client, including funding sources, counselor qualifications, possible impact on credit reports, and any costs of such program that will be paid by such client and how such costs will be paid;

(E) provide adequate counseling with respect to a client's credit problems that includes an analysis of such client's current financial condition, factors that caused such financial condition, and how such client can develop a plan to respond to the problems without incurring negative amortization of debt;

(F) provide trained counselors who receive no commissions or bonuses based on the outcome of the counseling services provided by such agency, and who have adequate experience, and have been adequately trained to provide counseling services to individuals in financial difficulty, including the matters described in subparagraph (E);

(G) demonstrate adequate experience and background in providing credit counseling; and

(H) have adequate financial resources to provide continuing support services for budgeting plans over the life of any repayment plan.

(d) The United States trustee (or the bankruptcy administrator, if any) shall only approve an instructional course concerning personal financial management—

(1) for an initial probationary period under subsection (b)(3) if the course will provide at a minimum—

(A) trained personnel with adequate experience and training in providing effective instruction and services;

(B) learning materials and teaching methodologies designed to assist debtors in understanding personal financial management and that are consistent with stated objectives directly related to the goals of such instructional course;

(C) adequate facilities situated in reasonably convenient locations at which such instructional course is offered, except that such facilities may include the provision of such instructional course by telephone or through the Internet, if such instructional course is effective;

(D) the preparation and retention of reasonable records (which shall include the debtor's bankruptcy case number) to permit evaluation of the effectiveness of such instructional course, including any evaluation of satisfaction of instructional course requirements for each debtor attending such instructional course, which shall be available for inspection and evaluation by the Executive Office for United States Trustees, the United States trustee (or the bankruptcy administrator, if any), or the chief bankruptcy judge for the district in which such instructional course is offered; and

(E) if a fee is charged for the instructional course, charge a reasonable fee, and provide services without regard to ability to pay the fee.

(2) for any 1-year period if the provider thereof has demonstrated that the course meets the standards of paragraph (1) and, in addition—

(A) has been effective in assisting a substantial number of debtors to understand personal financial management; and

(B) is otherwise likely to increase substantially the debtor's understanding of personal financial management.

(e) The district court may, at any time, investigate the qualifications of a nonprofit budget and credit counseling agency referred to in subsection (a), and request production of documents to ensure the integrity and effectiveness of such agency. The district court may, at any time, remove from the approved list under subsection (a) a nonprofit budget and credit counseling agency upon finding such agency does not meet the qualifications of subsection (b).

(f) The United States trustee (or the bankruptcy administrator, if any) shall notify the clerk that a nonprofit budget and credit counseling agency or an instructional course is no longer approved, in which case the clerk shall remove it from the list maintained under subsection (a).

(g) (1) No nonprofit budget and credit counseling agency may provide to a credit reporting agency information concerning whether a debtor has received or sought instruction concerning personal financial management from such agency.

(2) A nonprofit budget and credit counseling agency that willfully or negligently fails to comply with any requirement under this title with respect to a debtor shall be liable for damages in an amount equal to the sum of—

(A) any actual damages sustained by the debtor as a result of the violation; and

(B) any court costs or reasonable attorneys' fees (as determined by the court) incurred in an action to recover those damages.

Sec. 112. Prohibition on disclosure of name of minor children

The debtor may be required to provide information regarding a minor child involved in matters under this title but may not be required to disclose in the public records in the case the name of such minor child. The debtor may be required to disclose the name of such minor child in a nonpublic record that is maintained by the court and made available by the court for examination by the United States trustee, the trustee, and the auditor (if any) serving under section 586(f) of title 28, in the case. The court, the United States trustee, the trustee, and such auditor shall not disclose the name of such minor child maintained in such nonpublic record.

CHAPTER 3—CASE ADMINISTRATION

SUBCHAPTER I—COMMENCEMENT OF A CASE

Sec. 301. Voluntary cases

(a) A voluntary case under a chapter of this title is commenced by the filing with the bankruptcy court of a petition under such chapter by an entity that may be a debtor under such chapter.

(b) The commencement of a voluntary case under a chapter of this title constitutes an order for relief under such chapter.

Sec. 302. Joint cases

(a) A joint case under a chapter of this title is commenced by the filing with the bankruptcy court of a single petition under such chapter by an individual that may be a debtor under such chapter and such individual's spouse. The commencement of a joint case under a chapter of this title constitutes an order for relief under such chapter.

(b) After the commencement of a joint case, the court shall determine the extent, if any, to which the debtors' estates shall be consolidated.

Sec. 303. Involuntary cases

(a) An involuntary case may be commenced only under chapter 7 or 11 of this title, and only against a person, except a farmer, family farmer, or a corporation that is not a moneyed, business, or commercial corporation, that may be a debtor under the chapter under which such case is commenced.

(b) An involuntary case against a person is commenced by the filing with the bankruptcy court of a petition under chapter 7 or 11 of this title—

 (1) by three or more entities, each of which is either a holder of a claim against such person that is not contingent as to liability or the subject of a bona fide dispute as to liability or amount, or an indenture trustee representing such a holder, if such noncontingent, undisputed claims aggregate at least $10,000 more than the value of any lien on property of the debtor securing such claims held by the holders of such claims;

 (2) if there are fewer than 12 such holders, excluding any employee or insider of such person and any transferee of a transfer that is voidable under section 544, 545, 547, 548, 549, or 724(a) of this title, by one or more of such holders that hold in the aggregate at least $10,000 of such claims;

 (3) if such person is a partnership—

  (A) by fewer than all of the general partners in such partnership; or

  (B) if relief has been ordered under this title with respect to all of the general partners in such partnership, by a general partner in such partnership, the trustee of such a general partner, or a holder of a claim against such partnership; or

 (4) by a foreign representative of the estate in a foreign proceeding concerning such person.

(c) After the filing of a petition under this section but before the case is dismissed or relief is ordered, a creditor holding an unsecured claim that is not contingent, other than a creditor filing under subsection (b) of this section, may join in the petition with the same effect as if such joining creditor were a petitioning creditor under subsection (b) of this section.

(d) The debtor, or a general partner in a partnership debtor that did not join in the petition, may file an answer to a petition under this section.

(e) After notice and a hearing, and for cause, the court may require the petitioners under this section to file a bond to indemnify the debtor for such amounts as the court may later allow under subsection (i) of this section.

(f) Notwithstanding section 363 of this title, except to the extent that the court orders otherwise, and until an order for relief in the case, any business of the debtor may continue to operate, and the debtor may continue to use, acquire, or dispose of property as if an involuntary case concerning the debtor had not been commenced.

(g) At any time after the commencement of an involuntary case under chapter 7 of this title but before an order for relief in the case, the court, on request of a party in interest, after notice to the debtor and a hearing, and if necessary to preserve the property of the estate or to prevent loss to the estate, may order the United States trustee to appoint an interim trustee under section 701 of this title to take possession of the property of the estate and to operate any business of the debtor. Before an order for relief, the debtor may regain possession of property in the possession of a trustee ordered appointed under this subsection if the debtor files such bond as the court requires, conditioned on the debtor's accounting for and delivering to the trustee, if there is an order for relief in the case, such property, or the value, as of the date the debtor regains possession, of such property.

(h) If the petition is not timely controverted, the court shall order relief against the debtor in an involuntary case under the chapter under which the petition was filed. Otherwise, after trial, the court shall order relief against the debtor in an involuntary case under the chapter under which the petition was filed, only if—

  (1) the debtor is generally not paying such debtor's debts as such debts become due unless such debts are the subject of a bona fide dispute as to liability or amount; or

  (2) within 120 days before the date of the filing of the petition, a custodian, other than a trustee, receiver, or agent appointed or authorized to take charge of less than substantially all of the property of the debtor for the purpose of enforcing a lien against such property, was appointed or took possession.

(i) If the court dismisses a petition under this section other than on consent of all petitioners and the debtor, and if the debtor does not waive the right to judgment under this subsection, the court may grant judgment—

  (1) against the petitioners and in favor of the debtor for—

    (A) costs; or

    (B) a reasonable attorney's fee; or

  (2) against any petitioner that filed the petition in bad faith, for—

    (A) any damages proximately caused by such filing; or

    (B) punitive damages.

(j) Only after notice to all creditors and a hearing may the court dismiss a petition filed under this section—

  (1) on the motion of a petitioner;

  (2) on consent of all petitioners and the debtor; or

  (3) for want of prosecution.

(k) [Repealed.]

(l) (1) If—

    (A) the petition under this section is false or contains any materially false, fictitious, or fraudulent statement;

    (B) the debtor is an individual; and

(C) the court dismisses such petition,

the court, upon the motion of the debtor, shall seal all the records of the court relating to such petition, and all references to such petition.

(2) If the debtor is an individual and the court dismisses a petition under this section, the court may enter an order prohibiting all consumer reporting agencies (as defined in section 603(f) of the Fair Credit Reporting Act (15 U.S.C. 1681a(f))) from making any consumer report (as defined in section 603(d) of that Act) that contains any information relating to such petition or to the case commenced by the filing of such petition.

(3) Upon the expiration of the statute of limitations described in section 3282 of title 18, for a violation of section 152 or 157 of such title, the court, upon the motion of the debtor and for good cause, may expunge any records relating to a petition filed under this section.

Sec. 304. Repealed.

Sec. 305. Abstention

(a) The court, after notice and a hearing, may dismiss a case under this title, or may suspend all proceedings in a case under this title, at any time if—
   (1) the interests of creditors and the debtor would be better served by such dismissal or suspension; or
   (2) (A) a petition under section 1515 for recognition of a foreign proceeding has been granted; and
      (B) the purposes of chapter 15 of this title would be best served by such dismissal or suspension.

(b) A foreign representative may seek dismissal or suspension under subsection (a)(2) of this section.

(c) An order under subsection (a) of this section dismissing a case or suspending all proceedings in a case, or a decision not so to dismiss or suspend, is not reviewable by appeal or otherwise by the court of appeals under section 158(d), 1291, or 1292 of title 28 or by the Supreme Court of the United States under section 1254 of title 28.

Sec. 306. Limited appearance

An appearance in a bankruptcy court by a foreign representative in connection with a petition or request under section 303 or 305 of this title does not submit such foreign representative to the jurisdiction of any court in the United States for any other purpose, but the bankruptcy court may condition any order under section 303 or 305 of this title on compliance by such foreign representative with the orders of such bankruptcy court.

Sec. 307. United States trustee

The United States trustee may raise and may appear and be heard on any issue in any case or proceeding under this title but may not file a plan pursuant to section 1121(c) of this title.

Sec. 308. Debtor reporting requirements

(a) For purposes of this section, the term "profitability" means, with respect to a debtor, the amount of money that the debtor has earned or lost during current and recent fiscal periods.

(b) A small business debtor shall file periodic financial and other reports containing information including—

(1) the debtor's profitability;
(2) reasonable approximations of the debtor's projected cash receipts and cash disbursements over a reasonable period;
(3) comparisons of actual cash receipts and disbursements with projections in prior reports;
(4) (A) whether the debtor is—
    (i) in compliance in all material respects with postpetition requirements imposed by this title and the Federal Rules of Bankruptcy Procedure; and
    (ii) timely filing tax returns and other required government filings and paying taxes and other administrative expenses when due;
  (B) if the debtor is not in compliance with the requirements referred to in subparagraph (A)(i) or filing tax returns and other required government filings and making the payments referred to in subparagraph (A)(ii), what the failures are and how, at what cost, and when the debtor intends to remedy such failures; and
  (C) such other matters as are in the best interests of the debtor and creditors, and in the public interest in fair and efficient procedures under chapter 11 of this title.

SUBCHAPTER II—OFFICERS

Sec. 321. Eligibility to serve as trustee

(a) A person may serve as trustee in a case under this title only if such person is—
  (1) an individual that is competent to perform the duties of trustee and, in a case under chapter 7, 12, or 13 of this title, resides or has an office in the judicial district within which the case is pending, or in any judicial district adjacent to such district; or
  (2) a corporation authorized by such corporation's charter or bylaws to act as trustee, and, in a case under chapter 7, 12, or 13 of this title, having an office in at least one of such districts.
(b) A person that has served as an examiner in the case may not serve as trustee in the case.
(c) The United States trustee for the judicial district in which the case is pending is eligible to serve as trustee in the case if necessary.

Sec. 322. Qualification of trustee

(a) Except as provided in subsection (b)(1), a person selected under section 701, 702, 703, 1104, 1163, 1202, or 1302 of this title to serve as trustee in a case under this title qualifies if before five days after such selection, and before beginning official duties, such person has filed with the court a bond in favor of the United States conditioned on the faithful performance of such official duties.
(b) (1) The United States trustee qualifies wherever such trustee serves as trustee in a case under this title.
  (2) The United States trustee shall determine—
    (A) the amount of a bond required to be filed under subsection (a) of this section; and
    (B) the sufficiency of the surety on such bond.
(c) A trustee is not liable personally or on such trustee's bond in favor of the United States for any penalty or forfeiture incurred by the debtor.
(d) A proceeding on a trustee's bond may not be commenced after two years after the date on which such trustee was discharged.

Sec. 323. Role and capacity of trustee

(a) The trustee in a case under this title is the representative of the estate.

(b) The trustee in a case under this title has capacity to sue and be sued.

Sec. 324. Removal of trustee or examiner

(a) The court, after notice and a hearing, may remove a trustee, other than the United States trustee, or an examiner, for cause.

(b) Whenever the court removes a trustee or examiner under subsection (a) in a case under this title, such trustee or examiner shall thereby be removed in all other cases under this title in which such trustee or examiner is then serving unless the court orders otherwise.

Sec. 325. Effect of vacancy

A vacancy in the office of trustee during a case does not abate any pending action or proceeding, and the successor trustee shall be substituted as a party in such action or proceeding.

Sec. 326. Limitation on compensation of trustee

(a) In a case under chapter 7 or 11, the court may allow reasonable compensation under section 330 of this title of the trustee for the trustee's services, payable after the trustee renders such services, not to exceed 25 percent on the first $5,000 or less, 10 percent on any amount in excess of $5,000 but not in excess of $50,000, 5 percent on any amount in excess of $50,000 but not in excess of $1,000,000, and reasonable compensation not to exceed 3 percent of such moneys in excess of $1,000,000, upon all moneys disbursed or turned over in the case by the trustee to parties in interest, excluding the debtor, but including holders of secured claims.

(b) In a case under chapter 12 or 13 of this title, the court may not allow compensation for services or reimbursement of expenses of the United States trustee or of a standing trustee appointed under section 586(b) of title 28, but may allow reasonable compensation under section 330 of this title of a trustee appointed under section 1202(a) or 1302(a) of this title for the trustee's services, payable after the trustee renders such services, not to exceed five percent upon all payments under the plan.

(c) If more than one person serves as trustee in the case, the aggregate compensation of such persons for such service may not exceed the maximum compensation prescribed for a single trustee by subsection (a) or (b) of this section, as the case may be.

(d) The court may deny allowance of compensation for services or reimbursement of expenses of the trustee if the trustee failed to make diligent inquiry into facts that would permit denial of allowance under section 328(c) of this title or, with knowledge of such facts, employed a professional person under section 327 of this title.

Sec. 327. Employment of professional persons

(a) Except as otherwise provided in this section, the trustee, with the court's approval, may employ one or more attorneys, accountants, appraisers, auctioneers, or other professional persons, that do not hold or represent an interest adverse to the estate, and that are disinterested persons, to represent or assist the trustee in carrying out the trustee's duties under this title.

(b) If the trustee is authorized to operate the business of the debtor under section 721, 1202, or 1108 of this title, and if the debtor has regularly employed attorneys, accountants, or other professional persons on salary, the trustee may retain or replace such professional persons if necessary in the operation of such business.

(c) In a case under chapter 7, 12, or 11 of this title, a person is not disqualified for employment under this section solely because of such person's employment by or representation of a creditor, unless there is objection by another creditor or the United States trustee, in which case the court shall disapprove such employment if there is an actual conflict of interest.

(d) The court may authorize the trustee to act as attorney or accountant for the estate if such authorization is in the best interest of the estate.

(e) The trustee, with the court's approval, may employ, for a specified special purpose, other than to represent the trustee in conducting the case, an attorney that has represented the debtor, if in the best interest of the estate, and if such attorney does not represent or hold any interest adverse to the debtor or to the estate with respect to the matter on which such attorney is to be employed.

(f) The trustee may not employ a person that has served as an examiner in the case.

Sec. 328. Limitation on compensation of professional persons

(a) The trustee, or a committee appointed under section 1102 of this title, with the court's approval, may employ or authorize the employment of a professional person under section 327 or 1103 of this title, as the case may be, on any reasonable terms and conditions of employment, including on a retainer, on an hourly basis, on a fixed or percentage fee basis, or on a contingent fee basis. Notwithstanding such terms and conditions, the court may allow compensation different from the compensation provided under such terms and conditions after the conclusion of such employment, if such terms and conditions prove to have been improvident in light of developments not capable of being anticipated at the time of the fixing of such terms and conditions.

(b) If the court has authorized a trustee to serve as an attorney or accountant for the estate under section 327(d) of this title, the court may allow compensation for the trustee's services as such attorney or accountant only to the extent that the trustee performed services as attorney or accountant for the estate and not for performance of any of the trustee's duties that are generally performed by a trustee without the assistance of an attorney or accountant for the estate.

(c) Except as provided in section 327(c), 327(e), or 1107(b) of this title, the court may deny allowance of compensation for services and reimbursement of expenses of a professional person employed under section 327 or 1103 of this title if, at any time during such professional person's employment under section 327 or 1103 of this title, such professional person is not a disinterested person, or represents or holds an interest adverse to the interest of the estate with respect to the matter on which such professional person is employed.

Sec. 329. Debtor's transactions with attorneys

(a) Any attorney representing a debtor in a case under this title, or in connection with such a case, whether or not such attorney applies for compensation under this title, shall file with the court a statement of the compensation paid or agreed to be paid, if such payment or agreement was made after one year before the date of the filing of the petition, for services rendered or to be rendered in contemplation of or in connection with the case by such attorney, and the source of such compensation.

(b) If such compensation exceeds the reasonable value of any such services, the court may cancel any such agreement, or order the return of any such payment, to the extent excessive, to—

  (1) the estate, if the property transferred—

(A) would have been property of the estate; or

(B) was to be paid by or on behalf of the debtor under a plan under chapter 11, 12, or 13 of this title; or

(2) the entity that made such payment.

Sec. 330. Compensation of officers

(a) (1) After notice to the parties in interest and the United States Trustee and a hearing, and subject to sections 326, 328, and 329, the court may award to a trustee, a consumer privacy ombudsman appointed under section 332, an examiner, an ombudsman appointed under section 333, or a professional person employed under section 327 or 1103—

(A) reasonable compensation for actual, necessary services rendered by the trustee, examiner, ombudsman, professional person, or attorney and by any paraprofessional person employed by any such person; and

(B) reimbursement for actual, necessary expenses.

(2) The court may, on its own motion or on the motion of the United States Trustee, the United States Trustee for the District or Region, the trustee for the estate, or any other party in interest, award compensation that is less than the amount of compensation that is requested.

(3) In determining the amount of reasonable compensation to be awarded to an examiner, trustee under chapter 11, or professional person, the court shall consider the nature, the extent, and the value of such services, taking into account all relevant factors, including—

(A) the time spent on such services;

(B) the rates charged for such services;

(C) whether the services were necessary to the administration of, or beneficial at the time at which the service was rendered toward the completion of, a case under this title;

(D) whether the services were performed within a reasonable amount of time commensurate with the complexity, importance, and nature of the problem, issue, or task addressed;

(E) with respect to a professional person, whether the person is board certified or otherwise has demonstrated skill and experience in the bankruptcy field; and

(F) whether the compensation is reasonable based on the customary compensation charged by comparably skilled practitioners in cases other than cases under this title.

(4) (A) Except as provided in subparagraph (B), the court shall not allow compensation for—

(i) unnecessary duplication of services; or

(ii) services that were not—

(I) reasonably likely to benefit the debtor's estate; or

(II) necessary to the administration of the case.

(B) In a chapter 12 or chapter 13 case in which the debtor is an individual, the court may allow reasonable compensation to the debtor's attorney for representing the interests of the debtor in connection with the bankruptcy case based on a consideration of the benefit and necessity of such services to the debtor and the other factors set forth in this section.

(5) The court shall reduce the amount of compensation awarded under this section by the amount of any interim compensation awarded under section 331, and, if the amount of such interim compensation exceeds the amount of compensation awarded under this section, may order the return of the excess to the estate.

(6) Any compensation awarded for the preparation of a fee application shall be based on the level and skill reasonably required to prepare the application.

(7) In determining the amount of reasonable compensation to be awarded to a trustee, the court shall treat such compensation as a commission, based on section 326.

(b) (1) There shall be paid from the filing fee in a case under chapter 7 of this title $45 to the trustee serving in such case, after such trustee's services are rendered.

(2) The Judicial Conference of the United States—

(A) shall prescribe additional fees of the same kind as prescribed under section 1914(b) of title 28; and

(B) may prescribe notice of appearance fees and fees charged against distributions in cases under this title;

to pay $15 to trustees serving in cases after such trustees' services are rendered. Beginning 1 year after the date of the enactment of the Bankruptcy Reform Act of 1994, such $15 shall be paid in addition to the amount paid under paragraph (1).

(c) Unless the court orders otherwise, in a case under chapter 12 or 13 of this title the compensation paid to the trustee serving in the case shall not be less than $5 per month from any distribution under the plan during the administration of the plan.

(d) In a case in which the United States trustee serves as trustee, the compensation of the trustee under this section shall be paid to the clerk of the bankruptcy court and deposited by the clerk into the United States Trustee System Fund established by section 589a of title 28.

Sec. 331. Interim compensation

A trustee, an examiner, a debtor's attorney, or any professional person employed under section 327 or 1103 of this title may apply to the court not more than once every 120 days after an order for relief in a case under this title, or more often if the court permits, for such compensation for services rendered before the date of such an application or reimbursement for expenses incurred before such date as is provided under section 330 of this title. After notice and a hearing, the court may allow and disburse to such applicant such compensation or reimbursement.

Sec. 332. Consumer privacy ombudsman

(a) If a hearing is required under section 363(b)(1)(B), the court shall order the United States trustee to appoint, not later than 5 days before the commencement of the hearing, 1 disinterested person (other than the United States trustee) to serve as the consumer privacy ombudsman in the case and shall require that notice of such hearing be timely given to such ombudsman.

(b) The consumer privacy ombudsman may appear and be heard at such hearing and shall provide to the court information to assist the court in its consideration of the facts, circumstances, and conditions of the proposed sale or lease of personally identifiable information under section 363(b)(1)(B). Such information may include presentation of—

(1) the debtor's privacy policy;

(2) the potential losses or gains of privacy to consumers if such sale or such lease is approved by the court;

(3) the potential costs or benefits to consumers if such sale or such lease is approved by the court; and

(4) the potential alternatives that would mitigate potential privacy losses or potential costs to consumers.

(c) A consumer privacy ombudsman shall not disclose any personally identifiable information obtained by the ombudsman under this title.

Sec. 333. Appointment of patient care ombudsman

(a) (1) If the debtor in a case under chapter 7, 9, or 11 is a health care business, the court shall order, not later than 30 days after the commencement of the case, the appointment of an ombudsman to monitor the quality of patient care and to represent the interests of the patients of the health care business unless the court finds that the appointment of such ombudsman is not necessary for the protection of patients under the specific facts of the case.

(2) (A) If the court orders the appointment of an ombudsman under paragraph (1), the United States trustee shall appoint 1 disinterested person (other than the United States trustee) to serve as such ombudsman.

(B) If the debtor is a health care business that provides long- term care, then the United States trustee may appoint the State Long-Term Care Ombudsman appointed under the Older Americans Act of 1965 for the State in which the case is pending to serve as the ombudsman required by paragraph (1).

(C) If the United States trustee does not appoint a State Long- Term Care Ombudsman under subparagraph (B), the court shall notify the State Long-Term Care Ombudsman appointed under the Older Americans Act of 1965 for the State in which the case is pending, of the name and address of the person who is appointed under subparagraph (A).

(b) An ombudsman appointed under subsection (a) shall—

(1) monitor the quality of patient care provided to patients of the debtor, to the extent necessary under the circumstances, including interviewing patients and physicians;

(2) not later than 60 days after the date of appointment, and not less frequently than at 60-day intervals thereafter, report to the court after notice to the parties in interest, at a hearing or in writing, regarding the quality of patient care provided to patients of the debtor; and

(3) if such ombudsman determines that the quality of patient care provided to patients of the debtor is declining significantly or is otherwise being materially compromised, file with the court a motion or a written report, with notice to the parties in interest immediately upon making such determination.

(c) (1) An ombudsman appointed under subsection (a) shall maintain any information obtained by such ombudsman under this section that relates to patients (including information relating to patient records) as confidential information. Such ombudsman may not review confidential patient records unless the court approves such review in advance and imposes restrictions on such ombudsman to protect the confidentiality of such records.

(2) An ombudsman appointed under subsection (a)(2)(B) shall have access to patient records consistent with authority of such ombudsman under the Older Americans Act of 1965 and under non- Federal laws governing the State Long-Term Care Ombudsman program.

SUBCHAPTER III—ADMINISTRATION

Sec. 341. Meetings of creditors and equity security holders

(a) Within a reasonable time after the order for relief in a case under this title, the United States trustee shall convene and preside at a meeting of creditors.

(b) The United States trustee may convene a meeting of any equity security holders.

(c) The court may not preside at, and may not attend, any meeting under this section including any final meeting of creditors. Notwithstanding any local court rule, provision of a State constitution, any otherwise applicable nonbankruptcy law, or any other requirement that representation at the meeting of creditors under subsection (a) be by an attorney, a creditor holding a consumer debt or any representative of the creditor (which may include an entity or an employee of an entity and may be a representative for more than 1 creditor) shall be permitted to appear at and participate in the meeting of creditors in a case under chapter 7 or 13, either alone or in conjunction with an attorney for the creditor. Nothing in this subsection shall be construed to require any creditor to be represented by an attorney at any meeting of creditors.

(d) Prior to the conclusion of the meeting of creditors or equity security holders, the trustee shall orally examine the debtor to ensure that the debtor in a case under chapter 7 of this title is aware of—

  (1) the potential consequences of seeking a discharge in bankruptcy, including the effects on credit history;

  (2) the debtor's ability to file a petition under a different chapter of this title;

  (3) the effect of receiving a discharge of debts under this title; and

  (4) the effect of reaffirming a debt, including the debtor's knowledge of the provisions of section 524(d) of this title.

(e) Notwithstanding subsections (a) and (b), the court, on the request of a party in interest and after notice and a hearing, for cause may order that the United States trustee not convene a meeting of creditors or equity security holders if the debtor has filed a plan as to which the debtor solicited acceptances prior to the commencement of the case.

Sec. 342. Notice

(a) There shall be given such notice as is appropriate, including notice to any holder of a community claim, of an order for relief in a case under this title.

(b) Before the commencement of a case under this title by an individual whose debts are primarily consumer debts, the clerk shall give to such individual written notice containing—

  (1) a brief description of—

    (A) chapters 7, 11, 12, and 13 and the general purpose, benefits, and costs of proceeding under each of those chapters; and

    (B) the types of services available from credit counseling agencies; and

  (2) statements specifying that—

    (A) a person who knowingly and fraudulently conceals assets or makes a false oath or statement under penalty of perjury in connection with a case under this title shall be subject to fine, imprisonment, or both; and

    (B) all information supplied by a debtor in connection with a case under this title is subject to examination by the Attorney General.

(c) (1) If notice is required to be given by the debtor to a creditor under this title, any rule, any applicable law, or any order of the court, such notice shall contain the name, address, and last 4 digits of the taxpayer identification number of the debtor. If the notice concerns an amendment that adds a creditor to the schedules of assets and liabilities, the debtor shall include the full taxpayer identification number in the notice sent to that creditor, but the debtor shall include only the last 4 digits of the taxpayer identification number in the copy of the notice filed with the court.

(2) (A) If, within the 90 days before the commencement of a voluntary case, a creditor supplies the debtor in at least 2 communications sent to the debtor with the current account number of the debtor and the address at which such creditor requests to receive correspondence, then any notice required by this title to be sent by the debtor to such creditor shall be sent to such address and shall include such account number.

(B) If a creditor would be in violation of applicable nonbankruptcy law by sending any such communication within such 90- day period and if such creditor supplies the debtor in the last 2 communications with the current account number of the debtor and the address at which such creditor requests to receive correspondence, then any notice required by this title to be sent by the debtor to such creditor shall be sent to such address and shall include such account number.

(d) In a case under chapter 7 of this title in which the debtor is an individual and in which the presumption of abuse arises under section 707(b), the clerk shall give written notice to all creditors not later than 10 days after the date of the filing of the petition that the presumption of abuse has arisen.

(e) (1) In a case under chapter 7 or 13 of this title of a debtor who is an individual, a creditor at any time may both file with the court and serve on the debtor a notice of address to be used to provide notice in such case to such creditor.

(2) Any notice in such case required to be provided to such creditor by the debtor or the court later than 5 days after the court and the debtor receive such creditor's notice of address, shall be provided to such address.

(f) (1) An entity may file with any bankruptcy court a notice of address to be used by all the bankruptcy courts or by particular bankruptcy courts, as so specified by such entity at the time such notice is filed, to provide notice to such entity in all cases under chapters 7 and 13 pending in the courts with respect to which such notice is filed, in which such entity is a creditor.

(2) In any case filed under chapter 7 or 13, any notice required to be provided by a court with respect to which a notice is filed under paragraph (1), to such entity later than 30 days after the filing of such notice under paragraph (1) shall be provided to such address unless with respect to a particular case a different address is specified in a notice filed and served in accordance with subsection (e).

(3) A notice filed under paragraph (1) may be withdrawn by such entity.

(g) (1) Notice provided to a creditor by the debtor or the court other than in accordance with this section (excluding this subsection) shall not be effective notice until such notice is brought to the attention of such creditor. If such creditor designates a person or an organizational subdivision of such creditor to be responsible for receiving notices under this title and establishes reasonable procedures so that such notices receivable by such creditor are to be delivered to such person or such subdivision, then a notice provided to such creditor other than in accordance with this section (excluding this subsection) shall not be considered to have been brought to the attention of such creditor until such notice is received by such person or such subdivision.

(2) A monetary penalty may not be imposed on a creditor for a violation of a stay in effect under section 362(a) (including a monetary penalty imposed under section 362(k)) or for failure to comply with section 542 or 543 unless the conduct that is the basis of such violation or of such failure occurs after such creditor receives notice effective under this section of the order for relief.

Sec. 343. Examination of the debtor

The debtor shall appear and submit to examination under oath at the meeting of creditors under section 341(a) of this title. Creditors, any indenture trustee, any trustee or examiner in the case, or the United States trustee may examine the debtor. The United States trustee may administer the oath required under this section.

Sec. 344. Self-incrimination; immunity

Immunity for persons required to submit to examination, to testify, or to provide information in a case under this title may be granted under part V of title 18.

Sec. 345. Money of estates

(a) A trustee in a case under this title may make such deposit or investment of the money of the estate for which such trustee serves as will yield the maximum reasonable net return on such money, taking into account the safety of such deposit or investment.

(b) Except with respect to a deposit or investment that is insured or guaranteed by the United States or by a department, agency, or instrumentality of the United States or backed by the full faith and credit of the United States, the trustee shall require from an entity with which such money is deposited or invested—

(1) a bond—

(A) in favor of the United States;

(B) secured by the undertaking of a corporate surety approved by the United States trustee for the district in which the case is pending; and

(C) conditioned on—

(i) a proper accounting for all money so deposited or invested and for any return on such money;

(ii) prompt repayment of such money and return; and

(iii) faithful performance of duties as a depository; or

(2) the deposit of securities of the kind specified in section 9303 of title 31;

unless the court for cause orders otherwise.

(c) An entity with which such moneys are deposited or invested is authorized to deposit or invest such moneys as may be required under this section.

Sec. 346. Special provisions related to the treatment of State and local taxes

(a) Whenever the Internal Revenue Code of 1986 provides that a separate taxable estate or entity is created in a case concerning a debtor under this title, and the income, gain, loss, deductions, and credits of such estate shall be taxed to or claimed by the estate, a separate taxable estate is also created for purposes of any State and local law imposing a tax on or measured by income and such income, gain, loss, deductions, and credits shall be taxed to or claimed by the estate and may not be taxed to or claimed by the debtor. The preceding sentence shall not apply if the case is dismissed. The trustee shall make tax returns of income required under any such State or local law.

(b) Whenever the Internal Revenue Code of 1986 provides that no separate taxable estate shall be created in a case concerning a debtor under this title, and the income, gain, loss, deductions, and credits of an estate shall be taxed to or claimed by the debtor, such income, gain, loss, deductions, and credits shall be taxed to or claimed by the debtor under a State or local law imposing a tax on or measured by income and may not be taxed to or claimed by the estate. The trustee shall make such tax returns of income of corporations and of partnerships as are required under any State or local law, but with respect to partnerships, shall make such returns only to the extent such returns are also required to be made under such Code. The estate shall be liable for any tax imposed on such corporation or partnership, but not for any tax imposed on partners or members.

(c) With respect to a partnership or any entity treated as a partnership under a State or local law imposing a tax on or measured by income that is a debtor in a case under this title, any gain or loss resulting from a distribution of property from such partnership, or any distributive share of any income, gain, loss, deduction, or credit of a partner or member that is distributed, or considered distributed, from such partnership, after the commencement of the case, is gain, loss, income, deduction, or credit, as the case may be, of the partner or member, and if such partner or member is a debtor in a case under this title, shall be subject to tax in accordance with subsection (a) or (b).

(d) For purposes of any State or local law imposing a tax on or measured by income, the taxable period of a debtor in a case under this title shall terminate only if and to the extent that the taxable period of such debtor terminates under the Internal Revenue Code of 1986.

(e) The estate in any case described in subsection (a) shall use the same accounting method as the debtor used immediately before the commencement of the case, if such method of accounting complies with applicable nonbankruptcy tax law.

(f) For purposes of any State or local law imposing a tax on or measured by income, a transfer of property from the debtor to the estate or from the estate to the debtor shall not be treated as a disposition for purposes of any provision assigning tax consequences to a disposition, except to the extent that such transfer is treated as a disposition under the Internal Revenue Code of 1986.

(g) Whenever a tax is imposed pursuant to a State or local law imposing a tax on or measured by income pursuant to subsection (a) or (b), such tax shall be imposed at rates generally applicable to the same types of entities under such State or local law.

(h) The trustee shall withhold from any payment of claims for wages, salaries, commissions, dividends, interest, or other payments, or collect, any amount required to be withheld or collected under applicable State or local tax law, and shall pay such withheld or collected amount to the appropriate governmental unit at the time and in the manner required by such tax law, and with the same priority as the claim from which such amount was withheld or collected was paid.

(i) (1) To the extent that any State or local law imposing a tax on or measured by income provides for the carryover of any tax attribute from one taxable period to a subsequent taxable period, the estate shall succeed to such tax attribute in any case in which such estate is subject to tax under subsection (a).

(2) After such a case is closed or dismissed, the debtor shall succeed to any tax attribute to

which the estate succeeded under paragraph (1) to the extent consistent with the Internal Revenue Code of 1986.

(3) The estate may carry back any loss or tax attribute to a taxable period of the debtor that ended before the date of the order for relief under this title to the extent that—

(A) applicable State or local tax law provides for a carryback in the case of the debtor; and

(B) the same or a similar tax attribute may be carried back by the estate to such a taxable period of the debtor under the Internal Revenue Code of 1986.

(j) (1) For purposes of any State or local law imposing a tax on or measured by income, income is not realized by the estate, the debtor, or a successor to the debtor by reason of discharge of indebtedness in a case under this title, except to the extent, if any, that such income is subject to tax under the Internal Revenue Code of 1986.

(2) Whenever the Internal Revenue Code of 1986 provides that the amount excluded from gross income in respect of the discharge of indebtedness in a case under this title shall be applied to reduce the tax attributes of the debtor or the estate, a similar reduction shall be made under any State or local law imposing a tax on or measured by income to the extent such State or local law recognizes such attributes. Such State or local law may also provide for the reduction of other attributes to the extent that the full amount of income from the discharge of indebtedness has not been applied.

(k) (1) Except as provided in this section and section 505, the time and manner of filing tax returns and the items of income, gain, loss, deduction, and credit of any taxpayer shall be determined under applicable nonbankruptcy law.

(2) For Federal tax purposes, the provisions of this section are subject to the Internal Revenue Code of 1986 and other applicable Federal nonbankruptcy law.

Sec. 347. Unclaimed property

(a) Ninety days after the final distribution under section 726, 1226, or 1326 of this title in a case under chapter 7, 12, or 13 of this title, as the case may be, the trustee shall stop payment on any check remaining unpaid, and any remaining property of the estate shall be paid into the court and disposed of under chapter 129 of title 28.

(b) Any security, money, or other property remaining unclaimed at the expiration of the time allowed in a case under chapter 9, 11, or 12 of this title for the presentation of a security or the performance of any other act as a condition to participation in the distribution under any plan confirmed under section 943(b), 1129, 1173, or 1225 of this title, as the case may be, becomes the property of the debtor or of the entity acquiring the assets of the debtor under the plan, as the case may be.

Sec. 348. Effect of conversion

(a) Conversion of a case from a case under one chapter of this title to a case under another chapter of this title constitutes an order for relief under the chapter to which the case is converted, but, except as provided in subsections (b) and (c) of this section, does not effect a change in the date of the filing of the petition, the commencement of the case, or the order for relief.

(b) Unless the court for cause orders otherwise, in sections 701(a), 727(a)(10), 727(b), 728(a), 728(b),[6] 1102(a), 1110(a)(1), 1121(b), 1121(c), 1141(d)(4), 1146(a), 1146(b), 1201(a), 1221,

---

[6] *Sic.* Section 728 of this title has been repealed.

1228(a), 1301(a), and 1305(a) of this title, "the order for relief under this chapter" in a chapter to which a case has been converted under section 706, 1112, 1208, or 1307 of this title means the conversion of such case to such chapter.

(c) Sections 342 and 365(d) of this title apply in a case that has been converted under section 706, 1112, 1208, or 1307 of this title, as if the conversion order were the order for relief.

(d) A claim against the estate or the debtor that arises after the order for relief but before conversion in a case that is converted under section 1112, 1208, or 1307 of this title, other than a claim specified in section 503(b) of this title, shall be treated for all purposes as if such claim had arisen immediately before the date of the filing of the petition.

(e) Conversion of a case under section 706, 1112, 1208, or 1307 of this title terminates the service of any trustee or examiner that is serving in the case before such conversion.

(f) (1) Except as provided in paragraph (2), when a case under chapter 13 of this title is converted to a case under another chapter under this title—

(A) property of the estate in the converted case shall consist of property of the estate, as of the date of filing of the petition, that remains in the possession of or is under the control of the debtor on the date of conversion;

(B) valuations of property and of allowed secured claims in the chapter 13 case shall apply only in a case converted to a case under chapter 11 or 12, but not in a case converted to a case under chapter 7, with allowed secured claims in cases under chapters 11 and 12 reduced to the extent that they have been paid in accordance with the chapter 13 plan; and

(C) with respect to cases converted from chapter 13—

(i) the claim of any creditor holding security as of the date of the petition shall continue to be secured by that security unless the full amount of such claim determined under applicable nonbankruptcy law has been paid in full as of the date of conversion, notwithstanding any valuation or determination of the amount of an allowed secured claim made for the purposes of the case under chapter 13; and

(ii) unless a prebankruptcy default has been fully cured under the plan at the time of conversion, in any proceeding under this title or otherwise, the default shall have the effect given under applicable nonbankruptcy law.

(2) If the debtor converts a case under chapter 13 of this title to a case under another chapter under this title in bad faith, the property of the estate in the converted case shall consist of the property of the estate as of the date of conversion.

Sec. 349. Effect of dismissal

(a) Unless the court, for cause, orders otherwise, the dismissal of a case under this title does not bar the discharge, in a later case under this title, of debts that were dischargeable in the case dismissed; nor does the dismissal of a case under this title prejudice the debtor with regard to the filing of a subsequent petition under this title, except as provided in section 109(g) of this title.

(b) Unless the court, for cause, orders otherwise, a dismissal of a case other than under section 742 of this title—

(1) reinstates—

(A) any proceeding or custodianship superseded under section 543 of this title;

(B) any transfer avoided under section 522, 544, 545, 547, 548, 549, or 724(a) of this title, or preserved under section 510(c)(2), 522(i)(2), or 551 of this title; and

(C) any lien voided under section 506(d) of this title;

(2) vacates any order, judgment, or transfer ordered, under section 522(i)(1), 542, 550, or 553 of this title; and

(3) revests the property of the estate in the entity in which such property was vested immediately before the commencement of the case under this title.

Sec. 350. Closing and reopening cases

(a) After an estate is fully administered and the court has discharged the trustee, the court shall close the case.

(b) A case may be reopened in the court in which such case was closed to administer assets, to accord relief to the debtor, or for other cause.

Sec. 351. Disposal of patient records

If a health care business commences a case under chapter 7, 9, or 11, and the trustee does not have a sufficient amount of funds to pay for the storage of patient records in the manner required under applicable Federal or State law, the following requirements shall apply:

(1) The trustee shall—

(A) promptly publish notice, in 1 or more appropriate newspapers, that if patient records are not claimed by the patient or an insurance provider (if applicable law permits the insurance provider to make that claim) by the date that is 365 days after the date of that notification, the trustee will destroy the patient records; and

(B) during the first 180 days of the 365-day period described in subparagraph (A), promptly attempt to notify directly each patient that is the subject of the patient records and appropriate insurance carrier concerning the patient records by mailing to the most recent known address of that patient, or a family member or contact person for that patient, and to the appropriate insurance carrier an appropriate notice regarding the claiming or disposing of patient records.

(2) If, after providing the notification under paragraph (1), patient records are not claimed during the 365-day period described under that paragraph, the trustee shall mail, by certified mail, at the end of such 365-day period a written request to each appropriate Federal agency to request permission from that agency to deposit the patient records with that agency, except that no Federal agency is required to accept patient records under this paragraph.

(3) If, following the 365-day period described in paragraph (2) and after providing the notification under paragraph (1), patient records are not claimed by a patient or insurance provider, or request is not granted by a Federal agency to deposit such records with that agency, the trustee shall destroy those records by—

(A) if the records are written, shredding or burning the records; or

(B) if the records are magnetic, optical, or other electronic records, by otherwise destroying those records so that those records cannot be retrieved.

SUBCHAPTER IV—ADMINISTRATIVE POWERS

Sec. 361. Adequate protection

When adequate protection is required under section 362, 363, or 364 of this title of an interest of an entity in property, such adequate protection may be provided by—

(1) requiring the trustee to make a cash payment or periodic cash payments to such entity, to the extent that the stay under section 362 of this title, use, sale, or lease under section 363 of this title, or any grant of a lien under section 364 of this title results in a decrease in the value of such entity's interest in such property;

(2) providing to such entity an additional or replacement lien to the extent that such stay, use, sale, lease, or grant results in a decrease in the value of such entity's interest in such property; or

(3) granting such other relief, other than entitling such entity to compensation allowable under section 503(b)(1) of this title as an administrative expense, as will result in the realization by such entity of the indubitable equivalent of such entity's interest in such property.

Sec. 362. Automatic stay

(a) Except as provided in subsection (b) of this section, a petition filed under section 301, 302, or 303 of this title, or an application filed under section 5(a)(3) of the Securities Investor Protection Act of 1970, operates as a stay, applicable to all entities, of—

(1) the commencement or continuation, including the issuance or employment of process, of a judicial, administrative, or other action or proceeding against the debtor that was or could have been commenced before the commencement of the case under this title, or to recover a claim against the debtor that arose before the commencement of the case under this title;

(2) the enforcement, against the debtor or against property of the estate, of a judgment obtained before the commencement of the case under this title;

(3) any act to obtain possession of property of the estate or of property from the estate or to exercise control over property of the estate;

(4) any act to create, perfect, or enforce any lien against property of the estate;

(5) any act to create, perfect, or enforce against property of the debtor any lien to the extent that such lien secures a claim that arose before the commencement of the case under this title;

(6) any act to collect, assess, or recover a claim against the debtor that arose before the commencement of the case under this title;

(7) the setoff of any debt owing to the debtor that arose before the commencement of the case under this title against any claim against the debtor; and

(8) the commencement or continuation of a proceeding before the United States Tax Court concerning a corporate debtor's tax liability for a taxable period the bankruptcy court may determine or concerning the tax liability of a debtor who is an individual for a taxable period ending before the date of the order for relief under this title.

(b) The filing of a petition under section 301, 302, or 303 of this title, or of an application under section 5(a)(3) of the Securities Investor Protection Act of 1970, does not operate as a stay—

(1) under subsection (a) of this section, of the commencement or continuation of a criminal action or proceeding against the debtor;

(2) under subsection (a)—
  (A) of the commencement or continuation of a civil action or proceeding—
    (i) for the establishment of paternity;
    (ii) for the establishment or modification of an order for domestic support obligations;
    (iii) concerning child custody or visitation;
    (iv) for the dissolution of a marriage, except to the extent that such proceeding seeks to determine the division of property that is property of the estate; or
    (v) regarding domestic violence;
  (B) of the collection of a domestic support obligation from property that is not property of the estate;
  (C) with respect to the withholding of income that is property of the estate or property of the debtor for payment of a domestic support obligation under a judicial or administrative order or a statute;
  (D) of the withholding, suspension, or restriction of a driver's license, a professional or occupational license, or a recreational license, under State law, as specified in section 466(a)(16) of the Social Security Act;
  (E) of the reporting of overdue support owed by a parent to any consumer reporting agency as specified in section 466(a)(7) of the Social Security Act;
  (F) of the interception of a tax refund, as specified in sections 464 and 466(a)(3) of the Social Security Act or under an analogous State law; or
  (G) of the enforcement of a medical obligation, as specified under title IV of the Social Security Act;

(3) under subsection (a) of this section, of any act to perfect, or to maintain or continue the perfection of, an interest in property to the extent that the trustee's rights and powers are subject to such perfection under section 546(b) of this title or to the extent that such act is accomplished within the period provided under section 547(e)(2)(A) of this title;

(4) under paragraph (1), (2), (3), or (6) of subsection (a) of this section, of the commencement or continuation of an action or proceeding by a governmental unit or any organization exercising authority under the Convention on the Prohibition of the Development, Production, Stockpiling and Use of Chemical Weapons and on Their Destruction, opened for signature on January 13, 1993, to enforce such governmental unit's or organization's police and regulatory power, including the enforcement of a judgment other than a money judgment, obtained in an action or proceeding by the governmental unit to enforce such governmental unit's or organization's police or regulatory power;

(5) [Repealed.]

(6) under subsection (a) of this section, of the exercise by a commodity broker, forward contract merchant, stockbroker, financial institution, financial participant, or securities clearing agency of any contractual right (as defined in section 555 or 556) under any security agreement or arrangement or other credit enhancement forming a part of or related to any commodity contract, forward contract or securities contract, or of any contractual right (as defined in section 555 or 556) to offset or net out any termination value, payment amount, or other transfer obligation arising under or in connection with 1 or more such contracts, including any master agreement for such contracts;

(7) under subsection (a) of this section, of the exercise by a repo participant or financial participant of any contractual right (as defined in section 559) under any security

agreement or arrangement or other credit enhancement forming a part of or related to any repurchase agreement, or of any contractual right (as defined in section 559) to offset or net out any termination value, payment amount, or other transfer obligation arising under or in connection with 1 or more such agreements, including any master agreement for such agreements;

(8) under subsection (a) of this section, of the commencement of any action by the Secretary of Housing and Urban Development to foreclose a mortgage or deed of trust in any case in which the mortgage or deed of trust held by the Secretary is insured or was formerly insured under the National Housing Act and covers property, or combinations of property, consisting of five or more living units;

(9) under subsection (a), of—

(A) an audit by a governmental unit to determine tax liability;

(B) the issuance to the debtor by a governmental unit of a notice of tax deficiency;

(C) a demand for tax returns; or

(D) the making of an assessment for any tax and issuance of a notice and demand for payment of such an assessment (but any tax lien that would otherwise attach to property of the estate by reason of such an assessment shall not take effect unless such tax is a debt of the debtor that will not be discharged in the case and such property or its proceeds are transferred out of the estate to, or otherwise revested in, the debtor).

(10) under subsection (a) of this section, of any act by a lessor to the debtor under a lease of nonresidential real property that has terminated by the expiration of the stated term of the lease before the commencement of or during a case under this title to obtain possession of such property;

(11) under subsection (a) of this section, of the presentment of a negotiable instrument and the giving of notice of and protesting dishonor of such an instrument;

(12) under subsection (a) of this section, after the date which is 90 days after the filing of such petition, of the commencement or continuation, and conclusion to the entry of final judgment, of an action which involves a debtor subject to reorganization pursuant to chapter 11 of this title and which was brought by the Secretary of Transportation under section 31325 of title 46 (including distribution of any proceeds of sale) to foreclose a preferred ship or fleet mortgage, or a security interest in or relating to a vessel or vessel under construction, held by the Secretary of Transportation under chapter 537 of title 46 or section 109(h) of title 49, or under applicable State law;

(13) under subsection (a) of this section, after the date which is 90 days after the filing of such petition, of the commencement or continuation, and conclusion to the entry of final judgment, of an action which involves a debtor subject to reorganization pursuant to chapter 11 of this title and which was brought by the Secretary of Commerce under section 31325 of title 46 (including distribution of any proceeds of sale) to foreclose a preferred ship or fleet mortgage in a vessel or a mortgage, deed of trust, or other security interest in a fishing facility held by the Secretary of Commerce under chapter 537 of title 46;

(14) under subsection (a) of this section, of any action by an accrediting agency regarding the accreditation status of the debtor as an educational institution;

(15) under subsection (a) of this section, of any action by a State licensing body regarding the licensure of the debtor as an educational institution;

(16) under subsection (a) of this section, of any action by a guaranty agency, as defined in section 435(j) of the Higher Education Act of 1965 or the Secretary of Education regarding the eligibility of the debtor to participate in programs authorized under such Act;

(17) under subsection (a) of this section, of the exercise by a swap participant or financial participant of any contractual right (as defined in section 560) under any security agreement or arrangement or other credit enhancement forming a part of or related to any swap agreement, or of any contractual right (as defined in section 560) to offset or net out any termination value, payment amount, or other transfer obligation arising under or in connection with 1 or more such agreements, including any master agreement for such agreements;

(18) under subsection (a) of the creation or perfection of a statutory lien for an ad valorem property tax, or a special tax or special assessment on real property whether or not ad valorem, imposed by a governmental unit, if such tax or assessment comes due after the date of the filing of the petition;

(19) under subsection (a), of withholding of income from a debtor's wages and collection of amounts withheld, under the debtor's agreement authorizing that withholding and collection for the benefit of a pension, profit-sharing, stock bonus, or other plan established under section 401, 403, 408, 408A, 414, 457, or 501(c) of the Internal Revenue Code of 1986, that is sponsored by the employer of the debtor, or an affiliate, successor, or predecessor of such employer—

(A) to the extent that the amounts withheld and collected are used solely for payments relating to a loan from a plan under section 408(b)(1) of the Employee Retirement Income Security Act of 1974 or is subject to section 72(p) of the Internal Revenue Code of 1986; or

(B) a loan from a thrift savings plan permitted under subchapter III of chapter 84 of title 5, that satisfies the requirements of section 8433(g) of such title;

but nothing in this paragraph may be construed to provide that any loan made under a governmental plan under section 414(d), or a contract or account under section 403(b), of the Internal Revenue Code of 1986 constitutes a claim or a debt under this title;

(20) under subsection (a), of any act to enforce any lien against or security interest in real property following entry of the order under subsection (d)(4) as to such real property in any prior case under this title, for a period of 2 years after the date of the entry of such an order, except that the debtor, in a subsequent case under this title, may move for relief from such order based upon changed circumstances or for other good cause shown, after notice and a hearing;

(21) under subsection (a), of any act to enforce any lien against or security interest in real property—

(A) if the debtor is ineligible under section 109(g) to be a debtor in a case under this title; or

(B) if the case under this title was filed in violation of a bankruptcy court order in a prior case under this title prohibiting the debtor from being a debtor in another case under this title;

(22) subject to subsection (l), under subsection (a)(3), of the continuation of any eviction, unlawful detainer action, or similar proceeding by a lessor against a debtor involving residential property in which the debtor resides as a tenant under a lease or rental

agreement and with respect to which the lessor has obtained before the date of the filing of the bankruptcy petition, a judgment for possession of such property against the debtor;

(23) subject to subsection (m), under subsection (a)(3), of an eviction action that seeks possession of the residential property in which the debtor resides as a tenant under a lease or rental agreement based on endangerment of such property or the illegal use of controlled substances on such property, but only if the lessor files with the court, and serves upon the debtor, a certification under penalty of perjury that such an eviction action has been filed, or that the debtor, during the 30-day period preceding the date of the filing of the certification, has endangered property or illegally used or allowed to be used a controlled substance on the property;

(24) under subsection (a), of any transfer that is not avoidable under section 544 and that is not avoidable under section 549;

(25) under subsection (a), of—

  (A) the commencement or continuation of an investigation or action by a securities self regulatory organization to enforce such organization's regulatory power;

  (B) the enforcement of an order or decision, other than for monetary sanctions, obtained in an action by such securities self regulatory organization to enforce such organization's regulatory power; or

  (C) any act taken by such securities self regulatory organization to delist, delete, or refuse to permit quotation of any stock that does not meet applicable regulatory requirements;

(26) under subsection (a), of the setoff under applicable nonbankruptcy law of an income tax refund, by a governmental unit, with respect to a taxable period that ended before the date of the order for relief against an income tax liability for a taxable period that also ended before the date of the order for relief, except that in any case in which the setoff of an income tax refund is not permitted under applicable nonbankruptcy law because of a pending action to determine the amount or legality of a tax liability, the governmental unit may hold the refund pending the resolution of the action, unless the court, on the motion of the trustee and after notice and a hearing, grants the taxing authority adequate protection (within the meaning of section 361) for the secured claim of such authority in the setoff under section 506(a);

(27) under subsection (a) of this section, of the exercise by a master netting agreement participant of any contractual right (as defined in section 555, 556, 559, or 560) under any security agreement or arrangement or other credit enhancement forming a part of or related to any master netting agreement, or of any contractual right (as defined in section 555, 556, 559, or 560) to offset or net out any termination value, payment amount, or other transfer obligation arising under or in connection with 1 or more such master netting agreements to the extent that such participant is eligible to exercise such rights under paragraph (6), (7), or (17) for each individual contract covered by the master netting agreement in issue; and

(28) under subsection (a), of the exclusion by the Secretary of Health and Human Services of the debtor from participation in the medicare program or any other Federal health care program (as defined in section 1128B(f) of the Social Security Act pursuant to title XI or XVIII of such Act).

The provisions of paragraphs (12) and (13) of this subsection shall apply with respect to any such petition filed on or before December 31, 1989.

(c) Except as provided in subsections (d), (e), (f), and (h) of this section—
- (1) the stay of an act against property of the estate under subsection (a) of this section continues until such property is no longer property of the estate;
- (2) the stay of any other act under subsection (a) of this section continues until the earliest of—
  - (A) the time the case is closed;
  - (B) the time the case is dismissed; or
  - (C) if the case is a case under chapter 7 of this title concerning an individual or a case under chapter 9, 11, 12, or 13 of this title, the time a discharge is granted or denied;
- (3) if a single or joint case is filed by or against debtor who is an individual in a case under chapter 7, 11, or 13, and if a single or joint case of the debtor was pending within the preceding 1-year period but was dismissed, other than a case refiled under a chapter other than chapter 7 after dismissal under section 707(b)—
  - (A) the stay under subsection (a) with respect to any action taken with respect to a debt or property securing such debt or with respect to any lease shall terminate with respect to the debtor on the 30th day after the filing of the later case;
  - (B) on the motion of a party in interest for continuation of the automatic stay and upon notice and a hearing, the court may extend the stay in particular cases as to any or all creditors (subject to such conditions or limitations as the court may then impose) after notice and a hearing completed before the expiration of the 30-day period only if the party in interest demonstrates that the filing of the later case is in good faith as to the creditors to be stayed; and
  - (C) for purposes of subparagraph (B), a case is presumptively filed not in good faith (but such presumption may be rebutted by clear and convincing evidence to the contrary)—
    - (i) as to all creditors, if—
      - (I) more than 1 previous case under any of chapters 7, 11, and 13 in which the individual was a debtor was pending within the preceding 1-year period;
      - (II) a previous case under any of chapters 7, 11, and 13 in which the individual was a debtor was dismissed within such 1-year period, after the debtor failed to—
        - (aa) file or amend the petition or other documents as required by this title or the court without substantial excuse (but mere inadvertence or negligence shall not be a substantial excuse unless the dismissal was caused by the negligence of the debtor's attorney);
        - (bb) provide adequate protection as ordered by the court; or
        - (cc) perform the terms of a plan confirmed by the court; or
      - (III) there has not been a substantial change in the financial or personal affairs of the debtor since the dismissal of the next most previous case under chapter 7, 11, or 13 or any other reason to conclude that the later case will be concluded—
        - (aa) if a case under chapter 7, with a discharge; or

(bb) if a case under chapter 11 or 13, with a confirmed plan that will be fully performed; and

(ii) as to any creditor that commenced an action under subsection (d) in a previous case in which the individual was a debtor if, as of the date of dismissal of such case, that action was still pending or had been resolved by terminating, conditioning, or limiting the stay as to actions of such creditor; and

(4) (A) (i) if a single or joint case is filed by or against a debtor who is an individual under this title, and if 2 or more single or joint cases of the debtor were pending within the previous year but were dismissed, other than a case refiled under section 707(b), the stay under subsection (a) shall not go into effect upon the filing of the later case; and

(ii) on request of a party in interest, the court shall promptly enter an order confirming that no stay is in effect;

(B) if, within 30 days after the filing of the later case, a party in interest requests the court may order the stay to take effect in the case as to any or all creditors (subject to such conditions or limitations as the court may impose), after notice and a hearing, only if the party in interest demonstrates that the filing of the later case is in good faith as to the creditors to be stayed;

(C) a stay imposed under subparagraph (B) shall be effective on the date of the entry of the order allowing the stay to go into effect; and

(D) for purposes of subparagraph (B), a case is presumptively filed not in good faith (but such presumption may be rebutted by clear and convincing evidence to the contrary)—

(i) as to all creditors if—

(I) 2 or more previous cases under this title in which the individual was a debtor were pending within the 1-year period;

(II) a previous case under this title in which the individual was a debtor was dismissed within the time period stated in this paragraph after the debtor failed to file or amend the petition or other documents as required by this title or the court without substantial excuse (but mere inadvertence or negligence shall not be substantial excuse unless the dismissal was caused by the negligence of the debtor's attorney), failed to provide adequate protection as ordered by the court, or failed to perform the terms of a plan confirmed by the court; or

(III) there has not been a substantial change in the financial or personal affairs of the debtor since the dismissal of the next most previous case under this title, or any other reason to conclude that the later case will not be concluded, if a case under chapter 7, with a discharge, and if a case under chapter 11 or 13, with a confirmed plan that will be fully performed; or

(ii) as to any creditor that commenced an action under subsection (d) in a previous case in which the individual was a debtor if, as of the date of dismissal of such case, such action was still pending or had been resolved by terminating, conditioning, or limiting the stay as to such action of such creditor.

(d) On request of a party in interest and after notice and a hearing, the court shall grant relief from the stay provided under subsection (a) of this section, such as by terminating, annulling, modifying, or conditioning such stay—

(1) for cause, including the lack of adequate protection of an interest in property of such party in interest;

(2) with respect to a stay of an act against property under subsection (a) of this section, if—

(A) the debtor does not have an equity in such property; and

(B) such property is not necessary to an effective reorganization;

(3) with respect to a stay of an act against single asset real estate under subsection (a), by a creditor whose claim is secured by an interest in such real estate, unless, not later than the date that is 90 days after the entry of the order for relief (or such later date as the court may determine for cause by order entered within that 90-day period) or 30 days after the court determines that the debtor is subject to this paragraph, whichever is later—

(A) the debtor has filed a plan of reorganization that has a reasonable possibility of being confirmed within a reasonable time; or

(B) the debtor has commenced monthly payments that—

(i) may, in the debtor's sole discretion, notwithstanding section 363(c)(2), be made from rents or other income generated before, on, or after the date of the commencement of the case by or from the property to each creditor whose claim is secured by such real estate (other than a claim secured by a judgment lien or by an unmatured statutory lien); and

(ii) are in an amount equal to interest at the then applicable nondefault contract rate of interest on the value of the creditor's interest in the real estate; or

(4) with respect to a stay of an act against real property under subsection (a), by a creditor whose claim is secured by an interest in such real property, if the court finds that the filing of the petition was part of a scheme to delay, hinder, and defraud creditors that involved either—

(A) transfer of all or part ownership of, or other interest in, such real property without the consent of the secured creditor or court approval; or

(B) multiple bankruptcy filings affecting such real property.

If recorded in compliance with applicable State laws governing notices of interests or liens in real property, an order entered under paragraph (4) shall be binding in any other case under this title purporting to affect such real property filed not later than 2 years after the date of the entry of such order by the court, except that a debtor in a subsequent case under this title may move for relief from such order based upon changed circumstances or for good cause shown, after notice and a hearing. Any Federal, State, or local governmental unit that accepts notices of interests or liens in real property shall accept any certified copy of an order described in this subsection for indexing and recording.

(e) (1) Thirty days after a request under subsection (d) of this section for relief from the stay of any act against property of the estate under subsection (a) of this section, such stay is terminated with respect to the party in interest making such request, unless the court, after notice and a hearing, orders such stay continued in effect pending the conclusion of, or as a result of, a final hearing and determination under subsection (d) of this section. A hearing under this subsection may be a preliminary hearing, or may be consolidated with the final hearing under subsection (d) of this section. The court shall order such stay continued in effect pending the conclusion of the final hearing under subsection (d) of this section if there is a reasonable likelihood that the party opposing relief from such stay will prevail at the conclusion of such final hearing. If the hearing under this subsection is a preliminary hearing, then such final hearing shall be concluded not later than thirty days after the conclusion of such preliminary hearing, unless the 30-day period is extended with the consent of the parties in interest or for a specific time which the court finds is required by compelling circumstances.

(2) Notwithstanding paragraph (1), in a case under chapter 7, 11, or 13 in which the debtor is an individual, the stay under subsection (a) shall terminate on the date that is 60 days after a request is made by a party in interest under subsection (d), unless—

(A) a final decision is rendered by the court during the 60-day period beginning on the date of the request; or

(B) such 60-day period is extended—

(i) by agreement of all parties in interest; or

(ii) by the court for such specific period of time as the court finds is required for good cause, as described in findings made by the court.

(f) Upon request of a party in interest, the court, with or without a hearing, shall grant such relief from the stay provided under subsection (a) of this section as is necessary to prevent irreparable damage to the interest of an entity in property, if such interest will suffer such damage before there is an opportunity for notice and a hearing under subsection (d) or (e) of this section.

(g) In any hearing under subsection (d) or (e) of this section concerning relief from the stay of any act under subsection (a) of this section—

(1) the party requesting such relief has the burden of proof on the issue of the debtor's equity in property; and

(2) the party opposing such relief has the burden of proof on all other issues.

(h) (1) In a case in which the debtor is an individual, the stay provided by subsection (a) is terminated with respect to personal property of the estate or of the debtor securing in whole or in part a claim, or subject to an unexpired lease, and such personal property shall no longer be property of the estate if the debtor fails within the applicable time set by section 521(a)(2)—

(A) to file timely any statement of intention required under section 521(a)(2) with respect to such personal property or to indicate in such statement that the debtor will either surrender such personal property or retain it and, if retaining such personal property, either redeem such personal property pursuant to section 722, enter into an agreement of the kind specified in section 524(c) applicable to the debt secured by such personal property, or assume such unexpired lease pursuant to section 365(p) if the trustee does not do so, as applicable; and

(B) to take timely the action specified in such statement, as it may be amended before expiration of the period for taking action, unless such statement specifies the debtor's intention to reaffirm such debt on the original contract terms and the creditor refuses to agree to the reaffirmation on such terms.

(2) Paragraph (1) does not apply if the court determines, on the motion of the trustee filed before the expiration of the applicable time set by section 521(a)(2), after notice and a hearing, that such personal property is of consequential value or benefit to the estate, and orders appropriate adequate protection of the creditor's interest, and orders the debtor to deliver any collateral in the debtor's possession to the trustee. If the court does not so determine, the stay provided by subsection (a) shall terminate upon the conclusion of the hearing on the motion.

(i) If a case commenced under chapter 7, 11, or 13 is dismissed due to the creation of a debt repayment plan, for purposes of subsection (c)(3), any subsequent case commenced by the debtor under any such chapter shall not be presumed to be filed not in good faith.

(j) On request of a party in interest, the court shall issue an order under subsection (c) confirming that the automatic stay has been terminated.

(k) (1) Except as provided in paragraph (2), an individual injured by any willful violation of a stay provided by this section shall recover actual damages, including costs and attorneys' fees, and, in appropriate circumstances, may recover punitive damages.

(2) If such violation is based on an action taken by an entity in the good faith belief that subsection (h) applies to the debtor, the recovery under paragraph (1) of this subsection against such entity shall be limited to actual damages.

(l) (1) Except as otherwise provided in this subsection, subsection (b)(22) shall apply on the date that is 30 days after the date on which the bankruptcy petition is filed, if the debtor files with the petition and serves upon the lessor a certification under penalty of perjury that—

(A) under nonbankruptcy law applicable in the jurisdiction, there are circumstances under which the debtor would be permitted to cure the entire monetary default that gave rise to the judgment for possession, after that judgment for possession was entered; and

(B) the debtor (or an adult dependent of the debtor) has deposited with the clerk of the court, any rent that would become due during the 30-day period after the filing of the bankruptcy petition.

(2) If, within the 30-day period after the filing of the bankruptcy petition, the debtor (or an adult dependent of the debtor) complies with paragraph (1) and files with the court and serves upon the lessor a further certification under penalty of perjury that the debtor (or an adult dependent of the debtor) has cured, under nonbankrupcty[7] law applicable in the jurisdiction, the entire monetary default that gave rise to the judgment under which possession is sought by the lessor, subsection (b)(22) shall not apply, unless ordered to apply by the court under paragraph (3).

(3) (A) If the lessor files an objection to any certification filed by the debtor under paragraph (1) or (2), and serves such objection upon the debtor, the court shall hold a hearing within 10 days after the filing and service of such objection to determine if the certification filed by the debtor under paragraph (1) or (2) is true.

(B) If the court upholds the objection of the lessor filed under subparagraph (A)—

(i) subsection (b)(22) shall apply immediately and relief from the stay provided under subsection (a)(3) shall not be required to enable the lessor to complete the process to recover full possession of the property; and

(ii) the clerk of the court shall immediately serve upon the lessor and the debtor a certified copy of the court's order upholding the lessor's objection.

(4) If a debtor, in accordance with paragraph (5), indicates on the petition that there was a judgment for possession of the residential rental property in which the debtor resides and does not file a certification under paragraph (1) or (2)—

(A) subsection (b)(22) shall apply immediately upon failure to file such certification, and relief from the stay provided under subsection (a)(3) shall not be required to

---

[7] *Sic.*

enable the lessor to complete the process to recover full possession of the property; and

(B) the clerk of the court shall immediately serve upon the lessor and the debtor a certified copy of the docket indicating the absence of a filed certification and the applicability of the exception to the stay under subsection (b)(22).

(5) (A) Where a judgment for possession of residential property in which the debtor resides as a tenant under a lease or rental agreement has been obtained by the lessor, the debtor shall so indicate on the bankruptcy petition and shall provide the name and address of the lessor that obtained that pre-petition judgment on the petition and on any certification filed under this subsection.

(B) The form of certification filed with the petition, as specified in this subsection, shall provide for the debtor to certify, and the debtor shall certify—

(i) whether a judgment for possession of residential rental housing in which the debtor resides has been obtained against the debtor before the date of the filing of the petition; and

(ii) whether the debtor is claiming under paragraph (1) that under nonbankruptcy law applicable in the jurisdiction, there are circumstances under which the debtor would be permitted to cure the entire monetary default that gave rise to the judgment for possession, after that judgment of possession was entered, and has made the appropriate deposit with the court.

(C) The standard forms (electronic and otherwise) used in a bankruptcy proceeding shall be amended to reflect the requirements of this subsection.

(D) The clerk of the court shall arrange for the prompt transmittal of the rent deposited in accordance with paragraph (1)(B) to the lessor.

(m) (1) Except as otherwise provided in this subsection, subsection (b)(23) shall apply on the date that is 15 days after the date on which the lessor files and serves a certification described in subsection (b)(23).

(2) (A) If the debtor files with the court an objection to the truth or legal sufficiency of the certification described in subsection (b)(23) and serves such objection upon the lessor, subsection (b)(23) shall not apply, unless ordered to apply by the court under this subsection.

(B) If the debtor files and serves the objection under subparagraph (A), the court shall hold a hearing within 10 days after the filing and service of such objection to determine if the situation giving rise to the lessor's certification under paragraph (1) existed or has been remedied.

(C) If the debtor can demonstrate to the satisfaction of the court that the situation giving rise to the lessor's certification under paragraph (1) did not exist or has been remedied, the stay provided under subsection (a)(3) shall remain in effect until the termination of the stay under this section.

(D) tIf the debtor cannot demonstrate to the satisfaction of the court that the situation giving rise to the lessor's certification under paragraph (1) did not exist or has been remedied—

(i) relief from the stay provided under subsection (a)(3) shall not be required to enable the lessor to proceed with the eviction; and

(ii) the clerk of the court shall immediately serve upon the lessor and the debtor a certified copy of the court's order upholding the lessor's certification.

(3) If the debtor fails to file, within 15 days, an objection under paragraph (2)(A)—
(A) subsection (b)(23) shall apply immediately upon such failure and relief from the stay provided under subsection (a)(3) shall not be required to enable the lessor to complete the process to recover full possession of the property; and
(B) the clerk of the court shall immediately serve upon the lessor and the debtor a certified copy of the docket indicating such failure.

(n) (1) Except as provided in paragraph (2), subsection (a) does not apply in a case in which the debtor—
(A) is a debtor in a small business case pending at the time the petition is filed;
(B) was a debtor in a small business case that was dismissed for any reason by an order that became final in the 2-year period ending on the date of the order for relief entered with respect to the petition;
(C) was a debtor in a small business case in which a plan was confirmed in the 2-year period ending on the date of the order for relief entered with respect to the petition; or
(D) is an entity that has acquired substantially all of the assets or business of a small business debtor described in subparagraph (A), (B), or (C), unless such entity establishes by a preponderance of the evidence that such entity acquired substantially all of the assets or business of such small business debtor in good faith and not for the purpose of evading this paragraph.

(2) Paragraph (1) does not apply—
(A) to an involuntary case involving no collusion by the debtor with creditors; or
(B) to the filing of a petition if—
(i) the debtor proves by a preponderance of the evidence that the filing of the petition resulted from circumstances beyond the control of the debtor not foreseeable at the time the case then pending was filed; and
(ii) it is more likely than not that the court will confirm a feasible plan, but not a liquidating plan, within a reasonable period of time.

(o) The exercise of rights not subject to the stay arising under subsection (a) pursuant to paragraph (6), (7), (17), or (27) of subsection (b) shall not be stayed by any order of a court or administrative agency in any proceeding under this title.

Sec. 363. Use, sale, or lease of property

(a) In this section, "cash collateral" means cash, negotiable instruments, documents of title, securities, deposit accounts, or other cash equivalents whenever acquired in which the estate and an entity other than the estate have an interest and includes the proceeds, products, offspring, rents, or profits of property and the fees, charges, accounts or other payments for the use or occupancy of rooms and other public facilities in hotels, motels, or other lodging properties subject to a security interest as provided in section 552(b) of this title, whether existing before or after the commencement of a case under this title.

(b) (1) The trustee, after notice and a hearing, may use, sell, or lease, other than in the ordinary course of business, property of the estate, except that if the debtor in connection with offering a product or a service discloses to an individual a policy prohibiting the transfer of personally identifiable information about individuals to persons that are not affiliated with the debtor and if such policy is in effect on the date of the commencement of the case, then the trustee may not sell or lease personally identifiable information to any person unless—

(A) such sale or such lease is consistent with such policy; or

(B) after appointment of a consumer privacy ombudsman in accordance with section 332, and after notice and a hearing, the court approves such sale or such lease—

(i) giving due consideration to the facts, circumstances, and conditions of such sale or such lease; and

(ii) finding that no showing was made that such sale or such lease would violate applicable nonbankruptcy law.

(2) If notification is required under subsection (a) of section 7A of the Clayton Act in the case of a transaction under this subsection, then—

(A) notwithstanding subsection (a) of such section, the notification required by such subsection to be given by the debtor shall be given by the trustee; and

(B) notwithstanding subsection (b) of such section, the required waiting period shall end on the 15th day after the date of the receipt, by the Federal Trade Commission and the Assistant Attorney General in charge of the Antitrust Division of the Department of Justice, of the notification required under such subsection (a), unless such waiting period is extended—

(i) pursuant to subsection (e)(2) of such section, in the same manner as such subsection (e)(2) applies to a cash tender offer;

(ii) pursuant to subsection (g)(2) of such section; or

(iii) by the court after notice and a hearing.

(c) (1) If the business of the debtor is authorized to be operated under section 721, 1108, 1203, 1204, or 1304 of this title and unless the court orders otherwise, the trustee may enter into transactions, including the sale or lease of property of the estate, in the ordinary course of business, without notice or a hearing, and may use property of the estate in the ordinary course of business without notice or a hearing.

(2) The trustee may not use, sell, or lease cash collateral under paragraph (1) of this subsection unless—

(A) each entity that has an interest in such cash collateral consents; or

(B) the court, after notice and a hearing, authorizes such use, sale, or lease in accordance with the provisions of this section.

(3) Any hearing under paragraph (2)(B) of this subsection may be a preliminary hearing or may be consolidated with a hearing under subsection (e) of this section, but shall be scheduled in accordance with the needs of the debtor. If the hearing under paragraph (2)(B) of this subsection is a preliminary hearing, the court may authorize such use, sale, or lease only if there is a reasonable likelihood that the trustee will prevail at the final hearing under subsection (e) of this section. The court shall act promptly on any request for authorization under paragraph (2)(B) of this subsection.

(4) Except as provided in paragraph (2) of this subsection, the trustee shall segregate and account for any cash collateral in the trustee's possession, custody, or control.

(d) The trustee may use, sell, or lease property under subsection (b) or (c) of this section only—

(1) in accordance with applicable nonbankruptcy law that governs the transfer of property by a corporation or trust that is not a moneyed, business, or commercial corporation or trust; and

(2) to the extent not inconsistent with any relief granted under subsection (c), (d), (e), or (f) of section 362.

(e) Notwithstanding any other provision of this section, at any time, on request of an entity that has an interest in property used, sold, or leased, or proposed to be used, sold, or leased, by the trustee, the court, with or without a hearing, shall prohibit or condition such use, sale, or lease as is necessary to provide adequate protection of such interest. This subsection also applies to property that is subject to any unexpired lease of personal property (to the exclusion of such property being subject to an order to grant relief from the stay under section 362).

(f) The trustee may sell property under subsection (b) or (c) of this section free and clear of any interest in such property of an entity other than the estate, only if—

(1) applicable nonbankruptcy law permits sale of such property free and clear of such interest;

(2) such entity consents;

(3) such interest is a lien and the price at which such property is to be sold is greater than the aggregate value of all liens on such property;

(4) such interest is in bona fide dispute; or

(5) such entity could be compelled, in a legal or equitable proceeding, to accept a money satisfaction of such interest.

(g) Notwithstanding subsection (f) of this section, the trustee may sell property under subsection (b) or (c) of this section free and clear of any vested or contingent right in the nature of dower or curtesy.

(h) Notwithstanding subsection (f) of this section, the trustee may sell both the estate's interest, under subsection (b) or (c) of this section, and the interest of any co-owner in property in which the debtor had, at the time of the commencement of the case, an undivided interest as a tenant in common, joint tenant, or tenant by the entirety, only if—

(1) partition in kind of such property among the estate and such co-owners is impracticable;

(2) sale of the estate's undivided interest in such property would realize significantly less for the estate than sale of such property free of the interests of such co-owners;

(3) the benefit to the estate of a sale of such property free of the interests of co-owners outweighs the detriment, if any, to such co-owners; and

(4) such property is not used in the production, transmission, or distribution, for sale, of electric energy or of natural or synthetic gas for heat, light, or power.

(i) Before the consummation of a sale of property to which subsection (g) or (h) of this section applies, or of property of the estate that was community property of the debtor and the debtor's spouse immediately before the commencement of the case, the debtor's spouse, or a co-owner of such property, as the case may be, may purchase such property at the price at which such sale is to be consummated.

(j) After a sale of property to which subsection (g) or (h) of this section applies, the trustee shall distribute to the debtor's spouse or the co-owners of such property, as the case may be, and to the estate, the proceeds of such sale, less the costs and expenses, not including any compensation of the trustee, of such sale, according to the interests of such spouse or co-owners, and of the estate.

(k) At a sale under subsection (b) of this section of property that is subject to a lien that secures an allowed claim, unless the court for cause orders otherwise the holder of such claim may bid at such sale, and, if the holder of such claim purchases such property, such holder may offset such claim against the purchase price of such property.

(l) Subject to the provisions of section 365, trustee may use, sell, or lease property under subsection (b) or (c) of this section, or a plan under chapter 11, 12, or 13 of this title may provide for the use, sale, or lease of property, notwithstanding any provision in a contract, a lease, or applicable law that is conditioned on the insolvency or financial condition of the debtor, on the commencement of a case under this title concerning the debtor, or on the appointment of or the taking possession by a trustee in a case under this title or a custodian, and that effects, or gives an option to effect, a forfeiture, modification, or termination of the debtor's interest in such property.

(m) The reversal or modification on appeal of an authorization under subsection (b) or (c) of this section of a sale or lease of property does not affect the validity of a sale or lease under such authorization to an entity that purchased or leased such property in good faith, whether or not such entity knew of the pendency of the appeal, unless such authorization and such sale or lease were stayed pending appeal.

(n) The trustee may avoid a sale under this section if the sale price was controlled by an agreement among potential bidders at such sale, or may recover from a party to such agreement any amount by which the value of the property sold exceeds the price at which such sale was consummated, and may recover any costs, attorneys' fees, or expenses incurred in avoiding such sale or recovering such amount. In addition to any recovery under the preceding sentence, the court may grant judgment for punitive damages in favor of the estate and against any such party that entered into such an agreement in willful disregard of this subsection.

(o) Notwithstanding subsection (f), if a person purchases any interest in a consumer credit transaction that is subject to the Truth in Lending Act or any interest in a consumer credit contract (as defined in section 433.1 of title 16 of the Code of Federal Regulations (January 1, 2004), as amended from time to time), and if such interest is purchased through a sale under this section, then such person shall remain subject to all claims and defenses that are related to such consumer credit transaction or such consumer credit contract, to the same extent as such person would be subject to such claims and defenses of the consumer had such interest been purchased at a sale not under this section.

(p) In any hearing under this section—
  (1) the trustee has the burden of proof on the issue of adequate protection; and
  (2) the entity asserting an interest in property has the burden of proof on the issue of the validity, priority, or extent of such interest.

Sec. 364. Obtaining credit

(a) If the trustee is authorized to operate the business of the debtor under section 721, 1108, 1203, 1204, or 1304 of this title, unless the court orders otherwise, the trustee may obtain unsecured credit and incur unsecured debt in the ordinary course of business allowable under section 503(b)(1) of this title as an administrative expense.

(b) The court, after notice and a hearing, may authorize the trustee to obtain unsecured credit or to incur unsecured debt other than under subsection (a) of this section, allowable under section 503(b)(1) of this title as an administrative expense.

(c) If the trustee is unable to obtain unsecured credit allowable under section 503(b)(1) of this title as an administrative expense, the court, after notice and a hearing, may authorize the obtaining of credit or the incurring of debt—
  (1) with priority over any or all administrative expenses of the kind specified in section 503(b) or 507(b) of this title;

(2) secured by a lien on property of the estate that is not otherwise subject to a lien; or

(3) secured by a junior lien on property of the estate that is subject to a lien.

(d) (1) The court, after notice and a hearing, may authorize the obtaining of credit or the incurring of debt secured by a senior or equal lien on property of the estate that is subject to a lien only if—

(A) the trustee is unable to obtain such credit otherwise; and

(B) there is adequate protection of the interest of the holder of the lien on the property of the estate on which such senior or equal lien is proposed to be granted.

(2) In any hearing under this subsection, the trustee has the burden of proof on the issue of adequate protection.

(e) The reversal or modification on appeal of an authorization under this section to obtain credit or incur debt, or of a grant under this section of a priority or a lien, does not affect the validity of any debt so incurred, or any priority or lien so granted, to an entity that extended such credit in good faith, whether or not such entity knew of the pendency of the appeal, unless such authorization and the incurring of such debt, or the granting of such priority or lien, were stayed pending appeal.

(f) Except with respect to an entity that is an underwriter as defined in section 1145(b) of this title, section 5 of the Securities Act of 1933, the Trust Indenture Act of 1939, and any State or local law requiring registration for offer or sale of a security or registration or licensing of an issuer of, underwriter of, or broker or dealer in, a security does not apply to the offer or sale under this section of a security that is not an equity security.

Sec. 365. Executory contracts and unexpired leases

(a) Except as provided in sections 765 and 766 of this title and in subsections (b), (c), and (d) of this section, the trustee, subject to the court's approval, may assume or reject any executory contract or unexpired lease of the debtor.

(b) (1) If there has been a default in an executory contract or unexpired lease of the debtor, the trustee may not assume such contract or lease unless, at the time of assumption of such contract or lease, the trustee—

(A) cures, or provides adequate assurance that the trustee will promptly cure, such default other than a default that is a breach of a provision relating to the satisfaction of any provision (other than a penalty rate or penalty provision) relating to a default arising from any failure to perform nonmonetary obligations under an unexpired lease of real property, if it is impossible for the trustee to cure such default by performing nonmonetary acts at and after the time of assumption, except that if such default arises from a failure to operate in accordance with a nonresidential real property lease, then such default shall be cured by performance at and after the time of assumption in accordance with such lease, and pecuniary losses resulting from such default shall be compensated in accordance with the provisions of this paragraph;

(B) compensates, or provides adequate assurance that the trustee will promptly compensate, a party other than the debtor to such contract or lease, for any actual pecuniary loss to such party resulting from such default; and

(C) provides adequate assurance of future performance under such contract or lease.

(2) Paragraph (1) of this subsection does not apply to a default that is a breach of a provision relating to—

(A) the insolvency or financial condition of the debtor at any time before the closing of the case;

(B) the commencement of a case under this title;

(C) the appointment of or taking possession by a trustee in a case under this title or a custodian before such commencement; or

(D) the satisfaction of any penalty rate or penalty provision relating to a default arising from any failure by the debtor to perform nonmonetary obligations under the executory contract or unexpired lease.

(3) For the purposes of paragraph (1) of this subsection and paragraph (2)(B) of subsection (f), adequate assurance of future performance of a lease of real property in a shopping center includes adequate assurance—

(A) of the source of rent and other consideration due under such lease, and in the case of an assignment, that the financial condition and operating performance of the proposed assignee and its guarantors, if any, shall be similar to the financial condition and operating performance of the debtor and its guarantors, if any, as of the time the debtor became the lessee under the lease;

(B) that any percentage rent due under such lease will not decline substantially;

(C) that assumption or assignment of such lease is subject to all the provisions thereof, including (but not limited to) provisions such as a radius, location, use, or exclusivity provision, and will not breach any such provision contained in any other lease, financing agreement, or master agreement relating to such shopping center; and

(D) that assumption or assignment of such lease will not disrupt any tenant mix or balance in such shopping center.

(4) Notwithstanding any other provision of this section, if there has been a default in an unexpired lease of the debtor, other than a default of a kind specified in paragraph (2) of this subsection, the trustee may not require a lessor to provide services or supplies incidental to such lease before assumption of such lease unless the lessor is compensated under the terms of such lease for any services and supplies provided under such lease before assumption of such lease.

(c) The trustee may not assume or assign any executory contract or unexpired lease of the debtor, whether or not such contract or lease prohibits or restricts assignment of rights or delegation of duties, if—

(1) (A) applicable law excuses a party, other than the debtor, to such contract or lease from accepting performance from or rendering performance to an entity other than the debtor or the debtor in possession, whether or not such contract or lease prohibits or restricts assignment of rights or delegation of duties; and

(B) such party does not consent to such assumption or assignment; or

(2) such contract is a contract to make a loan, or extend other debt financing or financial accommodations, to or for the benefit of the debtor, or to issue a security of the debtor; or

(3) such lease is of nonresidential real property and has been terminated under applicable nonbankruptcy law prior to the order for relief.

(d) (1) In a case under chapter 7 of this title, if the trustee does not assume or reject an executory contract or unexpired lease of residential real property or of personal property of the debtor within 60 days after the order for relief, or within such additional time as the court, for cause, within such 60-day period, fixes, then such contract or lease is deemed rejected.

(2) In a case under chapter 9, 11, 12, or 13 of this title, the trustee may assume or reject an executory contract or unexpired lease of residential real property or of personal property of the debtor at any time before the confirmation of a plan but the court, on the request of any party to such contract or lease, may order the trustee to determine within a specified period of time whether to assume or reject such contract or lease.

(3) The trustee shall timely perform all the obligations of the debtor, except those specified in section 365(b)(2), arising from and after the order for relief under any unexpired lease of nonresidential real property, until such lease is assumed or rejected, notwithstanding section 503(b)(1) of this title. The court may extend, for cause, the time for performance of any such obligation that arises within 60 days after the date of the order for relief, but the time for performance shall not be extended beyond such 60-day period. This subsection shall not be deemed to affect the trustee's obligations under the provisions of subsection (b) or (f) of this section. Acceptance of any such performance does not constitute waiver or relinquishment of the lessor's rights under such lease or under this title.

(4) (A) Subject to subparagraph (B), an unexpired lease of nonresidential real property under which the debtor is the lessee shall be deemed rejected, and the trustee shall immediately surrender that nonresidential real property to the lessor, if the trustee does not assume or reject the unexpired lease by the earlier of—

(i) the date that is 120 days after the date of the order for relief; or

(ii) the date of the entry of an order confirming a plan.

(B) (i) The court may extend the period determined under subparagraph (A), prior to the expiration of the 120-day period, for 90 days on the motion of the trustee or lessor for cause.

(ii) If the court grants an extension under clause (i), the court may grant a subsequent extension only upon prior written consent of the lessor in each instance.

(5) The trustee shall timely perform all of the obligations of the debtor, except those specified in section 365(b)(2), first arising from or after 60 days after the order for relief in a case under chapter 11 of this title under an unexpired lease of personal property (other than personal property leased to an individual primarily for personal, family, or household purposes), until such lease is assumed or rejected notwithstanding section 503(b)(1) of this title, unless the court, after notice and a hearing and based on the equities of the case, orders otherwise with respect to the obligations or timely performance thereof. This subsection shall not be deemed to affect the trustee's obligations under the provisions of subsection (b) or (f). Acceptance of any such performance does not constitute waiver or relinquishment of the lessor's rights under such lease or under this title.

(e) (1) Notwithstanding a provision in an executory contract or unexpired lease, or in applicable law, an executory contract or unexpired lease of the debtor may not be terminated or modified, and any right or obligation under such contract or lease may not be terminated or modified, at any time after the commencement of the case solely because of a provision in such contract or lease that is conditioned on—

(A) the insolvency or financial condition of the debtor at any time before the closing of the case;

(B) the commencement of a case under this title; or

(C) the appointment of or taking possession by a trustee in a case under this title or a custodian before such commencement.

(2) Paragraph (1) of this subsection does not apply to an executory contract or unexpired lease of the debtor, whether or not such contract or lease prohibits or restricts assignment of rights or delegation of duties, if—

(A) (i) applicable law excuses a party, other than the debtor, to such contract or lease from accepting performance from or rendering performance to the trustee or to an assignee of such contract or lease, whether or not such contract or lease prohibits or restricts assignment of rights or delegation of duties; and

(ii) such party does not consent to such assumption or assignment; or

(B) such contract is a contract to make a loan, or extend other debt financing or financial accommodations, to or for the benefit of the debtor, or to issue a security of the debtor.

(f) (1) Except as provided in subsections (b) and (c) of this section, notwithstanding a provision in an executory contract or unexpired lease of the debtor, or in applicable law, that prohibits, restricts, or conditions the assignment of such contract or lease, the trustee may assign such contract or lease under paragraph (2) of this subsection.

(2) The trustee may assign an executory contract or unexpired lease of the debtor only if—

(A) the trustee assumes such contract or lease in accordance with the provisions of this section; and

(B) adequate assurance of future performance by the assignee of such contract or lease is provided, whether or not there has been a default in such contract or lease.

(3) Notwithstanding a provision in an executory contract or unexpired lease of the debtor, or in applicable law that terminates or modifies, or permits a party other than the debtor to terminate or modify, such contract or lease or a right or obligation under such contract or lease on account of an assignment of such contract or lease, such contract, lease, right, or obligation may not be terminated or modified under such provision because of the assumption or assignment of such contract or lease by the trustee.

(g) Except as provided in subsections (h)(2) and (i)(2) of this section, the rejection of an executory contract or unexpired lease of the debtor constitutes a breach of such contract or lease—

(1) if such contract or lease has not been assumed under this section or under a plan confirmed under chapter 9, 11, 12, or 13 of this title, immediately before the date of the filing of the petition; or

(2) if such contract or lease has been assumed under this section or under a plan confirmed under chapter 9, 11, 12, or 13 of this title—

(A) if before such rejection the case has not been converted under section 1112, 1208, or 1307 of this title, at the time of such rejection; or

(B) if before such rejection the case has been converted under section 1112, 1208, or 1307 of this title—

(i) immediately before the date of such conversion, if such contract or lease was assumed before such conversion; or

(ii) at the time of such rejection, if such contract or lease was assumed after such conversion.

(h) (1) (A) If the trustee rejects an unexpired lease of real property under which the debtor is the lessor and—

(i) if the rejection by the trustee amounts to such a breach as would entitle the lessee to treat such lease as terminated by virtue of its terms, applicable nonbankruptcy law, or any agreement made by the lessee, then the lessee under such lease may treat such lease as terminated by the rejection; or

(ii) if the term of such lease has commenced, the lessee may retain its rights under such lease (including rights such as those relating to the amount and timing of payment of rent and other amounts payable by the lessee and any right of use, possession, quiet enjoyment, subletting, assignment, or hypothecation) that are in or appurtenant to the real property for the balance of the term of such lease and for any renewal or extension of such rights to the extent that such rights are enforceable under applicable nonbankruptcy law.

(B) If the lessee retains its rights under subparagraph (A)(ii), the lessee may offset against the rent reserved under such lease for the balance of the term after the date of the rejection of such lease and for the term of any renewal or extension of such lease, the value of any damage caused by the nonperformance after the date of such rejection, of any obligation of the debtor under such lease, but the lessee shall not have any other right against the estate or the debtor on account of any damage occurring after such date caused by such nonperformance.

(C) The rejection of a lease of real property in a shopping center with respect to which the lessee elects to retain its rights under subparagraph (A)(ii) does not affect the enforceability under applicable nonbankruptcy law of any provision in the lease pertaining to radius, location, use, exclusivity, or tenant mix or balance.

(D) In this paragraph, "lessee" includes any successor, assign, or mortgagee permitted under the terms of such lease.

(2) (A) If the trustee rejects a timeshare interest under a timeshare plan under which the debtor is the timeshare interest seller and—

(i) if the rejection amounts to such a breach as would entitle the timeshare interest purchaser to treat the timeshare plan as terminated under its terms, applicable nonbankruptcy law, or any agreement made by timeshare interest purchaser, the timeshare interest purchaser under the timeshare plan may treat the timeshare plan as terminated by such rejection; or

(ii) if the term of such timeshare interest has commenced, then the timeshare interest purchaser may retain its rights in such timeshare interest for the balance of such term and for any term of renewal or extension of such timeshare interest to the extent that such rights are enforceable under applicable nonbankruptcy law.

(B) If the timeshare interest purchaser retains its rights under subparagraph (A), such timeshare interest purchaser may offset against the moneys due for such timeshare interest for the balance of the term after the date of the rejection of such timeshare interest, and the term of any renewal or extension of such timeshare interest, the value of any damage caused by the nonperformance after the date of such rejection, of any obligation of the debtor under such timeshare plan, but the timeshare interest purchaser shall not have any right against the estate or the debtor on account of any damage occurring after such date caused by such nonperformance.

(i) (1) If the trustee rejects an executory contract of the debtor for the sale of real property or for the sale of a timeshare interest under a timeshare plan, under which the purchaser is in possession, such purchaser may treat such contract as terminated, or, in the alternative, may remain in possession of such real property or timeshare interest.

(2) If such purchaser remains in possession—

(A) such purchaser shall continue to make all payments due under such contract, but may, offset against such payments any damages occurring after the date of the rejection of such contract caused by the nonperformance of any obligation of the debtor after such date, but such purchaser does not have any rights against the estate on account of any damages arising after such date from such rejection, other than such offset; and

(B) the trustee shall deliver title to such purchaser in accordance with the provisions of such contract, but is relieved of all other obligations to perform under such contract.

(j) A purchaser that treats an executory contract as terminated under subsection (i) of this section, or a party whose executory contract to purchase real property from the debtor is rejected and under which such party is not in possession, has a lien on the interest of the debtor in such property for the recovery of any portion of the purchase price that such purchaser or party has paid.

(k) Assignment by the trustee to an entity of a contract or lease assumed under this section relieves the trustee and the estate from any liability for any breach of such contract or lease occurring after such assignment.

(l) If an unexpired lease under which the debtor is the lessee is assigned pursuant to this section, the lessor of the property may require a deposit or other security for the performance of the debtor's obligations under the lease substantially the same as would have been required by the landlord upon the initial leasing to a similar tenant.

(m) For purposes of this section 365 and sections 541(b)(2) and 362(b)(10), leases of real property shall include any rental agreement to use real property.

(n) (1) If the trustee rejects an executory contract under which the debtor is a licensor of a right to intellectual property, the licensee under such contract may elect—

(A) to treat such contract as terminated by such rejection if such rejection by the trustee amounts to such a breach as would entitle the licensee to treat such contract as terminated by virtue of its own terms, applicable nonbankruptcy law, or an agreement made by the licensee with another entity; or

(B) to retain its rights (including a right to enforce any exclusivity provision of such contract, but excluding any other right under applicable nonbankruptcy law to specific performance of such contract) under such contract and under any agreement supplementary to such contract, to such intellectual property (including any embodiment of such intellectual property to the extent protected by applicable nonbankruptcy law), as such rights existed immediately before the case commenced, for—

(i) the duration of such contract; and

(ii) any period for which such contract may be extended by the licensee as of right under applicable nonbankruptcy law.

(2) If the licensee elects to retain its rights, as described in paragraph (1)(B) of this subsection, under such contract—

(A) the trustee shall allow the licensee to exercise such rights;

(B) the licensee shall make all royalty payments due under such contract for the duration of such contract and for any period described in paragraph (1)(B) of this subsection for which the licensee extends such contract; and

(C) the licensee shall be deemed to waive—

(i) any right of setoff it may have with respect to such contract under this title or applicable nonbankruptcy law; and

(ii) any claim allowable under section 503(b) of this title arising from the performance of such contract.

(3) If the licensee elects to retain its rights, as described in paragraph (1)(B) of this subsection, then on the written request of the licensee the trustee shall—

(A) to the extent provided in such contract, or any agreement supplementary to such contract, provide to the licensee any intellectual property (including such embodiment) held by the trustee; and

(B) not interfere with the rights of the licensee as provided in such contract, or any agreement supplementary to such contract, to such intellectual property (including such embodiment) including any right to obtain such intellectual property (or such embodiment) from another entity.

(4) Unless and until the trustee rejects such contract, on the written request of the licensee the trustee shall—

(A) to the extent provided in such contract or any agreement supplementary to such contract—

(i) perform such contract; or

(ii) provide to the licensee such intellectual property (including any embodiment of such intellectual property to the extent protected by applicable nonbankruptcy law) held by the trustee; and

(B) not interfere with the rights of the licensee as provided in such contract, or any agreement supplementary to such contract, to such intellectual property (including such embodiment), including any right to obtain such intellectual property (or such embodiment) from another entity.

(o) In a case under chapter 11 of this title, the trustee shall be deemed to have assumed (consistent with the debtor's other obligations under section 507), and shall immediately cure any deficit under, any commitment by the debtor to a Federal depository institutions regulatory agency (or predecessor to such agency) to maintain the capital of an insured depository institution, and any claim for a subsequent breach of the obligations thereunder shall be entitled to priority under section 507. This subsection shall not extend any commitment that would otherwise be terminated by any act of such an agency.

(p) (1) If a lease of personal property is rejected or not timely assumed by the trustee under subsection (d), the leased property is no longer property of the estate and the stay under section 362(a) is automatically terminated.

(2) (A) If the debtor in a case under chapter 7 is an individual, the debtor may notify the creditor in writing that the debtor desires to assume the lease. Upon being so notified, the creditor may, at its option, notify the debtor that it is willing to have the lease assumed by the debtor and may condition such assumption on cure of any outstanding default on terms set by the contract.

(B) If, not later than 30 days after notice is provided under subparagraph (A), the debtor notifies the lessor in writing that the lease is assumed, the liability under the lease will be assumed by the debtor and not by the estate.

(C) The stay under section 362 and the injunction under section 524(a)(2) shall not be violated by notification of the debtor and negotiation of cure under this subsection.

(3) In a case under chapter 11 in which the debtor is an individual and in a case under chapter 13, if the debtor is the lessee with respect to personal property and the lease is not assumed in the plan confirmed by the court, the lease is deemed rejected as of the conclusion of the hearing on confirmation. If the lease is rejected, the stay under section 362 and any stay under section 1301 is automatically terminated with respect to the property subject to the lease.

Sec. 366. Utility service

(a) Except as provided in subsections (b) and (c) of this section, a utility may not alter, refuse, or discontinue service to, or discriminate against, the trustee or the debtor solely on the basis of the commencement of a case under this title or that a debt owed by the debtor to such utility for service rendered before the order for relief was not paid when due.

(b) Such utility may alter, refuse, or discontinue service if neither the trustee nor the debtor, within 20 days after the date of the order for relief, furnishes adequate assurance of payment, in the form of a deposit or other security, for service after such date. On request of a party in interest and after notice and a hearing, the court may order reasonable modification of the amount of the deposit or other security necessary to provide adequate assurance of payment.

(c) (1) (A) For purposes of this subsection, the term "assurance of payment" means—

(i) a cash deposit;

(ii) a letter of credit;

(iii) a certificate of deposit;

(iv) a surety bond;

(v) a prepayment of utility consumption; or

(vi) another form of security that is mutually agreed on between the utility and the debtor or the trustee.

(B) For purposes of this subsection an administrative expense priority shall not constitute an assurance of payment.

(2) Subject to paragraphs (3) and (4), with respect to a case filed under chapter 11, a utility referred to in subsection (a) may alter, refuse, or discontinue utility service, if during the 30-day period beginning on the date of the filing of the petition, the utility does not receive from the debtor or the trustee adequate assurance of payment for utility service that is satisfactory to the utility.

(3) (A) On request of a party in interest and after notice and a hearing, the court may order modification of the amount of an assurance of payment under paragraph (2).

(B) In making a determination under this paragraph whether an assurance of payment is adequate, the court may not consider—

(i) the absence of security before the date of the filing of the petition;

(ii) the payment by the debtor of charges for utility service in a timely manner before the date of the filing of the petition; or

(iii) the availability of an administrative expense priority.

(4) Notwithstanding any other provision of law, with respect to a case subject to this subsection, a utility may recover or set off against a security deposit provided to the utility by the debtor before the date of the filing of the petition without notice or order of the court.

CHAPTER 5—CREDITORS, THE DEBTOR, AND THE ESTATE

SUBCHAPTER I—CREDITORS AND CLAIMS

Sec. 501. Filing of proofs of claims or interests

(a) A creditor or an indenture trustee may file a proof of claim. An equity security holder may file a proof of interest.

(b) If a creditor does not timely file a proof of such creditor's claim, an entity that is liable to such creditor with the debtor, or that has secured such creditor, may file a proof of such claim.

(c) If a creditor does not timely file a proof of such creditor's claim, the debtor or the trustee may file a proof of such claim.

(d) A claim of a kind specified in section 502(e)(2), 502(f), 502(g), 502(h) or 502(i) of this title may be filed under subsection (a), (b), or (c) of this section the same as if such claim were a claim against the debtor and had arisen before the date of the filing of the petition.

(e) A claim arising from the liability of a debtor for fuel use tax assessed consistent with the requirements of section 31705 of title 49 may be filed by the base jurisdiction designated pursuant to the International Fuel Tax Agreement (as defined in section 31701 of title 49) and, if so filed, shall be allowed as a single claim.

Sec. 502. Allowance of claims or interests

(a) A claim or interest, proof of which is filed under section 501 of this title, is deemed allowed, unless a party in interest, including a creditor of a general partner in a partnership that is a debtor in a case under chapter 7 of this title, objects.

(b) Except as provided in subsections (e)(2), (f), (g), (h) and (i) of this section, if such objection to a claim is made, the court, after notice and a hearing, shall determine the amount of such claim in lawful currency of the United States as of the date of the filing of the petition, and shall allow such claim in such amount, except to the extent that—

   (1) such claim is unenforceable against the debtor and property of the debtor, under any agreement or applicable law for a reason other than because such claim is contingent or unmatured;

   (2) such claim is for unmatured interest;

   (3) if such claim is for a tax assessed against property of the estate, such claim exceeds the value of the interest of the estate in such property;

   (4) if such claim is for services of an insider or attorney of the debtor, such claim exceeds the reasonable value of such services;

   (5) such claim is for a debt that is unmatured on the date of the filing of the petition and that is excepted from discharge under section 523(a)(5) of this title;

   (6) if such claim is the claim of a lessor for damages resulting from the termination of a lease of real property, such claim exceeds—

      (A) the rent reserved by such lease, without acceleration, for the greater of one year, or 15 percent, not to exceed three years, of the remaining term of such lease, following the earlier of—

         (i) the date of the filing of the petition; and

(ii) the date on which such lessor repossessed, or the lessee surrendered, the leased property; plus

(B) any unpaid rent due under such lease, without acceleration, on the earlier of such dates;

(7) if such claim is the claim of an employee for damages resulting from the termination of an employment contract, such claim exceeds—

(A) the compensation provided by such contract, without acceleration, for one year following the earlier of—

(i) the date of the filing of the petition; or

(ii) the date on which the employer directed the employee to terminate, or such employee terminated, performance under such contract; plus

(B) any unpaid compensation due under such contract, without acceleration, on the earlier of such dates;

(8) such claim results from a reduction, due to late payment, in the amount of an otherwise applicable credit available to the debtor in connection with an employment tax on wages, salaries, or commissions earned from the debtor; or

(9) proof of such claim is not timely filed, except to the extent tardily filed as permitted under paragraph (1), (2), or (3) of section 726(a) of this title or under the Federal Rules of Bankruptcy Procedure, except that a claim of a governmental unit shall be timely filed if it is filed before 180 days after the date of the order for relief or such later time as the Federal Rules of Bankruptcy Procedure may provide, and except that in a case under chapter 13, a claim of a governmental unit for a tax with respect to a return filed under section 1308 shall be timely if the claim is filed on or before the date that is 60 days after the date on which such return was filed as required.

(c) There shall be estimated for purpose of allowance under this section—

(1) any contingent or unliquidated claim, the fixing or liquidation of which, as the case may be, would unduly delay the administration of the case; or

(2) any right to payment arising from a right to an equitable remedy for breach of performance.

(d) Notwithstanding subsections (a) and (b) of this section, the court shall disallow any claim of any entity from which property is recoverable under section 542, 543, 550, or 553 of this title or that is a transferee of a transfer avoidable under section 522(f), 522(h), 544, 545, 547, 548, 549, or 724(a) of this title, unless such entity or transferee has paid the amount, or turned over any such property, for which such entity or transferee is liable under section 522(i), 542, 543, 550, or 553 of this title.

(e) (1) Notwithstanding subsections (a), (b), and (c) of this section and paragraph (2) of this subsection, the court shall disallow any claim for reimbursement or contribution of an entity that is liable with the debtor on or has secured the claim of a creditor, to the extent that—

(A) such creditor's claim against the estate is disallowed;

(B) such claim for reimbursement or contribution is contingent as of the time of allowance or disallowance of such claim for reimbursement or contribution; or

(C) such entity asserts a right of subrogation to the rights of such creditor under section 509 of this title.

(2) A claim for reimbursement or contribution of such an entity that becomes fixed after the commencement of the case shall be determined, and shall be allowed under subsection

(a), (b), or (c) of this section, or disallowed under subsection (d) of this section, the same as if such claim had become fixed before the date of the filing of the petition.

(f) In an involuntary case, a claim arising in the ordinary course of the debtor's business or financial affairs after the commencement of the case but before the earlier of the appointment of a trustee and the order for relief shall be determined as of the date such claim arises, and shall be allowed under subsection (a), (b), or (c) of this section or disallowed under subsection (d) or (e) of this section, the same as if such claim had arisen before the date of the filing of the petition.

(g) (1) A claim arising from the rejection, under section 365 of this title or under a plan under chapter 9, 11, 12, or 13 of this title, of an executory contract or unexpired lease of the debtor that has not been assumed shall be determined, and shall be allowed under subsection (a), (b), or (c) of this section or disallowed under subsection (d) or (e) of this section, the same as if such claim had arisen before the date of the filing of the petition.

(2) A claim for damages calculated in accordance with section 562 shall be allowed under subsection (a), (b), or (c), or disallowed under subsection (d) or (e), as if such claim had arisen before the date of the filing of the petition.

(h) A claim arising from the recovery of property under section 522, 550, or 553 of this title shall be determined, and shall be allowed under subsection (a), (b), or (c) of this section, or disallowed under subsection (d) or (e) of this section, the same as if such claim had arisen before the date of the filing of the petition.

(i) A claim that does not arise until after the commencement of the case for a tax entitled to priority under section 507(a)(8) of this title shall be determined, and shall be allowed under subsection (a), (b), or (c) of this section, or disallowed under subsection (d) or (e) of this section, the same as if such claim had arisen before the date of the filing of the petition.

(j) A claim that has been allowed or disallowed may be reconsidered for cause. A reconsidered claim may be allowed or disallowed according to the equities of the case. Reconsideration of a claim under this subsection does not affect the validity of any payment or transfer from the estate made to a holder of an allowed claim on account of such allowed claim that is not reconsidered, but if a reconsidered claim is allowed and is of the same class as such holder's claim, such holder may not receive any additional payment or transfer from the estate on account of such holder's allowed claim until the holder of such reconsidered and allowed claim receives payment on account of such claim proportionate in value to that already received by such other holder. This subsection does not alter or modify the trustee's right to recover from a creditor any excess payment or transfer made to such creditor.

(k) (1) The court, on the motion of the debtor and after a hearing, may reduce a claim filed under this section based in whole on an unsecured consumer debt by not more than 20 percent of the claim, if—

(A) the claim was filed by a creditor who unreasonably refused to negotiate a reasonable alternative repayment schedule proposed on behalf of the debtor by an approved nonprofit budget and credit counseling agency described in section 111;

(B) the offer of the debtor under subparagraph (A)—

(i) was made at least 60 days before the date of the filing of the petition; and

(ii) provided for payment of at least 60 percent of the amount of the debt over a period not to exceed the repayment period of the loan, or a reasonable extension thereof; and

(C) no part of the debt under the alternative repayment schedule is nondischargeable.

(2) The debtor shall have the burden of proving, by clear and convincing evidence, that—
(A) the creditor unreasonably refused to consider the debtor's proposal; and
(B) the proposed alternative repayment schedule was made prior to expiration of the 60-day period specified in paragraph (1)(B)(i).

Sec. 503. Allowance of administrative expenses

(a) An entity may timely file a request for payment of an administrative expense, or may tardily file such request if permitted by the court for cause.

(b) After notice and a hearing, there shall be allowed administrative expenses, other than claims allowed under section 502(f) of this title, including—

(1) (A) the actual, necessary costs and expenses of preserving the estate including—
(i) wages, salaries, and commissions for services rendered after the commencement of the case; and
(ii) wages and benefits awarded pursuant to a judicial proceeding or a proceeding of the National Labor Relations Board as back pay attributable to any period of time occurring after commencement of the case under this title, as a result of a violation of Federal or State law by the debtor, without regard to the time of the occurrence of unlawful conduct on which such award is based or to whether any services were rendered, if the court determines that payment of wages and benefits by reason of the operation of this clause will not substantially increase the probability of layoff or termination of current employees, or of nonpayment of domestic support obligations, during the case under this title;
(B) any tax—
(i) incurred by the estate, whether secured or unsecured, including property taxes for which liability is in rem, in personam, or both, except a tax of a kind specified in section 507(a)(8) of this title; or
(ii) attributable to an excessive allowance of a tentative carryback adjustment that the estate received, whether the taxable year to which such adjustment relates ended before or after the commencement of the case;
(C) any fine, penalty, or reduction in credit relating to a tax of a kind specified in subparagraph (B) of this paragraph; and
(D) notwithstanding the requirements of subsection (a), a governmental unit shall not be required to file a request for the payment of an expense described in subparagraph (B) or (C), as a condition of its being an allowed administrative expense;

(2) compensation and reimbursement awarded under section 330(a) of this title;

(3) the actual, necessary expenses, other than compensation and reimbursement specified in paragraph (4) of this subsection, incurred by—
(A) a creditor that files a petition under section 303 of this title;
(B) a creditor that recovers, after the court's approval, for the benefit of the estate any property transferred or concealed by the debtor;
(C) a creditor in connection with the prosecution of a criminal offense relating to the case or to the business or property of the debtor;
(D) a creditor, an indenture trustee, an equity security holder, or a committee representing creditors or equity security holders other than a committee appointed under section

1102 of this title, in making a substantial contribution in a case under chapter 9 or 11 of this title;

(E) a custodian superseded under section 543 of this title, and compensation for the services of such custodian; or

(F) a member of a committee appointed under section 1102 of this title, if such expenses are incurred in the performance of the duties of such committee;

(4) reasonable compensation for professional services rendered by an attorney or an accountant of an entity whose expense is allowable under subparagraph (A), (B), (C), (D), or (E) of paragraph (3) of this subsection, based on the time, the nature, the extent, and the value of such services, and the cost of comparable services other than in a case under this title, and reimbursement for actual, necessary expenses incurred by such attorney or accountant;

(5) reasonable compensation for services rendered by an indenture trustee in making a substantial contribution in a case under chapter 9 or 11 of this title, based on the time, the nature, the extent, and the value of such services, and the cost of comparable services other than in a case under this title;

(6) the fees and mileage payable under chapter 119 of title 28;

(7) with respect to a nonresidential real property lease previously assumed under section 365, and subsequently rejected, a sum equal to all monetary obligations due, excluding those arising from or relating to a failure to operate or a penalty provision, for the period of 2 years following the later of the rejection date or the date of actual turnover of the premises, without reduction or setoff for any reason whatsoever except for sums actually received or to be received from an entity other than the debtor, and the claim for remaining sums due for the balance of the term of the lease shall be a claim under section 502(b)(6);

(8) the actual, necessary costs and expenses of closing a health care business incurred by a trustee or by a Federal agency (as defined in section 551(1) of title 5) or a department or agency of a State or political subdivision thereof, including any cost or expense incurred—

(A) in disposing of patient records in accordance with section 351; or

(B) in connection with transferring patients from the health care business that is in the process of being closed to another health care business; and

(9) the value of any goods received by the debtor within 20 days before the date of commencement of a case under this title in which the goods have been sold to the debtor in the ordinary course of such debtor's business.

(c) Notwithstanding subsection (b), there shall neither be allowed, nor paid—

(1) a transfer made to, or an obligation incurred for the benefit of, an insider of the debtor for the purpose of inducing such person to remain with the debtor's business, absent a finding by the court based on evidence in the record that—

(A) the transfer or obligation is essential to retention of the person because the individual has a bona fide job offer from another business at the same or greater rate of compensation;

(B) the services provided by the person are essential to the survival of the business; and

(C) either—

(i) the amount of the transfer made to, or obligation incurred for the benefit of, the person is not greater than an amount equal to 10 times the amount of the mean transfer or obligation of a similar kind given to nonmanagement employees for any purpose during the calendar year in which the transfer is made or the obligation is incurred; or

(ii) if no such similar transfers were made to, or obligations were incurred for the benefit of, such nonmanagement employees during such calendar year, the amount of the transfer or obligation is not greater than an amount equal to 25 percent of the amount of any similar transfer or obligation made to or incurred for the benefit of such insider for any purpose during the calendar year before the year in which such transfer is made or obligation is incurred;

(2) a severance payment to an insider of the debtor, unless—

(A) the payment is part of a program that is generally applicable to all full-time employees; and

(B) the amount of the payment is not greater than 10 times the amount of the mean severance pay given to nonmanagement employees during the calendar year in which the payment is made; or

(3) other transfers or obligations that are outside the ordinary course of business and not justified by the facts and circumstances of the case, including transfers made to, or obligations incurred for the benefit of, officers, managers, or consultants hired after the date of the filing of the petition.

Sec. 504. Sharing of compensation

(a) Except as provided in subsection (b) of this section, a person receiving compensation or reimbursement under section 503(b)(2) or 503(b)(4) of this title may not share or agree to share—

(1) any such compensation or reimbursement with another person; or

(2) any compensation or reimbursement received by another person under such sections.

(b) (1) A member, partner, or regular associate in a professional association, corporation, or partnership may share compensation or reimbursement received under section 503(b)(2) or 503(b)(4) of this title with another member, partner, or regular associate in such association, corporation, or partnership, and may share in any compensation or reimbursement received under such sections by another member, partner, or regular associate in such association, corporation, or partnership.

(2) An attorney for a creditor that files a petition under section 303 of this title may share compensation and reimbursement received under section 503(b)(4) of this title with any other attorney contributing to the services rendered or expenses incurred by such creditor's attorney.

(c) This section shall not apply with respect to sharing, or agreeing to share, compensation with a bona fide public service attorney referral program that operates in accordance with non-Federal law regulating attorney referral services and with rules of professional responsibility applicable to attorney acceptance of referrals.

Sec. 505. Determination of tax liability

(a) (1) Except as provided in paragraph (2) of this subsection, the court may determine the amount or legality of any tax, any fine or penalty relating to a tax, or any addition to tax, whether or not previously assessed, whether or not paid, and whether or not contested before and adjudicated by a judicial or administrative tribunal of competent jurisdiction.

(2) The court may not so determine—

(A) the amount or legality of a tax, fine, penalty, or addition to tax if such amount or legality was contested before and adjudicated by a judicial or administrative tribunal of competent jurisdiction before the commencement of the case under this title;

(B) any right of the estate to a tax refund, before the earlier of—

(i) 120 days after the trustee properly requests such refund from the governmental unit from which such refund is claimed; or

(ii) a determination by such governmental unit of such request; or

(C) the amount or legality of any amount arising in connection with an ad valorem tax on real or personal property of the estate, if the applicable period for contesting or redetermining that amount under any law (other than a bankruptcy law) has expired.

(b) (1) (A) The clerk shall maintain a list under which a Federal, State, or local governmental unit responsible for the collection of taxes within the district may—

(i) designate an address for service of requests under this subsection; and

(ii) describe where further information concerning additional requirements for filing such requests may be found.

(B) If such governmental unit does not designate an address and provide such address to the clerk under subparagraph (A), any request made under this subsection may be served at the address for the filing of a tax return or protest with the appropriate taxing authority of such governmental unit.

(2) A trustee may request a determination of any unpaid liability of the estate for any tax incurred during the administration of the case by submitting a tax return for such tax and a request for such a determination to the governmental unit charged with responsibility for collection or determination of such tax at the address and in the manner designated in paragraph (1). Unless such return is fraudulent, or contains a material misrepresentation, the estate, the trustee, the debtor, and any successor to the debtor are discharged from any liability for such tax—

(A) upon payment of the tax shown on such return, if—

(i) such governmental unit does not notify the trustee, within 60 days after such request, that such return has been selected for examination; or

(ii) such governmental unit does not complete such an examination and notify the trustee of any tax due, within 180 days after such request or within such additional time as the court, for cause, permits;

(B) upon payment of the tax determined by the court, after notice and a hearing, after completion by such governmental unit of such examination; or

(C) upon payment of the tax determined by such governmental unit to be due.

(c) Notwithstanding section 362 of this title, after determination by the court of a tax under this section, the governmental unit charged with responsibility for collection of such tax may assess such tax against the estate, the debtor, or a successor to the debtor, as the case may be, subject to any otherwise applicable law.

Sec. 506. Determination of secured status

(a) (1) An allowed claim of a creditor secured by a lien on property in which the estate has an interest, or that is subject to setoff under section 553 of this title, is a secured claim to the extent of the value of such creditor's interest in the estate's interest in such property, or to the extent of the amount subject to setoff, as the case may be, and is an unsecured claim to the extent that the value of such creditor's interest or the amount so subject to setoff is less than the amount of such allowed claim. Such value shall be determined in light of the purpose of the valuation and of the proposed disposition or use of such property, and in conjunction with any hearing on such disposition or use or on a plan affecting such creditor's interest.

(2) If the debtor is an individual in a case under chapter 7 or 13, such value with respect to personal property securing an allowed claim shall be determined based on the replacement value of such property as of the date of the filing of the petition without deduction for costs of sale or marketing. With respect to property acquired for personal, family, or household purposes, replacement value shall mean the price a retail merchant would charge for property of that kind considering the age and condition of the property at the time value is determined.

(b) To the extent that an allowed secured claim is secured by property the value of which, after any recovery under subsection (c) of this section, is greater than the amount of such claim, there shall be allowed to the holder of such claim, interest on such claim, and any reasonable fees, costs, or charges provided for under the agreement or State statute under which such claim arose.

(c) The trustee may recover from property securing an allowed secured claim the reasonable, necessary costs and expenses of preserving, or disposing of, such property to the extent of any benefit to the holder of such claim, including the payment of all ad valorem property taxes with respect to the property.

(d) To the extent that a lien secures a claim against the debtor that is not an allowed secured claim, such lien is void, unless—

(1) such claim was disallowed only under section 502(b)(5) or 502(e) of this title; or

(2) such claim is not an allowed secured claim due only to the failure of any entity to file a proof of such claim under section 501 of this title.

Sec. 507. Priorities

(a) The following expenses and claims have priority in the following order:

(1) First:

(A) Allowed unsecured claims for domestic support obligations that, as of the date of the filing of the petition in a case under this title, are owed to or recoverable by a spouse, former spouse, or child of the debtor, or such child's parent, legal guardian, or responsible relative, without regard to whether the claim is filed by such person or is filed by a governmental unit on behalf of such person, on the condition that funds received under this paragraph by a governmental unit under this title after the date of the filing of the petition shall be applied and distributed in accordance with applicable nonbankruptcy law.

(B) Subject to claims under subparagraph (A), allowed unsecured claims for domestic support obligations that, as of the date of the filing of the petition, are assigned by a spouse, former spouse, child of the debtor, or such child's parent, legal guardian, or responsible relative to a governmental unit (unless such obligation is assigned voluntarily by the spouse, former spouse, child, parent, legal guardian, or responsible relative of the child for the purpose of collecting the debt) or are owed directly to or recoverable by a governmental unit under applicable nonbankruptcy law, on the condition that funds received under this paragraph by a governmental unit under this title after the date of the filing of the petition be applied and distributed in accordance with applicable nonbankruptcy law.

(C) If a trustee is appointed or elected under section 701, 702, 703, 1104, 1202, or 1302, the administrative expenses of the trustee allowed under paragraphs (1)(A), (2), and (6) of section 503(b) shall be paid before payment of claims under subparagraphs (A) and (B), to the extent that the trustee administers assets that are otherwise available for the payment of such claims.

(2) Second, administrative expenses allowed under section 503(b) of this title, and any fees and charges assessed against the estate under chapter 123 of title 28.

(3) Third, unsecured claims allowed under section 502(f) of this title.

(4) Fourth, allowed unsecured claims, but only to the extent of $10,000 for each individual or corporation, as the case may be, earned within 180 days before the date of the filing of the petition or the date of the cessation of the debtor's business, whichever occurs first, for—

(A) wages, salaries, or commissions, including vacation, severance, and sick leave pay earned by an individual; or

(B) sales commissions earned by an individual or by a corporation with only 1 employee, acting as an independent contractor in the sale of goods or services for the debtor in the ordinary course of the debtor's business if, and only if, during the 12 months preceding that date, at least 75 percent of the amount that the individual or corporation earned by acting as an independent contractor in the sale of goods or services was earned from the debtor.

(5) Fifth, allowed unsecured claims for contributions to an employee benefit plan—

(A) arising from services rendered within 180 days before the date of the filing of the petition or the date of the cessation of the debtor's business, whichever occurs first; but only

(B) for each such plan, to the extent of—

(i) the number of employees covered by each such plan multiplied by $10,000; less

(ii) the aggregate amount paid to such employees under paragraph (4) of this subsection, plus the aggregate amount paid by the estate on behalf of such employees to any other employee benefit plan.

(6) Sixth, allowed unsecured claims of persons—

(A) engaged in the production or raising of grain, as defined in section 557(b) of this title, against a debtor who owns or operates a grain storage facility, as defined in section 557(b) of this title, for grain or the proceeds of grain, or

(B) engaged as a United States fisherman against a debtor who has acquired fish or fish produce from a fisherman through a sale or conversion, and who is engaged in operating a fish produce storage or processing facility—

but only to the extent of $4,000 for each such individual.

(7) Seventh, allowed unsecured claims of individuals, to the extent of $1,800 for each such individual, arising from the deposit, before the commencement of the case, of money in connection with the purchase, lease, or rental of property, or the purchase of services,

for the personal, family, or household use of such individuals, that were not delivered or provided.

(8) Eighth, allowed unsecured claims of governmental units, only to the extent that such claims are for—

(A) a tax on or measured by income or gross receipts for a taxable year ending on or before the date of the filing of the petition—

(i) for which a return, if required, is last due, including extensions, after three years before the date of the filing of the petition;

(ii) assessed within 240 days before the date of the filing of the petition, exclusive of—

(I) any time during which an offer in compromise with respect to that tax was pending or in effect during that 240-day period, plus 30 days; and

(II) any time during which a stay of proceedings against collections was in effect in a prior case under this title during that 240-day period, plus 90 days.[8]

(iii) other than a tax of a kind specified in section 523(a)(1)(B) or 523(a)(1)(C) of this title, not assessed before, but assessable, under applicable law or by agreement, after, the commencement of the case;

(B) a property tax incurred before the commencement of the case and last payable without penalty after one year before the date of the filing of the petition;

(C) a tax required to be collected or withheld and for which the debtor is liable in whatever capacity;

(D) an employment tax on a wage, salary, or commission of a kind specified in paragraph (4) of this subsection earned from the debtor before the date of the filing of the petition, whether or not actually paid before such date, for which a return is last due, under applicable law or under any extension, after three years before the date of the filing of the petition;

(E) an excise tax on—

(i) a transaction occurring before the date of the filing of the petition for which a return, if required, is last due, under applicable law or under any extension, after three years before the date of the filing of the petition; or

(ii) if a return is not required, a transaction occurring during the three years immediately preceding the date of the filing of the petition;

(F) a customs duty arising out of the importation of merchandise—

(i) entered for consumption within one year before the date of the filing of the petition;

(ii) covered by an entry liquidated or reliquidated within one year before the date of the filing of the petition; or

(iii) entered for consumption within four years before the date of the filing of the petition but unliquidated on such date, if the Secretary of the Treasury certifies that failure to liquidate such entry was due to an investigation pending on such date into assessment of antidumping or countervailing duties or fraud, or if information needed for the proper appraisement or classification of such

---

[8] *Sic.* Period probably should be "; or".

merchandise was not available to the appropriate customs officer before such date; or

(G) a penalty related to a claim of a kind specified in this paragraph and in compensation for actual pecuniary loss.

An otherwise applicable time period specified in this paragraph shall be suspended for any period during which a governmental unit is prohibited under applicable nonbankruptcy law from collecting a tax as a result of a request by the debtor for a hearing and an appeal of any collection action taken or proposed against the debtor, plus 90 days; plus any time during which the stay of proceedings was in effect in a prior case under this title or during which collection was precluded by the existence of 1 or more confirmed plans under this title, plus 90 days.

(9) Ninth, allowed unsecured claims based upon any commitment by the debtor to a Federal depository institutions regulatory agency (or predecessor to such agency) to maintain the capital of an insured depository institution.

(10) Tenth, allowed claims for death or personal injury resulting from the operation of a motor vehicle or vessel if such operation was unlawful because the debtor was intoxicated from using alcohol, a drug, or another substance.

(b) If the trustee, under section 362, 363, or 364 of this title, provides adequate protection of the interest of a holder of a claim secured by a lien on property of the debtor and if, notwithstanding such protection, such creditor has a claim allowable under subsection (a)(2) of this section arising from the stay of action against such property under section 362 of this title, from the use, sale, or lease of such property under section 363 of this title, or from the granting of a lien under section 364(d) of this title, then such creditor's claim under such subsection shall have priority over every other claim allowable under such subsection.

(c) For the purpose of subsection (a) of this section, a claim of a governmental unit arising from an erroneous refund or credit of a tax has the same priority as a claim for the tax to which such refund or credit relates.

(d) An entity that is subrogated to the rights of a holder of a claim of a kind specified in subsection (a)(1), (a)(4), (a)(5), (a)(6), (a)(7), (a)(8), or (a)(9) of this section is not subrogated to the right of the holder of such claim to priority under such subsection.

Sec. 508. Effect of distribution other than under this title

If a creditor of a partnership debtor receives, from a general partner that is not a debtor in a case under chapter 7 of this title, payment of, or a transfer of property on account of, a claim that is allowed under this title and that is not secured by a lien on property of such partner, such creditor may not receive any payment under this title on account of such claim until each of the other holders of claims on account of which such holders are entitled to share equally with such creditor under this title has received payment under this title equal in value to the consideration received by such creditor from such general partner.

Sec. 509. Claims of codebtors

(a) Except as provided in subsection (b) or (c) of this section, an entity that is liable with the debtor on, or that has secured, a claim of a creditor against the debtor, and that pays such claim, is subrogated to the rights of such creditor to the extent of such payment.

(b) Such entity is not subrogated to the rights of such creditor to the extent that—

(1) a claim of such entity for reimbursement or contribution on account of such payment of such creditor's claim is—
 (A) allowed under section 502 of this title;
 (B) disallowed other than under section 502(e) of this title; or
 (C) subordinated under section 510 of this title; or

(2) as between the debtor and such entity, such entity received the consideration for the claim held by such creditor.

(c) The court shall subordinate to the claim of a creditor and for the benefit of such creditor an allowed claim, by way of subrogation under this section, or for reimbursement or contribution, of an entity that is liable with the debtor on, or that has secured, such creditor's claim, until such creditor's claim is paid in full, either through payments under this title or otherwise.

Sec. 510. Subordination

(a) A subordination agreement is enforceable in a case under this title to the same extent that such agreement is enforceable under applicable nonbankruptcy law.

(b) For the purpose of distribution under this title, a claim arising from rescission of a purchase or sale of a security of the debtor or of an affiliate of the debtor, for damages arising from the purchase or sale of such a security, or for reimbursement or contribution allowed under section 502 on account of such a claim, shall be subordinated to all claims or interests that are senior to or equal the claim or interest represented by such security, except that if such security is common stock, such claim has the same priority as common stock.

(c) Notwithstanding subsections (a) and (b) of this section, after notice and a hearing, the court may—
 (1) under principles of equitable subordination, subordinate for purposes of distribution all or part of an allowed claim to all or part of another allowed claim or all or part of an allowed interest to all or part of another allowed interest; or
 (2) order that any lien securing such a subordinated claim be transferred to the estate.

Sec. 511. Rate of interest on tax claims

(a) If any provision of this title requires the payment of interest on a tax claim or on an administrative expense tax, or the payment of interest to enable a creditor to receive the present value of the allowed amount of a tax claim, the rate of interest shall be the rate determined under applicable nonbankruptcy law.

(b) In the case of taxes paid under a confirmed plan under this title, the rate of interest shall be determined as of the calendar month in which the plan is confirmed.

SUBCHAPTER II—DEBTOR'S DUTIES AND BENEFITS

Sec. 521. Debtor's duties

(a) The debtor shall—
 (1) file—
  (A) a list of creditors; and
  (B) unless the court orders otherwise—
   (i) a schedule of assets and liabilities;
   (ii) a schedule of current income and current expenditures;

(iii) a statement of the debtor's financial affairs and, if section 342(b) applies, a certificate—
(I) of an attorney whose name is indicated on the petition as the attorney for the debtor, or a bankruptcy petition preparer signing the petition under section 110(b)(1), indicating that such attorney or the bankruptcy petition preparer delivered to the debtor the notice required by section 342(b); or
(II) if no attorney is so indicated, and no bankruptcy petition preparer signed the petition, of the debtor that such notice was received and read by the debtor;
(iv) copies of all payment advices or other evidence of payment received within 60 days before the date of the filing of the petition, by the debtor from any employer of the debtor;
(v) a statement of the amount of monthly net income, itemized to show how the amount is calculated; and
(vi) a statement disclosing any reasonably anticipated increase in income or expenditures over the 12-month period following the date of the filing of the petition;

(2) if an individual debtor's schedule of assets and liabilities includes debts which are secured by property of the estate—
(A) within thirty days after the date of the filing of a petition under chapter 7 of this title or on or before the date of the meeting of creditors, whichever is earlier, or within such additional time as the court, for cause, within such period fixes, the debtor shall file with the clerk a statement of his intention with respect to the retention or surrender of such property and, if applicable, specifying that such property is claimed as exempt, that the debtor intends to redeem such property, or that the debtor intends to reaffirm debts secured by such property;
(B) within 30 days after the first date set for the meeting of creditors under section 341(a), or within such additional time as the court, for cause, within such 30-day period fixes, the debtor shall perform his intention with respect to such property, as specified by subparagraph (A) of this paragraph; and
(C) nothing in subparagraphs (A) and (B) of this paragraph shall alter the debtor's or the trustee's rights with regard to such property under this title, except as provided in section 362(h);

(3) if a trustee is serving in the case or an auditor serving under section 586(f) of title 28, cooperate with the trustee as necessary to enable the trustee to perform the trustee's duties under this title;

(4) if a trustee is serving in the case or an auditor serving under section 586(f) of title 28, surrender to the trustee all property of the estate and any recorded information, including books, documents, records, and papers, relating to property of the estate, whether or not immunity is granted under section 344 of this title;

(5) appear at the hearing required under section 524(d) of this title;

(6) in a case under chapter 7 of this title in which the debtor is an individual, not retain possession of personal property as to which a creditor has an allowed claim for the purchase price secured in whole or in part by an interest in such personal property unless

the debtor, not later than 45 days after the first meeting of creditors under section 341(a), either—

(A) enters into an agreement with the creditor pursuant to section 524(c) with respect to the claim secured by such property; or

(B) redeems such property from the security interest pursuant to section 722; and

(7) unless a trustee is serving in the case, continue to perform the obligations required of the administrator (as defined in section 3 of the Employee Retirement Income Security Act of 1974) of an employee benefit plan if at the time of the commencement of the case the debtor (or any entity designated by the debtor) served as such administrator.

If the debtor fails to so act within the 45-day period referred to in paragraph (6), the stay under section 362(a) is terminated with respect to the personal property of the estate or of the debtor which is affected, such property shall no longer be property of the estate, and the creditor may take whatever action as to such property as is permitted by applicable nonbankruptcy law, unless the court determines on the motion of the trustee filed before the expiration of such 45-day period, and after notice and a hearing, that such property is of consequential value or benefit to the estate, orders appropriate adequate protection of the creditor's interest, and orders the debtor to deliver any collateral in the debtor's possession to the trustee.

(b) In addition to the requirements under subsection (a), a debtor who is an individual shall file with the court—

(1) a certificate from the approved nonprofit budget and credit counseling agency that provided the debtor services under section 109(h) describing the services provided to the debtor; and

(2) a copy of the debt repayment plan, if any, developed under section 109(h) through the approved nonprofit budget and credit counseling agency referred to in paragraph (1).

(c) In addition to meeting the requirements under subsection (a), a debtor shall file with the court a record of any interest that a debtor has in an education individual retirement account (as defined in section 530(b)(1) of the Internal Revenue Code of 1986) or under a qualified State tuition program (as defined in section 529(b)(1) of such Code).

(d) If the debtor fails timely to take the action specified in subsection (a)(6) of this section, or in paragraphs (1) and (2) of section 362(h), with respect to property which a lessor or bailor owns and has leased, rented, or bailed to the debtor or as to which a creditor holds a security interest not otherwise voidable under section 522(f), 544, 545, 547, 548, or 549, nothing in this title shall prevent or limit the operation of a provision in the underlying lease or agreement that has the effect of placing the debtor in default under such lease or agreement by reason of the occurrence, pendency, or existence of a proceeding under this title or the insolvency of the debtor. Nothing in this subsection shall be deemed to justify limiting such a provision in any other circumstance.

(e) (1) If the debtor in a case under chapter 7 or 13 is an individual and if a creditor files with the court at any time a request to receive a copy of the petition, schedules, and statement of financial affairs filed by the debtor, then the court shall make such petition, such schedules, and such statement available to such creditor.

(2) (A) The debtor shall provide—

(i) not later than 7 days before the date first set for the first meeting of creditors, to the trustee a copy of the Federal income tax return required under applicable law (or at the election of the debtor, a transcript of such return) for the most recent tax year ending immediately before the commencement of the case and for which a Federal income tax return was filed; and

(ii) at the same time the debtor complies with clause (i), a copy of such return (or if elected under clause (i), such transcript) to any creditor that timely requests such copy.

(B) If the debtor fails to comply with clause (i) or (ii) of subparagraph (A), the court shall dismiss the case unless the debtor demonstrates that the failure to so comply is due to circumstances beyond the control of the debtor.

(C) If a creditor requests a copy of such tax return or such transcript and if the debtor fails to provide a copy of such tax return or such transcript to such creditor at the time the debtor provides such tax return or such transcript to the trustee, then the court shall dismiss the case unless the debtor demonstrates that the failure to provide a copy of such tax return or such transcript is due to circumstances beyond the control of the debtor.

(3) If a creditor in a case under chapter 13 files with the court at any time a request to receive a copy of the plan filed by the debtor, then the court shall make available to such creditor a copy of the plan—

(A) at a reasonable cost; and

(B) not later than 5 days after such request is filed.

(f) At the request of the court, the United States trustee, or any party in interest in a case under chapter 7, 11, or 13, a debtor who is an individual shall file with the court—

(1) at the same time filed with the taxing authority, a copy of each Federal income tax return required under applicable law (or at the election of the debtor, a transcript of such tax return) with respect to each tax year of the debtor ending while the case is pending under such chapter;

(2) at the same time filed with the taxing authority, each Federal income tax return required under applicable law (or at the election of the debtor, a transcript of such tax return) that had not been filed with such authority as of the date of the commencement of the case and that was subsequently filed for any tax year of the debtor ending in the 3-year period ending on the date of the commencement of the case;

(3) a copy of each amendment to any Federal income tax return or transcript filed with the court under paragraph (1) or (2); and

(4) in a case under chapter 13—

(A) on the date that is either 90 days after the end of such tax year or 1 year after the date of the commencement of the case, whichever is later, if a plan is not confirmed before such later date; and

(B) annually after the plan is confirmed and until the case is closed, not later than the date that is 45 days before the anniversary of the confirmation of the plan;

a statement, under penalty of perjury, of the income and expenditures of the debtor during the tax year of the debtor most recently concluded before such statement is filed under this paragraph, and of the monthly income of the debtor, that shows how income, expenditures, and monthly income are calculated.

(g) (1) A statement referred to in subsection (f)(4) shall disclose—

(A) the amount and sources of the income of the debtor;

(B) the identity of any person responsible with the debtor for the support of any dependent of the debtor; and

(C) the identity of any person who contributed, and the amount contributed, to the household in which the debtor resides.

(2) The tax returns, amendments, and statement of income and expenditures described in subsections (e)(2)(A) and (f) shall be available to the United States trustee (or the bankruptcy administrator, if any), the trustee, and any party in interest for inspection and copying, subject to the requirements of section 315(c) of the Bankruptcy Abuse Prevention and Consumer Protection Act of 2005.

(h) If requested by the United States trustee or by the trustee, the debtor shall provide—

(1) a document that establishes the identity of the debtor, including a driver's license, passport, or other document that contains a photograph of the debtor; or

(2) such other personal identifying information relating to the debtor that establishes the identity of the debtor.

(i) (1) Subject to paragraphs (2) and (4) and notwithstanding section 707(a), if an individual debtor in a voluntary case under chapter 7 or 13 fails to file all of the information required under subsection (a)(1) within 45 days after the date of the filing of the petition, the case shall be automatically dismissed effective on the 46th day after the date of the filing of the petition.

(2) Subject to paragraph (4) and with respect to a case described in paragraph (1), any party in interest may request the court to enter an order dismissing the case. If requested, the court shall enter an order of dismissal not later than 5 days after such request.

(3) Subject to paragraph (4) and upon request of the debtor made within 45 days after the date of the filing of the petition described in paragraph (1), the court may allow the debtor an additional period of not to exceed 45 days to file the information required under subsection (a)(1) if the court finds justification for extending the period for the filing.

(4) Notwithstanding any other provision of this subsection, on the motion of the trustee filed before the expiration of the applicable period of time specified in paragraph (1), (2), or (3), and after notice and a hearing, the court may decline to dismiss the case if the court finds that the debtor attempted in good faith to file all the information required by subsection (a)(1)(B)(iv) and that the best interests of creditors would be served by administration of the case.

(j) (1) Notwithstanding any other provision of this title, if the debtor fails to file a tax return that becomes due after the commencement of the case or to properly obtain an extension of the due date for filing such return, the taxing authority may request that the court enter an order converting or dismissing the case.

(2) If the debtor does not file the required return or obtain the extension referred to in paragraph (1) within 90 days after a request is filed by the taxing authority under that paragraph, the court shall convert or dismiss the case, whichever is in the best interests of creditors and the estate.

Sec. 522. Exemptions

(a) In this section—

(1) "dependent" includes spouse, whether or not actually dependent; and

(2) "value" means fair market value as of the date of the filing of the petition or, with respect to property that becomes property of the estate after such date, as of the date such property becomes property of the estate.

(b) (1) Notwithstanding section 541 of this title, an individual debtor may exempt from property of the estate the property listed in either paragraph (2) or, in the alternative, paragraph (3) of this subsection. In joint cases filed under section 302 of this title and individual cases filed under section 301 or 303 of this title by or against debtors who are husband and wife, and whose estates are ordered to be jointly administered under Rule 1015(b) of the Federal Rules of Bankruptcy Procedure, one debtor may not elect to exempt property listed in paragraph (2) and the other debtor elect to exempt property listed in paragraph (3) of this subsection. If the parties cannot agree on the alternative to be elected, they shall be deemed to elect paragraph (2), where such election is permitted under the law of the jurisdiction where the case is filed.

(2) Property listed in this paragraph is property that is specified under subsection (d), unless the State law that is applicable to the debtor under paragraph (3)(A) specifically does not so authorize.

(3) Property listed in this paragraph is—

(A) subject to subsections (o) and (p), any property that is exempt under Federal law, other than subsection (d) of this section, or State or local law that is applicable on the date of the filing of the petition at the place in which the debtor's domicile has been located for the 730 days immediately preceding the date of the filing of the petition or if the debtor's domicile has not been located at a single State for such 730-day period, the place in which the debtor's domicile was located for 180 days immediately preceding the 730-day period or for a longer portion of such 180-day period than in any other place;

(B) any interest in property in which the debtor had, immediately before the commencement of the case, an interest as a tenant by the entirety or joint tenant to the extent that such interest as a tenant by the entirety or joint tenant is exempt from process under applicable nonbankruptcy law; and

(C) retirement funds to the extent that those funds are in a fund or account that is exempt from taxation under section 401, 403, 408, 408A, 414, 457, or 501(a) of the Internal Revenue Code of 1986.

If the effect of the domiciliary requirement under subparagraph (A) is to render the debtor ineligible for any exemption, the debtor may elect to exempt property that is specified under subsection (d).

(4) For purposes of paragraph (3)(C)and subsection (d)(12), the following shall apply:

(A) If the retirement funds are in a retirement fund that has received a favorable determination under section 7805 of the Internal Revenue Code of 1986, and that determination is in effect as of the date of the filing of the petition in a case under this title, those funds shall be presumed to be exempt from the estate.

(B) If the retirement funds are in a retirement fund that has not received a favorable determination under such section 7805, those funds are exempt from the estate if the debtor demonstrates that—

(i) no prior determination to the contrary has been made by a court or the Internal Revenue Service; and

(ii) (I) the retirement fund is in substantial compliance with the applicable requirements of the Internal Revenue Code of 1986; or

(II) the retirement fund fails to be in substantial compliance with the applicable requirements of the Internal Revenue Code of 1986 and the debtor is not materially responsible for that failure.

(C) A direct transfer of retirement funds from 1 fund or account that is exempt from taxation under section 401, 403, 408, 408A, 414, 457, or 501(a) of the Internal Revenue Code of 1986, under section 401(a)(31) of the Internal Revenue Code of 1986, or otherwise, shall not cease to qualify for exemption under paragraph (3)(C) or subsection (d)(12) by reason of such direct transfer.

(D) (i) Any distribution that qualifies as an eligible rollover distribution within the meaning of section 402(c) of the Internal Revenue Code of 1986 or that is described in clause (ii) shall not cease to qualify for exemption under paragraph (3)(C) or subsection (d)(12) by reason of such distribution.

(ii) A distribution described in this clause is an amount that -

(I) has been distributed from a fund or account that is exempt from taxation under section 401, 403, 408, 408A, 414, 457, or 501(a) of the Internal Revenue Code of 1986; and

(II) to the extent allowed by law, is deposited in such a fund or account not later than 60 days after the distribution of such amount.

(c) Unless the case is dismissed, property exempted under this section is not liable during or after the case for any debt of the debtor that arose, or that is determined under section 502 of this title as if such debt had arisen, before the commencement of the case, except—

(1) a debt of a kind specified in paragraph (1) or (5) of section 523(a) (in which case, notwithstanding any provision of applicable nonbankruptcy law to the contrary, such property shall be liable for a debt of a kind specified in section 523(a)(5));

(2) a debt secured by a lien that is—

(A) (i) not avoided under subsection (f) or (g) of this section or under section 544, 545, 547, 548, 549, or 724(a) of this title; and

(ii) not void under section 506(d) of this title; or

(B) a tax lien, notice of which is properly filed;

(3) a debt of a kind specified in section 523(a)(4) or 523(a)(6) of this title owed by an institution-affiliated party of an insured depository institution to a Federal depository institutions regulatory agency acting in its capacity as conservator, receiver, or liquidating agent for such institution; or

(4) a debt in connection with fraud in the obtaining or providing of any scholarship, grant, loan, tuition, discount, award, or other financial assistance for purposes of financing an education at an institution of higher education (as that term is defined in section 101 of the Higher Education Act of 1965 (20 U.S.C. 1001)).

(d) The following property may be exempted under subsection (b)(2) of this section:

(1) The debtor's aggregate interest, not to exceed $15,000 in value, in real property or personal property that the debtor or a dependent of the debtor uses as a residence, in a cooperative that owns property that the debtor or a dependent of the debtor uses as a residence, or in a burial plot for the debtor or a dependent of the debtor.

(2) The debtor's interest, not to exceed $2,400 in value, in one motor vehicle.

(3) The debtor's interest, not to exceed $400 in value in any particular item or $8,000 in aggregate value, in household furnishings, household goods, wearing apparel, appliances, books, animals, crops, or musical instruments, that are held primarily for the personal, family, or household use of the debtor or a dependent of the debtor.

(4) The debtor's aggregate interest, not to exceed $1,000 in value, in jewelry held primarily for the personal, family, or household use of the debtor or a dependent of the debtor.

(5) The debtor's aggregate interest in any property, not to exceed in value $800 plus up to $7,500 of any unused amount of the exemption provided under paragraph (1) of this subsection.

(6) The debtor's aggregate interest, not to exceed $1,500 in value, in any implements, professional books, or tools, of the trade of the debtor or the trade of a dependent of the debtor.

(7) Any unmatured life insurance contract owned by the debtor, other than a credit life insurance contract.

(8) The debtor's aggregate interest, not to exceed in value $8,000 less any amount of property of the estate transferred in the manner specified in section 542(d) of this title, in any accrued dividend or interest under, or loan value of, any unmatured life insurance contract owned by the debtor under which the insured is the debtor or an individual of whom the debtor is a dependent.

(9) Professionally prescribed health aids for the debtor or a dependent of the debtor.

(10) The debtor's right to receive—

  (A) a social security benefit, unemployment compensation, or a local public assistance benefit;

  (B) a veterans' benefit;

  (C) a disability, illness, or unemployment benefit;

  (D) alimony, support, or separate maintenance, to the extent reasonably necessary for the support of the debtor and any dependent of the debtor;

  (E) a payment under a stock bonus, pension, profitsharing, annuity, or similar plan or contract on account of illness, disability, death, age, or length of service, to the extent reasonably necessary for the support of the debtor and any dependent of the debtor, unless—

    (i) such plan or contract was established by or under the auspices of an insider that employed the debtor at the time the debtor's rights under such plan or contract arose;

    (ii) such payment is on account of age or length of service; and

    (iii) such plan or contract does not qualify under section 401(a), 403(a), 403(b), or 408 of the Internal Revenue Code of 1986.

(11) The debtor's right to receive, or property that is traceable to—

  (A) an award under a crime victim's reparation law;

  (B) a payment on account of the wrongful death of an individual of whom the debtor was a dependent, to the extent reasonably necessary for the support of the debtor and any dependent of the debtor;

  (C) a payment under a life insurance contract that insured the life of an individual of whom the debtor was a dependent on the date of such individual's death, to the extent reasonably necessary for the support of the debtor and any dependent of the debtor;

  (D) a payment, not to exceed $15,000, on account of personal bodily injury, not including pain and suffering or compensation for actual pecuniary loss, of the debtor or an individual of whom the debtor is a dependent; or

  (E) a payment in compensation of loss of future earnings of the debtor or an individual of whom the debtor is or was a dependent, to the extent reasonably necessary for the support of the debtor and any dependent of the debtor.

(12) Retirement funds to the extent that those funds are in a fund or account that is exempt from taxation under section 401, 403, 408, 408A, 414, 457, or 501(a) of the Internal Revenue Code of 1986.

(e) A waiver of an exemption executed in favor of a creditor that holds an unsecured claim against the debtor is unenforceable in a case under this title with respect to such claim against property that the debtor may exempt under subsection (b) of this section. A waiver by the debtor of a power under subsection (f) or (h) of this section to avoid a transfer, under subsection (g) or (i) of this section to exempt property, or under subsection (i) of this section to recover property or to preserve a transfer, is unenforceable in a case under this title.

(f) (1) Notwithstanding any waiver of exemptions but subject to paragraph (3), the debtor may avoid the fixing of a lien on an interest of the debtor in property to the extent that such lien impairs an exemption to which the debtor would have been entitled under subsection (b) of this section, if such lien is—

(A) a judicial lien, other than a judicial lien that secures a debt of a kind that is specified in section 523(a)(5); or

(B) a nonpossessory, nonpurchase-money security interest in any—

(i) household furnishings, household goods, wearing apparel, appliances, books, animals, crops, musical instruments, or jewelry that are held primarily for the personal, family, or household use of the debtor or a dependent of the debtor;

(ii) implements, professional books, or tools, of the trade of the debtor or the trade of a dependent of the debtor; or

(iii) professionally prescribed health aids for the debtor or a dependent of the debtor.

(2) (A) For the purposes of this subsection, a lien shall be considered to impair an exemption to the extent that the sum of—

(i) the lien;

(ii) all other liens on the property; and

(iii) the amount of the exemption that the debtor could claim if there were no liens on the property;

exceeds the value that the debtor's interest in the property would have in the absence of any liens.

(B) In the case of a property subject to more than 1 lien, a lien that has been avoided shall not be considered in making the calculation under subparagraph (A) with respect to other liens.

(C) This paragraph shall not apply with respect to a judgment arising out of a mortgage foreclosure.

(3) In a case in which State law that is applicable to the debtor—

(A) permits a person to voluntarily waive a right to claim exemptions under subsection (d) or prohibits a debtor from claiming exemptions under subsection (d); and

(B) either permits the debtor to claim exemptions under State law without limitation in amount, except to the extent that the debtor has permitted the fixing of a consensual lien on any property or prohibits avoidance of a consensual lien on property otherwise eligible to be claimed as exempt property;

the debtor may not avoid the fixing of a lien on an interest of the debtor or a dependent of the debtor in property if the lien is a nonpossessory, nonpurchase-money security interest in implements, professional books, or tools of the trade of the debtor or a dependent of the debtor or farm animals or crops of the debtor or a dependent of the debtor to the extent the value of such implements, professional books, tools of the trade, animals, and crops exceeds $5,000.

(4) (A) Subject to subparagraph (B), for purposes of paragraph (1)(B), the term "household goods" means—
(i) clothing;
(ii) furniture;
(iii) appliances;
(iv) 1 radio;
(v) 1 television;
(vi) 1 VCR;
(vii) linens;
(viii) china;
(ix) crockery;
(x) kitchenware;
(xi) educational materials and educational equipment primarily for the use of minor dependent children of the debtor;
(xii) medical equipment and supplies;
(xiii) furniture exclusively for the use of minor children, or elderly or disabled dependents of the debtor;
(xiv) personal effects (including the toys and hobby equipment of minor dependent children and wedding rings) of the debtor and the dependents of the debtor; and
(xv) 1 personal computer and related equipment.

(B) The term "household goods" does not include—
(i) works of art (unless by or of the debtor, or any relative of the debtor);
(ii) electronic entertainment equipment with a fair market value of more than $500 in the aggregate (except 1 television, 1 radio, and 1 VCR);
(iii) items acquired as antiques with a fair market value of more than $500 in the aggregate;
(iv) jewelry with a fair market value of more than $500 in the aggregate (except wedding rings); and
(v) a computer (except as otherwise provided for in this section), motor vehicle (including a tractor or lawn tractor), boat, or a motorized recreational device, conveyance, vehicle, watercraft, or aircraft.

(g) Notwithstanding sections 550 and 551 of this title, the debtor may exempt under subsection (b) of this section property that the trustee recovers under section 510(c)(2), 542, 543, 550, 551, or 553 of this title, to the extent that the debtor could have exempted such property under subsection (b) of this section if such property had not been transferred, if—

(1) (A) such transfer was not a voluntary transfer of such property by the debtor; and
(B) the debtor did not conceal such property; or

(2) the debtor could have avoided such transfer under subsection (f)(1)(B) of this section.

(h) The debtor may avoid a transfer of property of the debtor or recover a setoff to the extent that the debtor could have exempted such property under subsection (g)(1) of this section if the trustee had avoided such transfer, if—

(1) such transfer is avoidable by the trustee under section 544, 545, 547, 548, 549, or 724(a) of this title or recoverable by the trustee under section 553 of this title; and

(2) the trustee does not attempt to avoid such transfer.

(i) (1) If the debtor avoids a transfer or recovers a setoff under subsection (f) or (h) of this section, the debtor may recover in the manner prescribed by, and subject to the limitations of, section 550 of this title, the same as if the trustee had avoided such transfer, and may exempt any property so recovered under subsection (b) of this section.

(2) Notwithstanding section 551 of this title, a transfer avoided under section 544, 545, 547, 548, 549, or 724(a) of this title, under subsection (f) or (h) of this section, or property recovered under section 553 of this title, may be preserved for the benefit of the debtor to the extent that the debtor may exempt such property under subsection (g) of this section or paragraph (1) of this subsection.

(j) Notwithstanding subsections (g) and (i) of this section, the debtor may exempt a particular kind of property under subsections (g) and (i) of this section only to the extent that the debtor has exempted less property in value of such kind than that to which the debtor is entitled under subsection (b) of this section.

(k) Property that the debtor exempts under this section is not liable for payment of any administrative expense except—

(1) the aliquot share of the costs and expenses of avoiding a transfer of property that the debtor exempts under subsection (g) of this section, or of recovery of such property, that is attributable to the value of the portion of such property exempted in relation to the value of the property recovered; and

(2) any costs and expenses of avoiding a transfer under subsection (f) or (h) of this section, or of recovery of property under subsection (i)(1) of this section, that the debtor has not paid.

(l) The debtor shall file a list of property that the debtor claims as exempt under subsection (b) of this section. If the debtor does not file such a list, a dependent of the debtor may file such a list, or may claim property as exempt from property of the estate on behalf of the debtor. Unless a party in interest objects, the property claimed as exempt on such list is exempt.

(m) Subject to the limitation in subsection (b), this section shall apply separately with respect to each debtor in a joint case.

(n) For assets in individual retirement accounts described in section 408 or 408A of the Internal Revenue Code of 1986, other than a simplified employee pension under section 408(k) of such Code or a simple retirement account under section 408(p) of such Code, the aggregate value of such assets exempted under this section, without regard to amounts attributable to rollover contributions under section 402(c), 402(e)(6), 403(a)(4), 403(a)(5), and 403(b)(8) of the Internal Revenue Code of 1986, and earnings thereon, shall not exceed $1,000,000 in a case filed by a debtor who is an individual, except that such amount may be increased if the interests of justice so require.

(o) For purposes of subsection (b)(3)(A), and notwithstanding subsection (a), the value of an interest in—

(1) real or personal property that the debtor or a dependent of the debtor uses as a residence;

(2) a cooperative that owns property that the debtor or a dependent of the debtor uses as a residence;

(3) a burial plot for the debtor or a dependent of the debtor; or

(4) real or personal property that the debtor or a dependent of the debtor claims as a homestead;

shall be reduced to the extent that such value is attributable to any portion of any property that the debtor disposed of in the 10-year period ending on the date of the filing of the petition with the intent to hinder, delay, or defraud a creditor and that the debtor could not exempt, or that portion that the debtor could not exempt, under subsection (b), if on such date the debtor had held the property so disposed of.

(p) (1) Except as provided in paragraph (2) of this subsection and sections 544 and 548, as a result of electing under subsection (b)(3)(A) to exempt property under State or local law, a debtor may not exempt any amount of interest that was acquired by the debtor during the 1215-day period preceding the date of the filing of the petition that exceeds in the aggregate $125,000 in value in—

(A) real or personal property that the debtor or a dependent of the debtor uses as a residence;

(B) a cooperative that owns property that the debtor or a dependent of the debtor uses as a residence;

(C) a burial plot for the debtor or a dependent of the debtor; or

(D) real or personal property that the debtor or dependent of the debtor claims as a homestead.

(2) (A) The limitation under paragraph (1) shall not apply to an exemption claimed under subsection (b)(3)(A) by a family farmer for the principal residence of such farmer.

(B) For purposes of paragraph (1), any amount of such interest does not include any interest transferred from a debtor's previous principal residence (which was acquired prior to the beginning of such 1215-day period) into the debtor's current principal residence, if the debtor's previous and current residences are located in the same State.

(q) (1) As a result of electing under subsection (b)(3)(A) to exempt property under State or local law, a debtor may not exempt any amount of an interest in property described in subparagraphs (A), (B), (C), and (D) of subsection (p)(1) which exceeds in the aggregate $125,000 if—

(A) the court determines, after notice and a hearing, that the debtor has been convicted of a felony (as defined in section 3156 of title 18), which under the circumstances, demonstrates that the filing of the case was an abuse of the provisions of this title; or

(B) the debtor owes a debt arising from—

(i) any violation of the Federal securities laws (as defined in section 3(a)(47) of the Securities Exchange Act of 1934), any State securities laws, or any regulation or order issued under Federal securities laws or State securities laws;

(ii) fraud, deceit, or manipulation in a fiduciary capacity or in connection with the purchase or sale of any security registered under section 12 or 15(d) of the Securities Exchange Act of 1934 or under section 6 of the Securities Act of 1933;

(iii) any civil remedy under section 1964 of title 18; or

(iv) any criminal act, intentional tort, or willful or reckless misconduct that caused serious physical injury or death to another individual in the preceding 5 years.

(2) Paragraph (1) shall not apply to the extent the amount of an interest in property described in subparagraphs (A), (B), (C), and (D) of subsection (p)(1) is reasonably necessary for the support of the debtor and any dependent of the debtor.

Sec. 523. Exceptions to discharge

(a) A discharge under section 727, 1141, 1228(a), 1228(b), or 1328(b) of this title does not discharge an individual debtor from any debt—

(1) for a tax or a customs duty—

(A) of the kind and for the periods specified in section 507(a)(3) or 507(a)(8) of this title, whether or not a claim for such tax was filed or allowed;

(B) with respect to which a return, or equivalent report or notice, if required—

(i) was not filed or given; or

(ii) was filed or given after the date on which such return, report, or notice was last due, under applicable law or under any extension, and after two years before the date of the filing of the petition; or

(C) with respect to which the debtor made a fraudulent return or willfully attempted in any manner to evade or defeat such tax;

(2) for money, property, services, or an extension, renewal, or refinancing of credit, to the extent obtained by—

(A) false pretenses, a false representation, or actual fraud, other than a statement respecting the debtor's or an insider's financial condition;

(B) use of a statement in writing—

(i) that is materially false;

(ii) respecting the debtor's or an insider's financial condition;

(iii) on which the creditor to whom the debtor is liable for such money, property, services, or credit reasonably relied; and

(iv) that the debtor caused to be made or published with intent to deceive; or

(C) (i) for purposes of subparagraph (A)—

(I) consumer debts owed to a single creditor and aggregating more than $500 for luxury goods or services incurred by an individual debtor on or within 90 days before the order for relief under this title are presumed to be nondischargeable; and

(II) cash advances aggregating more than $750 that are extensions of consumer credit under an open end credit plan obtained by an individual debtor on or within 70 days before the order for relief under this title, are presumed to be nondischargeable; and

(ii) for purposes of this subparagraph—

(I) the terms "consumer", "credit", and "open end credit plan" have the same meanings as in section 103 of the Truth in Lending Act; and

(II) the term "luxury goods or services" does not include goods or services reasonably necessary for the support or maintenance of the debtor or a dependent of the debtor.

(3) neither listed nor scheduled under section 521(1) of this title, with the name, if known to the debtor, of the creditor to whom such debt is owed, in time to permit—

(A) if such debt is not of a kind specified in paragraph (2), (4), or (6) of this subsection, timely filing of a proof of claim, unless such creditor had notice or actual knowledge of the case in time for such timely filing; or

(B) if such debt is of a kind specified in paragraph (2), (4), or (6) of this subsection, timely filing of a proof of claim and timely request for a determination of dischargeability of such debt under one of such paragraphs, unless such creditor had notice or actual knowledge of the case in time for such timely filing and request;

(4) for fraud or defalcation while acting in a fiduciary capacity, embezzlement, or larceny;

(5) for a domestic support obligation;

(6) for willful and malicious injury by the debtor to another entity or to the property of another entity;

(7) to the extent such debt is for a fine, penalty, or forfeiture payable to and for the benefit of a governmental unit, and is not compensation for actual pecuniary loss, other than a tax penalty—

(A) relating to a tax of a kind not specified in paragraph (1) of this subsection; or

(B) imposed with respect to a transaction or event that occurred before three years before the date of the filing of the petition;

(8) unless excepting such debt from discharge under this paragraph would impose an undue hardship on the debtor and the debtor's dependents, for—

(A) (i) an educational benefit overpayment or loan made, insured, or guaranteed by a governmental unit, or made under any program funded in whole or in part by a governmental unit or nonprofit institution; or

(ii) an obligation to repay funds received as an educational benefit, scholarship, or stipend; or

(B) any other educational loan that is a qualified education loan, as defined in section 221(d)(1) of the Internal Revenue Code of 1986, incurred by a debtor who is an individual;

(9) for death or personal injury caused by the debtor's operation of a motor vehicle, vessel, or aircraft if such operation was unlawful because the debtor was intoxicated from using alcohol, a drug, or another substance;

(10) that was or could have been listed or scheduled by the debtor in a prior case concerning the debtor under this title or under the Bankruptcy Act in which the debtor waived discharge, or was denied a discharge under section 727(a)(2), (3), (4), (5), (6), or (7) of this title, or under section 14c(1), (2), (3), (4), (6), or (7) of such Act;

(11) provided in any final judgment, unreviewable order, or consent order or decree entered in any court of the United States or of any State, issued by a Federal depository institutions regulatory agency, or contained in any settlement agreement entered into by the debtor, arising from any act of fraud or defalcation while acting in a fiduciary capacity committed with respect to any depository institution or insured credit union;

(12) for malicious or reckless failure to fulfill any commitment by the debtor to a Federal depository institutions regulatory agency to maintain the capital of an insured depository institution, except that this paragraph shall not extend any such commitment which would otherwise be terminated due to any act of such agency;

(13) for any payment of an order of restitution issued under title 18, United States Code;

(14) incurred to pay a tax to the United States that would be nondischargeable pursuant to paragraph (1);

(14A) incurred to pay a tax to a governmental unit, other than the United States, that would be nondischargeable under paragraph (1);

(14B) incurred to pay fines or penalties imposed under Federal election law;

(15) to a spouse, former spouse, or child of the debtor and not of the kind described in paragraph (5) that is incurred by the debtor in the course of a divorce or separation or in connection with a separation agreement, divorce decree or other order of a court of record, or a determination made in accordance with State or territorial law by a governmental unit;

(16) for a fee or assessment that becomes due and payable after the order for relief to a membership association with respect to the debtor's interest in a unit that has condominium ownership, in a share of a cooperative corporation, or a lot in a homeowners association, for as long as the debtor or the trustee has a legal, equitable, or possessory ownership interest in such unit, such corporation, or such lot, but nothing in this paragraph shall except from discharge the debt of a debtor for a membership association fee or assessment for a period arising before entry of the order for relief in a pending or subsequent bankruptcy case;

(17) for a fee imposed on a prisoner by any court for the filing of a case, motion, complaint, or appeal, or for other costs and expenses assessed with respect to such filing, regardless of an assertion of poverty by the debtor under subsection (b) or (f)(2) of section 1915 of title 28 (or a similar non-Federal law), or the debtor's status as a prisoner, as defined in section 1915(h) of title 28 (or a similar non-Federal law);

(18) owed to a pension, profit-sharing, stock bonus, or other plan established under section 401, 403, 408, 408A, 414, 457, or 501(c) of the Internal Revenue Code of 1986, under— (A) a loan permitted under section 408(b)(1) of the Employee Retirement Income Security Act of 1974, or subject to section 72(p) of the Internal Revenue Code of 1986; or (B) a loan from a thrift savings plan permitted under subchapter III of chapter 84 of title 5, that satisfies the requirements of section 8433(g) of such title;

but nothing in this paragraph may be construed to provide that any loan made under a governmental plan under section 414(d), or a contract or account under section 403(b), of the Internal Revenue Code of 1986 constitutes a claim or a debt under this title; or

(19) that—

(A) is for—

(i) the violation of any of the Federal securities laws (as that term is defined in section 3(a)(47) of the Securities Exchange Act of 1934), any of the State securities laws, or any regulation or order issued under such Federal or State securities laws; or

(ii) common law fraud, deceit, or manipulation in connection with the purchase or sale of any security; and

(B) results, before, on, or after the date on which the petition was filed, from—

(i) any judgment, order, consent order, or decree entered in any Federal or State judicial or administrative proceeding;

(ii) any settlement agreement entered into by the debtor; or

(iii) any court or administrative order for any damages, fine, penalty, citation, restitutionary payment, disgorgement payment, attorney fee, cost, or other payment owed by the debtor.

For purposes of this subsection, the term "return" means a return that satisfies the requirements of applicable nonbankruptcy law (including applicable filing requirements). Such term includes a return prepared pursuant to section 6020(a) of the Internal Revenue Code of 1986, or similar State or local law, or a written stipulation to a judgment or a final order entered by a nonbankruptcy tribunal, but does not include a return made pursuant to section 6020(b) of the Internal Revenue Code of 1986, or a similar State or local law.

(b) Notwithstanding subsection (a) of this section, a debt that was excepted from discharge under subsection (a)(1), (a)(3), or (a)(8) of this section, under section 17a(1), 17a(3), or 17a(5) of the Bankruptcy Act, under section 439A[9] of the Higher Education Act of 1965, or under section 733(g)[10] of the Public Health Service Act in a prior case concerning the debtor under this title, or under the Bankruptcy Act, is dischargeable in a case under this title unless, by the terms of subsection (a) of this section, such debt is not dischargeable in the case under this title.

(c) (1) Except as provided in subsection (a)(3)(B) of this section, the debtor shall be discharged from a debt of a kind specified in paragraph (2), (4), or (6) of subsection (a) of this section, unless, on request of the creditor to whom such debt is owed, and after notice and a hearing, the court determines such debt to be excepted from discharge under paragraph (2), (4), or (6), as the case may be, of subsection (a) of this section.

(2) Paragraph (1) shall not apply in the case of a Federal depository institutions regulatory agency seeking, in its capacity as conservator, receiver, or liquidating agent for an insured depository institution, to recover a debt described in subsection (a)(2), (a)(4), (a)(6), or (a)(11) owed to such institution by an institution-affiliated party unless the receiver, conservator, or liquidating agent was appointed in time to reasonably comply, or for a Federal depository institutions regulatory agency acting in its corporate capacity as a successor to such receiver, conservator, or liquidating agent to reasonably comply, with subsection (a)(3)(B) as a creditor of such institution-affiliated party with respect to such debt.

(d) If a creditor requests a determination of dischargeability of a consumer debt under subsection (a)(2) of this section, and such debt is discharged, the court shall grant judgment in favor of the debtor for the costs of, and a reasonable attorney's fee for, the proceeding if the court finds that the position of the creditor was not substantially justified, except that the court shall not award such costs and fees if special circumstances would make the award unjust.

(e) Any institution-affiliated party of an insured depository institution shall be considered to be acting in a fiduciary capacity with respect to the purposes of subsection (a)(4) or (11).

Sec. 524. Effect of discharge

(a) A discharge in a case under this title—

(1) voids any judgment at any time obtained, to the extent that such judgment is a determination of the personal liability of the debtor with respect to any debt discharged under section 727, 944, 1141, 1228, or 1328 of this title, whether or not discharge of such debt is waived;

(2) operates as an injunction against the commencement or continuation of an action, the employment of process, or an act, to collect, recover or offset any such debt as a personal liability of the debtor, whether or not discharge of such debt is waived; and

(3) operates as an injunction against the commencement or continuation of an action, the

---

[9] *Sic.* Section 439A of the of the Higher Education Act of 1965 has been repealed.

[10] *Sic.* Section 733 of the Public Health Service Act has been repealed.

employment of process, or an act, to collect or recover from, or offset against, property of the debtor of the kind specified in section 541(a)(2) of this title that is acquired after the commencement of the case, on account of any allowable community claim, except a community claim that is excepted from discharge under section 523, 1228(a)(1), or 1328(a)(1), or that would be so excepted, determined in accordance with the provisions of sections 523(c) and 523(d) of this title, in a case concerning the debtor's spouse commenced on the date of the filing of the petition in the case concerning the debtor, whether or not discharge of the debt based on such community claim is waived.

(b) Subsection (a)(3) of this section does not apply if—

(1) (A) the debtor's spouse is a debtor in a case under this title, or a bankrupt or a debtor in a case under the Bankruptcy Act, commenced within six years of the date of the filing of the petition in the case concerning the debtor; and

(B) the court does not grant the debtor's spouse a discharge in such case concerning the debtor's spouse; or

(2) (A) the court would not grant the debtor's spouse a discharge in a case under chapter 7 of this title concerning such spouse commenced on the date of the filing of the petition in the case concerning the debtor; and

(B) a determination that the court would not so grant such discharge is made by the bankruptcy court within the time and in the manner provided for a determination under section 727 of this title of whether a debtor is granted a discharge.

(c) An agreement between a holder of a claim and the debtor, the consideration for which, in whole or in part, is based on a debt that is dischargeable in a case under this title is enforceable only to any extent enforceable under applicable nonbankruptcy law, whether or not discharge of such debt is waived, only if—

(1) such agreement was made before the granting of the discharge under section 727, 1141, 1228, or 1328 of this title;

(2) the debtor received the disclosures described in subsection (k) at or before the time at which the debtor signed the agreement;

(3) such agreement has been filed with the court and, if applicable, accompanied by a declaration or an affidavit of the attorney that represented the debtor during the course of negotiating an agreement under this subsection, which states that—

(A) such agreement represents a fully informed and voluntary agreement by the debtor;

(B) such agreement does not impose an undue hardship on the debtor or a dependent of the debtor; and

(C) the attorney fully advised the debtor of the legal effect and consequences of—

(i) an agreement of the kind specified in this subsection; and

(ii) any default under such an agreement;

(4) the debtor has not rescinded such agreement at any time prior to discharge or within sixty days after such agreement is filed with the court, whichever occurs later, by giving notice of rescission to the holder of such claim;

(5) the provisions of subsection (d) of this section have been complied with; and

(6) (A) in a case concerning an individual who was not represented by an attorney during the course of negotiating an agreement under this subsection, the court approves such agreement as—

(i) not imposing an undue hardship on the debtor or a dependent of the debtor; and

(ii) in the best interest of the debtor.

(B) Subparagraph (A) shall not apply to the extent that such debt is a consumer debt secured by real property.

(d) In a case concerning an individual, when the court has determined whether to grant or not to grant a discharge under section 727, 1141, 1228, or 1328 of this title, the court may hold a hearing at which the debtor shall appear in person. At any such hearing, the court shall inform the debtor that a discharge has been granted or the reason why a discharge has not been granted. If a discharge has been granted and if the debtor desires to make an agreement of the kind specified in subsection (c) of this section and was not represented by an attorney during the course of negotiating such agreement, then the court shall hold a hearing at which the debtor shall appear in person and at such hearing the court shall—

(1) inform the debtor—

(A) that such an agreement is not required under this title, under nonbankruptcy law, or under any agreement not made in accordance with the provisions of subsection (c) of this section; and

(B) of the legal effect and consequences of—

(i) an agreement of the kind specified in subsection (c) of this section; and

(ii) a default under such an agreement; and

(2) determine whether the agreement that the debtor desires to make complies with the requirements of subsection (c)(6) of this section, if the consideration for such agreement is based in whole or in part on a consumer debt that is not secured by real property of the debtor.

(e) Except as provided in subsection (a)(3) of this section, discharge of a debt of the debtor does not affect the liability of any other entity on, or the property of any other entity for, such debt.

(f) Nothing contained in subsection (c) or (d) of this section prevents a debtor from voluntarily repaying any debt.

(g) (1) (A) After notice and hearing, a court that enters an order confirming a plan of reorganization under chapter 11 may issue, in connection with such order, an injunction in accordance with this subsection to supplement the injunctive effect of a discharge under this section.

(B) An injunction may be issued under subparagraph (A) to enjoin entities from taking legal action for the purpose of directly or indirectly collecting, recovering, or receiving payment or recovery with respect to any claim or demand that, under a plan of reorganization, is to be paid in whole or in part by a trust described in paragraph (2)(B)(i), except such legal actions as are expressly allowed by the injunction, the confirmation order, or the plan of reorganization.

(2) (A) Subject to subsection (h), if the requirements of subparagraph (B) are met at the time an injunction described in paragraph (1) is entered, then after entry of such injunction, any proceeding that involves the validity, application, construction, or modification of such injunction, or of this subsection with respect to such injunction, may be commenced only in the district court in which such injunction was entered, and such court shall have exclusive jurisdiction over any such proceeding without regard to the amount in controversy.

(B) The requirements of this subparagraph are that—

(i) the injunction is to be implemented in connection with a trust that, pursuant to the plan of reorganization—

(I) is to assume the liabilities of a debtor which at the time of entry of the order for relief has been named as a defendant in personal injury, wrongful death, or property- damage actions seeking recovery for damages allegedly caused by the presence of, or exposure to, asbestos or asbestos- containing products;

(II) is to be funded in whole or in part by the securities of 1 or more debtors involved in such plan and by the obligation of such debtor or debtors to make future payments, including dividends;

(III) is to own, or by the exercise of rights granted under such plan would be entitled to own if specified contingencies occur, a majority of the voting shares of—

(aa) each such debtor;

(bb) the parent corporation of each such debtor; or

(cc) a subsidiary of each such debtor that is also a debtor; and

(IV) is to use its assets or income to pay claims and demands; and

(ii) subject to subsection (h), the court determines that—

(I) the debtor is likely to be subject to substantial future demands for payment arising out of the same or similar conduct or events that gave rise to the claims that are addressed by the injunction;

(II) the actual amounts, numbers, and timing of such future demands cannot be determined;

(III) pursuit of such demands outside the procedures prescribed by such plan is likely to threaten the plan's purpose to deal equitably with claims and future demands;

(IV) as part of the process of seeking confirmation of such plan—

(aa) the terms of the injunction proposed to be issued under paragraph (1)(A), including any provisions barring actions against third parties pursuant to paragraph (4)(A), are set out in such plan and in any disclosure statement supporting the plan; and

(bb) a separate class or classes of the claimants whose claims are to be addressed by a trust described in clause (i) is established and votes, by at least 75 percent of those voting, in favor of the plan; and

(V) subject to subsection (h), pursuant to court orders or otherwise, the trust will operate through mechanisms such as structured, periodic, or supplemental payments, pro rata distributions, matrices, or periodic review of estimates of the numbers and values of present claims and future demands, or other comparable mechanisms, that provide reasonable assurance that the trust will value, and be in a financial position to pay, present claims and future demands that involve similar claims in substantially the same manner.

(3) (A) If the requirements of paragraph (2)(B) are met and the order confirming the plan of reorganization was issued or affirmed by the district court that has jurisdiction

over the reorganization case, then after the time for appeal of the order that issues or affirms the plan—

(i) the injunction shall be valid and enforceable and may not be revoked or modified by any court except through appeal in accordance with paragraph (6);

(ii) no entity that pursuant to such plan or thereafter becomes a direct or indirect transferee of, or successor to any assets of, a debtor or trust that is the subject of the injunction shall be liable with respect to any claim or demand made against such entity by reason of its becoming such a transferee or successor; and

(iii) no entity that pursuant to such plan or thereafter makes a loan to such a debtor or trust or to such a successor or transferee shall, by reason of making the loan, be liable with respect to any claim or demand made against such entity, nor shall any pledge of assets made in connection with such a loan be upset or impaired for that reason;

(B) Subparagraph (A) shall not be construed to—

(i) imply that an entity described in subparagraph (A)(ii) or (iii) would, if this paragraph were not applicable, necessarily be liable to any entity by reason of any of the acts described in subparagraph (A);

(ii) relieve any such entity of the duty to comply with, or of liability under, any Federal or State law regarding the making of a fraudulent conveyance in a transaction described in subparagraph (A)(ii) or (iii); or

(iii) relieve a debtor of the debtor's obligation to comply with the terms of the plan of reorganization, or affect the power of the court to exercise its authority under sections 1141 and 1142 to compel the debtor to do so.

(4) (A) (i) Subject to subparagraph (B), an injunction described in paragraph (1) shall be valid and enforceable against all entities that it addresses.

(ii) Notwithstanding the provisions of section 524(e), such an injunction may bar any action directed against a third party who is identifiable from the terms of such injunction (by name or as part of an identifiable group) and is alleged to be directly or indirectly liable for the conduct of, claims against, or demands on the debtor to the extent such alleged liability of such third party arises by reason of—

(I) the third party's ownership of a financial interest in the debtor, a past or present affiliate of the debtor, or a predecessor in interest of the debtor;

(II) the third party's involvement in the management of the debtor or a predecessor in interest of the debtor, or service as an officer, director or employee of the debtor or a related party;

(III) the third party's provision of insurance to the debtor or a related party; or

(IV) the third party's involvement in a transaction changing the corporate structure, or in a loan or other financial transaction affecting the financial condition, of the debtor or a related party, including but not limited to—

(aa) involvement in providing financing (debt or equity), or advice to an entity involved in such a transaction; or (bb) acquiring or selling a financial interest in an entity as part of such a transaction.

(iii) As used in this subparagraph, the term "related party" means—

(I) a past or present affiliate of the debtor;

(II) a predecessor in interest of the debtor; or

(III) any entity that owned a financial interest in—

(aa) the debtor;

(bb) a past or present affiliate of the debtor; or

(cc) a predecessor in interest of the debtor.

(B) Subject to subsection (h), if, under a plan of reorganization, a kind of demand described in such plan is to be paid in whole or in part by a trust described in paragraph (2)(B)(i) in connection with which an injunction described in paragraph (1) is to be implemented, then such injunction shall be valid and enforceable with respect to a demand of such kind made, after such plan is confirmed, against the debtor or debtors involved, or against a third party described in subparagraph (A)(ii), if—

(i) as part of the proceedings leading to issuance of such injunction, the court appoints a legal representative for the purpose of protecting the rights of persons that might subsequently assert demands of such kind, and

(ii) the court determines, before entering the order confirming such plan, that identifying such debtor or debtors, or such third party (by name or as part of an identifiable group), in such injunction with respect to such demands for purposes of this subparagraph is fair and equitable with respect to the persons that might subsequently assert such demands, in light of the benefits provided, or to be provided, to such trust on behalf of such debtor or debtors or such third party.

(5) In this subsection, the term "demand" means a demand for payment, present or future, that—

(A) was not a claim during the proceedings leading to the confirmation of a plan of reorganization;

(B) arises out of the same or similar conduct or events that gave rise to the claims addressed by the injunction issued under paragraph (1); and

(C) pursuant to the plan, is to be paid by a trust described in paragraph (2)(B)(i).

(6) Paragraph (3)(A)(i) does not bar an action taken by or at the direction of an appellate court on appeal of an injunction issued under paragraph (1) or of the order of confirmation that relates to the injunction.

(7) This subsection does not affect the operation of section 1144 or the power of the district court to refer a proceeding under section 157 of title 28 or any reference of a proceeding made prior to the date of the enactment of this subsection.

(h) Application to Existing Injunctions.—For purposes of subsection (g)—

(1) subject to paragraph (2), if an injunction of the kind described in subsection (g)(1)(B) was issued before the date of the enactment of this Act, as part of a plan of reorganization confirmed by an order entered before such date, then the injunction shall be considered to meet the requirements of subsection (g)(2)(B) for purposes of subsection (g)(2)(A), and to satisfy subsection (g)(4)(A)(ii), if—

(A) the court determined at the time the plan was confirmed that the plan was fair and equitable in accordance with the requirements of section 1129(b);

(B) as part of the proceedings leading to issuance of such injunction and confirmation of such plan, the court had appointed a legal representative for the purpose of protecting the rights of persons that might subsequently assert demands described in subsection (g)(4)(B) with respect to such plan; and

(C) such legal representative did not object to confirmation of such plan or issuance of such injunction; and

(2) for purposes of paragraph (1), if a trust described in subsection (g)(2)(B)(i) is subject to a court order on the date of the enactment of this Act staying such trust from settling or paying further claims—

(A) the requirements of subsection (g)(2)(B)(ii)(V) shall not apply with respect to such trust until such stay is lifted or dissolved; and

(B) if such trust meets such requirements on the date such stay is lifted or dissolved, such trust shall be considered to have met such requirements continuously from the date of the enactment of this Act.

(i) The willful failure of a creditor to credit payments received under a plan confirmed under this title, unless the order confirming the plan is revoked, the plan is in default, or the creditor has not received payments required to be made under the plan in the manner required by the plan (including crediting the amounts required under the plan), shall constitute a violation of an injunction under subsection (a)(2) if the act of the creditor to collect and failure to credit payments in the manner required by the plan caused material injury to the debtor.

(j) Subsection (a)(2) does not operate as an injunction against an act by a creditor that is the holder of a secured claim, if—

(1) such creditor retains a security interest in real property that is the principal residence of the debtor;

(2) such act is in the ordinary course of business between the creditor and the debtor; and

(3) such act is limited to seeking or obtaining periodic payments associated with a valid security interest in lieu of pursuit of in rem relief to enforce the lien.

(k) (1) The disclosures required under subsection (c)(2) shall consist of the disclosure statement described in paragraph (3), completed as required in that paragraph, together with the agreement specified in subsection (c), statement, declaration, motion and order described, respectively, in paragraphs (4) through (8), and shall be the only disclosures required in connection with entering into such agreement.

(2) Disclosures made under paragraph (1) shall be made clearly and conspicuously and in writing. The terms “Amount Reaffirmed” and “Annual Percentage Rate” shall be disclosed more conspicuously than other terms, data or information provided in connection with this disclosure, except that the phrases “Before agreeing to reaffirm a debt, review these important disclosures” and “Summary of Reaffirmation Agreement” may be equally conspicuous. Disclosures may be made in a different order and may use terminology different from that set forth in paragraphs (2) through (8), except that the terms “Amount Reaffirmed” and “Annual Percentage Rate” must be used where indicated.

(3) The disclosure statement required under this paragraph shall consist of the following:

(A) The statement: “Part A: Before agreeing to reaffirm a debt, review these important disclosures:”;

(B) Under the heading "Summary of Reaffirmation Agreement", the statement: "This Summary is made pursuant to the requirements of the Bankruptcy Code";

(C) The "Amount Reaffirmed", using that term, which shall be—

(i) the total amount of debt that the debtor agrees to reaffirm by entering into an agreement of the kind specified in subsection (c), and

(ii) the total of any fees and costs accrued as of the date of the disclosure statement, related to such total amount.

(D) In conjunction with the disclosure of the "Amount Reaffirmed", the statements—

(i) "The amount of debt you have agreed to reaffirm"; and

(ii) "Your credit agreement may obligate you to pay additional amounts which may come due after the date of this disclosure. Consult your credit agreement.".

(E) The "Annual Percentage Rate", using that term, which shall be disclosed as—

(i) if, at the time the petition is filed, the debt is an extension of credit under an open end credit plan, as the terms "credit" and "open end credit plan" are defined in section 103 of the Truth in Lending Act, then—

(I) the annual percentage rate determined under paragraphs (5) and (6) of section 127(b) of the Truth in Lending Act, as applicable, as disclosed to the debtor in the most recent periodic statement prior to entering into an agreement of the kind specified in subsection (c) or, if no such periodic statement has been given to the debtor during the prior 6 months, the annual percentage rate as it would have been so disclosed at the time the disclosure statement is given to the debtor, or to the extent this annual percentage rate is not readily available or not applicable, then

(II) the simple interest rate applicable to the amount reaffirmed as of the date the disclosure statement is given to the debtor, or if different simple interest rates apply to different balances, the simple interest rate applicable to each such balance, identifying the amount of each such balance included in the amount reaffirmed, or

(III) if the entity making the disclosure elects, to disclose the annual percentage rate under subclause (I) and the simple interest rate under subclause (II); or

(ii) if, at the time the petition is filed, the debt is an extension of credit other than under an open end credit plan, as the terms "credit" and "open end credit plan" are defined in section 103 of the Truth in Lending Act, then—

(I) the annual percentage rate under section 128(a)(4) of the Truth in Lending Act, as disclosed to the debtor in the most recent disclosure statement given to the debtor prior to the entering into an agreement of the kind specified in subsection (c) with respect to the debt, or, if no such disclosure statement was given to the debtor, the annual percentage rate as it would have been so disclosed at the time the disclosure statement is given to the debtor, or to the extent this annual percentage rate is not readily available or not applicable, then

(II) the simple interest rate applicable to the amount reaffirmed as of the date the disclosure statement is given to the debtor, or if different simple interest rates apply to different balances, the simple interest rate applicable to each such balance, identifying the amount of such balance included in the amount reaffirmed, or

(III) if the entity making the disclosure elects, to disclose the annual percentage rate under (I) and the simple interest rate under (II).

(F) If the underlying debt transaction was disclosed as a variable rate transaction on the most recent disclosure given under the Truth in Lending Act, by stating "The interest rate on your loan may be a variable interest rate which changes from time to time, so that the annual percentage rate disclosed here may be higher or lower.".

(G) If the debt is secured by a security interest which has not been waived in whole or in part or determined to be void by a final order of the court at the time of the disclosure, by disclosing that a security interest or lien in goods or property is asserted over some or all of the debts the debtor is reaffirming and listing the items and their original purchase price that are subject to the asserted security interest, or if not a purchase-money security interest then listing by items or types and the original amount of the loan.

(H) At the election of the creditor, a statement of the repayment schedule using 1 or a combination of the following—

(i) by making the statement: "Your first payment in the amount of $___ is due on ___ but the future payment amount may be different. Consult your reaffirmation agreement or credit agreement, as applicable.", and stating the amount of the first payment and the due date of that payment in the places provided;

(ii) by making the statement: "Your payment schedule will be:", and describing the repayment schedule with the number, amount, and due dates or period of payments scheduled to repay the debts reaffirmed to the extent then known by the disclosing party; or

(iii) by describing the debtor's repayment obligations with reasonable specificity to the extent then known by the disclosing party.

(I) The following statement: "Note: When this disclosure refers to what a creditor 'may' do, it does not use the word 'may' to give the creditor specific permission. The word 'may' is used to tell you what might occur if the law permits the creditor to take the action. If you have questions about your reaffirming a debt or what the law requires, consult with the attorney who helped you negotiate this agreement reaffirming a debt. If you don't have an attorney helping you, the judge will explain the effect of your reaffirming a debt when the hearing on the reaffirmation agreement is held.".

(J) (i) The following additional statements:

"Reaffirming a debt is a serious financial decision. The law requires you to take certain steps to make sure the decision is in your best interest. If these steps are not completed, the reaffirmation agreement is not effective, even though you have signed it.

"1. Read the disclosures in this Part A carefully. Consider the decision to reaffirm carefully. Then, if you want to reaffirm, sign the reaffirmation agreement in Part B (or you may use a separate agreement you and your creditor agree on).

"2. Complete and sign Part D and be sure you can afford to make the payments you are agreeing to make and have received a copy of the disclosure statement and a completed and signed reaffirmation agreement.

"3. If you were represented by an attorney during the negotiation of your reaffirmation agreement, the attorney must have signed the certification in Part C.

"4. If you were not represented by an attorney during the negotiation of your reaffirmation agreement, you must have completed and signed Part E.

"5. The original of this disclosure must be filed with the court by you or your creditor. If a separate reaffirmation agreement (other than the one in Part B) has been signed, it must be attached.

"6. If you were represented by an attorney during the negotiation of your reaffirmation agreement, your reaffirmation agreement becomes effective upon filing with the court unless the reaffirmation is presumed to be an undue hardship as explained in Part D.

"7. If you were not represented by an attorney during the negotiation of your reaffirmation agreement, it will not be effective unless the court approves it. The court will notify you of the hearing on your reaffirmation agreement. You must attend this hearing in bankruptcy court where the judge will review your reaffirmation agreement. The bankruptcy court must approve your reaffirmation agreement as consistent with your best interests, except that no court approval is required if your reaffirmation agreement is for a consumer debt secured by a mortgage, deed of trust, security deed, or other lien on your real property, like your home.

"Your right to rescind (cancel) your reaffirmation agreement. You may rescind (cancel) your reaffirmation agreement at any time before the bankruptcy court enters a discharge order, or before the expiration of the 60-day period that begins on the date your reaffirmation agreement is filed with the court, whichever occurs later. To rescind (cancel) your reaffirmation agreement, you must notify the creditor that your reaffirmation agreement is rescinded (or canceled).

"What are your obligations if you reaffirm the debt? A reaffirmed debt remains your personal legal obligation. It is not discharged in your bankruptcy case. That means that if you default on your reaffirmed debt after your bankruptcy case is over, your creditor may be able to take your property or your wages. Otherwise, your obligations will be determined by the reaffirmation agreement which may have changed the terms of the original agreement. For example, if you are reaffirming an open end credit agreement, the creditor may be permitted by that agreement or applicable law to change the terms of that agreement in the future under certain conditions.

"Are you required to enter into a reaffirmation agreement by any law? No, you are not required to reaffirm a debt by any law. Only agree to reaffirm a debt if it is in your best interest. Be sure you can afford the payments you agree to make.

"What if your creditor has a security interest or lien? Your bankruptcy discharge does not eliminate any lien on your property. A 'lien' is often referred to as a security interest, deed of trust, mortgage or security deed. Even if you do not reaffirm and your personal liability on the debt is discharged, because of the lien your creditor may still have the right to take the security property if you do not pay the debt or default on it. If the lien is on an item of personal property that is exempt under your State's law or that the trustee has abandoned, you may be able to redeem the item rather than reaffirm the debt. To redeem, you make a single payment to the creditor equal to the current value of the security property, as agreed by the parties or determined by the court.".

(ii) In the case of a reaffirmation under subsection (m)(2), numbered paragraph 6 in the disclosures required by clause (i) of this subparagraph shall read as follows:

"6. If you were represented by an attorney during the negotiation of your reaffirmation agreement, your reaffirmation agreement becomes effective upon filing with the court.".

(4) The form of such agreement required under this paragraph shall consist of the following:

"Part B: Reaffirmation Agreement. I (we) agree to reaffirm the debts arising under the credit agreement described below.

"Brief description of credit agreement:

"Description of any changes to the credit agreement made as part of this reaffirmation agreement:

"Signature: Date:

"Borrower:

"Co-borrower, if also reaffirming these debts:

"Accepted by creditor:

"Date of creditor acceptance:".

(5) The declaration shall consist of the following:

(A) The following certification:

"Part C: Certification by Debtor's Attorney (If Any).

"I hereby certify that (1) this agreement represents a fully informed and voluntary agreement by the debtor; (2) this agreement does not impose an undue hardship on the debtor or any dependent of the debtor; and (3) I have fully advised the debtor of the legal effect and consequences of this agreement and any default under this agreement.

"Signature of Debtor's Attorney: Date: ".

(B) If a presumption of undue hardship has been established with respect to such agreement, such certification shall state that in the opinion of the attorney, the debtor is able to make the payment.

(C) In the case of a reaffirmation agreement under subsection (m)(2), subparagraph (B) is not applicable.

(6) (A) The statement in support of such agreement, which the debtor shall sign and date prior to filing with the court, shall consist of the following:

"Part D: Debtor's Statement in Support of Reaffirmation Agreement.

"1. I believe this reaffirmation agreement will not impose an undue hardship on my dependents or me. I can afford to make the payments on the reaffirmed debt because my monthly income (take home pay plus any other income received) is $___, and my actual current monthly expenses including monthly payments on post- bankruptcy debt and other reaffirmation agreements total $___, leaving $___ to make the required payments on this reaffirmed debt. I understand that if my income less my monthly expenses does not leave enough to make the payments, this reaffirmation agreement is presumed to be an undue hardship on me and must be reviewed by the court. However, this presumption may be overcome if I explain to the satisfaction of the court how I can afford to make the payments here: ___.

"2. I received a copy of the Reaffirmation Disclosure Statement in Part A and a completed and signed reaffirmation agreement.".

(B) Where the debtor is represented by an attorney and is reaffirming a debt owed to a creditor defined in section 19(b)(1)(A)(iv) of the Federal Reserve Act, the statement of support of the reaffirmation agreement, which the debtor shall sign and date prior to filing with the court, shall consist of the following:

"I believe this reaffirmation agreement is in my financial interest. I can afford to make the payments on the reaffirmed debt. I received a copy of the Reaffirmation Disclosure Statement in Part A and a completed and signed reaffirmation agreement.".

(7) The motion that may be used if approval of such agreement by the court is required in order for it to be effective, shall be signed and dated by the movant and shall consist of the following:

"Part E: Motion for Court Approval (To be completed only if the debtor is not represented by an attorney.). I (we), the debtor(s), affirm the following to be true and correct:

"I am not represented by an attorney in connection with this reaffirmation agreement.

"I believe this reaffirmation agreement is in my best interest based on the income and expenses I have disclosed in my Statement in Support of this reaffirmation agreement, and because (provide any additional relevant reasons the court should consider):

"Therefore, I ask the court for an order approving this reaffirmation agreement.".

(8) The court order, which may be used to approve such agreement, shall consist of the following:

"Court Order: The court grants the debtor's motion and approves the reaffirmation agreement described above.".

(l) Notwithstanding any other provision of this title the following shall apply:

(1) A creditor may accept payments from a debtor before and after the filing of an agreement of the kind specified in subsection (c) with the court.

(2) A creditor may accept payments from a debtor under such agreement that the creditor believes in good faith to be effective.

(3) The requirements of subsections (c)(2) and (k) shall be satisfied if disclosures required under those subsections are given in good faith.

(m) (1) Until 60 days after an agreement of the kind specified in subsection (c) is filed with the court (or such additional period as the court, after notice and a hearing and for cause, orders before the expiration of such period), it shall be presumed that such agreement is an undue hardship on the debtor if the debtor's monthly income less the debtor's monthly expenses as shown on the debtor's completed and signed statement in support of such agreement required under subsection (k)(6)(A) is less than the scheduled payments on the reaffirmed debt. This presumption shall be reviewed by the court. The presumption may be rebutted in writing by the debtor if the statement includes an explanation that identifies additional sources of funds to make the payments as agreed upon under the terms of such agreement. If the presumption is not rebutted to the satisfaction of the court, the court may disapprove such agreement. No agreement shall be disapproved without notice and a hearing to the debtor and creditor, and such hearing shall be concluded before the entry of the debtor's discharge.

(2) This subsection does not apply to reaffirmation agreements where the creditor is a credit union, as defined in section 19(b)(1)(A)(iv) of the Federal Reserve Act.

Sec. 525. Protection against discriminatory treatment

(a) Except as provided in the Perishable Agricultural Commodities Act, 1930, the Packers and Stockyards Act, 1921, and section 1 of the Act entitled "An Act making appropriations for the Department of Agriculture for the fiscal year ending June 30, 1944, and for other purposes," approved July 12, 1943, a governmental unit may not deny, revoke, suspend, or refuse to renew a license, permit, charter, franchise, or other similar grant to, condition such a grant to, discriminate with respect to such a grant against, deny employment to, terminate the employment of, or discriminate with respect to employment against, a person that is or has been a debtor under this title or a bankrupt or a debtor under the Bankruptcy Act, or another person with whom such bankrupt or debtor has been associated, solely because such bankrupt or debtor is or has been a debtor under this title or a bankrupt or debtor under the Bankruptcy Act, has been insolvent before the commencement of the case under this title, or during the case but before the debtor is granted or denied a discharge, or has not paid a debt that is dischargeable in the case under this title or that was discharged under the Bankruptcy Act.

(b) No private employer may terminate the employment of, or discriminate with respect to employment against, an individual who is or has been a debtor under this title, a debtor or bankrupt under the Bankruptcy Act, or an individual associated with such debtor or bankrupt, solely because such debtor or bankrupt—

(1) is or has been a debtor under this title or a debtor or bankrupt under the Bankruptcy Act;

(2) has been insolvent before the commencement of a case under this title or during the case but before the grant or denial of a discharge; or

(3) has not paid a debt that is dischargeable in a case under this title or that was discharged under the Bankruptcy Act.

(c) (1) A governmental unit that operates a student grant or loan program and a person engaged in a business that includes the making of loans guaranteed or insured under a student loan program may not deny a student grant, loan, loan guarantee, or loan insurance to a person that is or has been a debtor under this title or a bankrupt or debtor under the Bankruptcy Act, or another person with whom the debtor or bankrupt has been associated, because the debtor or bankrupt is or has been a debtor under this title or a bankrupt or debtor under the Bankruptcy Act, has been insolvent before the commencement of a case under this title or during the pendency of the case but before the debtor is granted or denied a discharge, or has not paid a debt that is dischargeable in the case under this title or that was discharged under the Bankruptcy Act.

(2) In this section, "student loan program" means any program operated under title IV of the Higher Education Act of 1965 or a similar program operated under State or local law.

Sec. 526. Restrictions on debt relief agencies

(a) A debt relief agency shall not—

(1) fail to perform any service that such agency informed an assisted person or prospective assisted person it would provide in connection with a case or proceeding under this title;

(2) make any statement, or counsel or advise any assisted person or prospective assisted person to make a statement in a document filed in a case or proceeding under this title, that is untrue and misleading, or that upon the exercise of reasonable care, should have been known by such agency to be untrue or misleading;

(3) misrepresent to any assisted person or prospective assisted person, directly or indirectly, affirmatively or by material omission, with respect to—

(A) the services that such agency will provide to such person; or

(B) the benefits and risks that may result if such person becomes a debtor in a case under this title; or

(4) advise an assisted person or prospective assisted person to incur more debt in contemplation of such person filing a case under this title or to pay an attorney or bankruptcy petition preparer fee or charge for services performed as part of preparing for or representing a debtor in a case under this title.

(b) Any waiver by any assisted person of any protection or right provided under this section shall not be enforceable against the debtor by any Federal or State court or any other person, but may be enforced against a debt relief agency.

(c) (1) Any contract for bankruptcy assistance between a debt relief agency and an assisted person that does not comply with the material requirements of this section, section 527, or section 528 shall be void and may not be enforced by any Federal or State court or by any other person, other than such assisted person.

(2) Any debt relief agency shall be liable to an assisted person in the amount of any fees or charges in connection with providing bankruptcy assistance to such person that such debt relief agency has received, for actual damages, and for reasonable attorneys' fees and costs if such agency is found, after notice and a hearing, to have—

(A) intentionally or negligently failed to comply with any provision of this section, section 527, or section 528 with respect to a case or proceeding under this title for such assisted person;

(B) provided bankruptcy assistance to an assisted person in a case or proceeding under this title that is dismissed or converted to a case under another chapter of this title because of such agency's intentional or negligent failure to file any required document including those specified in section 521; or

(C) intentionally or negligently disregarded the material requirements of this title or the Federal Rules of Bankruptcy Procedure applicable to such agency.

(3) In addition to such other remedies as are provided under State law, whenever the chief law enforcement officer of a State, or an official or agency designated by a State, has reason to believe that any person has violated or is violating this section, the State—

(A) may bring an action to enjoin such violation;

(B) may bring an action on behalf of its residents to recover the actual damages of assisted persons arising from such violation, including any liability under paragraph (2); and

(C) in the case of any successful action under subparagraph (A) or (B), shall be awarded the costs of the action and reasonable attorneys' fees as determined by the court.

(4) The district courts of the United States for districts located in the State shall have concurrent jurisdiction of any action under subparagraph (A) or (B) of paragraph (3).

(5) Notwithstanding any other provision of Federal law and in addition to any other remedy provided under Federal or State law, if the court, on its own motion or on the motion of the United States trustee or the debtor, finds that a person intentionally violated this section, or engaged in a clear and consistent pattern or practice of violating this section, the court may—

(A) enjoin the violation of such section; or

(B) impose an appropriate civil penalty against such person.

(d) No provision of this section, section 527, or section 528 shall—

(1) annul, alter, affect, or exempt any person subject to such sections from complying with any law of any State except to the extent that such law is inconsistent with those sections, and then only to the extent of the inconsistency; or

(2) be deemed to limit or curtail the authority or ability—

(A) of a State or subdivision or instrumentality thereof, to determine and enforce qualifications for the practice of law under the laws of that State; or

(B) of a Federal court to determine and enforce the qualifications for the practice of law before that court.

Sec. 527. Disclosures

(a) A debt relief agency providing bankruptcy assistance to an assisted person shall provide—

(1) the written notice required under section 342(b)(1); and

(2) to the extent not covered in the written notice described in paragraph (1), and not later than 3 business days after the first date on which a debt relief agency first offers to provide any bankruptcy assistance services to an assisted person, a clear and conspicuous written notice advising assisted persons that—

(A) all information that the assisted person is required to provide with a petition and thereafter during a case under this title is required to be complete, accurate, and truthful;

(B) all assets and all liabilities are required to be completely and accurately disclosed in the documents filed to commence the case, and the replacement value of each asset as defined in section 506 must be stated in those documents where requested after reasonable inquiry to establish such value;

(C) current monthly income, the amounts specified in section 707(b)(2), and, in a case under chapter 13 of this title, disposable income (determined in accordance with section 707(b)(2)), are required to be stated after reasonable inquiry; and

(D) information that an assisted person provides during their case may be audited pursuant to this title, and that failure to provide such information may result in dismissal of the case under this title or other sanction, including a criminal sanction.

(b) A debt relief agency providing bankruptcy assistance to an assisted person shall provide each assisted person at the same time as the notices required under subsection (a)(1) the following statement, to the extent applicable, or one substantially similar. The statement shall be clear and conspicuous and shall be in a single document separate from other documents or notices provided to the assisted person:

"IMPORTANT INFORMATION ABOUT BANKRUPTCY ASSISTANCE SERVICES FROM AN ATTORNEY OR BANKRUPTCY PETITION PREPARER.

"If you decide to seek bankruptcy relief, you can represent yourself, you can hire an attorney to represent you, or you can get help in some localities from a bankruptcy petition preparer who is not an attorney. THE LAW REQUIRES AN ATTORNEY OR BANKRUPTCY PETITION PREPARER TO GIVE YOU A WRITTEN CONTRACT SPECIFYING WHAT THE ATTORNEY OR BANKRUPTCY PETITION PREPARER WILL DO FOR YOU AND HOW MUCH IT WILL COST. Ask to see the contract before you hire anyone.

"The following information helps you understand what must be done in a routine bankruptcy case to help you evaluate how much service you need. Although bankruptcy can be complex, many cases are routine.

"Before filing a bankruptcy case, either you or your attorney should analyze your eligibility for different forms of debt relief available under the Bankruptcy Code and which form of relief is most likely to be beneficial for you. Be sure you understand the relief you can obtain and its limitations. To file a bankruptcy case, documents called a Petition, Schedules and Statement of Financial Affairs, as well as in some cases a Statement of Intention need to be prepared correctly and filed with the bankruptcy court. You will have to pay a filing fee to the bankruptcy court. Once your case starts, you will have to attend the required first meeting of creditors where you may be questioned by a court official called a 'trustee' and by creditors.

"If you choose to file a chapter 7 case, you may be asked by a creditor to reaffirm a debt. You may want help deciding whether to do so. A creditor is not permitted to coerce you into reaffirming your debts.

"If you choose to file a chapter 13 case in which you repay your creditors what you can afford over 3 to 5 years, you may also want help with preparing your chapter 13 plan and with the confirmation hearing on your plan which will be before a bankruptcy judge.

"If you select another type of relief under the Bankruptcy Code other than chapter 7 or chapter 13, you will want to find out what should be done from someone familiar with that type of relief.

"Your bankruptcy case may also involve litigation. You are generally permitted to represent yourself in litigation in bankruptcy court, but only attorneys, not bankruptcy petition preparers, can give you legal advice.".

(c) Except to the extent the debt relief agency provides the required information itself after reasonably diligent inquiry of the assisted person or others so as to obtain such information reasonably accurately for inclusion on the petition, schedules or statement of financial affairs, a debt relief agency providing bankruptcy assistance to an assisted person, to the extent permitted by nonbankruptcy law, shall provide each assisted person at the time required for the notice required under subsection (a)(1) reasonably sufficient information (which shall be provided in a clear and conspicuous writing) to the assisted person on how to provide all the information the assisted person is required to provide under this title pursuant to section 521, including—

(1) how to value assets at replacement value, determine current monthly income, the amounts specified in section 707(b)(2) and, in a chapter 13 case, how to determine disposable income in accordance with section 707(b)(2) and related calculations;

(2) how to complete the list of creditors, including how to determine what amount is owed and what address for the creditor should be shown; and

(3) how to determine what property is exempt and how to value exempt property at replacement value as defined in section 506.

(d) A debt relief agency shall maintain a copy of the notices required under subsection (a) of this section for 2 years after the date on which the notice is given the assisted person.

Sec. 528. Requirements for debt relief agencies

(a) A debt relief agency shall—

(1) not later than 5 business days after the first date on which such agency provides any bankruptcy assistance services to an assisted person, but prior to such assisted person's petition under this title being filed, execute a written contract with such assisted person that explains clearly and conspicuously—

(A) the services such agency will provide to such assisted person; and

(B) the fees or charges for such services, and the terms of payment;

(2) provide the assisted person with a copy of the fully executed and completed contract;

(3) clearly and conspicuously disclose in any advertisement of bankruptcy assistance services or of the benefits of bankruptcy directed to the general public (whether in general media, seminars or specific mailings, telephonic or electronic messages, or otherwise) that the services or benefits are with respect to bankruptcy relief under this title; and

(b) (1) An advertisement of bankruptcy assistance services or of the benefits of bankruptcy directed to the general public includes—

(A) descriptions of bankruptcy assistance in connection with a chapter 13 plan whether or not chapter 13 is specifically mentioned in such advertisement; and

(B) statements such as "federally supervised repayment plan" or "Federal debt restructuring help" or other similar statements that could lead a reasonable consumer to believe that debt counseling was being offered when in fact the services were directed to providing bankruptcy assistance with a chapter 13 plan or other form of bankruptcy relief under this title.

(2) An advertisement, directed to the general public, indicating that the debt relief agency provides assistance with respect to credit defaults, mortgage foreclosures, eviction proceedings, excessive debt, debt collection pressure, or inability to pay any consumer debt shall—

(A) disclose clearly and conspicuously in such advertisement that the assistance may involve bankruptcy relief under this title; and

(B) include the following statement: "We are a debt relief agency. We help people file for bankruptcy relief under the Bankruptcy Code." or a substantially similar statement.

SUBCHAPTER III—THE ESTATE

Sec. 541. Property of the estate

(a) The commencement of a case under section 301, 302, or 303 of this title creates an estate. Such estate is comprised of all the following property, wherever located and by whomever held:

(1) Except as provided in subsections (b) and (c)(2) of this section, all legal or equitable interests of the debtor in property as of the commencement of the case.

(2) All interests of the debtor and the debtor's spouse in community property as of the commencement of the case that is—

(A) under the sole, equal, or joint management and control of the debtor; or

(B) liable for an allowable claim against the debtor, or for both an allowable claim against the debtor and an allowable claim against the debtor's spouse, to the extent that such interest is so liable.

(3) Any interest in property that the trustee recovers under section 329(b), 363(n), 543, 550, 553, or 723 of this title.

(4) Any interest in property preserved for the benefit of or ordered transferred to the estate under section 510(c) or 551 of this title.

(5) Any interest in property that would have been property of the estate if such interest had been an interest of the debtor on the date of the filing of the petition, and that the debtor acquires or becomes entitled to acquire within 180 days after such date—

(A) by bequest, devise, or inheritance;

(B) as a result of a property settlement agreement with the debtor's spouse, or of an interlocutory or final divorce decree; or

(C) as a beneficiary of a life insurance policy or of a death benefit plan.

(6) Proceeds, product, offspring, rents, or profits of or from property of the estate, except such as are earnings from services performed by an individual debtor after the commencement of the case.

(7) Any interest in property that the estate acquires after the commencement of the case.

(b) Property of the estate does not include—

(1) any power that the debtor may exercise solely for the benefit of an entity other than the debtor;

(2) any interest of the debtor as a lessee under a lease of nonresidential real property that has terminated at the expiration of the stated term of such lease before the commencement of the case under this title, and ceases to include any interest of the debtor as a lessee under a lease of nonresidential real property that has terminated at the expiration of the stated term of such lease during the case;

(3) any eligibility of the debtor to participate in programs authorized under the Higher Education Act of 1965 (20 U.S.C. 1001 et seq.; 42 U.S.C. 2751 et seq.), or any accreditation status or State licensure of the debtor as an educational institution;

(4) any interest of the debtor in liquid or gaseous hydrocarbons to the extent that—

(A) (i) the debtor has transferred or has agreed to transfer such interest pursuant to a farmout agreement or any written agreement directly related to a farmout agreement; and

(ii) but for the operation of this paragraph, the estate could include the interest referred to in clause (i) only by virtue of section 365 or 544(a)(3) of this title; or

(B) (i) the debtor has transferred such interest pursuant to a written conveyance of a production payment to an entity that does not participate in the operation of the property from which such production payment is transferred; and

(ii) but for the operation of this paragraph, the estate could include the interest referred to in clause (i) only by virtue of section 365 or 542 of this title;

(5) funds placed in an education individual retirement account (as defined in section 530(b)(1) of the Internal Revenue Code of 1986) not later than 365 days before the date of the filing of the petition in a case under this title, but—

(A) only if the designated beneficiary of such account was a child, stepchild, grandchild, or stepgrandchild of the debtor for the taxable year for which funds were placed in such account;

(B) only to the extent that such funds—

(i) are not pledged or promised to any entity in connection with any extension of credit; and

(ii) are not excess contributions (as described in section 4973(e) of the Internal Revenue Code of 1986); and

(C) in the case of funds placed in all such accounts having the same designated beneficiary not earlier than 720 days nor later than 365 days before such date, only so much of such funds as does not exceed $5,000;

(6) funds used to purchase a tuition credit or certificate or contributed to an account in accordance with section 529(b)(1)(A) of the Internal Revenue Code of 1986 under a qualified State tuition program (as defined in section 529(b)(1) of such Code) not later than 365 days before the date of the filing of the petition in a case under this title, but—

(A) only if the designated beneficiary of the amounts paid or contributed to such tuition program was a child, stepchild, grandchild, or stepgrandchild of the debtor for the taxable year for which funds were paid or contributed;

(B) with respect to the aggregate amount paid or contributed to such program having the same designated beneficiary, only so much of such amount as does not exceed the total contributions permitted under section 529(b)(7) of such Code with respect to such beneficiary, as adjusted beginning on the date of the filing of the petition in a case under this title by the annual increase or decrease (rounded to the nearest tenth of 1 percent) in the education expenditure category of the Consumer Price Index prepared by the Department of Labor; and

(C) in the case of funds paid or contributed to such program having the same designated beneficiary not earlier than 720 days nor later than 365 days before such date, only so much of such funds as does not exceed $5,000;

(7) any amount—

(A) withheld by an employer from the wages of employees for payment as contributions—

(i) to—

(I) an employee benefit plan that is subject to title I of the Employee Retirement Income Security Act of 1974 or under an employee benefit plan which is a governmental plan under section 414(d) of the Internal Revenue Code of 1986;

(II) a deferred compensation plan under section 457 of the Internal Revenue Code of 1986; or

(III) a tax-deferred annuity under section 403(b) of the Internal Revenue Code of 1986;

except that such amount under this subparagraph shall not constitute disposable income as defined in section 1325(b)(2); or

(ii) to a health insurance plan regulated by State law whether or not subject to such title; or

(B) received by an employer from employees for payment as contributions—

(i) to—

(I) an employee benefit plan that is subject to title I of the Employee Retirement Income Security Act of 1974 or under an employee benefit plan which is a governmental plan under section 414(d) of the Internal Revenue Code of 1986;

(II) a deferred compensation plan under section 457 of the Internal Revenue Code of 1986; or

(III) a tax-deferred annuity under section 403(b) of the Internal Revenue Code of 1986;

except that such amount under this subparagraph shall not constitute disposable income, as defined in section 1325(b)(2); or

(ii) to a health insurance plan regulated by State law whether or not subject to such title;

(8) subject to subchapter III of chapter 5, any interest of the debtor in property where the debtor pledged or sold tangible personal property (other than securities or written or printed evidences of indebtedness or title) as collateral for a loan or advance of money given by a person licensed under law to make such loans or advances, where—

(A) the tangible personal property is in the possession of the pledgee or transferee;

(B) the debtor has no obligation to repay the money, redeem the collateral, or buy back the property at a stipulated price; and

(C) neither the debtor nor the trustee have exercised any right to redeem provided under the contract or State law, in a timely manner as provided under State law and section 108(b); or

(9) any interest in cash or cash equivalents that constitute proceeds of a sale by the debtor of a money order that is made—

(A) on or after the date that is 14 days prior to the date on which the petition is filed; and

(B) under an agreement with a money order issuer that prohibits the commingling of such proceeds with property of the debtor (notwithstanding that, contrary to the agreement, the proceeds may have been commingled with property of the debtor),

unless the money order issuer had not taken action, prior to the filing of the petition, to require compliance with the prohibition.

Paragraph (4) shall not be construed to exclude from the estate any consideration the debtor retains, receives, or is entitled to receive for transferring an interest in liquid or gaseous hydrocarbons pursuant to a farmout agreement.

(c) (1) Except as provided in paragraph (2) of this subsection, an interest of the debtor in property becomes property of the estate under subsection (a)(1), (a)(2), or (a)(5) of this section notwithstanding any provision in an agreement, transfer instrument, or applicable nonbankruptcy law—

(A) that restricts or conditions transfer of such interest by the debtor; or

(B) that is conditioned on the insolvency or financial condition of the debtor, on the commencement of a case under this title, or on the appointment of or taking possession by a trustee in a case under this title or a custodian before such commencement, and that effects or gives an option to effect a forfeiture, modification, or termination of the debtor's interest in property.

(2) A restriction on the transfer of a beneficial interest of the debtor in a trust that is enforceable under applicable nonbankruptcy law is enforceable in a case under this title.

(d) Property in which the debtor holds, as of the commencement of the case, only legal title and not an equitable interest, such as a mortgage secured by real property, or an interest in such a mortgage, sold by the debtor but as to which the debtor retains legal title to service or supervise the servicing of such mortgage or interest, becomes property of the estate under subsection (a)(1) or (2) of this section only to the extent of the debtor's legal title to such property, but not to the extent of any equitable interest in such property that the debtor does not hold.

(e) In determining whether any of the relationships specified in paragraph (5)(A) or (6)(A) of subsection (b) exists, a legally adopted child of an individual (and a child who is a member of an individual's household, if placed with such individual by an authorized placement agency for legal adoption by such individual), or a foster child of an individual (if such child has as the child's principal place of abode the home of the debtor and is a member of the debtor's household) shall be treated as a child of such individual by blood.

(f) Notwithstanding any other provision of this title, property that is held by a debtor that is a corporation described in section 501(c)(3) of the Internal Revenue Code of 1986 and exempt from tax under section 501(a) of such Code may be transferred to an entity that is not such a corporation, but only under the same conditions as would apply if the debtor had not filed a case under this title.

Sec. 542. Turnover of property to the estate

(a) Except as provided in subsection (c) or (d) of this section, an entity, other than a custodian, in possession, custody, or control, during the case, of property that the trustee may use, sell, or lease under section 363 of this title, or that the debtor may exempt under section 522 of this title, shall deliver to the trustee, and account for, such property or the value of such property, unless such property is of inconsequential value or benefit to the estate.

(b) Except as provided in subsection (c) or (d) of this section, an entity that owes a debt that is property of the estate and that is matured, payable on demand, or payable on order, shall pay such debt to, or on the order of, the trustee, except to the extent that such debt may be offset under section 553 of this title against a claim against the debtor.

(c) Except as provided in section 362(a)(7) of this title, an entity that has neither actual notice nor actual knowledge of the commencement of the case concerning the debtor may transfer property of the estate, or pay a debt owing to the debtor, in good faith and other than in the manner specified in subsection (d) of this section, to an entity other than the trustee, with the same effect as to the entity making such transfer or payment as if the case under this title concerning the debtor had not been commenced.

(d) A life insurance company may transfer property of the estate or property of the debtor to such company in good faith, with the same effect with respect to such company as if the case under this title concerning the debtor had not been commenced, if such transfer is to pay a premium or to carry out a nonforfeiture insurance option, and is required to be made automatically, under a life insurance contract with such company that was entered into before the date of the filing of the petition and that is property of the estate.

(e) Subject to any applicable privilege, after notice and a hearing, the court may order an attorney, accountant, or other person that holds recorded information, including books, documents, records, and papers, relating to the debtor's property or financial affairs, to turn over or disclose such recorded information to the trustee.

Sec. 543. Turnover of property by a custodian

(a) A custodian with knowledge of the commencement of a case under this title concerning the debtor may not make any disbursement from, or take any action in the administration of, property of the debtor, proceeds, product, offspring, rents, or profits of such property, or property of the estate, in the possession, custody, or control of such custodian, except such action as is necessary to preserve such property.

(b) A custodian shall—

(1) deliver to the trustee any property of the debtor held by or transferred to such custodian, or proceeds, product, offspring, rents, or profits of such property, that is in such custodian's possession, custody, or control on the date that such custodian acquires knowledge of the commencement of the case; and

(2) file an accounting of any property of the debtor, or proceeds, product, offspring, rents, or profits of such property, that, at any time, came into the possession, custody, or control of such custodian.

(c) The court, after notice and a hearing, shall—

(1) protect all entities to which a custodian has become obligated with respect to such property or proceeds, product, offspring, rents, or profits of such property;

(2) provide for the payment of reasonable compensation for services rendered and costs and expenses incurred by such custodian; and

(3) surcharge such custodian, other than an assignee for the benefit of the debtor's creditors that was appointed or took possession more than 120 days before the date of the filing of the petition, for any improper or excessive disbursement, other than a disbursement that has been made in accordance with applicable law or that has been approved, after notice and a hearing, by a court of competent jurisdiction before the commencement of the case under this title.

(d) After notice and hearing, the bankruptcy court—

(1) may excuse compliance with subsection (a), (b), or (c) of this section if the interests of creditors and, if the debtor is not insolvent, of equity security holders would be better served by permitting a custodian to continue in possession, custody, or control of such property, and

(2) shall excuse compliance with subsections (a) and (b)(1) of this section if the custodian is an assignee for the benefit of the debtor's creditors that was appointed or took possession more than 120 days before the date of the filing of the petition, unless compliance with such subsections is necessary to prevent fraud or injustice.

Sec. 544. Trustee as lien creditor and as successor to certain creditors and purchasers

(a) The trustee shall have, as of the commencement of the case, and without regard to any knowledge of the trustee or of any creditor, the rights and powers of, or may avoid any transfer of property of the debtor or any obligation incurred by the debtor that is voidable by—

(1) a creditor that extends credit to the debtor at the time of the commencement of the case, and that obtains, at such time and with respect to such credit, a judicial lien on all property on which a creditor on a simple contract could have obtained such a judicial lien, whether or not such a creditor exists;

(2) a creditor that extends credit to the debtor at the time of the commencement of the case, and obtains, at such time and with respect to such credit, an execution against the debtor that is returned unsatisfied at such time, whether or not such a creditor exists; or

(3) a bona fide purchaser of real property, other than fixtures, from the debtor, against whom applicable law permits such transfer to be perfected, that obtains the status of a bona fide purchaser and has perfected such transfer at the time of the commencement of the case, whether or not such a purchaser exists.

(b) (1) Except as provided in paragraph (2), the trustee may avoid any transfer of an interest of the debtor in property or any obligation incurred by the debtor that is voidable under applicable law by a creditor holding an unsecured claim that is allowable under section 502 of this title or that is not allowable only under section 502(e) of this title.

(2) Paragraph (1) shall not apply to a transfer of a charitable contribution (as that term is defined in section 548(d)(3)) that is not covered under section 548(a)(1)(B), by reason of section 548(a)(2). Any claim by any person to recover a transferred contribution described in the preceding sentence under Federal or State law in a Federal or State court shall be preempted by the commencement of the case.

Sec. 545. Statutory liens

The trustee may avoid the fixing of a statutory lien on property of the debtor to the extent that such lien—

(1) first becomes effective against the debtor—

(A) when a case under this title concerning the debtor is commenced;

(B) when an insolvency proceeding other than under this title concerning the debtor is commenced;

(C) when a custodian is appointed or authorized to take or takes possession;

(D) when the debtor becomes insolvent;

(E) when the debtor's financial condition fails to meet a specified standard; or

(F) at the time of an execution against property of the debtor levied at the instance of an entity other than the holder of such statutory lien;

(2) is not perfected or enforceable at the time of the commencement of the case against a bona fide purchaser that purchases such property at the time of the commencement of the case, whether or not such a purchaser exists, except in any case in which a purchaser is a purchaser described in section 6323 of the Internal Revenue Code of 1986, or in any other similar provision of State or local law;

(3) is for rent; or

(4) is a lien of distress for rent.

Sec. 546. Limitations on avoiding powers

(a) An action or proceeding under section 544, 545, 547, 548, or 553 of this title may not be commenced after the earlier of—

(1) the later of—

(A) 2 years after the entry of the order for relief; or

(B) 1 year after the appointment or election of the first trustee under section 702, 1104, 1163, 1202, or 1302 of this title if such appointment or such election occurs before the expiration of the period specified in subparagraph (A); or

(2) the time the case is closed or dismissed.

(b) (1) The rights and powers of a trustee under sections 544, 545, and 549 of this title are subject to any generally applicable law that—

(A) permits perfection of an interest in property to be effective against an entity that acquires rights in such property before the date of perfection; or

(B) provides for the maintenance or continuation of perfection of an interest in property to be effective against an entity that acquires rights in such property before the date on which action is taken to effect such maintenance or continuation.

(2) If—

(A) a law described in paragraph (1) requires seizure of such property or commencement of an action to accomplish such perfection, or maintenance or continuation of perfection of an interest in property; and

(B) such property has not been seized or such an action has not been commenced before the date of the filing of the petition; such interest in such property shall be perfected, or perfection of such interest shall be maintained or continued, by giving notice within the time fixed by such law for such seizure or such commencement.

(c) (1) Except as provided in subsection (d) of this section and in section 507(c), and subject to the prior rights of a holder of a security interest in such goods or the proceeds thereof, the rights and powers of the trustee under sections 544(a), 545, 547, and 549 are subject to the right of a seller of goods that has sold goods to the debtor, in the ordinary course of such seller's business, to reclaim such goods if the debtor has received such goods while insolvent, within 45 days before the date of the commencement of a case under this title, but such seller may not reclaim such goods unless such seller demands in writing reclamation of such goods—

(A) not later than 45 days after the date of receipt of such goods by the debtor; or

(B) not later than 20 days after the date of commencement of the case, if the 45-day period expires after the commencement of the case.

(2) If a seller of goods fails to provide notice in the manner described in paragraph (1), the seller still may assert the rights contained in section 503(b)(9).

(d) In the case of a seller who is a producer of grain sold to a grain storage facility, owned or operated by the debtor, in the ordinary course of such seller's business (as such terms are defined in section 557 of this title) or in the case of a United States fisherman who has caught fish sold to a fish processing facility owned or operated by the debtor in the ordinary course of such fisherman's business, the rights and powers of the trustee under sections 544(a), 545, 547, and 549 of this title are subject to any statutory or common law right of such producer or fisherman to reclaim such grain or fish if the debtor has received such grain or fish while insolvent, but—

(1) such producer or fisherman may not reclaim any grain or fish unless such producer or fisherman demands, in writing, reclamation of such grain or fish before ten days after receipt thereof by the debtor; and

(2) the court may deny reclamation to such a producer or fisherman with a right of reclamation that has made such a demand only if the court secures such claim by a lien.

(e) Notwithstanding sections 544, 545, 547, 548(a)(1)(B), and 548(b) of this title, the trustee may not avoid a transfer that is a margin payment, as defined in section 101, 741, or 761 of this title, or settlement payment, as defined in section 101 or 741 of this title, made by or to (or for the benefit of) a commodity broker, forward contract merchant, stockbroker, financial institution, financial participant, or securities clearing agency, or that is a transfer made by or to (or for the benefit of) a commodity broker, forward contract merchant, stockbroker, financial institution, financial participant, or securities clearing agency, in connection with a securities contract, as defined in section 741(7), commodity contract, as defined in section 761(4), or forward contract, that is made before the commencement of the case, except under section 548(a)(1)(A) of this title.

(f) Notwithstanding sections 544, 545, 547, 548(a)(1)(B), and 548(b) of this title, the trustee may not avoid a transfer made by or to (or for the benefit of) a repo participant or financial participant, in connection with a repurchase agreement and that is made before the commencement of the case, except under section 548(a)(1)(A) of this title.

(g) Notwithstanding sections 544, 545, 547, 548(a)(1)(B) and 548(b) of this title, the trustee may not avoid a transfer, made by or to (or for the benefit of) a swap participant or financial participant, under or in connection with any swap agreement and that is made before the commencement of the case, except under section 548(a)(1)(A) of this title.

(h) Notwithstanding the rights and powers of a trustee under sections 544(a), 545, 547, 549, and 553, if the court determines on a motion by the trustee made not later than 120 days after the date of the order for relief in a case under chapter 11 of this title and after notice and a hearing, that a return is in the best interests of the estate, the debtor, with the consent of a creditor and subject to the prior rights of holders of security interests in such goods or the proceeds of such goods, may return goods shipped to the debtor by the creditor before the commencement of the case, and the creditor may offset the purchase price of such goods against any claim of the creditor against the debtor that arose before the commencement of the case.

(i) (1) Notwithstanding paragraphs (2) and (3) of section 545, the trustee may not avoid a warehouseman's lien for storage, transportation, or other costs incidental to the storage and handling of goods.

(2) The prohibition under paragraph (1) shall be applied in a manner consistent with any State statute applicable to such lien that is similar to section 7-209 of the Uniform Commercial Code, as in effect on the date of enactment of the Bankruptcy Abuse Prevention and Consumer Protection Act of 2005, or any successor to such section 7-209.

(j) Notwithstanding sections 544, 545, 547, 548(a)(1)(B), and 548(b) the trustee may not avoid a transfer made by or to (or for the benefit of) a master netting agreement participant under or in connection with any master netting agreement or any individual contract covered thereby that is made before the commencement of the case, except under section 548(a)(1)(A) and except to the extent that the trustee could otherwise avoid such a transfer made under an individual contract covered by such master netting agreement.

Sec. 547. Preferences

(a) In this section—

(1) "inventory" means personal property leased or furnished, held for sale or lease, or to be furnished under a contract for service, raw materials, work in process, or materials used or consumed in a business, including farm products such as crops or livestock, held for sale or lease;

(2) "new value" means money or money's worth in goods, services, or new credit, or release by a transferee of property previously transferred to such transferee in a transaction that is neither void nor voidable by the debtor or the trustee under any applicable law, including proceeds of such property, but does not include an obligation substituted for an existing obligation;

(3) "receivable" means right to payment, whether or not such right has been earned by performance; and

(4) a debt for a tax is incurred on the day when such tax is last payable without penalty, including any extension.

(b) Except as provided in subsections (c) and (i) of this section, the trustee may avoid any transfer of an interest of the debtor in property—

(1) to or for the benefit of a creditor;

(2) for or on account of an antecedent debt owed by the debtor before such transfer was made;

(3) made while the debtor was insolvent;

(4) made—

(A) on or within 90 days before the date of the filing of the petition; or

(B) between ninety days and one year before the date of the filing of the petition, if such creditor at the time of such transfer was an insider; and

(5) that enables such creditor to receive more than such creditor would receive if—

(A) the case were a case under chapter 7 of this title;

(B) the transfer had not been made; and

(C) such creditor received payment of such debt to the extent provided by the provisions of this title.

(c) The trustee may not avoid under this section a transfer—

(1) to the extent that such transfer was—

(A) intended by the debtor and the creditor to or for whose benefit such transfer was made to be a contemporaneous exchange for new value given to the debtor; and

(B) in fact a substantially contemporaneous exchange;

(2) to the extent that such transfer was in payment of a debt incurred by the debtor in the ordinary course of business or financial affairs of the debtor and the transferee, and such transfer was—

(A) made in the ordinary course of business or financial affairs of the debtor and the transferee; or

(B) made according to ordinary business terms;

(3) that creates a security interest in property acquired by the debtor—

(A) to the extent such security interest secures new value that was—

(i) given at or after the signing of a security agreement that contains a description of such property as collateral;

(ii) given by or on behalf of the secured party under such agreement;

(iii) given to enable the debtor to acquire such property; and

(iv) in fact used by the debtor to acquire such property; and

(B) that is perfected on or before 30 days after the debtor receives possession of such property;

(4) to or for the benefit of a creditor, to the extent that, after such transfer, such creditor gave new value to or for the benefit of the debtor—

(A) not secured by an otherwise unavoidable security interest; and

(B) on account of which new value the debtor did not make an otherwise unavoidable transfer to or for the benefit of such creditor;

(5) that creates a perfected security interest in inventory or a receivable or the proceeds of either, except to the extent that the aggregate of all such transfers to the transferee caused a reduction, as of the date of the filing of the petition and to the prejudice of other creditors holding unsecured claims, of any amount by which the debt secured by such security interest exceeded the value of all security interests for such debt on the later of—

(A) (i) with respect to a transfer to which subsection (b)(4)(A)of this section applies, 90 days before the date of the filing of the petition; or

(ii) with respect to a transfer to which subsection (b)(4)(B) of this section applies, one year before the date of the filing of the petition; or

(B) the date on which new value was first given under the security agreement creating such security interest;

(6) that is the fixing of a statutory lien that is not avoidable under section 545 of this title;

(7) to the extent such transfer was a bona fide payment of a debt for a domestic support obligation;

(8) if, in a case filed by an individual debtor whose debts are primarily consumer debts, the aggregate value of all property that constitutes or is affected by such transfer is less than \$600; or

(9) if, in a case filed by a debtor whose debts are not primarily consumer debts, the aggregate value of all property that constitutes or is affected by such transfer is less than \$5,000.

(d) The trustee may avoid a transfer of an interest in property of the debtor transferred to or for the benefit of a surety to secure reimbursement of such a surety that furnished a bond or other obligation to dissolve a judicial lien that would have been avoidable by the trustee under subsection (b) of this section. The liability of such surety under such bond or obligation shall be discharged to the extent of the value of such property recovered by the trustee or the amount paid to the trustee.

(e) (1) For the purposes of this section—

(A) a transfer of real property other than fixtures, but including the interest of a seller or purchaser under a contract for the sale of real property, is perfected when a bona fide purchaser of such property from the debtor against whom applicable law permits such transfer to be perfected cannot acquire an interest that is superior to the interest of the transferee; and

(B) a transfer of a fixture or property other than real property is perfected when a creditor on a simple contract cannot acquire a judicial lien that is superior to the interest of the transferee.

(2) For the purposes of this section, except as provided in paragraph (3) of this subsection, a transfer is made—

(A) at the time such transfer takes effect between the transferor and the transferee, if such transfer is perfected at, or within 30 days after, such time, except as provided in subsection (c)(3)(B);

(B) at the time such transfer is perfected, if such transfer is perfected after such 30 days; or

(C) immediately before the date of the filing of the petition, if such transfer is not perfected at the later of—

(i) the commencement of the case; or

(ii) 30 days after such transfer takes effect between the transferor and the transferee.

(3) For the purposes of this section, a transfer is not made until the debtor has acquired rights in the property transferred.

(f) For the purposes of this section, the debtor is presumed to have been insolvent on and during the 90 days immediately preceding the date of the filing of the petition.

(g) For the purposes of this section, the trustee has the burden of proving the avoidability of a transfer under subsection (b) of this section, and the creditor or party in interest against whom recovery or avoidance is sought has the burden of proving the nonavoidability of a transfer under subsection (c) of this section.

(h) The trustee may not avoid a transfer if such transfer was made as a part of an alternative repayment schedule between the debtor and any creditor of the debtor created by an approved nonprofit budget and credit counseling agency.

(i) If the trustee avoids under subsection (b) a transfer made between 90 days and 1 year before the date of the filing of the petition, by the debtor to an entity that is not an insider for the benefit of a creditor that is an insider, such transfer shall be considered to be avoided under this section only with respect to the creditor that is an insider.

Sec. 548. Fraudulent transfers and obligations

(a) (1) The trustee may avoid any transfer (including any transfer to or for the benefit of an insider under an employment contract) of an interest of the debtor in property, or any obligation (including any obligation to or for the benefit of an insider under an employment contract) incurred by the debtor, that was made or incurred on or within 2 years before the date of the filing of the petition, if the debtor voluntarily or involuntarily—

(A) made such transfer or incurred such obligation with actual intent to hinder, delay, or defraud any entity to which the debtor was or became, on or after the date that such transfer was made or such obligation was incurred, indebted; or

(B) (i) received less than a reasonably equivalent value in exchange for such transfer or obligation; and

(ii) (I) was insolvent on the date that such transfer was made or such obligation was incurred, or became insolvent as a result of such transfer or obligation;

(II) was engaged in business or a transaction, or was about to engage in business or a transaction, for which any property remaining with the debtor was an unreasonably small capital;

(III) intended to incur, or believed that the debtor would incur, debts that would be beyond the debtor's ability to pay as such debts matured; or

(IV) made such transfer to or for the benefit of an insider, or incurred such obligation to or for the benefit of an insider, under an employment contract and not in the ordinary course of business.

(2) A transfer of a charitable contribution to a qualified religious or charitable entity or organization shall not be considered to be a transfer covered under paragraph (1)(B) in any case in which—

(A) the amount of that contribution does not exceed 15 percent of the gross annual income of the debtor for the year in which the transfer of the contribution is made; or

(B) the contribution made by a debtor exceeded the percentage amount of gross annual income specified in subparagraph (A), if the transfer was consistent with the practices of the debtor in making charitable contributions.

(b) The trustee of a partnership debtor may avoid any transfer of an interest of the debtor in property, or any obligation incurred by the debtor, that was made or incurred on or within 2 years before the date of the filing of the petition, to a general partner in the debtor, if the debtor was insolvent on the date such transfer was made or such obligation was incurred, or became insolvent as a result of such transfer or obligation.

(c) Except to the extent that a transfer or obligation voidable under this section is voidable under section 544, 545, or 547 of this title, a transferee or obligee of such a transfer or obligation that takes for value and in good faith has a lien on or may retain any interest transferred or may enforce any obligation incurred, as the case may be, to the extent that such transferee or obligee gave value to the debtor in exchange for such transfer or obligation.

(d) (1) For the purposes of this section, a transfer is made when such transfer is so perfected that a bona fide purchaser from the debtor against whom applicable law permits such transfer to be perfected cannot acquire an interest in the property transferred that is superior to the interest in such property of the transferee, but if such transfer is not so perfected before the commencement of the case, such transfer is made immediately before the date of the filing of the petition.

(2) In this section—

(A) "value" means property, or satisfaction or securing of a present or antecedent debt of the debtor, but does not include an unperformed promise to furnish support to the debtor or to a relative of the debtor;

(B) a commodity broker, forward contract merchant, stockbroker, financial institution, financial participant, or securities clearing agency that receives a margin payment, as defined in section 101, 741, or 761 of this title, or settlement payment, as defined in section 101 or 741 of this title, takes for value to the extent of such payment;

(C) a repo participant or financial participant that receives a margin payment, as defined in section 741 or 761 of this title, or settlement payment, as defined in section 741 of this title, in connection with a repurchase agreement, takes for value to the extent of such payment;

(D) a swap participant or financial participant that receives a transfer in connection with a swap agreement takes for value to the extent of such transfer; and

(E) a master netting agreement participant that receives a transfer in connection with a master netting agreement or any individual contract covered thereby takes for value to the extent of such transfer, except that, with respect to a transfer under any individual contract covered thereby, to the extent that such master netting agreement participant otherwise did not take (or is otherwise not deemed to have taken) such transfer for value.

(3) In this section, the term "charitable contribution" means a charitable contribution, as that term is defined in section 170(c) of the Internal Revenue Code of 1986, if that contribution—

(A) is made by a natural person; and

(B) consists of—

(i) a financial instrument (as that term is defined in section 731(c)(2)(C) of the Internal Revenue Code of 1986); or

(ii) cash.

(4) In this section, the term "qualified religious or charitable entity or organization" means—

(A) an entity described in section 170(c)(1) of the Internal Revenue Code of 1986; or

(B) an entity or organization described in section 170(c)(2) of the Internal Revenue Code of 1986.

(e) (1) In addition to any transfer that the trustee may otherwise avoid, the trustee may avoid any transfer of an interest of the debtor in property that was made on or within 10 years before the date of the filing of the petition, if—

(A) such transfer was made to a self-settled trust or similar device;

(B) such transfer was by the debtor;

(C) the debtor is a beneficiary of such trust or similar device; and

(D) the debtor made such transfer with actual intent to hinder, delay, or defraud any entity to which the debtor was or became, on or after the date that such transfer was made, indebted.

(2) For the purposes of this subsection, a transfer includes a transfer made in anticipation of any money judgment, settlement, civil penalty, equitable order, or criminal fine incurred by, or which the debtor believed would be incurred by—

(A) any violation of the securities laws (as defined in section 3(a)(47) of the Securities Exchange Act of 1934 (15 U.S.C. 78c(a)(47))), any State securities laws, or any regulation or order issued under Federal securities laws or State securities laws; or

(B) fraud, deceit, or manipulation in a fiduciary capacity or in connection with the purchase or sale of any security registered under section 12 or 15(d) of the Securities Exchange Act of 1934 (15 U.S.C. 78l and 78o(d)) or under section 6 of the Securities Act of 1933 (15 U.S.C. 77f).

Sec. 549. Postpetition transactions

(a) Except as provided in subsection (b) or (c) of this section, the trustee may avoid a transfer of property of the estate—

(1) that occurs after the commencement of the case; and

(2) (A) that is authorized only under section 303(f) or 542(c) of this title; or

(B) that is not authorized under this title or by the court.

(b) In an involuntary case, the trustee may not avoid under subsection (a) of this section a transfer made after the commencement of such case but before the order for relief to the extent any value, including services, but not including satisfaction or securing of a debt that arose before the commencement of the case, is given after the commencement of the case in exchange for such transfer, notwithstanding any notice or knowledge of the case that the transferee has.

(c) The trustee may not avoid under subsection (a) of this section a transfer of an interest in real property to a good faith purchaser without knowledge of the commencement of the case and for present fair equivalent value unless a copy or notice of the petition was filed, where a transfer of an interest in such real property may be recorded to perfect such transfer, before such transfer is so perfected that a bona fide purchaser of such real property, against whom applicable law permits such transfer to be perfected, could not acquire an interest that is superior to such interest of such good faith purchaser. A good faith purchaser without knowledge of the commencement of the case and for less than present fair equivalent value has a lien on the property transferred to the extent of any present value given, unless a copy or notice of the petition was so filed before such transfer was so perfected.

(d) An action or proceeding under this section may not be commenced after the earlier of—

(1) two years after the date of the transfer sought to be avoided; or

(2) the time the case is closed or dismissed.

Sec. 550. Liability of transferee of avoided transfer

(a) Except as otherwise provided in this section, to the extent that a transfer is avoided under section 544, 545, 547, 548, 549, 553(b), or 724(a) of this title, the trustee may recover, for the benefit of the estate, the property transferred, or, if the court so orders, the value of such property, from—

(1) the initial transferee of such transfer or the entity for whose benefit such transfer was made; or

(2) any immediate or mediate transferee of such initial transferee.

(b) The trustee may not recover under section (a)(2) of this section from—

(1) a transferee that takes for value, including satisfaction or securing of a present or antecedent debt, in good faith, and without knowledge of the voidability of the transfer avoided; or

(2) any immediate or mediate good faith transferee of such transferee.

(c) If a transfer made between 90 days and one year before the filing of the petition—

(1) is avoided under section 547(b) of this title; and

(2) was made for the benefit of a creditor that at the time of such transfer was an insider; the trustee may not recover under subsection (a) from a transferee that is not an insider.

(d) The trustee is entitled to only a single satisfaction under subsection (a) of this section.

(e) (1) A good faith transferee from whom the trustee may recover under subsection (a) of this section has a lien on the property recovered to secure the lesser of—

(A) the cost, to such transferee, of any improvement made after the transfer, less the amount of any profit realized by or accruing to such transferee from such property; and

(B) any increase in the value of such property as a result of such improvement, of the property transferred.

(2) In this subsection, "improvement" includes—

(A) physical additions or changes to the property transferred;

(B) repairs to such property;

(C) payment of any tax on such property;

(D) payment of any debt secured by a lien on such property that is superior or equal to the rights of the trustee; and

(E) preservation of such property.

(f) An action or proceeding under this section may not be commenced after the earlier of—

(1) one year after the avoidance of the transfer on account of which recovery under this section is sought; or

(2) the time the case is closed or dismissed.

Sec. 551. Automatic preservation of avoided transfer

Any transfer avoided under section 522, 544, 545, 547, 548, 549, or 724(a) of this title, or any lien void under section 506(d) of this title, is preserved for the benefit of the estate but only with respect to property of the estate.

Sec. 552. Postpetition effect of security interest

(a) Except as provided in subsection (b) of this section, property acquired by the estate or by the debtor after the commencement of the case is not subject to any lien resulting from any security agreement entered into by the debtor before the commencement of the case.

(b) (1) Except as provided in sections 363, 506(c), 522, 544, 545, 547, and 548 of this title, if the debtor and an entity entered into a security agreement before the commencement of the case and if the security interest created by such security agreement extends to property of the debtor acquired before the commencement of the case and to proceeds, products, offspring, or profits of such property, then such security interest extends to such proceeds, products, offspring, or profits acquired by the estate after the commencement of the case to the extent provided by such security agreement and by applicable nonbankruptcy law, except to any extent that the court, after notice and a hearing and based on the equities of the case, orders otherwise.

(2) Except as provided in sections 363, 506(c), 522, 544, 545, 547, and 548 of this title, and notwithstanding section 546(b) of this title, if the debtor and an entity entered into a security agreement before the commencement of the case and if the security interest created by such security agreement extends to property of the debtor acquired before the commencement of the case and to amounts paid as rents of such property or the fees, charges, accounts, or other payments for the use or occupancy of rooms and other public facilities in hotels, motels, or other lodging properties, then such security interest extends to such rents and such fees, charges, accounts, or other payments acquired by the estate after the commencement of the case to the extent provided in such security agreement, except to any extent that the court, after notice and a hearing and based on the equities of the case, orders otherwise.

Sec. 553. Setoff

(a) Except as otherwise provided in this section and in sections 362 and 363 of this title, this title does not affect any right of a creditor to offset a mutual debt owing by such creditor to the debtor that arose before the commencement of the case under this title against a claim of such creditor against the debtor that arose before the commencement of the case, except to the extent that—

(1) the claim of such creditor against the debtor is disallowed;

(2) such claim was transferred, by an entity other than the debtor, to such creditor—

(A) after the commencement of the case; or

(B) (i) after 90 days before the date of the filing of the petition; and

(ii) while the debtor was insolvent (except for a setoff of a kind described in section 362(b)(6), 362(b)(7), 362(b)(17), 362(b)(27), 555, 556, 559, 560, or 561); or

(3) the debt owed to the debtor by such creditor was incurred by such creditor—

(A) after 90 days before the date of the filing of the petition;

(B) while the debtor was insolvent; and

(C) for the purpose of obtaining a right of setoff against the debtor (except for a setoff of a kind described in section 362(b)(6), 362(b)(7), 362(b)(17), 362(b)(27), 555, 556, 559, 560, or 561).

(b) (1) Except with respect to a setoff of a kind described in section 362(b)(6), 362(b)(7), 362(b)(17), 362(b)(27), 555, 556, 559, 560, 561, 365(h), 546(h), or 365(i)(2) of this title, if a creditor offsets a mutual debt owing to the debtor against a claim against the debtor on or within 90 days before the date of the filing of the petition, then the trustee may recover from such creditor the amount so offset to the extent that any insufficiency on the date of such setoff is less than the insufficiency on the later of—

(A) 90 days before the date of the filing of the petition; and

(B) the first date during the 90 days immediately preceding the date of the filing of the petition on which there is an insufficiency.

(2) In this subsection, "insufficiency" means amount, if any, by which a claim against the debtor exceeds a mutual debt owing to the debtor by the holder of such claim.

(c) For the purposes of this section, the debtor is presumed to have been insolvent on and during the 90 days immediately preceding the date of the filing of the petition.

Sec. 554. Abandonment of property of the estate

(a) After notice and a hearing, the trustee may abandon any property of the estate that is burdensome to the estate or that is of inconsequential value and benefit to the estate.

(b) On request of a party in interest and after notice and a hearing, the court may order the trustee to abandon any property of the estate that is burdensome to the estate or that is of inconsequential value and benefit to the estate.

(c) Unless the court orders otherwise, any property scheduled under section 521(1) of this title not otherwise administered at the time of the closing of a case is abandoned to the debtor and administered for purposes of section 350 of this title.

(d) Unless the court orders otherwise, property of the estate that is not abandoned under this section and that is not administered in the case remains property of the estate.

Sec. 555. Contractual right to liquidate, terminate, or accelerate a securities contract

The exercise of a contractual right of a stockbroker, financial institution, financial participant, or securities clearing agency to cause the liquidation, termination, or acceleration of a securities contract, as defined in section 741 of this title, because of a condition of the kind specified in section 365(e)(1) of this title shall not be stayed, avoided, or otherwise limited by operation of any provision of this title or by order of a court or administrative agency in any proceeding under this title unless such order is authorized under the provisions of the Securities Investor Protection Act of 1970 or any statute administered by the Securities and Exchange Commission. As used in this section, the term "contractual right" includes a right set forth in a rule or bylaw of a derivatives clearing organization (as defined in the Commodity Exchange Act), a multilateral clearing organization (as defined in the Federal Deposit Insurance Corporation Improvement Act of 1991), a national securities exchange, a national securities association, a securities clearing agency, a contract market designated under the Commodity Exchange Act, a derivatives transaction execution facility registered under the Commodity Exchange Act, or a board of trade (as defined in the Commodity Exchange Act), or in a resolution of the governing board thereof, and a right, whether or not in writing, arising under common law, under law merchant, or by reason of normal business practice.

Sec. 556. Contractual right to liquidate, terminate, or accelerate a commodities contract or forward contract

The contractual right of a commodity broker, financial participant, or forward contract merchant to cause the liquidation, termination, or acceleration of a commodity contract, as defined in section 761 of this title, or forward contract because of a condition of the kind specified in section 365(e)(1) of this title, and the right to a variation or maintenance margin payment received from a trustee with respect to open commodity contracts or forward contracts, shall not be stayed, avoided, or otherwise limited by operation of any provision of this title or by the order of a court in any proceeding under this title. As used in this section, the term "contractual right" includes a right set forth in a rule or bylaw of a derivatives clearing organization (as defined in the Commodity Exchange Act), a multilateral clearing organization (as defined in the Federal Deposit Insurance Corporation Improvement Act of 1991), a national securities exchange, a national securities association, a securities clearing agency, a contract market designated under the Commodity Exchange Act, a derivatives transaction execution facility registered under the Commodity Exchange Act, or a board of trade (as defined in the Commodity Exchange Act) or in a resolution of the governing board thereof and a right, whether or not evidenced in writing, arising under common law, under law merchant or by reason of normal business practice.

Sec. 557. Expedited determination of interests in, and abandonment or other disposition of grain assets

(a) This section applies only in a case concerning a debtor that owns or operates a grain storage facility and only with respect to grain and the proceeds of grain. This section does not affect the application of any other section of this title to property other than grain and proceeds of grain.

(b) In this section—
  - (1) "grain" means wheat, corn, flaxseed, grain sorghum, barley, oats, rye, soybeans, other dry edible beans, or rice;
  - (2) "grain storage facility" means a site or physical structure regularly used to store grain for producers, or to store grain acquired from producers for resale; and
  - (3) "producer" means an entity which engages in the growing of grain.

(c) (1) Notwithstanding sections 362, 363, 365, and 554 of this title, on the court's own motion the court may, and on the request of the trustee or an entity that claims an interest in grain or the proceeds of grain the court shall, expedite the procedures for the determination of interests in and the disposition of grain and the proceeds of grain, by shortening to the greatest extent feasible such time periods as are otherwise applicable for such procedures and by establishing, by order, a timetable having a duration of not to exceed 120 days for the completion of the applicable procedure specified in subsection (d) of this section. Such time periods and such timetable may be modified by the court, for cause, in accordance with subsection (f) of this section.
  - (2) The court shall determine the extent to which such time periods shall be shortened, based upon—
    - (A) any need of an entity claiming an interest in such grain or the proceeds of grain for a prompt determination of such interest;
    - (B) any need of such entity for a prompt disposition of such grain;
    - (C) the market for such grain;
    - (D) the conditions under which such grain is stored;
    - (E) the costs of continued storage or disposition of such grain;
    - (F) the orderly administration of the estate;
    - (G) the appropriate opportunity for an entity to assert an interest in such grain; and
    - (H) such other considerations as are relevant to the need to expedite such procedures in the case.

(d) The procedures that may be expedited under subsection (c) of this section include—
  - (1) the filing of and response to—
    - (A) a claim of ownership;
    - (B) a proof of claim;
    - (C) a request for abandonment;

(D) a request for relief from the stay of action against property under section 362(a) of this title;

(E) a request for determination of secured status;

(F) a request for determination of whether such grain or the proceeds of grain—

(i) is property of the estate;

(ii) must be turned over to the estate; or

(iii) may be used, sold, or leased; and

(G) any other request for determination of an interest in such grain or the proceeds of grain;

(2) the disposition of such grain or the proceeds of grain, before or after determination of interests in such grain or the proceeds of grain, by way of—

(A) sale of such grain;

(B) abandonment;

(C) distribution; or

(D) such other method as is equitable in the case;

(3) subject to sections 701, 702, 703, 1104, 1202, and 1302 of this title, the appointment of a trustee or examiner and the retention and compensation of any professional person required to assist with respect to matters relevant to the determination of interests in or disposition of such grain or the proceeds of grain; and

(4) the determination of any dispute concerning a matter specified in paragraph (1), (2), or (3) of this subsection.

(e) (1) Any governmental unit that has regulatory jurisdiction over the operation or liquidation of the debtor or the debtor's business shall be given notice of any request made or order entered under subsection (c) of this section.

(2) Any such governmental unit may raise, and may appear and be heard on, any issue relating to grain or the proceeds of grain in a case in which a request is made, or an order is entered, under subsection (c) of this section.

(3) The trustee shall consult with such governmental unit before taking any action relating to the disposition of grain in the possession, custody, or control of the debtor or the estate.

(f) The court may extend the period for final disposition of grain or the proceeds of grain under this section beyond 120 days if the court finds that—

(1) the interests of justice so require in light of the complexity of the case; and

(2) the interests of those claimants entitled to distribution of grain or the proceeds of grain will not be materially injured by such additional delay.

(g) Unless an order establishing an expedited procedure under subsection (c) of this section, or determining any interest in or approving any disposition of grain or the proceeds of grain, is stayed pending appeal—

(1) the reversal or modification of such order on appeal does not affect the validity of any procedure, determination, or disposition that occurs before such reversal or modification, whether or not any entity knew of the pendency of the appeal; and

(2) neither the court nor the trustee may delay, due to the appeal of such order, any proceeding in the case in which such order is issued.

(h) (1) The trustee may recover from grain and the proceeds of grain the reasonable and necessary costs and expenses allowable under section 503(b) of this title attributable to preserving or disposing of grain or the proceeds of grain, but may not recover from such grain or the proceeds of grain any other costs or expenses.

(2) Notwithstanding section 326(a) of this title, the dollar amounts of money specified in such section include the value, as of the date of disposition, of any grain that the trustee distributes in kind.

(i) In all cases where the quantity of a specific type of grain held by a debtor operating a grain storage facility exceeds ten thousand bushels, such grain shall be sold by the trustee and the assets thereof distributed in accordance with the provisions of this section.

Sec. 558. Defenses of the estate

The estate shall have the benefit of any defense available to the debtor as against any entity other than the estate, including statutes of limitation, statutes of frauds, usury, and other personal defenses. A waiver of any such defense by the debtor after the commencement of the case does not bind the estate.

Sec. 559. Contractual right to liquidate, terminate, or accelerate a repurchase agreement

The exercise of a contractual right of a repo participant or financial participant to cause the liquidation, termination, or acceleration of a repurchase agreement because of a condition of the kind specified in section 365(e)(1) of this title shall not be stayed, avoided, or otherwise limited by operation of any provision of this title or by order of a court or administrative agency in any proceeding under this title, unless, where the debtor is a stockbroker or securities clearing agency, such order is authorized under the provisions of the Securities Investor Protection Act of 1970 or any statute administered by the Securities and Exchange Commission. In the event that a repo participant or financial participant liquidates one or more repurchase agreements with a debtor and under the terms of one or more such agreements has agreed to deliver assets subject to repurchase agreements to the debtor, any excess of the market prices received on liquidation of such assets (or if any such assets are not disposed of on the date of liquidation of such repurchase agreements, at the prices available at the time of liquidation of such repurchase agreements from a generally recognized source or the most recent closing bid quotation from such a source) over the sum of the stated repurchase prices and all expenses in connection with the liquidation of such repurchase agreements shall be deemed property of the estate, subject to the available rights of setoff. As used in this section, the term "contractual right" includes a right set forth in a rule or bylaw of a derivatives clearing organization (as defined in the Commodity Exchange Act), a multilateral clearing organization (as defined in the Federal Deposit Insurance Corporation Improvement Act of 1991), a national securities exchange, a national securities association, a securities clearing agency, a contract market designated under the Commodity Exchange Act, a derivatives transaction execution facility registered under the Commodity Exchange Act, or a board of trade (as defined in the Commodity Exchange Act) or in a resolution of the governing board thereof and a right, whether or not evidenced in writing, arising under common law, under law merchant or by reason of normal business practice.

Sec. 560. Contractual right to liquidate, terminate, or accelerate a swap agreement

The exercise of any contractual right of any swap participant or financial participant to cause the liquidation, termination, or acceleration of one or more swap agreements because of a condition of the kind specified in section 365(e)(1) of this title or to offset or net out any termination values or payment amounts arising under or in connection with the termination, liquidation, or acceleration of one or more swap agreements shall not be stayed, avoided, or otherwise limited by operation of any provision of this title or by order of a court or administrative agency in any proceeding under this title. As used in this section, the term "contractual right" includes a right set forth in a rule or bylaw of a derivatives clearing organization (as defined in the Commodity Exchange Act), a multilateral clearing organization (as defined in the Federal Deposit Insurance Corporation Improvement Act of 1991), a national securities exchange, a national securities association, a securities clearing agency, a contract market designated under the Commodity Exchange Act, a derivatives transaction execution facility registered under the Commodity Exchange Act, or a board of trade (as defined in the Commodity Exchange Act) or in a resolution of the governing board thereof and a right, whether or not evidenced in writing, arising under common law, under law merchant, or by reason of normal business practice.

Sec. 561. Contractual right to terminate, liquidate, accelerate, or offset under a master netting agreement and across contracts; proceedings under chapter 15

(a) Subject to subsection (b), the exercise of any contractual right, because of a condition of the kind specified in section 365(e)(1), to cause the termination, liquidation, or acceleration of or to offset or net termination values, payment amounts, or other transfer obligations arising under or in connection with one or more (or the termination, liquidation, or acceleration of one or more)—

(1) securities contracts, as defined in section 741(7);

(2) commodity contracts, as defined in section 761(4);

(3) forward contracts;

(4) repurchase agreements;

(5) swap agreements; or

(6) master netting agreements,

shall not be stayed, avoided, or otherwise limited by operation of any provision of this title or by any order of a court or administrative agency in any proceeding under this title.

(b)(1) A party may exercise a contractual right described in subsection (a) to terminate, liquidate, or accelerate only to the extent that such party could exercise such a right under section 555, 556, 559, or 560 for each individual contract covered by the master netting agreement in issue.

(2) If a debtor is a commodity broker subject to subchapter IV of chapter 7—

(A) a party may not net or offset an obligation to the debtor arising under, or in connection with, a commodity contract traded on or subject to the rules of a contract market designated under the Commodity Exchange Act or a derivatives transaction execution facility registered under the Commodity Exchange Act against any claim arising under, or in connection with, other instruments, contracts, or agreements listed in subsection (a) except to the extent that the party has positive net equity in the commodity accounts at the debtor, as calculated under such subchapter; and

(B) another commodity broker may not net or offset an obligation to the debtor arising under, or in connection with, a commodity contract entered into or held on behalf of a customer of the debtor and traded on or subject to the rules of a contract market designated under the Commodity Exchange Act or a derivatives transaction execution facility registered under the Commodity Exchange Act against any claim arising under, or in connection with, other instruments, contracts, or agreements listed in subsection (a).

(3) No provision of subparagraph (A) or (B) of paragraph (2) shall prohibit the offset of claims and obligations that arise under—

(A) a cross-margining agreement or similar arrangement that has been approved by the

Commodity Futures Trading Commission or submitted to the Commodity Futures Trading Commission under paragraph (1) or (2) of section 5c(c) of the Commodity Exchange Act and has not been abrogated or rendered ineffective by the Commodity Futures Trading Commission; or

(B) any other netting agreement between a clearing organization (as defined in section 761) and another entity that has been approved by the Commodity Futures Trading Commission.

(c) As used in this section, the term "contractual right" includes a right set forth in a rule or bylaw of a derivatives clearing organization (as defined in the Commodity Exchange Act), a multilateral clearing organization (as defined in the Federal Deposit Insurance Corporation Improvement Act of 1991), a national securities exchange, a national securities association, a securities clearing agency, a contract market designated under the Commodity Exchange Act, a derivatives transaction execution facility registered under the Commodity Exchange Act, or a board of trade (as defined in the Commodity Exchange Act) or in a resolution of the governing board thereof, and a right, whether or not evidenced in writing, arising under common law, under law merchant, or by reason of normal business practice.

(d) Any provisions of this title relating to securities contracts, commodity contracts, forward contracts, repurchase agreements, swap agreements, or master netting agreements shall apply in a case under chapter 15, so that enforcement of contractual provisions of such contracts and agreements in accordance with their terms will not be stayed or otherwise limited by operation of any provision of this title or by order of a court in any case under this title, and to limit avoidance powers to the same extent as in a proceeding under chapter 7 or 11 of this title (such enforcement not to be limited based on the presence or absence of assets of the debtor in the United States).

Sec. 562. Timing of damage measurement in connection with swap agreements, securities contracts, forward contracts, commodity contracts, repurchase agreements, and master netting agreements

(a) If the trustee rejects a swap agreement, securities contract (as defined in section 741), forward contract, commodity contract (as defined in section 761), repurchase agreement, or master netting agreement pursuant to section 365(a), or if a forward contract merchant, stockbroker, financial institution, securities clearing agency, repo participant, financial participant, master netting agreement participant, or swap participant liquidates, terminates, or accelerates such contract or agreement, damages shall be measured as of the earlier of—

(1) the date of such rejection; or

(2) the date or dates of such liquidation, termination, or acceleration.

(b) If there are not any commercially reasonable determinants of value as of any date referred to in paragraph (1) or (2) of subsection (a), damages shall be measured as of the earliest subsequent date or dates on which there are commercially reasonable determinants of value.

(c) For the purposes of subsection (b), if damages are not measured as of the date or dates of rejection, liquidation, termination, or acceleration, and the forward contract merchant, stockbroker, financial institution, securities clearing agency, repo participant, financial participant, master netting agreement participant, or swap participant or the trustee objects to the timing of the measurement of damages—

(1) the trustee, in the case of an objection by a forward contract merchant, stockbroker,

financial institution, securities clearing agency, repo participant, financial participant, master netting agreement participant, or swap participant; or

(2) the forward contract merchant, stockbroker, financial institution, securities clearing agency, repo participant, financial participant, master netting agreement participant, or swap participant, in the case of an objection by the trustee,

has the burden of proving that there were no commercially reasonable determinants of value as of such date or dates.

CHAPTER 7—LIQUIDATION

SUBCHAPTER I—OFFICERS AND ADMINISTRATION

Sec. 701. Interim trustee

(a) (1) Promptly after the order for relief under this chapter, the United States trustee shall appoint one disinterested person that is a member of the panel of private trustees established under section 586(a)(1) of title 28 or that is serving as trustee in the case immediately before the order for relief under this chapter to serve as interim trustee in the case.

(2) If none of the members of such panel is willing to serve as interim trustee in the case, then the United States trustee may serve as interim trustee in the case.

(b) The service of an interim trustee under this section terminates when a trustee elected or designated under section 702 of this title to serve as trustee in the case qualifies under section 322 of this title.

(c) An interim trustee serving under this section is a trustee in a case under this title.

Sec. 702. Election of trustee

(a) A creditor may vote for a candidate for trustee only if such creditor—

(1) holds an allowable, undisputed, fixed, liquidated, unsecured claim of a kind entitled to distribution under section 726(a)(2), 726(a)(3), 726(a)(4), 752(a), 766(h), or 766(i) of this title;

(2) does not have an interest materially adverse, other than an equity interest that is not substantial in relation to such creditor's interest as a creditor, to the interest of creditors entitled to such distribution; and

(3) is not an insider.

(b) At the meeting of creditors held under section 341 of this title, creditors may elect one person to serve as trustee in the case if election of a trustee is requested by creditors that may vote under subsection (a) of this section, and that hold at least 20 percent in amount of the claims specified in subsection (a)(1) of this section that are held by creditors that may vote under subsection (a) of this section.

(c) A candidate for trustee is elected trustee if—

(1) creditors holding at least 20 percent in amount of the claims of a kind specified in subsection (a)(1) of this section that are held by creditors that may vote under subsection (a) of this section vote; and

(2) such candidate receives the votes of creditors holding a majority in amount of claims specified in subsection (a)(1) of this section that are held by creditors that vote for a trustee.

(d) If a trustee is not elected under this section, then the interim trustee shall serve as trustee in the case.

Sec. 703. Successor trustee

(a) If a trustee dies or resigns during a case, fails to qualify under section 322 of this title, or is removed under section 324 of this title, creditors may elect, in the manner specified in section 702 of this title, a person to fill the vacancy in the office of trustee.

(b) Pending election of a trustee under subsection (a) of this section, if necessary to preserve or prevent loss to the estate, the United States trustee may appoint an interim trustee in the manner specified in section 701(a).

(c) If creditors do not elect a successor trustee under subsection (a) of this section or if a trustee is needed in a case reopened under section 350 of this title, then the United States trustee—

  (1) shall appoint one disinterested person that is a member of the panel of private trustees established under section 586(a)(1) of title 28 to serve as trustee in the case; or

  (2) may, if none of the disinterested members of such panel is willing to serve as trustee, serve as trustee in the case.

Sec. 704. Duties of trustee

(a) The trustee shall—

  (1) collect and reduce to money the property of the estate for which such trustee serves, and close such estate as expeditiously as is compatible with the best interests of parties in interest;

  (2) be accountable for all property received;

  (3) ensure that the debtor shall perform his intention as specified in section 521(2)(B) of this title;

  (4) investigate the financial affairs of the debtor;

  (5) if a purpose would be served, examine proofs of claims and object to the allowance of any claim that is improper;

  (6) if advisable, oppose the discharge of the debtor;

  (7) unless the court orders otherwise, furnish such information concerning the estate and the estate's administration as is requested by a party in interest;

  (8) if the business of the debtor is authorized to be operated, file with the court, with the United States trustee, and with any governmental unit charged with responsibility for collection or determination of any tax arising out of such operation, periodic reports and summaries of the operation of such business, including a statement of receipts and disbursements, and such other information as the United States trustee or the court requires;

  (9) make a final report and file a final account of the administration of the estate with the court and with the United States trustee;

  (10) if with respect to the debtor there is a claim for a domestic support obligation, provide the applicable notice specified in subsection (c);

  (11) if, at the time of the commencement of the case, the debtor (or any entity designated by the debtor) served as the administrator (as defined in section 3 of the Employee Retirement Income Security Act of 1974) of an employee benefit plan, continue to perform the obligations required of the administrator; and

(12) use all reasonable and best efforts to transfer patients from a health care business that is in the process of being closed to an appropriate health care business that—
(A) is in the vicinity of the health care business that is closing;
(B) provides the patient with services that are substantially similar to those provided by the health care business that is in the process of being closed; and
(C) maintains a reasonable quality of care.

(b) (1) With respect to a debtor who is an individual in a case under this chapter—
(A) the United States trustee (or the bankruptcy administrator, if any) shall review all materials filed by the debtor and, not later than 10 days after the date of the first meeting of creditors, file with the court a statement as to whether the debtor's case would be presumed to be an abuse under section 707(b); and
(B) not later than 5 days after receiving a statement under subparagraph (A), the court shall provide a copy of the statement to all creditors.

(2) The United States trustee (or bankruptcy administrator, if any) shall, not later than 30 days after the date of filing a statement under paragraph (1), either file a motion to dismiss or convert under section 707(b) or file a statement setting forth the reasons the United States trustee (or the bankruptcy administrator, if any) does not consider such a motion to be appropriate, if the United States trustee (or the bankruptcy administrator, if any) determines that the debtor's case should be presumed to be an abuse under section 707(b) and the product of the debtor's current monthly income, multiplied by 12 is not less than—
(A) in the case of a debtor in a household of 1 person, the median family income of the applicable State for 1 earner; or
(B) in the case of a debtor in a household of 2 or more individuals, the highest median family income of the applicable State for a family of the same number or fewer individuals.

(c)(1) In a case described in subsection (a)(10) to which subsection (a)(10) applies, the trustee shall—
(A)(i) provide written notice to the holder of the claim described in subsection (a)(10) of such claim and of the right of such holder to use the services of the State child support enforcement agency established under sections 464 and 466 of the Social Security Act for the State in which such holder resides, for assistance in collecting child support during and after the case under this title;
(ii) include in the notice provided under clause (i) the address and telephone number of such State child support enforcement agency; and
(iii) include in the notice provided under clause (i) an explanation of the rights of such holder to payment of such claim under this chapter;
(B) (i) provide written notice to such State child support enforcement agency of such claim; and
(ii) include in the notice provided under clause (i) the name, address, and telephone number of such holder; and
(C) at such time as the debtor is granted a discharge under section 727, provide written notice to such holder and to such State child support enforcement agency of—
(i) the granting of the discharge;
(ii) the last recent known address of the debtor;

(iii) the last recent known name and address of the debtor's employer; and

(iv) the name of each creditor that holds a claim that—

(I) is not discharged under paragraph (2), (4), or (14A) of section 523(a); or

(II) was reaffirmed by the debtor under section 524(c).

(2) (A) The holder of a, claim described in subsection (a)(10) or the State child support enforcement agency of the State in which such holder resides may request from a creditor described in paragraph (1)(C)(iv) the last known address of the debtor.

(B) Notwithstanding any other provision of law, a creditor that makes a disclosure of a last known address of a debtor in connection with a request made under subparagraph (A) shall not be liable by reason of making such disclosure.

Sec. 705. Creditors' committee

(a) At the meeting under section 341(a) of this title, creditors that may vote for a trustee under section 702(a) of this title may elect a committee of not fewer than three, and not more than eleven, creditors, each of whom holds an allowable unsecured claim of a kind entitled to distribution under section 726(a)(2) of this title.

(b) A committee elected under subsection (a) of this section may consult with the trustee or the United States trustee in connection with the administration of the estate, make recommendations to the trustee or the United States trustee respecting the performance of the trustee's duties, and submit to the court or the United States trustee any question affecting the administration of the estate.

Sec. 706. Conversion

(a) The debtor may convert a case under this chapter to a case under chapter 11, 12, or 13 of this title at any time, if the case has not been converted under section 1112, 1208, or 1307 of this title. Any waiver of the right to convert a case under this subsection is unenforceable.

(b) On request of a party in interest and after notice and a hearing, the court may convert a case under this chapter to a case under chapter 11 of this title at any time.

(c) The court may not convert a case under this chapter to a case under chapter 12 or 13 of this title unless the debtor requests or consents to such conversion.

(d) Notwithstanding any other provision of this section, a case may not be converted to a case under another chapter of this title unless the debtor may be a debtor under such chapter.

Sec. 707. Dismissal of a case or conversion to a case under chapter 11 or 13

(a) The court may dismiss a case under this chapter only after notice and a hearing and only for cause, including—

(1) unreasonable delay by the debtor that is prejudicial to creditors;

(2) nonpayment of any fees or charges required under chapter 123 of title 28; and

(3) failure of the debtor in a voluntary case to file, within fifteen days or such additional time as the court may allow after the filing of the petition commencing such case, the information required by paragraph (1) of section 521, but only on a motion by the United States trustee.

(b) (1) After notice and a hearing, the court, on its own motion or on a motion by the United States trustee, trustee (or bankruptcy administrator, if any), or any party in interest, may dismiss a case filed by an individual debtor under this chapter whose debts are primarily consumer debts, or, with the debtor's consent, convert such a case to a case under chapter 11 or 13 of this title, if it finds that the granting of relief would be an abuse of the provisions of this chapter. In making a determination whether to dismiss a case under this section, the court may not take into consideration whether a debtor has made, or continues to make, charitable contributions (that meet the definition of "charitable contribution" under section 548(d)(3)) to any qualified religious or charitable entity or organization (as that term is defined in section 548(d)(4)).

(2) (A) (i) In considering under paragraph (1) whether the granting of relief would be an abuse of the provisions of this chapter, the court shall presume abuse exists if the debtor's current monthly income reduced by the amounts determined under clauses (ii), (iii), and (iv), and multiplied by 60 is not less than the lesser of—

(I) 25 percent of the debtor's nonpriority unsecured claims in the case, or $6,000, whichever is greater; or

(II) $10,000.

(ii) (I) The debtor's monthly expenses shall be the debtor's applicable monthly expense amounts specified under the National Standards and Local Standards, and the debtor's actual monthly expenses for the categories specified as Other Necessary Expenses issued by the Internal Revenue Service for the area in which the debtor resides, as in effect on the date of the order for relief, for the debtor, the dependents of the debtor, and the spouse of the debtor in a joint case, if the spouse is not otherwise a dependent. Such expenses shall include reasonably necessary health insurance, disability insurance, and health savings account expenses for the debtor, the spouse of the debtor, or the dependents of the debtor. Notwithstanding any other provision of this clause, the monthly expenses of the debtor shall not include any payments for debts. In addition, the debtor's monthly expenses shall include the debtor's reasonably necessary expenses incurred to maintain the safety of the debtor and the family of the debtor from family violence as identified under section 309 of the Family Violence Prevention and Services Act,[11] or other applicable Federal law. The expenses included in the debtor's monthly expenses described in the preceding sentence shall be kept confidential by the court. In addition, if it is demonstrated that it is reasonable and necessary, the debtor's monthly expenses may also include an additional allowance for food and clothing of up to 5 percent of the food and clothing categories as specified by the National Standards issued by the Internal Revenue Service.

(II) In addition, the debtor's monthly expenses may include, if applicable, the continuation of actual expenses paid by the debtor that are reasonable and necessary for care and support of an elderly, chronically ill, or disabled household member or member of the debtor's immediate family (including parents, grandparents, siblings, children, and grandchildren of

---

[11] *Sic.* Section 309 of the Family Violence Prevention and Services Act has been redesignated as section 320 of the Act.

the debtor, the dependents of the debtor, and the spouse of the debtor in a joint case who is not a dependent) and who is unable to pay for such reasonable and necessary expenses.

(III) In addition, for a debtor eligible for chapter 13, the debtor's monthly expenses may include the actual administrative expenses of administering a chapter 13 plan for the district in which the debtor resides, up to an amount of 10 percent of the projected plan payments, as determined under schedules issued by the Executive Office for United States Trustees.

(IV) In addition, the debtor's monthly expenses may include the actual expenses for each dependent child less than 18 years of age, not to exceed $1,500 per year per child, to attend a private or public elementary or secondary school if the debtor provides documentation of such expenses and a detailed explanation of why such expenses are reasonable and necessary, and why such expenses are not already accounted for in the National Standards, Local Standards, or Other Necessary Expenses referred to in subclause (I).

(V) In addition, the debtor's monthly expenses may include an allowance for housing and utilities, in excess of the allowance specified by the Local Standards for housing and utilities issued by the Internal Revenue Service, based on the actual expenses for home energy costs if the debtor provides documentation of such actual expenses and demonstrates that such actual expenses are reasonable and necessary.

(iii) The debtor's average monthly payments on account of secured debts shall be calculated as the sum of—

(I) the total of all amounts scheduled as contractually due to secured creditors in each month of the 60 months following the date of the petition; and

(II) any additional payments to secured creditors necessary for the debtor, in filing a plan under chapter 13 of this title, to maintain possession of the debtor's primary residence, motor vehicle, or other property necessary for the support of the debtor and the debtor's dependents, that serves as collateral for secured debts;

divided by 60.

(iv) The debtor's expenses for payment of all priority claims (including priority child support and alimony claims) shall be calculated as the total amount of debts entitled to priority, divided by 60.

(B) (i) In any proceeding brought under this subsection, the presumption of abuse may only be rebutted by demonstrating special circumstances, such as a serious medical condition or a call or order to active duty in the Armed Forces, to the extent such special circumstances that justify additional expenses or adjustments of current monthly income for which there is no reasonable alternative.

(ii) In order to establish special circumstances, the debtor shall be required to itemize each additional expense or adjustment of income and to provide—

(I) documentation for such expense or adjustment to income; and

(II) a detailed explanation of the special circumstances that make such expenses or adjustment to income necessary and reasonable.

(iii) The debtor shall attest under oath to the accuracy of any information provided to demonstrate that additional expenses or adjustments to income are required.

(iv) The presumption of abuse may only be rebutted if the additional expenses or adjustments to income referred to in clause (i) cause the product of the debtor's current monthly income reduced by the amounts determined under clauses (ii), (iii), and (iv) of subparagraph (A) when multiplied by 60 to be less than the lesser of—

(I) 25 percent of the debtor's nonpriority unsecured claims, or $6,000, whichever is greater; or

(II) $10,000.

(C) As part of the schedule of current income and expenditures required under section 521, the debtor shall include a statement of the debtor's current monthly income, and the calculations that determine whether a presumption arises under subparagraph (A)(i), that show how each such amount is calculated.

(D) Subparagraphs (A) through (C) shall not apply, and the court may not dismiss or convert a case based on any form of means testing, if the debtor is a disabled veteran (as defined in section 3741(1) of title 38), and the indebtedness occurred primarily during a period during which he or she was—

(i) on active duty (as defined in section 101(d)(1) of title 10); or

(ii) performing a homeland defense activity (as defined in section 901(1) of title 32).

(3) In considering under paragraph (1) whether the granting of relief would be an abuse of the provisions of this chapter in a case in which the presumption in subparagraph (A)(i) of such paragraph does not arise or is rebutted, the court shall consider—

(A) whether the debtor filed the petition in bad faith; or

(B) the totality of the circumstances (including whether the debtor seeks to reject a personal services contract and the financial need for such rejection as sought by the debtor) of the debtor's financial situation demonstrates abuse.

(4) (A) The court, on its own initiative or on the motion of a party in interest, in accordance with the procedures described in rule 9011 of the Federal Rules of Bankruptcy Procedure, may order the attorney for the debtor to reimburse the trustee for all reasonable costs in prosecuting a motion filed under section 707(b), including reasonable attorneys' fees, if—

(i) a trustee files a motion for dismissal or conversion under this subsection; and

(ii) the court—

(I) grants such motion; and

(II) finds that the action of the attorney for the debtor in filing a case under this chapter violated rule 9011 of the Federal Rules of Bankruptcy Procedure.

(B) If the court finds that the attorney for the debtor violated rule 9011 of the Federal Rules of Bankruptcy Procedure, the court, on its own initiative or on the motion of a party in interest, in accordance with such procedures, may order—

(i) the assessment of an appropriate civil penalty against the attorney for the debtor; and

(ii) the payment of such civil penalty to the trustee, the United States trustee (or the bankruptcy administrator, if any).

(C) The signature of an attorney on a petition, pleading, or written motion shall constitute a certification that the attorney has—

(i) performed a reasonable investigation into the circumstances that gave rise to the petition, pleading, or written motion; and

(ii) determined that the petition, pleading, or written motion—

(I) is well grounded in fact; and

(II) is warranted by existing law or a good faith argument for the extension, modification, or reversal of existing law and does not constitute an abuse under paragraph (1).

(D) The signature of an attorney on the petition shall constitute a certification that the attorney has no knowledge after an inquiry that the information in the schedules filed with such petition is incorrect.

(5) (A) Except as provided in subparagraph (B) and subject to paragraph (6), the court, on its own initiative or on the motion of a party in interest, in accordance with the procedures described in rule 9011 of the Federal Rules of Bankruptcy Procedure, may award a debtor all reasonable costs (including reasonable attorneys' fees) in contesting a motion filed by a party in interest (other than a trustee or United States trustee (or bankruptcy administrator, if any)) under this subsection if—

(i) the court does not grant the motion; and

(ii) the court finds that—

(I) the position of the party that filed the motion violated rule 9011 of the Federal Rules of Bankruptcy Procedure; or

(II) the attorney (if any) who filed the motion did not comply with the requirements of clauses (i) and (ii) of paragraph (4)(C), and the motion was made solely for the purpose of coercing a debtor into waiving a right guaranteed to the debtor under this title.

(B) A small business that has a claim of an aggregate amount less than $1,000 shall not be subject to subparagraph (A)(ii)(I).

(C) For purposes of this paragraph—

(i) the term "small business" means an unincorporated business, partnership, corporation, association, or organization that—

(I) has fewer than 25 full-time employees as determined on the date on which the motion is filed; and

(II) is engaged in commercial or business activity; and

(ii) the number of employees of a wholly owned subsidiary of a corporation includes the employees of—

(I) a parent corporation; and

(II) any other subsidiary corporation of the parent corporation.

(6) Only the judge or United States trustee (or bankruptcy administrator, if any) may file a motion under section 707(b), if the current monthly income of the debtor, or in a joint case, the debtor and the debtor's spouse, as of the date of the order for relief, when multiplied by 12, is equal to or less than—

(A) in the case of a debtor in a household of 1 person, the median family income of the applicable State for 1 earner;

(B) in the case of a debtor in a household of 2, 3, or 4 individuals, the highest median family income of the applicable State for a family of the same number or fewer individuals; or

(C) in the case of a debtor in a household exceeding 4 individuals, the highest median family income of the applicable State for a family of 4 or fewer individuals, plus $525 per month for each individual in excess of 4.

(7) (A) No judge, United States trustee (or bankruptcy administrator, if any), trustee, or other party in interest may file a motion under paragraph (2) if the current monthly income of the debtor, including a veteran (as that term is defined in section 101 of title 38), and the debtor's spouse combined, as of the date of the order for relief when multiplied by 12, is equal to or less than—

(i) in the case of a debtor in a household of 1 person, the median family income of the applicable State for 1 earner;

(ii) in the case of a debtor in a household of 2, 3, or 4 individuals, the highest median family income of the applicable State for a family of the same number or fewer individuals; or

(iii) in the case of a debtor in a household exceeding 4 individuals, the highest median family income of the applicable State for a family of 4 or fewer individuals, plus $525 per month for each individual in excess of 4.

(B) In a case that is not a joint case, current monthly income of the debtor's spouse shall not be considered for purposes of subparagraph (A) if—

(i) (I) the debtor and the debtor's spouse are separated under applicable nonbankruptcy law; or

(II) the debtor and the debtor's spouse are living separate and apart, other than for the purpose of evading subparagraph (A); and

(ii) the debtor files a statement under penalty of perjury—

(I) specifying that the debtor meets the requirement of subclause (I) or (II) of clause (i); and

(II) disclosing the aggregate, or best estimate of the aggregate, amount of any cash or money payments received from the debtor's spouse attributed to the debtor's current monthly income.

(c) (1) In this subsection—

(A) the term "crime of violence" has the meaning given such term in section 16 of title 18; and

(B) the term "drug trafficking crime" has the meaning given such term in section 924(c)(2) of title 18.

(2) Except as provided in paragraph (3), after notice and a hearing, the court, on a motion by the victim of a crime of violence or a drug trafficking crime, may when it is in the best interest of the victim dismiss a voluntary case filed under this chapter by a debtor who is an individual if such individual was convicted of such crime.

(3) The court may not dismiss a case under paragraph (2) if the debtor establishes by a preponderance of the evidence that the filing of a case under this chapter is necessary to satisfy a claim for a domestic support obligation.

SUBCHAPTER II—COLLECTION, LIQUIDATION, AND DISTRIBUTION OF THE ESTATE

Sec. 721. Authorization to operate business

The court may authorize the trustee to operate the business of the debtor for a limited period, if such operation is in the best interest of the estate and consistent with the orderly liquidation of the estate.

Sec. 722. Redemption

An individual debtor may, whether or not the debtor has waived the right to redeem under this section, redeem tangible personal property intended primarily for personal, family, or household use, from a lien securing a dischargeable consumer debt, if such property is exempted under section 522 of this title or has been abandoned under section 554 of this title, by paying the holder of such lien the amount of the allowed secured claim of such holder that is secured by such lien in full at the time of redemption.

Sec. 723. Rights of partnership trustee against general partners

(a) If there is a deficiency of property of the estate to pay in full all claims which are allowed in a case under this chapter concerning a partnership and with respect to which a general partner of the partnership is personally liable, the trustee shall have a claim against such general partner to the extent that under applicable nonbankruptcy law such general partner is personally liable for such deficiency.

(b) To the extent practicable, the trustee shall first seek recovery of such deficiency from any general partner in such partnership that is not a debtor in a case under this title. Pending determination of such deficiency, the court may order any such partner to provide the estate with indemnity for, or assurance of payment of, any deficiency recoverable from such partner, or not to dispose of property.

(c) Notwithstanding section 728(c)[12] of this title, the trustee has a claim against the estate of each general partner in such partnership that is a debtor in a case under this title for the full amount of all claims of creditors allowed in the case concerning such partnership. Notwithstanding section 502 of this title, there shall not be allowed in such partner's case a claim against such partner on which both such partner and such partnership are liable, except to any extent that such claim is secured only by property of such partner and not by property of such partnership. The claim of the trustee under this subsection is entitled to distribution in such partner's case under section 726(a) of this title the same as any other claim of a kind specified in such section.

(d) If the aggregate that the trustee recovers from the estates of general partners under subsection (c) of this section is greater than any deficiency not recovered under subsection (b) of this section, the court, after notice and a hearing, shall determine an equitable distribution of the surplus so recovered, and the trustee shall distribute such surplus to the estates of the general partners in such partnership according to such determination.

---

[12] *Sic.* Section 728 of this title has been repealed.

Sec. 724. Treatment of certain liens

(a) The trustee may avoid a lien that secures a claim of a kind specified in section 726(a)(4) of this title.

(b) Property in which the estate has an interest and that is subject to a lien that is not avoidable under this title (other than to the extent that there is a properly perfected unavoidable tax lien arising in connection with an ad valorem tax on real or personal property of the estate) and that secures an allowed claim for a tax, or proceeds of such property, shall be distributed—

(1) first, to any holder of an allowed claim secured by a lien on such property that is not avoidable under this title and that is senior to such tax lien;

(2) second, to any holder of a claim of a kind specified in section 507(a)(1) (except that such expenses, other than claims for wages, salaries, or commissions that arise after the date of the filing of the petition, shall be limited to expenses incurred under chapter 7 of this title and shall not include expenses incurred under chapter 11 of this title), 507(a)(2), 507(a)(3), 507(a)(4), 507(a)(5), 507(a)(6), or 507(a)(7) of this title, to the extent of the amount of such allowed tax claim that is secured by such tax lien;

(3) third, to the holder of such tax lien, to any extent that such holder's allowed tax claim that is secured by such tax lien exceeds any amount distributed under paragraph (2) of this subsection;

(4) fourth, to any holder of an allowed claim secured by a lien on such property that is not avoidable under this title and that is junior to such tax lien;

(5) fifth, to the holder of such tax lien, to the extent that such holder's allowed claim secured by such tax lien is not paid under paragraph (3) of this subsection; and

(6) sixth, to the estate.

(c) If more than one holder of a claim is entitled to distribution under a particular paragraph of subsection (b) of this section, distribution to such holders under such paragraph shall be in the same order as distribution to such holders would have been other than under this section.

(d) A statutory lien the priority of which is determined in the same manner as the priority of a tax lien under section 6323 of the Internal Revenue Code of 1986 shall be treated under subsection (b) of this section the same as if such lien were a tax lien.

(e) Before subordinating a tax lien on real or personal property of the estate, the trustee shall—

(1) exhaust the unencumbered assets of the estate; and

(2) in a manner consistent with section 506(c), recover from property securing an allowed secured claim the reasonable, necessary costs and expenses of preserving or disposing of such property.

(f) Notwithstanding the exclusion of ad valorem tax liens under this section and subject to the requirements of subsection (e), the following may be paid from property of the estate which secures a tax lien, or the proceeds of such property:

(1) Claims for wages, salaries, and commissions that are entitled to priority under section 507(a)(4).

(2) Claims for contributions to an employee benefit plan entitled to priority under section 507(a)(5).

Sec. 725. Disposition of certain property

After the commencement of a case under this chapter, but before final distribution of property of the estate under section 726 of this title, the trustee, after notice and a hearing, shall dispose of any property in which an entity other than the estate has an interest, such as a lien, and that has not been disposed of under another section of this title.

Sec. 726. Distribution of property of the estate

(a) Except as provided in section 510 of this title, property of the estate shall be distributed—

(1) first, in payment of claims of the kind specified in, and in the order specified in, section 507 of this title, proof of which is timely filed under section 501 of this title or tardily filed on or before the earlier of—

(A) the date that is 10 days after the mailing to creditors of the summary of the trustee's final report; or

(B) the date on which the trustee commences final distribution under this section;

(2) second, in payment of any allowed unsecured claim, other than a claim of a kind specified in paragraph (1), (3), or (4) of this subsection, proof of which is—

(A) timely filed under section 501(a) of this title;

(B) timely filed under section 501(b) or 501(c) of this title; or

(C) tardily filed under section 501(a) of this title, if—

(i) the creditor that holds such claim did not have notice or actual knowledge of the case in time for timely filing of a proof of such claim under section 501(a) of this title; and

(ii) proof of such claim is filed in time to permit payment of such claim;

(3) third, in payment of any allowed unsecured claim proof of which is tardily filed under section 501(a) of this title, other than a claim of the kind specified in paragraph (2)(C) of this subsection;

(4) fourth, in payment of any allowed claim, whether secured or unsecured, for any fine, penalty, or forfeiture, or for multiple, exemplary, or punitive damages, arising before the earlier of the order for relief or the appointment of a trustee, to the extent that such fine, penalty, forfeiture, or damages are not compensation for actual pecuniary loss suffered by the holder of such claim;

(5) fifth, in payment of interest at the legal rate from the date of the filing of the petition, on any claim paid under paragraph (1), (2), (3), or (4) of this subsection; and

(6) sixth, to the debtor.

(b) Payment on claims of a kind specified in paragraph (1), (2), (3), (4), (5), (6), (7), or (8) of section 507(a) of this title, or in paragraph (2), (3), (4), or (5) of subsection (a) of this section, shall be made pro rata among claims of the kind specified in each such particular paragraph, except that in a case that has been converted to this chapter under section 1112, 1208, or 1307 of this title, a claim allowed under section 503(b) of this title incurred under this chapter after such conversion has priority over a claim allowed under section 503(b) of this title incurred under any other chapter of this title or under this chapter before such conversion and over any expenses of a custodian superseded under section 543 of this title.

(c) Notwithstanding subsections (a) and (b) of this section, if there is property of the kind specified in section 541(a)(2) of this title, or proceeds of such property, in the estate, such property or proceeds shall be segregated from other property of the estate, and such property or proceeds and other property of the estate shall be distributed as follows:

(1) Claims allowed under section 503 of this title shall be paid either from property of the kind specified in section 541(a)(2) of this title, or from other property of the estate, as the interest of justice requires.

(2) Allowed claims, other than claims allowed under section 503 of this title, shall be paid in the order specified in subsection (a) of this section, and, with respect to claims of a kind specified in a particular paragraph of section 507 of this title or subsection (a) of this section, in the following order and manner:
   (A) First, community claims against the debtor or the debtor's spouse shall be paid from property of the kind specified in section 541(a)(2) of this title, except to the extent that such property is solely liable for debts of the debtor.
   (B) Second, to the extent that community claims against the debtor are not paid under subparagraph (A) of this paragraph, such community claims shall be paid from property of the kind specified in section 541(a)(2) of this title that is solely liable for debts of the debtor.
   (C) Third, to the extent that all claims against the debtor including community claims against the debtor are not paid under subparagraph (A) or (B) of this paragraph such claims shall be paid from property of the estate other than property of the kind specified in section 541(a)(2) of this title.
   (D) Fourth, to the extent that community claims against the debtor or the debtor's spouse are not paid under subparagraph (A), (B), or (C) of this paragraph, such claims shall be paid from all remaining property of the estate.

Sec. 727. Discharge

(a) The court shall grant the debtor a discharge, unless—
   (1) the debtor is not an individual;
   (2) the debtor, with intent to hinder, delay, or defraud a creditor or an officer of the estate charged with custody of property under this title, has transferred, removed, destroyed, mutilated, or concealed, or has permitted to be transferred, removed, destroyed, mutilated, or concealed—
      (A) property of the debtor, within one year before the date of the filing of the petition; or
      (B) property of the estate, after the date of the filing of the petition;
   (3) the debtor has concealed, destroyed, mutilated, falsified, or failed to keep or preserve any recorded information, including books, documents, records, and papers, from which the debtor's financial condition or business transactions might be ascertained, unless such act or failure to act was justified under all of the circumstances of the case;
   (4) the debtor knowingly and fraudulently, in or in connection with the case—
      (A) made a false oath or account;
      (B) presented or used a false claim;
      (C) gave, offered, received, or attempted to obtain money, property, or advantage, or a promise of money, property, or advantage, for acting or forbearing to act; or
      (D) withheld from an officer of the estate entitled to possession under this title, any recorded information, including books, documents, records, and papers, relating to the debtor's property or financial affairs;
   (5) the debtor has failed to explain satisfactorily, before determination of denial of discharge under this paragraph, any loss of assets or deficiency of assets to meet the debtor's liabilities;
   (6) the debtor has refused, in the case—

(A) to obey any lawful order of the court, other than an order to respond to a material question or to testify;

(B) on the ground of privilege against self-incrimination, to respond to a material question approved by the court or to testify, after the debtor has been granted immunity with respect to the matter concerning which such privilege was invoked; or

(C) on a ground other than the properly invoked privilege against self-incrimination, to respond to a material question approved by the court or to testify;

(7) the debtor has committed any act specified in paragraph (2), (3), (4), (5), or (6) of this subsection, on or within one year before the date of the filing of the petition, or during the case, in connection with another case, under this title or under the Bankruptcy Act, concerning an insider;

(8) the debtor has been granted a discharge under this section, under section 1141 of this title, or under section 14, 371, or 476 of the Bankruptcy Act, in a case commenced within 8 years before the date of the filing of the petition;

(9) the debtor has been granted a discharge under section 1228 or 1328 of this title, or under section 660 or 661 of the Bankruptcy Act, in a case commenced within six years before the date of the filing of the petition, unless payments under the plan in such case totaled at least—

(A) 100 percent of the allowed unsecured claims in such case; or

(B) (i) 70 percent of such claims; and

(ii) the plan was proposed by the debtor in good faith, and was the debtor's best effort;

(10) the court approves a written waiver of discharge executed by the debtor after the order for relief under this chapter;

(11) after filing the petition, the debtor failed to complete an instructional course concerning personal financial management described in section 111, except that this paragraph shall not apply with respect to a debtor who is a person described in section 109(h)(4) or who resides in a district for which the United States trustee (or the bankruptcy administrator, if any) determines that the approved instructional courses are not adequate to service the additional individuals who would otherwise be required to complete such instructional courses under this section (The United States trustee (or the bankruptcy administrator, if any) who makes a determination described in this paragraph shall review such determination not later than 1 year after the date of such determination, and not less frequently than annually thereafter.); or

(12) the court after notice and a hearing held not more than 10 days before the date of the entry of the order granting the discharge finds that there is reasonable cause to believe that—

(A) section 522(q)(1) may be applicable to the debtor; and

(B) there is pending any proceeding in which the debtor may be found guilty of a felony of the kind described in section 522(q)(1)(A) or liable for a debt of the kind described in section 522(q)(1)(B).

(b) Except as provided in section 523 of this title, a discharge under subsection (a) of this section discharges the debtor from all debts that arose before the date of the order for relief under this chapter, and any liability on a claim that is determined under section 502 of this title as if such claim had arisen before the commencement of the case, whether or not a proof of claim based on any such debt or liability is filed under section 501 of this title, and whether or not a claim based on any such debt or liability is allowed under section 502 of this title.

(c) (1) The trustee, a creditor, or the United States trustee may object to the granting of a discharge under subsection (a) of this section.

(2) On request of a party in interest, the court may order the trustee to examine the acts and conduct of the debtor to determine whether a ground exists for denial of discharge.

(d) On request of the trustee, a creditor, or the United States trustee, and after notice and a hearing, the court shall revoke a discharge granted under subsection (a) of this section if—

(1) such discharge was obtained through the fraud of the debtor, and the requesting party did not know of such fraud until after the granting of such discharge;

(2) the debtor acquired property that is property of the estate, or became entitled to acquire property that would be property of the estate, and knowingly and fraudulently failed to report the acquisition of or entitlement to such property, or to deliver or surrender such property to the trustee;

(3) the debtor committed an act specified in subsection (a)(6) of this section; or

(4) the debtor has failed to explain satisfactorily—

(A) a material misstatement in an audit referred to in section 586(f) of title 28; or

(B) a failure to make available for inspection all necessary accounts, papers, documents, financial records, files, and all other papers, things, or property belonging to the debtor that are requested for an audit referred to in section 586(f) of title 28.

(e) The trustee, a creditor, or the United States trustee may request a revocation of a discharge—

(1) under subsection (d)(1) of this section within one year after such discharge is granted; or

(2) under subsection (d)(2) or (d)(3) of this section before the later of—

(A) one year after the granting of such discharge; and

(B) the date the case is closed.

Sec. 728. [Repealed.]

SUBCHAPTER III—STOCKBROKER LIQUIDATION

Sec. 741. Definitions for this subchapter

In this subchapter—

(1) "Commission" means Securities and Exchange Commission;

(2) "customer" includes—

(A) entity with whom a person deals as principal or agent and that has a claim against such person on account of a security received, acquired, or held by such person in the ordinary course of such person's business as a stockbroker, from or for the securities account or accounts of such entity—

(i) for safekeeping;

(ii) with a view to sale;

(iii) to cover a consummated sale;

(iv) pursuant to a purchase;

(v) as collateral under a security agreement; or

(vi) for the purpose of effecting registration of transfer; and

(B) entity that has a claim against a person arising out of -

(i) a sale or conversion of a security received, acquired, or held as specified in subparagraph (A) of this paragraph; or

(ii) a deposit of cash, a security, or other property with such person for the purpose of purchasing or selling a security;

(3) "customer name security" means security—

(A) held for the account of a customer on the date of the filing of the petition by or on behalf of the debtor;

(B) registered in such customer's name on such date or in the process of being so registered under instructions from the debtor; and

(C) not in a form transferable by delivery on such date;

(4) "customer property" means cash, security, or other property, and proceeds of such cash, security, or property, received, acquired, or held by or for the account of the debtor, from or for the securities account of a customer—

(A) including—

(i) property that was unlawfully converted from and that is the lawful property of the estate;

(ii) a security held as property of the debtor to the extent such security is necessary to meet a net equity claim of a customer based on a security of the same class and series of an issuer;

(iii) resources provided through the use or realization of a customer's debit cash balance or a debit item includible in the Formula for Determination of Reserve Requirement for Brokers and Dealers as promulgated by the Commission under the Securities Exchange Act of 1934; and

(iv) other property of the debtor that any applicable law, rule, or regulation requires to be set aside or held for the benefit of a customer, unless including such property as customer property would not significantly increase customer property; but

(B) not including—

(i) a customer name security delivered to or reclaimed by a customer under section 751 of this title; or

(ii) property to the extent that a customer does not have a claim against the debtor based on such property;

(5) "margin payment" means payment or deposit of cash, a security, or other property, that is commonly known to the securities trade as original margin, initial margin, maintenance margin, or variation margin, or as a mark-to-market payment, or that secures an obligation of a participant in a securities clearing agency;

(6) "net equity" means, with respect to all accounts of a customer that such customer has in the same capacity—

(A) (i) aggregate dollar balance that would remain in such accounts after the liquidation, by sale or purchase, at the time of the filing of the petition, of all securities positions in all such accounts, except any customer name securities of such customer; minus

(ii) any claim of the debtor against such customer in such capacity that would have been owing immediately after such liquidation; plus

(B) any payment by such customer to the trustee, within 60 days after notice under section 342 of this title, of any business related claim of the debtor against such customer in such capacity;

(7) "securities contract"—

(A) means—

(i) a contract for the purchase, sale, or loan of a security, a certificate of deposit, a mortgage loan, any interest in a mortgage loan, a group or index of securities, certificates of deposit, or mortgage loans or interests therein (including an interest therein or based on the value thereof), or option on any of the foregoing, including an option to purchase or sell any such security, certificate of deposit, mortgage loan, interest, group or index, or option, and including any repurchase or reverse repurchase transaction on any such security, certificate of deposit, mortgage loan, interest, group or index, or option (whether or not such repurchase or reverse repurchase transaction is a "repurchase agreement", as defined in section 101);

(ii) any option entered into on a national securities exchange relating to foreign currencies;

(iii) the guarantee (including by novation) by or to any securities clearing agency of a settlement of cash, securities, certificates of deposit, mortgage loans or interests therein, group or index of securities, or mortgage loans or interests therein (including any interest therein or based on the value thereof), or option on any of the foregoing, including an option to purchase or sell any such security, certificate of deposit, mortgage loan, interest, group or index, or option (whether or not such settlement is in connection with any agreement or transaction referred to in clauses (i) through (xi));

(iv) any margin loan;

(v) any extension of credit for the clearance or settlement of securities transactions;

(vi) any loan transaction coupled with a securities collar transaction, any prepaid forward securities transaction, or any total return swap transaction coupled with a securities sale transaction;

(vii) any other agreement or transaction that is similar to an agreement or transaction referred to in this subparagraph;

(viii) any combination of the agreements or transactions referred to in this subparagraph;

(ix) any option to enter into any agreement or transaction referred to in this subparagraph;

(x) a master agreement that provides for an agreement or transaction referred to in clause (i), (ii), (iii), (iv), (v), (vi), (vii), (viii), or (ix), together with all supplements to any such master agreement, without regard to whether the master agreement provides for an agreement or transaction that is not a securities contract under this subparagraph, except that such master agreement shall be considered to be a securities contract under this subparagraph only with respect to each agreement or transaction under such master agreement that is referred to in clause (i), (ii), (iii), (iv), (v), (vi), (vii), (viii), or (ix); or

(xi) any security agreement or arrangement or other credit enhancement related to any agreement or transaction referred to in this subparagraph, including any guarantee or reimbursement obligation by or to a stockbroker, securities clearing agency, financial institution, or financial participant in connection with any agreement or transaction referred to in this subparagraph, but not to exceed the damages in connection with any such agreement or transaction, measured in accordance with section 562; and

(B) does not include any purchase, sale, or repurchase obligation under a participation in a commercial mortgage loan;

(8) "settlement payment" means a preliminary settlement payment, a partial settlement payment, an interim settlement payment, a settlement payment on account, a final settlement payment, or any other similar payment commonly used in the securities trade; and

(9) "SIPC" means Securities Investor Protection Corporation.

Sec. 742. Effect of section 362 of this title in this subchapter

Notwithstanding section 362 of this title, SIPC may file an application for a protective decree under the Securities Investor Protection Act of 1970. The filing of such application stays all proceedings in the case under this title unless and until such application is dismissed. If SIPC completes the liquidation of the debtor, then the court shall dismiss the case.

Sec. 743. Notice

The clerk shall give the notice required by section 342 of this title to SIPC and to the Commission.

Sec. 744. Executory contracts

Notwithstanding section 365(d)(1) of this title, the trustee shall assume or reject, under section 365 of this title, any executory contract of the debtor for the purchase or sale of a security in the ordinary course of the debtor's business, within a reasonable time after the date of the order for relief, but not to exceed 30 days. If the trustee does not assume such a contract within such time, such contract is rejected.

Sec. 745. Treatment of accounts

(a) Accounts held by the debtor for a particular customer in separate capacities shall be treated as accounts of separate customers.

(b) If a stockbroker or a bank holds a customer net equity claim against the debtor that arose out of a transaction for a customer of such stockbroker or bank, each such customer of such stockbroker or bank shall be treated as a separate customer of the debtor.

(c) Each trustee's account specified as such on the debtor's books, and supported by a trust deed filed with, and qualified as such by, the Internal Revenue Service, and under the Internal Revenue Code of 1986, shall be treated as a separate customer account for each beneficiary under such trustee account.

Sec. 746. Extent of customer claims

(a) If, after the date of the filing of the petition, an entity enters into a transaction with the debtor, in a manner that would have made such entity a customer had such transaction occurred before the date of the filing of the petition, and such transaction was entered into by such entity in good faith and before the qualification under section 322 of this title of a trustee, such entity shall be deemed a customer, and the date of such transaction shall be deemed to be the date of the filing of the petition for the purpose of determining such entity's net equity.

(b) An entity does not have a claim as a customer to the extent that such entity transferred to the debtor cash or a security that, by contract, agreement, understanding, or operation of law, is—
   (1) part of the capital of the debtor; or
   (2) subordinated to the claims of any or all creditors.

Sec. 747. Subordination of certain customer claims

Except as provided in section 510 of this title, unless all other customer net equity claims have been paid in full, the trustee may not pay in full or pay in part, directly or indirectly, any net equity claim of a customer that was, on the date the transaction giving rise to such claim occurred—
   (1) an insider;
   (2) a beneficial owner of at least five percent of any class of equity securities of the debtor, other than—
      (A) nonconvertible stock having fixed preferential dividend and liquidation rights; or
      (B) interests of limited partners in a limited partnership;
   (3) a limited partner with a participation of at least five percent in the net assets or net profits of the debtor; or
   (4) an entity that, directly or indirectly, through agreement or otherwise, exercised or had the power to exercise control over the management or policies of the debtor.

Sec. 748. Reduction of securities to money

As soon as practicable after the date of the order for relief, the trustee shall reduce to money, consistent with good market practice, all securities held as property of the estate, except for customer name securities delivered or reclaimed under section 751 of this title.

Sec. 749. Voidable transfers

(a) Except as otherwise provided in this section, any transfer of property that, but for such transfer, would have been customer property, may be avoided by the trustee, and such property shall be treated as customer property, if and to the extent that the trustee avoids such transfer under section 544, 545, 547, 548, or 549 of this title. For the purpose of such sections, the property so transferred shall be deemed to have been property of the debtor and, if such transfer was made to a customer or for a customer's benefit, such customer shall be deemed, for the purposes of this section, to have been a creditor. .

(b) Notwithstanding sections 544, 545, 547, 548, and 549 of this title, the trustee may not avoid a transfer made before five days after the order for relief if such transfer is approved by the Commission by rule or order, either before or after such transfer, and if such transfer is—
   (1) a transfer of a securities contract entered into or carried by or through the debtor on behalf of a customer, and of any cash, security, or other property margining or securing such securities contract; or
   (2) the liquidation of a securities contract entered into or carried by or through the debtor on behalf of a customer.

Sec. 750. Distribution of securities

The trustee may not distribute a security except under section 751 of this title.

Sec. 751. Customer name securities

The trustee shall deliver any customer name security to or on behalf of the customer entitled to such security, unless such customer has a negative net equity. With the approval of the trustee, a customer may reclaim a customer name security after payment to the trustee, within such period as the trustee allows, of any claim of the debtor against such customer to the extent that such customer will not have a negative net equity after such payment.

Sec. 752. Customer property

(a) The trustee shall distribute customer property ratably to customers on the basis and to the extent of such customers' allowed net equity claims and in priority to all other claims, except claims of the kind specified in section 507(a)(2) of this title that are attributable to the administration of such customer property.

(b) (1) The trustee shall distribute customer property in excess of that distributed under subsection (a) of this section in accordance with section 726 of this title.

(2) Except as provided in section 510 of this title, if a customer is not paid the full amount of such customer's allowed net equity claim from customer property, the unpaid portion of such claim is a claim entitled to distribution under section 726 of this title.

(c) Any cash or security remaining after the liquidation of a security interest created under a security agreement made by the debtor, excluding property excluded under section 741(4)(B) of this title, shall be apportioned between the general estate and customer property in the same proportion as the general estate of the debtor and customer property were subject to such security interest.

Sec. 753. Stockbroker liquidation and forward contract merchants, commodity brokers, stockbrokers, financial institutions, financial participants, securities clearing agencies, swap participants, repo participants, and master netting agreement participants

Notwithstanding any other provision of this title, the exercise of rights by a forward contract merchant, commodity broker, stockbroker, financial institution, financial participant, securities clearing agency, swap participant, repo participant, or master netting agreement participant under this title shall not affect the priority of any unsecured claim it may have after the exercise of such rights.

SUBCHAPTER IV—COMMODITY BROKER LIQUIDATION

Sec. 761. Definitions for this subchapter

In this subchapter—

(1) "Act" means Commodity Exchange Act;

(2) "clearing organization" means a derivatives clearing organization registered under the Act;

(3) "Commission" means Commodity Futures Trading Commission;

(4) "commodity contract" means—

(A) with respect to a futures commission merchant, contract for the purchase or sale of a commodity for future delivery on, or subject to the rules of, a contract market or board of trade;

(B) with respect to a foreign futures commission merchant, foreign future;

(C) with respect to a leverage transaction merchant, leverage transaction;

(D) with respect to a clearing organization, contract for the purchase or sale of a commodity for future delivery on, or subject to the rules of, a contract market or board of trade that is cleared by such clearing organization, or commodity option traded on, or subject to the rules of, a contract market or board of trade that is cleared by such clearing organization;

(E) with respect to a commodity options dealer, commodity option;

(F) any other agreement or transaction that is similar to an agreement or transaction referred to in this paragraph;

(G) any combination of the agreements or transactions referred to in this paragraph;

(H) any option to enter into an agreement or transaction referred to in this paragraph;

(I) a master agreement that provides for an agreement or transaction referred to in subparagraph (A), (B), (C), (D), (E), (F), (G), or (H), together with all supplements to such master agreement, without regard to whether the master agreement provides for an agreement or transaction that is not a commodity contract under this paragraph, except that the master agreement shall be considered to be a commodity contract under this paragraph only with respect to each agreement or transaction under the master agreement that is referred to in subparagraph (A), (B), (C), (D), (E), (F), (G), or (H); or

(J) any security agreement or arrangement or other credit enhancement related to any agreement or transaction referred to in this paragraph, including any guarantee or reimbursement obligation by or to a commodity broker or financial participant in connection with any agreement or transaction referred to in this paragraph, but not to exceed the damages in connection with any such agreement or transaction, measured in accordance with section 562;

(5) "commodity option" means agreement or transaction subject to regulation under section 4c(b) of the Act;

(6) "commodity options dealer" means person that extends credit to, or that accepts cash, a security, or other property from, a customer of such person for the purchase or sale of an interest in a commodity option;

(7) "contract market" means a registered entity;

(8) "contract of sale", "commodity", "derivatives clearing organization", "future delivery", "board of trade", "registered entity", and "futures commission merchant" have the meanings assigned to those terms in the Act;

(9) "customer" means—

(A) with respect to a futures commission merchant—

(i) entity for or with whom such futures commission merchant deals and that holds a claim against such futures commission merchant on account of a commodity contract made, received, acquired, or held by or through such futures commission merchant in the ordinary course of such futures commission merchant's business as a futures commission merchant from or for the commodity futures account of such entity; or

(ii) entity that holds a claim against such futures commission merchant arising out of—

(I) the making, liquidation, or change in the value of a commodity contract of a kind specified in clause (i) of this subparagraph;

(II) a deposit or payment of cash, a security, or other property with such futures commission merchant for the purpose of making or margining such a commodity contract; or

(III) the making or taking of delivery on such a commodity contract;

(B) with respect to a foreign futures commission merchant—

(i) entity for or with whom such foreign futures commission merchant deals and that holds a claim against such foreign futures commission merchant on account of a commodity contract made, received, acquired, or held by or through such foreign futures commission merchant in the ordinary course of such foreign futures commission merchant's business as a foreign futures commission merchant from or for the foreign futures account of such entity; or

(ii) entity that holds a claim against such foreign futures commission merchant arising out of—

(I) the making, liquidation, or change in value of a commodity contract of a kind specified in clause (i) of this subparagraph;

(II) a deposit or payment of cash, a security, or other property with such foreign futures commission merchant for the purpose of making or margining such a commodity contract; or

(III) the making or taking of delivery on such a commodity contract;

(C) with respect to a leverage transaction merchant—

(i) entity for or with whom such leverage transaction merchant deals and that holds a claim against such leverage transaction merchant on account of a commodity contract engaged in by or with such leverage transaction merchant in the ordinary course of such leverage transaction merchant's business as a leverage transaction merchant from or for the leverage account of such entity; or

(ii) entity that holds a claim against such leverage transaction merchant arising out of—

(I) the making, liquidation, or change in value of a commodity contract of a kind specified in clause (i) of this subparagraph;

(II) a deposit or payment of cash, a security, or other property with such leverage transaction merchant for the purpose of entering into or margining such a commodity contract; or

(III) the making or taking of delivery on such a commodity contract;

(D) with respect to a clearing organization, clearing member of such clearing organization with whom such clearing organization deals and that holds a claim against such clearing organization on account of cash, a security, or other property received by such clearing organization to margin, guarantee, or secure a commodity contract in such clearing member's proprietary account or customers' account; or

(E) with respect to a commodity options dealer—

(i) entity for or with whom such commodity options dealer deals and that holds a claim on account of a commodity contract made, received, acquired, or held by or through such commodity options dealer in the ordinary course of such commodity options dealer's business as a commodity options dealer from or for the commodity options account of such entity; or

(ii) entity that holds a claim against such commodity options dealer arising out of—
(I) the making of, liquidation of, exercise of, or a change in value of, a commodity contract of a kind specified in clause (i) of this subparagraph; or
(II) a deposit or payment of cash, a security, or other property with such commodity options dealer for the purpose of making, exercising, or margining such a commodity contract;

(10) "customer property" means cash, a security, or other property, or proceeds of such cash, security, or property, received, acquired, or held by or for the account of the debtor, from or for the account of a customer—
(A) including—
(i) property received, acquired, or held to margin, guarantee, secure, purchase, or sell a commodity contract;
(ii) profits or contractual or other rights accruing to a customer as a result of a commodity contract;
(iii) an open commodity contract;
(iv) specifically identifiable customer property;
(v) warehouse receipt or other document held by the debtor evidencing ownership of or title to property to be delivered to fulfill a commodity contract from or for the account of a customer;
(vi) cash, a security, or other property received by the debtor as payment for a commodity to be delivered to fulfill a commodity contract from or for the account of a customer;
(vii) a security held as property of the debtor to the extent such security is necessary to meet a net equity claim based on a security of the same class and series of an issuer;
(viii) property that was unlawfully converted from and that is the lawful property of the estate; and
(ix) other property of the debtor that any applicable law, rule, or regulation requires to be set aside or held for the benefit of a customer, unless including such property as customer property would not significantly increase customer property; but
(B) not including property to the extent that a customer does not have a claim against the debtor based on such property;

(11) "foreign future" means contract for the purchase or sale of a commodity for future delivery on, or subject to the rules of, a board of trade outside the United States;

(12) "foreign futures commission merchant" means entity engaged in soliciting or accepting orders for the purchase or sale of a foreign future or that, in connection with such a solicitation or acceptance, accepts cash, a security, or other property, or extends credit to margin, guarantee, or secure any trade or contract that results from such a solicitation or acceptance;

(13) "leverage transaction" means agreement that is subject to regulation under section 19 of the Commodity Exchange Act, and that is commonly known to the commodities trade as a margin account, margin contract, leverage account, or leverage contract;

(14) "leverage transaction merchant" means person in the business of engaging in leverage transactions;

(15) "margin payment" means payment or deposit of cash, a security, or other property, that is commonly known to the commodities trade as original margin, initial margin, maintenance margin, or variation margin, including mark-to-market payments, settlement payments, variation payments, daily settlement payments, and final settlement payments made as adjustments to settlement prices;

(16) "member property" means customer property received, acquired, or held by or for the account of a debtor that is a clearing organization, from or for the proprietary account of a customer that is a clearing member of the debtor; and

(17) "net equity" means, subject to such rules and regulations as the Commission promulgates under the Act, with respect to the aggregate of all of a customer's accounts that such customer has in the same capacity—

(A) the balance remaining in such customer's accounts immediately after—

(i) all commodity contracts of such customer have been transferred, liquidated, or become identified for delivery; and

(ii) all obligations of such customer in such capacity to the debtor have been offset; plus

(B) the value, as of the date of return under section 766 of this title, of any specifically identifiable customer property actually returned to such customer before the date specified in subparagraph (A) of this paragraph; plus

(C) the value, as of the date of transfer, of—

(i) any commodity contract to which such customer is entitled that is transferred to another person under section 766 of this title; and

(ii) any cash, security, or other property of such customer transferred to such other person under section 766 of this title to margin or secure such transferred commodity contract.

Sec. 762. Notice to the Commission and right to be heard

(a) The clerk shall give the notice required by section 342 of this title to the Commission.

(b) The Commission may raise and may appear and be heard on any issue in a case under this chapter.

Sec. 763. Treatment of accounts

(a) Accounts held by the debtor for a particular customer in separate capacities shall be treated as accounts of separate customers.

(b) A member of a clearing organization shall be deemed to hold such member's proprietary account in a separate capacity from such member's customers' account.

(c) The net equity in a customer's account may not be offset against the net equity in the account of any other customer.

Sec. 764. Voidable transfers

(a) Except as otherwise provided in this section, any transfer by the debtor of property that, but for such transfer, would have been customer property, may be avoided by the trustee, and such property shall be treated as customer property, if and to the extent that the trustee avoids such transfer under section 544, 545, 547, 548, 549, or 724(a) of this title. For the purpose of such sections, the property so transferred shall be deemed to have been property of the debtor, and, if such transfer was made to a customer or for a customer's benefit, such customer shall be deemed, for the purposes of this section, to have been a creditor.

(b) Notwithstanding sections 544, 545, 547, 548, 549, and 724(a) of this title, the trustee may not avoid a transfer made before five days after the order for relief, if such transfer is approved by the Commission by rule or order, either before or after such transfer, and if such transfer is—
   (1) a transfer of a commodity contract entered into or carried by or through the debtor on behalf of a customer, and of any cash, securities, or other property margining or securing such commodity contract; or
   (2) the liquidation of a commodity contract entered into or carried by or through the debtor on behalf of a customer.

Sec. 765. Customer instructions

(a) The notice required by section 342 of this title to customers shall instruct each customer—
   (1) to file a proof of such customer's claim promptly, and to specify in such claim any specifically identifiable security, property, or commodity contract; and
   (2) to instruct the trustee of such customer's desired disposition, including transfer under section 766 of this title or liquidation, of any commodity contract specifically identified to such customer.

(b) The trustee shall comply, to the extent practicable, with any instruction received from a customer regarding such customer's desired disposition of any commodity contract specifically identified to such customer. If the trustee has transferred, under section 766 of this title, such a commodity contract, the trustee shall transmit any such instruction to the commodity broker to whom such commodity contract was so transferred.

Sec. 766. Treatment of customer property

(a) The trustee shall answer all margin calls with respect to a specifically identifiable commodity contract of a customer until such time as the trustee returns or transfers such commodity contract, but the trustee may not make a margin payment that has the effect of a distribution to such customer of more than that to which such customer is entitled under subsection (h) or (i) of this section.

(b) The trustee shall prevent any open commodity contract from remaining open after the last day of trading in such commodity contract, or into the first day on which notice of intent to deliver on such commodity contract may be tendered, whichever occurs first. With respect to any commodity contract that has remained open after the last day of trading in such commodity contract or with respect to which delivery must be made or accepted under the rules of the contract market on which such commodity contract was made, the trustee may operate the business of the debtor for the purpose of—
   (1) accepting or making tender of notice of intent to deliver the physical commodity underlying such commodity contract;
   (2) facilitating delivery of such commodity; or
   (3) disposing of such commodity if a party to such commodity contract defaults.

(c) The trustee shall return promptly to a customer any specifically identifiable security, property, or commodity contract to which such customer is entitled, or shall transfer, on such customer's behalf, such security, property, or commodity contract to a commodity broker that is not a debtor under this title, subject to such rules or regulations as the Commission may prescribe, to the extent that the value of such security, property, or commodity contract does not exceed the amount to which such customer would be entitled under subsection (h) or (i) of this section if such security, property, or commodity contract were not returned or transferred under this subsection.

(d) If the value of a specifically identifiable security, property, or commodity contract exceeds the amount to which the customer of the debtor is entitled under subsection (h) or (i) of this section, then such customer to whom such security, property, or commodity contract is specifically identified may deposit cash with the trustee equal to the difference between the value of such security, property, or commodity contract and such amount, and the trustee then shall—

  (1) return promptly such security, property, or commodity contract to such customer; or

  (2) transfer, on such customer's behalf, such security, property, or commodity contract to a commodity broker that is not a debtor under this title, subject to such rules or regulations as the Commission may prescribe.

(e) Subject to subsection (b) of this section, the trustee shall liquidate any commodity contract that—

  (1) is identified to a particular customer and with respect to which such customer has not timely instructed the trustee as to the desired disposition of such commodity contract;

  (2) cannot be transferred under subsection (c) of this section; or

  (3) cannot be identified to a particular customer.

(f) As soon as practicable after the commencement of the case, the trustee shall reduce to money, consistent with good market practice, all securities and other property, other than commodity contracts, held as property of the estate, except for specifically identifiable securities or property distributable under subsection (h) or (i) of this section.

(g) The trustee may not distribute a security or other property except under subsection (h) or (i) of this section.

(h) Except as provided in subsection (b) of this section, the trustee shall distribute customer property ratably to customers on the basis and to the extent of such customers' allowed net equity claims, and in priority to all other claims, except claims of a kind specified in section 507(a)(2) of this title that are attributable to the administration of customer property. Such distribution shall be in the form of—

  (1) cash;

  (2) the return or transfer, under subsection (c) or (d) of this section, of specifically identifiable customer securities, property, or commodity contracts; or

  (3) payment of margin calls under subsection (a) of this section.

  Notwithstanding any other provision of this subsection, a customer net equity claim based on a proprietary account, as defined by Commission rule, regulation, or order, may not be paid either in whole or in part, directly or indirectly, out of customer property unless all other customer net equity claims have been paid in full.

(i) If the debtor is a clearing organization, the trustee shall distribute—

  (1) customer property, other than member property, ratably to customers on the basis and to the extent of such customers' allowed net equity claims based on such customers' accounts other than proprietary accounts, and in priority to all other claims, except claims of a kind specified in section 507(a)(2) of this title that are attributable to the administration of such customer property; and

  (2) member property ratably to customers on the basis and to the extent of such customers' allowed net equity claims based on such customers' proprietary accounts, and in priority

to all other claims, except claims of a kind specified in section 507(a)(2) of this title that are attributable to the administration of member property or customer property.

(j) (1) The trustee shall distribute customer property in excess of that distributed under subsection (h) or (i) of this section in accordance with section 726 of this title.

(2) Except as provided in section 510 of this title, if a customer is not paid the full amount of such customer's allowed net equity claim from customer property, the unpaid portion of such claim is a claim entitled to distribution under section 726 of this title.

Sec. 767. Commodity broker liquidation and forward contract merchants, commodity brokers, stockbrokers, financial institutions, financial participants, securities clearing agencies, swap participants, repo participants, and master netting agreement participants

Notwithstanding any other provision of this title, the exercise of rights by a forward contract merchant, commodity broker, stockbroker, financial institution, financial participant, securities clearing agency, swap participant, repo participant, or master netting agreement participant under this title shall not affect the priority of any unsecured claim it may have after the exercise of such rights.

SUBCHAPTER V—CLEARING BANK LIQUIDATION

Sec. 781. Definitions

For purposes of this subchapter, the following definitions shall apply:

(1) Board.—The term "Board" means the Board of Governors of the Federal Reserve System.

(2) Depository institution.—The term "depository institution" has the same meaning as in section 3 of the Federal Deposit Insurance Act.

(3) Clearing bank.—The term "clearing bank" means an uninsured State member bank, or a corporation organized under section 25A of the Federal Reserve Act, which operates, or operates as, a multilateral clearing organization pursuant to section 409 of the Federal Deposit Insurance Corporation Improvement Act of 1991.

Sec. 782. Selection of trustee

(a) In General.—

(1) Appointment.—Notwithstanding any other provision of this title, the conservator or receiver who files the petition shall be the trustee under this chapter, unless the Board designates an alternative trustee.

(2) Successor.—The Board may designate a successor trustee if required.

(b) Authority of Trustee.—Whenever the Board appoints or designates a trustee, chapter 3 and sections 704 and 705 of this title shall apply to the Board in the same way and to the same extent that they apply to a United States trustee.

Sec. 783. Additional powers of trustee

(a) Distribution of Property Not of the Estate.—The trustee under this subchapter has power to distribute property not of the estate, including distributions to customers that are mandated by subchapters III and IV of this chapter.

(b) Disposition of Institution.—The trustee under this subchapter may, after notice and a hearing—

(1) sell the clearing bank to a depository institution or consortium of depository institutions (which consortium may agree on the allocation of the clearing bank among the consortium);

(2) merge the clearing bank with a depository institution;

(3) transfer contracts to the same extent as could a receiver for a depository institution under paragraphs (9) and (10) of section 11(e) of the Federal Deposit Insurance Act;

(4) transfer assets or liabilities to a depository institution; and

(5) transfer assets and liabilities to a bridge bank as provided in paragraphs (1), (3)(A), (5), and (6) of section 11(n) of the Federal Deposit Insurance Act, paragraphs (9) through (13) of such section, and subparagraphs (A) through (H) and subparagraph (K) of paragraph (4) of such section 11(n), except that—

(A) the bridge bank to which such assets or liabilities are transferred shall be treated as a clearing bank for the purpose of this subsection; and

(B) any references in any such provision of law to the Federal Deposit Insurance Corporation shall be construed to be references to the appointing agency and that references to deposit insurance shall be omitted.

(c) Certain Transfers Included.—Any reference in this section to transfers of liabilities includes a ratable transfer of liabilities within a priority class.

Sec. 784. Right to be heard

The Board or a Federal reserve bank (in the case of a clearing bank that is a member of that bank) may raise and may appear and be heard on any issue in a case under this subchapter.

CHAPTER 9—ADJUSTMENT OF DEBTS OF A MUNICIPALITY

[OMITTED]

CHAPTER 11—REORGANIZATION

SUBCHAPTER I—OFFICERS AND ADMINISTRATION

Sec. 1101. Definitions for this chapter

In this chapter—

(1) "debtor in possession" means debtor except when a person that has qualified under section 322 of this title is serving as trustee in the case;

(2) "substantial consummation" means—

(A) transfer of all or substantially all of the property proposed by the plan to be transferred;

(B) assumption by the debtor or by the successor to the debtor under the plan of the business or of the management of all or substantially all of the property dealt with by the plan; and

(C) commencement of distribution under the plan.

Sec. 1102. Creditors' and equity security holders' committees

(a) (1) Except as provided in paragraph (3), as soon as practicable after the order for relief under chapter 11 of this title, the United States trustee shall appoint a committee of creditors holding unsecured claims and may appoint additional committees of creditors or of equity security holders as the United States trustee deems appropriate.

(2) On request of a party in interest, the court may order the appointment of additional committees of creditors or of equity security holders if necessary to assure adequate representation of creditors or of equity security holders. The United States trustee shall appoint any such committee.

(3) On request of a party in interest in a case in which the debtor is a small business debtor and for cause, the court may order that a committee of creditors not be appointed.

(4) On request of a party in interest and after notice and a hearing, the court may order the United States trustee to change the membership of a committee appointed under this subsection, if the court determines that the change is necessary to ensure adequate representation of creditors or equity security holders. The court may order the United States trustee to increase the number of members of a committee to include a creditor that is a small business concern (as described in section 3(a)(1) of the Small Business Act), if the court determines that the creditor holds claims (of the kind represented by the committee) the aggregate amount of which, in comparison to the annual gross revenue of that creditor, is disproportionately large.

(b) (1) A committee of creditors appointed under subsection (a) of this section shall ordinarily consist of the persons, willing to serve, that hold the seven largest claims against the debtor of the kinds represented on such committee, or of the members of a committee organized by creditors before the commencement of the case under this chapter, if such committee was fairly chosen and is representative of the different kinds of claims to be represented.

(2) A committee of equity security holders appointed under subsection (a)(2) of this section shall ordinarily consist of the persons, willing to serve, that hold the seven largest amounts of equity securities of the debtor of the kinds represented on such committee.

(3) A committee appointed under subsection (a) shall—

(A) provide access to information for creditors who—

(i) hold claims of the kind represented by that committee; and

(ii) are not appointed to the committee;

(B) solicit and receive comments from the creditors described in subparagraph (A); and

(C) be subject to a court order that compels any additional report or disclosure to be made to the creditors described in subparagraph (A).

Sec. 1103. Powers and duties of committees

(a) At a scheduled meeting of a committee appointed under section 1102 of this title, at which a majority of the members of such committee are present, and with the court's approval, such committee may select and authorize the employment by such committee of one or more attorneys, accountants, or other agents, to represent or perform services for such committee.

(b) An attorney or accountant employed to represent a committee appointed under section 1102 of this title may not, while employed by such committee, represent any other entity having an adverse interest in connection with the case. Representation of one or more creditors of the same class as represented by the committee shall not per se constitute the representation of an adverse interest.

(c) A committee appointed under section 1102 of this title may—

(1) consult with the trustee or debtor in possession concerning the administration of the case;

(2) investigate the acts, conduct, assets, liabilities, and financial condition of the debtor, the operation of the debtor's business and the desirability of the continuance of such business, and any other matter relevant to the case or to the formulation of a plan;

(3) participate in the formulation of a plan, advise those represented by such committee of such committee's determinations as to any plan formulated, and collect and file with the court acceptances or rejections of a plan;

(4) request the appointment of a trustee or examiner under section 1104 of this title; and

(5) perform such other services as are in the interest of those represented.

(d) As soon as practicable after the appointment of a committee under section 1102 of this title, the trustee shall meet with such committee to transact such business as may be necessary and proper.

Sec. 1104. Appointment of trustee or examiner

(a) At any time after the commencement of the case but before confirmation of a plan, on request of a party in interest or the United States trustee, and after notice and a hearing, the court shall order the appointment of a trustee—

(1) for cause, including fraud, dishonesty, incompetence, or gross mismanagement of the affairs of the debtor by current management, either before or after the commencement of the case, or similar cause, but not including the number of holders of securities of the debtor or the amount of assets or liabilities of the debtor;

(2) if such appointment is in the interests of creditors, any equity security holders, and other interests of the estate, without regard to the number of holders of securities of the debtor or the amount of assets or liabilities of the debtor; or

(3) if grounds exist to convert or dismiss the case under section 1112, but the court determines that the appointment of a trustee or an examiner is in the best interests of creditors and the estate.

(b) (1) Except as provided in section 1163 of this title, on the request of a party in interest made not later than 30 days after the court orders the appointment of a trustee under subsection (a), the United States trustee shall convene a meeting of creditors for the purpose of electing one disinterested person to serve as trustee in the case. The election of a trustee shall be conducted in the manner provided in subsections (a), (b), and (c) of section 702 of this title.

(2) (A) If an eligible, disinterested trustee is elected at a meeting of creditors under paragraph (1), the United States trustee shall file a report certifying that election.

(B) Upon the filing of a report under subparagraph (A)—

(i) the trustee elected under paragraph (1) shall be considered to have been selected and appointed for purposes of this section; and

(ii) the service of any trustee appointed under subsection (d) shall terminate.

(C) The court shall resolve any dispute arising out of an election described in subparagraph (A).

(c) If the court does not order the appointment of a trustee under this section, then at any time before the confirmation of a plan, on request of a party in interest or the United States trustee, and after notice and a hearing, the court shall order the appointment of an examiner to conduct such an investigation of the debtor as is appropriate, including an investigation of any allegations of fraud, dishonesty, incompetence, misconduct, mismanagement, or irregularity in the management of the affairs of the debtor of or by current or former management of the debtor, if—

(1) such appointment is in the interests of creditors, any equity security holders, and other interests of the estate; or

(2) the debtor's fixed, liquidated, unsecured debts, other than debts for goods, services, or taxes, or owing to an insider, exceed $5,000,000.

(d) If the court orders the appointment of a trustee or an examiner, if a trustee or an examiner dies or resigns during the case or is removed under section 324 of this title, or if a trustee fails to qualify under section 322 of this title, then the United States trustee, after consultation with parties in interest, shall appoint, subject to the court's approval, one disinterested person other than the United States trustee to serve as trustee or examiner, as the case may be, in the case.

(e) The United States trustee shall move for the appointment of a trustee under subsection (a) if there are reasonable grounds to suspect that current members of the governing body of the debtor, the debtor's chief executive or chief financial officer, or members of the governing body who selected the debtor's chief executive or chief financial officer, participated in actual fraud, dishonesty, or criminal conduct in the management of the debtor or the debtor's public financial reporting.

Sec. 1105. Termination of trustee's appointment

At any time before confirmation of a plan, on request of a party in interest or the United States trustee, and after notice and a hearing, the court may terminate the trustee's appointment and restore the debtor to possession and management of the property of the estate and of the operation of the debtor's business.

Sec. 1106. Duties of trustee and examiner

(a) A trustee shall—

(1) perform the duties of the trustee, as specified in paragraphs (2), (5), (7), (8), (9), (10), (11), and (12) of section 704;

(2) if the debtor has not done so, file the list, schedule, and statement required under section 521(1) of this title;

(3) except to the extent that the court orders otherwise, investigate the acts, conduct, assets, liabilities, and financial condition of the debtor, the operation of the debtor's business and the desirability of the continuance of such business, and any other matter relevant to the case or to the formulation of a plan;

(4) as soon as practicable—

(A) file a statement of any investigation conducted under paragraph (3) of this subsection, including any fact ascertained pertaining to fraud, dishonesty, incompetence, misconduct, mismanagement, or irregularity in the management of the affairs of the debtor, or to a cause of action available to the estate; and

(B) transmit a copy or a summary of any such statement to any creditors' committee or equity security holders' committee, to any indenture trustee, and to such other entity as the court designates;

(5) as soon as practicable, file a plan under section 1121 of this title, file a report of why the trustee will not file a plan, or recommend conversion of the case to a case under chapter 7, 12, or 13 of this title or dismissal of the case;

(6) for any year for which the debtor has not filed a tax return required by law, furnish, without personal liability, such information as may be required by the governmental unit with which such tax return was to be filed, in light of the condition of the debtor's books and records and the availability of such information;

(7) after confirmation of a plan, file such reports as are necessary or as the court orders; and

(8) if with respect to the debtor there is a claim for a domestic support obligation, provide the applicable notice specified in subsection (c).

(b) An examiner appointed under section 1104(d) of this title shall perform the duties specified in paragraphs (3) and (4) of subsection (a) of this section, and, except to the extent that the court orders otherwise, any other duties of the trustee that the court orders the debtor in possession not to perform.

(c) (1) In a case described in subsection (a)(8) to which subsection (a)(8) applies, the trustee shall—

(A) (i) provide written notice to the holder of the claim described in subsection (a)(8) of such claim and of the right of such holder to use the services of the State child support enforcement agency established under sections 464 and 466 of the Social Security Act for the State in which such holder resides, for assistance in collecting child support during and after the case under this title; and

(ii) include in the notice required by clause (i) the address and telephone number of such State child support enforcement agency;

(B) (i) provide written notice to such State child support enforcement agency of such claim; and

(ii) include in the notice required by clause (i) the name, address, and telephone number of such holder; and

(C) at such time as the debtor is granted a discharge under section 1141, provide written notice to such holder and to such State child support enforcement agency of—

(i) the granting of the discharge;

(ii) the last recent known address of the debtor;

(iii) the last recent known name and address of the debtor's employer; and

(iv) the name of each creditor that holds a claim that—

(I) is not discharged under paragraph (2), (4), or (14A) of section 523(a); or

(II) was reaffirmed by the debtor under section 524(c).

(2) (A) The holder of a claim described in subsection (a)(8) or the State child enforcement support agency of the State in which such holder resides may request from a creditor described in paragraph (1)(C)(iv) the last known address of the debtor.

(B) Notwithstanding any other provision of law, a creditor that makes a disclosure of a last known address of a debtor in connection with a request made under subparagraph (A) shall not be liable by reason of making such disclosure.

Sec. 1107. Rights, powers, and duties of debtor in possession

(a) Subject to any limitations on a trustee serving in a case under this chapter, and to such limitations or conditions as the court prescribes, a debtor in possession shall have all the rights, other than the right to compensation under section 330 of this title, and powers, and shall perform all the functions and duties, except the duties specified in sections 1106(a)(2), (3), and (4) of this title, of a trustee serving in a case under this chapter.

(b) Notwithstanding section 327(a) of this title, a person is not disqualified for employment under section 327 of this title by a debtor in possession solely because of such person's employment by or representation of the debtor before the commencement of the case.

Sec. 1108. Authorization to operate business

Unless the court, on request of a party in interest and after notice and a hearing, orders otherwise, the trustee may operate the debtor's business.

Sec. 1109. Right to be heard

(a) The Securities and Exchange Commission may raise and may appear and be heard on any issue in a case under this chapter, but the Securities and Exchange Commission may not appeal from any judgment, order, or decree entered in the case.

(b) A party in interest, including the debtor, the trustee, a creditors' committee, an equity security holders' committee, a creditor, an equity security holder, or any indenture trustee, may raise and may appear and be heard on any issue in a case under this chapter.

Sec. 1110. Aircraft equipment and vessels

(a)(1) Except as provided in paragraph (2) and subject to subsection (b), the right of a secured party with a security interest in equipment described in paragraph (3), or of a lessor or conditional vendor of such equipment, to take possession of such equipment in compliance with a security agreement, lease, or conditional sale contract, and to enforce any of its other rights or remedies, under such security agreement, lease, or conditional sale contract, to sell, lease, or otherwise retain or dispose of such equipment, is not limited or otherwise affected by any other provision of this title or by any power of the court.

(2) The right to take possession and to enforce the other rights and remedies described in paragraph (1) shall be subject to section 362 if—

(A) before the date that is 60 days after the date of the order for relief under this chapter, the trustee, subject to the approval of the court, agrees to perform all obligations of the debtor under such security agreement, lease, or conditional sale contract; and

(B) any default, other than a default of a kind specified in section 365(b)(2), under such security agreement, lease, or conditional sale contract—

(i) that occurs before the date of the order is cured before the expiration of such 60-day period;

(ii) that occurs after the date of the order and before the expiration of such 60-day period is cured before the later of—

(I) the date that is 30 days after the date of the default; or

(II) the expiration of such 60-day period; and

(iii) that occurs on or after the expiration of such 60-day period is cured in compliance with the terms of such security agreement, lease, or conditional sale contract, if a cure is permitted under that agreement, lease, or contract.

(3) The equipment described in this paragraph—

(A) is—

(i) an aircraft, aircraft engine, propeller, appliance, or spare part (as defined in section 40102 of title 49) that is subject to a security interest granted by, leased to, or conditionally sold to a debtor that, at the time such transaction is entered into, holds an air carrier operating certificate issued pursuant to chapter 447 of title 49 for aircraft capable of carrying 10 or more individuals or 6,000 pounds or more of cargo; or

(ii) a vessel documented under chapter 121 of title 46 that is subject to a security interest granted by, leased to, or conditionally sold to a debtor that is a water carrier that, at the time such transaction is entered into, holds a certificate of public convenience and necessity or permit issued by the Department of Transportation; and

(B) includes all records and documents relating to such equipment that are required, under the terms of the security agreement, lease, or conditional sale contract, to be surrendered or returned by the debtor in connection with the surrender or return of such equipment.

(4) Paragraph (1) applies to a secured party, lessor, or conditional vendor acting in its own behalf or acting as trustee or otherwise in behalf of another party.

(b) The trustee and the secured party, lessor, or conditional vendor whose right to take possession is protected under subsection (a) may agree, subject to the approval of the court, to extend the 60-day period specified in subsection (a)(1).

(c) (1) In any case under this chapter, the trustee shall immediately surrender and return to a secured party, lessor, or conditional vendor, described in subsection (a)(1), equipment described in subsection (a)(3), if at any time after the date of the order for relief under this chapter such secured party, lessor, or conditional vendor is entitled pursuant to subsection (a)(1) to take possession of such equipment and makes a written demand for such possession to the trustee.

(2) At such time as the trustee is required under paragraph (1) to surrender and return equipment described in subsection (a)(3), any lease of such equipment, and any security agreement or conditional sale contract relating to such equipment, if such security agreement or conditional sale contract is an executory contract, shall be deemed rejected.

(d) With respect to equipment first placed in service on or before October 22, 1994, for purposes of this section—

(1) the term "lease" includes any written agreement with respect to which the lessor and the debtor, as lessee, have expressed in the agreement or in a substantially contemporaneous writing that the agreement is to be treated as a lease for Federal income tax purposes; and

(2) the term "security interest" means a purchase-money equipment security interest.

Sec. 1111. Claims and interests

(a) A proof of claim or interest is deemed filed under section 501 of this title for any claim or interest that appears in the schedules filed under section 521(1) or 1106(a)(2) of this title, except a claim or interest that is scheduled as disputed, contingent, or unliquidated.

(b) (1) (A) A claim secured by a lien on property of the estate shall be allowed or disallowed under section 502 of this title the same as if the holder of such claim had recourse against the debtor on account of such claim, whether or not such holder has such recourse, unless—

(i) the class of which such claim is a part elects, by at least two-thirds in amount and more than half in number of allowed claims of such class, application of paragraph (2) of this subsection; or

(ii) such holder does not have such recourse and such property is sold under section 363 of this title or is to be sold under the plan.

(B) A class of claims may not elect application of paragraph (2) of this subsection if—

(i) the interest on account of such claims of the holders of such claims in such property is of inconsequential value; or

(ii) the holder of a claim of such class has recourse against the debtor on account of such claim and such property is sold under section 363 of this title or is to be sold under the plan.

(2) If such an election is made, then notwithstanding section 506(a) of this title, such claim is a secured claim to the extent that such claim is allowed.

Sec. 1112. Conversion or dismissal

(a) The debtor may convert a case under this chapter to a case under chapter 7 of this title unless—

(1) the debtor is not a debtor in possession;

(2) the case originally was commenced as an involuntary case under this chapter; or

(3) the case was converted to a case under this chapter other than on the debtor's request.

(b) (1) Except as provided in paragraph (2) of this subsection, subsection (c) of this section, and section 1104(a)(3), on request of a party in interest, and after notice and a hearing, absent unusual circumstances specifically identified by the court that establish that the requested conversion or dismissal is not in the best interests of creditors and the estate, the court shall convert a case under this chapter to a case under chapter 7 or dismiss a case under this chapter, whichever is in the best interests of creditors and the estate, if the movant establishes cause.

(2) The relief provided in paragraph (1) shall not be granted absent unusual circumstances specifically identified by the court that establish that such relief is not in the best interests of creditors and the estate, if the debtor or another party in interest objects and establishes that—

(A) there is a reasonable likelihood that a plan will be confirmed within the timeframes established in sections 1121(e) and 1129(e) of this title, or if such sections do not apply, within a reasonable period of time; and

(B) the grounds for granting such relief include an act or omission of the debtor other than under paragraph (4)(A)—

(i) for which there exists a reasonable justification for the act or omission; and

(ii) that will be cured within a reasonable period of time fixed by the court.

(3) The court shall commence the hearing on a motion under this subsection not later than 30 days after filing of the motion, and shall decide the motion not later than 15 days after commencement of such hearing, unless the movant expressly consents to a continuance for a specific period of time or compelling circumstances prevent the court from meeting the time limits established by this paragraph.

(4) For purposes of this subsection, the term "cause" includes—

(A) substantial or continuing loss to or diminution of the estate and the absence of a reasonable likelihood of rehabilitation;
(B) gross mismanagement of the estate;
(C) failure to maintain appropriate insurance that poses a risk to the estate or to the public;
(D) unauthorized use of cash collateral substantially harmful to 1 or more creditors;
(E) failure to comply with an order of the court;
(F) unexcused failure to satisfy timely any filing or reporting requirement established by this title or by any rule applicable to a case under this chapter;
(G) failure to attend the meeting of creditors convened under section 341(a) or an examination ordered under rule 2004 of the Federal Rules of Bankruptcy Procedure without good cause shown by the debtor;
(H) failure timely to provide information or attend meetings reasonably requested by the United States trustee (or the bankruptcy administrator, if any);
(I) failure timely to pay taxes owed after the date of the order for relief or to file tax returns due after the date of the order for relief;
(J) failure to file a disclosure statement, or to file or confirm a plan, within the time fixed by this title or by order of the court;
(K) failure to pay any fees or charges required under chapter 123 of title 28;
(L) revocation of an order of confirmation under section 1144;
(M) inability to effectuate substantial consummation of a confirmed plan;
(N) material default by the debtor with respect to a confirmed plan;
(O) termination of a confirmed plan by reason of the occurrence of a condition specified in the plan; and
(P) failure of the debtor to pay any domestic support obligation that first becomes payable after the date of the filing of the petition.

(c) The court may not convert a case under this chapter to a case under chapter 7 of this title if the debtor is a farmer or a corporation that is not a moneyed, business, or commercial corporation, unless the debtor requests such conversion.

(d) The court may convert a case under this chapter to a case under chapter 12 or 13 of this title only if—
(1) the debtor requests such conversion;
(2) the debtor has not been discharged under section 1141(d) of this title; and
(3) if the debtor requests conversion to chapter 12 of this title, such conversion is equitable.

(e) Except as provided in subsections (c) and (f), the court, on request of the United States trustee, may convert a case under this chapter to a case under chapter 7 of this title or may dismiss a case under this chapter, whichever is in the best interest of creditors and the estate if the debtor in a voluntary case fails to file, within fifteen days after the filing of the petition commencing such case or such additional time as the court may allow, the information required by paragraph (1) of section 521, including a list containing the names and addresses of the holders of the twenty largest unsecured claims (or of all unsecured claims if there are fewer than twenty unsecured claims), and the approximate dollar amounts of each of such claims.

(f) Notwithstanding any other provision of this section, a case may not be converted to a case under another chapter of this title unless the debtor may be a debtor under such chapter.

Sec. 1113. Rejection of collective bargaining agreements

(a) The debtor in possession, or the trustee if one has been appointed under the provisions of this chapter, other than a trustee in a case covered by subchapter IV of this chapter and by title I of the Railway Labor Act, may assume or reject a collective bargaining agreement only in accordance with the provisions of this section.

(b) (1) Subsequent to filing a petition and prior to filing an application seeking rejection of a collective bargaining agreement, the debtor in possession or trustee (hereinafter in this section "trustee" shall include a debtor in possession), shall— (A) make a proposal to the authorized representative of the employees covered by such agreement, based on the most complete and reliable information available at the time of such proposal, which provides for those necessary modifications in the employees benefits and protections that are necessary to permit the reorganization of the debtor and assures that all creditors, the debtor and all of the affected parties are treated fairly and equitably; and

(B) provide, subject to subsection (d)(3), the representative of the employees with such relevant information as is necessary to evaluate the proposal.

(2) During the period beginning on the date of the making of a proposal provided for in paragraph (1) and ending on the date of the hearing provided for in subsection (d)(1), the trustee shall meet, at reasonable times, with the authorized representative to confer in good faith in attempting to reach mutually satisfactory modifications of such agreement.

(c) The court shall approve an application for rejection of a collective bargaining agreement only if the court finds that—

(1) the trustee has, prior to the hearing, made a proposal that fulfills the requirements of subsection (b)(1);

(2) the authorized representative of the employees has refused to accept such proposal without good cause; and

(3) the balance of the equities clearly favors rejection of such agreement.

(d) (1) Upon the filing of an application for rejection the court shall schedule a hearing to be held not later than fourteen days after the date of the filing of such application. All interested parties may appear and be heard at such hearing. Adequate notice shall be provided to such parties at least ten days before the date of such hearing. The court may extend the time for the commencement of such hearing for a period not exceeding seven days where the circumstances of the case, and the interests of justice require such extension, or for additional periods of time to which the trustee and representative agree.

(2) The court shall rule on such application for rejection within thirty days after the date of the commencement of the hearing. In the interests of justice, the court may extend such time for ruling for such additional period as the trustee and the employees' representative may agree to. If the court does not rule on such application within thirty days after the date of the commencement of the hearing, or within such additional time as the trustee and the employees' representative may agree to, the trustee may terminate or alter any provisions of the collective bargaining agreement pending the ruling of the court on such application.

(3) The court may enter such protective orders, consistent with the need of the authorized representative of the employee to evaluate the trustee's proposal and the application for rejection, as may be necessary to prevent disclosure of information provided to such representative where such disclosure could compromise the position of the debtor with respect to its competitors in the industry in which it is engaged.

(e) If during a period when the collective bargaining agreement continues in effect, and if essential to the continuation of the debtor's business, or in order to avoid irreparable damage to the estate, the court, after notice and a hearing, may authorize the trustee to implement interim changes in the terms, conditions, wages, benefits, or work rules provided by a collective bargaining agreement. Any hearing under this paragraph shall be scheduled in accordance with the needs of the trustee. The implementation of such interim changes shall not render the application for rejection moot.

(f) No provision of this title shall be construed to permit a trustee to unilaterally terminate or alter any provisions of a collective bargaining agreement prior to compliance with the provisions of this section.

Sec. 1114. Payment of insurance benefits to retired employees

(a) For purposes of this section, the term "retiree benefits" means payments to any entity or person for the purpose of providing or reimbursing payments for retired employees and their spouses and dependents, for medical, surgical, or hospital care benefits, or benefits in the event of sickness, accident, disability, or death under any plan, fund, or program (through the purchase of insurance or otherwise) maintained or established in whole or in part by the debtor prior to filing a petition commencing a case under this title.

(b) (1) For purposes of this section, the term "authorized representative" means the authorized representative designated pursuant to subsection (c) for persons receiving any retiree benefits covered by a collective bargaining agreement or subsection (d) in the case of persons receiving retiree benefits not covered by such an agreement.

(2) Committees of retired employees appointed by the court pursuant to this section shall have the same rights, powers, and duties as committees appointed under sections 1102 and 1103 of this title for the purpose of carrying out the purposes of sections 1114 and 1129(a)(13) and, as permitted by the court, shall have the power to enforce the rights of persons under this title as they relate to retiree benefits.

(c) (1) A labor organization shall be, for purposes of this section, the authorized representative of those persons receiving any retiree benefits covered by any collective bargaining agreement to which that labor organization is signatory, unless (A) such labor organization elects not to serve as the authorized representative of such persons, or (B) the court, upon a motion by any party in interest, after notice and hearing, determines that different representation of such persons is appropriate.

(2) In cases where the labor organization referred to in paragraph (1) elects not to serve as the authorized representative of those persons receiving any retiree benefits covered by any collective bargaining agreement to which that labor organization is signatory, or in cases where the court, pursuant to paragraph (1) finds different representation of such persons appropriate, the court, upon a motion by any party in interest, and after notice and a hearing, shall appoint a committee of retired employees if the debtor seeks to modify or not pay the retiree benefits or if the court otherwise determines that it is appropriate, from among such persons, to serve as the authorized representative of such persons under this section.

(d) The court, upon a motion by any party in interest, and after notice and a hearing, shall order the appointment of a committee of retired employees if the debtor seeks to modify or not pay the retiree benefits or if the court otherwise determines that it is appropriate, to serve as the authorized representative, under this section, of those persons receiving any retiree benefits not covered by a collective bargaining agreement. The United States trustee shall appoint any such committee.

(e) (1) Notwithstanding any other provision of this title, the debtor in possession, or the trustee if one has been appointed under the provisions of this chapter (hereinafter in this section "trustee" shall include a debtor in possession), shall timely pay and shall not modify any retiree benefits, except that—

(A) the court, on motion of the trustee or authorized representative, and after notice and a hearing, may order modification of such payments, pursuant to the provisions of subsections (g) and (h) of this section, or

(B) the trustee and the authorized representative of the recipients of those benefits may agree to modification of such payments,

after which such benefits as modified shall continue to be paid by the trustee.

(2) Any payment for retiree benefits required to be made before a plan confirmed under section 1129 of this title is effective has the status of an allowed administrative expense as provided in section 503 of this title.

(f) (1) Subsequent to filing a petition and prior to filing an application seeking modification of the retiree benefits, the trustee shall—

(A) make a proposal to the authorized representative of the retirees, based on the most complete and reliable information available at the time of such proposal, which provides for those necessary modifications in the retiree benefits that are necessary to permit the reorganization of the debtor and assures that all creditors, the debtor and all of the affected parties are treated fairly and equitably; and

(B) provide, subject to subsection (k)(3), the representative of the retirees with such relevant information as is necessary to evaluate the proposal.

(2) During the period beginning on the date of the making of a proposal provided for in paragraph (1), and ending on the date of the hearing provided for in subsection (k)(1), the trustee shall meet, at reasonable times, with the authorized representative to confer in good faith in attempting to reach mutually satisfactory modifications of such retiree benefits.

(g) The court shall enter an order providing for modification in the payment of retiree benefits if the court finds that—

(1) the trustee has, prior to the hearing, made a proposal that fulfills the requirements of subsection (f);

(2) the authorized representative of the retirees has refused to accept such proposal without good cause; and

(3) such modification is necessary to permit the reorganization of the debtor and assures that all creditors, the debtor, and all of the affected parties are treated fairly and equitably, and is clearly favored by the balance of the equities;

except that in no case shall the court enter an order providing for such modification which provides for a modification to a level lower than that proposed by the trustee in the proposal found by the court to have complied with the requirements of this subsection and subsection (f): Provided, however, That at any time after an order is entered providing for modification in the payment of retiree benefits, or at any time after an agreement modifying such benefits is made between the trustee and the authorized representative of the recipients of such benefits, the authorized representative may apply to the court for an order increasing those benefits which order shall be granted if the increase in retiree benefits sought is consistent with the standard set forth in paragraph (3): Provided further, That neither the trustee nor the authorized representative is precluded from making more than one motion for a modification order governed by this subsection.

(h) (1) Prior to a court issuing a final order under subsection (g) of this section, if essential to the continuation of the debtor's business, or in order to avoid irreparable damage to the estate, the court, after notice and a hearing, may authorize the trustee to implement interim modifications in retiree benefits.

(2) Any hearing under this subsection shall be scheduled in accordance with the needs of the trustee.

(3) The implementation of such interim changes does not render the motion for modification moot.

(i) No retiree benefits paid between the filing of the petition and the time a plan confirmed under section 1129 of this title becomes effective shall be deducted or offset from the amounts allowed as claims for any benefits which remain unpaid, or from the amounts to be paid under the plan with respect to such claims for unpaid benefits, whether such claims for unpaid benefits are based upon or arise from a right to future unpaid benefits or from any benefits not paid as a result of modifications allowed pursuant to this section.

(j) No claim for retiree benefits shall be limited by section 502(b)(7) of this title.

(k) (1) Upon the filing of an application for modifying retiree benefits, the court shall schedule a hearing to be held not later than fourteen days after the date of the filing of such application. All interested parties may appear and be heard at such hearing. Adequate notice shall be provided to such parties at least ten days before the date of such hearing. The court may extend the time for the commencement of such hearing for a period not exceeding seven days where the circumstances of the case, and the interests of justice require such extension, or for additional periods of time to which the trustee and the authorized representative agree.

(2) The court shall rule on such application for modification within ninety days after the date of the commencement of the hearing. In the interests of justice, the court may extend such time for ruling for such additional period as the trustee and the authorized representative may agree to. If the court does not rule on such application within ninety days after the date of the commencement of the hearing, or within such additional time as the trustee and the authorized representative may agree to, the trustee may implement the proposed modifications pending the ruling of the court on such application.

(3) The court may enter such protective orders, consistent with the need of the authorized representative of the retirees to evaluate the trustee's proposal and the application for modification, as may be necessary to prevent disclosure of information provided to such representative where such disclosure could compromise the position of the debtor with respect to its competitors in the industry in which it is engaged.

(l) If the debtor, during the 180-day period ending on the date of the filing of the petition—

(1) modified retiree benefits; and

(2) was insolvent on the date such benefits were modified;

the court, on motion of a party in interest, and after notice and a hearing, shall issue an order reinstating as of the date the modification was made, such benefits as in effect immediately before such date unless the court finds that the balance of the equities clearly favors such modification.

Sec. 1115. Property of the estate

(a) In a case in which the debtor is an individual, property of the estate includes, in addition to the property specified in section 541—
   (1) all property of the kind specified in section 541 that the debtor acquires after the commencement of the case but before the case is closed, dismissed, or converted to a case under chapter 7, 12, or 13, whichever occurs first; and
   (2) earnings from services performed by the debtor after the commencement of the case but before the case is closed, dismissed, or converted to a case under chapter 7, 12, or 13, whichever occurs first.

(b) Except as provided in section 1104 or a confirmed plan or order confirming a plan, the debtor shall remain in possession of all property of the estate.

Sec. 1116. Duties of trustee or debtor in possession in small business cases

In a small business case, a trustee or the debtor in possession, in addition to the duties provided in this title and as otherwise required by law, shall—

   (1) append to the voluntary petition or, in an involuntary case, file not later than 7 days after the date of the order for relief—
      (A) its most recent balance sheet, statement of operations, cash-flow statement, and Federal income tax return; or
      (B) a statement made under penalty of perjury that no balance sheet, statement of operations, or cash-flow statement has been prepared and no Federal tax return has been filed;
   (2) attend, through its senior management personnel and counsel, meetings scheduled by the court or the United States trustee, including initial debtor interviews, scheduling conferences, and meetings of creditors convened under section 341 unless the court, after notice and a hearing, waives that requirement upon a finding of extraordinary and compelling circumstances;
   (3) timely file all schedules and statements of financial affairs, unless the court, after notice and a hearing, grants an extension, which shall not extend such time period to a date later than 30 days after the date of the order for relief, absent extraordinary and compelling circumstances;
   (4) file all postpetition financial and other reports required by the Federal Rules of Bankruptcy Procedure or by local rule of the district court;
   (5) subject to section 363(c)(2), maintain insurance customary and appropriate to the industry;
   (6) (A) timely file tax returns and other required government filings; and
      (B) subject to section 363(c)(2), timely pay all taxes entitled to administrative expense priority except those being contested by appropriate proceedings being diligently prosecuted; and
   (7) allow the United States trustee, or a designated representative of the United States trustee, to inspect the debtor's business premises, books, and records at reasonable times, after reasonable prior written notice, unless notice is waived by the debtor.

SUBCHAPTER II—THE PLAN

Sec. 1121. Who may file a plan

(a) The debtor may file a plan with a petition commencing a voluntary case, or at any time in a voluntary case or an involuntary case.

(b) Except as otherwise provided in this section, only the debtor may file a plan until after 120 days after the date of the order for relief under this chapter.

(c) Any party in interest, including the debtor, the trustee, a creditors' committee, an equity security holders' committee, a creditor, an equity security holder, or any indenture trustee, may file a plan if and only if—

(1) a trustee has been appointed under this chapter;

(2) the debtor has not filed a plan before 120 days after the date of the order for relief under this chapter; or

(3) the debtor has not filed a plan that has been accepted, before 180 days after the date of the order for relief under this chapter, by each class of claims or interests that is impaired under the plan.

(d) (1) Subject to paragraph (2), on request of a party in interest made within the respective periods specified in subsections (b) and (c) of this section and after notice and a hearing, the court may for cause reduce or increase the 120-day period or the 180-day period referred to in this section.

(2) (A) The 120-day period specified in paragraph (1) may not be extended beyond a date that is 18 months after the date of the order for relief under this chapter.

(B) The 180-day period specified in paragraph (1) may not be extended beyond a date that is 20 months after the date of the order for relief under this chapter.

(e) In a small business case—

(1) only the debtor may file a plan until after 180 days after the date of the order for relief, unless that period is—

(A) extended as provided by this subsection, after notice and a hearing; or

(B) the court, for cause, orders otherwise;

(2) the plan and a disclosure statement (if any) shall be filed not later than 300 days after the date of the order for relief; and

(3) the time periods specified in paragraphs (1) and (2), and the time fixed in section 1129(e) within which the plan shall be confirmed, may be extended only if—

(A) the debtor, after providing notice to parties in interest (including the United States trustee), demonstrates by a preponderance of the evidence that it is more likely than not that the court will confirm a plan within a reasonable period of time;

(B) a new deadline is imposed at the time the extension is granted; and

(C) the order extending time is signed before the existing deadline has expired.

Sec. 1122. Classification of claims or interests

(a) Except as provided in subsection (b) of this section, a plan may place a claim or an interest in a particular class only if such claim or interest is substantially similar to the other claims or interests of such class.

(b) A plan may designate a separate class of claims consisting only of every unsecured claim that is less than or reduced to an amount that the court approves as reasonable and necessary for administrative convenience.

Sec. 1123. Contents of plan

(a) Notwithstanding any otherwise applicable nonbankruptcy law, a plan shall—

(1) designate, subject to section 1122 of this title, classes of claims, other than claims of a kind specified in section 507(a)(2), 507(a)(3), or 507(a)(8) of this title, and classes of interests;

(2) specify any class of claims or interests that is not impaired under the plan;

(3) specify the treatment of any class of claims or interests that is impaired under the plan;

(4) provide the same treatment for each claim or interest of a particular class, unless the holder of a particular claim or interest agrees to a less favorable treatment of such particular claim or interest;

(5) provide adequate means for the plan's implementation, such as—

(A) retention by the debtor of all or any part of the property of the estate;

(B) transfer of all or any part of the property of the estate to one or more entities, whether organized before or after the confirmation of such plan;

(C) merger or consolidation of the debtor with one or more persons;

(D) sale of all or any part of the property of the estate, either subject to or free of any lien, or the distribution of all or any part of the property of the estate among those having an interest in such property of the estate;

(E) satisfaction or modification of any lien;

(F) cancellation or modification of any indenture or similar instrument;

(G) curing or waiving of any default;

(H) extension of a maturity date or a change in an interest rate or other term of outstanding securities;

(I) amendment of the debtor's charter; or

(J) issuance of securities of the debtor, or of any entity referred to in subparagraph (B) or (C) of this paragraph, for cash, for property, for existing securities, or in exchange for claims or interests, or for any other appropriate purpose;

(6) provide for the inclusion in the charter of the debtor, if the debtor is a corporation, or of any corporation referred to in paragraph (5)(B) or (5)(C) of this subsection, of a provision prohibiting the issuance of nonvoting equity securities, and providing, as to the several classes of securities possessing voting power, an appropriate distribution of such power among such classes, including, in the case of any class of equity securities having a preference over another class of equity securities with respect to dividends, adequate provisions for the election of directors representing such preferred class in the event of default in the payment of such dividends;

(7) contain only provisions that are consistent with the interests of creditors and equity security holders and with public policy with respect to the manner of selection of any officer, director, or trustee under the plan and any successor to such officer, director, or trustee; and

(8) in a case in which the debtor is an individual, provide for the payment to creditors under the plan of all or such portion of earnings from personal services performed by the debtor after the commencement of the case or other future income of the debtor as is necessary for the execution of the plan.

(b) Subject to subsection (a) of this section, a plan may—

(1) impair or leave unimpaired any class of claims, secured or unsecured, or of interests;

(2) subject to section 365 of this title, provide for the assumption, rejection, or assignment of any executory contract or unexpired lease of the debtor not previously rejected under such section;

(3) provide for—

(A) the settlement or adjustment of any claim or interest belonging to the debtor or to the estate; or

(B) the retention and enforcement by the debtor, by the trustee, or by a representative of the estate appointed for such purpose, of any such claim or interest;

(4) provide for the sale of all or substantially all of the property of the estate, and the distribution of the proceeds of such sale among holders of claims or interests;

(5) modify the rights of holders of secured claims, other than a claim secured only by a security interest in real property that is the debtor's principal residence, or of holders of unsecured claims, or leave unaffected the rights of holders of any class of claims; and

(6) include any other appropriate provision not inconsistent with the applicable provisions of this title.

(c) In a case concerning an individual, a plan proposed by an entity other than the debtor may not provide for the use, sale, or lease of property exempted under section 522 of this title, unless the debtor consents to such use, sale, or lease.

(d) Notwithstanding subsection (a) of this section and sections 506(b), 1129(a)(7), and 1129(b) of this title, if it is proposed in a plan to cure a default the amount necessary to cure the default shall be determined in accordance with the underlying agreement and applicable nonbankruptcy law.

Sec. 1124. Impairment of claims or interests

Except as provided in section 1123(a)(4) of this title, a class of claims or interests is impaired under a plan unless, with respect to each claim or interest of such class, the plan—

(1) leaves unaltered the legal, equitable, and contractual rights to which such claim or interest entitles the holder of such claim or interest; or

(2) notwithstanding any contractual provision or applicable law that entitles the holder of such claim or interest to demand or receive accelerated payment of such claim or interest after the occurrence of a default—

(A) cures any such default that occurred before or after the commencement of the case under this title, other than a default of a kind specified in section 365(b)(2) of this title or of a kind that section 365(b)(2) expressly does not require to be cured;

(B) reinstates the maturity of such claim or interest as such maturity existed before such default;

(C) compensates the holder of such claim or interest for any damages incurred as a result of any reasonable reliance by such holder on such contractual provision or such applicable law;

(D) if such claim or such interest arises from any failure to perform a nonmonetary obligation, other than a default arising from failure to operate a nonresidential real property lease subject to section 365(b)(1)(A), compensates the holder of such claim or such interest (other than the debtor or an insider) for any actual pecuniary loss incurred by such holder as a result of such failure; and

(E) does not otherwise alter the legal, equitable, or contractual rights to which such claim or interest entitles the holder of such claim or interest.

Sec. 1125. Postpetition disclosure and solicitation

(a) In this section—

(1) "adequate information" means information of a kind, and in sufficient detail, as far as is reasonably practicable in light of the nature and history of the debtor and the condition of the debtor's books and records, including a discussion of the potential material Federal tax consequences of the plan to the debtor, any successor to the debtor, and a hypothetical investor typical of the holders of claims or interests in the case, that would enable such a hypothetical investor of the relevant class to make an informed judgment about the plan, but adequate information need not include such information about any other possible or proposed plan and in determining whether a disclosure statement provides adequate information, the court shall consider the complexity of the case, the benefit of additional information to creditors and other parties in interest, and the cost of providing additional information; and

(2) "investor typical of holders of claims or interests of the relevant class" means investor having—

(A) a claim or interest of the relevant class;

(B) such a relationship with the debtor as the holders of other claims or interests of such class generally have; and

(C) such ability to obtain such information from sources other than the disclosure required by this section as holders of claims or interests in such class generally have.

(b) An acceptance or rejection of a plan may not be solicited after the commencement of the case under this title from a holder of a claim or interest with respect to such claim or interest, unless, at the time of or before such solicitation, there is transmitted to such holder the plan or a summary of the plan, and a written disclosure statement approved, after notice and a hearing, by the court as containing adequate information. The court may approve a disclosure statement without a valuation of the debtor or an appraisal of the debtor's assets.

(c) The same disclosure statement shall be transmitted to each holder of a claim or interest of a particular class, but there may be transmitted different disclosure statements, differing in amount, detail, or kind of information, as between classes.

(d) Whether a disclosure statement required under subsection (b) of this section contains adequate information is not governed by any otherwise applicable nonbankruptcy law, rule, or regulation, but an agency or official whose duty is to administer or enforce such a law, rule, or regulation may be heard on the issue of whether a disclosure statement contains adequate information. Such an agency or official may not appeal from, or otherwise seek review of, an order approving a disclosure statement.

(e) A person that solicits acceptance or rejection of a plan, in good faith and in compliance with the applicable provisions of this title, or that participates, in good faith and in compliance with the applicable provisions of this title, in the offer, issuance, sale, or purchase of a security, offered or sold under the plan, of the debtor, of an affiliate participating in a joint plan with the debtor, or of a newly organized successor to the debtor under the plan, is not liable, on account of such solicitation or participation, for violation of any applicable law, rule, or regulation governing solicitation of acceptance or rejection of a plan or the offer, issuance, sale, or purchase of securities.

(f) Notwithstanding subsection (b), in a small business case—

(1) the court may determine that the plan itself provides adequate information and that a separate disclosure statement is not necessary;

(2) the court may approve a disclosure statement submitted on standard forms approved by the court or adopted under section 2075 of title 28; and

(3) (A) the court may conditionally approve a disclosure statement subject to final approval after notice and a hearing;

(B) acceptances and rejections of a plan may be solicited based on a conditionally approved disclosure statement if the debtor provides adequate information to each holder of a claim or interest that is solicited, but a conditionally approved disclosure statement shall be mailed not later than 25 days before the date of the hearing on confirmation of the plan; and

(C) the hearing on the disclosure statement may be combined with the hearing on confirmation of a plan.

(g) Notwithstanding subsection (b), an acceptance or rejection of the plan may be solicited from a holder of a claim or interest if such solicitation complies with applicable nonbankruptcy law and if such holder was solicited before the commencement of the case in a manner complying with applicable nonbankruptcy law.

Sec. 1126. Acceptance of plan

(a) The holder of a claim or interest allowed under section 502 of this title may accept or reject a plan. If the United States is a creditor or equity security holder, the Secretary of the Treasury may accept or reject the plan on behalf of the United States.

(b) For the purposes of subsections (c) and (d) of this section, a holder of a claim or interest that has accepted or rejected the plan before the commencement of the case under this title is deemed to have accepted or rejected such plan, as the case may be, if—

(1) the solicitation of such acceptance or rejection was in compliance with any applicable nonbankruptcy law, rule, or regulation governing the adequacy of disclosure in connection with such solicitation; or

(2) if there is not any such law, rule, or regulation, such acceptance or rejection was solicited after disclosure to such holder of adequate information, as defined in section 1125(a) of this title.

(c) A class of claims has accepted a plan if such plan has been accepted by creditors, other than any entity designated under subsection (e) of this section, that hold at least two-thirds in amount and more than one-half in number of the allowed claims of such class held by creditors, other than any entity designated under subsection (e) of this section, that have accepted or rejected such plan.

(d) A class of interests has accepted a plan if such plan has been accepted by holders of such interests, other than any entity designated under subsection (e) of this section, that hold at least two-thirds in amount of the allowed interests of such class held by holders of such interests, other than any entity designated under subsection (e) of this section, that have accepted or rejected such plan.

(e) On request of a party in interest, and after notice and a hearing, the court may designate any entity whose acceptance or rejection of such plan was not in good faith, or was not solicited or procured in good faith or in accordance with the provisions of this title.

(f) Notwithstanding any other provision of this section, a class that is not impaired under a plan, and each holder of a claim or interest of such class, are conclusively presumed to have accepted the plan, and solicitation of acceptances with respect to such class from the holders of claims or interests of such class is not required.

(g) Notwithstanding any other provision of this section, a class is deemed not to have accepted a plan if such plan provides that the claims or interests of such class do not entitle the holders of such claims or interests to receive or retain any property under the plan on account of such claims or interests.

Sec. 1127. Modification of plan

(a) The proponent of a plan may modify such plan at any time before confirmation, but may not modify such plan so that such plan as modified fails to meet the requirements of sections 1122 and 1123 of this title. After the proponent of a plan files a modification of such plan with the court, the plan as modified becomes the plan.

(b) The proponent of a plan or the reorganized debtor may modify such plan at any time after confirmation of such plan and before substantial consummation of such plan, but may not modify such plan so that such plan as modified fails to meet the requirements of sections 1122 and 1123 of this title. Such plan as modified under this subsection becomes the plan only if circumstances warrant such modification and the court, after notice and a hearing, confirms such plan as modified, under section 1129 of this title.

(c) The proponent of a modification shall comply with section 1125 of this title with respect to the plan as modified.

(d) Any holder of a claim or interest that has accepted or rejected a plan is deemed to have accepted or rejected, as the case may be, such plan as modified, unless, within the time fixed by the court, such holder changes such holder's previous acceptance or rejection.

(e) If the debtor is an individual, the plan may be modified at any time after confirmation of the plan but before the completion of payments under the plan, whether or not the plan has been substantially consummated, upon request of the debtor, the trustee, the United States trustee, or the holder of an allowed unsecured claim, to—

  (1) increase or reduce the amount of payments on claims of a particular class provided for by the plan;

  (2) extend or reduce the time period for such payments; or

  (3) alter the amount of the distribution to a creditor whose claim is provided for by the plan to the extent necessary to take account of any payment of such claim made other than under the plan.

(f) (1) Sections 1121 through 1128 and the requirements of section 1129 apply to any modification under subsection (a).

  (2) The plan, as modified, shall become the plan only after there has been disclosure under section 1125 as the court may direct, notice and a hearing, and such modification is approved.

Sec. 1128. Confirmation hearing

(a) After notice, the court shall hold a hearing on confirmation of a plan.

(b) A party in interest may object to confirmation of a plan.

Sec. 1129. Confirmation of plan

(a) The court shall confirm a plan only if all of the following requirements are met:

  (1) The plan complies with the applicable provisions of this title.

(2) The proponent of the plan complies with the applicable provisions of this title.

(3) The plan has been proposed in good faith and not by any means forbidden by law.

(4) Any payment made or to be made by the proponent, by the debtor, or by a person issuing securities or acquiring property under the plan, for services or for costs and expenses in or in connection with the case, or in connection with the plan and incident to the case, has been approved by, or is subject to the approval of, the court as reasonable.

(5) (A) (i) The proponent of the plan has disclosed the identity and affiliations of any individual proposed to serve, after confirmation of the plan, as a director, officer, or voting trustee of the debtor, an affiliate of the debtor participating in a joint plan with the debtor, or a successor to the debtor under the plan; and

(ii) the appointment to, or continuance in, such office of such individual, is consistent with the interests of creditors and equity security holders and with public policy; and

(B) the proponent of the plan has disclosed the identity of any insider that will be employed or retained by the reorganized debtor, and the nature of any compensation for such insider.

(6) Any governmental regulatory commission with jurisdiction, after confirmation of the plan, over the rates of the debtor has approved any rate change provided for in the plan, or such rate change is expressly conditioned on such approval.

(7) With respect to each impaired class of claims or interests—

(A) each holder of a claim or interest of such class—

(i) has accepted the plan; or

(ii) will receive or retain under the plan on account of such claim or interest property of a value, as of the effective date of the plan, that is not less than the amount that such holder would so receive or retain if the debtor were liquidated under chapter 7 of this title on such date; or

(B) if section 1111(b)(2) of this title applies to the claims of such class, each holder of a claim of such class will receive or retain under the plan on account of such claim property of a value, as of the effective date of the plan, that is not less than the value of such holder's interest in the estate's interest in the property that secures such claims.

(8) With respect to each class of claims or interests—

(A) such class has accepted the plan; or

(B) such class is not impaired under the plan.

(9) Except to the extent that the holder of a particular claim has agreed to a different treatment of such claim, the plan provides that—

(A) with respect to a claim of a kind specified in section 507(a)(2) or 507(a)(3) of this title, on the effective date of the plan, the holder of such claim will receive on account of such claim cash equal to the allowed amount of such claim;

(B) with respect to a class of claims of a kind specified in section 507(a)(1), 507(a)(4), 507(a)(5), 507(a)(6), or 507(a)(7) of this title, each holder of a claim of such class will receive—

(i) if such class has accepted the plan, deferred cash payments of a value, as of the effective date of the plan, equal to the allowed amount of such claim; or

(ii) if such class has not accepted the plan, cash on the effective date of the plan equal to the allowed amount of such claim;

(C) with respect to a claim of a kind specified in section 507(a)(8) of this title, the holder of such claim will receive on account of such claim regular installment payments in cash—

(i) of a total value, as of the effective date of the plan, equal to the allowed amount of such claim;

(ii) over a period ending not later than 5 years after the date of the order for relief under section 301, 302, or 303; and

(iii) in a manner not less favorable than the most favored nonpriority unsecured claim provided for by the plan (other than cash payments made to a class of creditors under section 1122(b)); and

(D) with respect to a secured claim which would otherwise meet the description of an unsecured claim of a governmental unit under section 507(a)(8), but for the secured status of that claim, the holder of that claim will receive on account of that claim, cash payments, in the same manner and over the same period, as prescribed in subparagraph (C).

(10) If a class of claims is impaired under the plan, at least one class of claims that is impaired under the plan has accepted the plan, determined without including any acceptance of the plan by any insider.

(11) Confirmation of the plan is not likely to be followed by the liquidation, or the need for further financial reorganization, of the debtor or any successor to the debtor under the plan, unless such liquidation or reorganization is proposed in the plan.

(12) All fees payable under section 1930 of title 28, as determined by the court at the hearing on confirmation of the plan, have been paid or the plan provides for the payment of all such fees on the effective date of the plan.

(13) The plan provides for the continuation after its effective date of payment of all retiree benefits, as that term is defined in section 1114 of this title, at the level established pursuant to subsection (e)(1)(B) or (g) of section 1114 of this title, at any time prior to confirmation of the plan, for the duration of the period the debtor has obligated itself to provide such benefits.

(14) If the debtor is required by a judicial or administrative order, or by statute, to pay a domestic support obligation, the debtor has paid all amounts payable under such order or such statute for such obligation that first become payable after the date of the filing of the petition.

(15) In a case in which the debtor is an individual and in which the holder of an allowed unsecured claim objects to the confirmation of the plan—

(A) the value, as of the effective date of the plan, of the property to be distributed under the plan on account of such claim is not less than the amount of such claim; or

(B) the value of the property to be distributed under the plan is not less than the projected disposable income of the debtor (as defined in section 1325(b)(2)) to be received during the 5-year period beginning on the date that the first payment is due under the plan, or during the period for which the plan provides payments, whichever is longer.

(16) All transfers of property of the plan shall be made in accordance with any applicable

provisions of nonbankruptcy law that govern the transfer of property by a corporation or trust that is not a moneyed, business, or commercial corporation or trust.

(b) (1) Notwithstanding section 510(a) of this title, if all of the applicable requirements of subsection (a) of this section other than paragraph (8) are met with respect to a plan, the court, on request of the proponent of the plan, shall confirm the plan notwithstanding the requirements of such paragraph if the plan does not discriminate unfairly, and is fair and equitable, with respect to each class of claims or interests that is impaired under, and has not accepted, the plan.

(2) For the purpose of this subsection, the condition that a plan be fair and equitable with respect to a class includes the following requirements:

(A) With respect to a class of secured claims, the plan provides—

(i) (I) that the holders of such claims retain the liens securing such claims, whether the property subject to such liens is retained by the debtor or transferred to another entity, to the extent of the allowed amount of such claims; and

(II) that each holder of a claim of such class receive on account of such claim deferred cash payments totaling at least the allowed amount of such claim, of a value, as of the effective date of the plan, of at least the value of such holder's interest in the estate's interest in such property;

(ii) for the sale, subject to section 363(k) of this title, of any property that is subject to the liens securing such claims, free and clear of such liens, with such liens to attach to the proceeds of such sale, and the treatment of such liens on proceeds under clause (i) or (iii) of this subparagraph; or

(iii) for the realization by such holders of the indubitable equivalent of such claims.

(B) With respect to a class of unsecured claims—

(i) the plan provides that each holder of a claim of such class receive or retain on account of such claim property of a value, as of the effective date of the plan, equal to the allowed amount of such claim; or

(ii) the holder of any claim or interest that is junior to the claims of such class will not receive or retain under the plan on account of such junior claim or interest any property, except that in a case in which the debtor is an individual, the debtor may retain property included in the estate under section 1115, subject to the requirements of subsection (a)(14) of this section.

(C) With respect to a class of interests—

(i) the plan provides that each holder of an interest of such class receive or retain on account of such interest property of a value, as of the effective date of the plan, equal to the greatest of the allowed amount of any fixed liquidation preference to which such holder is entitled, any fixed redemption price to which such holder is entitled, or the value of such interest; or

(ii) the holder of any interest that is junior to the interests of such class will not receive or retain under the plan on account of such junior interest any property.

(c) Notwithstanding subsections (a) and (b) of this section and except as provided in section 1127(b) of this title, the court may confirm only one plan, unless the order of confirmation in the case has been revoked under section 1144 of this title. If the requirements of subsections

(a) and (b) of this section are met with respect to more than one plan, the court shall consider the preferences of creditors and equity security holders in determining which plan to confirm.

(d) Notwithstanding any other provision of this section, on request of a party in interest that is a governmental unit, the court may not confirm a plan if the principal purpose of the plan is the avoidance of taxes or the avoidance of the application of section 5 of the Securities Act of 1933. In any hearing under this subsection, the governmental unit has the burden of proof on the issue of avoidance.

(e) In a small business case, the court shall confirm a plan that complies with the applicable provisions of this title and that is filed in accordance with section 1121(e) not later than 45 days after the plan is filed unless the time for confirmation is extended in accordance with section 1121(e)(3).

SUBCHAPTER III—POSTCONFIRMATION MATTERS

Sec. 1141. Effect of confirmation

(a) Except as provided in subsections (d)(2) and (d)(3) of this section, the provisions of a confirmed plan bind the debtor, any entity issuing securities under the plan, any entity acquiring property under the plan, and any creditor, equity security holder, or general partner in the debtor, whether or not the claim or interest of such creditor, equity security holder, or general partner is impaired under the plan and whether or not such creditor, equity security holder, or general partner has accepted the plan.

(b) Except as otherwise provided in the plan or the order confirming the plan, the confirmation of a plan vests all of the property of the estate in the debtor.

(c) Except as provided in subsections (d)(2) and (d)(3) of this section and except as otherwise provided in the plan or in the order confirming the plan, after confirmation of a plan, the property dealt with by the plan is free and clear of all claims and interests of creditors, equity security holders, and of general partners in the debtor.

(d) (1) Except as otherwise provided in this subsection, in the plan, or in the order confirming the plan, the confirmation of a plan—
  - (A) discharges the debtor from any debt that arose before the date of such confirmation, and any debt of a kind specified in section 502(g), 502(h), or 502(i) of this title, whether or not—
    - (i) a proof of the claim based on such debt is filed or deemed filed under section 501 of this title;
    - (ii) such claim is allowed under section 502 of this title; or
    - (iii) the holder of such claim has accepted the plan; and
  - (B) terminates all rights and interests of equity security holders and general partners provided for by the plan.

(2) A discharge under this chapter does not discharge a debtor who is an individual from any debt excepted from discharge under section 523 of this title.

(3) The confirmation of a plan does not discharge a debtor if—
  - (A) the plan provides for the liquidation of all or substantially all of the property of the estate;
  - (B) the debtor does not engage in business after consummation of the plan; and

(C) the debtor would be denied a discharge under section 727(a) of this title if the case were a case under chapter 7 of this title.

(4) The court may approve a written waiver of discharge executed by the debtor after the order for relief under this chapter.

(5) In a case in which the debtor is an individual—

(A) unless after notice and a hearing the court orders otherwise for cause, confirmation of the plan does not discharge any debt provided for in the plan until the court grants a discharge on completion of all payments under the plan;

(B) at any time after the confirmation of the plan, and after notice and a hearing, the court may grant a discharge to the debtor who has not completed payments under the plan if—

(i) the value, as of the effective date of the plan, of property actually distributed under the plan on account of each allowed unsecured claim is not less than the amount that would have been paid on such claim if the estate of the debtor had been liquidated under chapter 7 on such date; and

(ii) modification of the plan under section 1127 is not practicable; and

(C) unless after notice and a hearing held not more than 10 days before the date of the entry of the order granting the discharge, the court finds that there is no reasonable cause to believe that—

(i) section 522(q)(1) may be applicable to the debtor; and

(ii) there is pending any proceeding in which the debtor may be found guilty of a felony of the kind described in section 522(q)(1)(A) or liable for a debt of the kind described in section 522(q)(1)(B).

(6) Notwithstanding paragraph (1), the confirmation of a plan does not discharge a debtor that is a corporation from any debt—

(A) of a kind specified in paragraph (2)(A) or (2)(B) of section 523(a) that is owed to a domestic governmental unit, or owed to a person as the result of an action filed under subchapter III of chapter 37 of title 31 or any similar State statute; or

(B) for a tax or customs duty with respect to which the debtor—

(i) made a fraudulent return; or

(ii) willfully attempted in any manner to evade or to defeat such tax or such customs duty.

Sec. 1142. Implementation of plan

(a) Notwithstanding any otherwise applicable nonbankruptcy law, rule, or regulation relating to financial condition, the debtor and any entity organized or to be organized for the purpose of carrying out the plan shall carry out the plan and shall comply with any orders of the court.

(b) The court may direct the debtor and any other necessary party to execute or deliver or to join in the execution or delivery of any instrument required to effect a transfer of property dealt with by a confirmed plan, and to perform any other act, including the satisfaction of any lien, that is necessary for the consummation of the plan.

Sec. 1143. Distribution

If a plan requires presentment or surrender of a security or the performance of any other act as a condition to participation in distribution under the plan, such action shall be taken not later than five years after the date of the entry of the order of confirmation. Any entity that has not within such time presented or surrendered such entity's security or taken any such other action that the plan requires may not participate in distribution under the plan.

Sec. 1144. Revocation of an order of confirmation

On request of a party in interest at any time before 180 days after the date of the entry of the order of confirmation, and after notice and a hearing, the court may revoke such order if and only if such order was procured by fraud. An order under this section revoking an order of confirmation shall—

(1) contain such provisions as are necessary to protect any entity acquiring rights in good faith reliance on the order of confirmation; and

(2) revoke the discharge of the debtor.

Sec. 1145. Exemption from securities laws

(a) Except with respect to an entity that is an underwriter as defined in subsection (b) of this section, section 5 of the Securities Act of 1933 and any State or local law requiring registration for offer or sale of a security or registration or licensing of an issuer of, underwriter of, or broker or dealer in, a security do not apply to—

(1) the offer or sale under a plan of a security of the debtor, of an affiliate participating in a joint plan with the debtor, or of a successor to the debtor under the plan—

(A) in exchange for a claim against, an interest in, or a claim for an administrative expense in the case concerning, the debtor or such affiliate; or

(B) principally in such exchange and partly for cash or property;

(2) the offer of a security through any warrant, option, right to subscribe, or conversion privilege that was sold in the manner specified in paragraph (1) of this subsection, or the sale of a security upon the exercise of such a warrant, option, right, or privilege;

(3) the offer or sale, other than under a plan, of a security of an issuer other than the debtor or an affiliate, if—

(A) such security was owned by the debtor on the date of the filing of the petition;

(B) the issuer of such security is—

(i) required to file reports under section 13 or 15(d) of the Securities Exchange Act of 1934; and

(ii) in compliance with the disclosure and reporting provision of such applicable section; and

(C) such offer or sale is of securities that do not exceed—

(i) during the two-year period immediately following the date of the filing of the petition, four percent of the securities of such class outstanding on such date; and

(ii) during any 180-day period following such two-year period, one percent of the securities outstanding at the beginning of such 180-day period; or

(4) a transaction by a stockbroker in a security that is executed after a transaction of a kind specified in paragraph (1) or (2) of this subsection in such security and before the expiration of 40 days after the first date on which such security was bona fide offered to the public by the issuer or by or through an underwriter, if such stockbroker provides, at the time of or before such transaction by such stockbroker, a disclosure statement approved under section 1125 of this title, and, if the court orders, information supplementing such disclosure statement.

(b) (1) Except as provided in paragraph (2) of this subsection and except with respect to ordinary trading transactions of an entity that is not an issuer, an entity is an underwriter under section 2(11) of the Securities Act of 1933,[13] if such entity—

(A) purchases a claim against, interest in, or claim for an administrative expense in the case concerning, the debtor, if such purchase is with a view to distribution of any security received or to be received in exchange for such a claim or interest;

(B) offers to sell securities offered or sold under the plan for the holders of such securities;

(C) offers to buy securities offered or sold under the plan from the holders of such securities, if such offer to buy is—

(i) with a view to distribution of such securities; and

(ii) under an agreement made in connection with the plan, with the consummation of the plan, or with the offer or sale of securities under the plan; or

(D) is an issuer, as used in such section 2(11), with respect to such securities.

(2) An entity is not an underwriter under section 2(11) of the Securities Act of 1933 or under paragraph (1) of this subsection with respect to an agreement that provides only for—

(A) (i) the matching or combining of fractional interests in securities offered or sold under the plan into whole interests; or

(ii) the purchase or sale of such fractional interests from or to entities receiving such fractional interests under the plan; or

(B) the purchase or sale for such entities of such fractional or whole interests as are necessary to adjust for any remaining fractional interests after such matching.

(3) An entity other than an entity of the kind specified in paragraph (1) of this subsection is not an underwriter under section 2(11) of the Securities Act of 1933 with respect to any securities offered or sold to such entity in the manner specified in subsection (a)(1) of this section.

(c) An offer or sale of securities of the kind and in the manner specified under subsection (a)(1) of this section is deemed to be a public offering.

(d) The Trust Indenture Act of 1939 does not apply to a note issued under the plan that matures not later than one year after the effective date of the plan.

Sec. 1146. Special tax provisions

(a) The issuance, transfer, or exchange of a security, or the making or delivery of an instrument of transfer under a plan confirmed under section 1129 of this title, may not be taxed under any law imposing a stamp tax or similar tax.

(b) The court may authorize the proponent of a plan to request a determination, limited to questions of law, by a State or local governmental unit charged with responsibility for collection or determination of a tax on or measured by income, of the tax effects, under section 346 of this title and under the law imposing such tax, of the plan. In the event of an actual controversy, the court may declare such effects after the earlier of—

(1) the date on which such governmental unit responds to the request under this subsection; or

(2) 270 days after such request.

---

[13] *Sic.* Section 2(11) of the Securities Act of 1933 has been redesignated as section 2(a)(11) of the Act.

SUBCHAPTER IV—RAILROAD REORGANIZATION

Sec. 1161. Inapplicability of other sections

Sections 341, 343, 1102(a)(1), 1104, 1105, 1107, 1129(a)(7), and 1129(c) of this title do not apply in a case concerning a railroad.

Sec. 1162. Definition

In this subchapter, "Board" means the "Surface Transportation Board".

Sec. 1163. Appointment of trustee

As soon as practicable after the order for relief the Secretary of Transportation shall submit a list of five disinterested persons that are qualified and willing to serve as trustees in the case. The United States trustee shall appoint one of such persons to serve as trustee in the case.

Sec. 1164. Right to be heard

The Board, the Department of Transportation, and any State or local commission having regulatory jurisdiction over the debtor may raise and may appear and be heard on any issue in a case under this chapter, but may not appeal from any judgment, order, or decree entered in the case.

Sec. 1165. Protection of the public interest

In applying sections 1166, 1167, 1169, 1170, 1171, 1172, 1173, and 1174 of this title, the court and the trustee shall consider the public interest in addition to the interests of the debtor, creditors, and equity security holders.

Sec. 1166. Effect of subtitle IV of title 49 and of Federal, State, or local regulations

Except with respect to abandonment under section 1170 of this title, or merger, modification of the financial structure of the debtor, or issuance or sale of securities under a plan, the trustee and the debtor are subject to the provisions of subtitle IV of title 49 that are applicable to railroads, and the trustee is subject to orders of any Federal, State, or local regulatory body to the same extent as the debtor would be if a petition commencing the case under this chapter had not been filed, but—

(1) any such order that would require the expenditure, or the incurring of an obligation for the expenditure, of money from the estate is not effective unless approved by the court; and

(2) the provisions of this chapter are subject to section 601(b) of the Regional Rail Reorganization Act of 1973.

Sec. 1167. Collective bargaining agreements

Notwithstanding section 365 of this title, neither the court nor the trustee may change the wages or working conditions of employees of the debtor established by a collective bargaining agreement that is subject to the Railway Labor Act except in accordance with section 6 of such Act.

Sec. 1168. Rolling stock equipment

(a) (1) The right of a secured party with a security interest in or of a lessor or conditional vendor of equipment described in paragraph (2) to take possession of such equipment in compliance with an equipment security agreement, lease, or conditional sale contract, and to enforce any of its other rights or remedies under such security agreement, lease, or conditional sale contract, to sell, lease, or otherwise retain or dispose of such equipment, is not limited or otherwise affected by any other provision of this title or by any power of the court, except that right to take possession and enforce those other rights and remedies shall be subject to section 362, if—

(A) before the date that is 60 days after the date of commencement of a case under this chapter, the trustee, subject to the court's approval, agrees to perform all obligations of the debtor under such security agreement, lease, or conditional sale contract; and

(B) any default, other than a default of a kind described in section 365(b)(2), under such security agreement, lease, or conditional sale contract—

(i) that occurs before the date of commencement of the case and is an event of default therewith is cured before the expiration of such 60-day period;

(ii) that occurs or becomes an event of default after the date of commencement of the case and before the expiration of such 60-day period is cured before the later of—

(I) the date that is 30 days after the date of the default or event of the default; or

(II) the expiration of such 60-day period; and

(iii) that occurs on or after the expiration of such 60-day period is cured in accordance with the terms of such security agreement, lease, or conditional sale contract, if cure is permitted under that agreement, lease, or conditional sale contract.

(2) The equipment described in this paragraph—

(A) is rolling stock equipment or accessories used on rolling stock equipment, including superstructures or racks, that is subject to a security interest granted by, leased to, or conditionally sold to a debtor; and

(B) includes all records and documents relating to such equipment that are required, under the terms of the security agreement, lease, or conditional sale contract, that is to be surrendered or returned by the debtor in connection with the surrender or return of such equipment.

(3) Paragraph (1) applies to a secured party, lessor, or conditional vendor acting in its own behalf or acting as trustee or otherwise in behalf of another party.

(b) The trustee and the secured party, lessor, or conditional vendor whose right to take possession is protected under subsection (a) may agree, subject to the court's approval, to extend the 60-day period specified in subsection (a)(1).

(c) (1) In any case under this chapter, the trustee shall immediately surrender and return to a secured party, lessor, or conditional vendor, described in subsection (a)(1), equipment described in subsection (a)(2), if at any time after the date of commencement of the case under this chapter such secured party, lessor, or conditional vendor is entitled pursuant to subsection (a)(1) to take possession of such equipment and makes a written demand for such possession of the trustee.

(2) At such time as the trustee is required under paragraph (1) to surrender and return equipment described in subsection (a)(2), any lease of such equipment, and any security agreement or conditional sale contract relating to such equipment, if such security agreement or conditional sale contract is an executory contract, shall be deemed rejected.

(d) With respect to equipment first placed in service on or prior to October 22, 1994, for purposes of this section—
   (1) the term "lease" includes any written agreement with respect to which the lessor and the debtor, as lessee, have expressed in the agreement or in a substantially contemporaneous writing that the agreement is to be treated as a lease for Federal income tax purposes; and
   (2) the term "security interest" means a purchase-money equipment security interest.

(e) With respect to equipment first placed in service after October 22, 1994, for purposes of this section, the term "rolling stock equipment" includes rolling stock equipment that is substantially rebuilt and accessories used on such equipment.

Sec. 1169. Effect of rejection of lease of railroad line

(a) Except as provided in subsection (b) of this section, if a lease of a line of railroad under which the debtor is the lessee is rejected under section 365 of this title, and if the trustee, within such time as the court fixes, and with the court's approval, elects not to operate the leased line, the lessor under such lease, after such approval, shall operate the line.

(b) If operation of such line by such lessor is impracticable or contrary to the public interest, the court, on request of such lessor, and after notice and a hearing, shall order the trustee to continue operation of such line for the account of such lessor until abandonment is ordered under section 1170 of this title, or until such operation is otherwise lawfully terminated, whichever occurs first.

(c) During any such operation, such lessor is deemed a carrier subject to the provisions of subtitle IV of title 49 that are applicable to railroads.

Sec. 1170. Abandonment of railroad line

(a) The court, after notice and a hearing, may authorize the abandonment of all or a portion of a railroad line if such abandonment is—
   (1) (A) in the best interest of the estate; or
       (B) essential to the formulation of a plan; and
   (2) consistent with the public interest.

(b) If, except for the pendency of the case under this chapter, such abandonment would require approval by the Board under a law of the United States, the trustee shall initiate an appropriate application for such abandonment with the Board. The court may fix a time within which the Board shall report to the court on such application.

(c) After the court receives the report of the Board, or the expiration of the time fixed under subsection (b) of this section, whichever occurs first, the court may authorize such abandonment, after notice to the Board, the Secretary of Transportation, the trustee, any party in interest that has requested notice, any affected shipper or community, and any other entity prescribed by the court, and a hearing.

(d) (1) Enforcement of an order authorizing such abandonment shall be stayed until the time for taking an appeal has expired, or, if an appeal is timely taken, until such order has become final.
   (2) If an order authorizing such abandonment is appealed, the court, on request of a party in interest, may authorize suspension of service on a line or a portion of a line pending the determination of such appeal, after notice to the Board, the Secretary of Transportation, the trustee, any party in interest that has requested notice, any affected shipper or

community, and any other entity prescribed by the court, and a hearing. An appellant may not obtain a stay of the enforcement of an order authorizing such suspension by the giving of a supersedeas bond or otherwise, during the pendency of such appeal.

(e) (1) In authorizing any abandonment of a railroad line under this section, the court shall require the rail carrier to provide a fair arrangement at least as protective of the interests of employees as that established under section 11326(a) of title 49.

(2) Nothing in this subsection shall be deemed to affect the priorities or timing of payment of employee protection which might have existed in the absence of this subsection.

Sec. 1171. Priority claims

(a) There shall be paid as an administrative expense any claim of an individual or of the personal representative of a deceased individual against the debtor or the estate, for personal injury to or death of such individual arising out of the operation of the debtor or the estate, whether such claim arose before or after the commencement of the case.

(b) Any unsecured claim against the debtor that would have been entitled to priority if a receiver in equity of the property of the debtor had been appointed by a Federal court on the date of the order for relief under this title shall be entitled to the same priority in the case under this chapter.

Sec. 1172. Contents of plan

(a) In addition to the provisions required or permitted under section 1123 of this title, a plan—

(1) shall specify the extent to and the means by which the debtor's rail service is proposed to be continued, and the extent to which any of the debtor's rail service is proposed to be terminated; and

(2) may include a provision for—

(A) the transfer of any or all of the operating railroad lines of the debtor to another operating railroad; or

(B) abandonment of any railroad line in accordance with section 1170 of this title.

(b) If, except for the pendency of the case under this chapter, transfer of, or operation of or over, any of the debtor's rail lines by an entity other than the debtor or a successor to the debtor under the plan would require approval by the Board under a law of the United States, then a plan may not propose such a transfer or such operation unless the proponent of the plan initiates an appropriate application for such a transfer or such operation with the Board and, within such time as the court may fix, not exceeding 180 days, the Board, with or without a hearing, as the Board may determine, and with or without modification or condition, approves such application, or does not act on such application. Any action or order of the Board approving, modifying, conditioning, or disapproving such application is subject to review by the court only under sections 706(2)(A), 706(2)(B), 706(2)(C), and 706(2)(D) of title 5.

(c) (1) In approving an application under subsection (b) of this section, the Board shall require the rail carrier to provide a fair arrangement at least as protective of the interests of employees as that established under section 11326(a) of title 49.

(2) Nothing in this subsection shall be deemed to affect the priorities or timing of payment of employee protection which might have existed in the absence of this subsection.

Sec. 1173. Confirmation of plan

(a) The court shall confirm a plan if—

(1) the applicable requirements of section 1129 of this title have been met;

(2) each creditor or equity security holder will receive or retain under the plan property of a value, as of the effective date of the plan, that is not less than the value of property that each such creditor or equity security holder would so receive or retain if all of the operating railroad lines of the debtor were sold, and the proceeds of such sale, and the other property of the estate, were distributed under chapter 7 of this title on such date;

(3) in light of the debtor's past earnings and the probable prospective earnings of the reorganized debtor, there will be adequate coverage by such prospective earnings of any fixed charges, such as interest on debt, amortization of funded debt, and rent for leased railroads, provided for by the plan; and

(4) the plan is consistent with the public interest.

(b) If the requirements of subsection (a) of this section are met with respect to more than one plan, the court shall confirm the plan that is most likely to maintain adequate rail service in the public interest.

Sec. 1174. Liquidation

On request of a party in interest and after notice and a hearing, the court may, or, if a plan has not been confirmed under section 1173 of this title before five years after the date of the order for relief, the court shall, order the trustee to cease the debtor's operation and to collect and reduce to money all of the property of the estate in the same manner as if the case were a case under chapter 7 of this title.

CHAPTER 12—ADJUSTMENT OF DEBTS OF A FAMILY FARMER OR FISHERMAN WITH REGULAR ANNUAL INCOME

[OMITTED]

CHAPTER 13—ADJUSTMENT OF DEBTS OF AN INDIVIDUAL WITH REGULAR INCOME

[OMITTED]

CHAPTER 15—ANCILLARY AND OTHER CROSS-BORDER CASES

Sec. 1501. Purpose and scope of application

(a) The purpose of this chapter is to incorporate the Model Law on Cross-Border Insolvency so as to provide effective mechanisms for dealing with cases of cross-border insolvency with the objectives of—

(1) cooperation between—

(A) courts of the United States, United States trustees, trustees, examiners, debtors, and debtors in possession; and

(B) the courts and other competent authorities of foreign countries involved in cross-border insolvency cases;

(2) greater legal certainty for trade and investment;

(3) fair and efficient administration of cross-border insolvencies that protects the interests of all creditors, and other interested entities, including the debtor;

(4) protection and maximization of the value of the debtor's assets; and

(5) facilitation of the rescue of financially troubled businesses, thereby protecting investment and preserving employment.

(b) This chapter applies where—

(1) assistance is sought in the United States by a foreign court or a foreign representative in connection with a foreign proceeding;

(2) assistance is sought in a foreign country in connection with a case under this title;

(3) a foreign proceeding and a case under this title with respect to the same debtor are pending concurrently; or

(4) creditors or other interested persons in a foreign country have an interest in requesting the commencement of, or participating in, a case or proceeding under this title.

(c) This chapter does not apply to—

(1) a proceeding concerning an entity, other than a foreign insurance company, identified by exclusion in section 109(b);

(2) an individual, or to an individual and such individual's spouse, who have debts within the limits specified in section 109(e) and who are citizens of the United States or aliens lawfully admitted for permanent residence in the United States; or

(3) an entity subject to a proceeding under the Securities Investor Protection Act of 1970, a stockbroker subject to subchapter III of chapter 7 of this title, or a commodity broker subject to subchapter IV of chapter 7 of this title.

(d) The court may not grant relief under this chapter with respect to any deposit, escrow, trust fund, or other security required or permitted under any applicable State insurance law or regulation for the benefit of claim holders in the United States.

SUBCHAPTER I—GENERAL PROVISIONS

Sec. 1502. Definitions

For the purposes of this chapter, the term—

(1) "debtor" means an entity that is the subject of a foreign proceeding;

(2) "establishment" means any place of operations where the debtor carries out a nontransitory economic activity;

(3) "foreign court" means a judicial or other authority competent to control or supervise a foreign proceeding;

(4) "foreign main proceeding" means a foreign proceeding pending in the country where the debtor has the center of its main interests;

(5) "foreign nonmain proceeding" means a foreign proceeding, other than a foreign main proceeding, pending in a country where the debtor has an establishment;

(6) "trustee" includes a trustee, a debtor in possession in a case under any chapter of this title, or a debtor under chapter 9 of this title;

(7) "recognition" means the entry of an order granting recognition of a foreign main proceeding or foreign nonmain proceeding under this chapter; and

(8) "within the territorial jurisdiction of the United States", when used with reference to property of a debtor, refers to tangible property located within the territory of the United

States and intangible property deemed under applicable nonbankruptcy law to be located within that territory, including any property subject to attachment or garnishment that may properly be seized or garnished by an action in a Federal or State court in the United States.

Sec. 1503. International obligations of the United States

To the extent that this chapter conflicts with an obligation of the United States arising out of any treaty or other form of agreement to which it is a party with one or more other countries, the requirements of the treaty or agreement prevail.

Sec. 1504. Commencement of ancillary case

A case under this chapter is commenced by the filing of a petition for recognition of a foreign proceeding under section 1515.

Sec. 1505. Authorization to act in a foreign country

A trustee or another entity (including an examiner) may be authorized by the court to act in a foreign country on behalf of an estate created under section 541. An entity authorized to act under this section may act in any way permitted by the applicable foreign law.

Sec. 1506. Public policy exception

Nothing in this chapter prevents the court from refusing to take an action governed by this chapter if the action would be manifestly contrary to the public policy of the United States.

Sec. 1507. Additional assistance

(a) Subject to the specific limitations stated elsewhere in this chapter the court, if recognition is granted, may provide additional assistance to a foreign representative under this title or under other laws of the United States.

(b) In determining whether to provide additional assistance under this title or under other laws of the United States, the court shall consider whether such additional assistance, consistent with the principles of comity, will reasonably assure—

    (1) just treatment of all holders of claims against or interests in the debtor's property;
    (2) protection of claim holders in the United States against prejudice and inconvenience in the processing of claims in such foreign proceeding;
    (3) prevention of preferential or fraudulent dispositions of property of the debtor;
    (4) distribution of proceeds of the debtor's property substantially in accordance with the order prescribed by this title; and
    (5) if appropriate, the provision of an opportunity for a fresh start for the individual that such foreign proceeding concerns.

Sec. 1508. Interpretation

In interpreting this chapter, the court shall consider its international origin, and the need to promote an application of this chapter that is consistent with the application of similar statutes adopted by foreign jurisdictions.

Sec. 1509. Right of direct access

(a) A foreign representative may commence a case under section 1504 by filing directly with the court a petition for recognition of a foreign proceeding under section 1515.

(b) If the court grants recognition under section 1517, and subject to any limitations that the court may impose consistent with the policy of this chapter—

(1) the foreign representative has the capacity to sue and be sued in a court in the United States;

(2) the foreign representative may apply directly to a court in the United States for appropriate relief in that court; and

(3) a court in the United States shall grant comity or cooperation to the foreign representative.

(c) A request for comity or cooperation by a foreign representative in a court in the United States other than the court which granted recognition shall be accompanied by a certified copy of an order granting recognition under section 1517.

(d) If the court denies recognition under this chapter, the court may issue any appropriate order necessary to prevent the foreign representative from obtaining comity or cooperation from courts in the United States.

(e) Whether or not the court grants recognition, and subject to sections 306 and 1510, a foreign representative is subject to applicable nonbankruptcy law.

(f) Notwithstanding any other provision of this section, the failure of a foreign representative to commence a case or to obtain recognition under this chapter does not affect any right the foreign representative may have to sue in a court in the United States to collect or recover a claim which is the property of the debtor.

Sec. 1510. Limited jurisdiction

The sole fact that a foreign representative files a petition under section 1515 does not subject the foreign representative to the jurisdiction of any court in the United States for any other purpose.

Sec. 1511. Commencement of case under section 301 or 303

(a) Upon recognition, a foreign representative may commence—

(1) an involuntary case under section 303; or

(2) a voluntary case under section 301 or 302, if the foreign proceeding is a foreign main proceeding.

(b) The petition commencing a case under subsection (a) must be accompanied by a certified copy of an order granting recognition. The court where the petition for recognition has been filed must be advised of the foreign representative's intent to commence a case under subsection (a) prior to such commencement.

Sec. 1512. Participation of a foreign representative in a case under this title

Upon recognition of a foreign proceeding, the foreign representative in the recognized proceeding is entitled to participate as a party in interest in a case regarding the debtor under this title.

Sec. 1513. Access of foreign creditors to a case under this title

(a) Foreign creditors have the same rights regarding the commencement of, and participation in, a case under this title as domestic creditors.

(b) (1) Subsection (a) does not change or codify present law as to the priority of claims under section 507 or 726, except that the claim of a foreign creditor under those sections shall not be given a lower priority than that of general unsecured claims without priority solely because the holder of such claim is a foreign creditor.

(2) (A) Subsection (a) and paragraph (1) do not change or codify present law as to the allowability of foreign revenue claims or other foreign public law claims in a proceeding under this title.

(B) Allowance and priority as to a foreign tax claim or other foreign public law claim shall be governed by any applicable tax treaty of the United States, under the conditions and circumstances specified therein.

Sec. 1514. Notification to foreign creditors concerning a case under this title

(a) Whenever in a case under this title notice is to be given to creditors generally or to any class or category of creditors, such notice shall also be given to the known creditors generally, or to creditors in the notified class or category, that do not have addresses in the United States. The court may order that appropriate steps be taken with a view to notifying any creditor whose address is not yet known.

(b) Such notification to creditors with foreign addresses described in subsection (a) shall be given individually, unless the court considers that, under the circumstances, some other form of notification would be more appropriate. No letter or other formality is required.

(c) When a notification of commencement of a case is to be given to foreign creditors, such notification shall—

(1) indicate the time period for filing proofs of claim and specify the place for filing such proofs of claim;

(2) indicate whether secured creditors need to file proofs of claim; and

(3) contain any other information required to be included in such notification to creditors under this title and the orders of the court.

(d) Any rule of procedure or order of the court as to notice or the filing of a proof of claim shall provide such additional time to creditors with foreign addresses as is reasonable under the circumstances.

SUBCHAPTER III—RECOGNITION OF A FOREIGN PROCEEDING AND RELIEF

Sec. 1515. Application for recognition

(a) A foreign representative applies to the court for recognition of a foreign proceeding in which the foreign representative has been appointed by filing a petition for recognition.

(b) A petition for recognition shall be accompanied by—

(1) a certified copy of the decision commencing such foreign proceeding and appointing the foreign representative;

(2) a certificate from the foreign court affirming the existence of such foreign proceeding and of the appointment of the foreign representative; or

(3) in the absence of evidence referred to in paragraphs (1) and (2), any other evidence acceptable to the court of the existence of such foreign proceeding and of the appointment of the foreign representative.

(c) A petition for recognition shall also be accompanied by a statement identifying all foreign proceedings with respect to the debtor that are known to the foreign representative.

(d) The documents referred to in paragraphs (1) and (2) of subsection (b) shall be translated into English. The court may require a translation into English of additional documents.

Sec. 1516. Presumptions concerning recognition

(a) If the decision or certificate referred to in section 1515(b) indicates that the foreign proceeding is a foreign proceeding and that the person or body is a foreign representative, the court is entitled to so presume.

(b) The court is entitled to presume that documents submitted in support of the petition for recognition are authentic, whether or not they have been legalized.

(c) In the absence of evidence to the contrary, the debtor's registered office, or habitual residence in the case of an individual, is presumed to be the center of the debtor's main interests.

Sec. 1517. Order granting recognition

(a) Subject to section 1506, after notice and a hearing, an order recognizing a foreign proceeding shall be entered if—

  (1) such foreign proceeding for which recognition is sought is a foreign main proceeding or foreign nonmain proceeding within the meaning of section 1502;

  (2) the foreign representative applying for recognition is a person or body; and

  (3) the petition meets the requirements of section 1515.

(b) Such foreign proceeding shall be recognized—

  (1) as a foreign main proceeding if it is pending in the country where the debtor has the center of its main interests; or

  (2) as a foreign nonmain proceeding if the debtor has an establishment within the meaning of section 1502 in the foreign country where the proceeding is pending.

(c) A petition for recognition of a foreign proceeding shall be decided upon at the earliest possible time. Entry of an order recognizing a foreign proceeding constitutes recognition under this chapter.

(d) The provisions of this subchapter do not prevent modification or termination of recognition if it is shown that the grounds for granting it were fully or partially lacking or have ceased to exist, but in considering such action the court shall give due weight to possible prejudice to parties that have relied upon the order granting recognition. A case under this chapter may be closed in the manner prescribed under section 350.

Sec. 1518. Subsequent information

From the time of filing the petition for recognition of a foreign proceeding, the foreign representative shall file with the court promptly a notice of change of status concerning—

  (1) any substantial change in the status of such foreign proceeding or the status of the foreign representative's appointment; and

  (2) any other foreign proceeding regarding the debtor that becomes known to the foreign representative.

Sec. 1519. Relief that may be granted upon filing petition for recognition

(a) From the time of filing a petition for recognition until the court rules on the petition, the court may, at the request of the foreign representative, where relief is urgently needed to protect the assets of the debtor or the interests of the creditors, grant relief of a provisional nature, including—

  (1) staying execution against the debtor's assets;

  (2) entrusting the administration or realization of all or part of the debtor's assets located in

the United States to the foreign representative or another person authorized by the court, including an examiner, in order to protect and preserve the value of assets that, by their nature or because of other circumstances, are perishable, susceptible to devaluation or otherwise in jeopardy; and

(3) any relief referred to in paragraph (3), (4), or (7) of section 1521(a).

(b) Unless extended under section 1521(a)(6), the relief granted under this section terminates when the petition for recognition is granted.

(c) It is a ground for denial of relief under this section that such relief would interfere with the administration of a foreign main proceeding.

(d) The court may not enjoin a police or regulatory act of a governmental unit, including a criminal action or proceeding, under this section.

(e) The standards, procedures, and limitations applicable to an injunction shall apply to relief under this section.

(f) The exercise of rights not subject to the stay arising under section 362(a) pursuant to paragraph (6), (7), (17), or (27) of section 362(b) or pursuant to section 362(n) shall not be stayed by any order of a court or administrative agency in any proceeding under this chapter.

Sec. 1520. Effects of recognition of a foreign main proceeding

(a) Upon recognition of a foreign proceeding that is a foreign main proceeding—

(1) sections 361 and 362 apply with respect to the debtor and the property of the debtor that is within the territorial jurisdiction of the United States;

(2) sections 363, 549, and 552 apply to a transfer of an interest of the debtor in property that is within the territorial jurisdiction of the United States to the same extent that the sections would apply to property of an estate;

(3) unless the court orders otherwise, the foreign representative may operate the debtor's business and may exercise the rights and powers of a trustee under and to the extent provided by sections 363 and 552; and

(4) section 552 applies to property of the debtor that is within the territorial jurisdiction of the United States.

(b) Subsection (a) does not affect the right to commence an individual action or proceeding in a foreign country to the extent necessary to preserve a claim against the debtor.

(c) Subsection (a) does not affect the right of a foreign representative or an entity to file a petition commencing a case under this title or the right of any party to file claims or take other proper actions in such a case.

Sec. 1521. Relief that may be granted upon recognition

(a) Upon recognition of a foreign proceeding, whether main or nonmain, where necessary to effectuate the purpose of this chapter and to protect the assets of the debtor or the interests of the creditors, the court may, at the request of the foreign representative, grant any appropriate relief, including—

(1) staying the commencement or continuation of an individual action or proceeding concerning the debtor's assets, rights, obligations or liabilities to the extent they have not been stayed under section 1520(a);

(2) staying execution against the debtor's assets to the extent it has not been stayed under section 1520(a);

(3) suspending the right to transfer, encumber or otherwise dispose of any assets of the debtor to the extent this right has not been suspended under section 1520(a);

(4) providing for the examination of witnesses, the taking of evidence or the delivery of information concerning the debtor's assets, affairs, rights, obligations or liabilities;

(5) entrusting the administration or realization of all or part of the debtor's assets within the territorial jurisdiction of the United States to the foreign representative or another person, including an examiner, authorized by the court; (6) extending relief granted under section 1519(a); and

(7) granting any additional relief that may be available to a trustee, except for relief available under sections 522, 544, 545, 547, 548, 550, and 724(a).

(b) Upon recognition of a foreign proceeding, whether main or nonmain, the court may, at the request of the foreign representative, entrust the distribution of all or part of the debtor's assets located in the United States to the foreign representative or another person, including an examiner, authorized by the court, provided that the court is satisfied that the interests of creditors in the United States are sufficiently protected.

(c) In granting relief under this section to a representative of a foreign nonmain proceeding, the court must be satisfied that the relief relates to assets that, under the law of the United States, should be administered in the foreign nonmain proceeding or concerns information required in that proceeding.

(d) The court may not enjoin a police or regulatory act of a governmental unit, including a criminal action or proceeding, under this section.

(e) The standards, procedures, and limitations applicable to an injunction shall apply to relief under paragraphs (1), (2), (3), and (6) of subsection (a).

(f) The exercise of rights not subject to the stay arising under section 362(a) pursuant to paragraph (6), (7), (17), or (27) of section 362(b) or pursuant to section 362(n) shall not be stayed by any order of a court or administrative agency in any proceeding under this chapter.

Sec. 1522. Protection of creditors and other interested persons

(a) The court may grant relief under section 1519 or 1521, or may modify or terminate relief under subsection (c), only if the interests of the creditors and other interested entities, including the debtor, are sufficiently protected.

(b) The court may subject relief granted under section 1519 or 1521, or the operation of the debtor's business under section 1520(a)(3), to conditions it considers appropriate, including the giving of security or the filing of a bond.

(c) The court may, at the request of the foreign representative or an entity affected by relief granted under section 1519 or 1521, or at its own motion, modify or terminate such relief.

(d) Section 1104(d) shall apply to the appointment of an examiner under this chapter. Any examiner shall comply with the qualification requirements imposed on a trustee by section 322.

Sec. 1523. Actions to avoid acts detrimental to creditors

(a) Upon recognition of a foreign proceeding, the foreign representative has standing in a case concerning the debtor pending under another chapter of this title to initiate actions under sections 522, 544, 545, 547, 548, 550, 553, and 724(a).

(b) When a foreign proceeding is a foreign nonmain proceeding, the court must be satisfied that an action under subsection (a) relates to assets that, under United States law, should be administered in the foreign nonmain proceeding.

Sec. 1524. Intervention by a foreign representative

Upon recognition of a foreign proceeding, the foreign representative may intervene in any proceedings in a State or Federal court in the United States in which the debtor is a party.

SUBCHAPTER IV—COOPERATION WITH FOREIGN COURTS AND FOREIGN REPRESENTATIVES

Sec. 1525. Cooperation and direct communication between the court and foreign courts or foreign representatives

(a) Consistent with section 1501, the court shall cooperate to the maximum extent possible with a foreign court or a foreign representative, either directly or through the trustee.

(b) The court is entitled to communicate directly with, or to request information or assistance directly from, a foreign court or a foreign representative, subject to the rights of a party in interest to notice and participation.

Sec. 1526. Cooperation and direct communication between the trustee and foreign courts or foreign representatives

(a) Consistent with section 1501, the trustee or other person, including an examiner, authorized by the court, shall, subject to the supervision of the court, cooperate to the maximum extent possible with a foreign court or a foreign representative.

(b) The trustee or other person, including an examiner, authorized by the court is entitled, subject to the supervision of the court, to communicate directly with a foreign court or a foreign representative.

Sec. 1527. Forms of cooperation

Cooperation referred to in sections 1525 and 1526 may be implemented by any appropriate means, including—

(1) appointment of a person or body, including an examiner, to act at the direction of the court;

(2) communication of information by any means considered appropriate by the court;

(3) coordination of the administration and supervision of the debtor's assets and affairs;

(4) approval or implementation of agreements concerning the coordination of proceedings; and

(5) coordination of concurrent proceedings regarding the same debtor.

SUBCHAPTER V—CONCURRENT PROCEEDINGS

Sec. 1528. Commencement of a case under this title after recognition of a foreign main proceeding

After recognition of a foreign main proceeding, a case under another chapter of this title may be commenced only if the debtor has assets in the United States. The effects of such case shall be restricted to the assets of the debtor that are within the territorial jurisdiction of the United States and, to the extent necessary to implement cooperation and coordination under sections 1525, 1526, and 1527, to other assets of the debtor that are within the jurisdiction of the court under sections

541(a) of this title, and 1334(e) of title 28, to the extent that such other assets are not subject to the jurisdiction and control of a foreign proceeding that has been recognized under this chapter.

Sec. 1529. Coordination of a case under this title and a foreign proceeding

If a foreign proceeding and a case under another chapter of this title are pending concurrently regarding the same debtor, the court shall seek cooperation and coordination under sections 1525, 1526, and 1527, and the following shall apply:

(1) If the case in the United States pending at the time the petition for recognition of such foreign proceeding is filed—
   (A) any relief granted under section 1519 or 1521 must be consistent with the relief granted in the case in the United States; and
   (B) section 1520 does not apply even if such foreign proceeding is recognized as a foreign main proceeding.

(2) If a case in the United States under this title commences after recognition, or after the date of the filing of the petition for recognition, of such foreign proceeding—
   (A) any relief in effect under section 1519 or 1521 shall be reviewed by the court and shall be modified or terminated if inconsistent with the case in the United States; and
   (B) if such foreign proceeding is a foreign main proceeding, the stay and suspension referred to in section 1520(a) shall be modified or terminated if inconsistent with the relief granted in the case in the United States.

(3) In granting, extending, or modifying relief granted to a representative of a foreign nonmain proceeding, the court must be satisfied that the relief relates to assets that, under the laws of the United States, should be administered in the foreign nonmain proceeding or concerns information required in that proceeding.

(4) In achieving cooperation and coordination under sections 1528 and 1529, the court may grant any of the relief authorized under section 305.

Sec. 1530. Coordination of more than 1 foreign proceeding

In matters referred to in section 1501, with respect to more than 1 foreign proceeding regarding the debtor, the court shall seek cooperation and coordination under sections 1525, 1526, and 1527, and the following shall apply:

(1) Any relief granted under section 1519 or 1521 to a representative of a foreign nonmain proceeding after recognition of a foreign main proceeding must be consistent with the foreign main proceeding.

(2) If a foreign main proceeding is recognized after recognition, or after the filing of a petition for recognition, of a foreign nonmain proceeding, any relief in effect under section 1519 or 1521 shall be reviewed by the court and shall be modified or terminated if inconsistent with the foreign main proceeding.

(3) If, after recognition of a foreign nonmain proceeding, another foreign nonmain proceeding is recognized, the court shall grant, modify, or terminate relief for the purpose of facilitating coordination of the proceedings.

Sec. 1531. Presumption of insolvency based on recognition of a foreign main proceeding

In the absence of evidence to the contrary, recognition of a foreign main proceeding is, for the purpose of commencing a proceeding under section 303, proof that the debtor is generally not paying its debts as such debts become due.

Sec. 1532. Rule of payment in concurrent proceedings

Without prejudice to secured claims or rights in rem, a creditor who has received payment with respect to its claim in a foreign proceeding pursuant to a law relating to insolvency may not receive a payment for the same claim in a case under any other chapter of this title regarding the debtor, so long as the payment to other creditors of the same class is proportionately less than the payment the creditor has already received.

Deryck A. Palmer

Deryck Palmer, Co-Chairman of the Financial Restructuring Department of Cadwalader, Wickersham & Taft LLP, concentrates his practice in the representation of debtors as well as creditors under chapter 11 of the U.S. Bankruptcy Code, and has handled a wide variety of workout, corporate restructuring, and bankruptcy matters.

Recognized by *Turnarounds and Workouts* as one of the top "Outstanding Bankruptcy Lawyers" in the United States, Mr. Palmer serves as the Co-Vice-Chair of the American Bar Association's Business Bankruptcy Committee's Healthcare Working Group and is a member of both the New York State Bar Association Committee on Bankruptcy and Committee on Courts and the Community. He is also a former member of the Committee on Bankruptcy and Corporate Reorganization of the Association of the Bar of the City of New York.

Mr. Palmer lectures at many major law schools nationwide and is an Adjunct Professor of Law at New York Law School, teaching advanced topics in bankruptcy and corporate reorganization. He is co-author of *History of Bankruptcy Law in the Second Circuit* (Matthew Bender & Co., 1995) and *Restructuring: The Search for Value in a Troubled Enterprise* (Euromoney Books, 1993). In addition, he delivers numerous lectures each year on business reorganization topics, including an annual American Bar Association panel concerning current developments in the field.

Mr. Palmer is a member of the Bureau of National Affairs Advisory Board for the *Bankruptcy Law Reporter* and sits on the Board of Directors of Boys & Girls Harbor, Inc., INSOL International, Greater New York Councils Boy Scouts of America, Maplewood Village Alliance, Syracuse University, and The Cleveland Clinic Foundation. He is also a Fellow of the American College of Bankruptcy.

Mr. Palmer received his B.A. from Syracuse University and his J.D. from the University of Michigan. He recently received the *Chancellor's Citation for Exceptional Achievement* from Syracuse University, which recognizes outstanding contributions in scholarship, research, teaching, and creative work.

John J. Rapisardi

John Rapisardi, Co-Chairman of the Financial Restructuring Department of Cadwalader, Wickersham & Taft LLP, has more than twenty-five years of domestic and international restructuring experience across a variety of industries, including telecommunications, satellite, retail, healthcare, casinos, sports franchises, real estate, and manufacturing companies. Most recently, he is serving as outside counsel to the United States Department of Treasury and the Presidential Task Force on the (U.S.) Auto Industry.

Publications have consistently lauded Mr. Rapisardi's work. He was named as a highly recommended international restructuring counsel in *PLC Cross-border Restructuring and Insolvency Handbook*, recognized as one of the leading restructuring lawyers in the U.S. by *Chambers USA*, and included in *Best Lawyers in America*.

Mr. Rapisardi has advised investors of financial institutions and written extensively on the subject of lender rights and remedies under the new PRC bankruptcy law. He has also been the bi-monthly bankruptcy columnist for the *New York Law Journal* for the last ten years.

A Beta Gamma Sigma graduate from the College of Business Administration at Fordham University, Mr. Rapisardi received his LL.M. from New York University and J.D. from Pace University and served on the *Pace Law Review*.